1996

Science Annual

A Modern Science Anthology for the Family

1996

SCIENCE ANNUAL

STAFF

CONTRIBUTORS

TINA ADLER, General science editor, *Science News*
DESIGNER FATS

WILLIAM F. ALLMAN, Senior writer, *U.S. News & World Report*
BEYOND THE TOP QUARK

TERESA AUSTIN, Freelance engineering writer based in Teaneck, NJ
CIVIL ENGINEERING

DOUGLAS S. BARASCH, Freelance writer specializing in medical issues
THE MAINSTREAMING OF ALTERNATIVE MEDICINE

NANCY BERLINER, Freelance writer based in Boston, MA
THE CHANGING FACES ON MONEY

JAMES A. BLACKMAN, Professor of pediatrics, University of Virginia, Charlottesville, VA
ATTACK OF THE FLESH-EATING BACTERIA
ASK THE SCIENTIST: HUMAN SCIENCES

BRUCE BOWER, Behavioral sciences editor, *Science News*
BEHAVIORAL SCIENCES

LINDA J. BROWN, Freelance writer based in Bloomsbury, NJ
BUILDERS OF THE ANIMAL WORLD

GENE BYLINSKY, Editor, *Fortune* magazine
MANUFACTURING FOR REUSE

MICHAEL CARROLL, Journalist and artist specializing in astronomy
PLANETARY OCEANS

ANTHONY J. CASTAGNO, Energy consultant; manager, nuclear information, Northeast Utilities, Hartford, CT
ENERGY
IN MEMORIAM

THEODORE A. REES CHENEY, Associate professor, Fairfield University, Fairfield, CT
SAVING THE GREAT NORTHERN FOREST

RUTH COXETER, Assistant editor, *Business Week* magazine
coauthor, PRESSING MATTERS

PETER COY, Technology editor, *Business Week* magazine
coauthor, PRESSING MATTERS

DONNA HOOD CRECCA, Freelance writer based in West Islip, NY
PHYSICS ON THE FAIRWAY

DONALD W. CUNNINGHAM, Freelance writer based in Washington, DC
AUTOMOTIVE TECHNOLOGY
TRANSPORTATION

GODE DAVIS, Freelance science writer based in Warwick, RI
ASK THE SCIENTIST:
EARTH AND THE ENVIRONMENT
ASK THE SCIENTIST: TECHNOLOGY
OCEANOGRAPHY

JAMES A. DAVIS, Department of mathematics, University of Richmond, Richmond, VA
MATHEMATICS

JERRY DENNIS, Freelance writer; author of *A Place on the Water* (St. Martin's Press, 1993) and *It's Raining Frogs and Fishes* (HarperCollins, 1992)
THE CALL OF THE MERMAID
ENDANGERED SPECIES
ZOOLOGY

JARED DIAMOND, Contributing editor, *Discover* magazine
HOW TO TAME A WILD PLANT

TIMOTHY EGAN, Seattle bureau chief, *The New York Times*
DESERT SANCTUARY

DAVID S. EPSTEIN, Meteorologist and freelance writer
METEOROLOGY

DANIEL GOLEMAN, Behavioral science correspondent, *The New York Times*; coauthor, *The Creative Spirit* (NAL Dutton, 1993)
NAVIGATING THROUGH BLINDNESS

MARIA GUGLIELMINO, Registered dietitian and exercise physiologist
NUTRITION

JUDITH ANNE GUNTHER, Associate editor, *Popular Science*
MAKING MONEY

ERIN HYNES, Freelance science writer based in Austin, TX
BOTANY

VINOD JAIN, Freelance science writer based in Bowie, MD
CHEMISTRY

JAMES F. JEKEL, Professor of epidemiology and public health, Yale University School of Medicine, New Haven, CT
PUBLIC HEALTH

CHRISTOPHER KING, Managing editor, *Science Watch*, Institute for Scientific Information, Philadelphia, PA
PREHISTORIC CAVE PAINTINGS:
ARTWORK IN THE DARK
NOBEL PRIZES

LOUIS LEVINE, Department of biology, City College of New York, New York, NY
BIOLOGY
BIOTECHNOLOGY

LES LINE, Freelance writer based in Amenia, NY; former editor, *Audubon*; coauthor, *The Audubon Society Book of Water Birds* (Chanticleer Books, 1988)
HAVE WINGS, CAN'T FLY

RICHARD LIPKIN, Chemistry and material science editor, *Science News*
HOW COMPUTERS RECOGNIZE FACES
ELECTRONICS

THERESE A. LLOYD, Managing editor, *Oilfield Review*
PHYSICS

ELIZABETH MCGOWAN, Freelance writer based in New York City
TAKING THE LEAN OUT OF THE LEANING TOWER OF PISA

MARTIN M. MCLAUGHLIN, Freelance consultant; former vice president for education, Overseas Development Council
FOOD AND POPULATION

DENNIS L. MAMMANA, Resident astronomer, Reuben H. Fleet Space Theater and Science Center, San Diego, CA
FIRE AND ICE IN THE JOVIAN SKY
OTHER SUNS, OTHER WORLDS
ASK THE SCIENTIST:
ASTRONOMY AND SPACE SCIENCE
ASTRONOMY
SPACE SCIENCE

THOMAS H. MAUGH II, Science writer, *Los Angeles Times*
GENETICS

RICHARD MONASTERSKY, Earth sciences editor, *Science News*
RETHINKING THE RICHTER SCALE
GEOLOGY
PALEONTOLOGY
SEISMOLOGY
VOLCANOLOGY

M. ALEXANDRA NELSON, Freelance science and technology writer
DOTS OF ILLUSION

SUSAN NIELSEN, Freelance writer specializing in consumer issues
COMMUNICATION TECHNOLOGY
CONSUMER TECHNOLOGY

DANIEL PENDICK, Freelance writer specializing in earth science
UNDER THE VOLCANO

DAVID A. PENDLEBURY, Research analyst, Institute for Scientific Information, Philadelphia, PA
HAIL TO THE HALOGENS
GEOMETRIC PROGRESSIONS—THEY REALLY ADD UP!
ASK THE SCIENTIST: PHYSICAL SCIENCE

KATHRYN PHILLIPS, Freelance wildlife writer; author, *Tracking the Vanishing Frog: An Ecological Mystery* (St. Martin's Press, 1994)
SCHOOL SPIRIT

DEVERA PINE, Freelance science writer and editor based in Oley, PA
ASK THE SCIENTIST: PAST, PRESENT, AND FUTURE
AVIATION

FREDERIK POHL, Science-fiction writer, editor, and critic; author, *Mining the Oort* (Ballantine, 1993), *Stopping at Slowyear* (Bantam Books, 1992), and *Gateway* (Ballantine, 1987)
THE MAGIC OF SCIENCE FICTION

ABIGAIL W. POLEK, Freelance writer and editor based in Pennsylvania
SCIENCE EDUCATION

BRADLEY E. SCHAEFER, Astronomer, Yale University, New Haven, CT
ECLIPSES THAT SHAPED HISTORY

GOVERT SCHILLING, Science writer based in the Netherlands
THE ASTRONOMICAL NAME GAME

SETH SHOSTAK, Public programs scientist, Search for Extraterrestrial Intelligence (SETI) Institute, Mountain View, CA
CRACKS IN HEAVEN'S VAULT

NANCY SHUTE, Freelance writer based in Washington, DC
LIFE FOR LEFTIES

P.J. SKERRETT, Contributing editor, *Popular Science*; contributing writer, *Technology Review*
THE TIES THAT BIND

DAVA SOBEL, Investigative freelance journalist based in East Hampton, NY
SECRETS OF THE RINGS

JANE ELLEN STEVENS, Freelance wildlife and environment writer based in Northern California
BAMBOO IS BACK
ZEBRAS IN TURMOIL

DOUG STEWART, Freelance journalist based in Massachusetts
FIRES OF LIFE

JAY STULLER, Freelance writer based in San Francisco, CA
ON THE BEACH

FRANK M. SZIVOS, Freelance medical writer based in Fairfield, CT
VIRTUAL SURGERY: THE NEXT DIMENSION

JENNY TESAR, Freelance science and medical writer based in Bethel, CT; author, *Scientific Crime Investigation* (Watts, 1991) and *Global Warming* (Facts on File, 1991)
THE BALD EAGLE SOARS YET AGAIN
ASK THE SCIENTIST: ANIMALS AND PLANTS
HEALTH AND DISEASE

SCOTT WEIDENSAUL, Contributing editor, *Country Journal*; columnist, *The Philadelphia Inquirer*; author, *Mountains of the Heart: A Natural History of the Appalachians* (Fulcrum Publishing, 1994)
WOLF SONG

PETER S. WELLS, Professor of anthropology, University of Minnesota, Minneapolis, MN
ANTHROPOLOGY
ARCHAEOLOGY

JO ANN WHITE, Freelance writer and editor based in New Jersey
BOOK REVIEWS

ROBERT WISNER, Professor, Iowa State University; coeditor, *Marketing for Farmers*; author, *World Food Trade and U.S. Agriculture*
AGRICULTURE

CONTENTS

FEATURES

HUMAN SCIENCES 142

PAST, PRESENT, AND FUTURE 174

Features

Physical Sciences 216

Technology 248

REVIEWS

FEATURES

ANIMALS AND PLANTS

■ MOST DOLPHINS, INCLUDING THOSE AT LEFT, PASS THEIR DAYS NEAR THE SURFACE OF THE WATER. AS MAMMALS, DOLPHINS MUST BREATHE AIR EVERY FEW MINUTES. THIS REQUIREMENT PREVENTS THEM FROM CONSISTENTLY SWIMMING FAR BELOW THE SURFACE, ALTHOUGH SCIENTISTS HAVE RECORDED DOLPHINS MAKING RAPID DIVES TO DEPTHS GREATER THAN 1,000 FEET.

CONTENTS

THE BALD EAGLE SOARS

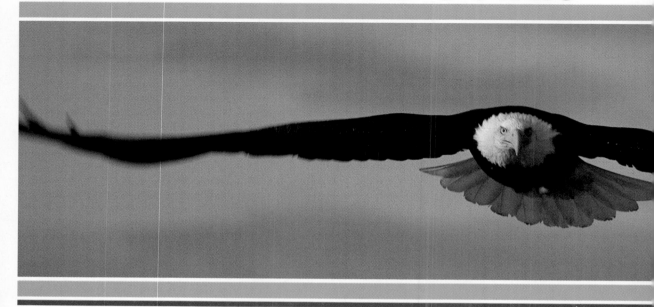

by Jenny Tesar

"There he goes!" The crowd falls silent as a magnificent bald eagle swoops down from high in a fir tree and snatches a perch from the rushing water below. Then, in a matter of seconds, with the hapless fish firmly secured in its talons, the eagle takes off again, this time in search of a private place where the giant bird can enjoy its meal in private.

Hidden in an unheated cabin, dozens of people watch the action through binoculars. So far on this wintry afternoon early in 1995, they have spotted 11 bald eagles near a dam on the Housatonic River in Connecticut. Some of the eagles soar high into the sky, while others play chasing games, locking their talons in midair. Still others stand on the river's edge, watching for perch, alewives, and other fish to surface. The presence of these eagles is a thrilling spectacle—a sight that for many years had disappeared, not only from the Housatonic River, but from most of the United States.

Historically, bald eagles were native to every U.S. state except Hawaii. At the time that Europeans began settling North America, perhaps as many as 75,000 bald eagles lived in what today are the Lower 48. But by 1963, researchers counted only 417 breeding pairs in that same area. Bird lovers and conservationists feared that one of the nation's proudest symbols would become extinct.

Fortunately, thanks to the collective efforts of government agencies, wildlife managers, and concerned citizens, bald eagles have come back from the brink to stage a dramatic recovery. By the spring of 1995, about 4,500 breeding pairs were tallied in the Lower 48; counting immature birds, the total population numbered around 25,000. This recovery demonstrates that humans can indeed learn, in the words of a Dakota Indian prayer, "to walk the soft earth as relatives to all that lives."

AGENTS OF DECLINE

Like every other member of the animal kingdom, bald eagles have a particular home, or habitat, to which they are best adapted. If that habitat is changed, it may no longer provide the resources needed by the species to survive. Animal habitats can be threatened by numerous forces. Some conditions, such as devastating storms and lengthy dry spells, are caused by Mother Nature. But in today's

YET AGAIN

world, some of the greatest menaces to animal habitats are created by humans.

One human activity that greatly harmed bald eagles was the destruction of nesting and wintering habitats. Bald eagles most commonly live in forested areas close to rivers and lakes, using old, tall trees near the water for nesting sites and perches. Many potential nesting habitats were lost as humans cut down forests to obtain wood for lumber, papermaking, fuel, and other uses. Further losses were suffered as large forests were cleared to make room for farms, housing tracts, industrial parks, roads, and other developments.

Noise created by human activities also endangered these fragile bird populations. Bald eagles are easily frightened; they do not like human contact, and avoid it whenever possible. If people disturb their habitats during nesting

The bald eagle is as much admired by Native American groups (right) as it was by the Founding Fathers, who declared the bird the U.S. national symbol in 1782. Today, the eagle's recovery from near extinction testifies to the success of the Endangered Species Act.

season—with such disruptions as snowmobiles, campsites, or construction—the eagles abandon their nests, a move that jeopardizes the entire reproductive cycle. Without heat from a brooding parent, the developing embryos in the deserted eggs die.

A number of other factors played into the bald eagle's decline. A surprising number have been electrocuted by flying into high-voltage power lines. Many more died of poisoning—either after feeding on the carcasses of wolves and coyotes that had been killed by strychnine bait or after eating waterfowl or game animals that had been brought down by lead shot. Others fell prey to human hunters, particularly during migration. Some eagles were killed accidentally, while others were shot because people mistakenly believed that the birds attacked farm animals.

CHEMICAL WARFARE

By far, the most catastrophic threat to bald eagles emerged in the late 1940s, when the pesticide DDT (dichlorodiphenyltrichloroethane) was introduced. DDT sprayed on farms and forests slowly seeped into groundwater and eventually into lakes and rivers, where it ultimately contaminated aquatic food chains. Further contamination occurred when marshes and coastal areas were sprayed

The bald eagle derives its name from the snowy white feathers of its head. Typically, a young eagle (second from right) does not develop its adult plumage until it is more than two years old.

thin, flaky shells that broke easily under the weight of the brooding parent. Even when eggs survived, pesticide residues often poisoned the embryos.

PCBs (polychlorinated biphenyls) were another group of chemicals that disrupted the eagles' hormonal system. These industrial chemicals, used in electrical transformers and capacitors, among other applications, entered the environment through leaks, spills, and vaporization. The PCBs built up in fish populations that were preyed upon by eagles, and then the chemicals caused birth defects and sterility in the birds.

RESPONDING TO A CRISIS

By the 1920s, years before the development of DDT and PCBs, forward-looking conservationists recognized that bald-eagle populations were declining as a result of human activities. As early as 1921, for example, an article titled "Threatened Extinction of the Bald Eagle" appeared in an issue of the journal *Ecology*. However, it wasn't until 1940 that the U.S. Congress passed the Bald Eagle Protection Act, which prohibited the possession, killing, and harming of these birds.

Despite such legislative efforts, the species continued to decline. In 1962, biologist Rachel Carson published *Silent Spring*; this book warned of the dangers of using pesticides indiscriminately, and described the lethal effect of DDT on egg production and chick survival. The book caused an uproar. Carson and her assertions were savagely maligned by chemical manufacturers and their supporters. Reviewing the book for *Chemical World News*, George C. Decker, an economic entomologist with the Illinois Natural History Survey, wrote, "I regard it as science fiction, to be read in the same way that the TV program *Twilight Zone* is to be

with DDT to control the mosquito population. The DDT was absorbed by protists and other small organisms. When fish and other animals fed on these organisms, the DDT was concentrated in their tissues. As bald eagles ate the contaminated animals, the DDT accumulated in their bodies. Rising levels of DDT did not kill the eagles directly, but instead interfered with their ability to reproduce. Absorbed DDT disrupts a mother eagle's hormonal system by inhibiting the production of calcium, a critical element in the manufacture of eggshells. As a result, some eggs were laid without shells; many others had

watched." Physician William B. Bean, writing in *Archives of Internal Medicine*, dismissed the book as "so much hogwash."

This criticism notwithstanding, many biologists were quick to support Carson, and added to the wealth of evidence presented in *Silent Spring*. Public concern was aroused, and soon government committees began holding hearings on the use of pesticides. In 1972, most uses of DDT were banned in the United States. Other contaminants also were phased out. PCBs were banned in 1978, and lead shot for hunting was replaced by steel shot.

The effects of banning these contaminants on water quality and wildlife have been dramatic. For example, according to the U.S. Environmental Protection Agency (EPA), levels of PCBs in trout in Lake Michigan fell from 23 parts per million (ppm) in 1974 to 3 ppm in 1994. Toxic residues in bald eagles and other birds of prey have also dropped significantly, and these birds are again producing eggs with normal shells.

Bald eagles also benefited when Congress enacted the Endangered Species Act in 1973. The act was designed to protect and restore populations of animals and plants whose survival is in jeopardy. Three primary mechanisms are used to accomplish this goal: species are listed as endangered (in danger of extinction) or threatened (likely to become endangered in the foreseeable future); habitat critical to a species' survival, including breeding and shelter areas, is conserved and improved; and a step-by-step recovery plan is developed.

On February 14, 1978, the bald eagle was listed as endangered in all but five of the lower 48 states; in Wisconsin, Michigan, Minnesota, Oregon, and Washington, it was listed as threatened. These designations publicized the bird's plight, influenced policy decisions, and made funds available.

A VARIETY OF INITIATIVES

One of the first steps undertaken under the Endangered Species Act was to find and map the locations of as many bald-eagle nests as possible. A protective zone was established around each nest: no logging, motor vehicles, or foot trails were allowed within 300 feet (90 meters) of a nest. For another 300 feet, logging was permitted only in winter, after the eagles had migrated south.

The expansion of protected lands, including the creation of wildlife refuges, preserved critical habitats, not only of bald eagles, but also of many other species. By 1994, the U.S. National Wildlife Refuge System contained roughly 91 million acres (37 million hectares) of secure habitat. This land included more than 310,000 acres (125,000 hectares) acquired specifically for the protection of listed species. Refuge staff carry out a variety of activities designed to aid species

The bald eagle is a formidable predator. In a typical hunting expedition, the bird uses its keen vision to spot prey thousands of feet below. Then, in a matter of seconds, the eagle swoops down from the sky and captures the hapless victim in its razor-sharp talons.

Bald eagles mate for life. Typically, a pair builds an enormous nest, or aerie, on a cliff or treetop (above). Year after year, the pair returns to the same nest, expanding it each time with sticks and grass.

disappeared. In these projects, young eaglets are reared by humans, then released when they appear to be ready to survive in the wild. Projects are judged to be successful when a wild breeding population is reestablished. The rationale and techniques of captive breeding can vary widely. In some cases, eggs are laid by captive eagles that are unable to survive in the wild. In other circumstances, eggs are removed from wild-eagle nests and hatched at a remote facility; if this is done at the right time, the parents will lay another clutch in the same season. Researchers have learned that incubating the eggs at an appropriate temperature and carefully monitoring the chicks as they learn to interact with one another and adjust to the outside environment are critical elements to the success of such programs.

A CHANGE OF STATUS

By the early 1990s, evidence was mounting that bald eagles were on the road to recovery. For the first time in the 20th century, Oklahoma had two active nests. In Virginia—which, in 1977, had 32 nesting pairs that produced 18 young—researchers in 1993 counted 151 pairs that produced 172 young.

recovery. For example, at Maryland's Blackwater National Wildlife Refuge, trappers are paid to kill nutrias—big brown South American rodents that, since their introduction into the United States, have been destroying wetlands. The nutria carcasses are then left in the wetlands to be found and eaten by bald eagles.

Other steps to protect bald eagles have been initiated. For example, high-voltage power poles and lines have been modified to reduce the number of eagles and other birds of prey killed by electrocution. Enforcement of protective laws has also been increased. People convicted of hunting bald eagles can face one-year prison terms and fines of $50,000.

Captive-breeding projects in at least 17 states have enabled wildlife managers to reintroduce bald eagles into historic habitats from which they had

The species began its spectacular recovery when the government banned several types of insecticides. Scientists have been able to follow this resurgence by banding young birds (above), a tracking technique that also provides considerable information about the eagle's habits. A banded nestling (left) can supply scientists with data for years.

Bald Facts About the Bald Eagle

The bald eagle (*Haliaeetus leucocephalus*) is a massive bird with a dark-brown body, a distinctive snow-white head and tail, and a great hooked bright-yellow beak. The two sexes have similar coloring, but females are larger and heavier than males. Fully grown males are 30 to 35 inches (76 to 89 centimeters) long and weigh roughly 9 pounds (4 kilograms); females are 34 to 43 inches (86 to 109 centimeters) long and weigh between 10 and 14 pounds (4.5 and 6.4 kilograms). Wingspans average 6 to 7 feet (about 2 meters).

The eyes of an eagle are among the biggest, relative to body size, of all land animals. Vision is the eagle's most important sense. It is so keen—about seven times sharper than human vision—that an eagle flying 2 miles (3.2 kilometers) above the ground can spot a rabbit moving through grass.

The plumage of male and female bald eagles is virtually identical. The female tends to be larger, however, sometimes weighing as much as 5 pounds more than her mate.

In addition to preying on small mammals such as rabbits and squirrels, bald eagles eat waterfowl and carrion, including roadkill. But their preferred food is fish. Much of the bald eagle's diet consists of dead or weakened fish gathered from the surface and shores of rivers and lakes. Eagles also are pirates that steal fish from other birds, especially ospreys. After an osprey catches a fish, it flies upward to a perch on which to dine. But if an eagle spies the flying osprey, it will give chase and harass the osprey until the fish is dropped. The eagle catches the fish in midair, leaving the osprey to renew its search for food.

Because fish comprise the bulk of their diet, bald eagles usually make their home in timbered areas along—or close to—shorelines. In warm climes, such as Florida, they remain in one locale all year; in northern areas, they migrate when their local waters are frozen over. The original breeding range stretches from central Alaska and northern Canada south to Baja California and the Gulf of Mexico. The wintering range is almost as large, beginning in southern Alaska and southern Canada and going south through the rest of the breeding range.

Bald eagles mate with a single companion for life. Their bulky nest, built high in a large tree, can be used for decades. Each breeding season, the eagles add more twigs, pine needles, mosses, and other materials. Eventually the nest may be 8 feet (2.4 meters) across, 12 feet (3.7 meters) deep, and weigh close to 2 tons!

A newly hatched eaglet is covered with a whitish down. The chick acquires its first brown plumage before it is able to fly. During the first four to five years, the plumage and bill remain brownish. Then, as the bird matures, its head and tail become white, and the bill turns yellow. Bald eagles enjoy a long life span—30 years or more.

In the summer of 1994, the U.S. Department of the Interior proposed that bald eagles be reclassified as threatened, but no longer endangered, in all parts of the Lower 48 except for sections of the Southwest, where the birds would remain classified as endangered. In celebration of this historic declassification, a female bald eagle named Hope, who had been nursed back to health after suffering a broken wing, was released at Blackwater National Wildlife Refuge. Mollie Beattie, director of the U.S. Fish and Wildlife Service, said: "As we honor our nation's independence on July 4, it is fitting to celebrate the return of the bird that symbolizes our country's freedom and fierce pride. All Americans can take pride in the eagle's recovery because it represents a fulfillment of our nation's commitment to protect our wild heritage."

More good news came later, when scientists reported that the bald-eagle population in the Southwest is not closed, or totally separate from other populations, as had been previously believed. Instead, researchers learned, there is some gene flow between bald eagles in and out of the region. These new findings precipitated proposals to upgrade the status of the Southwestern population to threatened. A final decision was expected sometime in 1995.

THE BATTLE CONTINUES

The bald eagle's new status under the Endangered Species Act indicates that the bird no longer is in immediate danger of extinction. Nonetheless, government officials stress that the species retains all of its legal protections under the act. Though conservationists expect the practical impact of the upgrading to be minimal, they have expressed concerns that enforcement of safeguards—particularly those against logging and development—may become less stringent.

Environmentalists also point out that although the bald eagle's future appears much brighter, many of the threats that gave the bird its endangered classification still remain. Illegal shootings of bald eagles remain common. The nation's steadily growing human population continues to introduce new threats to bald-eagle habitats. Traces of DDT continue to be found in eagle tissues, especially in the Southwest, where enormous amounts of the pesticide were sprayed on cotton fields. PCB residues in the mud at the bottom of the Great Lakes continue to enter food chains and work their way upward, in increasingly lethal concentrations.

Despite strong public support for the Endangered Species Act and other environmental programs, efforts are being made to weaken these protections. Loggers, property owners eager to develop their land, and other critics of environmental policies have strong allies in Congress and state legislatures. Each time that environmental laws face reauthorization and each time that funding for environmental programs is proposed, a contentious battle ensues.

We humans were responsible for the bald eagle's decline. We deserve much of the credit for the bird's escape from extinction. And we hold the bald eagle's future in our hands.

It is up to us to ensure that the bird that symbolizes America's freedom continues to fly free across the nation's skies. ◿

The success of captive-breeding programs has helped bald-eagle populations remain at a sustainable level. Most of the eagles returned to the wild have adapted well to their natural environment.

BUILDERS
OF THE ANIMAL WORLD

by Linda J. Brown

They design and build without the benefit of blueprints, hammers, or a single nail. Yet their creations are often complex, elegant, and precise. Some, like the beavers' dam or the 20-foot (6-meter)-high termites' mound, boldly declare themselves; others, such as the trap-door spider's underground burrow or the hummingbird's delicate 1-inch (2.5-centimeter)-wide nest, often go unnoticed. Here is a sampling of nature's finest builders.

BUSY AS A BEAVER

The largest rodent in the United States, the North American beaver *(Castor canadensis)*, which can weigh up to 70 pounds (38 kilograms), truly deserves its reputation as a master builder. "With the exception of humans, a single beaver can modify its environment more dramatically than any individual species in North America," writes the Wyoming Game and Fish Department. The instrument of this modification is, of course, the beaver's dam.

Master engineers, beavers redesign the landscape by building dams across streams. Constructed of sticks, mud, and rocks, the dams block the flow of water and create ponds where the beavers will live. Dams vary considerably in size, ranging from a few feet to several hundred feet in length, and 3 feet (1 meter) to 10 feet (3 meters) in height.

To build a dam, beavers drag branches to the selected site and lay them side to side, parallel to the current—with the tops faced downstream and the thickest ends pointed upstream. Often branch ends are thrust into the stream bottom to anchor the structure. Next the beavers pile on rocks, mud, and leaves; pack it all down; and fill in any leaks. "Then they'll start another layer. As the water rises, it serves as a level for their workmanship so they can build above the waterline,"

Animal builders have evolved the skills needed to help them adapt to their environment. Some zoological creations, like the termite mound above, are truly towering achievements.

The beaver (inset) is the master engineer of the animal kingdom. Using sticks, mud, and other simple building materials, the creature essentially redesigns the landscape, erecting dams (above) and building elaborate lodges.

says Bruce H. Smith, fisheries biologist and beaver expert at the Salmon/Challis National Forest in Salmon, Idaho. "That's how the dams end up being so level across the top." Smith notes that beavers are resourceful creatures, incorporating such unusual materials into their dams as cornstalks, sagebrush, cardboard boxes, and other various forms of debris pitched into creeks.

Benefits to the ecosystem from dams abound. "Beavers transform the whole bottom of the valley floor, turning it into a floodplain. That in turn affects the form, type, and rate of succession of the plant community. And all those niches created by the plant community constitute that much more of a diverse habitat for an entire host of other animals," says Smith. The ponds and channels created by dams also cause water tables to rise, slow spring runoff, provide new fish and bird habitats, and reduce soil erosion along stream banks. Beavers do not build dams if the water level remains high enough throughout the year for their den entrances to remain underwater.

When living on a large river or a stream with high banks, beavers usually dig dens and a network of tunnels in the bank. In shallow ponds, beavers build island lodges. Made of sticks cut to size and mud that cements the wood together, these dome-shaped structures may be as large as 30 feet (9 meters) in diameter, and may extend as much as 5 feet (1.5 meters) above the water. Able to easily withstand the weight of a human or even a bear, the lodge has one or two underwater entrances that open to a chamber above the water level where the beavers live. Family groups, which consist of parents and the young of the past two years, join forces to cut trees, build and repair dams and lodges, and store branches for their winter food supply.

STEP INTO MY PARLOR . . .

Although a spider's web appears fragile compared to a beaver's dam, spider silk is the world's strongest natural fiber for its weight. "Spiders use silk, not only to make webs for prey capture, but they use silk to make homes for themselves to live in; to line their burrows;

and to cover their eggs," says George Uetz, Ph.D., professor of biological sciences at the University of Cincinnati in Ohio.

Many of us are most familiar with the wheel-type "orb web." But that classic spider-web design does not even begin to describe the variety of webs woven by the world's 34,000 spider species.

The familiar orb web does, however, beautifully illustrate the spider's sophisticated handiwork. The web's characteristic feature is its symmetry: lines radiating from a central hub with a spiral overlay. The web contains both dry and sticky threads spun from different silk glands, which open through organs called spinnerets on the spider's abdomen. After setting up a foundation with the dry threads, the spider fills in the space with the sticky silken spokes that will snag its insect meals. When the hapless prey enters the nest, the vibrations caused by its struggle to escape are detected by the spider, which immediately rushes to the trapped creature and injects it with poison. The spider may sit in the center hub portion, waiting for its next victim, or it may hide outside the web (sometimes in a nest of several leaves tied together and lined with

silk), holding on to a signal line connected to the hub. Some orb weavers repair torn sections, while others simply weave a new web—a job that can take less than an hour!

The intriguing trap-door spider spends most of its life underground in a tube-shaped tunnel, which it digs and then coats with earth, saliva, and a silken lining. The tunnel opening remains closed with a strong, hinged lid made from layers of silk and soil particles. The lid design varies depending on species. Ranging from paper-thin to corklike, the lid may have edges that are smooth, scalloped, or toothed. Camouflaged on the outside with dirt and vegetation to blend with the surroundings, the trapdoor fits so tightly that rain and light cannot penetrate. At night when it hunts, the spider sits stone-still with the door ajar. When an insect passes by, the spider pounces and drags it inside.

Most spiders do not interact socially, although notable exceptions exist. *Metepeira incrassata*, Mexican spiders that Dr. Uetz has been studying, live in huge nets that are really solitary webs (numbering into the thousands) joined together. Often strung between trees or run along power lines, these interconnected webs can cover a distance longer than a football field. The structure shares a single framework, making it like an apartment complex with common walls. "Each spider still sits on its own web, has its own retreat, captures its own prey, and interacts somewhat aggressively with its neighbors, but they all cooperate in the maintenance of the common framework," says Dr. Uetz. *Anelosium eximius*, a spider of South and Central America, takes communal living a

The silken masterpiece (above) spun by the orb web spider is notable as much for its symmetry as it is for the speed with which it is built. Certain communal spiders weave elaborate interconnected webs (right) and then cooperate in the structure's maintenance.

step further. Thousands of family groups live in a huge net, which they jointly maintain; the creatures also cooperate in capturing prey.

FUNGUS FARMERS

Ants, with their highly developed social structure, exemplify community spirit. Perhaps none fashions a more unique nest than *Atta*, a genus of leaf-cutter ants found throughout Central and South America. Their nest structure and very existence revolve around their symbiotic relationship with fungi—an ancient alliance that began more than 50 million years ago.

With the precision of a drill team, the ants file out in columns to forage for leaves. They cut off crescent-shaped sections and return with them to their subterranean nest. There they use the pieces of leaves to make compost upon which fungus will grow. The ants carefully tend these fungus gardens and farm them for the tender fungal shoots, which they and their larvae then eat.

Nests begin quite small, with a queen and her mate digging a cavity perhaps 6 inches (15 centimeters) deep. The queen carries a bit of fungus from her parent nest to start her own garden. (Recent research published in the journal *Science* suggests that some *Atta* species have passed along and cultivated the same fungus for 25 million years.) The queen and male produce a brood, which develop into the soldier and worker ants of the colony. After three to five years of continued expansion, the leaf-cutter ants have created a massive nest, which can extend to a depth of 20 feet (6 meters), and can support more than 5 million residents. "There can be hundreds, if not thousands, of fungus chambers, each one about the size of a head of cabbage," says Ted Schultz of Cornell University,

Waiting to ambush its next victim, the trap-door spider (above) peeks from beneath the camouflaged lid of its silk-lined burrow.

Ithaca, New York, coauthor of the *Science* article. Interconnected by passageways, the fungus chambers are also linked to large waste chambers (10 times the size of the fungus chambers) around the periphery of the nest. "Every day, big portions of the spent fungus are removed and carted off to these waste chambers," says Schultz. Constant excavation also produces mounds of soil on the forest floor that may rise waist-high and take up an area as large as 20 feet (6 meters) square.

The success of these nests depends on finely tuned division of labor. "*Atta*, of all the ant species, has one of the most pronounced ranges of size of workers. The very smallest ones are only a few hundredths of an inch long, and the biggest ones are maybe four-tenths of an inch [1 centimeter] long," says Schultz. The largest ants, the nest defenders, sport strong jaw muscles; their bite can draw blood. "The only time you'll see these soldiers outside the nest is if there's an intruder interfering with the foraging columns. Then the soldiers will go out and fight," says Schultz. The second-largest workers, approximately housefly-sized, gather and cut leaves, trekking on paths kept scrupulously clean of debris. "These little highways are maybe 4 inches [10 centimeters] wide, and they go off in various directions into the forest with ants streaming out and coming back on them," says Schultz. In the nest, the pieces of leaves are passed to smaller and smaller ants. Each ant slices the leaf sections into tinier pieces. The smallest ants deposit the leaf pulp in the fungus gardens along with fecal droplets that contain enzymes to help the fungus "digest" the pulp. These ants also weed out foreign molds and bacteria, feed the ant larvae, and move the larvae around the nest.

TERMITE TERRITORY

Fungus gardens are not exclusive to ants. Various termite species produce fungus gardens using the wood that they eat and excrete in their nests. The fungus grows on these manure beds and in turn nourishes the termites. Nests of the large fungus-growing termites in Africa often stand over 6 feet (1.8 meters) high in conical shapes or with irregular vertical peaks.

While many termites build their nests in trees, underground, or right in the wood that they consume, the mound-building termites construct the showiest, most amazing nests. Built of soil, sand grains, and partially digested wood, which cements everything together, the mounds can be exceptionally hard and durable. "There are little mushroom-shaped ones and larger ones resembling columns, organ pipes, pyramids, steeples, and miniature mountain ranges. A termite hill may be more than 12 feet [3.7 meters] wide at the base and may tower some 20 feet [6 meters] into the air. On a scale of relative size, a human-made pyramid would have to be about 2.5 miles [4 kilometers] high," writes Walter Linsenmaier in his book *Insects of the World*.

The compass termites (*Amitermes meridionalis*) of Australia, for instance, build tall, wedgelike nests that reach a height of 13 feet (4 meters) and a length of 10 feet (3 meters), but are only a few inches thick. They position their mounds so that the long axis always is aligned north-south to absorb the hot rays of the midday Sun; the long, broad sides face east-west to soak up the cooler morning and evening Sun. "A traveler can quickly find his bearings by looking at the direction of these mounds," writes Karl von Frisch in his book *Animal Architecture*.

Inside termite mounds, construction styles vary by species, but all contain a series of complicated galleries, passageways, and nurseries that include some kind of ventilation system, whether it is ducts, tubelike chimneys, extremely porous walls, or more-complex designs. Most possess a royal cell with a special chamber for the queen and king. "The royal cell is normally about the size of a tennis ball or softball. It is very thick and heavily reinforced with small openings that other termites enter and leave from. Embedded within the royal cell is the royal chamber that houses the reproductives," says

The leaf-cutter ant (above) gathers bits of leaves for use in preparing a bed for a fungus garden (below), which the ants cultivate. The symbiotic relationship between the two species has existed for millions of years.

Barbara Thorne, assistant professor of entomology at the University of Maryland in College Park. "If an anteater, armadillo, or aardvark with sharp mammalian claws came along, it would be difficult for it to penetrate the royal cell and kill the reproductive element of the colony."

Built to last, a termite mound can remain active for several hundred years. "The lineage," says Thorne, "may continue within the same castle, which they pass on like an estate from generation to generation."

WINGED BUILDERS

Avian nests certainly do not endure for hundreds of years, but what they lack in longevity they make up for in incredible variety, ranging from simple scrapes in the ground to woven works of art.

Most birds try hard to keep their nests inconspicuous. This is true for the pied-billed grebe, an aquatic bird found in ponds, marshes, and lakes throughout most of the United States. This bird makes a floating nest of soggy, rotting vegetation, and anchors it to neighboring plants. The heap of brown sticks, reeds, and weeds blends quite well with the surroundings. Besides being nicely camouflaged, this type of nest serves other purposes. "Because the vegetation is rotting, it's sort of like a compost pile, and it's part of what warms the eggs," says Joan Dunning, author of *Secrets of the Nest*. Also, should the water level rise or fall, the grebe's nest can go with the flow without danger of being flooded.

Temperature is also a key consideration of the tiny ruby-throated hummingbird when she builds her spongy, padded nest.

A male weaverbird (bottom left) performs acrobatics in an attempt to attract a female to his intricately woven nest. In the large breeding colony below, many weaverbird nests dangle from a single tree.

The minuscule structure is designed to provide maximum warmth. "The female hummingbird builds her nest from materials that sound almost fairylike: over a core of bud scales bound to the branch with spider silk, she tamps milkweed fluff, fern down, thistledown, and fireweed into a contoured lining. The ruby-throat covers the outside

of her nest with gray-green lichens, which she binds into place with more spider silk and the web of tent caterpillars," writes Dunning. The nest affords a tight fit for her and her young, but the spider silk allows it to expand as the babies grow.

The many species of weaverbirds (family Ploceidae), found mainly in Africa and southern Asia, take weaving to an elevated level. Closed at the top, their nests hang from tree branches with entrances on the side or on the bottom at the end of a long flight tube. They work more or less like a basket weaver with grass blades or palm fronds, tying loose ends into the existing nest's mesh. They often breed in colonies, and it's not unusual to see numerous nests in one large tree. Other species of weaverbirds build roofed communal nests covered with entrances on the bottom. "They build this big nest of grasses that can reach a diameter of 16 feet [5 meters] or so, and they'll have 20 or 30 pairs nesting in that," says Martha Fisher, education assistant at the Cornell University Laboratory of Ornithology, Ithaca, New York.

WHO IS THE BEST BUILDER?

All animals—including human beings—are equipped with special talents that assist them in survival. Whether the result of intellect or instinct, expert construction skills allow animals and humans to successfully adapt to their environment.

Animals build for the same reasons that people do—to obtain food, to provide shelter, and to afford protection for their young and themselves. The tools and building materials may be different, but the form and function are the same. After all, there are more similarities than differences between a fisherman's net and a spider's web or between a bustling beehive and an urban apartment building.

So the next time you pass by a spider's web or spot a bird's nest, stop, take a closer look, and appreciate the achievements of these unassuming master builders.

Wolf Song

by Scott Weidensaul

I first heard the song of a wolf on a quiet evening in north-central Quebec, where the spruce forest, spangled with shimmering lakes and bogs, runs to the horizon and is empty of all things human.

Back at the camp after a long day of fishing, I sat on an overturned boat and listened to the loons as the Sun set and the darkness deepened. A few stars shone through the murk; a great horned owl hooted, mink frogs hammered out their courtship calls, and, in the shallows, I could hear the swish and swirl of pike chasing schools of minnows.

Then the wolf started, and it was as though every other sound ceased. I was electrified; my ears heard only the howl, coming from a point of land maybe half a mile away, rolling clear and insistent across the water. A second wolf joined the chorus, then a third, weaving harmonies that made the hairs on my neck stand erect.

Unless you are fortunate enough to live in a very wild place, you have to travel a long way, as I did, to hear the twilight chorus of the wolf. It wasn't always like this. Wolves were once found in almost every corner of North America, a preeminence that began to erode as the first Europeans arrived with guns and a bad attitude.

The eerie howl of the gray wolf, once heard throughout most of the United States, has since become the clarion call of an endangered species. Fortunately, the population and public standing of this often misunderstood creature are beginning to enjoy better days.

TWO SPECIES

North America has two species of wolves: the gray, or timber, wolf *(Canis lupus)* and the smaller red wolf *(C. rufus)*. Grays—which can be divided into more than 20 North American subspecies—best fit our mental image of a wolf, with their grizzled coat, broad muzzle, and great size (males of the largest Alaskan races may weigh 130 pounds [59 kilograms], with one giant tipping the scales at 175 pounds [79 kilograms]). They are lanky animals, long in the leg and built for running, able to maintain a ground-eating lope for miles, although they are not especially fast except in short bursts. A gray wolf's feet are enormous, serving as snowshoes in winter to spread its

The large paws of the gray wolf provide the species with great traction and agility in a variety of weather conditions, including snow and ice.

Wolves are skillful and hardworking big-game hunters. Wolf packs could not bring down such large animals as moose, caribou, and musk oxen (below) without precise teamwork.

The Social Animal

In the wild, most gray wolves live in packs—small family groups that usually consist of a mated pair and their grown offspring from the past several years. The dominant (or alpha) male runs the show, while his mate effectively cows the females in the pack. Ordinarily, only the alpha pair breed, producing an average of five or six pups.

Not surprisingly, pack size seems to be at least partially tied to the size of the prey the wolves hunt—a pack usually consists of only six or so in regions where deer are the main food, but 12 or more where the pack must tackle moose. Red wolves, on the other hand, generally hunt in pairs with just the offspring of the year. As social as the wolves of a pack may be with one another, they will attack outsiders infringing on their territory, driving them off or killing them. (That territory can range from 7 to 5,200 square miles [18 to 13,468 square kilometers]—the average being 50 square miles [144 square

Most wolves live in cohesive family units called packs. Members hunt, defend territory, raise pups, and socialize together.

kilometers]—depending on the amount of available prey and the time of the year.)

Wolves have a large vocabulary of body language and vocalizations. Tail position—high in dominant wolves, low or tucked in subordinates—is one method, as is the famous howl, which wolves can reportedly hear at distances of nearly 7 miles (11 kilometers). Howling may strengthen pack unity, and it serves as a territorial marker against intruders.

weight across snow and ice. Once, hiking along a braided stream in central Alaska, I came across the trail of a large (probably male) wolf. The paw prints, toes only slightly splayed from running, were nearly 6 inches (15 centimeters) across.

Smaller and slimmer than gray wolves, reds are much more coyotelike in their proportions, and usually weigh 50 or 60 pounds (22 or 27 kilograms). The coat usually has rich chestnut and russet tones on the head, back, and legs, although a black form was once common in the bottomland forests of the Southeast. In keeping with their size, red

wolves stick to small prey. They are able to take deer, but are more likely to hunt raccoons, opossums, muskrats, rabbits, and ground-dwelling birds.

PERSECUTION

In centuries past, it was hard to find a place that did not have wolves. The gray wolf was especially far-ranging—after humans, in fact, it was the world's most widespread land mammal, found on every continent save Antarctica and Australia. But its fall in North America was swift. One of the first acts of the Pilgrims of the Massachusetts

Gray-wolf pups form strong, often lifelong, bonds with their mother. The playful roughhousing that fills much of a pup's first months helps prepare the young wolf for the imminent and formidable business of predation.

Bay Colony was to set a bounty on wolves, and the persecution only gathered steam from there. By the beginning of the 20th century, grays were eliminated in the East, except for a few holdouts in the upper Great Lakes region, and, by the 1930s, they were gone from the West. Even national parks were denied them, on the grounds that they endangered so-called good animals like elk and deer. Meanwhile, red wolves were retreating to a few inaccessible swamps and thickets where Texas and Louisiana meet the Gulf. By World War II, the Lower 48 was virtually wolfless.

The reasons for such fierce persecution revolved around what wolves eat—or what we think they eat. Grays are hunters of large mammals—deer, caribou, Dall and bighorn sheep, elk, and moose. They do take livestock, usually only when native game is scarce (in populated areas, they will kill domestic dogs, perhaps seeing them as territorial rivals). But fears for human safety seem completely unjustified. The rare rabid wolf aside, no unprovoked attacks on humans have ever been documented on this continent.

The protection of game animals is often given as a reason to kill wolves, but this, too, rings hollow. Wolves, like most predators, are opportunists, and an adult gray wolf won't turn up its nose at a ground squirrel or lemming.

A wolf's greatest weapon against prey is its cooperative behavior. Hunting in groups, as early humans discovered, makes it possible to bring down animals far beyond the ability of a single individual. A lone wolf would stand no chance against even an immature moose, which can set up a lethal barrage of kicks. But a wolf pack will have some members feint to draw a moose's attention while others dart in to tear at its hindquarters.

Not that packs can slaughter at will—far from it. Studies on Isle Royale in Lake Superior have shown that more than 90 percent of the time, a moose responds so vigorously to an attack that the pack breaks it off almost immediately. Only when the wolves sense a weakness do they press in, wearing the moose down over a period of hours or even days.

Our beliefs about wolf predation have undergone some radical rethinking over the years, from perceiving them as efficient game killers that had to be eliminated to protect deer or caribou herds to seeing wolves as linchpins in a delicately balanced ecosystem that kept prey from overpopulating and stripping the land. Now that view has been replaced. Rather than controlling prey populations, wolves appear to be at their mercy, skimming the excess, but usually having little effect on their overall abundance.

BETTER TIMES AHEAD

Wolves' fortunes began to improve only when legal protection came to their aid in the 1960s and 1970s. By that time, outside of Alaska and Canada, where they remained common, gray wolves were found only in a small area of Minnesota and Michigan. To the south, the remaining handful of red wolves, whose race once roamed the Southeast and Gulf Coast, were being genetically swamped by invading coyotes, which were hybridizing them out of existence. In desperation, federal biologists captured anything that looked like a red wolf, weeded out the coyote-wolf hybrids, and kept the purebloods in captivity for breeding. The result, out of nearly 400 animals trapped and examined, was a meager 17 red wolves. Soon thereafter, the species was declared extinct in the wild.

Is the Red Wolf Really a Wolf?

Experts are split over the red wolf's pedigree. Some regard the animal as a distinct species, while others believe it is a coyote-wolf hybrid.

Just as red wolves were returning to the Smokies in 1991 came word that they may not be pure wolves at all. Scientists examining DNA samples determined that red wolves had no unique genetic material of their own—they have gray-wolf and coyote genes. That bolsters an old argument that red wolves are nothing more than a fertile hybrid between coyotes and grays.

But not everyone buys that line of reasoning. Some wolf experts note that fossil wolves are most similar to modern red wolves. And others point out that even in areas where gray wolves and coyotes hybridize, the result isn't an animal that looks or acts like a red wolf. Whatever its origins, *Canis rufus* remains a unique creature.

A Native Returns

Few animals have weathered a public-relations roller coaster like that experienced by the gray wolf. *Canis lupus* roamed through most of the United States for centuries until European settlers—swayed by age-old mythology and eager to develop ranching operations—initiated an aggressive program in the 19th century to eradicate the species. By 1930, only a few lone wolves remained in the lower 48 states.

In a dramatic turn of events (and reputation), this former outlaw has returned to some of its old haunts. In 1994, biologists began an ambitious program to restore wolves in the

Frank Church-River of No Return Wilderness in Idaho and in Yellowstone National Park, which straddles Wyoming, Montana, and Idaho.

Under the direction of the U.S. Fish and Wildlife Service, trappers caught 29 wolves in Canada and transported the animals to their new U.S. homes. In Idaho, the wolves were released directly into the wild. In Yellowstone, however, scientists kept the wolves in pens for two months, hoping to weaken a homing instinct that might draw them back to Canada. Biologists planned to release similar numbers of wolves in each of the next five years. Scientists hope that by the year 2002, populations of 100 wolves will prowl both regions.

With the wolf's return, Yellowstone—a park roughly the size of West Virginia—would become the largest complete ecosystem in the United States. Scientists were eager to observe how the reappearance of a top predator would transform the ecology of the region. Biologists anticipated that the wolf would present new challenges to other predators such as bears and cougars, lower the population and improve the health of ungulates like moose and elk, and trigger subtle changes in plant life and soil chemistry.

Such lofty intentions did not shield restoration efforts from opposition. Wolves have long been mythologized as demonic killers, typified by the villain of the tale of Little Red Riding Hood, and public fears about attacks remain. Western ranchers have voiced especially strong opposition to the return of the wolf. Ranchers and the politicians who represent them, arguing that a restored wolf population would feast on cattle and sheep, attempted to block the Yellowstone release in court. This effort ended in failure in January 1995.

The final restoration plan incorporated compromises to mollify ranchers and other opponents. Citizens were granted the right to kill any wolves preying on livestock, and a conservation group promised to compensate ranchers for livestock killed by wolves. While such concessions were not greeted with universal support, the path for a historic return was clear.

On March 24, six wolves—unaware of the political battles and scientific fanfare surrounding them—wandered out of their pen into Yellowstone's Lamar Valley. As the call of wolves echoed through the hills of Yellowstone for the first time in decades, supporters and opponents alike paused a moment, to hope and to listen. The wolf song had returned to the American West.

Peter A. Flax

Wolves live in well-defined social hierarchies and exhibit a complex system of behaviors to display their group status. The animals can draw from a wide palette of postures, vocalizations, and facial expressions to convey dominance or submission.

well that several were released into the wild—first on isolated barrier islands in the Southeast during the mid-1980s, then in 1987 in the Alligator River National Wildlife Refuge in coastal North Carolina. That introduction was so successful that, in 1991, red wolves were released in the Cades Cove area of the Great Smoky Mountains—the country's most popular national park. There were some grumbles from local farmers, but far from scaring people away, the wolves have become a focus of tourist interest, although visitors rarely see the secretive animals.

Their presence in the southern Appalachians ended nearly a century of exile. The red wolves sealed their return in 1993, when two of the pairs gave birth. Although some of the pups later died, such deaths are not unusual—and that the births occurred at all is good news for a race of hunters that has known only bad times for too long.

But from that nadir, the situation has steadily improved. The biggest change has been in public opinion. From seeing wolves as demons incarnate, or malicious stock killers, the average person is now more likely to view wolves in an almost spiritual light. Support for reintroducing wolves to Yellowstone National Park has been quite high, and only the stiff opposition of local ranchers and some Western politicians delayed the plan from going ahead sooner.

But while the Yellowstone debate continues to rage, the wolves may have already settled the issue. Gray wolves moved from Canada into Montana's Glacier National Park in the mid-1980s, and onto the eastern slope of the Rockies in 1993—the first time in 50 years that wolves had been in that area. Biologists still pressed for the Yellowstone reintroduction, however, despite wolf sightings in the park, knowing that it might take decades for a wild population to grow to stable levels.

Meanwhile, captive red wolves were reproducing so

When opportunity—or extreme hunger—presents itself, wolves demonstrate diverse dietary interests. Despite the wolf's outstanding hunting instincts and skills, most prospective meals manage to get away.

School Spirit

by Kathryn Phillips

Biologist John Hunter leads the way to a dimly lit room at the National Marine Fisheries Service lab in La Jolla, California. In a tank that resembles an aboveground swimming pool from some suburban backyard, 100, 200, maybe 300 silvery anchovies swim in the same direction with a beat-and-glide motion, side by side and one above another. Watching the fish swim with each other like mirror images is hypnotic, casting a dreamy spell over observers. Then Hunter breaks the spell by drumming on the side of the pool.

"Let's see if we can intensify things a little bit," he says. Quicker than you can say "June Taylor Dancers," the fish push away from Hunter's pounding hand, flee to the opposite side of the pool, and press together into a tight mass. The fish now look like commuters rushing to squeeze into the subway.

As far as these fish are concerned, Hunter is some kind of suspicious predator. At first glance, grouping together makes no sense, seemingly making a bigger catch for a hunter. Yet most schooling fish under attack do just what these anchovies do.

NOTHING FISHY

And they are not so dumb after all. Laboratory studies have found that, indeed, if you increase the density of the group of fish, some predators hesitate more, and their attack success goes down. A school can mean protection.

At least a fourth of the world's fish school. Some are hatchlings no larger than a paper clip, and others are adults the size of sofas. Fish school in fresh water and in the sea. Some school all their lives, and some only as juveniles or only as adults in mating season.

Exactly why fish that school do, and exactly how fish behave once they have joined a

school, has kept researchers busy for decades. Scientists are looking at schools as defense alliances, as hunting parties, and, in a few cases, as a way to find that special someone with whom to spawn. That research has become increasingly important as wildlife managers struggle to protect certain schooling species from being fished into near extinction.

SCHOOL STARTS

One unresolved question about schools concerns definition. "Obviously one fish is not a school; is two fish a school?" asks Julia K. Parrish, a zoologist at the University of Washington, Seattle, who has studied schooling in various ocean species. "I personally do not believe that two fish is a school, but there are definitely people who put two fish together and say they're studying schooling behavior.

"I think of a school as enough individuals to form a three-dimensional structure," she says, "so we're in the high tens to low hundreds as a minimum number." Some schools have millions of members, and span an area as large as a small town.

A number of researchers have avoided the difficulty by using the term "shoal" for all groups of fish, and then classifying them as either simple aggregations or schools. "Schools would be what you probably think of as a group of fish traveling together that turns with an impressive synchrony . . . rather like coordinated airplanes at air shows," says Tony Pitcher, director of the University of British Columbia Fisheries Center in Vancouver. True schools have distinct boundaries, Parrish notes. "There are lots of fish and then no fish. It's not that they sort of peter out."

Swimming in the middle of such a gathering is a surreal experience. "It's like being in an episode of *Star Trek*," adds Pitcher, who has snorkeled with herring. "You don't see the outside world, where you've been, or where you're going. And you're surrounded by quivering, moving silver bodies."

In a classic example of schooling, blue-striped snappers swim in unison as they slide by the wall of a coral reef near the South Pacific archipelago of Vanuatu. Zoologists believe that at least one-quarter of fish exhibit schooling behavior.

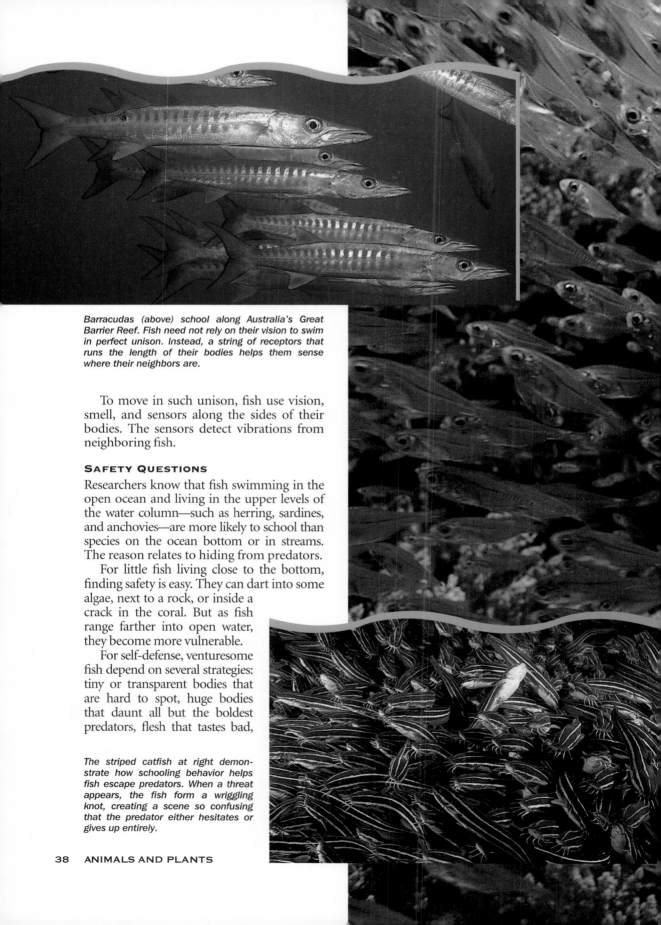

Barracudas (above) school along Australia's Great Barrier Reef. Fish need not rely on their vision to swim in perfect unison. Instead, a string of receptors that runs the length of their bodies helps them sense where their neighbors are.

To move in such unison, fish use vision, smell, and sensors along the sides of their bodies. The sensors detect vibrations from neighboring fish.

SAFETY QUESTIONS

Researchers know that fish swimming in the open ocean and living in the upper levels of the water column—such as herring, sardines, and anchovies—are more likely to school than species on the ocean bottom or in streams. The reason relates to hiding from predators.

For little fish living close to the bottom, finding safety is easy. They can dart into some algae, next to a rock, or inside a crack in the coral. But as fish range farther into open water, they become more vulnerable.

For self-defense, venturesome fish depend on several strategies: tiny or transparent bodies that are hard to spot, huge bodies that daunt all but the boldest predators, flesh that tastes bad,

The striped catfish at right demonstrate how schooling behavior helps fish escape predators. When a threat appears, the fish form a wriggling knot, creating a scene so confusing that the predator either hesitates or gives up entirely.

or skin that's hard to bite through. The ocean sunfish, for example, is a tough-skinned fish that lives as a loner. Schooling is right up there in the list of defenses. "If you school," Parrish explains, "the general thought is: get the other guy, not me. Safety in numbers."

HUNTING PARTIES

To avoid getting eaten is not the only reason to school. In some cases, it may be a good tactic for eating somebody else.

Around coral reefs, it is not uncommon to find schools of fish numbering fewer than 100, but including four or five different species. By cruising in a group, they overcome the territorial defenses of resident fish, and get feeding opportunities they could not find as individuals. These multi-species schools often hang together just for food, not defense. When a predator comes along, the group breaks up.

Among large, fast-moving, predatory species such as jacks and tuna, species move in schools in the open ocean as they look for smaller fish upon which to dine. "There definitely are cases where we think that fish are hunting cooperatively," Parrish notes. "There is some evidence that they herd their prey to a certain area and all attack."

NO SWEET SPOTS

If a school of tuna can be like a pride of lions, then is a school of herring like a herd of zebras avoiding those lions? Not exactly, Parrish has found. While the zebras in the center of a herd are safer from lion attack than those on the edges, within a school of fish, no place is really any safer than another.

Galloping along on land, mid-herd zebras are safer because danger moves in two dimensions instead of three. A lion cannot swoop up from below to snag its prey.

Also, the zebras can easily strike back. A lion attacking in the middle of all those pounding hooves would get kicked to death or at least run over. A tuna, however, is not

Some species of fish form schools of thousands or even millions of individuals. In the Red Sea, for example, silver sweepers (left) group together in vast numbers. Other fish prefer schools of only a few dozen; many species don't school at all.

going to hesitate about charging into the middle of a school. "If a tuna runs into a herring, it's not even going to be dented," Parrish says. "It's not even going to be a fender bender."

This size difference between predatory fish and their dinner—usually a big difference—may come about because fish do not have arms and legs. Parrish points out that lions don't have to swallow a zebra whole, but can steady it with their legs and paws while biting off chunks of meat. However, she says, "A tuna doesn't go up and take a bite out of a whale. It can't really rip off a piece." A tuna attacks species it can get into its mouth all at the same time, something a lot smaller than it is.

UNDER ATTACK

When a predator charges into a school, most fish react as the anchovies did when faced with John Hunter's tank pounding. They pull together, finding safety in numbers and, depending on the predator, taking advantage of the confusion effect.

The theory of the confusion effect assumes that certain predators, like sharpshooters, have to make visual contact with

Some experts argue that schooling behavior evolved as a means of giving individual fish reproductive access to others of their species.

their prey. By grouping together, the fish in a school present a confusing field of visual options. The muddle causes the predator to hesitate or even to give up.

Fish evolved bunching and other schooling behaviors as survival tricks. Nowadays, though,

the same behaviors "turn out to be absolutely disastrous" in the face of human fisheries, says Pitcher. When very few fish are left, grouping together makes them easier to catch. "With high-tech fisheries, we can find that last shoal, and fish every last fish out," he says.

The sardine population off the Pacific coast of North America, for example, has fallen to human efficiency. During the first half of this century, sardines supplied a thriving industry that built, among other places, Monterey, California's famous Cannery Row. But overfishing cut the sardine population from almost 4 million tons in the 1930s to less than 5,000 tons by the 1970s, notes John Hunter.

Populations dropped so much that there were not enough sardines to form their normal huge schools, and researchers found sardines joining anchovy schools. When sardines began to rebound, one of the early signs was that fishers and researchers found all-sardine schools again. Today the sardine population has reached 100,000 tons, still a fraction of its former size.

EASY MATING

Which brings us back to the idea that avoiding getting eaten cannot be the only reason for schooling. Some researchers believe that schools also boost the speed and efficiency with which fish find the right mate in a very large sea.

Some species clearly school for mating. Among certain types of groupers, individual fish spend most of the year alone in their territories, but like college students on spring break—when the Moon, the water, and the temperature are just right—they gather by the hundreds to school for a few days of courtship. Herring, however, swim in schools year-round, but during mating season move into shallow waters to spawn.

For most fish, experimental evidence is slim for mating as a key factor in schooling, Pitcher warns. Parrish adds, "People struggle with the relative importance of reproduction and food and predation." However, she hesitates to dismiss sex as a factor in the riddle of why fish school. "When you get down to it, reproduction is where it's at," she says. "You can avoid predators all your life, but if you don't mate, what's the point?"

BAMBOO IS BACK

by Jane Ellen Stevens

When interior designer Linda Garland left her London home to visit Bali, Indonesia, nearly 20 years ago, she fell in love with the island, the people—and the bamboo. Enthralled with the myriad ways the Balinese used the graceful plant in religious ceremonies, outrigger canoes, and houses, in utensils, chairs, and containers, she began designing bamboo furniture.

At first, Garland had no problems. She founded a factory on Bali, the first to use local species of giant bamboo, and brought the magic of the tropics to custom-designed furniture and interiors for international jet-setters such as rock star David Bowie. To protect her products from starch-loving powder post beetles that can destroy bamboo, she asked knowledgeable villagers to choose only the bamboo with the lowest starch content.

Good ideas get copied. Other bamboo furniture factories sprouted. To meet the demand, villagers began cutting bamboo regardless of starch content, and the powder post beetle emerged as an enduring pest. Garland's attempt to thwart it with an environmentally friendly treatment failed, and two shipments of furniture to wealthy customers in Fiji and Jamaica turned to dust. "It was a disaster," she says. Unwilling to use toxic pesticides, Garland reluctantly abandoned bamboo.

Bamboo (above) has emerged as a substitute for tropical hardwoods, concrete, steel, and other building materials—a development that has buoyed efforts to conserve this valuable plant.

Closely linked to bamboo for its survival, the endangered giant panda (left) dines on the plant— the bulk of its diet. The giant panda makes its home in China's dwindling bamboo forests.

bamboo, she fell down an Alice-in-Wonderland rabbit hole into a strange and astoundingly busy world. There, in the bamboo belt of Asia and South America, hundreds of scientists, engineers, architects, and environmentalists were turning ancient materials to new purposes, using bamboo to save rain forests, replenish watersheds destroyed by deforestation, reclaim land decimated by agriculture and mining, replace tropical woods in parquet flooring and iron rods in reinforced concrete, create construction materials for cars, and provide housing and income for the poor.

In her meandering through this new domain, Garland discovered that environmentally gentle treatments with materials such as boron salts had been proved effective against powder post beetles. Hopeful once more, she spent $200,000 of her own money to found the nonprofit Environmental Bamboo Foundation to promote the growth and use of bamboo.

New Hope in the Bamboo Belt

In 1993, however, the designer resumed her love affair with the ancient plant. Exasperated at the continued ravaging of Indonesia's rain forests, Garland still harbored a vague idea that bamboo might be a suitable substitute for the tropical hardwoods used in housing, furniture, and dozens of wood-pulp industries. Prospecting for information about

Now one of the goals of Garland's group is to help save the plants she had wanted to use so badly. In her quest, Garland found that demand has soared over the past 10 years, and is depleting certain kinds of bamboo stands as rapidly as rain forests. Some species have become extinct, but Garland and other experts say that if conservation starts now, the world's bamboo resources can grow back relatively quickly. She believes that bamboo—the plant that has carried generations of humans from cradle to grave, the plant that represents tenacity, endurance, and compromise to billions of people—may even be flexible enough to forgive humans their follies.

SPLENDOR IN THE GRASS

Even though some bamboo species' culms, or hollow woody stalks, are stronger than concrete, the world's approximately 1,250 species are members of the grass family. Some look like the thin reeds of tall field grass. Others, like the majestic giant bamboo that flourishes in remote Asian forests, grow as big around as a linebacker's thigh, and soar 197 feet (60 meters). A Japanese species of bamboo, *ma-dake*, is the fastest-growing plant in the world, shooting up 4 feet (1.2 meters) in 24 hours. People have said that they can hear it climbing.

Bamboos are versatile, with species thriving at sea level and at 13,000 feet (4,000 meters) up mountain slopes. In a band around Earth's belly, across mild-temperate, subtropical, and tropical zones, bamboo grows in the greatest abundance and variety from India through China, Japan to Korea, and from Thailand into Malaysia and Indonesia. South America hosts many species, but North America has only one indigenous type.

Bamboo sprouts naturally in the understory of forests. Shaded by the canopy, it waits for years until dying hardwoods crash to the ground, and then, like a voracious weed, the bamboo erupts in open clearings. Some types, such as the shrublike bamboo on the cold, windy upper slopes of Mount Fuji in Japan, proliferate in soils or climates inhospitable to other plants. Large natural stands, like the one in China where Garland rediscovered her fascination with bamboo,

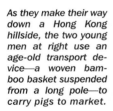
As they make their way down a Hong Kong hillside, the two young men at right use an age-old transport device—a woven bamboo basket suspended from a long pole—to carry pigs to market.

Bamboo flowering is synchronized. Plants of the same species blossom at the same time, even if they grow on opposite sides of the globe. Bamboos bloom only once every 20 to 120 years, depending on the species. A few have never been known to flower. Most bamboos give their all to producing seeds, and then collapse in a mass death. A new generation starts from the seeds.

probably were colonized after a catastrophe, such as a landslide or forest fire. Some of these huge stands have been managed for centuries as a sustainable harvest.

"The culms seem to go up to the sky forever and in all directions," says Garland, describing a walk through a forest of a species called *mao chu* in Angi Province of China, where people harvest bamboo for food, building materials, and agricultural and household implements. Unlike clumping bamboos, *mao chu* grow 5 feet (1.5 meters) apart. Culms 4 inches (10 centimeters) in diameter rise five stories high with feathery branches like huge quill pens. "Rays of filtered light were coming through all over the place," says Garland. "It was quiet, like walking through a room of people meditating."

Other than the studies of giant and red pandas eating bamboo, scientists know very little about the animals that live in these forests. "In Sumatra, if I found big bamboo

Straight and sturdy, bamboo is widely used for scaffolding at construction sites in Hong Kong. In some countries, bamboo is even replacing steel for reinforcing concrete.

forests, I found elephants," says Elizabeth Widjaja, an Indonesian botanist who headed the group of bamboo specialists for the World Conservation Union. "They eat the culm, and they even bleed from the silica crystals in the culm. But we don't know the relationship between elephants and bamboo. Also, I found orangutans in the bamboo forests. They're always eating young culms."

USES THROUGH THE AGES

The human relationship with bamboo is ancient and complex. Bamboo species have flourished for some 60 million years, and paleontologists suspect that early humans in Asia's bamboo country may have used the big grasses to fashion tools or household items, just as the first Europeans worked stone into useful shapes. Stone lasts; bamboo vanishes—we may never know if Stone Age contemporaries devised clever implements from culms. Yet the Age of Bamboo exists today with a vigor that has never been fully appreciated in the West.

Throughout history, half the world's population depended on bamboo: to shape into shelter, to eat, to hold food and drink, to form weapons, to feed livestock, to make water pipes for irrigating crops, to make ropes and bridges. "Bamboo is my brother," reads a Vietnamese proverb. According to Su Dongpo, a Chinese poet whose words have survived for nearly 1,000 years: "It is quite possible not to eat meat, but not to be without bamboo."

In the rich art of the East, bamboo is the paper, the brush, and the artist's subject. Bamboo is the flute from which musicians create melodies, the toy with which children create fantasies, and the prized fishing rods that serve anglers who spin tall tales. Lovers write romantic letters on bamboo stationery, wipe tears from their eyes with facial tissue made from its pulp, and seek comfort from its wine. People sleep on bamboo mats, behind bamboo walls, in bamboo homes. When the time comes for religious celebrations, the long, nodding stems evoke grace and humility in ceremonies.

Bamboo charcoal has been used in batteries, and it can be turned into diesel fuel.

Thomas Edison used a filament of carbonized bamboo to light his lamps, some of which still work to this day. Scientists have extracted natural preservatives from bamboo leaves, in which, for centuries, Asians have wrapped their food. The shoot of the yellow bamboo has been used to treat liver problems. The sap that hardens between nodes on some tropical bamboos is prescribed for asthma.

TECHNORENAISSANCE

Especially in the West, bamboo is often considered a poor man's timber, the stuff of baskets, mats, and tiny shacks for rural destitutes. Few Westerners realize that in Asia, industrial uses for bamboo have been booming. By the early 1980s, for instance, more than 300 paper mills in India and China used bamboo pulp to make paper and rayon.

Even so, much of today's industrial renaissance of bamboo is propelled by the West, especially by the Forestry and Environmental Program of Canada's International Development Research Center (IDRC). IDRC had a forestry program in Asia long before the center recognized the importance of bamboo. Now IDRC is in the forefront of bamboo research.

"In the 1980s, the IDRC noticed that bamboo was used so much by poor people that it mobilized funding for lots of small projects," says Trevor Williams, a geneticist and science adviser to the International Network for Bamboo and Rattan (INBAR). Since 1980, about $10 million from IDRC went to national research programs to fund more than 600 scientists and engineers in 14 nations.

These researchers found that, depending on the situation, fast-growing bamboo can

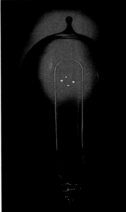

Bamboo's versatility has led to its use in many practical and decorative products. Strips of bamboo form the structural skeleton of the umbrellas above.

The bamboo-filament bulb (left), an early version of the electric lamp, proved less efficient than the carbon-filament bulb that became the industry standard. Both were developed for commercial use by Thomas Edison.

replace wood—including slow-maturing tropical hardwoods—as well as concrete and steel. Bamboo can be made into flooring, used as a reinforcement material in plastic composites, a replacement for iron in reinforced concrete, a filter in sewage-treatment plants, and pipe for water-supply systems. Engineers in Nanjing, China, developed a method for manufacturing plybamboo, a substitute for plywood, by softening, spreading, and planing culms. Engineers in India perfected an inexpensive

Standing at the edge of a bamboo grove in Nepal, a woman is dwarfed by the towering stalks. Bamboo is a fast-growing grass; in some species, new shoots reach full height in just a few months.

Although it will be many years before bamboo is a common building material globally, some countries are moving quickly to write standards for bamboo into their building codes. In Costa Rica, the National Bamboo Project has built 700 480-square-foot (45-square-meter) houses that use modern building materials and methods: a frame of bamboo connected by woven bamboo mesh onto which mortar is applied. The houses, each of which costs about $4,500, danced to the paroxysms of a magnitude-7.6 earthquake in 1991, while traditional brick and concrete houses crumbled. To meet the demand for rural housing, the project intends to build 1,000 houses per year "forever," says Jorge Gutierrez, an engineer who is vice president for research at the University of Costa Rica and technical adviser for the bamboo project.

method to produce plybamboo sheets by gluing together bamboo mats.

Today two dozen manufacturing plants make plybamboo and are stimulating cultivation of bamboo in marginal farms and wastelands. "By promoting bamboo, we don't destroy the forest," says Cherla Sastry, principal program officer for IDRC and executive director of INBAR in New Delhi. "It also brings extra income for women who are the traditional weavers of the bamboo mats that are glued together into plybamboo."

DANGEROUS SUCCESS

Today estimates of total global revenue generated from bamboo and its products range from $4.5 billion to $7 billion annually. But bamboo's usefulness is also its downfall. High demands have wiped out dozens of bamboo forests in India, Bangladesh, and Indonesia. Bamboo, in theory, can be a quick, renewable crop, but foresters must manage the stands wisely. "The demand for bamboo has led to over-exploitation," says Sastry.

Even more of a problem, says Elizabeth Widjaja, is that no one knows how much bamboo has been lost or how much remains. When governments inventoried their hardwood forests, they ignored the poor man's timber. Several bamboo species have become extinct, she says, although the status of many species is unknown.

Botanists traditionally ensure the diversity of species by establishing seed banks. But in a remarkable understatement, INBAR manager Paul Stinson notes: "Bamboo-seed production and its storage is a problem." Most crop plants produce an annual harvest of seeds that can be sequestered in cold storage for several years without damage. Yet bamboo's long growth periods before flowering complicate conservation, as do the short-lived seeds. No one is researching how to extend their lives. "It's not like growing a row of corn," laments Williams.

Scientists in India induced one species of bamboo to flower in a test tube, but the techniques need to be refined for other species, says Williams, in a process that will likely take years. Recent successes in tissue culture in China, India, and Thailand have opened new vistas. But until scientists can easily induce flowering, countries are struggling with maintaining collections of bamboo specimens.

Nevertheless, conservationists are making progress, albeit slowly, in replenishing the bamboo lost in the past couple of decades. During 1994, INBAR identified 10 species of bamboo to study, conserve, and promote as a cash crop; to restore degraded agricultural land; and to use in place of hardwoods. A patch of 4,940 cutover, eroding acres (2,000 hectares) in Bali is targeted for a reclamation experiment using a lush, fast-growing carpet of bamboo. But, explains Williams, since the rare bamboos are not all commercial species—major commodities that government forestry departments can work on—it will be up to nongovernmental organizations, such as Garland's Environmental Bamboo Foundation, to fill in the gaps by training people to grow, manage, and use local indigenous species.

In many Asian countries, bamboo has been of economic importance for centuries. Strips of bamboo can be used to make brooms—and thousands of other essential everyday items.

Garland is taking her task to heart. Her days are jam-packed with promoting the use and conservation of bamboo. With $250,000 in funding from the U.S. Agency for International Development (AID), she is setting up a training project for Indonesians to learn how to propagate and harvest bamboo sustainably. Garland has raised an additional $51,200 in grants from the Earth Love Foundation in England and the Connecticut-based Aid to Artisans.

A major project that she hopes to finish sometime in 1995, when her foundation plans to co-host the Fourth International Bamboo Congress, is a bamboo village where Western tourists can sit on bamboo furniture in a bamboo restaurant; dine on bamboo-shoot delicacies; and visit bamboo gardens, laboratories, artisans, and factories.

"Bamboo can benefit the poor and the environment," says Garland. "These are two things more or less forgotten in this world." As she muses, she relaxes a moment in her bamboo furniture, which she no longer worries will disintegrate.

ZEBRAS IN TURMOIL

by Jane Ellen Stevens

Early in the 19th century, the first Europeans to penetrate the interior of southern Africa found one animal that literally glittered on the sun-swept plains. This was the quagga, a type of zebra with chestnut body, white legs and tail, and cinnamon-and-cream stripes on head, neck, and chest. One British hunter of the 1840s wrote that quaggas at a distance sparkled like mica.

Named for its barking call, the quagga roamed South Africa by the thousands. However, as Europeans moved in, they killed quaggas mercilessly, using the hides for commerce and the meat for feeding servants. The last quagga died in the Amsterdam Zoo in 1883.

Ecologists, taxonomists, geneticists, and wildlife managers are struggling today to prevent two jeopardized species of zebra—the mountain and the Grevy's—from also going the way of the quagga. In addition, these scientists are endeavoring to ensure that the plains zebra, the only zebra species not facing immediate jeopardy, maintains its foothold on survival even as the burgeoning human population overruns wildlife habitat.

A TRIO OF PAINTED PONIES

Africa's three zebra species look much alike. The mountain zebra is the only slight eccentric, since it alone among zebras bears a loose fold of skin, called a dewlap, along its throat. Otherwise, all three fit a pattern—basic horse body with black-and-white stripes. The stripes vary in detail from one type of zebra to the next, but to the untrained eye, the differences are minimal.

Grevy's zebra, with the narrowest stripes, is the largest member of the zebra family. Large specimens weigh in at up to 1,000 pounds (450 kilograms). The Grevy's lives in semiarid scrubland and grassland in northern Kenya and south-central Ethiopia. Also native to Somalia, it has not been seen there since 1973, and biologists believe that the Grevy's is extinct in that part of its range.

Mountain zebras, the smallest at 440 pounds (200 kilograms), are found in isolated populations in southwestern Africa. They prefer broken or mountainous country, but also live on plateaus and flats,

Once roaming the plains of southern Africa by the thousands, the quagga (above), a type of plains zebra, is now extinct. Today, scientists are working to save the endangered mountain zebra and Grevy's zebra from a similar fate.

Plains zebras (facing page) form close family ties and travel in large herds for protection. Although not yet endangered, their numbers are declining from overhunting and competition with humans over grazing land and scarce water resources.

including the edges of deserts and in semi-arid and savanna grasslands.

The five subspecies of ponylike plains zebras, which average about 550 pounds (250 kilograms), range across the savannas and grasslands of eastern and southern Africa.

Zebras are generalized herbivores. They prefer grasses, but when pressed for food will eat the more digestible parts of trees and shrubs. Although the zebra's dietary adaptability may make it stiff competition for less flexible species such as antelope and cattle, under most conditions the zebra benefits other wild grazers.

Biologist Richard Bell, working at the Serengeti Research Institute in Tanzania, found that during July and August, when hundreds of thousands of animals move from Tanzania's Serengeti Plain to Kenya's Masai Mara National Reserve, zebras go first, followed by wildebeests, and then gazelles. Zebras clear off the tops of tall, coarse grasses, too difficult for other herbivores to digest. Wildebeests eat the shorter, more digestible blades of grass. And Thomson's gazelles, which require the highest protein content of all, nibble the shortest plants and new sprouts.

Zebras have another important nutritional role: they serve as food for a variety of predators and scavengers. They are the most important prey species for Serengeti lions, and rank second only to wildebeests as the kill of choice among the lions and hyenas of Tanzania's Ngorongoro Crater. Zebras are the biological foundation upon which the predators stand.

LIFE IN THE SOCIAL CLUB

Hans and Ute Klingel of the University of Braunschweig in Germany began their zebra research in the 1960s in Tanzania and Kenya, becoming the first biologists to look at a herd of plains zebras and see something other than a field of stripes. The herds, they found, are composed of hundreds of individual families, each consisting of one male with one to six females and offspring.

Family members bond strongly, and some relationships are lifelong. When traveling, family groups slow down for sick members. Together, they fend off predators. One observer found the remains of a zebra and an adult lion that had killed one another. Though inflicted with mortal wounds, the zebra had bitten the lion in the small of the

Competition for females often results in biting, kicking, and pushing matches between zebra stallions. Grevy's zebras (at left) are typically the most aggressive; they even fight over territorial borders.

Young males leave their families and join bachelor groups when about two or three years old. Elderly herd stallions sometimes join bachelor groups, too, when deposed by younger males. Often their sons go with them, staying in the bachelor herd until mature enough to begin their own families.

A WEAKER FAMILY STRUCTURE

Mountain-zebra family life is similar to that of plains zebras. Grevy's zebras, however, are another matter. They form no permanent bonds between adults. Instead of defending families, males defend their territories of 1 to 4 square miles (3 to 12 square kilometers)—the largest recorded among herbivores. They mark boundaries with dung piles heaped 16 inches (40 centimeters) high. Whereas plains stallions seek each other's company and go through friendly greeting ceremonies, Grevy's stallions fight along territorial boundaries. Females with young foals usually range across one or two male territories, says ecologist Mary Rowen, who studied Grevy's zebras in northern Kenya for two years. Other females range across many male territories, and males mate with the females they encounter.

Although the Grevy's only long-term relationship is between mare and offspring, they do establish temporary alliances, forming all-bachelor-male, all-female, or all-mother-and-offspring herds. These groupings sometimes keep their uniform composition even when they occasionally congregate into amalgams of up to 200 animals. Dominance hierarchies are weak or nonexistent, aside from the males' territorial belligerence.

Scientists can only speculate as to why the Grevy's social system differs so much from that of other zebra species. Presumably, restricted access to water in the desert areas inhabited by Grevy's zebras results in smaller

back, apparently severing the spinal cord, rendering a Pyrrhic victory, African style.

Sometimes zebras even try to save one another from biologists. The Klingels observed zebras trying to help family members that the researchers had tranquilized. Stallions tugged on drugged mares' necks to revive them, and even dragged them back to safety. Once the Klingels darted a four-year-old male that was still with his family, an unusual situation because males usually take off on their own when two or three years old. The animal, unfortunately, died. The herd stallion tried several times to revive him. Later, when hyenas began to eat the body, the distressed father left his family to spend six hours trotting through the herd, calling for his son.

When a plains-zebra female reaches a year and a half to two years old, she enters her first estrus. Nearby males take an immediate and active interest, attempting to run her off from her herd. The filly's father, like an overprotective dad, does his best to keep her at home, but eventually he loses her when the number of suitors exceeds his ability to mount a defense. While the herd stallion is frantically chasing off one interloper, another swoops in and makes off with the filly.

groups. Females with young stay near water sources, while females without young range more widely to areas with better forage.

All zebra species mate year-round, so offspring are born in all months, though the peak usually occurs during the rainy season. Gestation ranges from 11 to 14 months. At birth, a zebra foal weighs about 10 percent of its mother's weight and can double its weight in a month. If human babies were proportionally as large, women would give birth to 12-pound (5.5-kilogram) infants that would weigh 24 pounds (11 kilograms) a month later.

A baby zebra spends its first hour learning to walk and run. During the second hour, it begins bonding with its mother. For the first few days following a birth, a mother chases off any zebras that come within 10 feet (3 meters) of her foal, including members of her family. This allows the baby to learn its mother's voice, stripe pattern, and smell. If mother and offspring become separated before bonding occurs, the baby will follow any moving object, even a passing Land Rover.

POPULATIONS TAKE A PLUNGE

In addition to similarity of appearance and the practice of year-round mating, the three zebra species share another distinction: all have declined in this century. The most numerous today is the plains zebra—750,000 animals scattered across eastern and southern Africa. However, about 70 percent of these belong to a single subspecies, Grant's zebra. The other subspecies of plains zebra survive in substantially smaller numbers. For example, only one large population of the Upper Zambezi subspecies survives.

According to the Equid Specialist Group of the World

A pregnant female zebra (left) carries a baby inside her body for about one year. The mare gives birth, usually in the spring, to a single newborn; the foal typically weighs a formidable 55 to 88 pounds.

Shortly after birth, the young zebra learns to walk and nurse (below). The bond between mother and offspring is extremely strong. Within days, the foal can recognize its mother's stripe pattern, scent, and voice.

Conservation Union (International Union for the Conservation of Nature and Natural Resources, or IUCN), which monitors wild horses such as zebras and wild asses, the plains zebra as a species seems stable in protected areas, and stable or increasing on unprotected private lands in some of the more developed nations. Its biggest survival problem occurs on communally owned lands, where it is declining, sometimes rapidly. Even the Grant's has local problems. For example, since 1978, the number of Grant's zebras in Ethiopia has dropped from 9,000 to 2,000 animals. Though the total number of Grant's zebras has been stable or increasing in recent decades, the animal's range in eastern Africa has contracted by more than half since 1900.

About 8,100 mountain zebras remain in southern Africa. In the past, shooting for hides cut them down. In the early 1950s, more than 50,000 Hartmann's mountain zebras, one of two subspecies, lived in Namibia. Today the IUCN's Equid Specialist Group estimates that only 7,000 survive, and the IUCN lists the animal as vulnerable. The other subspecies, the Cape mountain zebra, sank to fewer than 100 animals by the late 1940s. Strong protection in national parks combined with reintroduction programs have brought that number up to about 600 today, still low enough to win endangered status for the Cape mountain zebra. Both subspecies remain jeopardized by drought and agricultural development.

Rarest of the species is the Grevy's, which numbers only 5,000 animals concentrated in a few areas. In 1980, perhaps 1,500 survived in Ethiopia, but they are probably dwindling. Populations in some parts of Kenya have fallen by up to 90 percent since the 1960s. A 1977 survey of Kenyan Grevy's zebras turned up an estimated 13,700 of the animals, while a more intensive 1988 survey found only an estimated 4,280, a 70 percent decline in 11 years. If this trend continues, the species will be extinct within 50 years. The IUCN lists the Grevy's as endangered.

The main challenge to the Grevy's survival is loss of habitat to domestic livestock. Fencing of water sources excludes the animals from pastures and water supplies. In

Thousands of plains animals travel in seasonal migrations in search of water and greener pastures. While others serve as lookouts, the zebras (facing page) enjoy a refreshing drink at the community watering hole.

northern Kenya, Rowen found that small changes in the environment, such as how far the animals must walk for water, affect infant survival. She discovered that offspring of females that give birth near bodies of water have a better chance of surviving than do offspring of mares that must walk long distances to drink. "Today there is an increasing human demand on water sources, making it more difficult for Grevy's to find safe water," says Rowen. Her work is helping Kenyan wildlife managers evaluate management of valuable water resources.

SAVING THE GENE POOL

Significant progress has been made toward implementing modern management for zebras. The IUCN's Equid Group completed an action plan for zebras and other wild horses in 1993, outlining programs designed to protect and recover beleaguered species. "The work has gone on despite the fact that zebras live in some of the world's most difficult political hot spots," says Patrick Duncan, chairman of the panel.

As part of a project to assure genetic diversity among surviving zebras, Oliver Ryder of the Center for Reproduction of Endangered Species in San Diego, California, and associate Ann Oakenfull are attempting to distinguish plains subspecies through DNA analysis of zebra blood samples gathered over eight years. Determining the amount of genetic variation that exists among isolated populations will help biologists determine which populations should receive management priority.

Ryder and Oakenfull also plan to identify sex roles in migration and gene flow. This work may provide wildlife managers with a model for population dynamics in other large herbivore herds, too.

Zebras represent an important food source for a variety of scavengers and predators—primarily lions, hyenas, leopards, and cheetahs. At left, a lioness guards her hard-won kill.

Much more needs to be learned to assure zebra survival. "We need to do social and economic as well as ecological research to develop good conservation plans," says Duncan. This includes determining how food and water shortages, predation, disease, restricted migration, and competition with livestock affect zebra populations.

One critical factor to zebra survival is the human element. Some Africans view zebras as competitive with livestock. As a result, farmers and ranchers put up fences on private land, cutting off zebra access to water, grazing areas, and migration routes. Some farmers shoot zebras that encroach on cropland.

Researchers hope to determine the effects of competition with livestock so that effective management plans can be developed. French researchers studying the interaction of zebras, wildebeests, impalas, kudu, and cattle on a 25,000-acre (10,000-hectare) spread in Zimbabwe may turn up some definitive answers.

Scientists believe that zebras will remain in jeopardy unless the animals in some way benefit the people with whom they share their range. The IUCN's action plan recommends raising zebras for meat and skins. "There is good economic potential in plains zebras," says Ryder. "They stand a good opportunity of working in ranch situations."

Zebras eat coarse grasses that grow on marginal lands where cattle do not do well, Duncan explains. Zebras are resistant to the cattle-killing trypanosomiasis disease transmitted by the tsetse fly. Several ranches in Kenya, South Africa, Zimbabwe, Botswana, and Namibia are already raising zebras for skins and food.

Wild zebras, too, can be economically important. In nations such as Kenya and Tanzania, zebras are a part of the economic base, drawing in tourist dollars. Nations that permit hunting charge shooters up to $1,000 each for the chance to bag a zebra.

Searching for a Lost Zebra

Perhaps nothing better underscores the importance of trying to protect vanishing wildlife than does an attempt by South African geneticists to reincarnate a lost subspecies. By crossbreeding plains zebras whose stripe patterns resemble those of the extinct quagga, the Quagga Experimental Breeding Committee hopes to create something that closely resembles the beast that once glittered on the South African plains. Sadly, geneticists may indeed produce a quagga look-alike, but this zebra-by-committee will not be the actual beast. Only quaggas can produce quaggas, says Ryder.

Have Wings, Can't Fly

by Les Line

T he odyssey of the egg began on a Madagascar hillside. Washed from its nest by torrential rains, the egg tumbled into a raging stream, where its thick shell bounced off rock after rock on a wild ride to the sea. The second leg of the egg's journey was tranquil by comparison: a 4,500-mile (7,200-kilometer) voyage on the currents of the Indian Ocean to the western shore of Australia. A storm tide rolled the egg high on a beach, and it was the safest of resting places. For as Earth's oceans retreated from the continents, the broad expanse of sand became a windblown dune nearly 0.6 mile (1 kilometer) inland.

Two thousand years later, three schoolchildren on Christmas holiday made an extraordinary discovery—and carted their treasure to show-and-tell when classes resumed. Thus, the elephant bird, a feathered colossus that has been extinct for centuries, leaped into world news in 1993.

LEGENDS AND LOST BIRDS

Imagine a bird's egg 13 inches (33 centimeters) long and 32 inches (81 centimeters) in circumference. An egg so huge that it could hold 12,000 hummingbird eggs, 180 chicken eggs, or 7 ostrich eggs. A bird's egg bigger than any dinosaur's egg ever found. Imagine, if you can, the 1,000-pound (450-kilogram) bird that laid that egg.

Imagine that bird flying! In the 13th century, Arab traders who had sailed to Madagascar told the Venetian traveler Marco Polo about "gryphon birds" that the natives called rocs. They were, he recounted, "so huge and bulky that one of them can pounce on an elephant and carry it up to a great height in the air."

Well, not really. We know from its 10-foot (3-meter)-tall skeleton that the great elephant bird was built like a steamroller and plodded over the Madagascar landscape on massive legs and feet. But it had only shriveled wings and neither talons nor hooked beak. The roc of Arab fable was an earthbound goliath that ate plants, not pachyderms.

Yet those vestigial wing bones suggest that, once upon a time, elephant birds (if not elephants) could indeed fly. They eventually lost that power as they adapted to a terrestrial lifestyle in a place free of predators. For the elephant bird and many others, it was a choice that worked well—until their paths crossed with humans and the animals they brought with them. Although flightless birds make up less than 1 percent of the avian world, they represent one-third of the 75 or more bird species that have become extinct over the past 400 years.

Only a few of the missing, however, were avian absurdities like the elephant bird or the dodo, a giant pigeon slaughtered by famished seafarers on nearby Mauritius Island. At the sublime end of the evolutionary scale, for instance, was a tiny gilded wren that had the misfortune to encounter a cat named Tibbles. Other flightless birds, among them a colorful gallinule and an owl-faced parrot, cling to the brink with help from conservationists.

A flock of ostriches, the largest living birds, gallops across the sandy plains of Africa. Although their wings are useless for flight, ostriches can maintain a steady pace for an extended period, thanks to their powerful legs. Always alert, the wary ostrich (facing page) relies on its keen eyesight, acute hearing, and fast footwork to escape predators.

King penguins (left) gather in large colonies to breed and raise their young; males and females share parenting responsibilities. Instead of for flying, penguins use their wings to propel them through the water.

ALIVE AND WELL

Some flightless species, however, have prospered. Seventeen wonderfully varied species of penguins have evolved from airborne ancestors to "fly" in another element: cold Antarctic waters. They share the seas off the tip of South America with flightless steamer ducks, massive waterfowl that churn the surface with wings and feet like a sidewheeler steaming through the water. On the Galápagos Islands, flightless cormorants—the largest members of this cosmopolitan aquatic family—spread their stunted wings to dry in the equatorial sun. And in tropical South America, no streamside would be complete without hoatzins, fantastic fowl that can swim better than they can fly even though they have long wings.

Then there are the elephant bird's living kin: rheas in South America, the African ostrich, Australia's emu, cassowaries on New Guinea, and the kiwis of New Zealand. They thrive, to a greater or lesser degree, in homelands that were joined 130 million years ago in a supercontinent called Gondwanaland—where the birds apparently had a common ancestor.

Current wisdom tells us this ostrichlike prototype from the Cretaceous period evolved into distinct families after the continents and their satellites, such as Madagascar, drifted apart. Progeny of this prototype share not only DNA but also the characteristic of a flat breastbone; a keel on the sternum to support powerful flight muscles became useless once the birds abandoned the skies. Scientists call the primitive members of this far-flung order "ratites," a term borrowed from a Latin word meaning "raft," since a flat-bottomed boat has no keel.

No one knows when the elephant bird vanished, but its fate was sealed when Indonesians and Africans arrived on Madagascar about the time our egg began its passage to present-day Perth, Australia. While clearing the forest habitat for crops, settlers hunted the immense birds and gathered their jumbo eggs for omelettes that could feed a whole village, saving the empty shells for bowls.

A few elephant birds probably survived into the 17th century, when the French planted their flag on the island, but no European ever ventured far enough into the interior to draw a picture of the bird. Eggs and bones are the only evidence of the creature's time on Earth. The elephant bird's extinction left the ostrich as the world's largest bird.

Below, a flightless cormorant spreads its stunted wings to dry its feathers after a sunset dive. Although unable to fly, this large seabird is a powerful swimmer and an excellent diver.

GOLD-MEDAL SPEED

If the elephant bird was as ponderous as its namesake, the ostrich is an Olympian runner. While a male ostrich may stand 9 feet (275 centimeters) tall and weigh as much as 330 pounds (150 kilograms), its powerful feet, long stride, and remarkable stamina can carry it over vast stretches of African plains at a steady 31 miles (50 kilometers) per hour.

Ostriches probably outdistance their ancestors at egg laying, too. It is hard to conceive of more than one elephant-bird egg to a nest. On the other hand, an ostrich nest—just a scrape in the sand—might hold five or six dozen eggs. In a typical ostrich breeding group, there is a territorial male; his "major hen," who starts a clutch; and several minor hens, who mate with roving males and add their eggs to the collection.

The dominant female recognizes her own eggs, eight or so in number, and arranges them in the middle. She knows that scavengers such as hyenas will steal the other hens' eggs at the edge of the nest first. The female ostrich, more cryptically colored than her mate, sits on the eggs by day; the male takes the night shift. Together, they care for the 20 or more chicks that hatch almost simultaneously at the vocal urging of the brooding hen.

In contrast, the male greater rhea of the South American pampas pays a steep price for the fleeting attention of up to a dozen females. After waiting in line to lay eggs in his nest, the harem sallies forth to find yet another nest to fill, leaving the male to rear their young without help. As in an ostrich nest, there are excess eggs that a brooding rhea cannot cover with his body. Flies that swarm over the rotting eggs feed the incubating male and newly hatched chicks.

Polyandry is the rule for the emu of arid Australia. A displaying female entices a male with a booming "e-moo, e-moo" sound that can be heard 1 mile (1.6 kilometers) away. After consorting for several months, she lays her eggs and runs off to find another male. For the next eight weeks, the male attends the nest without a break, neither eating nor drinking until the chicks hatch.

ENEMIES AND IDOLS

Such stoicism has not improved the emu's image with Australian farmers whose crops the birds ravage. In the 1930s, the Royal Artillery mobilized to western Australia to exterminate 20,000 emus with machine guns and grenades; the mortified soldiers managed to kill only a dozen of the well-camouflaged birds in the month of pursuit. Today high emu-proof fences protect grainfields.

On the other hand, New Guinea tribal people revere cassowaries, brawny and low-slung birds with shock-absorbing helmets

A well-camouflaged emu (above) tends to his nest, which holds a clutch of 8 to 12 green-black eggs deposited there by several hens. A dedicated father, the male incubates the eggs by himself—often going weeks without food or water.

and thornproof plumage. Some tribes consider cassowaries sacred. For others, roast cassowary is such a delicacy that a captive specimen can be traded for several pigs. The bird's razor-edged claws, which have eviscerated more than a few careless natives, make good tips for hunting arrows.

Not all ratites come so well armored. The nocturnal, bug-hunting kiwis of New Zealand are the odd lot of the ratite camp. Nearly blind, these shaggy and tailless birds rely on keen hearing to find their way

Single-wattled cassowaries (left) are large, flightless birds that live in New Guinea. They lead solitary lives, coming together only for breeding. Smooth, hairlike feathers and a helmeted head enable them to push easily through the dense forest. The brown-spotted kiwi (below) is a seldom-seen flightless bird from New Zealand. The nocturnal kiwi relies on its probing bill and sense of smell to find food on the forest floor.

through the dense forest, while nostrils at the tips of their long bills detect invertebrates hidden under the leaf litter.

Unlike their ostrichlike relatives, kiwis are monogamous and mate for life. Once again, however, it is the male who incubates the eggs in a well-concealed burrow, emerging after dark to feed. The kiwi egg is exceptional for its size: it contains a huge yolk on which chicks feed for 10 days after hatching. A pregnant kiwi—carrying an egg that represents one-fourth of her body weight—shuffles along with her belly dragging on the ground.

Over evolutionary time, the flight muscles and wings of the kiwi and its relatives withered away, while other earthbound birds simply lost the need to fly, but kept their wings. The peculiar hoatzin, a pheasantlike bird with an Aztec name and an offensive body odor, keeps its feet planted firmly near its favorite food, low-growing arum plants. Most of the space on the hoatzin's breast is claimed by a huge crop and gizzard, which are used to store the rubbery arum leaves and begin the digestive process. If the arum looks greener on the other side of a river, a hoatzin simply clambers to the top of a tree and glides down to the other side. If threatened, the hoatzin dives into the water.

FACING EXTINCTION

Another such parachutist, the huia, lived in New Zealand until overzealous collectors hastened the bird into extinction early in this century. Crow-sized and glossy black with orange wattles, mated huias foraged as a team because their bills were very different. The male chopped a hole in a tree with his chisel-shaped bill, then the female probed for wood-boring grubs with her long, curved bill.

No one has seen a huia since 1907, but there is a sliver of hope that it might endure, for two other "extinct" New Zealand birds have been granted a second chance. The owl parrot, or kakapo, is the largest and certainly oddest parrot on Earth: it nests and forages on the ground; male kakapos display like dancing grouse on a communal booming ground; and the bird is nocturnal. Indeed, the kakapo has the soft, silent plumage and facial disks of a predatory owl, although it eats ferns and fungi.

Dogs, ferrets, stoats, and rats brought by Europeans decimated kakapo numbers, and the bird was feared lost until 1977, when a small breeding population was discovered on cat-infested Stewart Island, New Zealand. Scientists have since moved all the birds to predator-free havens, but very few chicks have hatched, and the total kakapo population hovers around 50.

New Zealand's other will-o'-the-wisp is the takahe, a flightless member of the rail family. This brightly colored gallinule, known only from four museum specimens, had not been seen for

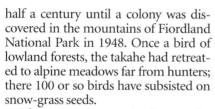

Hoatzins (above) are exotic-looking South American birds that nest in family groups near water. Better swimmers than fliers, hoatzins dive into the water when threatened. The kakapo (left), or owl parrot, is an endangered flightless bird of New Zealand. This nocturnal species nests and forages on the ground. The ground-dwelling takahe (below) is gathering grass for food and nesting material. A small population of these brightly colored, flightless birds lives in the alpine meadows of New Zealand.

half a century until a colony was discovered in the mountains of Fiordland National Park in 1948. Once a bird of lowland forests, the takahe had retreated to alpine meadows far from hunters; there 100 or so birds have subsisted on snow-grass seeds.

There are many riveting stories about the persecution, perseverance, and extinction of birds that stopped flying. None, however, is more poignant than the brief history of still another New Zealand bird, the Stephen Island wren. This island—little more than a dot of rock—was home to the world's only flightless songbird, a golden-brown sprite that emerged from its hole at dusk and scurried about in search of insects. The mouselike wren was discovered in 1894 by the lighthouse keeper's cat. "Tibbles" kept delivering specimens, which his owner duly sent off to museums until, a few months later, the supply ran out.

ASK THE SCIENTIST

► Are the yaks of Tibet related to oxen and other beasts of burden? How have they adapted to their high-altitude life in the Himalayas? Would they have trouble living at sea level?

Yaks are members of the cattle family, as are various animals commonly called oxen. (The animals called oxen in North America actually are large, castrated bulls.) Their adaptations for life at high elevations include large lungs and thick, hairy coats. "Yaks also are large animals, which helps them live on very rough vegetation such as coarse grasses; a big animal needs proportionately less good nutrition than a small animal because it has a lower metabolism," explains George Schaller, director for science at the Wildlife Conservation Society, Bronx, New York.

"Yaks can adapt to low altitudes to the extent that they are found in zoos, but they are not happy when it gets hot," says Schaller. "They have a hard time dissipating heat. Even if temperatures rise to 40° or 50° F [4° to 10° C], yaks will stand in icy rivers to cool off."

► During a recent visit to an arboretum, I saw a fantastic plant called a monkey-puzzle tree. Is the monkey-puzzle tree related to any North American species? Where do they grow naturally? Can they survive the harsh winters of the northern United States?

The monkey-puzzle tree, *Araucaria araucana*, is an ancient, primitive gymnosperm that is native to southern Chile; it is not related to any North American species. The

tree may reach heights of 150 feet (46 meters) or more. Its broad, sharp-pointed leaves overlap one another to densely cover the twisting branches.

"It got its common name because no one can figure out how a monkey can get up into the tree without killing itself," explains Adam Lifton-Schwerner, foreman of the Enid A. Haupt Conservatory at the New York Botanical Garden, Bronx, New York. "We had one here that fell on me; I was scratched up for weeks!"

Monkey-puzzle trees are popular ornamental trees in Southern California and in other subtropical areas of North America. They will not survive harsh northern winters, but they can be grown indoors as houseplants.

► Do dogs and cats see in color? How does their vision compare to that of a human with 20/20 eyesight? Do veterinarians perform eye surgery on pets?

"They have color vision, but they cannot discriminate as many different colors as we can," says Ellis Loew, associate professor of physiology at Cornell University's College of Veterinary Medicine. "Their resolution is poorer than ours in bright light because they have fewer cone cells. However, at some tasks—operating in dim light, for example—they are better than we are because their retinas are designed in a slightly different way."

Loew's colleague Ronald Riis, associate professor in comparative ophthalmology, has performed a wide variety of eye surgeries on pets. "We do everything on animals that is done on human eyes," he says.

Riis further notes, however, that "The one thing that is sometimes restrictive is the cost; many people are unable to afford some of the techniques that are available."

▶ *Do scientists yet understand why whales sometimes beach themselves or swim up rivers? Do manatees, dolphins, or other marine mammals ever do the same thing?*

"Single strandings are natural mortality; the animals get sick and die. But we don't know why mass strandings of whales—and manatees and dolphins—occur," says James Mead, curator of marine mammals at the Smithsonian Institution's National Museum of Natural History in Washington, D.C. "There have been as many theories suggested as there have been biologists who have worked on the problem. And none of these theories seem to have any basis in fact."

Mead notes that mass strandings occur in all parts of the world, and during all seasons of the year. Autopsies performed on the animals have found no evidence of medical problems. Interestingly, coastal species of whales do not mass-strand. The phenomenon has been seen only among ocean species, with pilot whales apparently having the strongest tendency to strand themselves.

▶ *Did ancient people build zoos to house exotic animals for display? What about aviaries? If so, how did they catch the creatures?*

Yes, ancient people collected wild animals for display, but this appears to have been done almost exclusively by—and for—the ruling classes. One of the earliest known collections was that of Queen Hatshepsut, who ruled Egypt in the 15th century B.C. "There is a record that she sent an expedition to what is believed to now be Somalia to bring back monkeys, leopards,

wild cattle, and exotic birds. These became part of the palace menagerie in the Egyptian capital," says Robert Hoage, chief of public affairs at the National Zoological Park in Washington, D.C., and editor of the soon-to-be-published book *New Worlds, New Animals: From Menagerie to Zoological Park in the 19th Century*.

There is no evidence that aviaries similar to those of today existed so long ago. Even in Greek and Roman times, captured birds probably were kept in small cages. Nor is there information on how animals were captured. "I assume that much of this was done with lures, snares, and pit traps," comments Hoage. "The ingenuity of the human mind for developing traps for animals is incredible!"

▶ *Every year, my mother-in-law and I have the same discussion: Is it better to prune rosebushes in the fall or in the spring? Do you have an opinion about our quandary?*

According to Leonard Veazey, head gardener for the American Rose Society, rosebushes are best pruned in the early spring, before they break dormancy: "As soon as the weather begins to warm up, you'll see the buds start to swell. That's a good time to prune, for it indicates that the canes will break out about two weeks later."

Veazey recommends that all dead wood, diseased wood, and spindly growth be removed. Nuisance canes, such as those that run into walls or come out over a walkway, should also be removed. In areas of the country where there is a problem with cane borers, cuts should be sealed with either a pruning sealer or a substance such as Elmer's glue.

"After the bushes start to bloom, you need to do what we call deadhead pruning," says Veazey. "When a bloom is spent, prune the cane no higher than the highest five-leaflet leaf. If you prune higher, or just snip off the end, you'll get a blind shoot and either a very small bloom or no bloom at all."

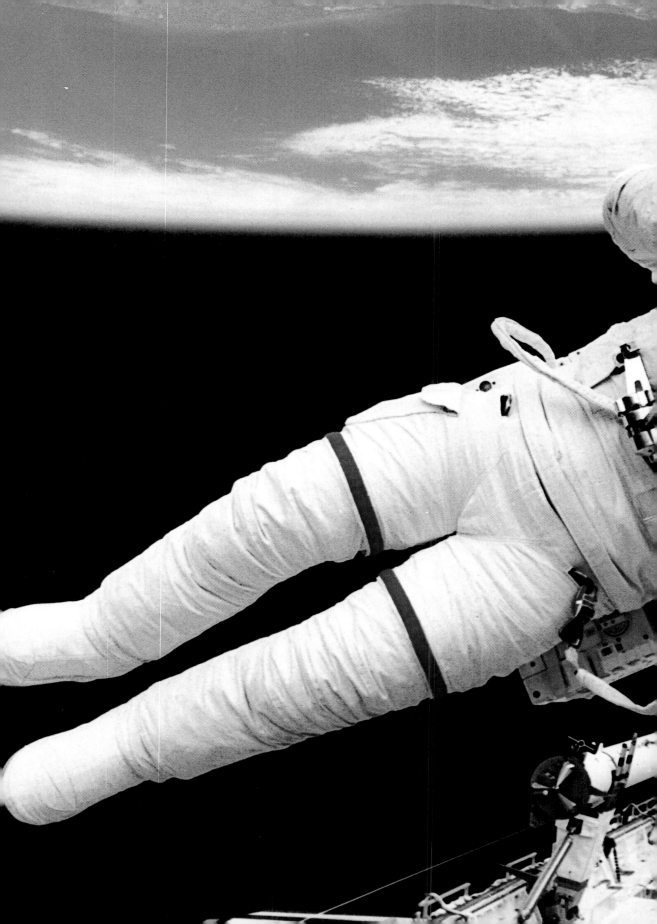

ASTRONOMY AND SPACE SCIENCE

■ RECENT ADVANCES IN SPACE-EX-PLORATION TECHNOLOGY INCLUDE A JET-POWERED RESCUE SYSTEM, SHOWN AT LEFT BEING TESTED BY A SPACE-SHUTTLE ASTRONAUT. THE BACKPACKLIKE DEVICE WOULD BE WORN DURING THE CONSTRUCTION AND OPERATION OF THE SPACE STA-TION, AND DURING OTHER UNTETHERED ACTIVITY OUTSIDE A SPACECRAFT.

CONTENTS

Fire
and
Ice
in the
Jovian
Sky

by Dennis L. Mammana

It was considered by many to be the most exciting week of modern astronomical history. Between July 16 and July 22, 1994, a fragmented comet named Shoemaker-Levy 9 (S/L-9) collided with the giant planet Jupiter, an event never before witnessed by human eyes, and one that captured the imaginations of scientists and the public.

Not only was Jupiter bombarded that week; so, too, were science museums and planetariums around our own planet—not by cometary debris, but by interested sky watchers. Astronomers at Griffith Observatory in Los Angeles, California, reported that as many as 10,000 people showed up there each day to peer through their telescopes at the cosmic fireworks.

Those with computer access to the Internet also got on the bandwagon—collecting information and images within minutes of

Jupiter (opposite) sports a chain of "cosmic black eyes," the sites at which fragments of Comet Shoemaker-Levy 9 collided with the giant planet in July 1994. Telescopes everywhere were focused on Jupiter to witness the weeklong bombardment.

their release by scientists. During impact week, the S/L-9 "Home Page" on the World Wide Web received 853 images of the show taken by 57 separate observatories, and 1,123,930 people logged on to receive 24.9 gigabytes of information.

Since no cosmic event of this magnitude or type had ever been observed before, astronomers and planetary scientists were absolutely giddy with excitement. They had nearly every telescope on Earth and in space aimed in the direction of Jupiter to collect, record, probe, measure, tabulate, and calibrate every piece of data they could.

What any one of these instruments would detect was anyone's guess. All scientists could do was use their knowledge of physics and mathematics, and rely on high-speed computer calculations, to speculate on the results of the impacts and whether they would be

When discovered, the comet had already been shattered by Jupiter's gravitational pull. In Hubble photographs taken two weeks before impact, the comet fragments resembled a glowing "string of pearls."

Tucson, Arizona, were using the 18-inch (0.5-meter) Schmidt Telescope on Palomar Mountain near San Diego, California, to scan the heavens in search of asteroids or comets passing overhead.

The weather was somewhat cloudy, and, since their photographic plates were expensive, the team decided to use plates that had previously been fogged by light. Through the broken clouds, the team aimed the telescope and began to make some exposures.

Once the team shoots and develops a pair of plates of the same celestial region, Carolyn Shoemaker, known affectionately to the group as "Ol' Eagle Eyes," begins to scan them with a stereomicroscope in search of objects that have changed their positions. On that night, she was examining a region about 4 degrees from Jupiter when something intriguing caught her eye.

"She came to a [fuzzy image about 1 minute of arc across]," recalls Gene Shoemaker, "then stopped, came back, and looked at it carefully. She sat up in her chair and said, 'I don't know what I've found here, but it looks like a squashed comet.' Later she wished she'd thought a bit longer and said something more poetic, but, in any case, she didn't. It kind of looked like a comet that somebody stepped on."

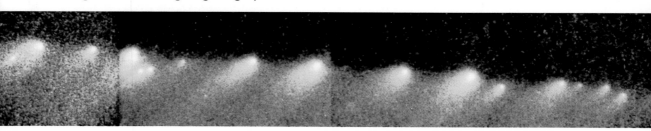

visible from Earth. After all, no one had ever seen such an event before. But now everyone was excited about the possibilities.

"HAVE YOU FOUND A COMET!"

All the cosmic hoopla began innocently enough on March 24, 1993. On that night, Eugene and Carolyn Shoemaker of the Lowell Observatory in Flagstaff, Arizona, and David H. Levy, an amateur astronomer from

In order to get an independent confirmation of their find, they called Jim Scotti, an astronomer at the University of Arizona in Tucson, who that night was working with the Spacewatch Telescope at the Kitt Peak National Observatory near Tucson. "I described to him what we were seeing," says Shoemaker, "[that] it was [near] Jupiter, and that its apparent motion on the sky mimicked [that] of Jupiter rather closely. He was immediately suspicious that we were seeing some kind of artifact on the film [caused by] some reflection of stray light from Jupiter, but he agreed that he would look.

"A couple of hours later, we called him again, and found an obviously excited guy on the other end of the line. 'Have you guys got a comet!' he exclaimed."

Since Scotti had the advantage of viewing the object with an electronic detector attached to a larger telescope, he could see many more details than the Shoemaker-Levy team. By adjusting the contrast on his computer monitor, he could see as many as 11

discrete pieces within the flattened comet. Nothing like it had ever been seen before.

A COMET ORBITING JUPITER

Within hours, word of the discovery was released, and astronomers around the world were gazing in amazement at the newly found multiple comet. Not only did it have a number of nuclei from which streamed tails of gas and dust, but it was in orbit, not around the Sun, which most comets orbit, but the planet Jupiter.

By calculating its orbit backward, astronomers determined that an otherwise normal

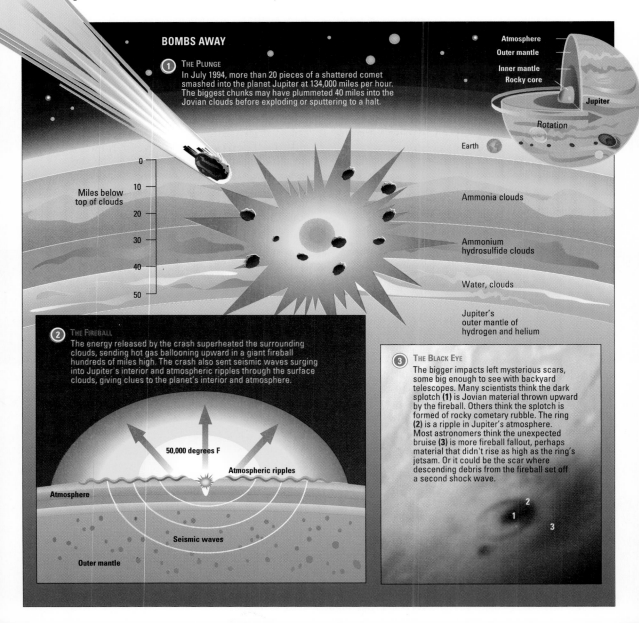

BOMBS AWAY

① **THE PLUNGE**
In July 1994, more than 20 pieces of a shattered comet smashed into the planet Jupiter at 134,000 miles per hour. The biggest chunks may have plummeted 40 miles into the Jovian clouds before exploding or sputtering to a halt.

Atmosphere
Outer mantle
Inner mantle
Rocky core
Jupiter
Rotation
Earth

Miles below top of clouds
0
10
20
30
40
50

Ammonia clouds

Ammonium hydrosulfide clouds

Water, clouds

Jupiter's outer mantle of hydrogen and helium

② **THE FIREBALL**
The energy released by the crash superheated the surrounding clouds, sending hot gas ballooning upward in a giant fireball hundreds of miles high. The crash also sent seismic waves surging into Jupiter's interior and atmospheric ripples through the surface clouds, giving clues to the planet's interior and atmosphere.

50,000 degrees F
Atmospheric ripples
Atmosphere
Seismic waves
Outer mantle

③ **THE BLACK EYE**
The bigger impacts left mysterious scars, some big enough to see with backyard telescopes. Many scientists think the dark splotch (1) is Jovian material thrown upward by the fireball. Others think the splotch is formed of rocky cometary rubble. The ring (2) is a ripple in Jupiter's atmosphere. Most astronomers think the unexpected bruise (3) is more fireball fallout, perhaps material that didn't rise as high as the ring's jetsam. Or it could be the scar where descending debris from the fireball set off a second shock wave.

2
1
3

comet had been orbiting Jupiter in a highly elliptical path for at least 20 years. But on July 7, 1992, when the comet reached its closest approach to the planet—about 60,000 miles (96,000 kilometers)—the planet's great gravitational pull tore the comet into pieces.

Comet S/L-9 was not the first comet ever to orbit Jupiter or even to break up. What made it unique was that it was the first ever to be *observed* while orbiting a planet.

"About two months after the discovery," recalls Shoemaker, "on May 22, it became possible to make a forecast that, on its next return to Jupiter, instead of just missing it narrowly, the comet would actually hit [the planet]. It was only about a two-thirds probability at that time, but as further positions [were determined, the probabilities] got better."

Now the questions came fast and furious. How large were the cometary fragments, and how fast were they moving? If S/L-9 did hit the planet, would it be an event we could see here on Earth? And what kind of effect would it have on the planet's atmosphere?

Over the next few months, astronomers and planetary scientists worked on answering these questions. "We were very lucky to have been able to find the comet so far ahead of time," says Shoemaker, "because it made it possible for observers around the world to lay plans for observing both the comet itself and the impact events which, by late December and early January 1994, we knew were going to happen the week of July 16–22."

Some scientists estimated that the parent nucleus of the comet (before breakup) was a chunk of dirty ice about 1.25 miles (2 kilometers) across, and that the individual icy fragments should be no larger than 0.33 mile (500 meters) across. Others suggested that the largest fragments could be as large as 1.8 to 2.5 miles (3 to 4 kilometers) across, which means that the original nucleus could have been at least 6.2 miles (10 kilometers) wide.

In 1993, the team of David Levy (left) and Carolyn and Eugene Shoemaker discovered the comet that now bears their names. Carolyn Shoemaker, a veteran comet hunter, holds the world record for comet discoveries.

Photos taken with the Hubble Space Telescope (HST) showed that the comet's train of nuclei—its "string of pearls," as one astronomer described it—was stretching, changing its length from about half the Earth-Moon distance at the time of its discovery, to more than 3 million miles (5 million kilometers) long by mid-July. They identified the multiple fragments with letters of the alphabet—with fragment "A" being the first expected to hit, followed by "B," "C," etc. (Several letters, including "I" and "O," were omitted to avoid confusion with the numbers "1" and "0.") In addition, the fragments themselves were evolving—some were apparently disintegrating or breaking up, while others were coming into view, adding an additional uncertainty to an otherwise confusing event.

Only a few predictions could be made with confidence. For example, the shattered comet would collide with Jupiter over a 5.6-day period in mid-July 1994. The first of its 21 fragments was expected to impact the planet on July 16, and the last on July 22. Unfortunately for Earthbound observers, the pieces would hit on the dark far side of Jupiter—about 5 to 9 degrees beyond the planet's sunlit side. They would disappear behind the limb of Jupiter only 5 to 15 seconds before impact. Then, about 8 to 18 minutes after each fragment hit, the impact points would rotate over the planet's horizon, entering sunlight and becoming visible to observers on Earth.

But the results of the impacts themselves, and the devastation they might cause in the Jovian atmosphere, were far from certain. "Many different theorists bent their lances on trying to calculate what would happen when a ball of ice plunges into the atmosphere of Jupiter at 130,000 miles per hour [60 kilometers per second] carrying a tremendous wallop

Dark, larger-than-Earth-sized impact scars (above) that dotted Jupiter's southern hemisphere quickly faded (inset). Information gained from the multiple impacts provided new knowledge about Jupiter, comets, and the origin of the solar system.

of energy," says Shoemaker. "A 1-kilometer-diameter ball of ice would carry much more energy than all the nuclear weapons in the world piled together and set off at one time."

Computer simulations were the only hope scientists had of getting a handle on the situation. They suggested that, at an altitude of 62 miles (100 kilometers) above the visible cloud decks of Jupiter, aerodynamic forces would overwhelm the material strength of the comet, beginning to squeeze it and tear it apart. Five seconds after entry, the comet fragment would deposit its kinetic energy of around 10^{28} ergs (equivalent to about 200,000 megatons of

dynamite) at 64 to 94 miles (100 to 150 kilometers) below the cloud layer. Bigger fragments would likely have more energy and go deeper, and would launch a hot plume thousands of miles above the Jovian cloud tops, and splash down into the stratosphere, enriching the region with such chemicals as water or ammonia, and producing haze.

Whether any of this would be visible, let alone happen in the first place, was anyone's guess. Would the impacts cause a long-term climate change in the giant planet's atmosphere? Would the intense light of the fireballs be reflected by the Jovian moons and be visible from Earth? Would the 21 nuclei survive their journey, or would they be so fragile that gravitational forces would pull them apart into thousands of smaller fragments, causing absolutely no effect at all? No one knew for sure, and debates raged among scientists.

STRIKE ONE!

On the evening of July 16, 1994, scientists were gathered at the headquarters of the National Aeronautics and Space Administration (NASA) to observe the results of the impact of fragment A. "That night," says Shoemaker, "I was upstairs giving a press conference, and these other people were downstairs watching the data coming in. Apparently, they were getting very excited while I had gone through all this theoretical jazz upstairs. Pretty soon, [Dr.] Heidi Hammel came upstairs and into the Press Room waving a picture in her hand, and showed what *actually* was happening at Jupiter. I can tell you there was joy in Mudville!"

The photo showed a "bruise," larger than the entire Earth, in the upper atmosphere of the giant planet. Was this cometary material left behind as the chunk plunged through the atmosphere, or was it material dredged up from deep within the Jovian clouds? No one knew, but with 20 more fragments still to hit, scientists were excited beyond words. And they began to update their observation programs to capture as much data as possible.

Over the following week, many more fragments impacted Jupiter, and many more photos were made available to the scientific and public communities alike. We learned that S/L-9, though much debated, was probably cometary in origin, rather than being a broken-up asteroid. The HST Faint-Object Spectrograph found evidence in the Jovian atmosphere for sulfur-bearing compounds as well as ammonia, silicon, magnesium, and iron, some of which could have been left behind by the impacting bodies themselves.

Hubble's Wide-Field/Planetary Camera (WF/PC) made global maps of Jupiter to track changes in the dark debris caught up in the high-speed winds at Jupiter's cloud tops. Over time, easterly and westerly jet streams turned the original dark "blobs" at the impact sites into striking "curlicue" features.

But scientists were interested in more than just visible effects. For example, about four days before impact, at a distance of 2.3 million miles (3.7 million kilometers) from Jupiter, fragment G apparently penetrated Jupiter's powerful magnetic field. HST's Faint-Object Spectrograph recorded dramatic changes at the magnetosphere crossing that provided a rare opportunity to gather more clues on the comet's true composition. Hubble also detected an unusual amount of auroral activity in Jupiter's northern hemisphere immediately following impact of the K fragment in the planet's southern hemisphere, possibly caused by an electromagnetic disturbance that traveled along magnetic field lines from one hemisphere to the other.

THE VIEW FROM DEEP SPACE

Voyager 2 and Galileo were the only two spacecraft in direct view of the nightside impact points. From its distant location 3.8 billion miles (6.1 billion kilometers) away, Voyager 2, launched in August 1977 and now leaving the solar system after exploring the giant outer planets, used its ultraviolet spectrometer and its planetary radio astronomy instrument to detect and measure emissions stimulated by the impacts.

From its vantage point in space en route to Jupiter, the Galileo spacecraft had the only "close-up" view of the collisions on the dark side of the giant planet. Even so, Galileo was about 153 million miles (246 million kilometers) from Jupiter during impact week. Because of problems with its high-gain antenna, the spacecraft could not transmit data immediately to Earth. Instead, Galileo gathered observational data and stored the data on the spacecraft's onboard tape recorder for later transmittal with its low-gain antenna. Since information could be sent only at the unbelievably slow rate of 10 bits of data per second (or 10 baud), several months were required to receive it all. Since the impacts in July 1994, Galileo has transmitted images showing sequences of explosive plumes thousands of miles above the Jovian cloud tops, proving the predictions of scientists before the collisions.

The third major spacecraft to turn its eye toward Jupiter during impact week was Ulysses, the joint NASA/European Space Agency (ESA) mission to study the poles of the Sun. During July, while in the midst of its southern passage around the Sun, the craft was about 250 million miles (400 million kilometers) from our star, and about twice that distance from Jupiter. Its combined radio and plasma-wave instrument searched for impact-related radio emissions from Jupiter's magnetosphere.

WHAT A WEEK!

"We've been privileged to witness one of the primary processes that has shaped our own planet," says Shoemaker, "the impact process that has delivered the environment for life on Earth—it's delivered the water, the carbon, the other chemical constituents which are the building blocks of life and, I believe, probably the starting organic compounds—that is, the amino acids as well, during much more intense bombardment of comets early in the history of the solar system."

During the week, millions of people worldwide turned their eyes skyward—many for the first time—and witnessed one of the greatest astronomical events in history. They got to see firsthand the dark spots and streaks left behind by one of the most exciting events in modern astronomical history. And many experienced for the first time the wonder of scientific exploration and discovery.

Cracks In Heaven's Vault

by Seth Shostak

The ancients beheld the starry beauty of the night sky, and concluded that the heavens must be perfect in their construction. But modern astronomy tells a different tale. Lurking between the crystal white brilliance of the stars are places, terrible places, where space and time are twisted and mingled, and where the universe itself is punctured and bent. These are black holes, the cracks in heaven's vault.

No one has seen a black hole. By their very nature, no light escapes their tortured interiors, so they can't be observed directly. But these dark cosmic denizens can be revealed by the action of their enormous gravitational fields. In 1994, astronomers using the Hubble Space Telescope (HST) found compelling evidence for a massive black hole occupying the center of the nearby galaxy M87. Hidden within its maw is the mass of a few billion Suns.

While this discovery caused great popular excitement, most astronomers were more gratified than amazed. For decades, massive black holes have been the suspects in a major astronomical mystery: what powers such violent and energetic objects as quasars and radio galaxies? To find a massive black hole lurking in the center of M87 was akin to hearing the butler confess.

Unlike most of the objects known to populate the universe, black holes were first discovered, not with a telescope, but with a blackboard. Their existence was a possibility that dawned slowly, the result of thinking about how stars die.

WHITE DWARFS AND NEUTRON STARS

Stars are giant balls of hot, turbulent gas—gas that would soon evaporate into space if it weren't for gravity's inexorable inward tug.

But it is self-evident that the nuclear fires that keep a star burning must ultimately wane. When that happens, gravity's pull begins to overwhelm the forces that keep stars bloated. A dying star must inevitably collapse under its own weight. But collapse to what? For a Sun-like star, the final implosion will suddenly halt as the star shrinks to a ball no bigger than the Earth. The resulting stellar corpse is known as a white dwarf.

What are white dwarfs made of? In fact, they are composed of ordinary atoms, but atoms in which gravity has squeezed out virtually all the room between nuclei and electrons. The electrons no longer follow nice orbits around their nuclei, but wander from nucleus to nucleus, making an electron "gas." The pressure of the gas is enormous, and it is what keeps the white dwarfs from collapsing further. This is the strange fate that awaits many of the stars of our galaxy, including the Sun.

In 1930, while en route to England, a 19-year-old Indian student, Subrahmanyan Chandrasekhar, deliberated further the properties of white dwarfs. His fellow shipboard passengers arrived with tans and improved shuffleboard skills, but the young Chandrasekhar had something else to show for his time at sea. He had worked out the disconcerting fact that for dying stars larger than about 1.4 times the mass of the Sun, the pressure of an electron gas will not withstand the force of gravitational collapse.

Astronomers have long sought to prove the existence of black holes—objects so powerful and compact that matter and light cannot escape them. Finally, in 1994, conclusive evidence of a black hole was found inside an immense disk of swirling gases in a galaxy 50 million light-years away.

Thus, an expiring star only somewhat larger than Sol, of which there are many, will shrivel to a white dwarf, and keep on shrinking!

This fearsome prognosis was revised only two years later, to everyone's relief, after the discovery of the neutron. In 1932, the Russian physicist L. D. Landau showed that squeezing a white dwarf will force the electrons to combine with the protons of the nuclei, producing a ball of solidly packed neutrons only 5 miles across. The atomic forces of the neutrons, compressed to a density of 10 billion tons per spoonful, will be sufficient to thwart gravity's compulsion to collapse.

J. Robert Oppenheimer worked out the details of such "neutron stars" immediately

prior to the Second World War (before gaining wider fame as the father of the atomic bomb), although their physical discovery did not take place until three decades later. In 1968, Jocelyn Bell and Antony Hewish in Cambridge, England, observed clocklike radio pulses coming from the sky. These "pulsars" were soon recognized as the rotating neutron residues of massive stars, the pathological corpses predicted by Oppenheimer.

Practically all stars are destined to become either white dwarfs or neutron stars. But after massive stars is grim. They will collapse indefinitely. They will be crushed to the size of a pinhead and smaller.

POINT OF NO RETURN

The macabre consequences of such a choking concentration of matter, a black hole, can be divined from Einstein's general theory of relativity. An important aspect of this theory is that gravity warps the otherwise-smooth fabric of space. Beams of light, which we think of as traveling in straight

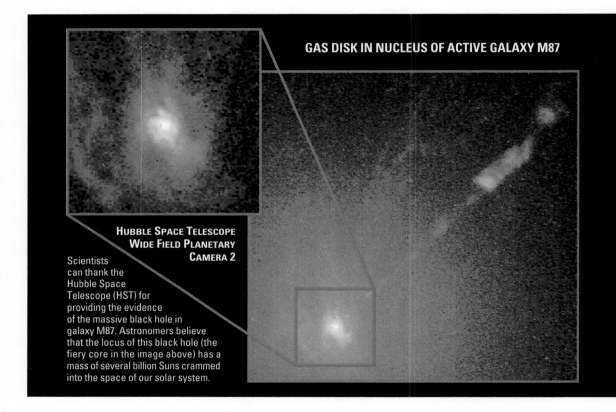

GAS DISK IN NUCLEUS OF ACTIVE GALAXY M87

HUBBLE SPACE TELESCOPE WIDE FIELD PLANETARY CAMERA 2

Scientists can thank the Hubble Space Telescope (HST) for providing the evidence of the massive black hole in galaxy M87. Astronomers believe that the locus of this black hole (the fiery core in the image above) has a mass of several billion Suns crammed into the space of our solar system.

Oppenheimer's work, theoreticians were vaguely troubled by the fate of the remaining few that won't—stars whose burned-out bodies are larger than three Suns. Simply put, these bodies can't exist. Even the fierce nuclear forces of compacted neutrons cannot withstand their gravity. Such stellar behemoths can be found in the Galaxy, and the theoreticians realized that the fate of these lines, bend slightly near sources of gravity, such as Earth or the Sun. From the light beam's point of view, it always proceeds along the shortest path to wherever it's going. It is space itself that has been warped.

In 1916, the German astronomer Karl Schwarzschild worked out the warping caused by an infinitely small concentration of mass. Schwarzschild was simply looking for a solution to Einstein's equations. The term "black hole" was still 40 years in the future. But the bizarre solution worked out by Schwarzschild turns out to describe the behavior of a simple, nonrotating black hole.

Schwarzschild found that there is a sphere around the crushed mass within which gravity's pull is so enormous that light is irresistibly turned back toward the center. The size of the sphere is given by the "Schwarzschild radius," which is directly proportional to the mass of a star. Light cannot escape from this sphere; a region of space has been bent in upon itself, and cut off from the rest of the universe. To put it another way, irrespective of what is happening to the condensed material at its core, a black hole emits no light. Trying to uncover a black hole with a flashlight or by bouncing handballs off it would be a waste of time. The Schwarzschild radius marks a point of no return for either light or handballs. Once they get closer, they are irretrievably lost. Black holes are truly black.

Which makes them very hard to find.

A Beastly Black Hole

Fortunately for those who hunt for these defects in the universe, some black holes are greedily feeding on their neighbors. Imagine two stars that orbit one another, a rather common situation in our galaxy. If one of these two stellar buddies happens to be especially hefty, it will eventually die and collapse to an invisible black hole. But the gravity of the dead star will continue to rip material off of its hapless partner. As the gas spirals fatefully inward toward the Schwarzschild radius, it will be squeezed and heated to millions of degrees by the black hole's gravitational field. X rays and gamma rays will stream from the incandescent gas, thereby betraying the dead star's presence.

This is more than a hypothetical scenario. Astronomers have found a handful of X-ray-emitting systems that look suspiciously like two stars, one of which is visible and one of which is a black hole. But the exciting news from the Hubble Space Telescope did not announce another such stellar-sized black-hole candidate. The Hubble team had found evidence for something

bigger. Much bigger. Crouching at the center of M87, according to Hubble, is the mother of all black holes: a Brobdingnagian beast with 2 billion times the mass of a star.

For nearly three decades, astronomers have pressed a search for such supermassive black holes. Their quest is motivated by the puzzling behavior of so-called "active galaxies," stellar conglomerations that are not content to simply fill the sky with the soft glow of starlight. Good examples are the radio galaxies, which somehow manage to squirt jets of high-speed particles from their innermost regions millions of light-years into space. Others are the quasars, intensely bright galaxies seen at great distances, radiating hundreds of times as much light as the Milky Way. Astronomers have observed that the energy for these hyperactive galaxies is generated in a tiny bit of space in their central cores. But what engine powers them?

Massive black holes have long been the prime suspect. According to Walter Jaffe, an active-galaxies specialist working at Leiden University in the Netherlands, "There's simply no other way to explain the very large amount of energy that comes from the central regions of active galaxies. We think that material falling into a massive black hole and radiating before it disappears within the Schwarzschild radius is the most efficient way of generating energy." Indeed, to produce energy by sucking material toward a black hole is dozens of times more efficient than nuclear fusion, the energy source of both the Sun and the hydrogen bomb. For this reason, astronomers have desperately sought evidence for titanic black holes. Finding such evidence would finally confirm their best guess as to what's under the hood of active galaxies.

M87 has long been a favorite hunting ground for this evidence. It is a huge, nearly spherical swarm of a trillion stars or more, and a well-known radio galaxy. It also has a famous luminous finger, or jet, extending from its core—a suspicious trail leading away from a secret powerhouse in M87's interior. For a dozen years, astronomers have trained their telescopes on the galaxy's center, hoping to find tell-tale signs of its hidden energy source. A few clues have turned up, primarily indications that the material near the center is

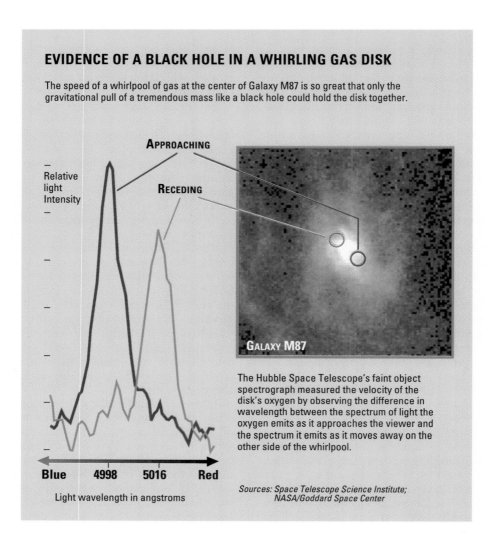

EVIDENCE OF A BLACK HOLE IN A WHIRLING GAS DISK

The speed of a whirlpool of gas at the center of Galaxy M87 is so great that only the gravitational pull of a tremendous mass like a black hole could hold the disk together.

Relative light Intensity

APPROACHING

RECEDING

GALAXY M87

The Hubble Space Telescope's faint object spectrograph measured the velocity of the disk's oxygen by observing the difference in wavelength between the spectrum of light the oxygen emits as it approaches the viewer and the spectrum it emits as it moves away on the other side of the whirlpool.

Blue   4998   5016   Red

Light wavelength in angstroms

Sources: Space Telescope Science Institute;
NASA/Goddard Space Center

in rapid movement. According to Newton's laws of motion, the more massive the object, the faster the speed of the bodies orbiting it. Rapid motion may mean a beastly black hole.

But this evidence is merely suggestive, not conclusive. Astronomers have been unable to scrutinize the innermost regions of M87 because the vision of ground-based telescopes is inevitably blurred by Earth's turbulent atmosphere. The Hubble Telescope was shot into space to beat that rap. So when the telescope was finally repaired, one of the first objects on its observing list was M87.

The results were stunning. At the center of M87 was a disk of hot gas 60 light-years (1 light-year equals 5.8 trillion miles or 9.4

trillion kilometers) from that galaxy's core, spiraling at over 680 miles (1,100 kilometers) per second, or over 2 million miles (3.2 million kilometers) per hour. Only one thing could keep this hell-bent-for-leather gas in place: the gravitational pull of several billion stars. But there are only a few stars visible in the core. The mass is there, but the light is not, and that's a perfect description of a supermassive black hole.

Does this wrap up the case? Holland Ford, one of the team leaders for the Hubble experiment, has little doubt: "I think it does. I think the data are speaking to it. When I show people the pictures and observations, and compare those to what you would predict

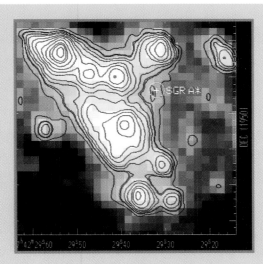

New data indicate that a black hole is growing at the center of the Milky Way. Infared images of Sagittarius A Star (SGR A*), a body in this region, show intense radiation emissions that are suggestive of a fast-spinning gas disk (and a black hole) like that detected in galaxy M87.

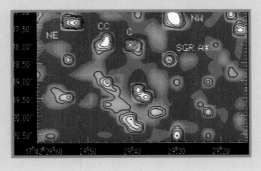

for a simple disk rotating about a 2-billion-solar-mass black hole, it looks pretty convincing." Of course, a devil's advocate might suggest that the central mass is composed of a dense cluster of neutron stars, or even tens of billions of dim, ordinary stars. "But the problem is that these would quickly collide, producing a massive black hole anyway," according to Ford.

Cannibalized Galaxies

The fuel for M87's black hole is probably hot gas that was spewed into space by exploding stars in the galaxy's younger days. Some of this ancient gas naturally falls to the center of the M87 galaxy, where it is now being eaten

at the rate of one star's worth every millennium. The hole is growing rather slowly.

It may be that the amount of activity in galaxies depends entirely on how fast they are fed. In the early days of the universe, galaxies were more numerous. Large ones frequently devoured their smaller neighbors. Consequently, even pint-sized central black holes would quickly bulk up on a diet of cannibalized galaxies. The energetic side effects of this youthful feeding frenzy are visible to us now when we look back in time at distant quasars, the intrinsically brightest objects in the cosmos.

How common are massive black holes? Walter Jaffe thinks, "There is certainly one per radio galaxy. So that's 5 to 10 percent of all galaxies, or billions in the visible universe." Holland Ford is more cautious, but basically agrees: "We all want to know. At present, I'm agnostic about it. We're going to observe other galaxies like M87, but also some nonradio objects. We're going to look at the Andromeda galaxy, for which there's already some evidence for a massive black hole. I think that all active galaxies have massive black holes, and it may be that *every* galaxy has them."

And that would include ours. Indeed, the Milky Way has long been suspected of hosting a modest central black hole with the mass of a million Suns. This suspicion has recently been bolstered with observations by astronomers at the University of Arizona in Tucson, who found evidence of a fast-spinning gas disk near the Milky Way's center.

Assuming our galaxy has a massive black hole, it is still 30,000 light-years distant, and neither a threat to us nor a likely destination for one of our space probes. Nonetheless, the theoretical work of the astrophysicists who first uncovered these objects with blackboards and ballpoints allows us to consider the fantastic possibilities for a voyager willing to take the plunge into a massive black hole.

Unlike the simple black holes described by Schwarzschild, a massive black hole would be rotating. "The geometry of a rotating black hole is horribly complex," explains Vincent Icke, a cosmologist working at both Leiden and the University of Amsterdam. "Space and time are so strangely curved, the paths taken by light begin to defy imagination."

VISIT TO A BLACK HOLE

Imagine for a moment falling toward the center of M87. Approaching the core, you see a growing black disk in front of you surrounded by an asymmetric halo of blue light—light from the rest of the universe now trapped in orbit about the black hole. Until you pass the Schwarzschild radius of M87, about 100 million miles (160 million kilometers) from the collapsed central mass, you can still send reports back to friends who have declined to make the trip. But the universe behind you closes off quickly. You are now lost as far as the familiar world is concerned.

If your path is precisely aimed at the crushed material in the hole's center, you have no hope and very little future. You'll

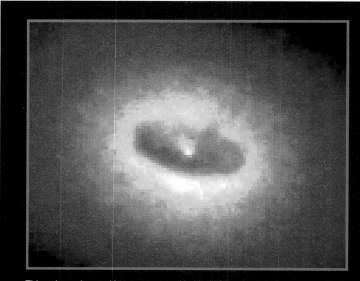

This color-enhanced image, captured by the HST, reveals evidence of a black hole and a surrounding gaseous whirlpool in the core of another distant galaxy. With such observations becoming increasingly common, some scientists believe that the universe may contain millions, or even billions, of black holes.

get about 10 minutes to consider the meaning of it all before you, too, will join the crushed remains of a few billion Suns. But if your path aims slightly to the side of the center, your fate is more bizarre. You might chance to go to another world, or another part of our world.

"Geometrically, it's possible to connect Schwarzschild horizons in a rotating black hole, but the future and past have been swapped," according to Icke. "What would happen to you is that you would pass through the Schwarzschild radius in our universe, becoming incommunicado from your brethren, but would emerge in another universe, where you would suddenly spring forth, suddenly appear.

"And technically, it's possible for both of these locales to be in the same universe, provided they are very far apart spatially. That's called a wormhole." In other words, you could reappear in our familiar universe of stars and galaxies, but a few billion light-years from M87 and other known astronomical landmarks.

That's a disturbing thought. Is it really possible that a 10-minute trip through a massive black hole would take you to another universe, or another region of our own universe? Both Icke and his co-worker Ed van den Heuvel, a specialist in compact objects, are skeptical. According to van den Heuvel, "The wormhole is a purely mathematical type of solution to Einstein's equations which is not forbidden, but it's unclear whether it's really physically possible. Based on a hunch and physical intuition, it's my feeling that it may be pretty difficult to come out the wormhole, either in our universe or in another. After all, when you come out, you could suddenly be standing next to some other guy. That's not a nice thing to do to someone."

Indeed not. But the fact that such a possibility can even be considered is strong testament to the baroque properties of the universe, properties brought to light by a few people curious about how stars die.

Other Suns, Other Worlds

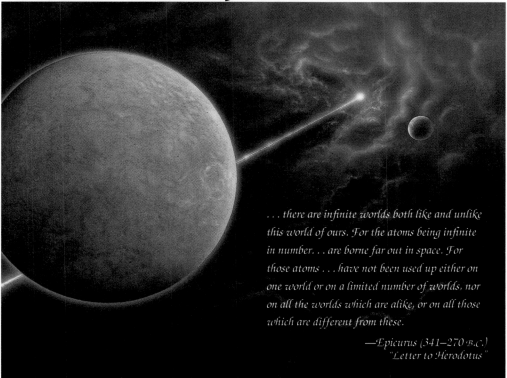

. . . there are infinite worlds both like and unlike this world of ours. For the atoms being infinite in number. . . are borne far out in space. For those atoms . . . have not been used up either on one world or on a limited number of worlds, nor on all the worlds which are alike, or on all those which are different from these.

—Epicurus (341–270 B.C.)
"Letter to Herodotus"

by Dennis L. Mammana

In his Letter to Herodotus more than two millennia ago, the famous Greek thinker Epicurus expressed his view that our familiar world is not the only one that exists— that beyond the world we know as Earth must lie others just waiting to be discovered.

At first glance, it might seem that Epicurus was millennia ahead of his time, pondering and teaching the existence of other planets in orbit around distant stars. But to the ancients, the expression "world" meant something completely different than it does today. "In Greek and Roman times, other 'worlds' meant other systems invisible to us," explains historian Michael J. Crowe of the University of Notre Dame in Indiana. "They weren't identified by planets or stars. Instead, each would be a whole system like ours—an Earth, a Sun, and planets going around it, and a starry ball where all the stars are just points on a huge vault like a planetarium roof."

While the idea that other suns are home to other worlds has its roots in antiquity, only recently has technology caught up with the dream, and is now enabling scientists to search for such systems.

FIRST CLUES

The first half of the 20th century saw astronomical discoveries come at a prodigious rate. Astronomers learned that the Milky Way was part of an immense universe of galaxies that were racing apart as if hurled from a huge cosmic fireball perhaps 15 billion years ago. They found that the universe radiates in wavelengths not visible to the human eye—infrared, radio, and X rays—

Scientists have taken great leaps forward in the age-old quest to find planets outside of our solar system. After decades of disappointing failures, astronomers have reported irrefutable evidence of a planetary system in a constellation some 1,500 light-years away.

and that special instruments could be built to detect these signals. And they learned of the existence of a ninth planet in the solar system—Pluto—a world so distant and faint that its light was detected only after an intense nine-month search. With an entirely new universe coming into view, surely, it seemed, the discovery of planets and planetary systems in orbit around other stars could not be far behind.

That is why, on April 18, 1963, at an astronomical conference in Tucson, Ari-

He determined that he could explain its irregular motion if an orbiting planet were tugging gravitationally on the star. Indeed, only six years later, Van de Kamp proposed an even more startling possibility—that the star was orbited, not by a single planet, but by two in circular, coplanar orbits. Now, it seemed, there was potentially an entire system of worlds orbiting Barnard's star.

But such was not to be the case, for it was not long before Van de Kamp's former student, Robert Harrington, found a strange dis-

Medieval astronomers (left) were able to identify and measure the movements of neighboring planets and stars, but they lacked the technology to find even such relatively nearby bodies as Uranus and Neptune.

For millennia, humans have pondered whether Earth-like worlds exist. The ancient Greeks, for example, believed that other habitable planetary systems were concealed in the distant heavens.

zona, when the distinguished astronomer Peter Van de Kamp, Ph.D., of Swarthmore College's Sproul Observatory stood before his colleagues with news of yet another discovery, the imagination of the world was piqued. It was here that Van de Kamp announced the discovery of a new planet. But this body was unlike any that had been found before, for it was 9,000 times more distant than Pluto, and orbiting another star.

Van de Kamp never actually saw the planet itself, but instead deduced its presence mathematically. For two and a half decades, he had watched its parent star—known as Barnard's star—wobble across the starry background.

continuity in the data that suggested the star's motion. Harrington showed that this irregularity was caused, not by an orbiting planet tugging on the star, but by a change in the telescope optics that occurred around 1949. When the data were compared with those taken before the change, the discontinuity appeared in the paths of the star's motions and produced the illusion of wobbles—wobbles that Van de Kamp had interpreted as evidence of extrasolar planets.

Rather than giving up completely, Van de Kamp put away all of the photographs he had taken before 1950, and continued to gather data on the star. And again, in 1978, Van de

Kamp made an announcement. This time, he described two bodies in orbit around Barnard's star—one with a mass of 0.8 Jupiter, orbiting every 11.7 years in a nearly circular orbit some 240 million miles (400 million kilometers) out, and the other with a mass of 0.4 Jupiter, orbiting every 20 years or more at a distance of 340 million miles (568 million kilometers).

Unfortunately, most astronomers today believe that Van de Kamp's "planets" were merely an illusion—an effect of less-than-per-

fect optics, inefficient measurement techniques, and, perhaps, an overly enthusiastic desire to find planets in the first place. Yet Van de Kamp's tireless work inspired astronomers to look to the stars in an entirely new way—as a potential home to planets and planetary systems beyond our own. Scientists realized that such a discovery would not be easy. It would have to be left to a new generation of astronomers, one armed with a revolutionary new arsenal of optics and electronic detectors.

MORE CLUES . . .

New understanding began unexpectedly with the launching of the InfraRed Astro-

nomical Satellite (IRAS) in 1983. In its first-ever infrared study of the heavens, IRAS found 50 or 60 stars that immediately caught astronomers' attention. These stars seemed to emit more infrared radiation than was expected from theory.

In astronomers' search for an explanation, one scenario kept surfacing: that the infrared "excess" was most likely emitted by a shell or disk of dusty material around each star and stretching outward 20 billion miles (33 billion kilometers). Because many of the stars involved were relatively young (less than 1 billion years old), astronomers believed they had found primordial solar systems in the process of forming.

Although these disks proved to be remarkable finds, they marked only the beginning. Soon astronomers put powerful ground-based instruments to work on the problem. In mid-1984, Bradford Smith of the University of Arizona in Tucson and Richard Terrile of the California-based Jet Propulsion Laboratory (JPL) armed themselves with a list of these "infrared-excess" stars and set out to see their disks. The astronomers' plan was to block the light of each tiny star image with a modified corona-graph, and use sensitive electronic detectors to record their images.

With their equipment attached to the 100-inch (2.5-meter) telescope at Las Campanas Observatory in Chile, the astronomers began with a five-minute exposure of the star Beta Pictoris. After the photograph was processed with special computer-enhancement techniques, scientists had an image of remarkable detail. Extending outward on both sides of the circular occulting mask were streaks of light—nearly 1 minute of arc from end to end. At the distance of

Beta Pictoris, this corresponds to a disk 37 billion miles (62 billion kilometers) across—10 times larger than our solar system.

Astronomers believe that the Beta Pictoris system may be only a few hundred million years old at most—a relative youngster compared to our own solar system—but old enough that planet building may have already begun within the system's disk. "This in itself doesn't firmly prove we have a solar system here," says Smith. "But based on the accepted model of how our own solar system formed, the particles should collide, stick together, and start building planets. The circumstantial evidence is very strong."

DIRECT EVIDENCE?

The first "direct" evidence also came in 1984, with the giant reflector telescopes at the Kitt Peak National Observatory near Tucson, Arizona. Donald McCarthy and Frank Low of the University of Arizona, and Ronald Probst of the National Optical Astronomy Observatory, set out to find unseen companion stars that made their presence known through the wobblings of their parent stars.

The astronomers used a new technique called speckle interferometry to reduce the blurring effects of our turbulent atmosphere so as to produce images many times sharper than otherwise possible. The key was to use the technique with infrared radiation so that the glare of the main star would not overwhelm that of the companion. As expected, the technique worked, and the researchers found most of the companion stars they were seeking. But one object, in orbit about the faint star Van Biesbroeck 8 (VB8) in the constellation Ophiuchus, immediately caught their attention.

At a distance of 21 light-years from Earth, the object—designated VB8-B—lay only 1 arc second from its parent star—the size of a dime as seen from a distance of nearly 2 miles (3.2 kilometers). It was much too faint and cool to be a star. It appeared instead to be the first real planetary body found in orbit around another sun.

From the faint flickers of light received, the scientists deduced conditions on the body. "We guess that it would have about the same size as Jupiter, but may be 10 to 30 times its mass, and [have] a temperature of about 1,100° C," says McCarthy. "Otherwise, we would expect it to be very similar to Jupiter—the same gaseous composition without a rocky surface to stand on. And it is revolving around a red-dwarf star every few decades at about the same distance as Jupiter is from our Sun."

McCarthy and his colleagues were concerned with checking and rechecking their results before making an announcement. Once the story hit the press, newspaper and magazine articles began accumulating on McCarthy's shelves. And then other astronomers pounced; some of them were upset with the decision to call the newly found object a planet.

"It had never occurred to me that you couldn't call this thing a planet," explains McCarthy. "It was an object that's not massive enough to generate energy by nuclear fusion, and it's revolving around a star. It's just a large Jupiter, guys! But that's not what everyone thought. I quickly found out that there were

The 33-foot Keck Telescopes atop Hawaii's Mauna Kea are expected to play an important role in the search for other worlds. NASA researchers plan to train the Kecks, the world's largest optical telescopes, on nearby stars to identify subtle indications of orbiting planets.

a wide variety of definitions of the word 'planet' floating around among astronomers."

VB8-B was unlike any star ever seen, yet unlike any planet in the solar system. For lack of a better description, scientists classified it as a "substellar object"—a peculiar missing link between stars and planets. Where the dividing line was between these bodies, however, was anyone's guess.

During the next few years, VB8-B went the way of Barnard's star's companions a decade earlier. Several independent teams of astronomers from Europe and the United States aimed telescopes toward VB8 with hopes of seeing its mysterious companion, but no one could find a trace of the body. McCarthy also went back to the telescope to take another look, but, despite a painstakingly careful search, he could not find it either. For all practical purposes, the body had simply vanished.

The first confirmed extrasolar planetary system orbits a pulsar—a collapsed star that emits conic beams, or pulses, of energy at regular intervals. The illustration above shows how planets may form in a type of binary system in which an ordinary star circles a pulsar (top). In a later evolutionary stage, the star grows into a massive red giant (bottom left). As it expands, the strong gravitational force of the pulsar pulls the red giant's outer layers into its orbit. Eventually, the orbiting particles coalesce into a planet (bottom right).

What could have happened to VB8-B? One of the most popular explanations today is that the body had never existed in the first place—that the original observations somehow had fallen victim to the Earth's wavering and unpredictable atmosphere or to the observational technique that astronomers used to find VB8-B.

AT LONG LAST . . . PLANETS?

Despite another extrasolar planetary disappointment, astronomers grew even more inspired, for they were armed with ever-more-powerful telescopic instrumentation and observational strategies. It was not long before an all-out race began to find planets in orbit around other stars. Yet, despite such intense efforts, no one could prove convincingly the existence of a single planet in orbit around another star. Until 1992, that is.

While working with a powerful radio telescope at the Arecibo Observatory in Puerto Rico, astrophysicists Alex Wolszczan from Pennsylvania State University in State College and Dale Frail from the National Radio Astronomy Observatory detected something rather unusual coming from the pulsar B1257+12.

Pulsars are remnants of supernova explosions—the deaths of massive stars that blast their atmospheres into space and leave behind a hot, dense core—a neutron star. With barely the diameter of a large city, these stellar corpses rotate extremely rapidly, and send pulses of radiation outward like beacons from a lighthouse. As the beams sweep past our line of sight here on Earth, astronomers detect them as pulses: hence the name "pulsars." Since pulsars radiate with periods that can be timed to within an accuracy of 10 millionths of a second, even the slightest outside effect on their motions can be measured accurately. And that is exactly what Wolszczan and Frail found: sometimes the pulses arrived several milliseconds earlier or later than one would expect from a single, isolated pulsar.

Astrophysicist Alex Wolszczan (below) and colleagues found convincing proof of new planets by studying unusual radio signals emitted by a distant pulsar. Many scientists have grown confident that new worlds—perhaps even some showing signs of life—will be identified.

The scientists argued that this variation was caused by at least two orbiting planets tugging on the pulsar—away from Earth, then toward Earth. And after continuing their observations, Wolszczan's team found evidence of one more planet. All of the three bodies appeared to be interacting gravitationally on each other and on their parent pulsar.

What made this discovery so unusual was that the planets orbited the remnant of a supernova explosion—a star that may have originally existed as part of a binary system. After the supernova of one star, the companion star spilled some of its material onto the pulsar, helping to spin the pulsar to its current rotational period of about 6 milliseconds.

These findings raised many questions. Where did the planets come from in this turbulent environment? If they existed in the original binary system (something astronomers do not yet understand), would they have survived the supernova explosion? And what caused the companion star to disappear, and how did this apocalypse contribute to the planet-making process?

While their origin is still a mystery, it seems likely that these planets mark the first extrasolar planetary system ever to have been confirmed. And if planets can form, not just at the birth of stars, but at their deaths as well, the universe may be literally teeming with planets—a prospect that excites modern astronomers tremendously.

"There are methods being applied right now that use technology like never before," says Donald McCarthy. "And in the next 10 or 20 years—when you throw the Hubble Space Telescope on top of that—we're going to see a lot of these things popping out all over the place. It's the beginning of a whole new field, and it's going to be fantastic."

The philosophical implications of these discoveries may be even more staggering than the scientific revelations. "A lot of the population, including many scientists, believe that our solar system is unique, that something peculiar happened here to form planets," says Bradford Smith. "These discoveries show that if there is only one more solar system out there, there surely must be others."

If such assertions prove to be correct, then a glance at the nighttime sky may encompass, not only thousands of stars, but possibly thousands of planets and even—who knows—some civilizations like our own.

Only time will tell if Epicurus' vision was correct!

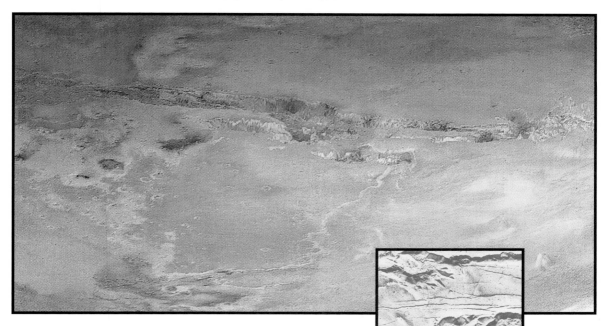

Planetary Oceans

by Michael Carroll

W here oceans exist, astronomers calculated, living things will prosper. Thus, they hoped mightily to find seas on the surfaces of our planetary siblings in this solar system. As the view of those planets enlarged with grander telescopes, radiointerferometry, and missile-aided observations, they were disappointed.

OLD HOPES DRY OUT

Astronomers first speculated that Venus—Earth's twin in size and proximity to the Sun—was an oceanic planet. Early telescopes showed scientists a cloud-enshrouded world, one that must have been supported by swamps. Research has demonstrated that Venus is far from swampland. With daytime temperatures hot enough to melt lead, and a carbon dioxide (CO_2) atmosphere some 90 times as thick as the air we breathe on Earth, liquid water cannot exist on the surface of Venus.

Next, astronomers theorized that Mars was a watery planet. Smaller than Earth and half again as far from the Sun, this cold little world sports polar ice caps similar to Earth's.

The caps can be seen to retreat in the local summer and expand again in winter. When the caps disappear, darkness sweeps across the face of the Red Planet in a wave. It seemed to scientists that Mars held great forests that were greening with the waters of melting ices. But Mars is a desert world, far drier than the most hostile deserts of Earth. The cyclical waves of darkness come, not from flowering jungles, but from blowing dust. Mars' rarefied atmosphere is equivalent in pressure to Earth's at an altitude of 100,000 feet (30,500 meters). Summer temperatures scarcely climb above the freezing point of water at the warm equator. These conditions dictate that any Martian water instantly freezes or boils away explosively in the low pressure.

One of the distinct peculiarities of the solar system is that Earth is the only planet with liquid water on its surface. A search from

The Viking image of Mars (above) shows the canyons, volcanoes, and plains of the Martian surface. Features resembling ancient riverbeds (inset) add support to the theory that water once flowed on the Red Planet.

Earth is the only planet in our solar system with life-giving water on its surface. Any water on nearby planets would instantly freeze or boil away—preventing the existence of life as we know it.

Mercury to Pluto reveals not a single ocean like the ones that touch the shores of Earth. Beyond Mars, there are planets with plenty of water, but it is all frozen. In fact, the largest moons of Jupiter and Saturn are gigantic balls of ice with rocky cores. Their interiors may contain strange mixtures of water and methane or ammonia, but no watery surf washes across their frigid beaches.

For astronomers, this series of discoveries came as a grave disappointment. "All life on Earth requires liquid water," says Chris McKay of the National Aeronautics and Space Administration's (NASA's) Ames Research Center. McKay is a biologist who has been studying microbiology in the world's most barren places. "I've studied the polar plateau and the Greenland ice sheet. There are no organisms in these places except at the boundaries where liquid water exists."

On Earth now—witness to toxic ocean dumping and international squabbles over the oceans' wealth—it is a sobering thought that our planet has the only active hydrologic cycle in this highly diverse planetary system.

LIQUID ON DISTANT MOONS?

Bizarre oceanic masses may yet exist on the planetary moons of some of our neighbors, but these oceans at best are truly exotic and very alien. Researchers estimate that an ocean may exist below the surface of Jupiter's moon Europa. Europa's spectrum and density imply that the little moon is covered by a crust of ice and water more than 50 miles (80 kilometers) deep.

Oceans teem with life here on Earth thanks to the energy of the Sun. It seems inconceivable that anything could survive beneath dozens of miles of shadowy ice. But in 1977, the deep-sea submersible *Alvin* changed our ideas of just where life can live. In that year, the *Alvin* made its historic dive to the bottom of the Galápagos Rift Zone, some 9,200 feet (2,800 meters) below sea level. The site is bathed in eternal darkness; the water temperature is near freezing at a pressure of 2 tons per square inch. Pilot Jack Donnelly turned on the submarine's floodlights to see an oasis of living creatures unknown to science. This life was dependent, not on the Sun, but on internal chemicals that erupt from volcanoes on the ocean floor. Europa may have similar energy sources, fired by the gravitational pull of nearby Jupiter and its massive moons. What life may have evolved there is anyone's guess.

Europa's ocean is not visible, since it is covered with an ice crust, but we will undoubtedly have a better idea of the Europan ocean's structure when NASA's Galileo spacecraft arrives at Jupiter late in 1995. The craft is expected to return high-resolution images of Europa and the other moons of Jupiter. Perhaps someday we will be able to send space-age divers to explore the depths of this Jovian moon.

Many of the moons of the outer planets have water ice as a major constituent. Two of Jupiter's other large moons, Ganymede and Callisto, are thought to be nearly 45 percent water ice, but their geology shows us that liquid water, if it exists, is far below the surface. Many of Saturn's moons show fairly pure water ice on their surfaces, and one, Enceladus, seems to have had some kind of flooding in its past. Enceladus is associated with the faint "E" ring of Saturn, which is a fine mist of ice particles encircling the ringed world. This ring may be evidence of active geysers on Enceladus today, but subsurface water probably exists only in the form of small ponds or lakes.

AN EXOTIC OCEAN

Another exotic ocean may exist beneath the bright-orange haze of Saturn's planet-sized moon Titan. This ocean is not made of water, but rather, a mixture of liquid ethane, propane, methane, and liquid nitrogen. Jonathan Lunine of the Lunar and Planetary Laboratory at the University of Arizona in Tucson explains how the scientific community has

As the Sun ages and swells, Earth's oceans will dry up and, on neighboring planets, frozen oceans beneath the surface will be released. Scientists may yet discover liquid water on distant worlds beyond our solar system.

struggled to understand the nature of Titan's surface: "With the Voyager spacecraft encounters, we saw enough methane in the lower atmosphere to indicate that it was pretty close to the saturation point. People were saying, 'Maybe there's a pure-methane ocean on the surface.' But when we realized that there wasn't enough methane in the atmosphere to support that, we started to think that maybe there wasn't any methane liquid on the surface at all. Then the idea came up that if you mix the methane with some of the byproducts of methane from the atmosphere (like ethane), and also with the nitrogen that makes up the bulk of the atmosphere, you could have an ocean of methane at the surface that didn't require such a high humidity of methane in the atmosphere."

Further research brought about updated models for Titan involving a hydrocarbon sludge raining out of the atmosphere onto an icy surface. These hydrocarbons result from sunlight acting upon methane to break it up. The resulting molecules recombine with others to create organic material that falls to the surface. The landscape was also thought to be partially covered by oceans of up to 0.6 mile (1 kilometer) in depth. "When you get oceans beyond 1 kilometer deep," says Lunine, "you're probably covering all the craters completely, so at this point, some were envisioning a global ocean. That's where things stood until people began looking at Titan with radar." Radar studies in 1989 indicated that Titan had a smooth surface with several rough "continents," but the smooth areas carried the radar signature of a hard surface rather than an ocean.

The radar data forced many to suggest that dry land dominates the landscape below the orange haze of Titan, but the radar data are enigmatic. Lunine sums up the situation in this way: "I would say that the chemistry we saw through Voyager still argues for large areas covered with substantial seas, and other terrain that is dry and covered by solid organic material which has rained out of the sky." Perhaps we will know 10 years from now, when NASA's Cassini Saturn mission delivers the European Space Agency's (ESA's) Huygens probe into the ruddy and still-mysterious fog of Titan.

NEPTUNE'S HIDDEN SEAS

Beyond Saturn, and out even beyond Uranus, lies the blue giant Neptune. It was once thought that nitrogen, which makes up most of Earth's air, existed as oceans or lakes on Neptune's moon Triton. Triton is so cold that many of the gases we normally breathe would there turn into a pool of liquid or a block of solid ice. When the Voyager spacecraft visited Triton, the probe discovered that Triton's nitrogen seas are actually underground. Sometimes the ice cracks, and nitrogen geysers burst into the thin air of Neptune's strange moon. The southern latitudes of Triton are covered by a veneer of frozen nitrogen.

Researchers believe that sunlight filters in through the nitrogen ice, which is clearer than water ice. As the sunlight reaches the interior of the ice, it warms the lower layers. This process is called a "solid-state greenhouse effect." The nitrogen ice vaporizes, building up pockets of gas that eventually explode onto the surface. Miniature seas of liquid nitrogen may rest throughout the inner layers of Triton's ice cap. Evidence of liquid eruptions can be seen in locations all across the face of Triton that we have seen through the eyes of Voyager, but understanding the true nature of these eruptions must await further investigation.

Other mysterious seas may exist at the heart of the giant worlds: Jupiter, Saturn, Uranus, and Neptune. Under the unimaginable pressures beneath hundreds of miles of atmosphere, seas of metallic liquid hydrogen may slosh in an eternal night. Envisioning such a sea at the heart of Jupiter, astronomer William K. Hartmann describes it as "a world sea 114 times the area of the entire planet Earth." The pressures are so great that they have not even been duplicated in the laboratory, but mathematical models point to superdense liquid cores within these colossal worlds. We can only guess.

CHANGING TIMES

Earth's oceans are unique in the solar system today, but our planetary neighbors may once have held great watery systems. Because many spacecraft have drawn near Mars, scientists have a pretty clear idea of its surface details. At the edge of the great Martian plains appear to be dried-up river valleys. Planetary geologist Vic Baker and others feel that a huge ocean may have glistened across these plains in past epochs, when the air of Mars was warmer and thicker. "The existence of [an ancient] ocean is not essential," says Baker in a recent paper, "but it is a probable element in the hydrological cycling responsible for the widespread valley networks." Although it is an arctic wasteland today, Mars may have been much more like Earth long ago. While the issue of long-term oceanic bodies on the Red Planet is controversial, according to Cornell's Steven Squyres: "I think we all agree that conditions on early Mars were significantly different from those of today." Mars may have had thundershowers and blizzards that were much like our own weather.

Even our broiling neighbor Venus once may have been cooled by oceans. It is so close to the Sun, and Venus' geologic cycles are so different from ours, that its oceans could not keep it cool. Soon the Venusian oceans boiled away, leaving carbon dioxide permanently in the atmosphere, and resulting in the furnace that Venus is today. Active volcanism in the past few hundred million years has erased any evidence of ancient oceans.

In the distant future, our Sun will swell up, becoming what is known as a red-giant star. In old age, stars similar to our Sun burn up most of their hydrogen fuel in the nuclear fires at their core, converting it to helium. As the helium begins to fuse into heavier materials such as carbon, the core heats the outer layers of the star. As this process causes our older Sun to swell, it will engulf Mercury and, most probably, Venus. In 4 billion years, scientists estimate, our oceans will be long gone, replaced by molten rock. Mars may enjoy a brief season wherein water inventories currently locked in permafrost will be freed to bolster the atmosphere and form lakes and oceans. Later the moons of Jupiter and Saturn will turn into wet worlds, with deep oceans covering their entire surfaces.

The study of other planets proves that nothing lasts forever. When our Sun grows old, our own life-giving oceans will disappear. That such fragile and unique conditions provide Earth with oceans might inspire us to show more respect for this resource that covers most of our home planet.

The Astronomical Name Game

by Govert Schilling

Joseph and Mary were lucky: an angel appeared to Joseph in a dream and told him which name to give their son. But astronomers rarely, if ever, experience such divine assistance in naming comets, asteroids, planetary satellites, or craters. And the problem gets worse every year as more objects are discovered, and space probes find ever more details on the surfaces of planets, moons, and asteroids.

In 1991, for instance, the Galileo spacecraft revealed numerous craters on the asteroid Gaspra, a lump of rock between the orbits of Mars and Jupiter measuring all of 9.3 miles (15 kilometers) across. However, the astronomers took inspiration from Grigory Neujmin, the Russian astronomer who discovered the asteroid in 1916, and named it Gaspra after a health resort in the Crimea. The craters on the asteroid will all bear names of other spas around the world, including Bath (England), Aix (France), and Spa (Belgium). Galileo also discovered a small satellite in orbit around asteroid Ida; this is now officially called Dactyl.

These are just some of the hundreds of new names approved by the 23rd General Assembly of the International Astronomical

Union (IAU) held at The Hague in the Netherlands in August 1994. "It's a time-consuming business," laments Brian Marsden, director of the IAU's Minor Planet Center in Cambridge, Massachusetts. In 1994, Marsden became chairman of the Small Bodies Task Group of the Working Group on Planetary System Nomenclature of the IAU, which is responsible for dreaming up names for newly discovered astronomical objects of all sorts.

LITERAL MINEFIELD

Nevertheless, naming things is fun. Marsden—himself a walking encyclopedia of hundreds of obscure numbers, designations, and proper names—could talk about it for hours. And it's instructive, too. Did you know that the surname of the French painter Rosa Bonheur, when transcribed in the Russian Cyrillic alphabet, is exactly the same as that of Yelena Bonner, the Russian political activist and widow of Andrei Sakharov? Well, it is, and for the Russian member of the IAU working group, this was reason enough to protest against naming a crater on Venus after Bonheur. So the IAU decreed that the crater be named Rosa Bonheur to avoid confusion.

Thousands of new names on Venus were necessary after the Magellan spacecraft mapped the planet in extreme detail between 1990 and 1993. Because Venus was the Roman goddess of love, the IAU decided that all the new surface features should be named after women. The scientists involved in the Magellan project came up with a large number of suggestions for names, but not enough. So many were needed that the IAU put announcements in astronomy magazines asking for more ideas from readers.

Among the hundreds of new names that the union approved in August are those of Austen (for the English novelist Jane Austen), Fossey (for Dian Fossey of *Gorillas in the Mist* fame), Akiko (Yosano, a Japanese poet), Aksentyeva (Zinaida, a Soviet geophysicist and astronomer), Kaikilani (first female ruler of Hawaii), and Martinez (Maria, a Pueblo artist).

The solar system has become a veritable *Who's Who*—not only of astronomy, but also of the other sciences and the arts. Craters on the Moon are named after scientists, while on the planet Mercury you'll find writers, painters, and composers—from Dickens, Dürer, and Dvořák to Rilke, Rubens, and Rameau.

Mars, though, is more reminiscent of an atlas, with a large number of small craters named after towns and cities on Earth, such as Amsterdam and Aspen. Whether or not you will be honored with a crater in space is usually not decided during your lifetime, however. "You have to be dead to have a lunar crater," acknowledges Marsden. But if you want a taste of immortality before your death, you can do it without being a brilliant scientist or an influential artist. You could try to discover a comet.

COMET CULTURE

Marsden sighs when the subject of comet nomenclature comes up. He is not a supporter of the current system of naming comets after their discoverers. "Of course, it's an important stimulus to amateur astronomers, who discover new comets visually by scanning the skies with their telescopes," says Marsden. What makes him uncomfortable, though, is the frequency with which comets are now named after teams of people.

The most famous of these are Eugene and Carolyn Shoemaker, who, together with amateur astronomer David Levy, have discovered a large number of comets. The comet Shoemaker-Levy 9, which crashed into Jupiter in July 1994, was their twelfth.

"Carolyn Shoemaker wants every member of the team to be honored in the name of the comet," says Marsden, "although she does the actual discovery by meticulously scanning the photographs." A couple of months ago, she discovered a comet while studying a photographic film back at her home institute in Flagstaff, Arizona, and when David Levy was "hundreds, if not thousands, of miles away," according to Marsden. Nevertheless, she insisted his name be included, because he was a member of the team that made the photographs. "You might as well include the name of the builder of the telescope," exclaims Marsden.

Unlike the case with asteroids, the International Astronomical Union does not have official rules for numbering and naming comets. Instead, the tradition has grown up of naming them after their discoverer. The "team problem," says Marsden, started in the late 1920s, when a new comet was announced by two astronomers, Schwassmann and Wachmann. The pair worked at the same observatory in Hamburg, Germany, and they set the precedent. "The comet was named Schwassmann-Wachmann. Maybe that was a crucial mistake," Marsden says.

"In 1939, three names—of independent discoverers—were used for the first time, with Comet Jurlof-Achmarof-Hassel." That set another precedent, notes Marsden. Ever since, triple-name comets have littered the solar system, not to mention the astronomical literature. For instance, there are Honda-Mrkós-Pajdušáková, Tuttle-Giacobini-Kresák, Du Toit-Neujmin-Delporte, and Tago-Sato-Kosaka, to list just a few.

In September 1994, to Marsden's relief, the IAU approved a new system of comet designations (numbers and letters), which became effective at the beginning of January 1995. The IAU has also set up a committee to establish clear guidelines for comet nomenclature in order to ensure fairness and simplicity. "In any case, the importance of comet names will be played down," explains Marsden. "Preference will be given to alphanumeric designations, and names will be put in parentheses."

FIGURE IT OUT

For instance, Comet Maury, which was discovered in August 1985, would be called 115P/1985 Q1 (Maury): it is the 115th known short-periodic comet, and the first one to be discovered in the second half of August 1985—short-periodic comets complete an orbit of the Sun in less than 200 years, and the 24 half-months are designated A through Y, skipping I because of possible confusion with the numeral 1. A second sighting of the comet in May 1994 (1994 Jl) has firmly established its periodicity. "In the future, the comet could simply be called 115P (Maury)," says Marsden.

This system of nomenclature is almost exactly the opposite to the one used for

After the Magellan probe yielded precise maps of Venus, scientists who name celestial objects decided that newly discovered features on the planet would honor women. Spanish Queen Isabella I (facing page), jazz vocalist Billie Holiday (center), and aviatrix Amelia Earhart (near left) were among those immortalized with Venusian namesakes.

asteroids—for which names are preferred, and numbers, which indicate how many well-cataloged asteroids were known when the orbit of the latest one was defined, are put in parentheses. For instance, Gaspra and Ida are officially known as (951) Gaspra and (243) Ida. But the provisional designation system is similar to the system for naming comets: immediately after their discovery, asteroids are called something like 1968 HB (the second asteroid discovered in the second half of April 1968). Only when their orbits are firmly established do they receive an official number and name.

Asteroids (or minor planets, as Marsden calls them) are not named after their discoverers, but by them. More than 4,000 names are in use, from classical ones like (26) Proserpina and (43) Ariadne to modern ones like (2907) Sagan and, yes, (1877) Marsden. You do not have to be dead to "have" an asteroid, although it might help: more than 200 letters from fans recently resulted in naming asteroid (3834) Zappafrank, after rock musician Frank Zappa, who died in December 1993.

Asteroid names follow many rules. Political or military names are not allowed; a name should preferably be a pronounceable

The 1993 death of eccentric rock star Frank Zappa inspired hundreds of fans to lobby for the dedication of a galactic memorial in his name. Asteroid Zappafrank, and many other oddly named objects, now tour outer space.

single word, and should be no longer than 16 characters. "We like to twiddle around with names—to be imaginative," admits Marsden. He is especially fond of "whimsical" names, like the ones suggested by Swiss astronomer Paul Wild. For instance, 1968 HB was named (2138) Swissair, because HB is the international code for this airline. Asteroid (2037), also discovered by Wild, was named Tripaxeptalis, with asteroids (679) Pax and (291) Alice in mind: 2037 = 3 x 679 = 7 x 291; "three times Pax and seven times Alice" became "Latinized" to Tripaxeptalis.

Many astronomers name their minor planets after their own family members. There is a complete Shoemaker dynasty up there, with (2074) Shoemaker and (4446) Carolyn surrounded by four parents, an aunt, an uncle, a brother, a sister, three children, a son-in-law, a daughter-in-law, and a grandchild. Twenty-five Nobel laureates have found their way into the heavens, as well as nearly every president and general secretary of the IAU.

Of course, special numbers warrant special names. Minor planet (1000) Piazzi is named after the discoverer of the first asteroid (in 1801); (2000) Herschel honors the first astronomer to discover a new planet; (5000) IAU was a present by the IAU to, well, the IAU. During 1994, the orbit of asteroid 1987 UN was confirmed so that it could become (6000) United Nations. Minor planet (2001) is not called Clarke or Kubrick, as you might expect, but Einstein.

According to Marsden, the names of minor planets are an interesting reflection of centuries of human society and culture. Browsing through Lutz D. Schmadel's *Dictionary of Minor Planet Names* proves him right—every single page turns up new surprises. Of course, the same holds true for the thousands of names on the surfaces of the Moon, Mercury, Venus, Mars, and the satellites of the giant planets. Joel Russell of the U.S. Geological Survey (USGS) in Flagstaff is currently completing the first edition of the *Gazetteer of Planetary Nomenclature*, which will probably also be published in electronic form. Although Joseph, Mary, and Jesus do not appear in its pages, the gazetteer may well become the bible of the astronomical name game. ◢

SECRETS OF THE RINGS

by Dava Sobel

Galileo mistook Saturn's strange markings for a pair of moons. Other early astronomers thought the planet spat out giant clouds of vaporous breath that clung close by; still others suggested that Saturn was shaped like an egg, and that two black blotches on its surface made it look like a double-handled cup.

It was Christian Huygens who first realized that Saturn's odd "appendages" might in fact be a ring, which he supposed was a solid, shiny strip. Still cautious about this conclusion, however, he hedged his bets by publishing his idea in the form of an anagram. At the end of his 1656 pamphlet announcing his discovery of Saturn's moon Titan, Huygens added a coded message that, unscrambled, read: "It is surrounded by a thin flat ring, nowhere touching, and inclined to the ecliptic." Not until the end of the 19th century did James Clerk Maxwell correctly suggest that a solid ring would shatter under the gravitational strains of orbit; he concluded that the ring must consist of a dense collection of countless separate small particles, all orbiting Saturn the way the planets orbit the Sun.

A MYSTERIOUS COSMIC SPECIES

Today the sprawling, sparkling Saturnian rings continue to surprise astronomers lured into their beguiling maze. During the past 10 years, for example, many scientists have been forced to abandon the long-established notion that the rings of Saturn are as ancient and enduring as the solar system itself. It now appears that the rings could not have formed along with the planet 4.5 billion years ago. Rather, they are a recent addition no more

The dramatic rings of Saturn have intrigued astronomers for centuries. The rings are not solid structures; rather, they are composed of millions of tiny particles that orbit the planet within a plane no more than 1.2 miles thick.

than 100 million years old. Furthermore, the same processes that created them are already sowing the seeds of their destruction. This makes the rings a passing fancy that will disappear before the next 100 million years go by. In all likelihood, Saturn has fathered several generations of rings over the course of its lifetime.

Once considered unique, Saturn's rings now represent merely the most spectacular specimens of a cosmic species known to circle every giant world—from Jupiter's diffuse, dusty halo, to the narrow, dark hoops of Uranus, to the demi-rings that appear to trace a line of dashes around Neptune. The presence of so many different systems suggests that rings sprout as a normal part of a giant planet's life cycle.

"I'm interested in all the ring systems," says Jeffrey Cuzzi of the National Aeronautics and Space Administration's (NASA's) Ames Research Center in Mountain View, California, who was drawn to his work by the confounding beauty of Saturn's rings. "I like to think of them as a family. Everybody is an individual, yet because of the resemblances, you can understand each one better by knowing something about the others."

To decipher the mysteries encoded in the rings, astronomers are currently scrutinizing these planetary sidekicks with every available means. They view them through ground-based, airborne, and space telescopes—both by the light that rings reflect from the Sun and in the silhouettes created whenever a ringed planet passes against the backdrop of a bright star. Some are planning future spacecraft encounters with Jupiter and Saturn for close-up study, while others content themselves with mental modeling, such as programming supercomputers to mimic ring behavior.

For now, the ice-bright rings of Saturn reign as lord of all the ring systems. Though Huygens took them for a single shining

The fine strands of Saturn's outlying F ring appear braided, perhaps as a result of the gravitational pull of two small, unseen moons.

body, within 20 years, Gian Domenico Cassini, using a superior telescope, found a gap. There were two rings, he insisted in 1675, with a dark lane between them that is still known today as the Cassini division. Even now, the most conspicuous features of Saturn's ring system, seen from a distance, remain the bright A ring; the even brighter, broader B ring that lies inside, just across the Cassini division; and the dim C ring, first seen in 1850, which reaches from the B ring's inner margin almost to the cloud tops of the planet. More recently, the Voyager and Pioneer missions confirmed the existence of three additional outlying rings (E, G, and F) and the vanishingly faint innermost D ring.

ANATOMY OF THE RINGS

Close scrutiny reveals at least 100,000 individual ringlets, each a little different from the next, shaped by the pulling of the planet and its many moons on the rich fabric of the ring particles. Picture the system as a spinning superhighway, divided into myriad narrow lanes. With modern radar and spacecraft, the ring particles resolve into red-tinged snowballs that range in size from sand grains to enormous boulders. Large satellites that lie beyond the ring system carve features within it, such as the scimitar-sharp edges and scalloped hems. Tiny moonlets embedded within the rings may knot them, braid them, clump them, and cut slices out of them.

Rings, most researchers agree, are moons gone to pieces—or captured comets, caught on the fly and then torn to shreds by competing gravitational forces. If you scooped up all the scattered particles of ice and dust in the glittering ring system of Saturn and packed them together, you could mold a moon about the size of Saturn's moon Mimas—a little under 250 miles (400 kilometers) in diameter. Such a satellite probably existed quite close to the planet 100 million years ago. Then along came a comet or another big body on a collision course and blasted the moon to bits.

This ill-fated moon lay within Saturn's Roche limit—named for the 19th-century French mathematician Edouard Roche, and defined as the region close to a planet where competing gravitational forces are strong enough to shatter unstable satellites or prevent them from forming in the first place. Within the Roche limit, destructive tidal forces dominate other effects. Tidal forces pull those parts of an orbiting body that are relatively close to the planet more strongly than the parts farther away; as a result, the satellite—held together only by the weak glue of its own gravity—may literally be pulled to pieces.

Outside the Roche limit, particles of a pulverized moon may regroup themselves bit by bit until they eventually fashion a born-again moon. Just such a series of calamitous events may have befallen Uranus' moon Miranda, and could explain why this particular satellite looks like an accident victim whose parts have been haphazardly sewn together. Miranda, some astronomers say, apparently formed, broke apart on impact, reassembled itself, suffered a subsequent impact, pulled itself together again, and so on—perhaps as many as five or six times since the solar system was young. Other ring researchers have reason to discount this scenario, but like all aspects of ring evolution, the real history of Miranda remains a matter for informed speculation.

HOW SATURN'S RINGS WERE FORMED

The moon that became Saturn's rings was too close to the massive planet to pull itself back together. Once it was smashed to bits, the pieces—large and small—all went into orbit in a cloud of debris. These particles eventually fell into a disk around the planet's equator. Orbits of particles at angles to the disk plane inevitably crossed, leading to frequent collisions. Only ring lanes more or less parallel to one another were able to survive for long. And even then, the particles continued (and continue) to bump and jostle one another, spreading themselves into concentric rings of varying diameters, like the grooves of a phonograph record.

Today the great circle spreads out into a disk more than 180,000 miles (290,000 kilometers) wide but scarcely 60 feet (18 meters) high, making it many orders of magnitude flatter than a pancake. Ring researchers compare it to a sheet of tissue paper spread across a football field.

Computer enhancement highlights the color differences between the rings of Saturn. The variations indicate differences in composition.

"You could never get another massive ring like this one around Saturn by bashing up a moon," observes Carolyn Porco of the Lunar and Planetary Laboratory at the University of Arizona in Tucson. "The only satellite left that's big enough to do it is Mimas, and Mimas lies far outside the Roche limit. But at Uranus and Neptune, you still have plenty of food for the ring machine. If you broke up all the satellites within the Roche limit of Neptune, you'd get a ring system that would not look too terribly different from Saturn's." That hasn't happened yet because nothing has smashed into one of these moons, but nothing precludes such an encounter in the future.

A photograph that shows "all" of Saturn's rings (above) belies the fact that the ring system includes at least 100,000 individual ringlets.

No one is certain, of course, that Saturn's rings were formed by a single large moon. They could just as well have formed from a group of three small satellites that were smashed, creating the current three-main-ring design. Some astronomers argue that the rings originated from a large comet that passed too close to Saturn and got ripped apart by tidal forces.

It could happen again, even today. Catastrophic events are hardly relegated to the solar system's distant past. In mid-1992, a comet known as Shoemaker-Levy 9 split into at least a dozen pieces after a close brush with Jupiter. These strung-out pieces crash-landed on Jupiter during July 1994 in a great burst of fireworks. But had the comet's path been a little different, its debris might have remained in Jupiter's orbit, perhaps developing into a stunning, substantive new ring.

"Mechanisms that are going on in the solar system today can explain how we got rings in the first place," notes Porco. "This is one of the arguments supporting the idea that the rings could be young."

SIGNS OF YOUTH

The dazzling brightness of Saturn's rings is another convincing indication of youth. Even though the rings of Saturn glisten with water ice and are therefore intrinsically brighter than the coal-black boulders that encircle Uranus, they still look eerily new, almost like a brand-new pair of tennis shoes. And that strikes astronomers as odd.

"We think the rings would look much darker if they were very old," says Cuzzi. "In computer models, we start off with nice clean rings of water ice, then dirty them up with comet crud." It does not take very long, on planetary time scales, for this dark, cometary dirt to scatter among the ice particles and turn the simulated rings the same color as Saturn's—about 100 million years.

Cuzzi's current research is focused on interpreting the varying shades of red in the Saturnian rings. Most "comet crud"—the pervasive debris that eventually dirties almost everything in space—is reddish. Scientists think it's either organic material or iron-bearing minerals, or some combination of both. In Earth's atmosphere, the sprinkling of space dust causes meteors, or shooting stars. Saturn probably comes in for an even heavier pelting, since the planet's greater mass attracts more material its way.

Whatever the nature of the reddish dust, Cuzzi can account for the gradations in shade by the effects of meteoroid bombardment. "Once dirt gets into the rings, it stays there and mixes in with the other material," he says, in a process he calls pollution transport. Dark dirt, distributed throughout the broad but thin ring plane, never disappears from view. The rings just grow dingier as time goes by. In the latest-generation computer model, just as in actual images of Saturn's rings, color deepens in a broad swath throughout the ring span. The areas with the least amount of material—the gaps, such as the Cassini division, and the tenuous areas, such as the C ring—have the fewest places for the dirt to hide, and tend to get darkest fastest.

Aside from causing color changes, the rain of debris could also add enough mass to the ring system to topple it before it reached an advanced old age. The new material landing among the ring particles lacks the angular momentum of the already orbiting particles; since the amount of angular momentum in a system always stays the same, other particles must sink to lower orbits, picking up speed, to compensate (just as a spinning ice skater's speed increases as he pulls in his arms). The effect is that ring particles slowly but inexorably begin to fall from the sky. Since we still see the rings, however, we can assume that they are too young to have accumulated an overdose of extra mass.

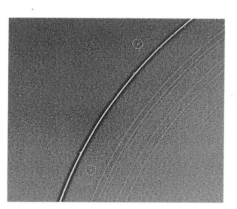

Gravity from two "shepherd" moons, Cordelia and Ophelia, forces the particles of Uranus' outermost ring into a narrow lane.

"If our estimate of the frequency of meteoroid hits is correct," Cuzzi says, "it's hard to understand how the rings could be more than 100 million years old." That estimate will be checked when the next outer-planet mission mounted by NASA and the European Space Agency (ESA), scheduled for launch in 1997, reaches Saturn in 2004. The double spacecraft, named for Huygens and Cassini, will measure the gross amount and individual particle size of infalling meteoroid material, as well as its velocity and electric charge. Once Huygens separates to land on Titan, Cassini will sail for at least four years among the rings and moons of Saturn; the craft is expected to send back some 500,000 images defining the stark geometry of the Saturn system and perhaps revealing the forces that shape it.

PAST AND PRESENT MOONS

Porco, who leads the Cassini imaging effort, would not be at all surprised to stumble on a few new moons that are too tiny or too embedded in the ring system to be detected from afar. Saturn's rings are not only the ruined remains of former moons (or comets); they also owe some of their fancy structure to the action of existing moons—at least 18 at last count—that orbit around and among the ring particles. Obvious ring features, such as the crisp margins and the dark Cassini division, which are readily seen through an amateur's small telescope, look sculpted by an outside hand. In a way, they are.

"You wouldn't expect a bunch of orbiting particles to create such sharp features," says California Institute of Technology (Caltech) theoretician Peter Goldreich, explaining why he and Scott Tremaine, now director of the Canadian Institute for Theoretical Astrophysics in Toronto, Ontario, first took on the ring margins as a thorny problem in dynamics. Something had to be confining particles, preventing them from following their natural tendency to spread out.

Physicists had long suspected that an important clue to the identity of that "something" lay in the respective positions of the Cassini division and the moon Mimas, which orbits about 60,000 miles (96,500 kilometers) outside the ring. The satellite travels at a slower pace than the ring particles, owing to its greater distance from Saturn. As Kepler showed in his laws of planetary motion, orbital speed depends on distance, with the closest bodies circling the fastest. Thus, at Saturn, the ring particles race ahead of the outlying moons. And the ring particles near the Cassini division travel almost precisely twice as fast as Mimas. Every time the moon orbits once around the planet, the particles shoot around twice. They fall directly under the moon's influence twice each go-around—once when Mimas is halfway through its appointed round, and once at the finish. At both these points, Mimas pulls on the particles harder than usual. Since the pull always comes at the same two points in the orbit, it gains strength over time—just as a child on a swing goes higher faster if always pushed at exactly the same place in the swing's arc. Even very gentle pushes in the right place can, over time, create a huge momentum, sufficient to propel the child right over the top. Similarly, Mimas has shoved the particles out of the Cassini division.

"Other investigators had considered the interactions of satellites with individual particles," says Goldreich, "but those effects would be too small to open gaps or maintain edges." Goldreich and Tremaine realized that the satellites were resonating instead with vast collections of particles that moved together fluidly, like molecules of water in an ocean wave. The particles, held together by their own mutual gravitational attractions, would not only feel the rhythmic tugging of the moons, but also transmit the disturbance outward through the ring plane, from the resonant orbits toward the outer fringes of the rings.

Indeed, Goldreich and Tremaine predicted that if they could get close to Saturn's rings, they would actually see these disturbances moving across the rings in spiral waves of compression and rarefaction not unlike sound waves. This bold prediction was verified when Voyager II photographed more than 30 spiral-density waves in the A ring that looked like the alternating light and dark stripes of a spinning pinwheel. The waves begin at the resonant orbits, then spiral out through thick and thin regions of the ring; some die out, while others crash on the ring's scalloped shores.

It is no accident that this pattern bears an uncanny resemblance to the spiral arms of the Milky Way. The rings may be built from the same blueprints, although, in the case of our galaxy, the sources of the gravitational tugging remain unknown. Planetary rings also provide a handy model for the proto-planetary disk that circled our Sun and condensed into planets 4.5 billion years ago; the current planetary orbits would correspond to density concentrations of ages past.

THE SHEPHERD MOONS

Other features in the rings demand different explanations. For example, two tiny Saturnian moons, discovered during a spacecraft flyby, orbit on either side of the planet's thin, outlying F ring. These newfound moons define the ring's shape by keeping the particles, which would otherwise tend to spread out, confined between them in a narrow strip—the way a couple of yapping dogs hold a flock of sheep together. The moons' names are Pandora and Prometheus, but they are more often called shepherd moons. Goldreich and Porco showed that two other shepherd moons, Cordelia and Ophelia, serve as ring bearers to the outermost ring of Uranus—which looks, in Porco's description, "as though someone took a brush and carefully painted between the lines."

The mechanism behind the herding involves both gravitational forces and complex exchanges of angular momentum between moons and ring particles. In brief, it works like this: the shepherd moon outside the ring moves more slowly than the ring particles, which in turn are outpaced by the fast inner moon. The outer moon pulls on the particles as they whiz by, producing a bulge in the ring, but since the particles are moving faster, the bulge quickly gets ahead of the moon and pulls it forward. This increase in speed boosts the satellite's angular momentum, pushing it into a higher orbit. Since the ring particles must lose as much momentum as the moon gains (to conserve angular momentum), they fall into lower orbits. Meanwhile, on the inside track, the moon's gravity raises a bulge in the ring, which lags *behind* the moon. The bulge slows the moon down, robbing it of angular momentum. That same momentum is gained by the ring particles, which respond by jumping into higher orbits. Caught between the inner moon and the outer moon, the particles are focused into a narrow band.

FAINT RINGS, STRONG CURIOSITY

When Neptune's rings were spotted by Voyager II in 1989, they looked like scattered arcs, like broken lines that did not wholeheartedly embrace the planet. Closer investigation, however, revealed that these arcs are very dense regions of quite tenuous rings that do, in fact, make full circles around

Of all the ringed planets, Jupiter has the most insubstantial set of rings. The main ring is a conglomeration of dust flanked on the inside by a cloudlike halo, and on the outside by a faint "gossamer ring."

Neptune. Porco speculates that the inclination of the orbit of the moon Galatea, tilted slightly in relation to the orbit of the ring particles, might be pulling them into clumps, creating the rich clusters that from afar appear to be isolated ring arcs.

Jupiter's rings are more ephemeral still—so insubstantial that many ring investigators scorn the system as "fluff" too tenuous to trifle with. The largest planet seems to have the frailest ring system of all. Over time, encounters with space debris have pulverized the ring particles to a powder barely detectable except by the closest scrutiny. Jupiter's thin main dust ring is flanked on the inside by a thick, cloudlike halo that

reaches halfway to the planet, and on the outside by a faint "gossamer ring," discovered and named by Joseph Burns of Cornell University in Ithaca, New York.

With this faint ring, as with perfume, Burns argues, a small amount of material can raise a high level of interest. The amount is so small, in fact, that gravity seems to play a rather small role in the Jovian ring dynamics. Instead, the rings seem organized around electromagnetic effects: the minuscule bits of dust dance to electric forces created within Jupiter's enormous magnetic field. Conspicuous by their absence are any ring features that could be attributed to gravitational resonances or shepherding. Although Jupiter has a large retinue of satellites, they can't seem to get a grip on the gossamer ring.

Somewhere buried in the dust, Burns believes, are the remains of the moons that spawned the system. If the rings were merely dust through and through, with no larger bodies shrouded within, the dust would dissipate quickly—in less than three years. Something keeps replenishing the dust particles, and the most likely candidates are small moons under constant meteoroid bombardment.

In this regeneration process, with crumbling remnant moons feeding a waning ring, the Jovian system shows its only family resemblance to the other systems. Old or young, all the rings consist of ancient materials, recycled through the solar system's tumultuous activity.

"The ring systems are a little bit like poppies on the hill," muses Cuzzi. "You come back next year to the same place, and you'll still see poppies on the hillside, but they're not the poppies you saw last year. In the same way, the rings of the planets may not be the same rings that were there a million years ago—or 10 million or 100 million years ago. They're just the most recent incarnation. And the process just keeps on going."

ASK THE SCIENTIST

To a person standing on the surface of Saturn, would the rings seem to cast a shadow on the planet's surface? What would the rings look like from underneath?

A person standing at the cloudtops of Saturn (there is no known surface) would see the rings span the sky from east to west. From the planet's equator, the rings would appear as a thin line overhead, while from higher northern or southern latitudes, they would appear as a thicker band. During sunset or sunrise, when the Sun's light shines upon them from a steep angle, a hypothetical Saturnian observer might see sparkling reflections from the millions of icy moonlets. And when the rings are lit from behind—at Saturnian noon—their myriad ice crystals might create a beautiful halo around the Sun. In addition, as the moonlets drift by on their orbits around the planet, they would create many eclipses that would cause the Sun and stars to blink off and on many times each day.

Is outer space by and large a vacuum? What is its temperature? Is it warmer closer to a star?

Though people often think of space as a vacuum, astronomers find that it is filled with all kinds of material—stars and planets, gas atoms and molecules, and microscopic particles of dust. In Earth's neighborhood, about eight atoms of material per cubic centimeter (1 cubic centimeter equals about one teaspoonful) of space are found, on the average. Between the stars, there may be only about one atom per cubic centimeter, and one dust grain for every 100,000 cubic centimeters. And, in the thick interstellar clouds known as nebulas, scientists believe there are more than 100,000 molecules per cubic centimeter. Even with this matter, space is closer to a vacuum than any human-made one.

The temperatures of space vary considerably as well. Clouds of dense molecules can have temperatures hovering only 10° above absolute zero (-460° F, -273° C), while the outer regions of ionized-gas clouds can soar to more than 10,000° above absolute zero. Temperatures are higher the closer one gets to a star. This is why temperatures at Mercury are hundreds of degrees above zero, while those at Pluto are hundreds of degrees below zero.

Since Mars has two moons, does that mean that it has twice as many eclipses as Earth? Are we able to detect eclipses on other planets?

Scientists are indeed able to detect eclipses occurring on other planets. One of the easiest is Jupiter, whose four largest moons (the Galilean moons) frequently block sunlight and cast shadows onto the planet's cloudtops. These eclipses are visible as dark spots moving slowly across the creamy white disk of the planet—even to viewers using small backyard telescopes.

The two moons of Mars, Phobos and Deimos, also pass in front of the Sun, but do not create eclipses as we know them. Since, from Mars, these two moons appear smaller than the Sun, a hypothetical Martian observer could often see them in silhouette against the solar disk. Phobos would appear as a tiny speck, and would take less than 30 seconds to cross the disk, while Deimos would fill nearly two-thirds of the solar disk, and would require nearly two minutes to complete its transit.

▶ *What sort of rest-room facilities do space-shuttle astronauts have at their disposal? How do they compare with the facilities on, say, Apollo missions? Is human waste recycled during space missions?*

The space shuttle uses a toilet similar to those on Earth, but with a vacuum "flush" that is turned on before it is used. Liquid waste is ultimately dumped overboard along with water from the orbiter's fuel cells. The Apollo missions were different in that astronauts used bags instead of toilets, and returned samples to Earth for medical study. Only the Russian Salyut and Mir missions have experimented with recycled liquid human waste to produce water, but, although the water is suitable for drinking, no cosmonaut has yet cared to try it.

▶ *My brother insists that the Sun is actually closer to Earth during the winter than during the summer. Would that mean that in the Southern Hemisphere, the Sun is closer during the summer (the northern winter)?*

Because Earth's orbit is not circular but slightly elliptical, Earth is actually closer to the Sun in January than in July. This means that residents of our planet's northern hemisphere are closer to the Sun in winter, while those of the Southern Hemisphere are closer during the summer. Since Earth's distance from the Sun varies by only about 3 percent, it does not contribute much to seasonal temperature differences. The temperature variations are due, instead, to the tilt of Earth's axis—about 23.45 degrees to the plane of its orbit. In the summer months, the tilt creates longer days that allow the

atmosphere and surface a chance to heat up significantly, and shorter nights that prevent the heat from escaping quickly.

▶ *Is it possible that a heavenly body exists that is made entirely of gold, or silver, or some other precious metal? Are there ways of determining the metallic composition of nearby planets?*

Metals are precious because they are very rare on Earth. From analyzing the spectrum of light reflecting off nearby planets, and that emanating from the stars, astronomers can learn that such chemical elements are rare in space as well. These, along with every other element, are forged in the interior of stars, particularly during stellar explosions known as supernovas. They are then tossed outward into space, where they can interact with other elements to make other stars, planets, and even life itself. Stars and planets could never accumulate enough of these rare commodities to be entirely composed of them.

▶ *Has the United States ever attempted to land a spacecraft on the planet Mercury? Are astronomers particularly interested in Mercury? I rarely read anything about it in the news.*

Astronomers are quite interested in the planet Mercury, the innermost and second-smallest planet of our solar system. No spacecraft have ever landed on this world, but several have passed by and photographed its cratered surface. Mariner 10, which made three close approaches in 1974 and 1975, found that Mercury's daytime temperatures can reach 806° F (430° C) and, at night, plunge to -274° F (-170° C). Mariner revealed an ancient, heavily cratered terrain that resembles the appearance of our Moon, and an immense impact basin that may have been formed by a collision 3.8 billion years ago.

Earth
and the
Environment

■ THE AWESOME POWER OF NATURE
IS PERHAPS BEST ILLUSTRATED BY A
TORNADO—A DARK, RAPIDLY ROTAT-
ING FUNNEL-SHAPED COLUMN OF AIR
THAT HANGS FROM A THUNDER-
STORM CLOUD. IN ITS BRIEF LIFETIME,
A TORNADO CAN GENERATE WINDS
UP TO 500 MILES PER HOUR AND
CAUSE CATASTROPHIC DAMAGE. THE
UNITED STATES HAS MORE TORNA-
DOES PER YEAR THAN ANY OTHER
PLACE ON EARTH.

CONTENTS

Desert Sanctuary

by Timothy Egan

I n November 1994, soon after the U.S. Congress created the largest single expanse of parkland and protected wilderness in the lower 48 states with the passage of the California Desert Protection Act, a curious couple pulled into the Mojave Desert outpost of Cima, California, population 15.

What the visitors saw, about 120 miles (192 kilometers) south of the newly upgraded Death Valley National Park, in one of the driest places on Earth, was a cluster of sunbaked cows, a handwritten sign blasting the federal government, and another one adver-

tising beer and soda. Behind a fence, a few abandoned cars were perched on blocks.

"They wanted to know where was the land that had just been added to the national-park system," recalls Irene Ausmus, the Cima postmistress. "I told them they were in it. Boy, were they surprised."

The 1994 passage of the California Desert Protection Act extended federal stewardship to an extraordinary expanse of wilderness. The area's arid climate belies a world full of life, where the gnarled Joshua tree (above) and hundreds of other exotic plants and animals thrive.

HISTORIC LEGISLATION

As one of its last acts, on October 8, the 103rd Congress ended a decade of wrangling over 9 million acres (3.6 million hectares) of Southern California desert, and created two new national parks (Death Valley and Joshua Tree), a large preserve (Mojave), and a huge patchwork of wilderness.

More than 90 mountain ranges, some reaching 11,000 feet (3,350 meters) above the desert floor; 2,000 kinds of plants and animals unique to a world where rain is a phantom; sand dunes as high as 700 feet (213 meters); and a host of archaeological treasures were given protected status under the new law.

Death Valley, upgraded from a monument, is now the largest national park in the contiguous United States—containing more than 3 million acres (1.2 million hectares), nearly 1 million acres more than Yellowstone National Park in Wyoming.

But these parks and wilderness areas will not be strictly nature sanctuaries. In a flurry of amendments intended to accommodate proponents of property rights, Congress essentially wrote a dozen cattle ranchers, several miners, a large corporate property owner, and assorted dry-country loners into the new park system—freezing a snapshot of desert commerce into the ageless tableau of dunes, cinder cones, and Joshua-tree forests.

MIXING BUSINESS AND PLEASURE

But never, perhaps, has such an eclectic mix of people, business, and landowners been written into a park as was done in the California desert.

Hunting, prohibited in virtually every other national park except under special circumstances, will be allowed in the Mojave National Preserve. Grazing of domestic cattle, which now goes on in a limited fashion in only one small park in Nevada, will be permitted throughout much of the protected desert land. A couple of working mines will continue operations.

As a result, the newest additions to the national-park system not only contain some of the oldest trees in the world, the hottest place

Campers, climbers, and other nature lovers in the Golden State have cause for celebration with the long-anticipated creation of the Mojave National Preserve and two new national parks—Death Valley and Joshua Tree.

on the planet, and California's only known dinosaur tracks, but also feature a desert cowboy named Clay Overson and a Death Valley prospector who goes by the name of Sparrow.

The question, as the Mojave Desert prepares for a surge of visitors, is whether all these users can get along, or whether they will undermine the special features of land that is supposed to be set aside for the ages.

When the Desert Protection Act was signed by President Clinton on October 31, it enshrined two sometimes conflicting tenets of American thought: the national-park idea—created with Yellowstone in 1872, and since copied around the world—and a reverence for private property.

A NEW SENSE OF WILDERNESS

National parks try to preserve something unique and wondrous. The United States has no shortage of cows, so, park supporters argue, why let them wander through some of the most fragile land in the country? Ranchers and other desert-property users argued that much of the desert parkland is no different than any other shank of the Mojave. But having lost that argument, they

The imperiled desert tortoise became an unlikely player in legislative debates after scientists found that off-road vehicles were threatening the reptile's habitat.

Unpredictable desert rains often presage the arrival of colorful wildflowers, including ground-hugging wooly daisies (top left); spindly, scarlet-blossomed ocotillos and fragrant, lemon-yellow cholla blooms (middle left); and the yawning flowers of the mound cactus (bottom left).

The sandy, windswept Kelso Dunes are only one of many quiet, otherworldly hideaways in the newly created Mojave National Preserve. The controversial decision to classify the area as a preserve allows limited hunting, business operations, and private landholding to continue.

now fear that the National Park Service will be a heavy-handed regulator.

In the past, national parks have been drawn around everything from army bases to gold mines, usually with the provision that "inappropriate" activities will be phased out. An Indian war once passed through Yellowstone, astonishing tourists.

Senator Dianne Feinstein, the California Democrat who is the chief architect of the new law, said the ranchers were part of "our Western heritage," and she agreed to a provision that allowed grazing inside the new parks for perpetuity.

Under the new law, almost 90 percent of Death Valley is classified as wilderness, which prohibits development and road building. At the same time, several hundred people—including about 30 members of the Timbisha Shoshone tribe, whose ancestors have been here for hundreds of years—will live year-round in an oasis surrounding a golf course inside the new park. It is an island of private land once advertised as an area said to have "all the advantages of hell without any of the inconveniences."

Entering the park from the east, a visitor may be overwhelmed by the vistas, the clarity of the air, the sense of solitude, and all the sunset-colored rings of exposed geology. But only a few miles from that entrance is a working borax mine and a nearly aban-

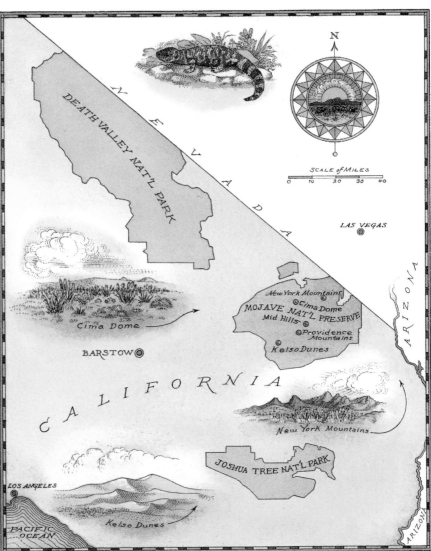

The decade-long battle to preserve the California desert brought new or upgraded government protection to more than 9 million acres of precious wilderness (see map).

doned workers' village protected by four vocal, large-toothed dogs.

Originally, the Billie Mine and the near ghost town of Ryan were supposed to be part of the park, but they were later drawn out of it, a distinction that will be difficult to discern for anyone setting out to explore the park.

PRESERVING AN EXOTIC REFUGE

Most people who study the desert are happy simply to have the broad new federal protection for the area.

"The Mojave is not quite ready for the critical list," says Charles Douglas, Ph.D., a professor of biology at the University of Nevada at Las Vegas, "but it's been approaching it."

Dr. Douglas says that new communities sprouting in the desert have drained water from springs that a variety of animals, including bighorn sheep, depended on. And off-road vehicles have ripped up the habitat of desert tortoises, a threatened species.

With passage of the desert act, the government has a chance to avoid some mistakes of the past that have led to traffic jams and excessive commercial development at other national parks, some park advocates say.

"This may well be the last major park area created in the nation," says Norbert Riedy, an official with the Wilderness Society who has been working on the California desert issue since 1986. "I look at this as an opportunity to build a park for the 21st century. But we also should look down the road, 200 to 500 years from now, when these public lands will be the backyard of millions of people."

By this view, the desert wilderness will be best appreciated as a refuge for urban-harried

humanity. As Edward Abbey wrote in *Desert Solitaire*, his tribute to arid America, "Out there is a different world, older and greater and deeper by far than ours, a world which surrounds and sustains the little world of man."

Abbey wrote his book in 1968, when the predominant view of the desert was still that of a wasteland, a place to dump nuclear garbage and to use as a target range for new weapons. Now more than 22 million people, mostly in the Los Angeles metropolitan area, live within half a day's drive of one of the new desert parks. And the fastest-growing city in the United States is a Mojave Desert mecca, Las Vegas, Nevada, just two hours from most of the new parkland.

Joshua Tree, which has been upgraded to a national park from a national monument, with its exotic yuccas and slabs of perfect climbing rocks, has seen attendance double over the past decade, to more than 1.4 million people a year. More than 1 million people visited Death Valley last year, a record. But for all the Mojave's newfound popularity, for its cattle and mines, it remains a place where people find solitude.

"You will be able to go there and experience what it was like in the Garden of Eden," says Peter Burk, a Barstow, California, librarian who first came up with the idea of a park in the eastern Mojave 15 years ago.

SOME NATIVES ARE RESTLESS

At the same time, some of the desert dwellers encircled by the new parks are restless. They want to continue doing what they have always done—riding off-road, shooting guns, and exploring new mining claims—unimpeded by new regulations that come with national-park status. Some of these activities will be allowed, but under significant restrictions.

"If you live around here and use the desert, you don't want to have a

Death Valley is now the largest national park in the lower 48 states. Well-known as the hottest place on Earth, this massive wilderness also contains fertile oases and kaleidoscopic geography (above).

Many desert inhabitants have mechanisms to survive in the unforgiving conditions. The hedgehog cactus (right) overcomes its arid habitat by storing water in its stem.

park ranger holding your hand, or be unable to camp anywhere but in an asphalt parking lot," says Mike Smith, who lives in Twentynine Palms, California, just outside Joshua Tree.

In December 1994, a leader of a group opposed to federal protection of more land told about 100 people who live near the Mojave preserve to fight the National Park Service every step of the way as the land was put under new guidelines.

The cattlemen, miners, and hunters who operate within the new additions to the park

The stark contrasts and startling beauty of the California desert attract sightseers from around the world. Government officials and many concerned citizens hope to preserve this unique and awe-inspiring landscape as a sanctuary for future generations.

system "are the last vestiges of our pioneering spirit in this country," says Chuck Cushman, director of the American Land Rights Association, which represents property owners surrounded by federal land.

Connie Connely is one of those people whose new landlord will be the Park Service. Her father was a prospector who built his house on land leased from the government, inside what is now the Mojave preserve.

The land is 1.4 million acres (570,000 hectares) of rust-colored mountain ranges, odd-shaped lava formations, and wind-sculptured dunes wedged between the two new national parks. It also contains high-voltage transmission lines, dune-buggy roads, and natural-gas lines.

"I guess I'm just a hermit type," Connely says, adding that she lives in the desert because of the peace. But since the area became part of the park, she sees a lot more people, particularly on weekends.

"Ran into a bunch of people here the other day looking for turtles," Connely says. "They said they came out here to see their new park. *Their* new park! I said it's my park, too. I'm part of it."

PRESERVING CONTROVERSY

Actually, the east Mojave was supposed to be a national park, like Joshua Tree and Death Valley, under the terms of earlier legislation passed by Congress. It was changed to a preserve to allow hunting, after heavy lobbying by the National Rifle Association (NRA). In an average year, hunters there kill about 25 deer and 5 sheep.

But in trying to accommodate a handful of hunters, Congress may have hurt the potential for big tourist dollars.

"There are more deer killed on the George Washington Parkway every year than will be shot in the Mojave," says Martin Hayden, a lobbyist for the Sierra Club, referring to the roadway in the Virginia suburbs of Washington. "People don't know what a preserve is, and by downgrading it, you cost the economy around there a lot of money."

Still, Hayden and other environmentalists are ecstatic about the desert act. "This is a gift to our grandchildren," he says.

On the Beach

by Jay Stuller

There is a powerful allure that draws us to the boundary between land and sea. With a trained eye, one can observe the forces that shape a beach. It is a place that envelops the senses, inducing anxious minds into a state of tranquillity. While part of an endless continuum, each ocean wave rolling up onto the shore has just enough individuality to prevent the sight from growing monotonous. Breakers generate a sound so soothing that its rhythms must somehow mimic the womb.

A Battle Between Land and Sea

It is therefore ironic that a beach, this tonic for emotional peace, is a by-product of powerful violence. Grinding rocks into granules of sand, ocean waves also tear down towering cliffs and swallow small islands whole. Giving way in places, the land rearranges itself in others to blunt the onslaught. Every beach is a battlefield upon which this struggle for supremacy between terra firma and sea is waged. The land, of course, has endured for billions of years and will surely hold for billions more. Of late, however, the sea appears to have an upper hand.

In January 1992, all along the length of a new seawall at Ocean City, Maryland, it took the storm-whipped ocean less than one day to swipe more than half of the sand laid down by the U.S. Army Corps of Engineers just six months before. The beach "replenishment" project had cost $45 million; the repairs added an additional $12 million.

At Chatham on Massachusetts' Cape Cod, a 1987 storm breached a barrier spit, leaving a narrow gash that within months widened to 1 mile (1.6 kilometers). Ordinary ocean surf striking the once-sheltered main shoreline scoured away 75 feet (23 meters) of land in one year, and only enormous rock revetments prevent further recession. Similar problems plague beaches all along the eastern coast of the United States.

The Threat of Coastal Erosion

Meanwhile, chunks of England are crumbling into the North Sea. Cliffs along the Yorkshire coast—and with them farm and residential land—are claimed at a rate of some 9 feet (2.7 meters) annually. Many of Britain's 1,100 miles (1,770 kilometers) of seawalls and other coastal defenses are failing.

What's more, sea levels have risen by about 1 foot (30 centimeters) over the past century, be it from the thermal expansion of warming seas or from melting polar ice caps. Since people are drawn to coastlines and seem to be compelled to erect houses, hotels, and other structures as close as possible, much is at stake. Should the rising trend continue, beaches and development around the world are clearly menaced.

As the transition area between land and sea, beaches are as much a place of beauty and serenity as they are the scene of destructive natural forces. The question of how or whether to protect human structures built in this battle zone of nature has emerged as a contentious issue.

How best to respond to the threat of beach erosion is a matter of profound and increasingly contentious public policy. Notes Rutherford H. Platt, a professor of geography and planning law at the University of Massachusetts at Amherst, in a recent issue of *Environment Magazine*: "The prevailing responses to coastal erosion have been either to ignore it or to safeguard shorefront development with engineered, or 'hard,' shore protection projects, such as sea walls, revetments, groins and jetties, or breakwaters."

For one thing, such defenses are costly, and taxpayers usually foot the bill. In 1991, the United Kingdom spent 58 million pounds on such maintenance and construction. In the United States, at least $10 million is spent annually on beach-replenishment projects, and even more on hard structures.

There is also growing evidence suggesting that hard defenses exacerbate erosion—at the site of a seawall or jetty, and perhaps more so on adjacent, unprotected beaches. That is the argument of Orrin Pilkey, Ph.D., a geologist at Duke University in Durham, North Carolina, who contends that if we are to preserve the recreational and environmental value of beaches, we must leave the land and sea to find their own equilibrium. "The Maginot Line approach," he says, "is turning America's beaches into an endangered species." Perhaps better said, though, is that what's endangered are beaches as we know them.

BEACHES AS WE KNOW THEM

Myriad physiographic forms take shape on the boundary between land and sea. Whatever exists in the intertidal area between surf and dry land is a beach. To envision the future of coastal features, one must first understand the forces and materials that help fashion these areas. With such knowledge, one can "read" a beach; look into wave patterns and have an idea of what lurks below the surf line's water; know whether a beach is growing, shrinking, or is in balance.

The concept of a beach is hardly universal. The expanses of coarse, light-colored sand that typify Southern California and Eastern Seaboard beaches set popular American standards. In Great Britain, much of the coast is covered with "shingle," or flat stones. The fabled French beach at Cannes is mostly pebbles. Hawaii has jet-black beaches with sand that once was volcanic lava; elsewhere on the Big Island are shores of fine white sand, created from ground-up coral reefs.

Great variety exists on the continental U.S. coastline. While the light-colored and soft sand in Southern California comes from weathered quartz and feldspar, many beaches in Washington State are green or dark gray. The product of weathered basalt, these shore zones are often hard and flat. What is on a

Seashores derive their distinctive character from a variety of colorful materials. Black sands, like those of some Greek islands (left), are typically of volcanic origin. The rock-ribbed shores of Nova Scotia (bottom left) provide evidence of the glacial influence on eastern Canada's geology. The popular American image of soft, light-colored sandy beaches can be found in North Carolina (below) and elsewhere on the East and West coasts.

beach, then, be it soft sand or boulders, is generally dictated by local geology.

THE RISE AND FALL OF LAND

For all that it does to coastal topography, the ocean's erosive force is a gnat compared to the elephant of tectonic-plate movement. The shifting of giant pieces of planetary crust can cause the land to rise or fall relative to sea level. Moreover, the weight of an ice sheet can cause land to sink, as is happening in Greenland. When ice retreats, the land will rebound, which—10,000 years after the last great Ice Age—is still occurring in parts of North America. Indeed, while many of England's problems are due to subsidence of its south and east coasts, the island is tilting, causing the northern part to rise. As Willard Bascom noted in his book *Waves and Beaches*, a government survey in the early 1900s—conducted after property owners complained about losing land—found that the United Kingdom actually gained about 900 acres (365 hectares) of new land annually.

Coasts are often classified by whether they are rising or submerging. Bascom points to Puget Sound as an example of "drowned topography"—land that, relative to sea level, is sinking. In areas where the topography was once mostly hilly, one finds beaches that are irregular in length, narrow, and often rocky. The very existence of a seaside cliff is a clue that erosion is at work on drowning topography. Conversely, the broad, long, and straight beaches from New Jersey to Florida indicate a coast that has been stable for a long time, or at least where the battle between land and sea is generally in balance. Whether land is rising or subsiding, winds, ocean currents, and waves keep beaches in perpetual motion.

Physical forces are constantly creating the stuff that goes into a beach. On a cliff-lined coast, for example, waves are hurled at cracks in the wall. The pressure of water and compressed air widens the splits and breaks off pieces. Following waves grind the pieces together to eventually create sand. The

Many waterfront homeowners—including those in Malibu, California (right)—can testify to the powerful and capricious nature of stormy seas. In an effort to protect beaches and buildings, communities spend millions of dollars building structures such as jetties (bottom right) and replenishing beaches with newly dredged sand (below).

chemical reaction of salt water and oxygen also weathers, or breaks down, rocks that are in occasional contact with seawater.

Yet another source of beach material is sediment from the weathering of inland rocks, which is washed into rivers and carried to sea. Sediment is usually the source of marshlike beach areas, flat and muddy expanses of intertidal ground. But sedimentary sand is also critical to beaches farther from a river outlet. For example, since its completion upon the River Volta in 1966, Ghana's Akosombo Dam has trapped so much silt that the neighboring nation of Togo has lost about 10,000 houses to coastal erosion—homes on beachfronts that would otherwise have been replenished and protected by the Volta's sand.

READING A BEACH

Most sand movement around a beach takes place in the surf zone and just beyond, where waves and currents hold the particles in suspension until the weight of the grains causes them to sink. However, as each wave breaks upon the shore, it carries with it a thin film of sand. As a wave retreats, it takes sand back into the surf zone. It is usually impossible to perceive whether the process is building up or stripping away a beach.

It is easier to see what's happening after a storm. A vertical cut in the berm—or the high point of the beach—and a steeper face indicates that large waves have claimed a healthy amount of sand. The sand often does not go far. Offshore the waves may be breaking in a slightly different place than on the previous day. What was part of the beach face has settled into a bar, the subsurface feature on which waves initially break.

In winter, the berm on a typical beach is tall and narrow, and its face steep. The offshore bars are large. In summer, berms appear lower in profile, but are much wider. In fact, what most folks sit on at the beach—what we consider a beach—is the berm.

The reason that sand is stripped off by strong waves and put back by milder ones is a function of wave energy. Big waves expend a lot of energy on the beach, and have the power to hold more sand particles in suspension than do smaller waves. Milder summer waves have enough energy to pick up sand from a bar and carry it shoreward, but since they lack the power to suspend the particles for long, the summer waves leave more upon the berm than they can carry away. If the amount of sand in a beach environment remains constant, this process will repeat itself year after year.

SMALL WONDERS IN THE SAND

There are numerous minor features one can observe on a beach, especially after a high tide. While declaiming that these have "no great geological or engineering importance," Bascom describes the small wonders as "swash marks, backwash marks, rills, cusps, domes, pinholes, and ripple marks."

Swash marks are the forward line of sand grains left by the farthest reach of each wave. As the tide rises, the swash marks move up the beach, as each king wave erases the standard set by its predecessor. With the tide in retreat, swash marks form a pattern of intersecting, curving arcs.

While some wave water seeps into the beach, water sliding down the face leaves backwash marks, little crisscrossed valleys that form small diamonds in the sand. Rill marks are left by streams of water that seep back out of the sand. Looking much like the patterns created by river deltas, the main streams branch out into numerous rivulets.

Cusps are evenly spaced depressions, crescent-shaped and concave to seaward, which form on the edge of the berm facing the sea. "Of all the curiosities of the shore," writes Bascom, "these are surely the most puzzling." Bascom concludes that cusps are sculpted when neither the erosive nor building force of a wave has command.

When water sinks into dry sand and displaces the air below, it can leave a mark of a phantom clam, or a pinhole. Sand domes, or miniature mounds, are formed by the same process. Sand subjected to slow-moving water forms into small waves of parallel ridges and troughs, or ripples, the same effect seen in stream bottoms.

CURRENT EVENTS

A larger beach feature that is easily observed is the formation that produces rip currents. When waves cross an underwater sandbar in rapid succession, they pile water into the zone between the bar and the beach. Since the incoming water keeps the zone's contents from flowing back evenly, a current forms as gravity draws the water to the lowest point of the bar. This gouges out a channel. What passes through is a powerful flow, or rip current. The process also generates feeder currents inside the bar, which make the rip even stronger. From shore, the presence of a breach in the bar is obvious; while waves break normally on either side of it, the outgoing current makes the wave coming into it grow too steep too fast, destabilizing it into a frothy foam. Surfers use the rip to get out past the breakers; poor swimmers get caught in it, panic, and sometimes drown.

Such mechanics are part of a larger system called "littoral transport," or the movement of sand by wave-generated currents. When waves hit a shore straight on, they merely move sand up and down the beach face. When waves arrive at an angle, they can establish a strong current just beyond the surf zone; running parallel to the beach, the current can carry large volumes of sand.

Were a beach left to its own devices, sand would tend to be redistributed fairly evenly along a coast. Such self-preservation is also at work on barrier islands. If a sandy spit is breached and eroded, the island usually "rolls over" and re-forms, giving way in the weakest point and growing larger in a more protected area. Of course, homeowners are disinclined to roll with the redistribution process, and instead opt for protection with groins, jetties, and seawalls.

CAN SHORELINES BE PROTECTED?

While coastal engineers claim that their structures do more good than harm, problems often seem to arise around hard barriers. So says Pilkey, whose book *The Beaches Are Moving: The Drowning of America's Shoreline* has brought attention to his cause, which he has been accused of espousing as more religion than science.

Pilkey has little charity for individuals whose homes might tumble into the sea.

His argument is to "save beaches, not buildings," and tough luck to anyone who won't move back from an encroaching ocean. Except for those places where massive development warrants protection—such as Miami, Florida; and New Jersey—Pilkey feels that hard structures are too costly, will fall to a rising sea, and make the problems worse anyway.

As Pilkey and William Neal, a professor of geology at Grand Valley State University in Allendale, Michigan, wrote in *Issues in Science and Technology*, some seawalls "are built so far seaward—in the surf zone below the high tide line—that their location alone results in the immediate loss of beach area." A more common practice in decades past, this is the reason Miami lost much of its recreational beaches in the 1960s.

Pilkey and Neal also contend that seawalls play an active role in sand removal. "We think that during storms the presence of a seawall may concentrate the scouring power of waves breaking in the surf zone," they write, "because the waves have less room to expend their energy than they do when rolling over a natural beach."

Groins and jetties that extend into the surf zone, claim the pair, are "robbing Peter to pay Paul." For example, if the current is moving north to south, sand will tend to pile up on the north side of a groin. However, on the south side of the structure, waves will scour the beach and carry the sand far away. Without any "littoral drift" replenishing the south side, that area of beach can go quickly, opening up more land to erosion.

Beach "nourishment," or piling on sand dredged from offshore, is another form of coastal-protection management. Miami Beach has used it for years. But the "soft" solution is costly—about $1 million per mile (1.6 kilometers)—and temporary. Replenished beaches usually last less than five years; a big storm can take them out at any time.

Even the best-built structures cannot always withstand the encroachment of the sea. Many in the scientific community now advocate a restrained approach to coastal protection in which beaches are allowed to find their own equilibrium.

BEACHES VERSUS BUILDINGS

Abandoning coastal habitations is yet another option, though hardly practical where there are cities, nor popular with seaside homeowners. The question may come down to a taxpayer decision: Do we continue to invest in hard protections and compensate those who must move, or write them off as individuals who had the joy of living near the sea, but must now pay the price?

In Great Britain, there is growing interest in "managed retreat." The British government apparently has a list of 40 areas where, as an experiment, the sea will be allowed to have its way. The first to go could be a small North Sea peninsula called Spurn Head. The sandy ground has been kept safe by seawalls for about 150 years. The walls are crumbling. Engineers figure that winds and waves will dismantle Spurn Head piece by piece. They also expect that it will re-form, perhaps as an island, a little to the west.

Herein is the benefit of allowing the sea to have its way. Erosion does claim hard land, and at a high cost to property owners. But it is a process that also creates broad, soft, and sandy beaches.

What we surrender to Neptune is ultimately given back—often in a more sublime and invaluable form.

Rethinking the Richter Scale

by Richard Monastersky

Seismologists, as a rule, tend to keep their cool, even when the ground heaves beneath their feet and buildings collapse around them. But these days, earthquake experts are scurrying for cover at the mere mention of two words. Such is the fallout over use of the term "Richter scale"—a household phrase that lies at the heart of a brewing controversy about conveying earthquake information to the public.

The rhetoric has reached such a pitch that one newspaper columnist pilloried the agency in charge of disseminating earthquake information. "A kick in the butt is what someone ought to give the U.S. Geological Survey [(USGS)] for its dithering about how to define the magnitude of earthquakes," wrote Keay Davidson in the *San Francisco Examiner* following a large Bolivian tremor on June 8, 1994.

Although the question "How strong was it?" will continue to be asked after any significant quake, the traditional Richter-scale answer is rapidly losing ground to more-accurate ways of expressing earthquake magnitude.

SEISMOLOGICAL SEMANTICS

Davidson is by no means alone. Reporters, editors, and many seismically sensitive members of the public are having trouble sorting out how scientists measure earthquakes. Much to their dismay, people are learning that seismologists typically do not use the Richter scale to judge quake size.

It's almost like hearing that Santa Claus doesn't exist.

"What's going on is that we're just recovering from decades of telling a white lie, that's all," says seismologist Thomas H. Heaton, half in jest. Heaton is president of the Seismological Society of America and a USGS researcher in Pasadena, California.

In one sense, the flap boils down to semantics. While seismologists generally do not use the original Richter magnitude scale, the measuring systems currently in vogue represent extensions of the type that Charles Richter developed nearly 60 years ago. That explains why some scientists continue to use the term when addressing the press.

But the recent brouhaha goes beyond the question of the name itself. According to seismologists who frequently get up in front of the television cameras, the problems now surfacing reflect a deep-seated misunderstanding about earthquakes—one that has important consequences for how the public and even engineers respond to seismic hazards.

"The public gets extremely confused after they've been through a heavy shake, and they're frightened," says Heaton. "Then you say, 'Oh, by the way, we're expecting an 8, and that is 50 times bigger.' What they now imagine is 50 times the intensity of the ground motion they just felt, and they realize that nothing can survive it. At that point, they just stop talking about it."

SIZE VERSUS INTENSITY

It's only fitting that Davidson and other news reporters feel such a strong connection to the Richter scale, because journalists played an important role in the system's origin. "[Richter] introduced it because he was tired of the newsmen asking him about the

Journalists, needing a gauge by which to convey the relative size of an earthquake to their audience, did much to make the Richter scale a household term.

relative size of earthquakes," recalls veteran seismologist Bruce A. Bolt from the University of California, Berkeley.

Prior to Richter's work, researchers in the United States had no way of judging an earthquake's absolute size, which remains the same no matter where it is measured. Instead, they dealt with a concept called intensity, which describes the strength of shaking at a particular location. Because tremors fade with distance from the epicenter, the intensity of a single quake varies considerably from point to point.

Richter defined seismic magnitude in terms of a particular type of recording device, called a Wood-Anderson seismograph, situated at a standard distance of 62 miles (100 kilometers) from an earthquake's epicenter.

Richter also appropriated from astronomy the idea of a logarithmic scale—based on powers of 10—to accommodate the incredible range of earthquake sizes. (The smallest detectable tremors equal the energy of a brick dropped off a table, while monster quakes surpass the largest nuclear explosions.) By Richter's original definition, a shake of magnitude 1.0 would cause the arm of the Wood-Anderson machine to swing one-thousandth of a millimeter. A magnitude-2.0 temblor would make the arm swing 10 times as much, or one-hundredth of a millimeter.

In 1906, the year of the great San Francisco, California, earthquake (above), scientists had no reliable way to express the quake's strength. The Richter scale was not introduced until 1935.

FREQUENCY OF EARTHQUAKE OCCURRENCE
(BASED ON OBSERVATIONS SINCE 1990)

DESCRIPTOR	MAGNITUDE	ANNUAL AVERAGE
Great	8.0 and higher	1
Major	7.0–7.9	18
Strong	6.0–6.9	120
Moderate	5.0–5.9	800
Light	4.0–4.9	6,200 (estimated)
Minor	3.0–3.9	49,000 (estimated)
Very minor	less than 3.0	Mag. 2.0–3.0: about 1,000/day
		Mag. 1.0–2.0: about 8,000/day

In the early 1930s, Japanese seismologist Kiyoo Wadati devised a method of comparing the sizes of quakes. He would take seismic recordings of various shocks, and set them on an equal footing by factoring in the distance between the recording station and the earthquake.

But this method was not easily grasped by laypeople, especially the reporters of quake-plagued Southern California. In 1935, Richter dressed up the Japanese method to create an earthquake index—a simple numerical scale much like the stellar magnitudes used by his astronomical colleagues at the California Institute of Technology (Caltech) in Pasadena.

In theory, the scale had no upper limit. But in practice, magnitudes could not top 7.0. "You would never see an earthquake bigger than magnitude 7 [on the original magnitude scale], or at least we hope you never would, because everything would be dead," Heaton says.

Of course, scientists rarely had a Wood-Anderson seismograph stationed exactly 62 miles from an earthquake. But by comparing the arrival of slow versus fast seismic waves at a recording station, they could calculate what one of the devices would have detected at the standard distance.

The magnitude index, as originally defined, could measure only Southern California earthquakes, because Richter calibrated the scale for the crust there. What's more, the index worked only for jolts within a few hundred miles of a Wood-Anderson seismometer.

A MULTITUDE OF M'S

Recognizing these limitations, Caltech's Beno Gutenberg and Richter devised a more general magnitude measurement to handle distant earthquakes. To avoid confusion, they denoted the new magnitude M_S, because it depended on measurements of surface waves rippling through the Earth's crust with a period of about 20 seconds. The original magnitude scale—based on waves with periods of 0.1 to 3.0 seconds—became known as M_L, or local magnitude.

Even the new and improved magnitude formula had problems, however, because deep earthquakes do not produce many surface waves. So Gutenberg and Richter invented m_b, measured from body waves, which travel through the planet's interior. This yardstick proved helpful in distinguishing nuclear explosions from actual earthquakes.

In the 1970s, earthquake experts realized that all existing magnitude methods underestimated the energy of truly large earthquakes. To circumvent this limitation, Hiroo Kanamori, a successor of Richter and Gutenberg at Caltech, created a magnitude scale, M_W, that quantifies the total amount of seismic-wave energy released in an earthquake.

But because such calculations are difficult, scientists usually approximate the energy by computing a quantity called "seismic moment," determined from long-period vibrations. In the case of great earthquakes, these vibrations have cycles longer than 200 seconds. Seismologists therefore refer to M_W as the moment magnitude.

M_W differs from all other types of magnitude in that it measures the earthquake source, Kanamori says. The Richter magnitude and most others gauge only the strength of vibrations sensed at Earth's surface. But to calculate moment magnitude, seismologists use the long-period waves to decipher the dimensions of the fault rupture that produced the quake.

In other words, moment magnitude measures the cause rather than the effect.

Although researchers have developed more than a dozen other ways of calculating earthquake magnitude, moment magnitude remains the figure of choice among scientists, especially for earthquakes larger than magnitude 6.5.

Confused?

With M_L, M_S, m_b, M_W, and a litany of other M's floating around, it's no wonder that many seismologists took the easy way out over the years by giving reporters what they thought the media wanted. When pressed for details, researchers typically simplified the issue by calling any magnitude a Richter magnitude, even though this term applies only to the local magnitudes determined by Richter's original formulation.

"The problem is that seismologists have used the term 'Richter scale' in a very loose way, and now it's catching up with them. We didn't use it among ourselves, because it doesn't mean anything," Heaton says.

American seismologist Charles Richter (above) simplified a complex Japanese method of comparing earthquakes to develop the relatively straightforward numerical scale that bears his name.

Sizing Up Seismicity

Chief Waverly Person (above) and other seismologists at the National Earthquake Center prefer to express earthquake strength in terms of magnitude rather than intensity.

When Charles Richter invented the concept of seismic magnitude, he made it easy to compare earthquakes. Anyone who can count to 10 will recognize that a magnitude-7.0 shock packs a bigger punch than a 6.0 quake. But the question "How much bigger?" is not so easily answered.

In the original definition of magnitude, a 1-point increase meant that peak waves recorded by a Wood-Anderson seismometer jumped by a factor of 10. So far, so good. But not all seismometers respond to seismic waves equally. Some measure different frequencies, and some are more sensitive than others. So newer instruments do not respond the way Wood-Andersons did in their era.

Delving even deeper, what does the seismometer measure anyway? It does not translate directly into the strength of the shaking felt by humans or buildings, because seismometers measure one band of frequencies, whereas we feel a different range of waves.

An increase of one unit in magnitude therefore does not translate cleanly to 10 times more shaking. In fact, the force of the ground motion close to a tremor's epicenter rises much less than a factor of 10.

Going from a magnitude-6.5 to a 7.5 jolt, the jerky shaking close to the quake may increase in strength only by a factor of 1.5 (equal to a 50 percent boost). On the other hand, a seismograph stationed halfway around the globe may measure a 10-fold difference in the surface waves that have managed to travel that far.

In terms of energy, magnitude units rise even faster. A step of one full unit increases the energy by roughly 33 times, so a magnitude-7.0 quake unleashes approximately 1,000 times the energy released by a magnitude-5.0 temblor.

Is there an easier way? Some feel that the logarithmic magnitude scale is just too difficult for the public to comprehend. "It's made a lot of confusion," says Thomas H. Heaton, president of the Seismological Society of America. "To be honest, I think Richter did us a disservice. We spend as much time explaining to the public what a logarithm is as anything else. Why not just say 1, 10, and 10 million?"

Seismologists themselves compare earthquakes using seismic moments, which represent the length of the fault rupture multiplied by the amount of rock movement and then again by the stiffness of the rock. But moments are expressed in unwieldy numbers, such as 2×10^{27} newton meters—clearly not an appealing figure for the public.

Pat Jorgenson, a U.S. Geological Survey (USGS) spokeswoman in Menlo Park, California, says she would prefer to discuss quakes in terms of something people can comprehend. "When the comet hit Jupiter this summer, it was reported that this was equivalent to so many atomic bombs. Why can't we report earthquakes like that?"

In that vein, a magnitude-1.0 earthquake would equal roughly 6 ounces of TNT. For a magnitude 5.0, think of 1,000 tons of TNT. A quake of magnitude 7.2 corresponds to a million tons of explosive—which is a little less than the energy locked in the swirling winds of a typical hurricane. The largest recorded earthquake, of moment magnitude 9.5 in Chile in 1960, equaled about 3 billion tons of TNT.

SEISMIC SOPHISTICATION

These days, earthquake experts hope to clean up the magnitude morass in their dealings with the public. The USGS put out a statement in July 1994 explaining how the newer measurements do not renounce the Richter scale, but rather, extend the original magnitude both to greater distances and to larger earthquakes.

At the USGS's National Earthquake Information Center in Golden, Colorado, director Waverly J. Person says his staff balances the need for timeliness with the desire to report moment magnitudes, which take an hour or two to compute.

Immediately after an earthquake, the center releases a preliminary measurement, which could be a surface-wave magnitude, a body-wave magnitude, or even a local magnitude (similar to Richter's original formulation, except that modern seismographs have replaced Wood-Anderson ones). After determining the moment magnitude, the scientists release this number, which may fall above or below the preliminary one.

As for the use of the term "Richter scale," the USGS has dodged any decision. "The question of labeling these magnitudes as 'Richter scale' is a matter of tradition, semantics, and personal perspective. The USGS has no official scientific position on the use of the term," declares the July statement.

The USGS' Heaton, who works across the street from Richter's old Pasadena office, says he wants to avoid the term entirely. "You probably wouldn't catch us using the term 'Richter magnitude' around here."

Other seismologists note that while the public feels comfortable with the term, they often lack even a basic understanding of what it means. Several scientists tell tales of people asking to see the Richter scale.

"It seems to be a popular misconception that it's actually a piece of equipment, like a bathroom scale," says Roger Musson of the British Geological Survey in Edinburgh, Scotland. "Things have come to such a pass in today's press that I had an inquiry recently from the *Sunday Times*, no less, asking for a picture of the Richter scale. I said this was a bit like asking for a picture of kilometers."

Others describe the wild rumors that circulate after an earthquake. In the case of the January 17, 1994, Northridge, California, jolt, the reports of different earthquake magnitudes—M_S 6.6 versus M_W 6.7—confused many Angelenos, prompting speculation that the USGS was underestimating the magnitude to save the federal government from spending disaster-relief money.

As journalists get more seismically sophisticated, they may head off some of the confusion. The Associated Press (AP) recently retired the term "Richter scale" in favor of the phrases "preliminary magnitude" and "moment magnitude."

QUAKES AND THEIR EQUIVALENTS

MAGNITUDE	ENERGY RELEASED (IN MILLIONS OF ERGS)	ROUGH EQUIVALENT
-2.0	630	100-watt lightbulb left on for a week
0	630,000	1-ton car going 25 miles per hour
2.0	630,000,000	Amount of energy in a lightning bolt
4.0	630,000,000,000	Seismic waves from 1 kiloton of explosives
6.0	630,000,000,000,000	Hiroshima atomic bomb
8.0	630,000,000,000,000,000	1980 eruption of Mount St. Helens Largest recorded quake, M_W 9.5, Chile, 1960
10.0	630,000,000,000,000,000,000	Annual U.S. energy consumption

But simply tidying the terminology will not, on its own, help people better understand the size of an earthquake. After all, how can one number convey the power of something equivalent to a colossal nuclear explosion?

Even moment magnitude does not suffice, says its inventor. "The problem is, everyone thinks that a single number determines everything. It's almost like asking how big you are," says Kanamori. "The question is whether you are asking height, weight, or width. Depending on how you measure a person, the answer can be very different. In the case of earthquakes, it's even more complex."

Fires of Life

by Doug Stewart

From the skies over south Florida's Big Cypress National Preserve, a helicopter routinely drops small incendiary devices into the dry grass. War games for the National Park Service, perhaps? Training grounds for a fire department? Actually, the point here is just what it appears to be: setting fires. Airborne rangers routinely torch the park in order to nourish it.

The idea, says Big Cypress wildlife biologist Deborah Jansen, is "to replicate lightning strikes as closely as possible." Fires are essential to keeping open the wet prairie that covers parts of the 700,000-acre (280,000-hectare) preserve. Explains Jansen: "When fire comes through, it brings in new growth, which is more palatable than older vegetation to the deer and feral hogs we have." Well-fed deer and hogs make for well-fed Florida panthers. Only 30 to 50 of the endangered felines are thought to exist; 15 stalk Big Cypress and its environs.

That searing flames could help rescue a tiny band of animals from extinction may not seem terribly logical to nonbiologists, especially those of us raised to equate big fires with the ecology of Hell. Every summer, residents of the drier parts of the country, especially in the West, gird themselves for the home-threatening forest fires and brushfires that seem to strike every year.

FLAMES OF REJUVENATION

Yet to ecopyrologists (those who study the ecology of fire), nature without fire, in most places, would be unnatural indeed. A good number of the Earth's species evolved in concert with lightning-caused fires, and many depend on flames for their survival. Biologists are now struggling to temper civilized humankind's tendency to battle any and all fires, a tactic that can bring an unwanted stillness to once-thriving wildlife habitats.

U.S. Forest Service botanist Larry Stritch recalls a sad patch of flora in the rolling oak-hickory woodlands and savanna of Illinois' Shawnee National Forest a few years back. "There were prairie wildflowers that were barely hanging on among the leaf litter, not even blooming," he says. Some of the prairie grasses were tall-grass varieties in name only.

Within a month after the second of two controlled, low-intensity fires burned away much of the shrubby understory, the scene changed dramatically. "There was a solid carpet of flowers, forbs, and grasses everywhere you stepped," Stritch says. "Sunlight was actually hitting the ground." Postfire rains had soaked the soil with a flood of nutrients from the ash of burned plants. Seeds that had lain dormant just under-

ground for years had sprouted in profusion. Botanists tallied 63 new plant species.

So-called edge species, found where fields border woodlands, now thrive throughout the area's parklike mixture of clearings and groves. Sparrows and butterflies flit in and out of the sunlight beneath the patchy woodland canopy, and wild turkeys have appeared for the first time within memory. Goldfinches are drawn by the reappearance of thistle, which yields puffy down that the birds use to build their nests. "We're amazed by the number of species that came back," Stritch says.

AN EVOLVING LANDSCAPE

Controlled burns like these would not be needed in wildlife habitats around the nation if natural fires had not been stamped out whenever possible for nearly a century. Over time, fire suppression changes a landscape. Grassy clearings close up. Swamps fill in with vegetation and dry out. Once-open areas under trees can turn into a nearly impenetrable tangle of young trees and woody brush known as a "dog-hair thicket."

As vegetation becomes more uniform over large areas, some animals lose elements of their ecological niches, just as the goldfinch loses its thistle. A savanna that once hosted herds of elk, bison, and deer—along with bears, wolves, and a multitude of birds and insects—ultimately becomes home mostly to ravens, squirrels, porcupines, and a few other deep-woods birds and rodents.

Most wildlife biologists and park managers would agree that a given landscape is healthier when it supports abundant and diverse numbers of species rather than just a few. (Of course, an arid or frigid place probably will not naturally support the same number of species as, say, a Florida forest.) And fire can be the key to maintaining that diversity.

SMOKEY BEAR AND BAMBI

"What most people know about fire is what they've learned from Smokey Bear and *Bambi*," says Don Despain, a research biologist for the National Biological Survey (NBS) in Wyoming. "Smokey Bear was not an ecologist—he was mostly interested in lumber." As for *Bambi*, the 1942 cartoon in which animals flee in terror as a wall of flame chases them, "*Bambi* was a fairy tale." Yes, animals avoid fire, but there is no evidence that they run for their lives to avoid being engulfed. For one thing, that is not how most fires burn; the massive but mostly slow-moving fires in Wyoming's Yellowstone National Park in 1988 burned for months.

Crews fighting forest fires have reported deer and elk darting away from a fire line, but the animals were probably fleeing the people, not the fire. Even the hottest flames rarely incinerate huge, unbroken swaths of forest; rather, they leave a mosaic of burned patches—killing some plants

The brilliant flowers (left) that sprouted from the ashes of a large 1988 wildfire in Yellowstone National Park (far left) attest to the rejuvenating powers of fire. Scientists have identified a surprising number of plants and animals that actually depend on flames for their survival.

Despite folklore to the contrary, few animals are killed by wildfires. Bison (left) and other large mammals have little trouble evading a typical blaze; smaller creatures can usually escape harm in underground burrows.

risk that the litter will eventually fuel "crown fires." These are unusually hot and fast-moving burns that can engulf entire trees in flames, killing whole stands of trees at once.

A Burning Debate

Knowing the importance of fire in regeneration, the National Park Service quietly adopted a policy in the early 1970s of letting natural fires burn themselves out, within limits. The policy drew criticism in 1988, when fires swept parts of Yellowstone. The criticism was worsened by press coverage of the fires that was itself overheated. "Sea of Fire Engulfs Once-Splendid Park," screamed the *Milwaukee Journal* in a typical headline. Governor Thomas Kean of New Jersey announced he was rushing 1,000 evergreen seedlings to the supposedly devastated park.

As it happened, no reseeding was necessary. To the contrary, the fire rejuvenated the forests, as cooler heads knew it would. Measuring the "seed rain" dropped by trees in several areas after the fires passed through, the NBS' Despain came up with 50,000 to 1 million seeds per acre (20,000 to 400,000 seeds per hectare). "The system is well adjusted to fires," he says. "All those forests are still there. Some of them are just in a different stage of development." As for wildlife, he says, very few animals died.

According to surveys after the fires, no grizzlies were killed, only one black bear, and a handful of hoofed animals other than elk. About 300 elk did die of smoke inhalation, but that number is barely one-tenth the normal winter die-off for Yellowstone's huge elk herds. (Similarly, it is often said that the droughts that lead to fires end up killing far more animals than the fires do.) In all, says Despain, the most seriously affected animal population was probably

and trees, scarring others, leaving many untouched—depending on variables such as vegetation, terrain, and weather.

Like elk, most large mammals can easily sidestep such an approaching fire. Mice, rabbits, and badgers, meanwhile, can wait it out in their burrows. Soil is a superb insulator: when the surface of the ground is 2,000° F (1,095° C), the soil 4 inches (10 centimeters) below may be no warmer than 100° F (38° C). A bigger threat for small animals when they emerge is the sudden absence of the foliage and forest litter that once hid them from predators.

In fact, many plants and animals not only survive, but thrive, after a fire. The lodgepole pines of the western United States are sometimes called a "fire species" because they depend on regular fires to propagate. Intense heat speeds the release of their seeds by melting a resin that can hold their cones shut for decades. In some of the dry western states, moreover, deadwood piles up year after year without rotting. Periodic ground fires dispose of this accumulating tinder without harming the thick-barked trees, and this lessens the

the park's pinecone-eating red squirrels, which lost some of their food to fire.

CLOSER TO HOME

In wilderness parks and other remote public areas, land managers can let natural wildfires burn. But in places where the native biota share their habitat with an influx of home-owners, as in the chaparral country of coastal Southern California, there is no such choice: wildfires *must* be fought. In chaparral country, or Mediterranean scrub forest, summers are long, hot, and dry. Dense thickets of oily-leaved plants are almost explosively flamma-ble, and, for centuries, fires have swept through the area perhaps every 8 or 10 years. In the fall of 1993, wind-fanned fires in the mountains east and west of Los Angeles, many of them apparently set by arsonists, destroyed dozens of homes and left many of the hillsides as black as a charcoal briquette, and seemingly as lifeless.

Especially hard hit were parts of the Santa Monica Mountains National Recreation Area, which encompasses large amounts of privately owned land as well as wilderness

areas. After one fire, says ranger Jacquie Stiv-er, visitors thought the area looked "blown up." But, she says, "Within a week, there were already green shoots—a week!"

After two months, Stiver and her col-leagues counted 35 plant species growing on the blackened hillsides. Local fire species such as laurel sumac, purple needle grass, and coast golden bush do not even need rain to resprout from their unburned roots. Seeds lying just underground are, like roots, largely unscathed by fire; mice, rabbits, and quail emerge to feed on them while the terrain is still smoking. Local raptors like golden eagles, red-shouldered hawks, and great horned owls swoop in to dine on the seedeaters.

In the long term, as in other environ-ments, fire helps restore diversity to chapar-ral country. "Without fire, large, woody chaparral shrubs become dominant," says Ray Sauvajot, an ecologist at the Santa Mon-ica Recreation Area. "When fire comes through, the landscape opens up incredibly. A lot of plants that couldn't germinate before because of competition from other plants, lack of light, and lack of water do so

Periodic wildfires help preserve the fragile ecosystem in Florida's Everglades National Park. After a fire dies, cordgrass and other plants send up fresh growth that lures white-tailed deer and feral hogs to the area. These species, in turn, help sustain the endangered Florida panther (inset).

Burning Issues

The summer of 1994 will long be remembered as one of the fieriest to hit the western United States in decades. Wildfires raged through the region, leaving 4 million acres (1.6 million hectares) in ashes and killing 26 firefighters. The autumn rains that ultimately brought the destructive season to an end did not extinguish the controversy over how to prevent such deadly fires in the future. Indeed, scientists, government officials, loggers, and homeowners have entered into a fierce debate over the nation's policies on protecting the Western wilderness.

Most observers agree that decades of aggressive development have altered the fabric of many Western ecosystems. The once-unpeopled woodlands of the West are among the nation's fastest-growing regions. Thousands of houses—highly combustible fuel to wildfires—have been built in places where fire is a part of nature. In areas where officials once let brushfires burn or set controlled blazes to remove fire-prone undergrowth, firefighters must now wage an all-out battle to save human structures. The most lethal fire of 1994, which erupted near Glenwood Springs, Colorado, was a painful case in point: 14 lives were lost protecting a housing subdivision.

A century of intense fire fighting has left forests overcrowded with flammable trees, a legacy that forebodes more fiery summers. And while attention has been lavished on developing equipment and techniques to contain a blaze, few resources have been applied to thinning the dense vegetation that is likely to cause a disastrous fire.

The concerned parties are far from agreement over how to prevent catastrophic fires in the future. Many scientists advocate setting more controlled burns to reduce the stockpile of forest fuels. Opponents maintain that efforts to fight fire with fire degrade air quality and endanger people and houses. The timber industry also complains that controlled fires consume salable lumber, and further asserts that selective logging would curtail the buildup of combustible fuels. Environmentalists counter that timber operations often damage forest ecosystems and that loggers will pursue valuable trees over more-volatile species.

In 1994 alone, the federal government spent about $600 million fighting wildfires—creating another burning controversy. Some officials argue that the government should not have to bail out people who insist on living in known fire zones and, instead, should tighten building codes and take other steps to limit wilderness development.

Few experts think that government regulations can clear the pall of smoke from the West. "Wildfires will continue as long as there are wildlands," asserts fire historian Stephen Pyne. And until opponents can agree on a plan to better protect our forests, more and more brave firefighters will be needed to save homes—and lives—from the inevitable flames of summer.

Peter A. Flax

after a fire." From two to five years after a fire, herbaceous, or nonwoody, plants enjoy a revival, "which provides a tremendous food source for deer and other herbivores," says Sauvajot. Farther up the food chain, bobcats and coyotes profit in turn.

Many local homeowners understandably do not view conflagrations in terms of ecological benefit. A particularly shrill debate has erupted over an endangered rodent, the Stephens' kangaroo rat. Property owners in much of Riverside County, California, are enjoined from disturbing the animal's habitat of Mediterranean grassland—notably from cutting firebreaks around their dwellings with tractor-drawn, ground-chewing discs that slice through the rodents' burrows. Mowing flammable vegetation is fine, but mowing is more laborious, so many homeowners prefer discing. As a result, many did neither, and some homes went up in flames. "I'm now homeless, and it all began with a little rat," one resident complained in the *Los Angeles Times* in November 1993.

Local wildlife managers and environmentalists dispute the idea that fires can be blamed on the kangaroo rats. "If every kangaroo rat in this area were destroyed tomorrow, the fires would still come," asserts Anne Dennis of the local Sierra Club chapter. Not only that, fire officials say that most of the fires were so intense that neither firebreaks nor firefighters could have stopped them. U.S. Interior Secretary Bruce Babbitt, among others, has suggested that people flocking to build in this arid region need to understand the risks they take living in a fire-prone landscape—a landscape that fire ecologist Richard Minnich of the University of California, Riverside, has likened to a "lake of gasoline."

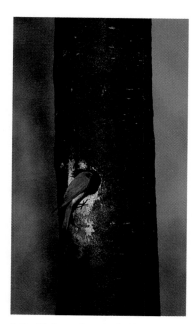

A bluebird's nesting site inside a charred tree illustrates one of the more inventive ways that wildlife can thrive in the aftermath of a forest fire.

POPCORN WITHOUT A POPPER

By contrast, when fire crackles through the Virginia habitat of the Peter's Mountain mallow, hardly anyone notices. This rare plant grows on a mountainside in a preserve owned by the nonprofit Nature Conservancy. A pink-blossomed perennial related to the hollyhock, Peter's Mountain mallow *(Iliamna corei)* was discovered in 1927, when some 50 plants were counted. "By 1980, there were four," says Caren Caljouw of Virginia's Department of Conservation and Recreation. "By the early 1990s, those same four plants were just hanging on." Heavy grazing by deer and feral goats had taken a toll, but even with these animals fenced out, the plants continued to decline. Then researchers in 1988 found that the site's soil was embedded with mallow seeds. Unlike most seeds, these "will not germinate unless the hard seed coat is cracked," says Caljouw. Only then can moisture reach the seed itself. "And the most natural way for the seed coat to crack is for fire to pass over the seedbed."

Until the 1940s, the site had been swept by wildfires every 7 to 10 years, but fire suppression turned the Peter's Mountain mallow seeds into popcorn without a popper. Then test plots were burned over in 1992, and, soon after, ecologists discovered 14 seedlings poking up from the ash. A hotter burn in 1993, followed by three weeks of rain, thrilled the scientists by producing 500 more seedlings. The moral of the story, according to Caljouw, is that "we can't just lock these places up if we want to protect them."

Not long ago, Don Despain of the National Biological Survey was studying a poster of Smokey Bear featuring wildflowers. He recalls, "I thought, 'Good grief, at least half of those species do better *after* a fire.'"

But for a last-minute change in plans, Harry Glicken would have perished on May 17, 1980, when the explosive collapse of Mount St. Helens Volcano obliterated the observation post he had manned until the day before. A decade later, however, his luck ran out. Glicken lost his life during an eruption of Mount Unzen, a volcano on Japan's Kyushu Island.

On June 3, 1991, Glicken went into an evacuated area on Unzen's eastern flank with French volcanologists Maurice and Katia Krafft to shoot close-up footage of the eruption for an educational film on volcanic hazards. Late that afternoon, the volcano unleashed a mammoth torrent of ash, rocky debris, and 500° F (260° C) gases that raced down the Mizunashi River to Kita-Kamikoba, a residential district of nearby Shimabara City nestled at the foot of Unzen's summit cone. This pyroclastic flow blew through the evacuated zone like a hurricane, killing the three volcanologists and 40 Japanese citizens.

A GROWING THREAT

Since that day, nine more volcanologists have died at volcanoes in Ecuador, Indonesia, and Colombia. By far the worst incident occurred at Colombia's Galeras Volcano in January 1993, when an unexpected shower of debris killed six scientists and three tourists.

Globally, the threat of volcanic disaster has grown in proportion to the population of the developing world, where many of the world's most dangerous active volcanoes are located. The number of people at risk from eruptions may reach 500 million by the turn of the century, according to U.S. Geological Survey (USGS) volcanologists Robert Tilling and Peter Lipman.

Typical volcanic hazards include earthquakes, explosive emissions of ash and debris, rivers of mud called lahars, rampaging lava, and pyroclastic flows—ground-hugging mixtures of hot gas, ash, and rocky debris that can race downhill at more than 100 miles (160 kilometers) per hour. To reduce the human toll, volcanologists rush to volcanoes that are showing signs of life, set up monitoring devices, and attempt to warn local residents of impending doom.

GEOLOGY IN THE PRESENT TENSE

But an eruption is also an opportunity to study an ultraviolent process that has shaped the contours of the planet and cooked up most of its foundational rock. In this sense, volcanology is geology in the present tense—the study of a world in the making.

Mount Unzen has created such an opportunity. For three years, Japanese scientists have monitored the volcano with seismometers, heat-sensitive cameras, microphones, advanced imaging radar systems, and video

UNDER
THE VOLCANO

by Daniel Pendick

cameras. Unzen's frequent, highly destructive pyroclastic flows have received the most attention. Efforts to harvest new information from them range from the ordinary to the ingenious. For example, one group of volcanologists has used microphones to record the low-frequency growl of moving pyroclastic flows, whose acoustic signature comes in part from colliding particles of debris. By comparing these sounds to the laboratory-generated clacking of different-sized steel balls, the scientists have extracted information about the size and distribution of particles in the flows.

Studies like these may lead to better ways of anticipating the risks presented by Mount

Unzen and volcanoes like it. "The motivation behind studying the dynamics of these things is prediction—to be able to get people out of the way," says USGS volcanologist Rick Hoblitt, who studied pyroclastic flows at Mount St. Helens.

At Unzen, pyroclastic flows are born at the edges of the volcano's 300-foot (90-meter)-high summit lava dome, a plug of congealed magma that began forming near the 4,485-

People living in Japan's Shimabara City (above) or in other communities that lie in the shadow of a volcano rely on scientists to warn them of the possibility of an eruption.

foot (1,360-meter) summit in May 1991. Riddled with cracks and gas-filled pores, this clot of silica-rich lava hangs precariously over the Mizunashi and Oshigadani river valleys on Unzen's eastern flank.

Hawaii is subject to relatively frequent volcanic eruptions (above). The lava flows that accompany eruptions in Hawaii and elsewhere cause a great deal of property damage (right) and are responsible for most of the deaths associated with volcanoes.

Periodically, huge masses of lava 200 to 300 feet (60 to 90 meters) high crumble from the dome and disintegrate on Unzen's steep summit slope. Hot gases formerly trapped in the lava escape, helping to convert these avalanches into slippery, highly mobile pyroclastic flows and more-dilute "ash hurricanes," or pyroclastic surges. These flows and surges follow Unzen's river valleys toward outlying areas of Shimabara City, a community of 45,000 whose center lies just a few miles from Unzen's summit.

STUDYING LAVA FLOWS

Unzen's unique combination of cliff-hanging topography and steady magma supply has spawned more than 7,000 pyroclastic flows since 1991, creating the best natural laboratory in the world to study this phenomenon.

Studying this phenomenon is important because it is one of the deadliest of volcanic events. Worldwide, pyroclastic flows and surges have been responsible for the majority of deaths and injuries from eruptions in the 20th century. The death toll includes

nearly all 29,000 residents of St. Pierre, a city that was obliterated by a pyroclastic flow and surge during the 1902 eruption of Martinique's Mont Pelee—the deadliest volcanic eruption in the past 100 years.

Although Mount Unzen is today an excellent place to study pyroclastic flows, it has been known for relatively gentle lava flows. During its last eruption before the 1991 event, a vent opened up on the volcano's northeast flank in 1792 and disgorged about 20 million cubic yards (15 million cubic meters) of runny lava. According to Kazuya Ohta, director of the Shimabara Earthquake and Volcano Observatory, 18th-century tourists would climb Unzen's wooded slope to drink sake and watch the lava spew.

When disaster struck in the past, it came, not from Unzen, but from nearby Mount Mayuyama. One month after the Unzen lava flow of 1792, powerful earthquakes loosened the eastern slope of Mayuyama, a now-extinct volcanic cone just east of Fugendake, the currently active cone that makes up part of Mount Unzen. Mayuyama's flank collapsed, unleashing a massive landslide that rode over Shimabara City and into the Ariake Sea. Some 15,000 people died from the landslide and the tsunami it caused. This was the worst volcanic disaster in Japan's history.

Until recently, however, the people of the Shimabara Peninsula have mostly lived in harmony with their volcanoes. After the Shimabara catastrophe, Mount Unzen again became the centerpiece of local tourism. Tourists traveled to Unzen-Amakusa National Park, 50 minutes by bus from Nagasaki, to watch the azaleas bloom on the volcano's fertile slopes or to visit the area's hot-spring resorts.

UNZEN AWAKES

But all that changed in November 1989, when something big and dangerous awoke beneath the Shimabara Peninsula. Scientists from the Shimabara Earthquake and Volcano Observatory detected earthquake swarms 12 miles (19 kilometers) beneath Chijiwa Bay, a semicircular body of water west of Unzen. These earthquakes—a sign that magma was on the move—began to migrate east toward Unzen. In the spring of 1991, the volcano swelled with magma. Finally, on May 24, it began to grow a lava dome and cast off pyroclastic flows.

Evacuations were ordered for areas at risk, including Kita-Kamikoba, a village on the Mizunashi River. But on June 3, despite official warnings, some journalists and residents stayed to watch the pyroclastic flows rip down the Mizunashi River. Police and firefighters were also on hand, as were Glicken and the Kraffts. The scene was set for Japan's worst volcanic accident in 60 years.

At 4:09 P.M., Unzen's lava dome collapsed, leaving behind a horseshoe-shaped depression 450 feet (140 meters) across. A flood of debris traveled a surprising 2.5 miles (4 kilometers) down the Mizunashi River Valley, smashing houses, snapping trees, and tossing cars around like toys. Those in the path of the flow did not stand a chance.

PERSISTENT MYSTERIES

For all the destruction flows and surges have caused, volcanologists still do not fully understand their inner workings. "Our understanding of what's going on inside these things is pretty primitive," admits Hoblitt.

One reason is that a pyroclastic flow's inner machinery is so hard to see. Outwardly, it looks like a rolling mass of billowing gray ash tumbling down the side of a volcano at racecar speed. But hidden inside the curtains of ash lies a complex, multilayered creature

During an eruption, Mount Unzen casts an alarming glow over Shimabara City (top). Thanks to the ability of scientists to predict the path of the pyroclastic flow, endangered residents can be evacuated; little can be done to protect property (above).

that behaves more like a dense, hot fluid than a simple gravity-driven rockfall. A generic pyroclastic flow has three basic components. The basal flow carries the largest, heaviest chunks of debris. Often, but not always, a more dilute, fluidlike surge develops over the basal flow. Finally, a buoyant, billowing column of the finest ash rises from the flow, towering hundreds of feet into the air.

These parts do not necessarily stay together, and that is what makes pyroclastic

came when the towering ash column over the main flow collapsed, generating an ash hurricane that charged ahead 0.5 mile (0.8 kilometer) at a speed of nearly 200 miles (320 kilometers) per hour.

ANTICIPATING VOLCANIC BEHAVIOR

To USGS volcanologist James Riehle, the widespread destruction wrought by the June 3 flow highlighted the limitations of relying on a volcano's past behavior to pre-

Mount St. Helens' violent 1980 eruption (above) killed 57 people, devastated 220 square miles, and caused $1 billion in damage. The Washington state volcano is still considered to be one of the most hazardous volcanoes in the world.

flows so lethal and unpredictable. "There's an interplay between the pyroclastic flow and the path it follows," Hoblitt says. When it reaches a steep slope or rides off a cliff, the flow accelerates and ingests more air, which causes it to inflate. "Conditions being right, the surge can separate from the main flow."

These conditions apparently existed the day of the Kita-Kamikoba disaster, according to a study by the Geological Survey of Japan. Takahiro Yamamoto, Shinji Takarada, and Shigeru Suto carefully mapped the debris and devastation along the Mizunashi River, and concluded that individual pyroclastic surges peeled off the basal flow four times. The final surge—the lethal blow to residents of Kita-Kamikoba as well as to Glicken and the two French volcanologists—

dict future hazards. "The volcanologists who went up to Unzen made the reasonable assumption that the pyroclastic flows would pretty much continue to go where they'd gone before," he says. "Then a rogue flow came down and killed them."

Traditionally, Riehle explains, volcanologists have relied on the geologic record of past eruptions to predict the likely size and range of pyroclastic flows that could occur during future eruptions. In addition, the location of river valleys and other key topographical features suggests directions that flows might take. Volcanologists use this information to create "hazard maps," which indicate the areas most likely to be attacked.

However, these maps cannot explain why one flow behaves differently than another in the same area, Riehle says. "To get at why some flows go farther than others requires that you think about the factors that govern the movement of the flows themselves."

Jonathan Fink and Susan Kieffer, volcanologists at Arizona State University in Tempe, have created a theoretical model that could help researchers do just that. Like other pyroclastic-flow models, this one is composed of equations that approximate the basic motions and properties of pyroclastic flows.

Fink and Kieffer developed their model to explore the process that sets pyroclastic flows in motion at crumbling lava domes. Their work suggests that the explosive release of gas—mostly water vapor—that accompanies a dome collapse can boost the initial energy of the debris significantly, creating unusually destructive and far-ranging flows like the one that flattened Kita-Kamikoba. If Fink and Kieffer are right, the appearance of especially water-rich magma could presage trouble.

At present, however, pyroclastic-flow models are better at explaining past events than predicting the future. To improve prediction, says Riehle, "first we have to create a theoretical model that reproduces what you see in nature."

THE QUEST FOR REALISM

Partly because of the deaths at Kita-Kamikoba, U.S. and Japanese researchers have decided to give top priority to developing models that add that needed realism to simulations of dome collapses and pyroclastic flows, says Chris Newhall of the USGS, who helped organize a March 1993 meeting of volcanologists from both countries. If researchers can develop more-realistic models, they might be able to predict how far a volcano's pyroclastic flows are likely to run. Newhall cautions, however, that the inherent complexity of volcanoes may limit the predictive power of pyroclastic-flow models.

For example, the size of the lava chunks that peel off Unzen's dome helps determine the ultimate size of the pyroclastic flows. And anything from the number of internal cracks in the dome to the strength of local seismic tremors can affect what comes off the dome or whether it will collapse completely. "It's very difficult to know up front what the conditions are at a dome, whether at Unzen or any other volcano," Newhall says. "So really, the models will define a spectrum of possible outcomes."

By using the Dante II robot (above) and other remote-controlled devices, scientists can enjoy a certain measure of safety when conducting research within a volcanic crater.

Given the uncertainties of predicting what a volcano might throw at people living nearby, the only way to ensure safety is to assume that the worst will happen, and to evacuate everybody at risk when a volcano stirs, Newhall says. This option probably saved many lives during the 1991 eruption of Mount Pinatubo in the Philippines when thousands were evacuated from nearby settlements.

Unfortunately, large-scale evacuation is not practical in Japan. In this crowded land of perpetual volcanism, people cannot possibly leave every time a volcano raises hell.

"Our reaction when we have a restless volcano is to get people out of the way and discourage development in areas vulnerable to volcanic hazards," says Hoblitt. "In Japan, they don't have that option." ◪

Saving the Great Northern Forest

by Theodore A. Rees Cheney

There rides astride the northern parts of Maine, New Hampshire, Vermont, and New York a huge and beautiful natural resource—a forest the combined size of Vermont, New Hampshire, Massachusetts, Connecticut, and Rhode Island. This splendid mix of evergreen spruces and firs, white birches, and many-hued maples, often referred to as the Great Northern Forest,

covers 26 million acres (10.5 million hectares). The region is a haven for the many types of wildlife that inhabit its woodlands and its thousands of lakes and streams.

Only about 1 million people live and work within the Great Northern Forest, but 70 million more can reach it within a day's drive. Therein lies a problem.

Millions of urbanites hope to visit, own vacation homes, or even move into this vast forested paradise, especially along the shores of its 7,700 ponds and lakes. Others would prefer to live along one of the 67,000 miles (107,803 kilometers) of rocky, roaring streams that run through the almost 23 million acres (9.3 million hectares) of timberlands. Therein lies another problem.

Only 15 percent of this wild and wonderful world is owned by state or federal governments for use by the people—not for sale. Public lands include Maine's Baxter State Park, New York's Adirondack State Park, and the White and Green Mountain national forests of New Hampshire and Vermont, respectively. Together, this area comprises less than 4 million acres (1.6 million hectares) of the Northern Forest.

Most of the Northern Forest is held privately—primarily by timber companies. The uncertain future of the large timber industry and the sale of private land to developers are at the heart of the Northern Forest controversy. Public- and private-interest groups are grappling with such issues as private-property rights, public access to wilderness areas, and environmental protection.

AN ALARM IS SOUNDED

In December 1982, the possibility that large-scale growth could indeed happen in the Northern Forest became apparent when Sir John Goldsmith, an English financier, purchased Diamond International Corporation—a giant forest-products company with assets that included 1 million acres (405,000 hectares) of land within the Northern Forest. Huge tracts of timberland had often changed hands before; this time, however, the exchange of land was not between two timber companies. Only six years later, a group of land

Each year, thousands of visitors flock to see the dazzling autumn foliage, crystal-clear waters, and rich wildlife of the Great Northern Forest, a wooded paradise that is now the focus of a raging controversy between private-interest concerns and environmental groups.

developers bought all 90,000 acres (36,450 hectares) that Goldsmith had put up for sale from the million acres he had bought in northern New Hampshire and Vermont. The developers planned to subdivide the acreage to sell as small vacation lots.

Fearing such development, New Hampshire bought back from the developers some 40,000 acres (16,200 hectares) called the Nash Stream Tract. The state paid some $12 million for the land, about $4 million of which came from federal sources. New Hampshire now owns and manages the tract's recreational and timber use; the federal government is responsible for all other development rights. The tract lies north of the northernmost part of the White Mountain National Forest, which includes 724,000 acres (293,220 hectares) of protected woodland.

Although already too developed to be included within the definition of the Northern Forest, the Lakes District (a group of several lakes in central New Hampshire) begins just south of the White Mountain National Forest. A prime example of overdevelopment is Lake Winnipesaukee. Its 183 miles (295 kilometers) of shoreline are lined with summer homes and, increasingly, with year-round retirees from southern New England.

The sparkling blue bodies of water in the Lakes District, with their modern developments, condominiums, marinas, and mills stand as precursory testaments to what could likely happen farther north.

AN ENVIRONMENTAL LEADER

Like its neighbors, Vermont has abundant forests, mountains, and lakes. Although broken up administratively into several state parks, state forests, and the Green Mountain National Forest, an almost continuous forest runs from Quebec in the north to the Vermont/Massachusetts border in the south. Much of the forestland is owned by paper and timber companies.

A particularly wild region of the state is the Northeast Kingdom, a dense forest

The Great Northern Forest (depicted in the map) includes millions of acres of public and private lands. Many environmentalists fear that the forest's wilderness areas (below) will become crowded vacation spots (right) unless land-use restrictions are implemented.

More than 5,000 pristine ponds and lakes and 67,000 miles of rock-strewn brooks help make the Northern Forest a haven for wildlife and a restful retreat for tourists.

that covers 1.28 million acres (518,400 hectares) in the northeastern corner of Vermont. Although only the Vermont section is called the Northeast Kingdom, the forest extends in nature eastward across the panhandle of New Hampshire. Again, like most of the region, it is owned by paper and timber companies.

In response to increased development and pressures on natural resources, Vermont's legislature passed the Vermont Land Use and Development Law in 1970. Under this law, prospective land developers must adhere to explicit, detailed guidelines designed to protect the environment and maintain the integrity of Vermont towns. This comprehensive law establishes Vermont as a national leader in protecting its environment.

On the federal level, Senator Patrick Leahy (D-Vt.) is seeking legislation in Congress to designate Lake Champlain as America's sixth Great Lake, making it eligible for the same federal assistance now given the other five Great Lakes. Lake Champlain is cradled in a valley between New York's Adirondack Mountains and Vermont's Green Mountains. The lake is still considered in good ecological condition, yet rapid growth along its shoreline makes it a "ticking time bomb," according to some experts. Vermont, New York, and Quebec are working together to find effective ways to defuse the problem on a regional basis.

FORESIGHT IN ADIRONDACKS

Much of the Northern Forest in New York State is included in Adirondack State Park, which

ST. LAWRENCE RIVER

QUEBEC

NEW BRUNSWICK

Allagash Wilderness Waterway

Baxter State Park

Moosehead Lake

Proposed Maine Woods Reserve

MILLINOCKET

MAINE

BANGOR

AUGUSTA

White Mountain National Forest

Acadia National Park

PORTLAND

NEW HAMPSHIRE

Lake Winnipesaukee

CONCORD

N

PRIVATE LAND

STATE OR FEDERAL LAND

SCALE OF MILES

0   50   100

Visitors to Maine's Mount Katahdin (above) or to any of the forest's parks, historical sites, or private recreation centers can enjoy a variety of outdoor activities. At left, a wilderness ranger assists backpackers embarking on a challenging trek.

encompasses nearly one-fifth of the state's total land area, making it the largest park in the Lower 48. The Adirondack Park covers an area about the size of Vermont.

The Adirondack Council (representatives from the Sierra Club, the Wilderness Society, and other voluntary citizen groups), in its first *2020 Vision Report*, said, "Today the people of New York own title to the finest vestiges of wilderness in the northeastern United States. This splendid natural legacy is testimony to the foresight of our forebears. How fully and quickly we seize the opportunities to complete the Adirondack Wilderness System will be a test of this generation's foresight. One thing is certain: time is of the essence. Once wilderness is subdivided and developed, it is wilderness no more."

Some 57 percent of the Adirondack Park is privately owned, used mainly for forestry, agriculture, and outdoor recreation. The park

is occupied by only 130,000 permanent and 210,000 seasonal residents, but 9 million people visit it annually.

Forty-three percent of the Adirondack Park is the state-owned Adirondack Forest Preserve, which the state constitution has protected since 1894: "[It] shall be forever kept as wild forest land." Within the Adirondack Forest Preserve are 16 "wilderness areas." Motorized vehicles and equipment are banned from the designated wilderness areas to help preserve wildlife and to retain the quiet and solitude of nature for those who recreate within it. Motorized vehicles are allowed to roam rather freely, however, within 1.3 million acres (526,500 hectares) of areas designated as "wild forest."

The present 16 wilderness areas occupy about 45 percent of the land within the Adirondack Forest Preserve. The council has proposed adding a new wilderness area, the Bob Marshall Great Wilderness, of 409,000 acres (165,645 hectares) in the western portion of the park. This large area would be of sufficient size and remoteness to sustain populations of most wildlife species native to

The Northern Forest has year-round appeal for sports enthusiasts. During the winter months, its hillsides are dotted with downhill skiers, snowmobilers, and cross-country skiers (left).

the Adirondacks, including reintroduced wolves, moose, and possibly even cougars. "The Bob" would encompass 441 lakes and ponds, and more than 70 miles (112 kilometers) of already designated "wild rivers." If created, "the Bob" would be the largest "wilderness area" in the eastern United States north of the Everglades.

CRISIS IN MAINE

Fifteen million acres (6,075,000 hectares) of the Northern Forest are part of Maine's vast forest system, which covers nearly 90 percent of the total land area of the state. Not surprisingly, the timber industry has always been of key economic importance to the state. During the lumber industry's heyday in the 1800s, 410 sawmills were in operation at or above Bangor on Maine's Penobscot River, making this area the undisputed lumber capital of the world. Today, however, opting for short-term profits, many timber companies are shifting from sustainable logging to massive clear-cutting. Now an increasing amount of privately held timberland is being offered for sale to developers. This activity threatens the integrity of the Northern Forest because so few of Maine's forests are protected public lands. A notable exception is the 200,000-acre (81,000-hectare) Baxter State Park, named

for former Governor Percival Baxter, who wanted the area kept as close as possible to the way it was when naturalist Henry David Thoreau hiked it in the mid-1800s. When the legislature could not agree on whether to keep these lands out of the hands of the paper and timber industry, Baxter bought the acreage himself, donating it to the people as a state park.

Many streams still run wild through the Northern Forest in Maine, but only the Allagash has been designated as an official Wilderness Waterway. The Allagash runs through apparent wilderness for 100 miles (161 kilometers), but the thousands of canoeists who camp along its beautiful evergreen shores occasionally hear huge trucks and monster machines clear-cutting the forest just out of sight. Except for a narrow strip of protected land along the river, the timber belongs to paper and lumber companies.

Although Baxter State Park and much of the timber-company lands surrounding it are available to the public for hiking, hunting, camping, cross-country skiing, and snowmobiling, many people would like to see much more of Maine's wilderness protected and preserved. They believe that the Northern Forest is most threatened in Maine because the timber industry is the state's principal landowner.

The Wilderness Society has proposed a plan to create a Maine Woods Reserve that would include Baxter State Park within its 2.7 million acres (1.1 million hectares). The society says its goal is to keep the area as wild as it is currently by preventing the kind of rapid development now occurring around Greenville at the southern tip of Moosehead Lake. This largest lake in Maine carries that name because it is thought to resemble in outline the large, antlered head of Maine's most beloved wild animal.

A small but dedicated private organization, *RESTORE: The North Woods*, proposes a

3.2-million-acre (1.3-million-hectare) area that would become the Maine Woods National Park. This newest national park would exceed the area of Yellowstone National Park by 1 million acres (405,000 hectares).

Others propose a 1 million-acre area, including the St. John River, the Allagash Wilderness Waterway, Baxter State Park, the Maine Woods, and other lands as far west as the Rangeley Lakes. They would name it the Thoreau Regional Wilderness Reserve, after Henry David Thoreau, who wrote about the region's wild and beautiful rivers. Thoreau also canoed through many of the hundreds of lakes and ponds, most of which even today can be reached only by canoe or floatplane.

Although the concept of the Great Northern Forest stops at the United States-Canada border, the forest itself continues in nature well into New Brunswick, Canada. This extension encompasses the same kind of woodlands and streams. Unfortunately, it also faces many of the same problems as the Maine woods. The New Brunswick forests are disappearing under the attack of the chain saw even more rapidly than are Maine's.

OTHER THREATS

Land sales to developers are not the only threats to land preservation. The military services continue to show great interest in setting aside remote areas for their specialized purposes. Because the Northern Forest greatly resembles Siberia's taiga forest, the U.S. Air Force flies its largest bombers at treetop levels—under radar range—across silent forests occupied mainly by deer, moose, and bear. The U.S. Marines practice assault tactics within Reid State Park, Maine. In 1990, the Army National Guard asked to expand its

Canoeists gliding along a river enjoy the serenity of the seemingly untouched wilderness (right). A narrow ribbon of forest along the Allagash conceals the extensive clear-cutting that has occurred beyond the river's edge (below).

training-activities area in Maine from 181,000 acres (73,305 hectares) to 711,000 acres (287,955 hectares).

In addition, the military has a radar installation, which includes horizontal banks of antennas up to 5,000 feet (1,525 meters) long, near Moscow, Maine. Originally devised to protect our shores from treetop attack by Soviet bombers, the facility is now claimed to protect us from treetop flights of drug suppliers from Central and South America.

Ironically, another threat comes from a new technological development favored by ecologically concerned citizens—wind

The survival of the wolf, bald eagle, black bear (right), and other species may depend on the establishment of large reserves within the confines of the Northern Forest.

power. One wind-power corporation proposes to create in Maine the world's largest wind-driven generating facility in the world. Unfortunately, the company wants to build its power plant in Maine's Kibby Range, one of the only remaining roadless areas east of the Mississippi that exceeds 100,000 acres (40,500 hectares). The proposal includes 630 wind-power turbines on the peaks, connected by 75 miles (121 kilometers) of new woodland and crest-line roads. Each of the two hundred ten 80-foot (24-meter) towers will support three gigantic whirling blades. Although wind-generated energy is essentially pollution-free, the construction of the necessary structures, and their enduring presence in the forests, will take a heavy toll on this pristine wilderness and on the animals that inhabit it.

LOOKING AHEAD

Many people feel that all these wonders of wilderness that allow biodiversity to thrive and provide spaces for recreational activities should be kept available for future generations. New York State showed great foresight when it decided that the huge forest preserve within the giant Adirondack Park should remain forever as a wild forest. New Hampshire has its White Mountain National Forest, Vermont its Green Mountains, but Maine has very little in the way of publicly owned lands. For this reason, activists believe that Maine, in particular, must address the issue of protecting its wild forests that are in the private, and sometimes unpredictable, hands of the timber industry.

Private ownership of wilderness by forest-products companies is not inappropriate, especially when they allow the public to hunt, fish, hike, canoe, and ski on their lands, as they have done over the years. Problems arise, however, when the timber companies sell their great tracts to other types of businesses—the development companies. These groups often subdivide an area into smaller

and smaller (as small as a house lot) units for development. When a large tract of land goes from zero human inhabitants to thousands of families, all the "civilization problems" come with the newcomers: chain saws, snowmobiles, cars, trucks, buses, motorboats, air pollution, noise pollution, stream and lake pollution—much of what the people came there in the first place to avoid.

Organizations like the Wilderness Society, the Sierra Club, and the Audubon Society try hard to find ways to minimize the impact of possible future large-tract land sales, but it is a difficult process. The Diamond International Corporation's sale of its lands to developers rang the emergency bell.

Few people believed that sales the size of the Diamond transaction would ever happen. Between 1976 and 1990, more than half the lands in the proposed Maine Woods National Park changed hands. This year, a major paper company is preparing to sell 800,000 acres (324,000 hectares) of timberland in Maine, and 200,000 acres (81,000 hectares) in New Hampshire, Vermont, and New York.

Since the Diamond sale, there has been extensive regional concern about the future of the Great Northern Forest. Several private and public groups have studied and debated the situation with the hope of creating acceptable conservation and development strategies. A solution agreeable to the public- and private-interest groups has not been found. With each passing day, the face of the Great Northern Forest changes forever. ◪

ASK THE SCIENTIST

▶ *What is an artesian well? How does it work? Are all wells of the artesian variety?*

The name "artesian" derives from the French province of Artois. As early as the 12th century A.D., the province was known for its artesian ("of Artois") wells, in which water rose under pressure from a porous stratum of rock (or aquifer) overlaid by impermeable rock. Once an artesian well is sunk into an artesian basin, water flows upward toward the surface by itself and does not have to be pumped, at least not entirely. Probably the largest artesian basin in the world is Queensland's Great Artesian Basin in Australia, covering an area of over 600,000 square miles (1.5 million square kilometers). Some of the wells in this basin are up to 4,600 feet (1,400 meters) deep, while many other wells discharge groundwater so hot that it must be stored in cooling ponds before livestock can drink it. The largest artesian aquifer in the United States is thought to sit beneath North and South Dakota and several other Great Plains states. Because naturally occurring artesian basins are relatively rare, most wells are not of the artesian variety.

▶ *Were most or all mountain peaks at one time volcanoes? Has a volcano occurred in the Appalachian Mountains in modern times? What about the Alps?*

Technically, a mountain and a volcano are not the same thing—one is a bulge in the Earth's crust; the other is a fissure—thus, a mature volcano like Mount St. Helens in Washington is a mountain with a volcano in it. And while many so-called "young" mountains (still measured in thousands, perhaps millions, of years) may have volcanoes, not all do. For instance, no true volcanoes occur in the Himalayas or the Alps, because these young mountain ranges are formed in such a way that volcanic eruptions are suppressed. As for the Appalachians, true volcanoes do not occur in old ranges. Volcanoes occur exclusively in regions (called belts) around Earth where the planetary crust has recently been wrinkled or cracked.

▶ *Are tsunamis and tidal waves the same thing? Does one or the other always form after an earthquake? What is the tallest tsunami/tidal wave on record?*

The Japanese word *tsunami*, which means "harbor wave," refers to seismic sea waves. Although seismic sea waves are commonly called "tidal waves," they have nothing to do with tides or tide-producing forces. In fact, tsunamis have everything to do with earthquakes—particularly those exceeding a magnitude of 6.5—and may be caused by the displacement of tremendous volumes of water through such earthquake-related mechanisms as vertical faulting or great mudslides on the seafloor. Tsunami waves exceeding 200 feet (60 meters) in height have been known to occur; in 1737, for example, explorer George S. Eiby reported such a wave breaking off the southern tip of Kamchatka, a peninsula in the Russian Far East.

The imprecise term "tidal wave" also refers to storm-created sea waves. Such storm surges, including those associated with hurricanes and other tropical cyclones, are influenced by tides and tide-producing forces. In a hurricane storm surge, extremely low air pressure under a hurricane causes the ocean underneath it to rise. The higher tide, pushed by strong winds, forms a storm "surge." Probably the tallest and most destructive such "tidal wave" occurred in November 1970 during a tropical cyclone in the bathtub-shaped Bay of Bengal. The resultant surge exceeded 30 feet (9 meters) in height, and drowned an estimated 200,000 to 300,000 people in Bangladesh.

Is it true that the Sahara Desert was once a fertile area with sufficient rainfall to sustain plant life? Has the Sahara always been a desert in modern times?

The vast Sahara is the world's largest desert. It covers more than a quarter of the African continent, an area greater than 3 million square miles (7.7 million square kilometers) and as large as the continental United States. But parts of the Sahara once teemed with plant *and* animal life—and people, too! As recently as 8,000 to 10,000 years ago, according to N. C. Pollock, lecturer emeritus in geography at Oxford University in England, extensive areas of the present-day Sahara—including today's Egyptian desert—once supported a savanna vegetation with nomadic herdspeople and a wide variety of fauna and flora. In fact, the southward spread of the Quaternary ice sheet in Europe caused much higher rainfall in the Sahara than there is now. Where, today, only disconnected dry wadis (riverbeds) and a desert landscape remain, in antiquity, the region contained a large and integrated system of rivers rivaling the Niger and the Nile.

With the final retreat of the ice sheet in Europe and the establishment of a semi-permanent dome of dry, sinking air over the region, the Sahara became increasingly arid. Although elephants and other animals wandered happily in oases, such as those in the Atlas Mountains of modern-day Morocco and Algeria, well into the Christian era, the abundant life began to disappear, retreating to the edges of the rapidly expanding desert.

The Sahara has remained a desert in modern times. A few remnants of the wetter past are still found in the central Sahara's plateau region (also called the Ahaggar), where oases manage to support some meager plant life. Most of the Sahara's current inhabitants—some 2 million people—maintain permanent homes at these upland oases or pursue a nomadic lifestyle in the Sahel, a large grasslands region along the southern margins of the desert.

What is the difference between quarrying and strip-mining? Why do quarries so often seem to fill up with water?

Quarrying and strip-mining are both so-called "surface" methods of mining, but most of their similarities end there. Quarrying is generally employed for the removal of stone (such as marble, sandstone, granite, and limestone) and residual deposits. It can be performed on a small or huge scale, but tends to be a localized mining operation.

Strip-mining is used to extract near-surface, flat, or gently inclined sedimentary ore beds such as coal, bauxite, clay, or phosphate. It generally occurs over much-more-extensive areas. Environmentalists universally decry the practice of strip-mining because it tends to transform the land into a sterile wasteland, especially where sulfur associated with coal-bearing formations enters nearby streams to become sulfuric acid.

Because the rocks surrounding a quarry-excavated area are often permeable (and may be adjacent to spring-fed aquifers), and because excavation usually occurs below the existing water table (where groundwater tends to collect), quarries often fill up with water unless the water is pumped out.

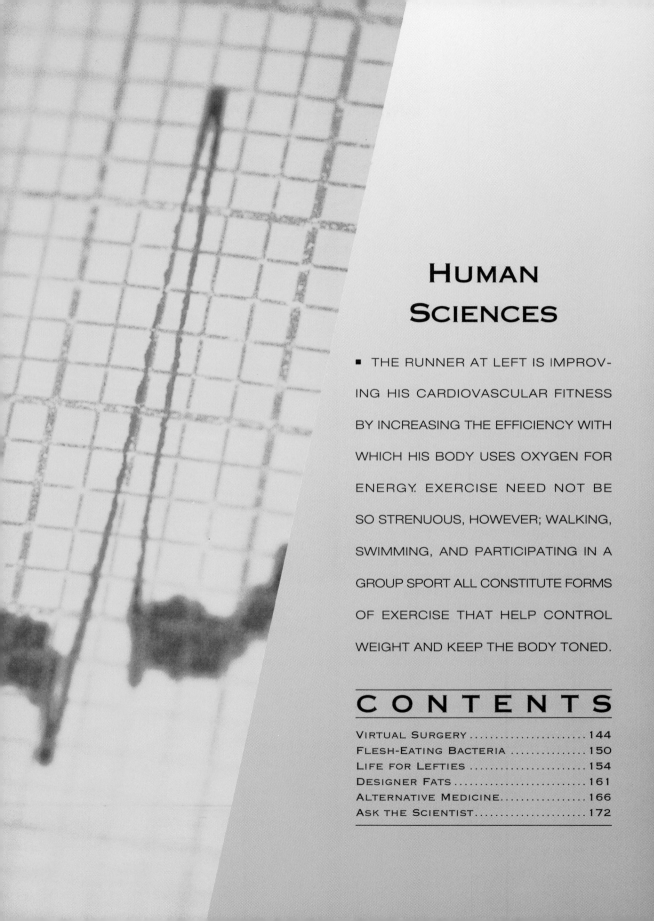

HUMAN SCIENCES

■ THE RUNNER AT LEFT IS IMPROV-
ING HIS CARDIOVASCULAR FITNESS
BY INCREASING THE EFFICIENCY WITH
WHICH HIS BODY USES OXYGEN FOR
ENERGY. EXERCISE NEED NOT BE
SO STRENUOUS, HOWEVER; WALKING,
SWIMMING, AND PARTICIPATING IN A
GROUP SPORT ALL CONSTITUTE FORMS
OF EXERCISE THAT HELP CONTROL
WEIGHT AND KEEP THE BODY TONED.

CONTENTS

VIRTUAL SURGERY:
THE NEXT DIMENSION

by Frank M. Szivos

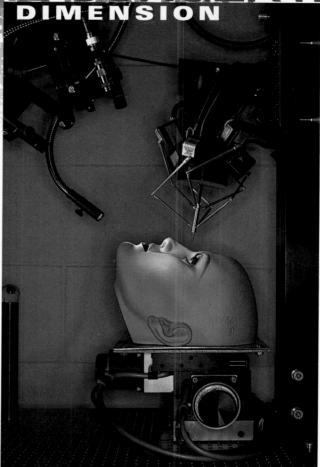

The surgical resident inserts a specialized tube called a laparoscope (a fiber-optic instrument with a camera and surgical tool mounted on it) through a keyhole-sized incision in the abdomen. Guided only by an image appearing on a monitor, he carefully maneuvers the laparoscope through the patient's body. By means of a joystick similar to those used for video games, the instrument is directed to the gallbladder, the target of the search.

The resident feels the tension of slicing through the gallbladder, and sees the blood oozing from the incision. After an hour or so of cutting and suturing, he completes the laparoscopic cholecystectomy—a minimally invasive procedure in which the gallbladder is surgically removed through a small incision in the abdomen.

If this had been a real operation, the patient would now be resting comfortably, the operation a success. But the surgical resident has just completed a "virtual" operation on a computer-simulated abdomen.

In the virtual-reality surgery just described, the three-dimensional (3-D) computer graphics precisely replicated the abdomen and gallbladder. Even the bleeding and the tactile sensation of cutting through tissue were simulated by computer to create the precise conditions that the surgeon will ultimately face in the operating room.

Virtual-surgery systems have also been developed to simulate eye and prostate surgery,

Doctors use virtual-reality surgical simulators to learn new techniques and practice difficult procedures. Above, a surgeon's motions are exactly duplicated by robotic arms that "perform" delicate eye surgery.

as well as various laparoscopic procedures in the abdomen and chest cavity. As these systems become more refined, virtual reality will likely emerge as an invaluable teaching tool in the education and training of surgeons.

A VIRTUAL-REALITY EXPLOSION

Virtual surgery traces its origins to the late 1980s. Back then, computer technology spawned a type of high-tech arcade video game in which the player wears special headgear that contains two tiny video screens.

The screens produce slightly different images for each eye, creating a 3-D effect that makes the wearer actually seem to be in the computer-generated scene. The creators of this "virtual-reality" technology soon realized that it had countless applications beyond the arcade.

At about the same time that virtual reality began making a sensation, a new type of surgery called laparoscopy was rapidly replacing traditional methods for performing television monitor. The laparoscopic trainee must therefore develop an extraordinary level of remote-control eye-hand coordination before ever reaching the operating room. For years, doctors have had to rely on simple Nintendo or Sega video games in an effort to gain the needed dexterity.

Researchers demonstrate a "virtual cadaver" program that enables doctors wearing special headgear and "data" gloves to manipulate the anatomy of a human leg.

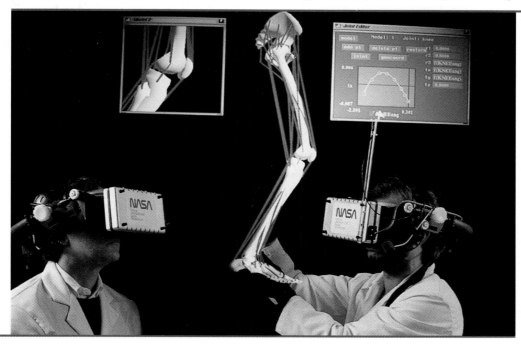

certain chest, abdominal, and pelvic operations. Medical schools and teaching hospitals were, unfortunately, at a loss for how best to teach laparoscopic techniques to their students and staff. By definition, laparoscopic surgery is minimally invasive, and requires the doctors to work within an exceedingly confined area of, say, the abdomen or the chest cavity. The vast majority of a laparoscopic operation is performed via remote control; aside from the initial incision, virtually every cut and suture is performed by surgical instruments manipulated by means of a joystick. Visual access to the surgical site is limited to a two-dimensional image on a

SIMULATED SURGERY

As it turned out, the medical profession discovered a way to train laparoscopic surgeons by observing the methods used to train airplane pilots. For the past three decades, military and commercial pilots have received extensive training via flight simulators. The simulators accelerate the learning process by duplicating, nearly exactly, the conditions that pilots will face—without ever leaving the ground. Flight simulators, of course, require less-complex computerization than do simulators depicting the interaction of internal organs that can be cut, stretched, reattached, and otherwise manipulated. For

OPERATING ON DIGITAL PATIENTS

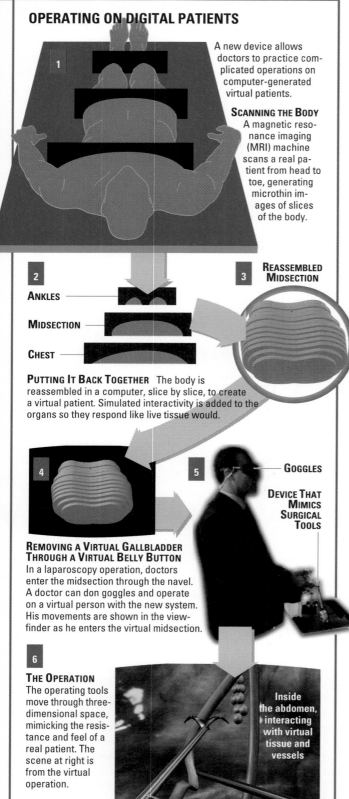

A new device allows doctors to practice complicated operations on computer-generated virtual patients.

SCANNING THE BODY
A magnetic resonance imaging (MRI) machine scans a real patient from head to toe, generating microthin images of slices of the body.

2

ANKLES

MIDSECTION

CHEST

3 REASSEMBLED MIDSECTION

PUTTING IT BACK TOGETHER The body is reassembled in a computer, slice by slice, to create a virtual patient. Simulated interactivity is added to the organs so they respond like live tissue would.

4

5

GOGGLES

DEVICE THAT MIMICS SURGICAL TOOLS

REMOVING A VIRTUAL GALLBLADDER THROUGH A VIRTUAL BELLY BUTTON
In a laparoscopy operation, doctors enter the midsection through the navel. A doctor can don goggles and operate on a virtual person with the new system. His movements are shown in the viewfinder as he enters the virtual midsection.

6

THE OPERATION
The operating tools move through three-dimensional space, mimicking the resistance and feel of a real patient. The scene at right is from the virtual operation.

Inside the abdomen, interacting with virtual tissue and vessels

Source:
High Techsplanations,
Rockville, MD

REPRESENTATIONS OF MEDICAL INSTRUMENTS

surgery simulators, researchers turned to virtual reality to create (or, more correctly, replicate) the high-definition visual component and the tactile sensations that a doctor needs to experience when practicing laparoscopic surgery. Before long, it was evident that virtual-reality systems would someday become an indispensable training tool for laparoscopic surgeons.

"It's exciting stuff," says James "Butch" Rosser, Jr., M.D., director of Yale University Medical School's Endoscopic and Laparoscopic Training Center in New Haven, Connecticut. "Virtual reality has a definite place and use in the future," he says, noting that "we'll need an entire squadron of Jedi Knights to deliver surgical health care for the 21st century."

Kevin McGovern, executive vice president of Cine-Med, a medical-education company in Woodbury, Connecticut, agrees wholeheartedly, describing virtual-reality surgery as "the most radically different phenomenon since the onset of general anesthesia." As for virtual surgery's application to training laparoscopic surgeons, McGovern is quick to point out that before laparoscopy, "surgery meant exposing the body." And while laparoscopy minimizes the exposure, it requires that the physician learn an entirely new set of skills—"highly technical skills," says McGovern, "that practicing surgery using virtual reality can develop."

In traditional surgery, doctors must train on animals and cadavers. In virtual surgery, the need for this costly and sometimes controversial practice is eliminated, comments Keith Green, Ph.D., D.Sc., a physiologist at the Medical College of Georgia in Augusta. Perhaps more important, he adds, virtual surgery permits surgeons to practice a technique as much as they like before operating on flesh-and-blood patients. Finally, the virtual system provides a harm-free environment designed to give surgeons feedback and to alert them if they make an error.

"With virtual surgery, no one gets hurt," Green explains. "If a surgeon makes a mistake, he resets the machine and starts over."

Colin Bethel, M.D., a pediatric surgical resident at Yale-New Haven Hospital, enthusiastically supports Green's position. "Virtual surgery is exciting and a lot of fun to work with," Bethel says. "It really improves your depth perception and increases the dexterity of your nondominant hand." He notes that the proficiency of the nondominant hand (the less-used hand; for example, the left hand of a right-handed individual) is especially important for laparoscopy, since this type of surgery requires both hands to manipulate the joysticks.

Bethel also finds that "there's an incredible learning curve [practicing on a virtual-reality system]. After Dr. Rosser's two-day course [on laparoscopic CD-ROM training], I came out of there doing things I didn't think were possible."

After experimenting with virtual-surgery systems several times, Daniel Passeri, M.D., a vascular surgeon for 15 years at St. Vincent's Medical Center in Bridgeport, Connecticut, became an enthusiastic advocate of virtual surgery.

"I've tried a simulator, and it was incredible," he says. "It felt like a Disney ride as I looked into the abdominal cavity." Passeri is quick to point out that in laparoscopic surgery, "doctors are used to seeing things

Surgical Boot Camp

As prototypes of virtual surgery are refined, James "Butch" Rosser, Jr., M.D., director of Yale University Medical School's Endoscopic and Laparoscopic Training Center in New Haven, Connecticut, has addressed the immediate need for more-sophisticated surgical-training methods. By tapping available computer and CD-ROM technology to train surgeons in delicate laparoscopic procedures, Rosser has developed a laparoscopic simulator that uses cartoonlike two-dimensional graphics that are inexpensive to produce and effective as a training tool. Although it lacks the three-dimensional, realistic appearance of sophisticated virtual surgery, the system works. As he sees it, CD-ROM simulation has "real" value in the present critical need to train surgeons in new laparoscopic techniques. "Virtual surgery could be as long as four or five years off," Rosser says. "My need is now. I have to train doctors to work in the two-dimensional world they operate in and see on the television monitor."

Rosser calls his course "laparoscopic boot camp." During three days of intense training, surgeons learn new skills that are demanded by laparoscopic procedures. Rosser has devised three drills—the Slam Dunk, the Cobra Rope, and the Terrible Triangle—to develop intricate laparoscopic surgical skills.

In the Slam Dunk, surgeons manipulate joysticks that maneuver surgical arms equipped with clamps to pick up dried peas and drop them into an opening about 0.25 inch (0.6 centimeter) wide. The Cobra Rope requires surgeons to grab a thin piece of rope with clamps on designated marked areas. And in the Terrible Triangle, perhaps the most demanding, a surgeon must manipulate a surgical arm mounted with a hook at the end to pick up a metal triangle and place it in a small circle. Surgeons are timed in all three drills, and are forced to use their nondominant hand.

"We try to call on the surgeons' competitive natures," Rosser says. "There's a great deal of rooting for each other. But doctors are timed, and we rank them on a board. It brings the most out of them. The course is very intense, and they come out of it with sharper skills for the demanding minimally invasive surgery that is becoming more prevalent. Think of it. A patient can have a gallbladder removed and go home the next day," marvels Rosser. "That takes surgical skills different from the skills of open surgery."

in only two dimensions on the television monitor. The three dimensions [of virtual surgery] make it more interesting. For the first time," he exclaims, "I could see the back side of the liver."

A SOFTWARE REVOLUTION

Doctors are not alone in recognizing the potential of virtual-surgery systems. Many universities and pharmaceutical companies have offered support to individuals and companies specializing in virtual-reality research. One such beneficiary is High Techsplanations of Rockville, Maryland, a virtual-reality-products manufacturer that has received technical and financial support.

As part of a joint venture with a pharmaceutical and a medical-equipment firm, High Techsplanations has created a virtual-reality program to illustrate a pelvic lymph-node dissection. The program, which was demonstrated at the 1995 American Urological Association Conference in San Francisco, California, drew the attention of many delegates. High Techsplanations has also designed a prostate-surgery simulator that creates a 3-D image of the prostate gland and the surrounding anatomy. As the surgeon manipulates a simulated scalpel, the system indicates if a mistake is made, and suggests how to correct the error.

"The response is tremendous," says Rhonda Roy, a company spokesperson. "Universities and pharmaceutical companies see the advantages of virtual reality. The benefits are limitless."

In the meantime, Cine-Med has jumped into the race to develop medical virtual-reality models. The Connecticut medical-training company is perfecting a virtual-reality model of the human heart. Cardiologists with first-hand exposure to the virtual heart describe the experience as akin to being on a roller-coaster ride through the heart's chambers and arteries. The virtual-reality heart even gives physicians an inside look at the physiology of a heart attack and other cardiac problems. "This is a never-before-seen simulation," McGovern says. "It's quite amazing even for the most experienced doctors."

Taking virtual surgery a step further, Cine-Med is developing a virtual clinic with CAT-scan and MRI capabilities, that would allow a patient to be repeatedly scanned while surgery is in progress. In the virtual clinic, a computer registers the position of the surgeon's instruments, and includes their exact location in the 3-D image viewed by the surgeon and radiologist.

TELESURGERY: LONG-DISTANCE DOCTORING

Perhaps the most ambitious application of virtual surgery is telesurgery (also called tele-robotics, telepresence, or teleoperation)—a virtual-reality surgical system that sounds more like fantasy than reality. Imagine

Using a virtual-reality computer program, an operator can direct radiation to a lung tumor (in yellow) by moving a three-dimensional mouse. Below, the user views a 3-D image of the lungs and tumor.

undergoing surgery at the "hands" of a tele-robot that is receiving instructions from a surgeon miles away!

In telesurgery, a remote-controlled robot is operated by a human surgeon who manipulates "master" surgical instruments, which appear to extend into a 3-D image of the human body. The image, displayed on a viewing screen and in the virtual-reality headwear worn by the doctor, looks and feels like human tissue. To enhance the sense of touch, the system is equipped with position and force sensors and even sound effects. Robotic "slave" instruments precisely mimic the motions of the surgeon's hand

perform microsurgical procedures that were previously beyond their abilities.

Hunter's system is not intended to replace surgeons, but
rather to enhance surgery. For
example, a distinct benefit is the
speed of the computer system,
which can move in unison with
a blinking eye, a beating heart, or
a squirming patient. The computer also senses a surgeon's
involuntary hand tremor, and
removes it from the message being sent to the robot arm. In fact,
the computer can even adjust
for a bumpy ambulance ride!

and perform the actual surgery on either a
human or a computer-generated patient.

Once perfected, telerobotic technology
will enable military surgeons at field hospitals behind the front lines to perform life-
saving emergency surgery on wounded
soldiers as they are being evacuated. Closer
to home, small towns and remote communities will have easier access to the services
of surgical specialists, who typically practice
at large urban hospitals.

Currently more than 10 research groups in
the United States and Europe are developing
telesurgical systems. A leader in the field is Ian
Hunter, Ph.D., a mechanical-engineering professor at the Massachusetts Institute of Technology's (MIT's) Department of Mechanical
Engineering in Cambridge. Hunter and his
colleagues developed a telesurgical system that
specializes in microsurgery. Using digitized
maps of the human body, they designed a
prototype virtual environment for eye surgery
that includes a teleoperated microrobot.

The system's computer scales down the
surgeon's actual movements by a factor of
up to 1 million. Instantaneously, the microrobot arm replicates the surgeon's movements, but on a microscopic scale. Using
the system, human surgeons will be able to

FROM THE DRAWING BOARD

Researchers anticipate several more years of
development before a complete telesurgery
system becomes commercially available. Fortunately, some of the tools that can be applied
to telesurgery already exist.

The virtual-surgery systems that simulate
delicate eye surgery and certain laparoscopic
procedures in the abdomen and chest are already in production. Medical engineers anticipate that these systems will reach the market
by 1996. Initially such systems are expected
to be costly, ranging in price from $50,000 to
$150,000. As with many new technologies,
however, the price is expected to drop quickly.

Passeri shares the view of many doctors
and hospital administrators who recognize
the benefits of virtual surgery, but can't justify
its steep price tag in today's economic climate.
Commenting on his firsthand virtual-surgery
experience, he says, "I liked it; it's easier to learn
on. But I don't think it's worth the anticipated
cost right now." Others, such as McGovern,
think virtual surgery is worth the price.

"Virtual surgery is changing medicine. It's
wild stuff," exclaims McGovern. In his opinion, virtual surgery will prove to be one of
the most important medical breakthroughs
in this century.

ATTACK OF THE FLESH-EATING BACTERIA

A strain of streptococcus bacteria (left) has been implicated in the outbreak of necrotizing fasciitis, a condition most notable for the destruction of flesh. Sessions in an infrared chamber (below) may help promote scar-free healing.

by James A. Blackman, M.D., M.P.H.

Phyllis Parker, a high-school geography teacher in Lexington, Virginia, was making good progress in her postholiday cleaning. But just as she began returning Christmas ornaments to the attic, she felt a pain on the right side of her chest. Then she noticed that at the site of her pain, the skin had turned a fiery red. Three days later, she lay near death in the intensive-care unit at the University of Virginia Hospital in Charlottesville.

Parker was fighting an infection caused by a usually innocuous bacterium called Group A streptococcus (plural: streptococci). Fortunately, her doctors recognized the problem early enough. Her life was saved thanks to massive doses of penicillin.

Not everyone is so lucky. The Centers for Disease Control and Prevention (CDC) in Atlanta estimates that about 10,000 to 15,000 severe strep infections occur each year in the United States, with 2,000 to 3,000 resulting in death. Given that the population of the United States is about 260 million people, 2,000 to 3,000 is a fairly small percentage. However, a seeming increase in these numbers has sparked a recent panic in the United States and around the world.

LURID HEADLINES

In the spring of 1994, an outbreak of necrotizing fasciitis, a gangrenous condition in which muscle tissue is rapidly destroyed, was reported in Gloucestershire, England. Lurid reports that the flesh of previously healthy people had been eaten away by the disease became the grist for some hot-selling British tabloid newspapers, which featured such inflammatory headlines as: "Killer Bug Ate My Face" and "Flesh-eating Bug Kills Young Mother."

One week later, papers in the United States revealed that two unrelated patients hospitalized in Norwalk, Connecticut, were also suffering from this virulent form of streptococcus-A infection. Subsequently, additional cases were reported in New York City, California, Florida, Michigan, several European nations, Australia, and New Zealand. In Ontario, Canada, 17 cases of severe Group A strep infection were reported in early 1994, compared to nine in all of 1993. The outbreak continued into 1995, with eight cases in Virginia's Shenandoah Valley. Five of these patients, whose ages ranged from 28 to 83, died.

The sensational coverage of the disease prompted the public to make hundreds of panicked calls to hospitals, public-health agencies, physicians, and pharmacists, asking about this mysterious and gruesome illness. Many people feared the emergence of a full-scale epidemic. Parents were worried about the potential consequences of every cut and scrape on their children. Pharmacists noted that customers were asking much more about first aid for wounds, and were purchasing more antiseptics.

WHEN STREP GETS MEAN

The most common serious illness caused by Group A streptococci is streptococcal pharyngitis (strep throat), a condition marked by fever and swollen lymph nodes in the neck. Sometimes the bug is involved in a localized skin infection called impetigo. These diseases are typically treated with oral penicillin. In fact, about 10 to 15 percent of people carry the strep-A germ around in their throat or on their skin without any symptoms whatsoever (though they can pass it to others, who may then develop a sore throat).

In some people, however, this same organism causes serious trouble when it deeply penetrates the tissue. About 50 percent of severe cases of strep can be traced to a wound infection. Once strep takes up residence in such a lesion, the bacteria multiply, and release a toxin that destroys surrounding tissue, allowing more bacterial growth with further toxin spread. What begins as a tiny area of redness can quickly develop into a large area of blackened, dead tissue under the surface.

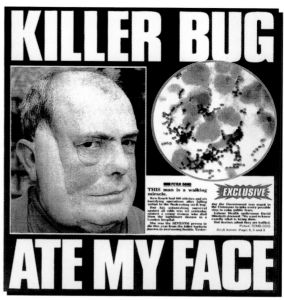

The disfigurement that can accompany necrotizing fasciitis led to sensational tabloid coverage of the condition, replete with lurid photographs of worst-case scenarios.

THE INFECTION UNFOLDS

When invasive Group A strep strikes, the illness can be fast-moving. Within 24 hours, the patient develops flulike symptoms, including a high fever and chills. Over the next day or two, these conditions worsen; a rash and severely swollen lymph nodes may develop as well.

Steve Hillman of southern Florida noticed a pimple on his backside one evening. He and his wife thought nothing of it until two days later, when it had grown into a black-and-purple boil. By that time, Steve was extremely ill. His blood pressure was dropping, and many of his organs—including his kidneys, liver, and lungs—were failing. The massive effort to save him included surgery to remove the bacteria-infested dead tissue, life-support systems to support his circulation and breathing, and a whopping dose of penicillin. The doctors assert that if Hillman had waited only a few more hours before seeking medical attention, he almost certainly would have died.

Why does the usually innocuous Group A strep germ turn ugly? Researchers, though puzzled, are beginning to discover what makes some infections with strep so deadly. Apparently, certain strains damage tissue by secreting a protein called pyrogenic exotoxin

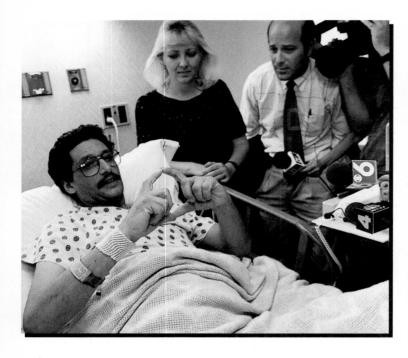

Usually, invasive streptococcus A initially manifests itself with flulike symptoms. For Steve Hillman (left), however, the first symptom was a fairly large lesion on his backside.

creator of the Muppets, died suddenly in 1990 because of toxic shock associated with a strep-induced pneumonia.

A SECOND SUSPECT EMERGES

The most visually horrifying aspect of severe Group A strep infections is the rapid and extensive tissue destruction. Scientists now suspect that this condition may be caused largely by a second bacteria-produced substance called exotoxin B, an enzyme that destroys tissue by breaking down protein. Researchers led by James Todd, M.D., of the University of Colorado Medical Center in Denver found that strains of Group A strep associated with necrotizing fasciitis secrete abnormally high amounts of cysteine protease (another name for exotoxin B).

A, which acts as a "superantigen." Ordinary antigens are protein fragments that, if foreign to the body, stimulate the immune system to mount a search-and-destroy mission in order to rid the body of the invaders. In contrast, superantigens trigger an out-of-control immune response in which cytokines—chemicals that carry signals between cells—are massively overproduced. The legions of cytokines damage the lining of blood vessels so that fluid leaks out into tissue, and blood flow is reduced, leading to tissue death from lack of oxygen. This chain reaction may account for the toxic-shock reaction that accompanies invasive strep infection with or without necrotizing fasciitis. Researchers believe that Jim Henson, the

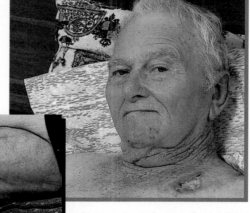

In an untreated case of necrotizing fasciitis, the flesh destruction can be quite severe; virtually any part of the body can be affected. Fortunately, most cases can be cured with antibiotics, especially if administered early in the course of the infection.

Strep expert Patrick Schlievert, Ph.D., a microbiologist at the University of Minnesota in Minneapolis, believes that bacteria may enter the bloodstream through a cut, but eventually become trapped in an area of poor blood flow, such as a bruise, where they are protected from the immune system. The bacteria then begin churning out both toxins. Exotoxin B starts creating an area of dead cells. As that area grows, the organisms have more room to expand. As the bacteria multiply, more toxins are produced, and more tissue dies. When such a destructive cycle ensues, sometimes only amputation of the affected tissue can stop the spread of infection and prevent certain death.

Other experts disagree with this scenario. They believe that the toxins do not destroy tissue directly, but rather, somehow spur the victim's immune system to do the job for them.

NEW DISEASE OR OLD?

Based on studies of streptococcus toxic-shock syndrome, Dennis Stevens, M.D., of the Veterans Affairs Medical Center in Boise, Idaho, feels that streptococcus A is becoming more virulent. Older medical literature indicates that in the past, most patients survived necrotizing fasciitis, even before the emergence of antibiotic therapy. In contrast, the recent British outbreak of Group A strep killed about 70 percent of its victims, despite antibiotic treatment.

Although this ailment has received a great deal of news coverage, it is "nothing new," according to the Centers for Disease Control and Prevention. CDC officials state that the actual incidence of severe streptococcus-A infection in the past several years is comparable to what it had been in previous years. Public-health authorities in Great Britain agree. They admit that the cluster of cases in Gloucestershire was unusual. However, they cite the fact that the number of cases of systemic infection in all of the United Kingdom has remained unchanged, and that the various subtypes of Group A strep are typical of those encountered routinely. These facts should allay any concern about an AIDS-like epidemic caused by a rampant, mutant strain of strep.

The recent clusters of cases probably represent a recurring biological cycle, not a new phenomenon. The scarlet-fever epidemics of

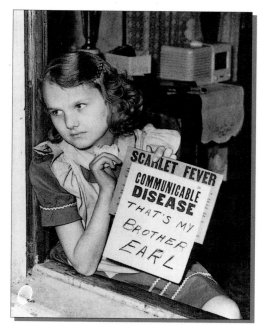

Before the discovery of antibiotics, strep infections often led to scarlet fever. Doctors could do little more than to impose a quarantine on the household in which the infection occurred.

the 1930s and 1940s were caused by invasive strep A, and, at the time, there were reports of necrotizing fasciitis. After completing its deadly run through the population, the outbreak subsided as victims either developed an immunity to the bacterium or died. Most medical experts agree that a modern-day epidemic is unlikely, due to much-improved treatments. While certain strains of strep are developing a resistance to some antibiotics, drugs such as penicillin are still effective in most cases, particularly if they are administered early in the course of the disease. However, some strains have gained resistance to erythromycin, a commonly used alternative for patients allergic to penicillin.

Researchers welcome the heightened public interest in Group A streptococcus, particularly if this attention helps convey information about the symptoms and treatment of the disease. But they also warn people not to fall prey to journalistic sensationalism. "I think a lot of the hype makes it seem like this is something where everyone is in danger," says Benjamin Schwartz, an infectious-disease specialist at the Centers for Disease Control. "And that is not the case. The disease is still very, very rare."

Life for Lefties

by Nancy Shute

General H. Norman Schwarzkopf, relaxing in his Florida office, is telling me one of his war stories. Deep in the Arabian desert during the 1991 Persian Gulf conflict, he was faced with a situation he knew would test his skills to the utmost: eating dinner.

Saudi Arabian tribesmen had invited the commander of the U.S. forces to a banquet. "You're out in the desert. They bring forth these huge communal plates of food," he says. "You reach into the plate and wad the food into a ball.

"You only eat with your right hand," the general continues. "The left hand is polluted. It's a Muslim custom." But

The tools of everyday life can be quite nettlesome—or even perilous—to lefties. Scientists are only beginning to understand the causes and inherent hazards of left-handedness.

Schwarzkopf knew something that, for him, transformed the meal from a festivity into a trial: he is left-handed. Each time he began to relax, his left hand would reach for the food. How was he to avoid a diplomatic faux pas? "It was so awkward that I literally sat on my left hand," the general says, laughing.

With his dominant hand imprisoned, the general could give no offense. But he still had the problem of a right hand untutored in the fine motor skills that this meal called for. "I would never quite get my ball wadded up enough and would dribble rice down my front as I tried to get it down my mouth," Schwarzkopf admits. His hosts graciously ignored his dining habits, and the alliance continued.

A CHALLENGED MINORITY

The general's dilemma is just one example of the challenges that beset the 10 to 15 percent of humankind who are left-handed. Persecuted for centuries as spawn of the Devil, and teased for being maladroit, lefties are just now hearing that the world really may be out to get them.

"Lefties Die Nine Years Earlier," world headlines gasped in 1991, when psychologists Stanley Coren and Diane Halpern published their findings. Left-handers have a shorter life span, the researchers concluded, not only because a world designed for right-handers makes lefties more accident-prone, but because the physiology of many left-handers makes them more susceptible to

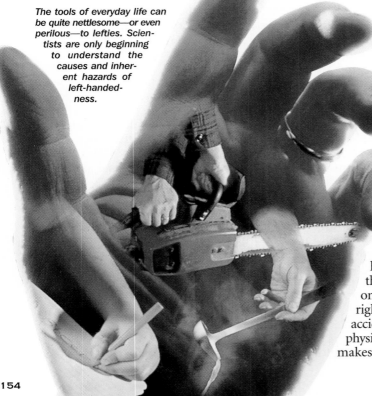

disease. Although lefties howled in outrage, the controversy has led to new awareness of the odd lot of left-handers. More right-handers are getting a grip on left-handers' experiences, and scientists are beginning to understand that left-handers really are different, but not in the ways long imagined.

A SINISTER REPUTATION

As if right-handed tools were not enough for left-handers to deal with, there is a question of reputation. Throughout

prayer wheels, and swearing on the Bible. The Muslim aversion to the left hand that confounded General Schwarzkopf is prevalent in the Middle East and Asia; it is based in practicality as well as tradition, as the left hand is commonly used for toilet hygiene.

Given the world's right-handed bias, it is a wonder that anyone would remain a left-hander, but the number of left-handers seems to have been consistent through the millennia regardless of social pressures to switch. People have been puzzling for

Since ancient times, the left side of the body has been associated with darkness and evil. The canons of Islam, Christianity, and Judaism, for example, contain many distinctions between the saintly right and the sinister left.

history, the left side of the body has been associated with darkness, ill fortune, and evil spirits; while the right has been linked to light, luck, and virtue. The Bible, the Talmud, and the Koran are rife with distinctions between saintly righties and sinister lefties. Buddha sends his adherents down the right-hand path to Nirvana; Satan sits to God's left and is often portrayed as left-handed.

Language, too, reflects these rightward leanings. From the Latin *sinister* ("left") to our own "left-handed compliments," the left is synonymous with bad news. The English word "left" comes from the Anglo-Saxon *lyft*, which means "weak" or "broken"; the *Oxford English Dictionary* catalogs a spate of unflattering synonyms for "left-handed," from "defective" and "doubtful" to "illegitimate." Even the Gypsies use the Roman word for left-handed, *bongo*, to refer to an evil person.

Social and ritual gestures follow suit; the right hand is used for shaking hands, saluting, making the sign of the cross, spinning

just about as long over why left-handers exist, with great minds from Plato to Rousseau pondering whether handedness was innate or learned. Theories abound. As late as the 1940s, New York psychiatrist Abram Blau blamed left-handedness on toddlers' tantrums.

Genetics appears to be a factor in handedness, but not an overriding one. While about 90 percent of children born to right-handed parents are right-handed, fewer than half of the children of two left-handers grow up to be lefties. Even identical twins may have opposite dominant hands. It may well be that at some point in our evolution, the human neurological system decided that it was more efficient to specialize for performing fine motor skills, be they chucking rocks or penning a sonata. And that specialization is almost always right-handed.

The initial encounter a young left-hander has with society's rightward bias often occurs when trying to use a pair of scissors—only one of countless products that are designed with right-handers in mind.

LIFE ON THE LEFT

All left-handers know that they are different, different in ways that can make everyday life seem like a trip to a foreign country without a phrase book. Lefties have roughly the first year or two of their lives to prepare for the obstacle course they will encounter; until they are a couple of years old, infants frequently use both hands interchangeably. It is when children begin to master fine motor skills that a dominant hand emerges.

Most little lefties first run afoul of civilization's rightward bias when they enter school. The first big shock is usually scissors. If you pick up an average pair, especially a cheap pair (which grade-school-issue scissors invariably are), you will notice as you open and close them that, in addition to the downward pressure, there is also a little bit of forward pressure in the thumb and a little backward pressure in the fingers. Those pressures push the thumb blade against the finger blade when they cross below the pivot point—which makes them cut.

If you put the same pair of scissors in the left hand, and use the exact same motion with your thumb and fingers, the thumb blade will be pushed away from the finger blade, resulting in the paper simply bending between the slightly separated blades as they cross. To get the scissors to cut, you must push with your fingers and pull with your thumb; it feels awkward, and it is. Staring around the classroom, rubbing a sore thumb to the accompaniment of singing scissors on all sides, the young left-hander may well wonder if his or her ragged construction-paper tree is not the result of mere clumsiness.

Many older left-handers remember writing as the biggest hurdle they faced in school. Well into the 20th century, American schools forced pupils to write right-handed through scolding or knuckle rapping. Left-handed kids paid a price for holding firm; many are the lefties who got demerits in first grade for smudged papers, or who spent backbreaking hours taking high-school lecture notes at right-handed desks. Even today, many lefty youngsters report that their parents still have to take them to three or four sports stores before they can find a proper fielder's glove.

In fact, many lefties learn sports right-handed because they're mimicking the movements of their right-handed instructor. John Diana, a Long Island, New York, sports enthusiast, spent years searching for left-handed instruction manuals. "I ruined all my wife's golf books," he confesses; everyplace the instructions said "right" and "left," he glued tiny "left" and "right" labels in their place.

Furniture designer Chris Weiland, a left-hander, teaches woodworking techniques at

The right-handed world has become increasingly accommodating to the long-tormented left-handed minority. Few schools still try to force lefties to write with their nondominant hands or to use right-handed desks.

Indiana University of Pennsylvania. "I show them how to use hand tools right-handed," says Weiland. "Then I change over to my dominant hand. I actually show them both ways." Power tools are a different matter. "You have to learn to use most of them right-handed for safety reasons," he says. "Left-handers seem to be a lot more cautious

Left-handed sporting enthusiasts often must go to great lengths to learn how to putt, drive, serve, or bat properly; indeed, most instructors and how-to books cater to the right-handed masses.

and perceptive," Weiland adds, speaking of watching his lefty students work right-handed with machines where one false move could mean the loss of a finger.

A SILENT KILLER?

According to Stanley Coren, the psychologist from the University of British Columbia in Vancouver who so upset left-handers with his pronouncements on their early demise, it is those kinds of adjustments that make life so dangerous for lefties. Lefties are five times more likely to die in accidents than righties, he says, because the world refuses to accommodate them. "The ergonomic and human-factors people say that there aren't enough left-handers out there; they'll just have to learn."

Coren first became intrigued with laterality while studying perception in the 1970s. Over the years, he noticed something odd: although 13 percent of the population of 20-year-olds were left-handed, only 5 percent among 50-year-olds were, and 1 percent of octogenarians. Where were the old left-handers?

In 1988 Coren and Diane Halpern, a psychologist at California State University in San Bernardino, analyzed the life spans of 2,271 baseball players, as recorded in the *Baseball Encyclopedia*. They found that, on average, right-handers live eight months longer than lefties, a small but intriguing difference. But it was their 1991 study, reported in a five-paragraph letter to the *New England Journal of Medicine*, that made Coren and Halpern infamous among left-handers.

They polled relatives of 2,000 people in Southern California who had died recently, asking if the deceased had been left-handed.

The researchers tabulated a mean age of death for right-handers at 75; for left-handers at 66—a difference of nine years! Left-handedness, it seemed, was a silent killer. "Don't Wait for Lefty," a *New York Times* headline announced; "He's Dead." The researchers' phones rang with entreaties from talk-show schedulers and threats from distraught lefties.

But other researchers say Coren and Halpern's study took too small a snapshot to be reliable. Marcel Salive, an epidemiologist at the National Institute on Aging, ran numbers through the computer from a six-year study of elderly Bostonians, and came to the conclusion that death rates were almost the same for lefties and righties. The lack of aged lefties, Salive speculates, may well be due to switching in the earlier part of the century.

"That's the first thing we thought of," Coren counters, noting that the percentage of lefties has proved constant through the centuries, despite cultural pressure to switch. But he admits the nine-year difference may be off base. Coren and Salive can agree that the question of lefty life span deserves a deeper look.

ONE-SIDED DANGERS ABOUND

For their part, lefties say they do have problems with the world, but that those problems are more often niggling aggravations than life-threatening accidents. "We get a lot of complaints about camcorders, hair dryers, telephones—the controls are on the right, and the cord is on the left," says Kim Kipers, editor of *Lefthander Magazine*.

For a lefty, the most mundane tasks can turn dangerous. "The kitchen can be a nightmare for the left-hander," says John Diana. Beyond the usual aggravations—potato peelers, ladles, corkscrews—knives can be downright dangerous because, like scissors, the problem is not obvious. The one-sided serration of a typical bagel knife carries it slightly to the right as it slices toward the bottom—away from the hand that is holding the bagel. Put that same knife in the left hand, and it will try its best to home in on the right middle finger.

Even the yard can be treacherous. Gardening writer Allen Lacy, who puts out a newsletter called *Home Ground*, has had run-ins with garden tools worthy of a Stephen King novel. After a few strokes with a sharp-bladed hand weeder, left-handed Lacy realized it might prove more dangerous to him than to the weeds. "The blade curves to the right," he says. "You could eviscerate yourself with no trouble at all."

Add to the list a power lawn mower that threatened to nibble Lacy's toes when he stood on the machine's right-hand side to pull the starting cord (a necessity in order to get the body's strength behind the pull), and a nylon-cord trimmer with the exhaust pipe on the right. "I used it for about five minutes, and realized it was seriously dangerous. The hot exhaust pipe was right next to my body."

A disproportionate number of famed artists have been left-handed. One such lefty, rock-music icon Jimi Hendrix (above), performed his trademark playing style on a right-handed guitar strung upside down.

LEARNING TO ADAPT

But are these encounters enough to kill left-handers? Calls to the Occupational Safety and Health Administration (OSHA) and a group of other federal agencies charged with tracking health and safety turned up no evidence of maimed or dying lefties. On the other hand, officials admit that this may be because they never ask if accident victims are left-handed.

Industrial designers say it is not that they have not noticed lefties. "We make a conscious effort to make tools ambidextrous," says Douglas Spranger, president of Human Factors Industrial Design Incorporated, a New York City firm that has invented hundreds of specialized hand tools, from surgical staplers to a new mascara wand for Lancôme. "Left-handers are 15 percent of our target market. Every manufacturer is concerned with it." But, Spranger concedes, "We [designers] tend to favor the right-handed user. Notice the numerical keypad on your computer. It's not on the left."

So why aren't lefties incapacitated? "More often than not, left-handers adapt to a right-handed world," Spranger says. "The bottom line is, you left-handed folks have adapted to a much larger range of tasks than we right-handers. We're the functional cripples in this world."

If lefties have learned to adapt, it is also true that the world is lightening up on them. School-teachers are more tolerant of left-handed writers, and right-handed desks are becoming a thing of the past. Specialty shops and catalogs hawk left-handed scissors and ladles, garden shears, and many other tools. John Diana, the Long Island golfer, dealt with his frustrations by opening a lefty mail-order business that offers high-quality lefty corkscrews and knives, among other products. He has also written *The Left-Hander's Guide and Reference Manual*, which explains, with illustrations, the left-handed way to golf, bowl, and play tennis and baseball.

DIFFERENT BRAINS?

But as Coren points out, even if the world were to ban right-handed tools, left-handers would still face another risk: their own physiology. We have known for more than 100 years that the human brain is laterally differentiated: the left side usually controls the right side of the body and houses language skills; the right hemisphere usually controls the left side and tends to handle spatial tasks. Nineteenth-century researchers figured that left-handers must be right-brain-dominant, the mirror image of a right-hander.

Alas, it is not that simple. We now know that although 97 percent of right-handers are left-brain-dominant for language, so are 68 percent of left-handers. Less than 20 percent of lefties are "right-brained" for language; there is no scientific support for the popular notion that lefties are innately more "right-brained"—intuitive and artistic—or that righties are more rigid and rational.

But scientists do know that lefties' brains are different from righties', with less specialization between hemispheres and more crossovers between the two. In recent years, researchers also have documented that non-right-handers suffer a higher incidence of certain health problems, including learning disabilities, migraine, depression, allergies, and autoimmune disorders such as rheumatoid arthritis and ulcerative colitis. What the researchers could not figure out was why.

One intriguing theory comes from the late Norman Geschwind, an eminent Harvard neurobiologist who hypothesized that imbalances in testosterone levels during gestation may affect the fetus' immune system and also slow the development of the left-brain hemisphere, making it less specialized. That could account for health problems, increased non-right-handedness, and even the fact that men are more often left-handed and suffer more learning disabilities than women.

Some scientists believe that half of all left-handers may be "pathological" left-handers, nudged away from right-handedness by hormone levels or stresses such as premature birth. But the realization that you or your child's left-handedness is pathological is not as awful as it sounds. Coren foresees the day when recognizing left-handers' physiological

No activity favors left-handers more than the national pastime. Many batters have great difficulty spotting and hitting pitches from Seattle Mariner Randy Johnson (above) and other southpaw fireballers.

differences will prompt customized treatments. "It could be helpful," says Mark Hallett, clinical director of the National Institute of Neurological Disorders and Stroke. "Problems like dyslexia sometimes are missed in children. Left-handedness may be a sign that there's a little bit of brain damage. It's always worth looking into."

GOOD SPORTS

Fortunately, it is not all bad news for lefties; there are some jobs where sinistrality comes in handy. In no place are lefties considered more precious than in the game of baseball. Nineteenth-century sportswriters gave lefty pitchers the sobriquet "southpaw," after the westward-facing pitcher's mound in a Chicago ballpark. The sport favors left-handed pitchers because they face the runner on first base, and left-handed hitters because they stand two steps closer to first.

Still, those small advantages do not account for the mystique surrounding left-handed ballplayers. Ted Williams, Ty Cobb, and "Shoeless Joe" Jackson are remembered, not only as great hitters, but as great lefty hitters. Babe Ruth persevered in playing lefty even though, while at St. Mary's Industrial School for boys in Baltimore, Maryland, he was so poor that he played with a righty's mitt, yanking it off to make a left-handed throw.

In 1992, the U.S. political arena was poised for an unstoppable turn to the left. For the first time in history, all major presidential candidates—Bill Clinton, H. Ross Perot, and George Bush—were lefties.

Left-handed pitchers, from former greats like Sandy Koufax and Steve Carlton to the Seattle Mariners' Randy Johnson, are even more valued, especially for their much-vaunted ability to throw to lefty batters. (Among major-league pitchers, nearly one-third are lefties.) Johnson throws at about 95 miles (150 kilometers) per hour; to the lefty hitter, his curveball looks like it is coming straight for the head before it breaks to the right, over the plate. A lot of teams just bench their left-handed hitters when Johnson is pitching.

Lefties also fare well in tennis, boxing, and fencing, thanks in large part to the element of surprise; their opponents spend most of their playing time fending off the assaults of righties. Rod Laver, Jimmy Connors, Martina Navratilova, and John McEnroe are just a few of the many left-handed tennis players who have excelled. But lefties are banned from playing left-handed in polo and jai alai; those sports have deemed a left-handed ambush too dangerous.

LEGENDARY LEFTIES

Lefties are also quick to point out that a disproportionately large number of architects, chess masters, mathematicians, and artists are left-handed; consider Leonardo, Raphael, Holbein, Klee, and Picasso. Musicians Bob Dylan, Ringo Starr, and Paul McCartney are lefties. Jimi Hendrix was, too; he strung his guitar upside down. Harpo Marx and Charlie Chaplin were left-handed; Chaplin played a custom-made lefty violin.

And left-handers seem to have growing influence in politics. Presidents Truman, Ford, and Bush were all left-handed, as is President Clinton. In 1992, for the first time, all major presidential contenders, including H. Ross Perot, were confirmed lefties.

Stanley Coren, for one, is cheered by the lefties' new visibility. He envisions a day when all tools that cannot be designed for ambidextrous use are widely available in left- and right-compatible versions. "One of the things I tried to do is to point out that left-handers are a minority," Coren says, as we talk in his small, book-crammed office. "They need high-quality tools to conduct their business. They need penknives with a left-sided opening notch." At that, Coren fishes a Swiss Army knife out of his pocket and hands it to me. I reach to open it, and—oops! All these years of opening knives, and I had never noticed that I have to reach my left hand across the blade to find the right-handed notch.

FIGHTING BACK WITH HUMOR

It is an experience every lefty can relate to. General Schwarzkopf tells me that his mother, a proud ambidexter, insisted that her boy Norman not be switched in school. The U.S. Army was another matter. "When I first came into the military, we were still using the old M-1 rifle," the general, now retired, says. "The M-1 was designed for right-handed shooters. All the hot brass was thrown in your face, because it all ejected on the right." The young West Point cadet learned to fire the M-1 right-handed.

But the Army was not done with Schwarzkopf yet. "All the holsters were right-handed holsters. If you ever had to use your pistol, you were out of luck," he recalls. "Swords were the same thing. You carried the saber on your left side. I had to learn to be a right-handed swordsman."

Like most lefties, however, the general learned to adjust, fighting back only with humor. "For years," laughs Schwarzkopf, "I had a sign on my desk saying: 'Everyone is born left-handed. You turn right-handed when you commit your first sin.' And I believe it!"

Designer Fats

by Tina Adler

You take a spoonful of your favorite ice cream. Mmmm. It melts slowly on your tongue and fills your mouth with its smooth, flavorful sweetness. Yum!

Then you glance at the fat content listed on the container and remember what your doctor said about your cholesterol. Whoops.

So you buy some guilt-free, fat-free frozen dessert and take a bite. Whoops again. It tastes odd, and it feels weird on the tongue, too.

looks department, too, by adding sheen and holding color. In the important category of texture, fat can make food tender, flaky, or creamy. It helps the body absorb fat-soluble vitamins and feel full.

In most reduced-fat food, various combinations of water, air, proteins, starches, and carbohydrates mimic fat. But the shortcomings of these fake-fat mixtures have forced food chemists to look beyond fat mimetics.

Some companies are spending considerable research sums restructuring fat molecules to formulate "better" fats—

Low-fat and nonfat foods appear to have taken over grocery store aisles as fat's reputation for clogging arteries and adding calories has made it an outlaw in many kitchens. In fact, reduced-fat items made up almost 7 percent of new processed foods introduced in 1993.

FORMING BETTER FATS

Companies trying to replicate fat's role in food have a big job. The substance plays a key part in making what we eat taste good. It can even mask bad flavors. It helps in the

those that satisfy without saturated fats and calories.

"[These] are designer fats more than fat replacers," says George H. Pauli of the U.S. Food and Drug Administration (FDA).

In a duel over flavor and texture, fats would win hands down over the fat substitutes currently on the market. Researchers hope soon to develop an alternative that will mimic fat's desirable attributes—and be nutritious to boot.

Not long ago, many food experts thought someone would produce a miracle fat alternative—the NutraSweet of the fat industry, says Karen A. Penichter of FMC Corporation, a chemical and machinery producer in Philadelphia, Pennsylvania. But none has come along, and, she predicts, probably none will. "There is not one panacea," agrees Leora C. Hatchwell of NSC Technologies, a research-and-development division of NutraSweet Company in Mount Prospect, Illinois. Instead, companies rely on mixtures of familiar ingredients to get the fat effect.

"One of the oldest fat substitutes is air," points out Michael F. Jacobson, executive director of the Center for Science in the Public Interest (CSPI) in Washington, D.C. Water is also popular.

THE INGREDIENTS OF FAKE FATS

Various modified starches and gums, as well as proteins that manufacturers chop into tiny pieces, make up the bulk of fake fats, according to a December 1993 report on the food sciences from the National Academy of Sciences (NAS) Institute of Medicine.

For example, McDonald's restaurants use carrageenan, extracted from red algae and mixed with water,

to help retain juices in their McLean Deluxe reduced-fat hamburgers, says Penichter, whose company makes carrageenan.

One of the earliest products designed to replace fat is a whey-protein concentrate called Simplesse, manufactured by NutraSweet and approved by the FDA in 1989. Its many microparticles, which range in diameter from 0.1 micrometer to 3 micrometers (1 micrometer equals 0.00004 inch), give foods the creaminess of fat, researchers say. People perceive particles smaller than 0.1 micrometer as watery, and those larger than 5 micrometers as powdery or chalky, according to NutraSweet.

Most of these common alternatives to fat, including Simplesse, have one major drawback in the eyes of the industry, however. They fail to stand up to the intense heat needed to fry foods. Also, although companies claim their nonfat or low-fat delicacies taste as good as their full-fat cousins, "fat-free" often means a gustatory catastrophe, according to some food experts.

"We have managed to simulate the texture of fat, but we haven't been able to work out the flavor," says Hatchwell, a flavor-applications expert. The problem lies not so much in the effects of the fat substitutes on flavor as in the absence of fat.

Most aroma chemicals, which greatly influence flavor, are soluble in fat and escape only gradually when consumed. That's how sinfully rich ice creams

Designer fats simply can't take the heat. Natural fats, on the other hand, stand up well to the high temperatures needed to fry potatoes, chicken, and other foods.

Fats provide the eater with a more satisfying sensation of fullness than do fat substitutes. But even when eaten in moderation, fatty foods can create a distinct feeling of sluggishness.

impart their scrumptious raspberry or chocolate tastes. But when people eat nonfat frozen desserts, they "get slapped in the face with the flavor, and then [the flavor] is gone," explains Hatchwell.

The taste of cheese depends largely on the by-products of its resident microbes, which "chew up and spit out" the fat. In the absence of fat, the microbes consume carbohydrates and proteins. "Then you get a very offensive flavor," she warns.

Hatchwell finds most foods with fat replacements "disappointing," although some brands of low-fat yogurt, cream cheese, and sour cream taste O.K., she says.

From a health standpoint, Jacobson and other researchers say, many of the ingredients used to mimic fat, such as emulsifiers and thickening agents, are safe. Whether they actually help consumers eat less fat has yet to be determined.

PROMISING PRODUCTS

Companies say that the designer fats now under development will help solve the problems facing today's fat substitutes. One group of stand-ins sounds good on paper, food scientists say. Called sucrose polyesters, they cannot be digested; hence, they provide neither fat nor calories. Yet these synthetic fats can be substituted for traditional grease and butter in many uses, even frying.

"Sucrose polyesters are the great hope of the diet-food industry," notes Jacobson.

Olestra, a sucrose polyester made by Procter & Gamble Company, is currently under review by the FDA for use as a food additive. It "is a really novel, new kind of thing," according to the FDA's Pauli.

The agency's decision on Olestra "will be very precedent-setting," predicts J. Bruce German of the University of California, Davis. Olestra would constitute the first true substitute for a major human nutrient approved by the FDA, he says. Other companies developing similar fake fats are eagerly awaiting the word from the FDA on Olestra.

Conventional fats consist of one to three fatty acids attached to glycerol. Olestra has six to eight fatty acids, all derived from vegetable oils, attached to sucrose. Enzymes in the human body fail to break down the sucrose bond, so the fatty acids pass through the body undigested, ignoring such comfortable resting places as the hips and paunch. Olestra has been evaluated in 100 animal studies and 25 clinical trials, the results of which show the product to be safe, the company claims.

"It's a very safe material, and could make a difference, especially with fried foods," contends Joseph F. Borzelleca of the Medical College of Virginia in Richmond. He reviewed Procter & Gamble data on Olestra a few years ago.

But is it a magic bullet? Probably not.

No one knows whether Olestra will inspire people to reduce their intake of real fat. Why people crave the substance remains largely a mystery, but fat's metabolic effects, which Olestra fails to produce, may be part of it, German suspects.

In addition, products made with nondigestible fatty acids could trap fat-soluble vitamins or drugs, such as oral contraceptives, in the gut and prevent the body from absorbing them, Borzelleca suggests. However, Procter & Gamble asserts that Olestra does not interfere with drug absorption, he says. The company states that it will supplement foods with vitamins if needed.

German wonders about the leftovers. Farmers reuse commercial cooking oils in animal feed, and nondigestible fats may not go over well with them. "Thinner cows are not what we're after," he points out.

MOLECULAR TINKERING

Rather than designing entirely new fatlike compounds, some companies are simply tinkering with the cholesterol and calorie content of existing fats. For example, the Nabisco Foods Group in East Hanover, New Jersey, has created a new family of low-calorie fats called Salatrim. The company intends to use Salatrim first in chocolate, and eventually in ice cream, puddings, yogurt, and baked goods, explains Nabisco's Robert E. Smith. The product cannot stand up to frying, however.

Because Salatrim is made from ingredients already in use, Nabisco does not consider it a new food additive. The company has asked the FDA to approve the remodeled fat as "generally recognized as safe," which involves less review than a new additive would.

Salatrim has 5 calories per gram, as opposed to traditional fat's 9 calories, according to studies in the February 1994 *Agricultural and Food Chemistry*. Like most dietary fats, Salatrim consists of three fatty acids attached to a glycerol molecule. But the product includes primarily long-chain stearic acid, which the body absorbs poorly, and either acetic, propionic, or butyric short-chain acids, which have fewer calories than other fatty acids, the studies report. And unlike other highly saturated fatty acids, stearic acid doesn't interfere with the body's ability to remove cholesterol.

Salatrim has no adverse effects on health, according to studies by Nabisco. Smith would not comment on whether the company had done taste tests.

It "certainly looks like an innocuous substance to me," says Jacobson. But German questions whether Salatrim will deliver everything its proponents predict. "It's not clear that this will really translate into a significant calorie reduction," he warns. Animal studies that show Salatrim has fewer calories than regular fat may not apply to humans, who are better fat absorbers.

Consumers are likely to buy foods containing Salatrim only if they are convinced that those items are more healthful than others. "I don't believe the FDA would permit [a company] to suggest [a person's] diet would be healthier with this in it," German says.

BUILDING A NEW FAT

Nowadays companies proudly label their goods "cooked in vegetable oil." But this oil is often partially hydrogenated vegetable shortening, according to a study done during 1993 by the CSPI. Margarines are also partially hydrogenated oils. The problem? Partial hydrogenation produces *trans* fatty acids—unsaturated fats that raise concentrations of cholesterol in the blood, studies conducted since 1990 reveal.

Two scientists from Brandeis University in Waltham, Massachusetts, have helped to create a new fat called Appetize, which they say is not partially hydrogenated, yet stands up to commercial frying, works well as a spread, can be put in dairy goods, and has less cholesterol than normal fats. One drawback for dieters: Appetize comes with as many calories as normal fat. On the other hand, it has only about 8 milligrams of cholesterol per 100 grams, compared with milk fat's 250 milligrams and beef fat's 100 milligrams, according to Richard D. Kiley, president of Source Food Technology in Burnsville, Minnesota, which licenses the product.

To make Appetize, the researchers first strip the cholesterol from butter, beef tallow, or lard. They then mix this revised animal fat with various polyunsaturated vegetable oils that contain linoleic acid, which studies suggest lowers cholesterol, says one of Appetize's inventors, K. C. Hayes.

In a recent study, hamsters that dined on Appetize had lower cholesterol

For the foreseeable future, natural fats will continue to take the blue ribbon in every category from taste and feel to touch and texture. The search is on for a new designer fat to stage an upset victory.

concentrations than those eating fats found in the typical American diet or in the American Heart Association's (AHA's) recommended diet, both of which contain *trans* fats, according to a Source Food Technology brochure.

Late in 1994, Kiley and his colleagues expected to complete their first study of how Appetize affects cholesterol in humans. The volunteers in the study were 30 nuns from a convent in Minnesota. The company, which did not ask the FDA to review its product, is proceeding with plans to market Appetize.

A HARD ACT TO FOLLOW

Any avid dieter has surely wondered why so many no-fat foods contain real sugar, and why sugar-free foods come full of real fat. "It's very, very difficult to take [both] sugar and fat out of a product," explains Ofori J. Amankonah of the Kelco Division of Merck & Company in San Diego, California. Fat and sugar don't actually interact, but they both play such key roles in making what we eat taste, feel, and look good that manufacturers can let only one go at a time.

Food experts and their employers, who have millions of dollars riding on their ability to create designer fats, stand in awe of the real thing. Their appreciation surpasses that of consumers, who extol the virtues of ice cream, chocolate, or pastry, but may neglect to credit the butterfat buried deep inside.

"Fat is great stuff," Hatchwell says, with a note of respect in her voice.

"As long as you are not an artery," quips colleague Angela Miraglio, as a reminder of at least one reason that researchers are making such an effort to fake out fat lovers.

THE MAINSTREAMING OF
ALTERNATIVE MEDICINE

by Douglas S. Barasch

There was little more that doctors could do for Catherine Bettez. Afflicted for nearly 10 years with lymphocytic hypophysitis, a rare, incurable disease of the endocrine system that depresses immunity, the 43-year-old woman had become increasingly debilitated by pain and depression, conditions that persisted despite medication. Acknowledging their limitations, her endocrinologist and her psychiatrist referred her to another kind of healer—a practitioner whose treatments were meditation and yoga.

"It seemed off-the-wall," says Bettez, a former proofreader in Westminster, Massachusetts. "I'm going to sit around and meditate, and that's going to make me feel better?"

Because the healer her physicians recommended was not some robed mystic, but a professor of medicine at the University of Massachusetts in Worcester, she decided to enroll in his program. Since completing it, Bettez reports, she has been able to cut down on Naprosyn, an anti-inflammatory medication that helps alleviate her pain, and to stop taking Ativan for her depression.

In recent years, unconventional therapies such as meditation, acupuncture, and homeopathy have begun to gain a foothold in American medicine. Catherine Bettez is one of millions of patients who have been treated with such methods, and her physicians are among the thousands of doctors who either refer patients to practitioners of alternative medicine or use elements of it themselves.

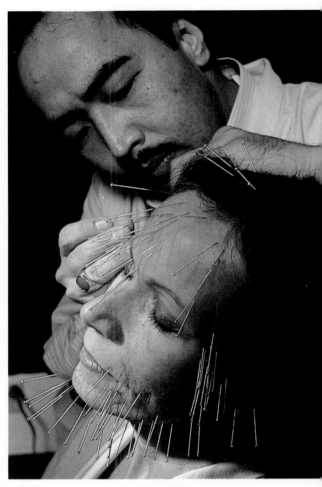

Alternative forms of medicine, including acupuncture (above), are gaining acceptance, especially now that patients and health-care professionals are discovering the benefits of non-Western treatments.

A NEW APPROACH

During 1992, the National Institutes of Health (NIH) established an Office for the Study of Unconventional Medical Practices (soon after renamed the Office of Alternative Medicine) to investigate a wide range of treatments, including herbal medicine and massage therapy. In the following two years, the NIH spent roughly $13 million to study such nonconventional treatments. Harvard Medical School in Boston, Massachusetts, introduced a course on unorthodox medicine. Similar courses and lectures are also available to medical students at Georgetown University, the University of Louisville, the University of Arizona, and the University of Massachusetts. David M. Eisenberg, M.D., an instructor of medicine who persuaded Harvard to offer the course after having studied acupuncture in China, says his purpose was not only to introduce students to the theory and practice of alternative treatments, but also "to train students to think rigorously about them."

Acupuncture, a mainstay of Chinese medicine for thousands of years, came to Westerners' attention during the early 1970s, when China opened its doors to the modern world. American doctors were intrigued by the use of acupuncture as a surgical anesthetic, and researchers found that it works by inducing nerve cells to produce endorphins, the body's natural painkillers. Scientists have also found evidence to support the view, held by many cultures, that illness can be brought on not only by external forces, like viruses, but by one's state of mind. Stress seems to weaken the immune system, and happiness to strengthen it. Personality traits such as impatience increase the risk of heart disease. Studies show that meditation and other holistic ("mind-body") therapies confer various benefits, including reduced pain and, for infertile women, a higher conception rate.

Many physicians now speak of a transition from the narrow biomedical model of Western medicine to a "biopsychosocial" one. With this approach, doctors would continue to marshal the tools of Western medicine to do what it does best: save the life of a patient who is acutely ill or in critical condition, by pumping him full of antibiotics when he has pneumonia, for example, or by mending his skull after it has been shattered in a car accident. Doctors would also draw on holistic techniques to help prevent killer illnesses such as heart disease, diabetes, and cancer, and to treat chronic conditions such as pain, hypertension, and anxiety—problems that often do not yield to high-tech medicine. Patients would then have the healer's touch and, if necessary, the magnetic resonance imaging (MRI).

Under the direction of Jon Kabat-Zinn, M.D., a professor of medicine at the Stress Reduction Clinic at the University of Massachusetts Medical Center, the clinic has taught Buddhist meditation and yoga to thousands of patients, most of whom have been referred

Alternative-Medicine Lexicon

Acupuncture—An ancient Chinese practice that involves inserting thin needles into the body at various points and manipulating them to relieve pain or treat illness.

Biofeedback—A technique for teaching people to become aware of their heart rate, blood pressure, temperature, and other involuntary body functions in order to control them by a conscious mental effort.

Herbal medicine—The use of balms and medications prepared from flowers, leaves, and other parts of plants.

Homeopathy—A medical system based on the idea of treating disease by using minute, highly diluted doses of the very substances that, in large doses, can cause it.

Hypnotherapy—A method of inducing a trancelike state characterized by extreme suggestibility in order to help patients relax, control pain, and overcome addictions such as smoking.

Naturopathy—An approach to treating illness with diet, exercise, and other "natural" means, rather than with drugs or surgery.

Guided imagery—The use of mental imagery to facilitate the healing process.

by physicians. At one recent class, there were 30 patients whose ailments included AIDS, muscular dystrophy, hypertension, chronic back pain, anxiety disorder, gastrointestinal distress, coronary-artery disease, and cancer.

Follow-up studies show that most patients who go through Kabat-Zinn's eight-week program feel much better than they did before, regardless of their illnesses. "They're taking people that the system is not helping.

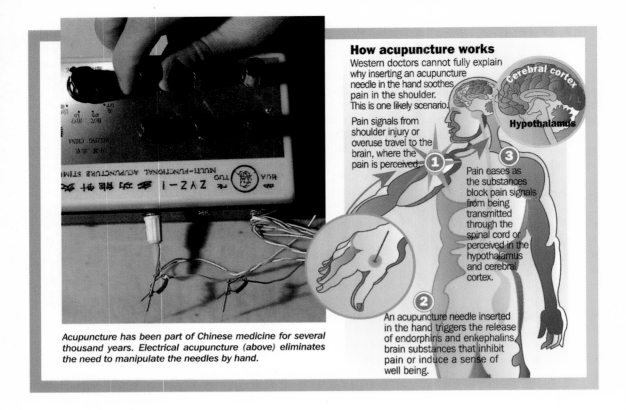

How acupuncture works

Western doctors cannot fully explain why inserting an acupuncture needle in the hand soothes pain in the shoulder. This is one likely scenario.

Pain signals from shoulder injury or overuse travel to the brain, where the pain is perceived. **1**

Cerebral cortex

Hypothalamus

3 Pain eases as the substances block pain signals from being transmitted through the spinal cord or perceived in the hypothalamus and cerebral cortex.

2 An acupuncture needle inserted in the hand triggers the release of endorphins and enkephalins, brain substances that inhibit pain or induce a sense of well being.

Acupuncture has been part of Chinese medicine for several thousand years. Electrical acupuncture (above) eliminates the need to manipulate the needles by hand.

They're taking the toughest patients and having significant outcomes," says John K. Zawacki, M.D., a gastroenterologist at the University of Massachusetts Medical Center.

THE RELAXATION RESPONSE

About 40 miles (64 kilometers) east, at Deaconess Hospital in Boston, is the Harvard-affiliated Mind/Body Medical Institute, founded in 1988 by Herbert Benson, M.D., a cardiologist at Harvard Medical School. The institute uses meditation, repetitive exercise, and yoga to achieve what Dr. Benson calls "the relaxation response," a physiological state characterized by lowered blood pressure, heart rate, respiration, and metabolism that was the subject of his best-selling book.

The institute offers programs for cardiac risk reduction and rehabilitation, infertility, insomnia, chronic pain, AIDS, and cancer. Cures are not promised. Patients can, however, hope for a reduction in symptoms, or at least a greater ability to cope with serious medical conditions as well as with treatments (such as chemotherapy) that can be both psychologically and physically debilitating.

Dr. Benson has demonstrated the success of his methods in several clinical studies.

One of his studies, published during 1991 in the journal *Fertility and Sterility*, showed that women receiving medical treatment for infertility who also went through his infertility program had about a 35 percent conception rate, compared with a roughly 17 percent rate among women who received only traditional medical treatment. Another 1991 study, in the *Clinical Journal of Pain*, found that after going through Dr. Benson's chronic-pain program, people no longer felt the need to go to the doctor as often—in fact, the number of visits was reduced by an average of 38 percent. And another study, published in the *Journal of Cardiopulmonary Rehabilitation*, found that patients who had completed his hypertension program showed reductions in blood pressure, anxiety, and depression.

Relaxation techniques as well as other alternative therapies such as biofeedback are now routinely taught to patients at medical centers and doctors' offices around the country. More than 2,000 physicians use acupuncture in conjunction with conventional medicine, according to the American Academy of Medical Acupuncture, and 5,000 use hypnotherapy, according to the American

Society of Clinical Hypnosis. Dana Ullman, a board member of the National Center for Homeopathy, estimates that more than 1,000 doctors practice homeopathy.

COSTS AND COVERAGE

Alternative therapies have a reputation for being less expensive than conventional medicine, since practitioners prescribe fewer drugs and recommend fewer diagnostic tests and other costly interventions. But the fees charged by practitioners of unconventional medicine can be high because they typically spend more time with patients than regular doctors do. An initial consultation with a physician, a nurse, or some other certified practitioner of homeopathy costs $60 to $300, depending on the location, although the visit lasts about an hour and a half, says William Shevin, president of the National Center for Homeopathy. Subsequent half-hour visits range from $45 to $80. Acupuncturists charge $50 to $100, says Joseph M. Helms, M.D., president of the American Academy of Medical Acupuncture. Jon Kabat-Zinn's stress-reduction program runs $565 for nine sessions, and Dr. Benson's programs cost an average of $1,000 for 10 classes.

Insurance reimbursement for unconventional medicine varies by the policy, the therapy, the practitioner, and the geographic region. Catherine Bettez' insurance policy covered most of the fee for Kabat-Zinn's relaxation program, and another patient, Ken Hokanson, says his policy covered all of it. At least six states—California, Florida, Montana, Nevada, New Mexico, and Oregon—require insurers to reimburse patients who see licensed acupuncturists for pain relief. And in Alaska, the services of licensed naturopaths, practitioners who treat disease with such nonmedical approaches as diet and exercise, must be covered.

Some insurance companies impose their own standards. The American Western Life Insurance Company in California, a $60 million insurer with 300,000 clients, recently launched a "wellness and preventative care health plan," which reimburses patients for alternative therapies such as homeopathy, herbal medicine, shiatsu massage, acupressure, acupuncture, guided imagery, hypnotherapy, and biofeedback.

But American Western is clearly the exception. Many major companies, including the Prudential Insurance Company of

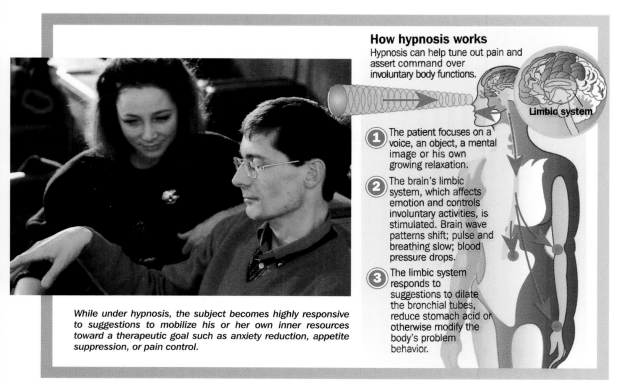

How hypnosis works
Hypnosis can help tune out pain and assert command over involuntary body functions.

Limbic system

1 The patient focuses on a voice, an object, a mental image or his own growing relaxation.

2 The brain's limbic system, which affects emotion and controls involuntary activities, is stimulated. Brain wave patterns shift; pulse and breathing slow; blood pressure drops.

3 The limbic system responds to suggestions to dilate the bronchial tubes, reduce stomach acid or otherwise modify the body's problem behavior.

While under hypnosis, the subject becomes highly responsive to suggestions to mobilize his or her own inner resources toward a therapeutic goal such as anxiety reduction, appetite suppression, or pain control.

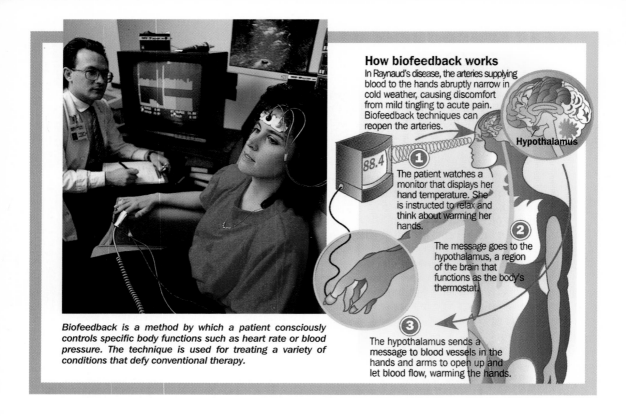

How biofeedback works

In Raynaud's disease, the arteries supplying blood to the hands abruptly narrow in cold weather, causing discomfort from mild tingling to acute pain. Biofeedback techniques can reopen the arteries.

Hypothalamus

1 The patient watches a monitor that displays her hand temperature. She is instructed to relax and think about warming her hands.

2 The message goes to the hypothalamus, a region of the brain that functions as the body's thermostat.

3 The hypothalamus sends a message to blood vessels in the hands and arms to open up and let blood flow, warming the hands.

Biofeedback is a method by which a patient consciously controls specific body functions such as heart rate or blood pressure. The technique is used for treating a variety of conditions that defy conventional therapy.

America and the John Hancock Mutual Life Insurance Company, two multibillion-dollar insurers, cover alternative therapies only if a medical doctor or a licensed practitioner performs them. A therapy must also be deemed medically necessary by the insurance company's own doctors. "It has to be documented to be an effective and safe intervention, not just prescribed by a doctor or provided by a physician," says I. Steven Udvarhelyi, M.D., vice president of medical services at Prudential, which covers meditation, biofeedback, acupuncture, and shiatsu massage, but not hypnotherapy. "We base our coverage decisions on a careful and extensive review of the medical literature. We also consider the consensus opinion within the medical community."

SUPPORTING STUDIES

The medical community's willingness to accept some alternative therapies has been strengthened by a few groundbreaking studies. In 1990, Dean Ornish, M.D., director of the Preventive Medicine Research Institute in Sausalito, California, published a study in the *Lancet* showing that techniques such as yoga and meditation, when used in conjunction with a low-fat diet, can reverse coronary heart disease, actually reducing the amount of plaque in the arteries. A year earlier, also in the *Lancet*, David Spiegel, M.D., a psychiatrist at Stanford University School of Medicine in California, demonstrated that women with metastatic breast cancer who got medical care as well as "psychosocial treatment"—including support groups and self-hypnosis—survived twice as long as patients who received only medical care. These studies "added significantly to the cumulative evidence that emotions and behaviors can influence physical health," says Halsted R. Holman, M.D., a professor of medicine at Stanford.

Scores of other studies have suggested a link between emotions or attitudes and physical health. For example, a report in the *New England Journal of Medicine* found that stress increases a person's chances of catching a cold. Other research has shown that particular alternative therapies are effective against certain ailments. Homeopathic remedies can relieve headaches, colds, flu, and allergies, according to several European studies. And an article in the *Lancet* concluded that a traditional Chinese herbal therapy reduces the symptoms of dermatitis.

As the scientific evidence supporting various unconventional treatments accumulates, some physicians predict nothing less than the transformation of American medicine, from a biomedical model to a biopsychosocial one. Joel Elkes, M.D., professor emeritus of psychiatry at the University of Louisville, in Kentucky, believes that within 25 years, mind-body techniques will permeate medical practice, from primary care to the treatment of such illnesses as cancer and heart disease. The integration of approaches such as meditation, yoga, acupuncture, and biofeedback with drugs and surgery, he says, "will be as important to medicine as the discovery of antibiotics."

"I think that's possible," says Arnold S. Relman, M.D., former editor of the *New England Journal of Medicine,* who now teaches at Harvard Medical School. "But it all depends on whether we can get more scientific evidence."

SKEPTICS ABOUND

Like Dr. Relman, other gatekeepers of American medicine remain skeptical about much of the research on alternative treatments. Marcia Angell, M.D., executive editor of the *New England Journal of Medicine,* thinks many of the studies have been poorly designed and "characterized by exuberant interpretation."

Naturopaths prescribe nonmedical therapies such as herbs and vitamins to treat illness. At a naturopathic center in India (below), patients seem to benefit from being wrapped in leaves.

Some scientists studying the interaction between the mind and the body are themselves skeptics, who say their work is often erroneously used by practitioners—including many physicians—as justification for alternative therapies.

"I resent being cited as the scientific basis for protocols and approaches that have never been tested scientifically," says David L. Felten, M.D., a leading researcher in the new field of psychoneuroimmunology, the study of the connection between the mind and the body's susceptibility to disease. Dr. Felten, a professor of neurobiology and anatomy at the University of Rochester School of Medicine and Dentistry in New York, who received a MacArthur fellowship in 1983, has been working out the "hardwiring" of mind-body communication. His research has helped uncover a fascinating network of communication pathways between the body's endocrine, immune, and nervous systems—a sort of physiological Rosetta stone. This network reveals that neurotransmitters, immune cells, and hormones act as messengers between our thoughts and emotions and our immune defenses.

What everyone wants to know is which alternative therapies really work. Many medical practices that are widely accepted today met stiff opposition from the medical establishment when they were first introduced. Doctors initially doubted the need to wash their hands before performing surgery to prevent infection, for example, and also doubted the benefits of anesthesia. More recently, the value of acupuncture has been questioned. "People thought acupuncture was way-out, spooky, flimflam, a few generations ago," Dr. Relman says. "But there appears to be convincing evidence that it can relieve or prevent pain, and now it's more respected."

Some of the resistance to alternative therapies is giving way as more scientists study them. "The champions of alternative medicine shouldn't expect to be believed unless they meet rigorous standards," he adds. "But on the other side, the traditional biomedical establishment ought not to prejudge. All biases and prejudices ought to fall before the evidence."

ASK THE SCIENTIST

▶ *What causes hiccups? Are there any diseases for which hiccups are the main symptom? Has anyone ever died from uncontrollable hiccups?*

Hiccups are forceful, involuntary gulps of air caused by sudden, downward contractions of the diaphragm. Short bouts of hiccups are often associated with stomach distention, alcohol intake, or a quick swallow of a carbonated beverage. Usually they arise out of the blue.

Prolonged bouts of hiccups, although rare, can be quite disabling, causing fatigue, depression, weight loss, and sleep deprivation. The longest episode recorded in the *Guinness Book of Records* afflicted Charles Osborne of Anthon, Iowa. While slaughtering a hog in 1922, he started hiccupping; the bout continued until his death 69 years later. Osborne led a fairly normal life, although he did experience some trouble keeping his false teeth in.

No one knows what causes hiccups, but they usually resolve spontaneously or with simple remedies (holding one's breath, swallowing a spoonful of sugar). In severe cases, medications are sometimes effective.

▶ *What causes a person to vomit? Why does the urge to vomit persist even after there is nothing left to throw up? Why is one so exhausted after an episode of vomiting?*

Vomiting, the means by which the stomach rids itself of its contents, is usually preceded by a sensation of nausea. This uncomfortable feeling is caused by irritative impulses to the vomiting center in the brain's medulla oblongata. These impulses arise from the gastrointestinal tract (with stomach flu or too much rich food), from the motion receptors in the inner ear (seasickness), or from the cerebral cortex (watching someone else vomit or smelling something very noxious).

Minutes before the actual act of vomiting, the intestines begin reverse rhythmic contractions that propel food and digestive juices backward toward the stomach. Once these intestinal contents reach and distend the duodenum (the first part of the small intestine), the strongest impulse to vomit reaches the brain.

Then comes a strong downward contraction of the diaphragm, along with simultaneous contraction of all the abdominal muscles to exert a squeezing action around the stomach. The one-way valve at the top of the stomach relaxes, and out it comes. Retching will continue, even though the stomach is empty, until the inciting impulses cease. After prolonged episodes of vomiting, most people are exhausted and have sore abdominal muscles from the repeated spasms.

▶ *Do a man's nipples serve any physiological function? Is there any truth to the story that the father of a motherless child can sometimes nurse the baby?*

The human embryo begins life with the potential to become male or female depending on the sex chromosomes. Two X chromosomes direct the embryo to develop uniquely female structures; one X and one Y result in male organs. Males retain remnant structures of the female that have no reproductive or child-rearing functional importance, such as the breasts.

Stimulated by estrogen and progesterone at puberty and then during pregnancy, the woman's breasts enlarge and develop the structures required to produce and excrete milk. There have been reports that with hormone administration and direct stimulation of the nipples, nonpregnant women have been able to breast-feed infants.

However, while certain diseases cause men's breasts to enlarge and even secrete a small amount of milky material, they cannot produce sufficient milk to nurse a baby. The experience of breast-feeding has been simulated for men by an artificial breast that is worn on the chest. The infant sucks on an artificial nipple connected to a pouch of milk.

▶ *Do people actually turn yellow when they have yellow fever? Do they turn scarlet when they have scarlet fever? Are either of these diseases common anymore? Do any diseases make your skin change color?*

Any disease that blocks the liver from excreting bile into the intestines will cause the skin and the normally white parts of the eye to turn yellow, a condition called jaundice. In addition to chronic alcohol abuse and hepatitis, yellow fever is such a disease. Still prevalent in tropical areas of Africa and South America, yellow fever is caused by an arbovirus carried by mosquitoes. The disease gets its name because jaundice commonly appears after the third day of the illness. Symptoms can be mild or severe, but include high fever, vomiting of blood, muscle pains, and even coma. An immunization is available for people traveling to areas where the disease is endemic .

The term scarlet fever arose from the reddish color of the skin caused by the bright-red rash associated with this disease. Caused by toxins released by Group A streptococcus, scarlet fever is rare today because infections with this organism, usually of the throat, are treated with penicillin, aborting the scarlet-fever manifestations. Before this antibiotic was available, there were large epidemics of this disease, with high fatality rates.

One other more-common cause of skin-color change is not a disease at all. Excessive intake of carotene (a form of vitamin A), found in yellow and orange vegetables such as squash and carrots, produces high carotene blood levels. Especially in fair-skinned infants and toddlers, this can lead to carotenosis, in which the skin (but not the whites of the eyes) becomes deep yellow-orange, especially on the palms and soles. This is not dangerous, and does not require a reduction in the ingestion of these healthful foods.

▶ *When I exercise particularly strenuously, I sometimes develop a "stitch" in my side. It usually goes away eventually. Should I be concerned? What causes this sensation?*

Athletes are familiar with the common entity known as a "stitch in the side." Typically the pain develops on one side, usually the right, with deep inspiration at peak exercise. These attacks are always short-lived, lasting no more than a few minutes.

Theories about what causes these pains range from gas in the colon on the right, to gas in the stomach on the left, to spasm of the respiratory muscles. In any case, lying on one's back with upraised arms usually shortens the duration of the pain. It is uncommon for the pain to return after a rest of 10 to 15 minutes. If the pain does recur regularly, further medical evaluation is warranted.

James A. Blackman, M.D.

PAST, PRESENT, AND FUTURE

■ THE INTERNATIONALIZATION OF AR-
CHITECTURAL STYLES IS A COMPARA-
TIVELY RECENT PHENOMENON. NOT
LONG AGO, ARCHITECTURE WAS TO
SOME DEGREE A MANIFESTATION OF A
CULTURE'S UNIQUE HERITAGE. IN TOKYO
(LEFT) AND MANY OTHER MODERN
CITIES, THE UBIQUITOUS GLASS TOWER
COEXISTS WITH HIGHLY CRAFTED ARTI-
FACTS FROM EARLIER GENERATIONS.

CONTENTS

PREHISTORIC CAVE PAINTINGS:

by Christopher King

The explorers knew they were onto something when they felt the draft. It was December 18, 1994. Two men and one woman were searching through the rocky gorges in the Ardèche region of southern France, near the town of Vallon-Pont-d'Arc, when they felt a sensation that all cavers must dream about: a draft of air rising up out of the ground. "For us," one of the men would say later, "that's a sign that there is something else."

Something else indeed. The trio of explorers spent the rest of the day clearing

debris from the entrance to a narrow hole. Returning to the site a week later, on Christmas Eve, the team ventured into the tunnel that they had made. Soon their helmet lights began to play on markings on the walls—images unmistakably made by human hands. As the team lowered themselves on a rope, they realized that they were entering a great cavern through the ceiling. And their lights illuminated even more human markings and drawings on the cave walls. Seeing the images, the cavers began to shout with excitement.

A STUNNING DISCOVERY

It didn't take long for these shouts to travel around the world. Officials from the French Ministry of Culture were quickly called in, along with the nation's leading archaeologists. Their inspection of the cave produced

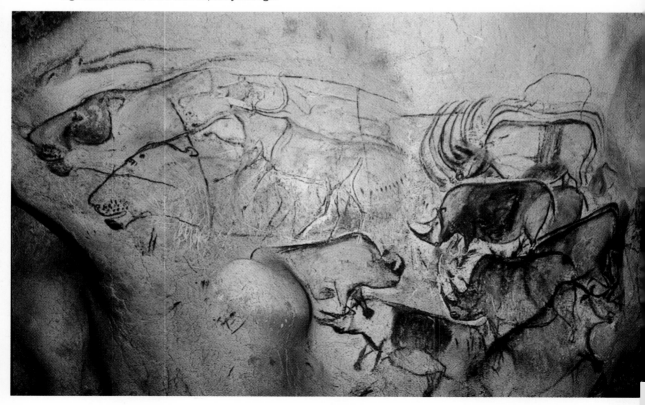

In 1994, an astonishing treasure trove of Stone Age art was discovered in a French cave known as Chauvet. The hundreds of well-preserved paintings and engravings were rendered more than 30,000 years ago.

ARTWORK IN THE DARK

an immediate conclusion: the three explorers had made one of the greatest archaeological finds of the century.

In four great halls, each up to 70 yards (64 meters) long and 40 yards (37 meters) wide, the walls are covered with more than 300 paintings and engravings, all apparently undisturbed since prehistoric artists rendered them more than 30,000 years ago. In vivid colors of red and brown, the wildlife of the Stone Age comes to life: bison and wild horses gallop, long-extinct mammoths lumber about, woolly rhino face off with one another as if in combat. In many cases, the artists made skillful use of the natural bulges and projections of rock in the cave, giving the animals a three-dimensional appearance. To rock-art specialists, the most-intriguing images of all are those of bears, lions, hyenas, and even a panther—all predatory, meat-eating creatures that have rarely been seen in previously discovered cave art. As Jean Clottes, an expert in rock painting with the French Ministry of Culture, observed to a reporter, "This is going to change our outlook."

Aside from the animals, other tantalizing images fill the cave. Dots and other strange geometric forms adorn the walls, along with the shapes of human hands held against the stone and outlined with pigment. On a flat rock sits a bear skull, apparently placed there deliberately. Was this some kind of altar? Thousands of years before recorded history, did this place serve as a cathedral, a sacred hall of reverence and worship? Or was its purpose darker—a place of dread and terror in which the young were initiated into secret cults?

In all, the painting and other works in the newly found cave—now being called Chauvet, after one of its discoverers—promise to provide new insights into prehistoric art. Equally significant is the opportunity to examine the untouched artifacts of human activity that lie on the floor of the cave—including bones, flint knives, and the remains of fireplaces. This material undoubtedly holds clues to the social and spiritual lives of the people who made the art. With the first priority being to safeguard

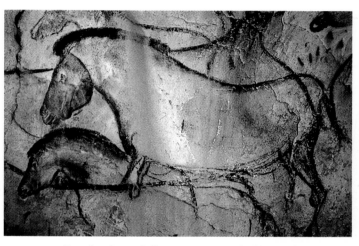

The chambers of Chauvet are graced with colorful murals of horses (above), lions, bears, and bison, as well as the first prehistoric images of panthers and owls ever found.

conditions in the cave, the work at Chauvet has just begun. The effort to understand prehistoric cave art, however, has been going on for more than a century.

HUNDREDS OF PAINTED CAVES

The rich new trove of art within Chauvet represents just one of more than 200 painted caves that have been discovered in France and neighboring Spain in the past 100 years or so. The opening to the first such cave—called Altamira after the farm on which it was found (the name means "high lookout" in Spanish)—was discovered accidentally by Marcelino Sanz de Sautuola in the Cantabrian Mountains of northern Spain in 1868. When Sautuola explored the cave 11 years later, he discovered, with the aid of his sharp-eyed five-year-old daughter, a large ceiling painting of two dozen bison. Throughout the cave were other paintings: of horses, a wolf,

Lascaux, in the Dordogne region of France, four teenage boys were wandering through the woods, looking for a lost dog. Examining a cranny in the rocks, the boys uncovered a descending passageway, which they decided to explore. After lowering themselves down, they entered a large cavern and, with their flashlights, saw markings on the walls. "Intrigued by these designs," wrote one of the boys later, "we began to inspect the walls carefully, and to our great surprise discovered there many figures of animals of a respectable size…We went through the whole cave, making discovery after discovery…Our excitement was indescribable."

The boys had discovered the cave of Lascaux, Europe's other great repository of Stone Age art. To experts in prehistoric life, the works of Lascaux, painted some 17,000 years ago, have become as familiar as the permanent collection of a great museum. On the limestone walls, in shades of red, black, and yellow, dynamic images of wild cattle seem to stampede toward the inner recesses of the cave. Two passageways break off from this main hall. Throughout the cave, pictures of horses, deer, bison, musk oxen, and other animals have been found, along with dots, squares, boomerang shapes, and other inexplicable geometric forms. Many scenes depict images of the hunt, with animals staggering from spear wounds.

One of Lascaux's most famous images is in a remote recess of the cave known as the Shaft. A crudely drawn human, with a bird-like face and four fingers on each hand, falls before a mortally wounded, charging bison. For decades, scientists have debated the meaning of these images. Does this scene record an actual incident from a hunt? Is the human figure meant to be a man, or is it something else?

A half-century after its discovery, its treasures now thoroughly documented, Lascaux still inspires wonder and debate among

The discoverers of Chauvet pose beneath the limestone palisades (above) that hid the cave's entrance for millennia. The cliffs are located in a region of southern France long known to contain Stone Age settlements.

boars, and deer. Crowds of people soon came to view the cave. Ironically, the 19th-century historians who viewed Altamira's art refused at first to accept that it was authentically prehistoric—they believed that primitive hands could not have created such works.

As more caves were discovered and as archaeology grew more sophisticated, Altamira took its place as the "Sistine Chapel of prehistoric art," a title that it held, unchallenged, until a September day in 1940. On that occasion, in the limestone hills of

scholars of prehistory—as do all the other painted caves. Careful scientific study has brought an increasing store of knowledge about the lives of the artists and the means by which they created their art. More elusive has been the answer to broader questions. Why did people create art thousands of

theories about the prehistoric development of art. Most known sites of cave art, including Altamira and Lascaux, have been traced back to late in the Upper Paleolithic, roughly 20,000 years ago to 10,000 years ago.

This was the time of the Ice Age. Europe was a very different place. Glaciers covered

Chauvet contains the greatest collection of Stone Age art found since the Lascaux cave (above) was uncovered in 1940. Scientists are comparing paintings from the two sites to learn how art evolved in prehistoric times.

years ago? What function or place did such images have in their lives?

THE AGE OF REINDEER

The first signs of human art appeared at the start of the Upper Paleolithic era, some 35,000 years ago. Radiocarbon dating indicates that some of the artwork in Chauvet is at least 30,000 years old—more than 3,000 years older than any other known paintings. These findings surprised many scientists and may force them to rethink long-held

Scandinavia and most of Britain. To the south, the terrain varied: a mix of tundra, forest, and rocky hills. But through it all swept vast herds of wildlife, including reindeer, horses, bison, and mammoths. And, existing in small groups, living off the plentiful game that vastly outnumbered them, humans.

These humans were the Cro-Magnons and their descendants, the first physically modern humans, who appeared some 35,000 years ago, replacing the more primitive Neanderthals. Scientific evidence indicates that Cro-Magnons were nomadic hunter-gatherers, living out in the open in tent encampments as they followed game. In the winter, they wrapped themselves in clothes made from reindeer fur, the same material that covered their tents. There is evidence that some groups took shelter in caves during the winter months. Significantly, however, archaeological studies suggest that these early humans did not live in the caves in which artwork has been found.

These were skilled toolmakers and able hunters. Yet, clearly, there was more to their

paints to the cave walls. The simplest tool, of course, was the artist's own finger. Sticks, perhaps mashed or crushed at one end, also could have served as paintbrushes, as could tufts of horsehair. To apply broader strokes, the artists might have used "sponges" of fur. There are even suggestions that prehistoric artists used a kind of spray-painting, by mixing pigments with saliva in their mouths and spitting the colors onto the cave walls

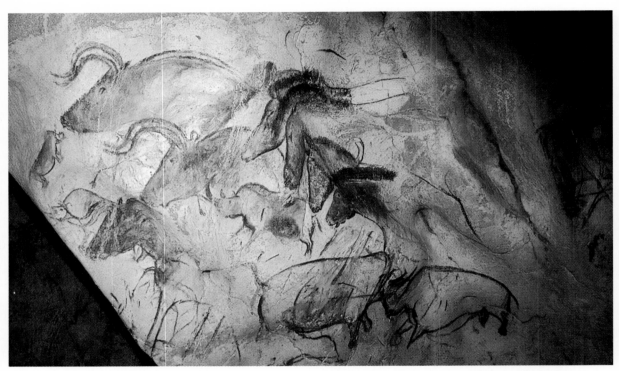

The pictures of Chauvet are clearly the work of talented and resourceful artists. In many cases, the painters skillfully used the natural bulges of the rock to impart a three-dimensional appearance to the illustrations.

lives than a struggle for food. They had the time, the means, and the inclination to make art. Using minerals from the caves themselves or from other sources, the painters had a range of colors and methods to work with: ochers, for example, for creating shades from yellow to red; iron oxides, such as limonite and hematite, for shades of brown; and manganese dioxide for blacks. These pigments would then be mixed with a binder, such as water, blood, or animal grease.

Prehistoric artists also appeared to have a choice of instruments for applying the

through a hollow reed. Experts believe that the hand stencils in Chauvet were created by this method.

One more tool was essential for painting and engraving within the caves: light. Early versions of the artists' lamps appear quite simple—essentially rocks with a bowl-shaped hollow in which grease was burned. As time passed, the technology and artistry of the lamps grew more sophisticated. One lamp found at Lascaux was made of delicately polished sandstone, with an engraved handle and a large hollow to hold grease and wicks made of juniper or some other conifer. Modern experiments using such lamps have demonstrated that they emitted a light equivalent to two or three candles. Equipped with such lamps, prehistoric artists ventured farther and farther into caves—upwards of 1 mile (1.6 kilometers) in some cases.

Archaeologists have never before seen prehistoric images of carnivores in such numbers. Among the cave's more unusual drawings are images of woolly rhino locked in battle (right) and puzzling creatures that resemble hyenas (above).

Apparently, the making of cave art often involved the efforts of many people. Some of the paintings at Lascaux are more than 10 feet (3 meters) above the cave floor. Given the difficulty of reaching such heights and the remnants of wood found in the caves, archaeologists have surmised that artists used a form of scaffolding in creating these images. Young trees were felled with flint axes, branches were cut off, and the wood was carried into the caves. These and other complex efforts—including the tasks of gathering and preparing paints, carrying tools for applying the paint, and bringing sufficient quantities of grease for the lamps—indicate that creating art was an important aspect of group life. Were some of the caverns, such as Lascaux's Great Hall of Bulls, intended as sacred temples, to be relatively open and accessible to large numbers of people?

Yet many examples of cave painting suggest the opposite: an artist making a solitary journey to a remote, inaccessible site, hastily creating artwork on a wall, and departing. The Shaft at Lascaux, bearing the famous image of a birdlike hunter apparently about to be gored by a bison, is one such example. Indeed, some sites seem to have been selected for their extreme inaccessibility.

THE SEARCH FOR MEANING

As long as archaeologists have explored the caves, they have attempted to formulate theories to explain or interpret messages in the art. One of the century's great experts in Ice Age art was the French priest Abbé Henri Breuil. His interpretation, which was widely accepted for decades, was that the paintings were inextricably tied to the hunting by which the people survived. To the prehistoric hunters, Breuil believed, making images of animals was a way of working magic over them. This magic would ensure that the game remained plentiful and that the hunt would be successful. Painting was part of a prehunt ritual performed in the sacred location of the caves.

In more-recent years, however, this "hunting magic" theory has been largely rejected. For one thing, archaeologists have found no evidence that ancient hunters faced any shortages of game or were preoccupied with anxiety about the availability of food. And excavations of campsites and caves have indicated that the most common prey for Ice Age hunters was the reindeer, a relatively rare image in cave art. Why should the artists want to work magic over animals that were seldom hunted?

Some observers have offered more-complex interpretations of Ice Age art. French scholar André Leroi-Gourhan, for example, developed classifications of images and objects to show the common features and shared meanings of artwork from many different sites. In his view, the art was a symbolic

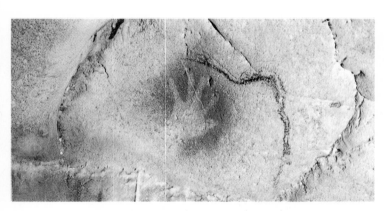

Several silhouetted handprints were found on the walls of Chauvet. Scientists hope that further study will reveal the meaning of these markings—and shed new light on the mysterious lives of their ancient creators.

expression of prehistoric society itself, reflecting a division of the world into the male and the female. Proponents of this interpretation point to the group of female bison depicted on the ceiling at Altamira. The way the animals are grouped, and the fact that their attitudes suggest that they are giving birth, could be interpreted to correspond to the social organization of a prehistoric hunter-gatherer group. In such a society, women remained grouped in the central location of an encampment while the men were absent for extended periods during their hunts.

Although experts continue to develop new theories and to update old ones, the frustrating fact remains that the meaning of

prehistoric paintings and symbols can only be guessed at. The rarity of human images in cave art constitutes one more puzzle piece. Scholars still debate the meaning of the bird-headed man at Lascaux and, from other caves, strange images of creatures that seem half-man, half-beast. Are these symbolic depictions of the unity between humans and nature? Or are they actual pictures of holy men—"shamans" or "sorcerers"—garbed in animal costumes and dancing in a trancelike state as they conduct secret rituals within the caves?

"Cro-Magnon cave art was probably meant to be seen by very few people under conditions of extreme difficulty and dread," writes art critic Robert Hughes, discussing the newly found Chauvet cave. Evidence suggests that many caves were sites of initiation. Footprints indicate that young people, including small children, were brought into the caves to view the paintings. Such an experience—to be led through the consuming darkness, with the flicker of light and shadow on the walls producing the sudden appearance of great beasts—can only be imagined.

Chauvet introduced its own store of new questions. Why are predatory animals featured so prominently? Why are there some 40 pictures of rhino? What was the symbolic or spiritual importance of the rhino and the other animals? What is the significance of the stenciled outlines of human hands?

As experts set about answering these and other questions, the first order of business is to protect the art and the cave floor. The Lascaux and Altamira caves were initially turned into bustling tourist attractions, and the humidity and algae that accompanied the attendant crowds seriously degraded the paintings. Today those great caves are closed to the public (although visitors can tour replicas nearby). As science is brought to bear at Chauvet, and at the still-hidden caves that await discovery, the mysteries of prehistoric cave art will undoubtedly be brought further and further into the light.

In 1989, close to 1 million visitors huffed and puffed their way up the 294 steps of its spiral staircase. Their destination? The top of Italy's Leaning Tower of Pisa, a structure world renowned as much for its ethereal beauty as for its tantalizing tilt. If the unwitting tourists had known the precarious condition of the tipsy 12th-century campanile, many might have opted to view it from a safe distance.

Back then, many failed to realize that the eight-tiered tower—which leans more than 17 feet (5.3 meters) off the perpendicular—was in such bad shape, though some experts worried that it was teetering toward the breaking point. The Italian government's policy toward the structure was more or less

Taking the Lean Out of the Leaning Tower of Pisa

by Elizabeth McGowan

benign neglect—if it ain't broke, let's debate it some more. This bureaucratic inertia was exacerbated by a turf war between the Ministry of Fine Arts and Ancient Monuments and the Ministry of Public Buildings and Works about which ministry had jurisdiction over the tower. Though many suggestions for reducing the tilt had been submitted to Italian authorities over the years, official discussions about an actual plan of action typically ended up in stalemate.

The Leaning Tower of Pisa began to tilt almost as soon as its construction commenced in the 12th century. Today, tourists flock to the landmark, all but unaware that scientists are racing against time to save the structure from collapsing.

STANDING ON BORROWED TIME

It wasn't until a 500-year-old vertical tower in the northern Italian town of Pavia toppled in February 1989, killing four bystanders, that government officials decided it was time to get serious about the Pavia tower's Pisa cousin. A study by a specially appointed committee revealed that the Leaning Tower of Pisa was well on its way to becoming the Shattered Rubble of Pisa.

"The trends in the tower were all in the direction of failure, both in the foundation and structural support, as well as in the architectural features," explains Gerald Leonards, Ph.D., professor emeritus of soil mechanics at Purdue University in West Lafayette, Indiana. "In my opinion, the tower was on borrowed time. I'm not talking centuries; I'm talking days, months, at best years."

"The tower was on the cliff edge," concurs John Burland, Ph.D., D.Sc., professor of soil mechanics at London's Imperial College in Britain.

When news of the special committee's report hit Rome that the famous Pisan landmark was close to becoming history, Italy's then public-works minister, Giovanni Prandini, grabbed the jurisdictional reins. In January 1990, he ordered the tower closed

indefinitely. The public outcry caused the Italian Parliament to appoint an international commission of experts, including Drs. Leonards and Burland, to devise a plan to stabilize the tower. The commission includes members with geotechnical, structural, and architectural-restoration expertise, as well as archaeologists and art historians. Dr. Burland, for example, recently acted as an expert consultant for the construction of an extension of the London subway system, and is perhaps best known for ensuring that construction of an underground garage at the Houses of Parliament did not harm Big Ben. Dr. Leonards—who, as far back as the 1960s, had submitted a proposal to stabilize the tower—is widely hailed as an expert on the strength and consolidation of clay soils, the type on which the tower is built.

Despite the impressive credentials of the appointed commission, Pisans were outraged by what they considered a unilateral decision to close their beloved *la Torre Pendente*, part of a complex of structures, including a cathedral and a baptistery, that grace the grassy expanse of the Piazza dei Miracoli, one of the most beautiful squares in all of Europe.

"To Pisans, the piazza is symbolic of the entire life cycle," explains Rita Mannella, deputy counsel for the Italian Consulate in New York City and a native of Pisa. "The baptistery is associated with birth, the church and tower are life and connection with God, the lawn is where you go with your first boyfriend, and the cemetery represents death. It's very much a part of the people. It's not just for tourists."

Without tourists, however, the city of Pisa stood to lose billions of lire in revenue from the millions who come each year to view the tower, the major local attraction. Prior to the tower's closing, an annual 1 million people paid $3 apiece to climb to the top of the landmark, from which a young Galileo is said to have dropped balls to demonstrate his theory of the speed of falling objects. Pisan hotels and restaurants counted on tower-viewing visitors to fill their rooms, and tourist purchases kept roofs over the heads of legions of souvenir sellers.

Responding to word of the tower's closing, local newspapers blasted Rome with charges of tyranny. Giacomino Granchi, a Socialist who was then mayor of Pisa, accused Public Works Minister Prandini, a Christian Democrat, of seeking gratuitous publicity for himself and his party. And the word on the street was that reports of the tower's impending demise were greatly exaggerated. "Pisans simply dismissed the idea that the tower was in danger," recalls Dr. Burland. "They said, 'The tower cannot die; it's on the Piazza dei Miracoli [the Field of Miracles].'"

CRYING WOLF?

The collective denial was not surprising—over the years, the dazzling white tower has exhibited an uncanny ability to defy gravity, surviving misguided restoration projects, numerous earthquake tremors, even World War II shelling that destroyed medieval galleries and frescoes in the cemetery a mere stone's throw away.

Locals had also been hearing cry-wolf predictions of the tower's collapse practically since its foundations were laid by Bonnano the Pisan on what proved to be unstable ground. Work on the Romanesque-style marble cylinder, designed to be a freestanding bell tower for the cathedral, began in 1173. There were problems from the start. "The tower wobbled around quite a bit during construction," explains Dr. Burland. "By the time its fourth story was completed in 1178, the tower was tipping northward, opposite to the way it's tipping now." This finding is based on an interpretation of the variations in height of the exterior stone blocks in relation to a presumed plan that the builders followed to compensate for apparent tilting.

For reasons political or economic—but not architectural, according to Dr. Burland—construction stopped on the tower for almost 100 years, picking up again in 1272. This time, the fickle tower switched sides and

The leaning tower is the campanile, or bell tower, of the cathedral of Pisa, Italy. Other structures in the magnificent complex of buildings include the baptistery (foreground) and the cathedral itself.

swung southward, the direction to which it leans today. To coax the tower into a more upright position, the builders bent the building's axis northward, using thicker stones on one side of the tower than on the other.

In 1298, the first tower safety commission on record met to discuss the stability of the structure. Two master stonemasons and a master carpenter measured the ever-increasing tilt with a plumb line, and reassured locals that the tower was not going to crash. Unfortunately, the measured tilt angle was not recorded.

Work on the tower did not resume until 1360, when a belfry was added atop the six round-arched galleries to complete the structure. By this point, the southward tilt was so pronounced that architect Tommaso Pisano incorporated a dramatic architectural correction that is visible to the naked eye: viewed from the outside, the top tier of the cylinder lies off-center to the lower shaft. Inside the structure, six steps lead to the bell chamber on the south side, only four on the north, a clever compensation for the off-kilter addition.

"The builders had incredible skill," says Dr. Leonards, who has been studying the tower for more than 30 years with a fascination he describes as akin to love. "Given our present technology, we would be very hard pressed to make such a circular tower with such precise dimensions."

Using crude tools including a plumb line, a level, and probably a template, the builders, says Dr. Leonards, "attempted to account for the fact that the structure would probably lean some more when they built the eighth story. They predicted how much it would yield, how much it would lean, and adjusted for it. In addition to the compensating wedge, the builders offset the belfry northward (away from the tilt) and used heavier stones on the north side than on the south,

in an effort to provide a counterbalancing moment. This is what we call the observational method, which we think is very modern, but actually was done centuries ago."

As the builders foresaw, the addition of the belfry did indeed result in an accelerated tilt. "After the top was put on, the tower *really* took off, ending up at an inclination of about 5 degrees to the south," says Dr. Burland. Until about 1930, the tilt increased by an average of 0.025 inch (0.65 millimeter) per year; after 1930, the rate doubled to an alarming 0.047 inch (1.2 millimeters) per year.

Innumerable suggestions have been advanced for reinforcing the leaning tower. Some of the ideas, while vividly demonstrated (above), would prove distinctly unrealistic to implement.

Adding to the strain on the nearly 16,000-ton tower is the fact that its masonry, like that of all buildings, expands and contracts depending on the weather. "Our instruments show that the tower actually follows a sort of elliptical orbit. In the summer, the ellipsis is mainly east-west; in the winter, it becomes much more of a circle," explains Professor Burland. "We are not sure how much that contributes to the problem, but it's certainly not beneficial."

REMEDIES GALORE

Over the decades, hundreds of tower aficionados from all over the world have submitted suggestions, some complete with models and blueprints, for stabilizing *la Torre Pendente*. Some of the more imaginative have included attaching a blimp-sized helium balloon to the belfry to buoy the cylinder from above; constructing an identical tower leaning in the opposite direction to prop up the existing tower; and erecting a giant statue of Saint Daniel, Pisa's patron saint, so that the statue would support the tower with its outstretched hand.

In 1838, an architect "almost administered the coup de grâce to the tower," says Dr. Burland. "For some reason, he decided that the general public should have the opportunity to view the beauty of the tower foundations. He excavated a walkway around them, and the tower tipped about a half a degree."

The tower again teetered sharply to the south in 1934, when Benito Mussolini ordered about 100 tons of grout injected into the tower's foundation. Though Mussolini has been blamed for many evils, Dr. Burland believes he may have gotten a bum rap for that one. "There's no doubt the tower moved quite a bit at that time," Burland explains, "but our research is showing that it may not have been due entirely to the grouting operation."

The tower took another lurch during a drought in the 1970s, when water was pumped from the lower strata of sand in the Piazza dei Miracoli area, tipping the entire piazza to the southwest and accelerating the southward tilt of the tower.

It is little wonder, then, that the appointment of yet another meddling commission, the 14th this century, was greeted by Pisans with less than enthusiasm.

"The local people and the Italian press were very skeptical," recalls Dr. Leonards, the only non-European on the current 13-member commission. "We've gone through a period of considerable criticism, ridiculing cartoons, and lots of interviews in the newspapers with well-known figures in science and engineering who disagreed with some of the approaches the commission was discussing."

Adding to the difficulties has been "having to make long-term decisions in a short-term political atmosphere," according to Dr. Burland. Since the commission was appointed under a temporary law, its mandate must be reconfirmed every few months. The plug on the project, therefore, can be pulled at any time.

ARCHITECTURAL CATCH-22S

Despite the obstacles, the commission has set about solving a problem that might be considered an architectural Catch-22—straightening the tower enough so that it does not fall down, but not so much that its appearance is altered significantly. After all, "The goal is to preserve this incomparable historic monument, not to change it in any observable way," says Dr. Leonards.

The group meets every two months in Pisa and operates by consensus. Dr. Leonards explains the process. "We have a formal meeting with minutes and simultaneous translations, English to Italian, Italian to English. We keep debating and debating, but we generally resolve our differences. In the intervening months, we each have our assignments, and there are lots of faxes going back and forth. We're a very active commission."

The commission's first task was to temporarily stabilize the tower while they researched a permanent solution. In 1992, the lowest cornice of the building, where stresses are greatest, was fitted with a sort of architectural corset—12 tensioned steel wires shrouded in plastic to blend in with the color of the masonry. The wires, according to Dr. Burland, "act a little like the bands around a barrel to keep the barrel from bursting. The term 'corset' implies some great mass of iron, but it's actually very delicate and nonintrusive."

Similar to a patient in intensive care, the building was also equipped with ultrasensitive instrumentation, which monitors how the tower reacts to everything from temperature and moisture to groundwater conditions and Earth tremors—a mouse probably couldn't run across the floor without scientists knowing about it.

Next, 600 tons of lead weights were placed on the uptilted foundations at the tower's north side to counterbalance the lean.

In August 1993, the high-tech equipment registered a high-impact finding, what the

Over the years, scientific articles (left) have argued the effectiveness of various reinforcement schemes. One method already implemented involves placing lead weights on the uptilted foundation at the tower's north side (above).

experts hailed as the "first good news for the Leaning Tower of Pisa in 800 years." Thanks to the lead counterweights, the tower had not only stabilized, but its tilt had decreased! Only a tad (0.30 inch; 7.8 millimeters), it was true, but it was a tad in the right direction. By September 1994, the ante was upped to 0.50 inch (1.3 centimeters).

A promising start, but the experts say there is still a long way to go—before their work is done, the commission hopes to reduce the lean by between 4 and 14 inches (10 and 35 centimeters).

STAYING THE COURSE

At this writing, construction has begun to install a prestressed concrete ring around the lower portion of the tower foundation in preparation for the installation of an underground network of 10 tensioned cable anchors. The anchors will apply a larger counterbalancing moment than that of the lead weights—which were intended to provide a safety margin for installing the anchors, and are not exactly pleasing to the eye.

The commission's initial successes have not silenced all of its detractors, however. One of the most vocal, Piero Pierotti, Ph.D., a professor of medieval-architecture history at the University of Pisa, argues that the lead counterweights and underground cables might prove dangerous in an earthquake,

since the tower lies in a seismic zone, and that more research should have been conducted before these techniques were implemented. He also maintains that the underground cable network under construction is "very intrusive and is not reversible."

A better method to straighten the tilt, Dr. Pierotti believes, would be to remove some of the ground below the tower—a method, he says, "that was proposed by experts in geotechnics 30 years ago and accepted, but not effected by the present commission." The committee is scheduled to hold a symposium sponsored by the United Nations Educational, Scientific, and Cultural Organization (UNESCO) in the fall of 1995, to update the scientific and academic communities on its work.

For the most part, however, criticism of the project has decreased, and the commission is staying its course. While the cable network is under construction, the team is directing its research at the root of the tower's problems: the unstable foundation soils and the integrity of the tower's architectural and structural support.

"A generic solution is to induce what we call 'controlled subsidence' on the north side of the tower," explains Dr. Burland. "A lot of people say, 'Why don't you just jack up the south side?' Well, actually, that's working against gravity. If you can very gently cause

Once in place, the 600 tons of lead (above) began to counter-balance the tower's tilt ever so gradually. At present, only workers are allowed inside the tower and its arcades (right); tourists have been denied entry to the tower since 1990.

the ground to settle on the north side, it would cradle the foundation northward. That's the whole secret."

Toward that end, two techniques are under serious study. The first, called "under-excavation," is a procedure that is currently being used to stabilize the Metropolitan Cathedral in Mexico City. This method involves inserting casings into the ground through which the clay can very gradually be extracted while the reaction of the tower is carefully monitored. Scientists are starting a full-scale trial of this system, experimenting with drilling technology on a large foundation built expressly for this purpose on a part of the piazza where the soil is similar to that under the tower.

The second approach, the "pressing slab" technique, involves loading the ground on the north side of the tower with an articulated slab that will be pressed down via ground anchors. "Consolidating the soil on the north side will hopefully cause the tower to lean northward," explains Dr. Leonards, who believes this technique holds promise, but cautions that it is still in the numerical-analysis phase. Simulations using models in a centrifuge are also under way.

BEATING THE ODDS

Which of the two methods—if either of them—will end up being implemented as the permanent solution to the instability of the tower remains to be seen. "It's too early to tell," says Dr. Leonards. But once a method is decided upon, he predicts, it can be executed within a year.

That, of course, is contingent on whether the Italian Parliament renews the decree of the commission, which expires on December 1, 1995. Dr. Leonards, for one, is confident that the work of the commission on what he considers to be the "most aesthetically pleasing tower ever constructed in the history of mankind" will continue "as long as we keep doing good things."

By most reports, Pisans, the commission's toughest audience, seem to have accepted the necessity of reducing the lean of their Leaning Tower. Pisa Mayor Piero Floriani, a strong supporter of the international team, says he is pleased with their progress and has been reassured by the head of the commission that once the work is completed, the tower, "in a restricted manner, will open once again to the public."

Though some of the mayor's constituents still attribute the tower's longevity to a miracle, most are now putting their money on modern science. With the rest of the world, they await the day when the seven bells in the lopsided campanile, now silent, will ring the news that, once again, their beloved *la Torre Pendente* has beaten the odds. ◩

The Call of the Mermaid

by Jerry Dennis

When I saw my first manatee heave the water of a Florida canal and float at the surface like a porcine bather in a Renaissance painting, I naturally thought of mermaids. Anyone who has seen a manatee knows that it takes a real stretch of the imagination to think it looks *anything* like the half-human mermaid of popular culture. The loaflike, almost hairless mammal more closely resembles a giant insect larva than Daryl Hannah in *Splash* or the statue of Hans Christian Andersen's Little Mermaid overlooking the harbor in Copenhagen, Denmark.

Legends of mermaids may have arisen from the stories of ancient sailors—lonely men who mistook the distant sighting of a manatee or seal for a beautiful woman with the tail of a fish.

High on a cliff along a treacherous stretch of the Rhine River, Lorelei sang with such an enchanting voice that boatmen passing below grew distracted—and crashed into the rocks.

Perhaps it was their long months at sea, but ancient mariners saw *something* womanlike out there; and scientists considered manatees and their relatives plausible enough candidates for the honor to name their order Sirenia, for the Sirens, who were the mythological forerunners of mermaids. The subject gets strange, gets absolutely psychological, when you note how often sirens and mermaids of old lured innocent sailors to their deaths, something a gentle manatee would never do.

MERMAIDS OF MYTH

Legends of mermaids and mermen (folklorists group them as merfolk) go way back. For ages, it was believed that every creature on land had a counterpart in the sea. There were horses and seahorses, dogs and dogfish, and snakes and eels. Why not men and mermen, women and mermaids?

A Babylonian fertility goddess named Atargatis, who dates back to about 5000 B.C., was an early prototype of the mermaid and was personified as both good and destruc-

Through the ages, a mermaid has often presaged catastrophe for the mariner who sights her. A rich body of folklore provides guidance on how to handle oneself in the presence of a mermaid.

tive, a contradictory nature that would later be standard in most mermaid legends. The Greek writer Lucian, in the 2nd century A.D., described a drawing of Atargatis in distinctly mermaid terms: "In the upper half she is a woman, but from the waist to the lower extremities runs in the tail of a fish."

Atargatis evolved into Aphrodite and Venus, the Greek and Roman goddesses of

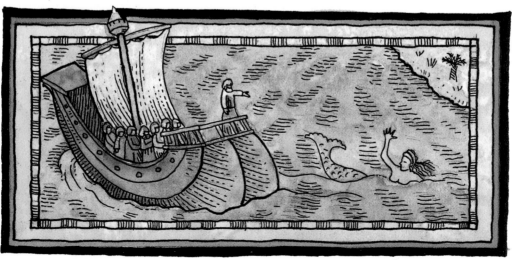

The Danish people honored fairy-tale author Hans Christian Andersen by placing a statue of one of his most beloved characters, the Little Mermaid, on a rock overlooking Copenhagen harbor.

crew from the Sirens by having himself lashed to the mast and ordering his men to plug their ears with wax.

By the Middle Ages, European folklore had brought mermaids down to Earth, making them mortal like elves and fairies, and giving them a variety of magical powers. In many folktales, it was bad luck to accept a gift from a mermaid, and if she was offended (by, say, a human who refused to accept a gift), she would cause floods and other natural disasters. For a mariner to merely glimpse a mermaid was an omen of shipwreck, but you could never be sure you had actually seen one. Sometimes mermaids would assume human form and prowl the shores. Sometimes men married them. It took a crafty human to betroth a mermaid: he had to steal her cap, comb, or mirror, and as long as he kept it hidden, she was forced to remain his wife. If she found her possession, however, she escaped immediately back into the sea.

Other versions of the legend include a German mermaid named Lorelei, who stationed herself on a cliff 433 feet (132 meters) above a narrow, twisting section of the Rhine River and sang in a voice so lovely it distracted boaters and caused them to crash into the rocks. Gerald Lyon, in his 1481 bestiary *Créatures Moralisées*, described a mermaid luring mariners to their deaths. As a ship passed, she would frolic in the sea beside it and call up to sailors to join her in the water. When a man dove in, the maiden changed into a monster and devoured him.

love, respectively. In these later forms, she was without a fishlike tail, which was attributed instead to the Tritons, Aphrodite's male escorts in the sea, and their female companions, the Tritonids.

The Sirens of Greek mythology were another probable source of mermaid legends. Those carnivorous sea nymphs had the heads of women and the bodies of birds; and they inhabited certain Mediterranean islands, where they would sing and play such beautiful music that passing sailors were irresistibly drawn to them. Once the mariners ventured near, their ships would be wrecked on rocks, and the men devoured. Jason and the Argonauts avoided that disaster by listening instead to the lovely lyre music of Orpheus, which was loud enough to drown out the Sirens. Odysseus saved his ship and

In Greek mythology, the music of the Sirens invariably drew mariners to their doom. Jason and the Argonauts avoided that fate by listening instead to the lyre music of Orpheus, which was loud enough to drown out the Sirens.

Eyewitness Accounts

• During Christopher Columbus' first voyage to the New World, while sailing east from his new settlement on the island of Hispaniola, he reported the sighting of "three sirens that rose high out of the sea, but were not as beautiful as they are represented." Many commentators have assumed he saw manatees; some have theorized a trio of the now-extinct Caribbean monk seals rose in the water to watch the strange sight of the *Niña* under sail.

• Another West Indies mermaid was reported by Captain John Smith in the 17th century. The captain admitted being smitten with the animal, and noted it had "large eyes, rather too round, a finely shaped nose, a little too short, well-formed ears, rather too long, and her long green hair imparted to her an original character." But when the mermaid swam near Smith, he was startled to see that she "gave way to fish" below the waist.

• While sailing up the Hudson River in 1609, Henry Hudson filed this report in his journal: "This evening one of our company, looking overboard, saw a mermaid, and, calling up some of the company to see her, one more of the crew came up, and by that time she was close to the ship's side, looking earnestly on the men. A little after that a sea came and overturned her. From the navel upward, her back and breasts were like a woman's, as they saw her; her body was as big as one of us, her skin very white, and long hair hanging down her back, of color black. In her going down they saw her tail, which was like the tail of a porpoise, speckled like a mackerel."

• A Captain Whitbourne, sailing to North America in 1610, claimed he saw a mermaid as he approached St. John's, Newfoundland. The creature swam toward his ship, "looking cheerfully as if it had been a woman, by the Face, Eyes, Nose, Mouth, Ears, Neck and Forehead." It then tried to scramble aboard a nearby boat and was promptly clobbered on the head with an oar. Whitbourne concluded by saying, "Whether it were a mermaid or no . . . I leave it for others to judge."

SIRENIANS AND SEALS

Most of us know, of course, that mermaids don't exist and that they never did. Unlike the Loch Ness monster, Sasquatch, and extraterrestrial visitors, merfolk seldom inspire true believers to argue for their existence. Attempts at rational explanations usually center on manatees, dugongs, seals, and walruses. That makes sense, claim debunkers, because these aquatic mammals are vaguely human in appearance and are found in many of the waters where merfolk sightings have been most common. But reports of dugongs and manatees nursing their calves in distinctly human fashion—floating on their backs with the young cradled on their bellies—are simply wrong. Sirenians nurse their young underwater, with the calves suspended beneath them, much as dolphins and whales do.

In Ireland and Scotland, where belief in mermaids and fairies has diminished in recent decades, many of their supernatural powers have been transferred to seals. According to folklore, seals are capable of talking, prophesying, weeping, singing, and giving aid to shipwrecked or stranded mariners, and can periodically remove their skin and go ashore to walk about in human form. It is thought that the seal remains in its human form as long as it is out of its skin, and that if someone should discover the skin, the seal must do whatever it is bid to do, including marrying a human and bearing him children.

Like a lot of legendary creatures, mermaids are complex. Horace Beck, author of *Folklore of the Sea*, says their complexity is a result of being a "fractured mythology" glued together from many sources. Perhaps, too, these mermaid legends are like the oceans themselves: beautiful, mysterious, and lethal. Maybe it is only our feelings about the sea that are complicated. The call of the sea might be very different from the call of a siren or a mermaid, but both are difficult to ignore, and both can have dire consequences.

FERTILE MIXTURES

The world is big enough to hide wonders. The seas, especially, are crammed with oddities even stranger than a naked, humanlike animal with a finned tail. The potential for such wonders excites our imagination. We love any story sensational enough to raise the hair on our necks, and we are so eager to believe outlandish tales that we're willing to pay for the privilege of being misinformed. Newspaper tabloids sell in the millions by blaring lurid headlines that almost nobody believes. In the 19th century, Japan supported a thriving industry of bogus mermaids manufactured from stuffed monkey skins sewn to fish tails and sold to gullible sailors. P. T. Barnum, of "There's a sucker born every minute" fame, used a similar ruse during the 1870s to separate thousands of credulous yokels from their paychecks. They rushed to stand in line to see a shriveled and naked wonder of the sea that Barnum was shrewd enough to keep hidden in a private viewing room.

An Englishman by the name of Robert Hawker pulled off a truly spectacular hoax in 1825 by stripping naked, wrapping the lower half of his body in an oilskin tail, and swimming to a prominent rock off the shore of Cornwall. He spent several nights on the rock, combing seaweed from his hair, looking into a mirror, and singing. His performance was convincing enough to attract enormous crowds. Hawker ended the hoax by singing a mighty rendition of "God Save the King," and diving from the rock and out of sight.

Where there is mythological smoke, there's psychological fire. Perhaps, in the case of mermaids and sea monsters, that fire is fueled by our strong and contradictory feelings about the oceans. The sea inspires us and terrifies us. It is both unimaginably rich with life and dreadfully indifferent to death. Stand on its shore at night, and it seems as vast and terrifying as the universe itself. We love it, and it scares the hell out of us.

Such a fertile mix of emotions demands symbols we can grab onto. Besides, we like a good story. This one has all the elements of a blockbuster: half-naked women, men in mortal struggle with their urges, the sea a compelling background setting the mood and tone, providing music and rhythm, its motion a rocking cadence as pervasive and assuring as the beating of our own hearts.

Though we seem capable of finding explanations for every inexplicable phenomenon, we don't always try very hard. I suspect that most of us are secretly glad to find questions that can't be answered and mysteries that can't be solved. Mermaids don't exist, but what a wonder it would be if they did.

The occasional appearance of mermaids in contemporary decorative motifs bears testimony to the unique way in which mermaids personify the romantic nature of the sea.

How to Tame a Wild Plant

by Jared Diamond

Part of the fun of hiking in the woods is the treat of coming across a bush chock full of wild berries. Even those of us who are city dwellers know that some plants, like wild strawberries and blueberries, are safe to eat—they are sufficiently similar to their domesticated kin that we can easily recognize them. More-adventurous hikers may eat mushrooms, too, although with caution, aware that many species can be poisonous. But not even the most ardent nut lover among us will eat wild almonds; their lousy taste keeps us away, which is fortunate, since eating just a few dozen of the wild nuts would result in ingesting enough cyanide to kill the eater.

All of the modern crops that we grow and eat today had to arise from just such wild plants. Until the advent of farming, every plant eaten by every human on Earth was wild. But what caveman ever got the idea of "domesticating" a wild plant, and how was the transformation accomplished? That question seems especially puzzling for the many crops, like almonds, whose wild progenitors are lethal or bad-tasting, or others, like corn,

In ancient times, wild plants chosen for domestication had attributes useful to humans. Olives, for example, have been cultivated for their fruit and oil from antiquity (above) to modern times (below).

that look drastically different from their wild ancestors. After all, the first farmers didn't have any existing crop as a model to inspire them to develop other ones. They could not have been conscious that, whatever they were doing, there was a tasty result ahead.

A Plant's Point of View

As far as plants are concerned, we humans are just one of thousands of animal species that unconsciously "domesticate" them.

Like all animal species, plant species must spread their offspring to suitable areas where they can thrive and pass on their parents' genes. Young animals generally disperse by walking or flying. Because plants do not have that option, they must somehow hitchhike. Some plant seeds disperse by blowing in the wind or floating on water. Many other plant species, though, trick an animal into carrying their seeds, by

Ancient drawings (above) illustrate the variety of crops that early Egyptians cultivated. Today's large, fluffy cotton bolls (below) are the end product of thousands of years of selective growing practices.

enclosing them within a tasty fruit and advertising the fruit's ripeness by its color or smell. The hungry animal plucks and swallows the fruit, walks or flies off, and later defecates or spits out the seeds somewhere far from the parent tree. Seeds can thereby be carried for thousands of miles.

Wild strawberries offer a good example of hitchhiking tactics. When strawberry seeds are still young and not yet ready to be planted, the surrounding fruit is green and sour. When the seeds finally mature, the berries turn red and sweet. The change in the berries' color serves as a signal to birds which then pluck the strawberries, fly off, and eventually spit out or defecate the seeds.

Naturally, strawberry plants did not set out with a conscious intent of attracting birds only when their seeds were ready to be dispersed. Nor did birds set out with the intent of domesticating strawberries. Rather, strawberry plants evolved through natural selection. The sweeter and redder the final strawberry, the more birds dispersed its ripe seeds; the greener and more sour the young strawberry, the fewer birds destroyed the seeds by eating berries before the seeds were ready.

Many other plants have fruits adapted to being eaten and dispersed by particular animals. Just as strawberries are adapted to birds, acorns are adapted to squirrels, and mangoes to bats. No one would describe this unconscious, evolutionary process as domestication; likewise, the early stages of crop evolution were unintentional also. They involved wild plants developing characteristics that attracted humans to eat and disperse their fruit.

EARLY HUMAN LABORATORIES

Our ancestors unintentionally sowed some wild seeds in many places. As we know from our current practices, when we gather edible plants and bring them home, some inevitably spill, either en route or at our houses. Some fruit rots while still containing perfectly good seeds, and gets thrown, uneaten, into the garbage. Of the fruit that we actually take into our mouths, some varieties contain seeds so tiny that they are always swallowed and defecated, but others have seeds large enough to spit out. Thus, our ancestors' garbage dumps undoubtedly joined their latrines to form the first agricultural-research laboratories.

At whichever such "lab" the seeds ended up, they tended to come from certain individual plants—namely, the individuals that humans preferred to eat for one reason or another. Eventually, when the first farmers began to sow seeds intentionally, they would sow seeds from those individual plants that they had chosen to gather.

What precisely were their criteria? One, of course, was size. As a result of such selection, many crop plants have much bigger fruits than their wild ancestors. Peas, apples, sunflowers, strawberries, and corn provide examples of colossal crops dwarfing their progenitors.

Another obvious criterion was taste. Many wild seeds evolved to be bitter, bad-tasting, or actually poisonous to deter animals from eating them. Thus, natural selection acts oppositely on seeds and on fruits. Plants whose fruits are tasty get their seeds dispersed by animals, but the seed within the fruit has to be bad-tasting. Otherwise the animal would also chew up the seed, and it could not sprout.

Almonds provide a striking example of the evolution and de-evolution of bitter seeds.

The Pilgrims (above) learned how to plant corn from Native Americans. Modern-day corn, with its long ears and plump, sweet kernels (below), does not even resemble its spindly wild ancestor.

Most wild-almond seeds contain an intensely bitter chemical called amygdalin, which breaks down to yield the poison cyanide. A snack of wild almonds can kill a person foolish enough to ignore the warning of the bitter taste. Since the first stage in unconscious domestication involves gathering seeds to eat, how on Earth did domestication of wild almonds ever get started?

The explanation is that occasional individual almond trees have a mutation in a single gene that prevents them from synthesizing the bitter-tasting amygdalin. Such trees die out in the wild without leaving any progeny, because birds discover and eat all their seeds. But curious or hungry children of early farmers would also have sampled and noticed those nonbitter almond trees, and the nonbitter almond seeds are the ones ancient farmers would have planted—at first unintentionally in their garbage heaps, and later intentionally, by 3000 B.C., in their orchards. Lima beans, potatoes, and eggplants are among the many other familiar crops whose wild ancestors were bitter or poisonous, and of which occasional sweet individuals must have sprouted around the latrines and garbage heaps of ancient hikers.

Human hunter-gatherers also went after wild plants with fleshy or seedless fruits. Their preferences ultimately selected, not only for big pumpkins and squashes weighing 700 pounds (320 kilograms) or more (the world's largest fruit), but also ones consisting of far more flesh than seeds. Cultivated bananas were selected long ago to be all flesh and no seed, thereby inspiring modern agricultural scientists to develop seedless oranges, grapes, and watermelons as well. Seedlessness provides a good example of how human selection can completely reverse the evolutionary purpose of a wild fruit, which is to serve as a vehicle for dispersing seeds.

Many plants were similarly selected for oily fruits or seeds. Among the earliest fruit trees domesticated in the Mediterranean world were olives, which were first cultivated around 4000 B.C., not just for edible fruit, but, more important, to obtain olive oil. Thus, crop olives are not only bigger but also oilier than wild ones. Ancient farmers selected sesame, mustard, poppies, and flax as well for oily seeds. Finally, some plants were chosen for their fibers. In this way, cotton came to be domesticated and used to weave textiles. The fibers, called lint, are hairs on the cotton seeds, and early farmers of both the Americas and the Old World selected cotton for long lint. In flax, the fibers come instead from the stem, and plants were selected for long, straight stems.

INVISIBLE MECHANISMS

By consciously harvesting wild plants with visible qualities such as fruit size, bitterness, and fleshiness, ancient peoples unconsciously dispersed the plants and launched them on the road to domestication. In addition, though, there were changes that could not have involved such conscious choices, because in these cases, the plant features being selected for were invisible. For instance, many wild plants have specialized mechanisms that scatter seeds, but thereby make them unavailable to humans.

A clear example involves peas, whose seeds—the peas we eat—come enclosed in a pod. Wild peas have to get out of the pod if they are to germinate. To that end, pea plants evolved a gene that makes the pod explode, shooting the peas onto the ground. But occasionally there are pods of mutant peas that do not explode. In the wild, the mutant peas would die entombed in their pod; only the popping pods would pass on their genes. But, conversely, the only pods available to humans to harvest would be the nonpopping ones left on the plant, making them the progenitors of crops. Thus, as soon as humans began bringing wild peas home to eat—spilling some, throwing spoiled ones away—there was immediate selection for that single-gene mutant, even though hunter-gatherers were unaware of the difference between popping and nonpopping pods.

Another type of change was even less visible to ancient hikers, and involved the speed with which certain seeds germinate. For annual plants growing in an unpredictable

For centuries, crop cultivation required extremely intensive labor. Medieval farmers, for example, used such simple tools as the hand-held scythe (above) to harvest grain. By contrast, today's mechanical harvesters (below) make short work of acres of wheat.

climate, it could be lethal if all the seeds sprouted quickly and simultaneously—all might be killed by a single drought or frost, leaving no seeds to propagate the species. Many annual plants, therefore, have evolved to hedge their bets by means of germination inhibitors, which make seeds initially dormant, and spread out their germination over several years. In that way, even if most seedlings are killed by a bout of bad weather, some seeds will be left to germinate later.

A common bet-hedging adaptation is to enclose the seeds in a thick coat; this is the mechanism used by wild wheat, barley, peas, flax, and sunflowers, among many other plants. While such late-sprouting seeds still have the opportunity to germinate in the wild, consider what must have happened as farming developed. Occasional mutant individuals among wild plants lacked thick seed coats or other inhibitors of germination.

Early farmers would have ensured good conditions by tilling and watering the soil, then sowing seeds. Mutant seeds that immediately sprouted would grow into plants whose seeds were then harvested and planted the next year. Seeds that did not immediately sprout yielded no harvest. Early farmers would not have noticed the difference. But the result of this cycle of sow, grow, harvest, sow would have selected immediately and unconsciously for the mutants.

FARMING THROUGH THE CENTURIES

Curiously, some plants were domesticated long ago, others not until the Middle Ages, while still others have proved immune to all our activities. How can we account for these vast differences in ease of domestication?

It turns out that the earliest Near Eastern crops—cereals and legumes such as wheat, barley, and peas, domesticated around 10,000 years ago—arose from wild ancestors that offered many advantages. They were already edible and productive in the wild. They were easily grown, merely by sowing or planting. They grew quickly, and could be harvested within a few months of sowing, a big advantage to people still on the borderline between being nomadic hunters and settled villagers. They could be readily stored, unlike many later crops such as strawberries and lettuce. They were mostly self-pollinating, which meant that the crop varieties could pass on their own desirable genes unchanged, instead of having to hybridize with other varieties less useful to humans. Finally, their wild ancestors required very little genetic change to convert them into a crop: for instance, in peas, just a few mutations, such as the one for nonpopping pods.

A next stage in the Near East included the first fruit and nut crops, domesticated around 4000 B.C.; among these were olives, figs, dates, pomegranates, and grapes. Compared with the cereals and legumes, they had the disadvantage of not starting to yield food until at least three years after planting, and not reaching full production for as long as a decade. Thus, growing these crops was possible only for people who were committed to the settled village life and were no longer seminomadic. However, these early fruit and nut crops were

still the easiest such crops to cultivate. Unlike later tree domesticates, they could be grown directly by planting cuttings or even seeds. Cuttings had the advantage that, once ancient farmers had found or developed a productive tree, all its descendants remained identical to it.

A third stage included fruit trees that proved much harder to cultivate, among them apples, pears, plums, and cherries. These trees cannot be grown from cuttings. It is also a waste of effort to grow them from seed, since the offspring of even an outstanding individual tree of those species is highly variable and yields mostly worthless fruit. Instead, those trees must be grown by the difficult technique of grafting, developed in China long after the beginnings of agriculture. Such problems delayed the domestication of these fruit trees until around classical times. From the outset, their cultivation was a highly conscious enterprise, carried out according to explicit rules that the Romans described in encyclopedic treatises.

By Roman times, almost all of today's leading crops were being cultivated somewhere in the world. The few later additions have remained of relatively minor importance. Naturally, modern plant breeders are still making improvements in ancient crops. But early

Modern agriculture goes far beyond simple selection of favorable natural variations. Biotechnology is now being used to artificially select, and in some cases design or accentuate, desirable crop features.

farmers succeeded in at least initially domesticating most plants worth domesticating.

PROMINENT FAILURES

Still, our list of triumphs lacks many wild plants that, notwithstanding their value as food, we never succeeded in domesticating. Notable among these failures of ours are oak trees, whose acorns were the staple food of California Indians and a fallback food for European peasants in famine times due to crop failure. Acorns are nutritionally valuable, being rich in starch and oil. Like many otherwise-edible wild foods, acorns do contain bitter tannins, but acorn lovers learned to deal with tannins in the same way that they dealt with bitter chemicals in almonds and other wild plants: either by grinding and leaching the acorns to remove the tannins, or by harvesting acorns from the occasional mutant individual oak tree low in tannins.

Granted, oak trees are not the simplest plant to cultivate, because they cannot be started from cuttings. But that minor obstacle did not prevent us from domesticating dozens of other species posing the same problem. Why, then, have we failed to domesticate such a prized food source?

As it happens, oak trees have three strikes against them. First, their slow growth would exhaust the patience of most farmers. Sown wheat yields a crop within a few months; a planted almond grows into a nut-bearing tree in three or four years; but a planted acorn may not become productive for a decade or more. Second, oak trees evolved to make acorns of a size and taste suitable for squirrels, which bury, dig up, and eat acorns. Oaks grow from the occasional acorn that a squirrel buries and forgets. With billions of squirrels spreading acorns to virtually any spot suitable for oak trees to grow, we humans never stood a chance of selecting oaks for the acorns we wanted. Finally, perhaps the most important difference between almonds and acorns is that bitterness is controlled by a single dominant gene in almonds, but appears to be controlled by many genes in oaks. If an ancient farmer planted almonds from the occasional nonbitter-mutant-almond tree, the laws of genetics dictate that half the nuts from the resulting tree would be equally nonbitter. But if that same farmer planted acorns from a nonbitter oak, almost all the resulting acorns would still be bitter. That alone would kill the enthusiasm of any would-be acorn farmer who had defeated the squirrels and remained patient.

Just as squirrels gave us trouble with acorns, robins and other berry-loving birds thwarted our efforts to fully tame strawberries and raspberries. Yes, the Romans did tend wild strawberries in their gardens. But with billions of European thrushes defecating wild strawberry seeds in every possible place (including Roman gardens), strawberries remained the little berries that thrushes wanted, not the big berries that humans wanted. Only with the recent development of protective nets and greenhouses were we finally able to defeat the thrushes and redesign strawberries and raspberries according to our own standards.

NATURAL SELECTION

Those standards eventually led to today's gigantic supermarket berries. But it is important to remember that the differences between those berries and their tiny wild ancestors arose out of natural variation among the wild plants themselves, and that the resulting evolution of wild plants into crops was an unconscious process. It followed simply and inevitably from our selecting among wild-plant individuals.

In his great book *Origin of Species*, Charles Darwin began with a lengthy account of how our domesticated plants and animals arose through artificial selection by humans.

"I have seen great surprise expressed in horticultural works," he wrote, "at the wonderful skill of gardeners, in having produced such splendid results from such poor materials; but the art has been simple, and as far as the final result is concerned, has been followed almost unconsciously. It has consisted in always cultivating the best-known variety, sowing its seeds, and, when a slightly better variety chanced to appear, selecting it, and so onwards."

Those principles of crop development by artificial selection still serve as our most understandable model of the origin of species by natural selection.

A total solar eclipse is one of the most beautiful spectacles the sky has to offer; it can also be an awesome and ominous celestial event. Despite its rarity, a solar eclipse can have a large enough impact to change the course of history.

The best-known example of a solar eclipse affecting a historical event occurred during a war between the Lydians and the Medes in 585 B.C. Darkness fell in the middle of a pitched battle, and both sides became eager to make peace. The Greek historian Herodotus tells us that the year of the eclipse had been predicted by Thales of Miletus. But the contribution of Thales is under a modern cloud because of the vagueness of the claim and the lack of a framework for predictions even in later times.

Solar eclipses have changed history in many other instances, and these often center on little-known stories involving famous people.

MUHAMMAD

The prophet Muhammad, founder of Islam, was born in Mecca in the Year of the Elephant, A.D. 569–70. His birth year got its name from an invasion by the Abyssinians, who used elephants in the assault. The army was miraculously driven off when a flock of birds dropped stones on the troops, causing an epidemic similar to smallpox.

The Year of the Elephant was also memorable (and datable) because of its solar eclipse. In ancient times, the births

ECLIPSES THAT SHAPED HISTORY

by Bradley E. Schaefer

The rarity and spectacle of a total solar eclipse led people in earlier times to exaggerate the significance of these seemingly ominous celestial events.

and deaths of leaders were often associated with celestial omens, and Muhammad's beginning was no exception. However, Islamic theology does not accept that the eclipse was sent by God as an omen of the prophet's birth, a doctrine that is based on another solar eclipse closely tied to Muhammad.

The Prophet's infant son, Ibrahim, died tragically on January 22, 632. The Sun was eclipsed on that day, and some Meccans claimed it was a sign from God. Muhammad quickly corrected them, declaring, "The Sun and Moon are signs of God and do not eclipse for the death or birth of any man." Islamic legal scholars have used this statement to reject astrology.

A third solar eclipse related to Muhammad occurred 39 years after his death. In 661, Muawiya became leader of the empire after a revolt against Ali (the Prophet's cousin, second convert, and son-in-law). The son of Muhammad's chief Meccan enemy, Muawiya decided to transfer the Prophet's pulpit from Medina to his capital in Damascus, Syria. But as his men were removing it, the sky darkened such that stars could be seen. This was taken as a sign of divine displeasure, and the relic remained in Medina as a symbol of Muawiya's failure.

Solar eclipses marked the year of Muhammad's birth, the death day of his son, and the day many years later when rebels sought to remove his pulpit from Medina.

TECUMSEH

At the start of the 19th century, America was vigorously expanding west of the Appalachian Mountains. This land was occupied by many diverse Indian tribes who did not have the population base or technological skills to hold back the advancing settlers. Moreover, the tribes seldom acted in concert or with long-term goals. But this was not always true.

Tecumseh was a warrior of the Shawnee tribe in the Ohio River Valley who had the necessary vision. He realized that all tribes in the area would be killed or pushed out unless they formed a united front and protected each other. To this end, he worked tirelessly to create an Indian confederation. He was aided by the logic of his arguments, his great diplomatic powers, and his brother, Tenskwatawa.

The Shawnee Prophet, as Tenskwatawa was called, preached religious revival with a strong rejection of all white customs, particularly the drinking of alcohol. He attracted many followers because Indian society was collapsing, and his call for a return to traditional practices promised to stem the tide of change. Thus, both brothers were attempting to preserve Indian lands and culture.

Any leader of a religion that supports the existence of miracles is always in a precarious position should he be challenged to perform one. William Henry Harrison, governor of the Indiana Territory, demanded that Tenskwatawa provide "some proofs at least of his being the messenger of the Deity." Tecumseh learned of an upcoming eclipse from members of an expedition to the area who were preparing for the event. He induced his brother to announce that on the morning of June 16, 1806, the Great Spirit would take the Sun in hand and hide it from the world. On the appointed morning, a large gathering in Greenville, Ohio, saw the prophet's promise come true. Then he saved the world from perpetual night by ordering the Great Spirit to release the Sun.

Backed by such a dramatic effect, the prophet became a powerful leader in the territory. The two brothers traveled from tribe to tribe, winning converts and organizing the confederation. For a time, the alliance successfully held back the white settlers, and a capital, called Prophetstown, was built near Indiana's Tippecanoe River. The confederation later collapsed, however, when Harrison led a strong army against the town, and, in a rash night assault, Tenskwatawa made his warriors an ill-conceived promise of immunity from death. Their loss at Tippecanoe on November 7, 1811, was decisive, and the prophet's followers turned on him. Tecumseh was killed during a large battle in Ontario in 1813, and the defeated tribes were soon transported across the Mississippi River. The confederation forged by two brothers of vision and a solar eclipse could not survive failed prophecies and the loss of its leaders.

NAT TURNER

The treatment of the American Indians and black slaves reflects the most despicable episodes in U.S. history. Kidnapped Africans were transported to the New World and forced to work long hours under squalid conditions for no reward. Any such situation is inherently unstable, so the slave masters lived in deep fear of an uprising by their chattels.

The best-known slave rebellion in America centered on the charismatic figure of Nat Turner. He was born in 1800 in Southampton County, Virginia, where he learned to read from his master's son. His literacy was unusual because slave owners knew that education could lead to revolt. Turner channeled his energy into religious devotion, and became a preacher for his fellow blacks, who came to call him The Prophet. In 1828, Turner had a vision that he would lead his people to freedom. He slowly gathered his forces by recruiting an inner circle of roughly 20 trusted friends.

But first, Turner had to await a sign from God. A solar eclipse on February 12, 1831, appeared to Turner as a black angel occulting a white one. This omen symbolized black overcoming white, so the time for revolt had come.

The slaves planned to murder farmers for their weapons; gather recruits from nearby farms; march on the armory in Jerusalem, Virginia; then head for the Great Dismal Swamp, where capture would be difficult. The revolt was set for the Fourth of July, both as a symbol of freedom and because the slaves were allowed greater movement on that holiday. However, the uprising was delayed when

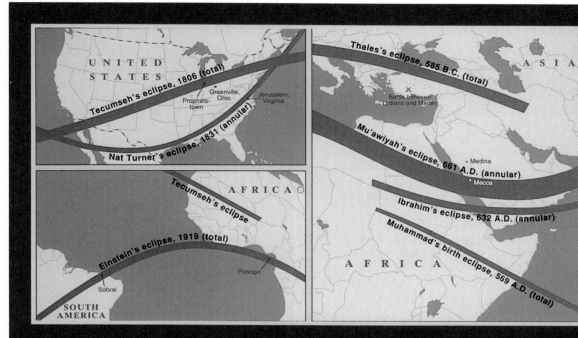

In 585 B.C., an eclipse during a battle between the Lydians and the Medes led both sides to sue for peace, fearing heavenly wrath. Divine intervention played no role in a series of eclipses more than 1,000 years later (right map), all associated with Muhammad. In 1806, brothers Tecumseh and Tenskwatawa of the Shawnee tribe, using foreknowledge of an upcoming solar eclipse, claimed to potential allies that the Great Spirit was going to hide the Sun. The eclipse convinced the other tribes to follow

the brothers into a confrontation with white settlers (above right). The path of Tecumseh's eclipse intersected the path of another eclipse 25 years later (upper-left map), during which Nat Turner, a Virginia slave, claimed to have seen a black angel overcome a white angel. Turner interpreted his vision as a divine signal to launch a slave rebellion (right). No supernatural intervention is associated with Einstein's eclipse (bottom-left map); rather, its significance rests with its scientific importance.

Turner became ill, forcing the group to await another sign. It arrived on August 13th, when the Sun appeared dim, with green-and-blue coloring. Then Turner saw what was likely a naked-eye sunspot group (the year 1831 was just after a maximum of the sunspot cycle).

The revolt started on the night of the 21st with the murder of Turner's owners. The march on Jerusalem was stopped the next morning by a small band of militia, and the revolt soon degenerated into a rout with the capture and execution of the slaves. A total of 60 whites and perhaps 200 slaves (many innocent of rebellion) were killed in the uprising. Turner remained in hiding for 70 days until he, too, was caught and hanged.

ALBERT EINSTEIN

In 1905, Albert Einstein wrote three papers, each worthy of a Nobel Prize, that explained Brownian motion, the photoelectric effect,

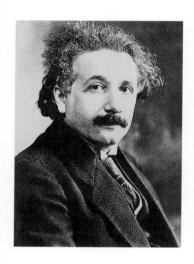

Albert Einstein (left) hypothesized that light bends when it travels near a massive object, a theory proven by British astronomer Arthur Eddington during observations of an eclipse in 1919. In this century, scientists have greatly increased their understanding of the Sun by studying eclipses like the one photographed in La Paz, Mexico, in 1991 (right).

and special relativity. The success from the papers transformed him from an obscure patent clerk into one of the top scientists in the tiny field of physics. He followed this phenomenal start with many strong advances in the field, including the discoveries of Bose-Einstein statistics, stimulated emission, the cosmological constant, and the Einstein-Rosen-Podolsky paradox.

By far Einstein's most famous and influential work after 1905 was his general theory of relativity, which describes the distortion of space-time in a strong gravitational field. He completed his formulation of the theory between 1913 and 1916, and, during this time, he predicted a previously unknown phenomenon that, if observed, would validate his work. He believed that the curvature of space near a massive object like the Sun would bend light that passed close by. Thus, for example, a star seen near the edge of the Sun during an eclipse would

appear to have shifted by 1.75 arc seconds from its usual place. A German expedition to the Crimea, in present-day Ukraine, was mounted for the August 21, 1914, total solar eclipse to test the prediction. But that was not a good time to be a German national in Russian territory—no photographs were exposed, and the team was interned for a month until an exchange was arranged.

During World War I, scientific ideas were precariously swapped between Germany and the Allies. When English astronomer Arthur Eddington received Einstein's paper on general relativity, he immediately realized its importance. He mounted an eclipse expedition of his own for the May 29, 1919, event. The planning started at the height of the war, when prospects were darkest for the Allies. This British test of a German's theory was a great display of internationalism in science, and served to quash attempts to boycott German scientists after the war.

To guard against clouds, Eddington had two observing sites—one on Príncipe Island off the west coast of Africa, and one in Sobral, Brazil. On Príncipe, eclipse day began with heavy rain; it stopped by noon, but the Sun was glimpsed only after first contact. In a routine familiar to many amateurs, Eddington took 16 photographs through scattered clouds and glanced up only twice. The results confirmed Einstein's theory exactly.

The news was announced on November 6, 1919, at a meeting of the Royal Astronomical Society. The packed audience realized it was present at the shifting of humankind's worldview. The international press trumpeted the discovery and lionized Einstein as the epitome of genius. It is doubtful he would have progressed from being a renowned physicist to the legendary scientist without the dramatic fanfare that followed the eclipse.

ECLIPSES AND RELIGION

The first three cases of solar eclipses affecting history mentioned here involve figures

Legend holds that Saint Patrick was inadvertently assisted in his efforts to convert Ireland to Christianity by a total eclipse that frightened the local pagans.

thought to be prophets, who used the phenomenon, deliberately or otherwise, for religious purposes. Other prophets have done the same. Saint Patrick is reputed to have used a great darkness to convert the Irish pagans in the 5th century, and, in 1884, the Mahdi used a solar eclipse to demoralize the defenders of Khartoum. Eclipses have been linked to the deaths of religious figures, including those of Saint Olaf at the Battle of Stiklestad, and of Jesus Christ, who had three hours of darkness during his Crucifixion. Both Christians and Muslims have prophecies of eclipses associated with Judgment Day in their Holy Scripture.

Eclipses have probably been associated so closely with religion because they occur in the heavens—the abode of the gods, where mortals cannot intervene. What better place to look for divine signs? Fear of eclipses may have developed because Sun worship is such a strong part of humankind's past, making an eclipse a terrifying symbol of the death of a god.

In modern society, the association between eclipses and religion is largely gone. If preachers tried to capitalize on an eclipse today, they would be laughed at. Now that we know what causes eclipses and can predict when they will occur, the fear is gone. A predictable event does not break harmony, but instead, is a manifestation of order in the universe. In the past century, eclipses have changed from signs of God to the tools of science. As we have seen, the 1919 eclipse was used to confirm general relativity. These events not only allow astronomers to better study the Sun, but also permit multitudes of amateur astronomers to view the solar corona and prominences. Even Ibrahim's eclipse has been used to quantify the acceleration of the Earth's rotation.

This attitude shift reflects a change in our worldview. No longer is religion the only model for all thought; science has become a guiding paradigm for art, philosophy, and even commerce—mainly because science delivers miracles, and its prophecies come true. The 1919 eclipse was used to confirm the highest doctrine and to raise a new "prophet." In a sense, science has become a new religion, with eclipses as one of its rituals.

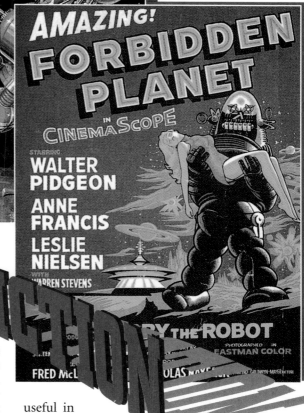

THE MAGIC OF
SCIENCE FICTION

by Frederik Pohl

S cience fiction has come a long way since the days of my youth, when readers were likely to hide a magazine inside a copy of the *Police Gazette*. Now science-fiction books often turn up on the *New York Times* best-seller list, and science-fiction films are well represented among the blockbusters from Hollywood. Nevertheless, when one scientist wants to denounce another's theories, the killing blow is often to describe them as "mere science fiction."

"Scientifiction" Emerges

Hugo Gernsback would have hated that. Gernsback, a Luxembourg-born inventor, began a career as a magazine publisher after coming to America in 1904. In April 1926, he brought out the world's first true science-fiction magazine, *Amazing Stories*, making him the godfather of modern science fiction (the field's principal awards, the Hugos, are named after him). Gernsback cared deeply about science, especially insofar as it was useful in creating new technologies. The way to write Gernsback science fiction was to imagine some invention and build a story around it. Better still, imagine a whole flock of inventions, as Gernsback himself did in his most famous novel, *Ralph 124C41+*. *Ralph* envisions developments such as television, radar, and space travel.

Gernsback's influence was Jules Verne, and, indeed, he acknowledged his debt by

Science fiction gained a mainstream audience in the 1920s with the introduction of Amazing Stories, *the first of the sci-fi magazines. By the 1950s,* Forbidden Planet *and other science-fiction films had become enormously popular.*

decorating the contents page of his magazine with a picture of Verne's tomb at Amiens. Verne prided himself on the technological accuracy of his novels, decrying the free-ranging imagination of the upstart H. G. Wells; Verne contrasted the sensible way he transported his own characters to the Moon (fired out of a giant cannon) with the imaginary antigravity shield Wells employed for the same journey. There was nothing "mere" about the science in Gernsback or Verne science fiction. Rather, it was the fiction part that was relatively unimportant, though it did provide a lot of exciting action.

Yet Gernsback's ambition extended far beyond getting his scientific and technological facts straight. He believed that what he called "scientifiction" served a socially useful purpose. It would, he thought, educate its readers in scientific facts, and inspire them to researches and inventions of their own. He wasn't entirely wrong.

FANS WHO MADE HISTORY

The honor roll of figures in contemporary science is filled with people who were addicted to science fiction in their youth. Stephen Hawking, current occupant of the chair once held by Isaac Newton at Cambridge University in England, is one, confessing that he spent his first few university years reading science fiction rather than his texts; Marvin Minsky, who won the Japan Prize a couple of years ago for his lifelong contributions to the study of artificial intelligence, is another. Minsky credits such science-fiction stories as Isaac Asimov's *I, Robot* and Jack Williamson's *The Humanoids* with awakening his interest in the prospect of intelligent robots. In fact, one of his first projects at the Artificial Intelligence Laboratory at the Massachusetts Institute of Technology (MIT) in Cambridge was to attempt to program Asimov's "three laws of robotics" into an actual computer.

Then there were the teenagers at New York's Bronx High School of Science in the 1950s. Among them was Sheldon Glashow, who, with two others, formed an active fan

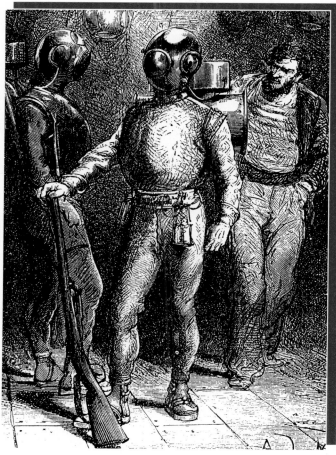

French novelist Jules Verne is almost universally considered the father of science fiction. An engraving from his 1870 classic 20,000 Leagues Under the Sea portrays with amazing accuracy the equipment needed for humans to explore the ocean floor.

group, putting out the school's science-fiction "fanzine" and taking part in campus dramatizations of science-fiction stories. "I went from comic books to science fiction, which probably was as important as anything else in getting me interested in science," Glashow reminisces. A decade or so later, he and Steven Weinberg, who had also belonged to the fan group, developed the "WSG electroweak" theory, which unites electromagnetism with the weak force that governs some nuclear interactions. Their partner in the WSG model was Abdus Salam of the International Center for Theoretical Physics in Trieste, Italy, and for that work the three shared a Nobel Prize in 1979.

Indeed, the influence of science fiction on actual scientists may have been even greater than Gernsback imagined, at least in some areas. Leo Szilard partly credits H. G. Wells' early science-fiction story about atomic energy, "The World Set Free," with the inspiration that led him directly to the Manhattan Project—and the world to its present nuclear anxieties. Living in London at the time, Szilard had read a newspaper statement by one of the grand old men of English science to the effect that nuclear power was a fantasy. Later that day, while Szilard was waiting for a traffic light to change, Wells' visionary story popped into his mind, along with the notion that a neutron chain reaction could release surplus energy from fissioning atoms. A few years later, Szilard and others built a primi-

Human travel to the Moon was a favorite topic among early science-fiction writers. In a popular Jules Verne story, a Moon-bound spaceship (below) escapes Earth's gravity by being fired out of a giant cannon.

tive nuclear reactor under the Stagg Field grandstand in Chicago, Illinois, based on just such a concept.

Even more concretely, the world's space programs were sparked largely by such science-fiction fans as rocket engineer Wernher von Braun, who during World War II kept up a subscription to his favorite magazine, *Astounding Science Fiction*, through a mail drop in neutral Sweden. Less traditional disciplines like futurology and the search for extraterrestrial intelligence have even deeper roots in science fiction. The National Aeronautics and Space Administration's (NASA's) Search for Extraterrestrial Intelligence (SETI) program could hardly have been imagined without the suggestion in 1,000 science-fiction stories that there might well be some extraterrestrial intelligences out there to search for, and futurology has often made great use of specific science-fiction stories. At the Hudson Institute futurological think tank, the late Herman Kahn, a leading figure in forecasting methodology, assigned a postdoctoral student to the task of reading through the entire works of such science-fiction writers as A. E. Van Vogt and listing their predictions.

Like von Braun, many scientists maintain their interest in science fiction throughout their lives, and some have gone so far as to write science fiction of their own. Leo Szilard published a volume of short stories called *The Voice of the Dolphin*; wry, satirical commentaries on the politics and social institutions of the 20th century, they are also indisputably science fiction. Cosmologist Fred Hoyle's first science-fiction novel, *The Black Cloud*, which speculated about intelligent life arising in an interstellar gas cloud, gave him so much pleasure that he went on to add a string of other novels. Astronomer Carl Sagan's best-selling novel *Contact* reflects his interest in communication with aliens, and Marvin Minsky's science-fiction technothriller, written in collaboration with science-fiction writer Harry Harrison, fleshes out speculation about storing human intelligence in machines.

Even O. R. Frisch, codiscoverer of the neutron fission reaction, once ventured into science fiction to make a political point about nuclear power; his short essay "Report on the Feasibility of Coal-Burning Power Stations" is a deadpan joke, set in an alternate world where technology has taken some different paths. The "report" describes the

The novels of H.G. Wells frequently veered in the direction of science fiction. In The Shape of Things to Come (1933), later made into a film (above), Wells predicted many of the dangers that ultimately came to threaten the world during the 20th century.

horrendous dangers of generating electricity by burning fossil fuel, and argues that impractically immense balloons would be needed to capture the dangerous stack emissions.

Indeed, quite a few of science fiction's most prolific writers are scientists in their day jobs. Some are mathematicians like the late Eric Temple Bell, who wrote many swashbuckling science fantasies in the 1930s under the pseudonym of John Taine, and Vernor Vinge of San Diego State University in California, whose A Fire Upon the Deep—a wonderfully inventive account of struggles between superhuman intelligences—won a Best Novel Hugo Award in 1993. Edward E.

("Doc") Smith, whose galaxy-ranging 1929 novel The Skylark of Space paved the way for the film Star Wars and all its kin, had a doctorate in chemistry and an occupational specialty in food chemistry, particularly grains. And Isaac Asimov held a doctorate in biochemistry—although, as anyone who knew Asimov or his works can testify, his primary field of expertise was actually everything.

RECONCILING IMAGINATION WITH DOCTRINE

Since science fiction does tend to incorporate phenomena no one has ever experienced, writers need to take some liberties, however devoted they may be to scientific accuracy. And that raises the question of just how many liberties they can take. Yoji Kondo, director of NASA's Extreme Ultraviolet Explorer research satellite, and, under his pen name of Eric Kotani, coauthor of the science-fiction novel Delta Pavonis and others, formalized the rules of the game in a paper delivered to the 1994 meeting of the American Association for the Advancement of Science (AAAS):

- Where a known natural law applies, the story must be consistent with that law.
- Where a known law is ambiguous or not explicit, the author may fudge, again within the constraints of well-established laws.
- Where no known natural law exists, an author may exercise his or her imagination, provided the extrapolation does not contradict other well-established laws.
- If the plot requires that the preceding rules be bent or broken, the author may do so, but must explain why. One might say that a new theory has superseded the old, or that a theory has proven incomplete or wrong.

Even before Kondo spelled out the rules, science-fiction writers, or at least the best of them, tried to reconcile their imaginations with current scientific doctrine. Of course, "current" sometimes means what's in that morning's *New York Times*. Particularly in astronomy, any new discovery is sure to turn up in some story, possibly many of them, almost overnight. Clyde Tombaugh discovered Pluto in 1930, and by the beginning of 1931, Stanton A. Coblents' *Into Plutonian Depths* was already in print. When Edwin Hubble announced the expansion of the universe, Edmond Hamilton published a story within months explaining what caused the expansion. (It was because all the other stars and galaxies were fleeing Earth, which, they had discovered, had developed the terrible disease of organic life.)

But even the most conscientious authors run into trouble when scientific opinions change. A generation or two ago, science-fiction stories were filled with inhabitants of planets in our solar system—ETs such as squat, immensely strong Jovians and willowy, sunburned-black creatures from the planet Mercury—for better telescopes and visiting spacecraft had not yet ruled out the possibility that beings like these existed. If Ray Bradbury and, particularly, Edgar Rice Burroughs allowed their characters to have adventures with Martians, they were not out of line with many leading scientists. The canals of Mars were not invented by Burroughs, but largely endorsed by such eminent astronomers as Percival Lowell. So pervasive was the assumption that Mars might be inhabited that the scientific literature of the late 19th century contains dozens of schemes for opening up a dialogue with Martians.

As scientists have shown that this solar system's planets are unlikely habitats for intelligent aliens, writers have gone farther afield to supply their fiction with such beings. Granted, Einstein's speed limit for space travel—the speed of light—is now canonical, yet thanks to the speculations of astrophysicists and cosmologists like Kip Thorne and Stephen

Hawking, characters can hop from star to star in an afternoon through "space warps" or "wormholes" between black holes and white ones. Or they can rely on that wonderfully useful theoretical particle, the tachyon.

The tachyon was originally proposed by Gerald Feinberg, Sheldon Glashow's boy-

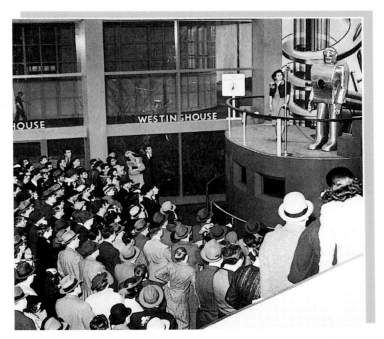

The 1939 World's Fair in New York City included exhibits of robots (above), television, and other futuristic concepts that, until that time, had been exclusively the province of science-fiction writers.

hood classmate at the Bronx High School of Science and the third member of the science-fiction fan group to which Glashow and Steven Weinberg belonged. Feinberg's tachyon obeys Einstein's laws in every respect: the speed of light is its limiting velocity, just as with all other particles. But Feinberg found a loophole in Einstein's equations: for the tachyon, the speed of light is a *lower* limit. It can never travel that slowly, but it can go as fast as anyone could wish. Indeed, the less energetic the tachyon, the faster it will go.

Unfortunately, even in theory, tachyons cannot propel a spaceship built of normal matter, but that doesn't make them useless for science fiction. Like any stream of particles, tachyons might carry information—perhaps coded assembly instructions that could be used to build an exact duplicate of something from Earth around the star Alpha Centauri, or, for that matter, somewhere in the Andromeda nebula. That something might even be a copy of a person, once the problems of locating and identifying every molecule in the human body are solved.

Another stratagem for interstellar travel is Einstein's phenomenon of time dilation, in which, at speeds close to that of light, time passes so slowly that voyagers can cross a galaxy before lunch. And then there's "frozen sleep." The basic concept of immortality through freezing was proposed in the early 1960s by Robert C. W. Ettinger, a science teacher from the Detroit, Michigan, area. Will it work? The jury is out. But for the purposes of science fiction, the possibility alone is enough. Star travelers can be popped into the deep freeze on takeoff, and defrosted when they've reached their destination—10 years later or 1,000.

The guest appearance of acclaimed physicist Stephen Hawking (right) on Star Trek: The Next Generation testifies to the attention given to scientific accuracy by the writers of the science-fiction television series.

The worlds these characters can visit have also become more interesting with the help of scientific speculation. Freeman Dyson's notion that an advanced civilization might solve its energy needs by enclosing its star in a vast, energy-trapping shell has inspired a number of science-fiction stories, notably Larry Niven's *Ringworld*. Even Fred Hoyle's steady-state universe, a cosmology now known to be unlikely, was good while it lasted, giving science-fiction writers—including Jack Williamson and myself in *The Reefs of Space*—the opportunity to create some colorful settings. The theory was that the universe had neither beginning nor end, but continually increased through the sponta-

neous creation of new matter, and we proposed that this new matter out in space might form itself into complex structures inhabited by unearthly creatures.

PREVENTING FUTURE SHOCK

To be sure, science fiction includes reams of comics and pulp adventures and an endless flood of monster movies and silly TV shows. Yet even in film and television, there are some who try to keep their honor bright. For instance, the producers of *Star Trek* now employ a scientist full-time to check their scripts for scientific howlers. Perhaps that newfound care is why, in a 1993 episode, Stephen Hawking himself did a guest shot on the show, in the company of holographic simulations of Albert Einstein and Isaac Newton.

Interestingly, though, science fiction is not fiction about science, despite all the attention writers often lavish on the science in their tales. Indeed, some of the best—the works of such masters as Harlan Ellison and Ray Bradbury—have no detectable science in them at all. Science fiction is about something much more fundamental, as Arthur C. Clarke must have realized when he said that he wrote science fiction "because no other kind of literature concerns itself with reality."

The foremost reality that science fiction deals with is change, which could be the reason for the growing interest in the genre in the 20th century, when the world has experienced more change than ever before. When science plays a significant part in science fiction, as it surely does, it is primarily as one of the instruments of change. Science fiction is the sovereign prophylactic against future shock, so that if you read enough of it, nothing will take you entirely by surprise.

Not that science-fiction writers intend to predict the future. The idea is simply to investigate possibilities—sometimes with the goal of sounding a warning, as George Orwell did in *1984*. When Ray Bradbury was asked whether he expected the future to be like the nasty one he described in *Fahrenheit 451*, he answered, "I don't try to predict the future. All I want to do is prevent it."

ARMCHAIR FUN

So what, in the final analysis, is this thing called science fiction? There isn't a good answer. Many attempts have been made to define it, but none are entirely satisfactory. The best one I know is by the late English science-fiction writer John Phillifent, who once wrote me in some elation to say that he had finally figured out what distinguishes science fiction from all other kinds of writing. Every science-fiction story, he said, is written by

With its depictions of 1980 New York as a city of mile-high skyscrapers and personal rocket ships, the 1930 sci-fi musical Just Imagine *represents a flagrant example of inaccurate predictions on the part of the writer.*

means of the "science-fiction method," analogous to the "scientific method"—the orderly system of information gathering and theory formulation that distinguishes science from random anecdote. Unfortunately, Phillifent died without ever specifying just what that science-fiction method was, but I nevertheless believe he was right. There is such a method, and science-fiction writers have been employing it all along, whether consciously aware of it or not. It consists of looking at the world around us in all its parts, taking some of those parts out and replacing them with invented ones, and then putting the model back together and writing a story to show how it works.

Sometimes that process is socially useful. Science fiction does demand that its readers develop a larger perspective on the planet—demands that they ponder "the view from a distant star," in astronomer Harlow Shapley's phrase. And there may soon be even more proof for Hugo Gernsback's claims about science fiction as pedagogy. In another paper delivered to the AAAS meeting, Hal Coyle, now in the science-education department of the Harvard-Smithsonian Institute for Astrophysics, described how he used *Star Trek* to help convey scientific concepts to high school students in his first postgraduate job as a science teacher. Klingons and other aliens opened the door to a discussion of evolution, and the starship *Enterprise*'s great speed and maneuverability sparked interest in Einstein's theory of relativity and Newton's laws of motion. The planets the ship visited helped students understand stellar types and the scale of the universe.

But none of that would have worked if it had not been for science fiction's other major trait. It may teach. It may inspire. Still, most of all, what it does for many millions of people around the world is to let them explore, from their armchairs, places and times they can never visit in the flesh. It is, in short, fun.

Ask the Scientist

▶ *Who were the ancient Macedonians? Were any famous personalities of ancient times Macedonian? Are the ancient Macedonians the ancestors of the people who live in the modern-day Republic of Macedonia?*

The ancient civilization of Macedonia began with an Indo-European tribe that, sometime during the 7th century B.C., settled in what is now part of northern Greece. Perhaps the best-known personality of ancient Macedonia was Alexander III—commonly known as Alexander the Great, says Carolyn S. Snively, Ph.D., associate professor of classics at Gettysburg College in Gettysburg, Pennsylvania. Alexander the Great took over the throne of Macedonia in 336 B.C., after his father, Philip II, died. Alexander led the Macedonians on great military quests, conquering the Persian Empire, Egypt, and Syria, and traveling as far as India.

The philosopher Aristotle is also associated with Macedonia, according to Dr. Snively. Aristotle was born in a Greek colony in Macedonia in 384 B.C., and may have tutored Alexander the Great.

By the time the Romans took it over in the 2nd century B.C., ancient Macedonia extended north of Greece to the modern-day Republic of Macedonia (in the former Yugoslavia). The inhabitants of modern Macedonia are not descended from their ancient namesakes.

▶ *Did the religion practiced by the Druids really include tree worship? Did the Druids build temples or churches? When did the religion cease to exist?*

Druidism was the religion practiced by the ancient Celts, a tribe of people who inhabited Ireland, Britain, and Gaul, an ancient country that comprised what are now modern France and Belgium. The priests, or Druids, of this religion were men of high standing in these societies.

Since the Celts did not keep a written record of their religious practices, our knowledge of Druidism is sketchy. For instance, it is not clear whether the Druids actually worshiped trees. However, it is known that oak trees were sacred in the religion, and that religious ceremonies were often held in oak forests. In fact, the word "druid" may be derived from *daur*, which is Celtic for "oak tree." Mistletoe was also sacred in the religion.

The Druids apparently did not build churches or temples: historians once attributed ancient stone monuments such as Stonehenge to the Druids, but it is now known that these predate the Druid culture.

When the Romans took over Britain and Gaul, they suppressed the Druid religion. In Ireland, which never fell under Roman rule, Druidism lasted until approximately A.D. 500.

▶ *Why are the Pygmies of Africa so short? Do Pygmies still adhere to a traditional way of life? Is the term "Pygmy" still considered correct?*

Scientists believe that the short stature of the Pygmies may be due to nothing more than genetics, random chance, and the isolation of a population: "The Pygmies may be descendants of a group of people who for one reason or another became separated from other populations," says Robert Kelly, Ph.D., associate professor and chair of the Department of Anthropology at the University of Louisville in Kentucky. "By sheer chance, that isolated population could have included individuals whose genes code for shortness. Those genes by chance could have become dominant." Since the Pygmies were isolated, the dominant shortness genes would be passed from generation to generation. Previously, some scientists had suggested that the Pygmies' height was an adaption to the equatorial climate they lived in. However, most populations of people who live at the equator are tall and thin—a body type that most efficiently dissipates heat—so it is unlikely that the Pygmies' build has anything to do with climate, Dr. Kelly says.

For the most part, Pygmies live much the same way they did 100 years ago: in camps in the forest, hunting and gathering some of their food, and getting the rest of the food they need in exchange for working the farms of their agricultural neighbors.

Finally, "Pygmy" is still the correct term for these groups of people, though the word is usually paired with the name of the particular group of Pygmies, such as the Efe Pygmies, the Aka Pygmies, and the Mbuti Pygmies.

▶ *My history teacher says that World War II had a big impact on the native peoples living in the South Pacific. He said that one effect was the development of "cargo cults." Exactly what is a cargo cult?*

World War II had a huge impact on the native peoples of the South Pacific, says Lin Poyer, Ph.D., associate professor in the Department of Anthropology at the University of Cincinnati in Ohio.

When the war ended, the locals who had been working on the coasts of the South Pacific islands began returning to their relatively isolated villages in the highlands. They took with them their new view of the world and the visions of the goods and war

materials that they had seen or enjoyed. These goods—"cargo"—soon became part of the local religious rituals as people prayed for the return of the times of plenty that the war had brought, says Poyer. Since the rituals took a cult form—people made model airplanes and used them to "entice" real airplanes to come and give them cargo, for instance—the rituals became known as "cargo cults." Eventually the cargo cults, combined with the sense of independence and ability to achieve what the black American troops had inspired, led to the formation of several independent nations in the South Pacific.

▶ *Is there any evidence that, through time, the outward appearance of humans has changed substantially in historical times? Are people really taller now than they used to be?*

The only substantial change in appearance that scientists have been able to document has been an increase in height. For instance, says Lynne Schepartz, Ph.D., research professor of anthropology at the University of Cincinnati, anthropological studies of immigrant populations have shown an increase in stature from one generation to the next. Scientists believe that the change is the result of better nutrition in childhood: at the turn of the century, the native countries of most immigrants were depressed areas where food was scarce or expensive. This change in height has been documented, not only among the U.S. population, but in several populations around the world, for the past few generations.

In addition to better nutrition, some scientists speculate that humans are getting taller as a result of the increased proliferation of stimuli such as artificial lights. Experiments with lab rats show, for instance, that stimulation such as prolonging the hours of the day with artificial light promotes growth. It is not clear whether artificial light exerts a similar effect on humans, however.

PHYSICAL SCIENCES

■ THE ARRANGEMENT OF ATOMS AND MOLECULES UNIQUE TO EACH SUBSTANCE DETERMINES IN LARGE PART THE METHODS BY WHICH A SPECIFIC MATERIAL CAN BE MANIPULATED. IN MANY INDUSTRIAL SETTINGS, COMPUTERS ARE USED TO ACCELERATE THE CALCULATION OF PARAMETERS NEEDED TO WORK A MATERIAL FOR A SPECIFIED APPLICATION.

CONTENTS

BEYOND THE TOP QUARK

by William F. Allman

Call it Physics for the Next Millennium. Just as researchers were announcing in April 1994 the first compelling evidence of the existence of the "top quark"—the final subatomic building block of the atom and a key element in the scientific world's reigning model of physical reality—a flurry of new books were heralding a new age in physics, an age in which the ordinary understanding of reality is being turned on its head and inside out.

Never have researchers conjured up a world so weird: it is a universe where space exists in 10 dimensions, where one can travel through time into the past, where holes in the fabric of space and time pop up and serve as shortcuts to other parts of the universe, and where the visible universe may be only one of myriad mini-universes that coexist like so many soap bubbles in a cosmic froth.

NO FANTASY FRINGE

Such notions no doubt would have shocked Albert Einstein, yet the new research is in fact a legacy of the great theorist's work. At universities and research labs around the world, Einstein's theories of space and time are being stretched and refined by the brightest minds in science today, some of whom will undoubtedly garner Nobel prizes for their

A new theory challenges our understanding of reality by suggesting that the universe includes not only the familiar dimensions of space and time, but also additional dimensions of hyperspace, which cannot yet be detected.

soberminded efforts to make the ordinary world seem very strange indeed. "Most people think of physicists as people who wear white smocks and work with tuning forks or study friction," says Michio Kaku, a physicist at the City University of New York in New York City and author of *Hyperspace: A Scientific Odyssey Through Parallel Universes, Time Warps, and the 10th Dimension.* "But in fact, we make our living discovering things that blow people's minds."

Much of the new research stems from the intellectual effort to make the cluttered and chaotic universe tidier and more elegant. The so-called Standard Model—the mathematical formulation that predicts, among other things, the existence of the newly found quark—contains some 60 different particles with a broad variety of properties. Though a tremendous achievement of modern science, this theoretical model is simply too complicated to be the ultimate description of reality, says Kaku. "It's like using Scotch tape to pull together a mule, a whale, a tiger, and a giraffe." Many physicists today assume that there must be a deeper, more comprehensive theory that unites all the phenomena in the universe, from light to gravity to quarks.

There is now tremendous excitement over a theory that may achieve that goal, but it is a theory that requires a kind of multidimensional thinking that even many scientists are unaccustomed to. Kaku uses a carp pond as an analogy for the new physics, with the fish being analogous to earthbound cosmologists. If carp were to observe rain splattering the pond's surface, for example, they might construct theories explaining the motion of the ripples in the water—yet never realize that what they observed was caused by actions in an unseen world beyond their grasp.

A 10-DIMENSIONAL UNIVERSE?

Similarly, physicists such as Kaku are exploring the notion that the universe contains higher dimensions—known as hyperspace—

and that many of the long-standing problems in theoretical physics can be simplified with such a view. For nearly a century, for instance, physicists have wondered how light can display the properties of a wave traveling through water, even though light is capable of traveling through empty space where there exists no medium in which to ripple. But if physicists regard the universe as having, not the familiar four dimensions—three of space and one of time—but instead, an additional spatial dimension, then the properties of light emerge naturally from the equations describing this five-dimensional world. Adding even more dimensions gives rise to still other forces of nature. Indeed, the number of dimensions that appears to best explain nature is 10; physicists say the world merely seems four-dimensional to us because the other six dimensions, present during the Big Bang, are now inaccessible—like rain clouds to a carp.

According to the new physics, time travel is theoretically possible. Shortcuts to parallel universes or other parts of our own universe may exist via "wormholes"— openings in the fabric of space and time.

The Missing Piece in a Cosmic Puzzle

The announcement on April 26, 1994, of evidence of the so-called top quark had physicists both congratulating one another and breathing a huge sigh of relief. By finding in their powerful atom smasher faint traces of the elusive subatomic particle, an international team of hundreds of scientists at the Fermi National Accelerator Laboratory (Fermilab) in Batavia, Illinois, ended the long search for the last puzzle piece in the so-called Standard Model of matter. Failure to find the last of matter's basic building blocks, and thus to confirm the reigning theory of physical reality, would have meant embarrassment of cosmic proportions.

For nearly a century, physicists have known that all matter is made up of atoms, and that these atoms themselves are constructed from particles such as protons and neutrons. Decades ago, physicist Murray Gell-Mann of the California Institute of Technology (Caltech) in Pasadena proposed a theory that protons, neutrons, and other known subatomic particles were

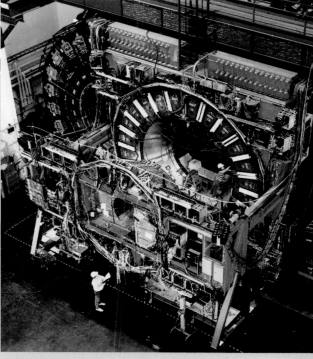

Researchers using Fermilab's powerful atom smasher (above) detected the elusive subatomic particle called the top quark. Its discovery confirms the current theory of physical reality known as the Standard Model.

made of even smaller particles that he dubbed quarks. He took the whimsical name from a line in the James Joyce masterwork *Finnegans Wake*: "three quarks for Muster Mark."

The notion of a 10-dimensional universe may be impossible for ordinary folks to comprehend, but it is a key part of a newly ascendant model of the universe known as the "superstring" theory. This theory holds that all matter and energy are the result of the vibration of infinitesimally small loops that are some 100 billion billion times smaller than a proton. These strings are the fundamental blocks that make up the entire universe, according to the new physicists, who say that a 10-dimensional universe arises naturally from superstring equations. Though there are still many issues to resolve, many scientists feel that this new model is the most promising hope for a "Theory of Everything," in which all of the

properties of the universe can be folded into one set of equations.

PONDERING TIME TRAVEL

Resolving superstring theory will help settle the hot debate now going on in scholarly journals over the possibility of time travel. Several years ago, physicist Kip Thorne and his colleagues at the California Institute of Technology (Caltech) in Pasadena proposed that Einstein's equations describing space and time allowed for the possibility of tunnels in the fabric of space. These "wormholes" could theoretically connect one part of the universe with another, or even loop around to bring a time traveler to a point in the universe's past.

NATURE'S FLAVORS

Gell-Mann's theory, for which he won a Nobel Prize, posited that quarks come in six different "flavors"—known as up, down, charm, strange, bottom, and top—which combine to create subatomic particles. A proton, for instance, is made up of two up quarks and one down quark. But until recently, only the first five quarks had been found, holding out the nagging concern that the Standard Model might be flawed. An international team of physicists, using a particle accelerator at the European Center for Nuclear Research (CERN) near Geneva, Switzerland, previously claimed that it had found the top quark, but subsequent attempts to confirm the discovery were unsuccessful.

The difficulty in hunting the top quark is that, like some other particles in the cosmic zoo, it exists only for a near-infinitesimal fraction of a second. Thus, its presence must be inferred from the unique signature of the other "daughter" particles into which it rapidly decays. Indeed, the Fermilab team based its announcement on finding only 12 such signature "events" among literally billions of collisions.

The top quark is so massive (at least within the realm of subatomic particles) that it could be detected only by re-creating, in an atom smasher, the huge energies that existed in the early universe following the Big Bang. The more massive a particle is, the more energy needed to create it, and the Fermilab has the only machine capable of producing such energies. The proposed Superconducting Super Collider (SSC) would have had more power, but the half-finished project was permanently canceled by the U.S. Congress during 1993.

Even without a new atom smasher, physicists still have new opportunities to probe deeper into the fundamental mysteries of nature. Construction of a new gravity-wave detector, which will search for ripples in space-time that are evidence of black holes, has already begun in the United States, and Fermilab is retrofitting its accelerator to give it greater power. Most important, there remain the simple tools of paper, pencil, mathematics, and the human mind, which can intellectually create bizarre—but real—worlds that machines may never detect.

Though no one has actually seen a wormhole, they are theoretically possible because, as Einstein established, gravity twists and bends the structure of space itself. Around huge chunks of matter—such as the superdense collapsed stars that form a black hole—the surrounding space could be bent in such a way that a wormhole might open up, allowing a time traveler to slip through. Other physicists, including Stephen Hawking, have since weighed in on the issue, suggesting that the radiation surrounding such a wormhole would annihilate a time traveler, or that the energy arising from activating a wormhole might cause it to collapse, or that the hole might open and close too quickly to allow anyone to pass through. In his new book, *Black Holes and Time Warps: Einstein's Outrageous Legacy*, Thorne points out that one of the biggest problems for humans wishing to travel through time is that the amount of energy needed to produce a wormhole is beyond the scope of anything known today. "Even if a wormhole could be created," says Thorne, "it would be as far beyond our present technology as space travel is to an amoeba." Still, when Newton described his laws of force and motion three centuries ago, he possessed the theoretical tools to calculate the energy required to go to the Moon, even though he lived in the era of the horse and buggy.

The biggest objection to time travel may arise from common sense rather than theory. Physicist Hawking, whose collection of essays *Black Holes and Baby Universes* came out late in 1993, argues that time travel must not be possible, since if it were, modern civilization would already have been overrun by tourists from the future. More troubling for many physicists is the "grandfather paradox": if time travel were possible, what would happen if someone traveled back in time and murdered his grandfather, thereby preventing his own birth?

In the alternative reality of bubble universes, many parallel universes—one of which is our own—simultaneously exist independently of one another in a difficult-to-fathom foamlike matrix.

THE MULTIVERSE

One way around this difficulty, argue a growing number of physicists, is to look to the concept of "multiple worlds." In the shadowy world of quantum mechanics, particles can be described only as a collection of probabilities. Scientists can say with precision, for example, that a given particle will decay within 20 minutes, but there is no way of predicting exactly when in that 20-minute span the decay will actually occur; this uncertainty is an intrinsic property of the particle. To escape this apparent randomness, some researchers suggest that in fact all the possible scenarios exist simultaneously, but in multiple, parallel universes that are independent of each other. Thus, in one universe, the particle will decay after one minute; in another, after two minutes; and so on. In the same way, it might be possible for people to travel through time and slay their grandfathers, but these events would merely trigger the creation of a parallel universe where the person was not born, leaving the other, more familiar, universe intact.

The concept of multiple universes—or the "multiverse," as the new theorists call it—may help physicists answer the question of what happened at the instant of Creation. "Theologians sometimes come up to you and say, 'Nyaah, nyaah, you may know what happened at the beginning of the Big Bang, but what was there *before* the Big Bang?'" says Kaku. Indeed, the physical conditions at the instant of the universe's creation do not conform to Einstein's theories, but the possibility of a 10-dimensional universe offers one explanation, suggests Kaku. The primordial 10-dimensional universe was unstable, he believes, and so began to "boil," creating bubbles of space and time that expanded to create the Big Bang. The result, according to this theory, was a foamlike matrix of mini-universes, one of which is our own.

The idea that these mini-universes might be connected to each other via wormholes gives Kaku hope that some future civilization might escape the Big Crunch, the theoretically possible collapse of the universe in the far distant future. As the conflagration looms, he suggests, some technologically advanced civilization that has the power to harness hyperspace might use its knowledge to transport society into another dimension. Such speculation is bound to raise eyebrows among some of his colleagues, but Kaku is looking forward, not back. "The finding of the last quark marked the end of the old era of physics," he says. "And the beginning of the new."

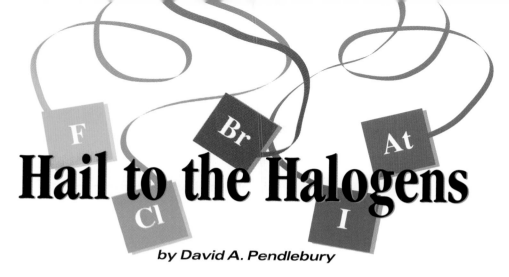

Hail to the Halogens

by David A. Pendlebury

You may not recognize the name "halo-gens," but you most certainly know them. In fact, you live with them every day. For example: What do you use to whiten your wash? What is the coating on your frying pan? What do you use to flavor your fish? If you answered chlorine bleach, Teflon, and table salt, then you know the halogens—or, more precisely, the halogen compounds.

WHAT IS A HALOGEN?

The halogens are an intriguing group of non-metallic elements occupying column VIIA in the periodic table. The halogen family has five members: fluorine (F), chlorine (Cl), bromine (Br), iodine (I), and the exceedingly rare astatine (At). As family members, they share certain characteristics and types of behavior. For example, the halogens are highly reactive, which means they tend to combine with other elements and molecules to form compounds. In fact, the halogens are so reactive that they are never found in their elemental form in nature.

It is instructive to compare the halogen family with its next-door neighbors to the right in the periodic table, the noble-gas family, which occupies column VIIIA. Speaking metaphorically, members of the halogen family are extremely social and look for every opportunity to get together with other elements. By contrast, members of the noble-gas family prefer to stay at home, aloof from other elements. The halogens cannot help running all over town, just as the noble gases cannot manage to get themselves off the couch. The difference in their behavior derives from essential differences in their atomic structure and electron configuration.

Orbiting around the core, or nucleus, of every element are rings, or shells, of electrons. The number of electrons in the outermost shell (called valence electrons) determines how easily one element can combine with another to form a compound. The most stable arrangement for an element is one in which there are eight valence electrons. In this arrangement, called the octet, there is no impetus to form compounds by giving electrons up to—or by taking electrons from—other elements or compounds. The noble-gas elements (with the exception of helium) all have eight electrons in their outermost shells; hence, they are essentially non-reactive, or inert. The halogens, on the other hand, all have seven electrons in their outermost shell, so there is room for one more electron. Since all elements attempt, when forming compounds, to move toward the most stable configuration of eight valence electrons, the halogens attempt to gain an electron. When successful, a stable ion is formed with a negative charge of 1.

All the halogens are oxidizing agents, which means they want to gain electrons. Elements classified as metals tend to lose electrons easily, so metals readily combine with the halogens to form compounds known as salts. The most familiar of these is sodium chloride (NaCl), ordinary table salt. In fact, the name "halogen" derives from two Greek roots meaning "salt" and "producer." When halogens form compounds with other elements, the compound is called a halide. Halides include fluorides, chlorides, bromides, iodides, and astatides.

The members of the halogen family were discovered at different times and by different

I A											
1 H	II A										
3 Li	4 Be										
11 Na	12 Mg	III B	IV B	V B	VI B	VII B	VIII B			I B	II B
19 K	20 Ca	21 Sc	22 Ti	23 V	24 Cr	25 Mn	26 Fe	27 Co	28 Ni	29 Cu	30 Zn
37 Rb	38 Sr	39 Y	40 Zr	41 Nb	42 Mo	43 Tc	44 Ru	45 Rh	46 Pd	47 Ag	48 Cd
55 Cs	56 Ba	57 *La	72 Hf	73 Ta	74 W	75 Re	76 Os	77 Ir	78 Pt	79 Au	80 Hg
87 Fr	88 Ra	89 †Ac	104 ‡Db	105 ‡Jl	106 ‡Rf	107 ‡Bh	108 ‡Hn	109 ‡Mt			

*Lanthanides

58 Ce	59 Pr	60 Nd	61 Pm	62 Sm	63 Eu	64 Gd	65 Tb

†Actinides

90 Th	91 Pa	92 U	93 Np	94 Pu	95 Am	96 Cm	97 Bk

investigators beginning in the late 18th century. The first halogen to be isolated was chlorine, in 1774; the last was astatine, in 1940. While, as mentioned, none are found as single atoms in nature, the halogens can be produced in diatomic form (a compound of two atoms of the same halogen, such as F_2) through various methods, such as electrolysis. When in this "pure" form, all the halogens give off a strong, unpleasant odor; in this state, they are also destructive to human tissue, a property that led to their use as poisonous gas in chemical warfare. But the halogens have also been exploited for many beneficial purposes, such as for the purification of water and, in diluted form, as antiseptics.

FLUORINE

A mineral compound of fluorine, called fluorspar, was known for hundreds of years before the isolation of fluorine itself in 1886.

Texts on metallurgical processes from the 16th century mention fluorspar (CaF_2), which was used as a cleansing agent, or flux, in certain metal-making and -refining processes. The word for this mineral derives from the Latin root for the verb "to flow." The word "fluorescence" is also related to this process; when fluorspar is warmed, it gives off a bluish glow. Today fluorspar and other fluorine-containing minerals continue to be the chief source of fluorine.

As other members of the halogen family were first identified, there was much speculation about the existence of the element that eventually came to be called fluorine. In the late 18th century, French chemist Antoine Lavoisier suggested that "fluoric acid" in minerals such as fluorspar could be a new element. In 1813, British chemist Sir Humphry Davy suggested the name fluorine for this missing element. But it was not until 1886 that Henri

III A	IV A	V A	VI A	VII A	VIII A
					2 He
5 B	6 C	7 N	8 O	9 F	10 Ne
13 Al	14 Si	15 P	16 S	17 Cl	18 Ar
31 Ga	32 Ge	33 As	34 Se	35 Br	36 Kr
49 In	50 Sn	51 Sb	52 Te	53 I	54 Xe
81 Tl	82 Pb	83 Bi	84 Po	85 At	86 Rn

‡Provisional Names

66 Dy	67 Ho	68 Er	69 Tm	70 Yb	71 Lu
98 Cf	99 Es	100 Fm	101 ‡Md	102 ‡No	103 ‡Lr

Moissan of France was finally able to isolate fluorine, a feat accomplished by electrolyzing a solution of potassium fluoride in hydrogen fluoride at -58° F (-50° C). So spectacular was this achievement that Moissan was awarded the 1906 Nobel Prize in Chemistry.

Fluorine's extreme reactivity kept it out of the hands of chemists long after its existence was suspected. Fluorine is the most reactive of all the elements, and it forms compounds with almost any element. Its electron configuration consists of two shells. The closer one to the nucleus contains two electrons. The next, outer, shell holds seven electrons. Since this second shell is positioned so closely to the positively charged nucleus, fluorine has great attractive force and combines readily with other elements and molecules.

At room temperature, fluorine is a pale-yellow gas. Compounds of fluorine—the fluorides—are used for many purposes. The small amounts of fluorine found in groundwater come from dissolved minerals. Nowadays minute amounts of fluorine are typically added to community water sources at a concentration of 1 part per million (ppm). Fluorinated water has the beneficial effect of hardening tooth enamel, thus preventing tooth decay. Fluorine is also added to toothpaste and mouthwash for the same purpose. At slightly higher concentrations, however, fluorine can be toxic. The practice of adding fluorine to water is therefore not without controversy. Individuals and groups have vociferously objected to the additive, citing detrimental health consequences.

Industrially, fluorine and fluorides are used in the production of aluminum and steel. Hydrofluoric acid, created by carefully combining fluorine and hydrogen, is used to etch glass with designs or lettering and to create frosted lightbulbs.

Fluorine has a great affinity for carbon, and the combination creates compounds that are amazingly stable and durable. One such well-known compound is Teflon, which is a trademark for a variety of tetrafluoroethylenes. Another well-known product of fluorocarbon chemistry is Freon (most commonly CCl_2F_2), a trade name for a refrigerant and a propellant used in aerosol-spray cans. The commercial use of Freons, however, has been scaled back greatly since the 1987 signing of the international treaty known as the Montreal Protocol, which curtails their use worldwide. In the 1970s and 1980s, researchers implicated these fluorocarbons in the progressive destruction of atmospheric ozone.

The release of chlorofluorocarbons and their increasing concentration has also been cited as contributing to the greenhouse effect and global warming. Increasingly, industrial firms around the world use safer hydrofluorocarbons as substitute refrigerants and propellants for aerosol sprays.

The extreme reactivity of fluorine was exploited in March 1995, when terrorists released poisonous gas in the Tokyo subway system. Ten citizens died, and thousands were injured or sickened. The gas released was identified as sarin, a fluoride compound. Sarin is one of the most toxic members of the fluorophosphate family; it kills by causing respiratory paralysis rather than by burning.

Fluorine added to water, toothpaste, or mouthwash helps harden tooth enamel and, therefore, reduces dental decay. Nonetheless, the element's potential toxicity has made its use in public water supplies controversial.

CHLORINE

Like the other halogens, chlorine is not found in elemental form in nature, but only in compounds called chlorides. The most familiar of these, of course, is sodium chloride—salt—which is found as crystals in dried lake beds and in seawater.

In 1774, Carl Wilhelm Scheele, a Swedish chemist, became the first to isolate chlorine, although he did not recognize the importance of his discovery at the time. He heated hydrochloric acid (then called muriatic acid) with an oxidizing agent and obtained a foul-smelling, choking yellow-greenish gas. It was not until 1810 that Sir Humphry Davy showed that the gas, which he called chlorine, was an element. Davy chose this name from the Greek word for the color yellow-green.

Chlorine is extremely reactive, but not quite so much as the lighter element fluorine. The element chlorine has three electron shells—one more than fluorine. The innermost shell contains two orbiting electrons, the middle shell holds eight (the octet arrangement), while the third and outermost shell has the seven orbiting electrons that are the hallmark of the halogens.

Today chlorine is the most abundant of the halogens produced and used by industry. There are various techniques for capturing chlorine, including electrolysis and oxidation methods. Chlorine is used as a bleaching agent, not only in the wash, but also for whitening paper pulp or newsprint. The bleach added to your laundry is typically sodium hypochlorite (NaOCl) in 5-percent solution. Other industrial uses of chlorine include the production of dyes, the manufacture of explosives, and in certain metallurgical processes, such as those used to recover precious and semiprecious metals from ores (although several other methods are now in use). A combination of chlorine with carbon has created a class of useful compounds known as carbon tetrachlorides. These compounds are used to make dry-cleaning fluids, some solvents, and the material ejected by fire extinguishers.

Another chloride compound much in use is the plastic polyvinyl chloride, known as PVC. This versatile polymer material will not corrode or degrade for decades, and it can be fashioned into a variety of specific

Because it kills harmful bacteria, chlorine is regularly used to purify swimming-pool water and public water supplies. Chlorine is also used to treat sewage.

Bromine-containing halogen lamps are replacing incandescent light bulbs in streetlamps and automobile headlights. The longer-lasting halogen lamps produce a whiter, brighter light than do traditional bulbs—and use less energy to boot.

shapes. These characteristics make it ideal for certain uses in environments exposed to water, such as for pipes, window frames, to shield and insulate wiring, and even for garden furniture. PVC, notes chemist and science writer John Emsley, is a "superb electric insulator, it is flexible, it is tough, it is scratch-resistant, it does not crack, and it does not catch fire easily... and [it is] cheap to make."

Hydrochloric acid (HCl), which is used in laboratories and manufacturing processes, is a hydrogen chloride preparation, typically 40 percent HCl in water. Humans produce HCl in the stomach to break down and digest food.

Chlorine is also an effective germicide. It is added to swimming-pool water as well as to drinking water to kill bacteria, for example. Chlorine is also exploited in the treatment of sewage. And while chlorine has contributed materially to improving human health through better sanitation, its properties have also been harnessed to harm humans. In 1917, during World War I, chlorine gas was used by German troops against Allied forces, causing over 20,000 casualties and 5,000 fatalities. When the gas comes in contact with humans, it burns the eyes and throat, causes tightening in the chest, and results in blistering of the skin. Mustard gas,

which is a chloride ($C_4H_8Cl_2S$), was used in the Iran-Iraq war during the 1980s, and by Iraq's Saddam Hussein against Kurds living in northern Iraq.

Ironically, just after World War I, inhalation of very low concentrations (1 ppm) of chlorine gas in a specially built chamber was considered an effective treatment for colds. Thirty times this concentration constitutes a lethal dose within 30 minutes. Chlorine-gas exposure is, needless to say, no longer prescribed for treating the common cold.

BROMINE

The word for the element bromine, the next member of the halogen family, derives from the Greek word for "stench" or "foul odor." Whereas fluorine and chlorine, when isolated, are gases at room temperature, bromine is a reddish-brown liquid, and it does have a strong, unpleasant smell. French chemist Antoine J. Balard discovered the element in 1826 when he extracted the dark-red liquid from brine. Seawater is still a major source of bromine. In both its liquid and its gaseous form, bromine is highly corrosive and will produce painful burns on the skin.

Bromine is slightly less reactive than its cousins fluorine and chlorine. Bromine has four electron shells around its nucleus, which hold 2, 8, 18, and 7 electrons, respectively.

In medicine, bromide compounds have a sedating effect on the central nervous system. In years past, bromides, especially potassium bromide (KBr), were prescribed as tranquilizers. Bromides are now seldom used for this purpose, however, owing to mental disturbances associated with continual use. The stomach-settling product Bromo Seltzer is a vestige of this chapter in medical history. Another bromine-containing compound that retains an important role in medicine is halothane. This compound ($C_2HBrClF_3$), which includes the halogens bromine, chlorine, and fluorine, is used as a general anesthetic. Halothane was introduced in the 1950s, and replaced ether, which had been used for more than a century.

Industrial applications for bromides include: ethylene dibromide ($C_2H_4Br_2$), used as an antiknock additive for leaded gasoline; silver bromide (AgBr), a light-sensitive material used in photographic film, paper, and processing; and methyl bromide (CH_3Br), a flame-retardant compound.

One of the more recent industrial uses of halogens—and of bromine in particular—is in halogen lamps, invented by scientists at the General Electric Company (GE). Halogen lights have several advantages over traditional incandescent lamps: they produce a whiter, brighter light that burns hotter but actually uses less energy, and part of the halogen lamp's efficient design allows it to last longer and to keep the inside face of the bulb cleaner. Halogen lamps are increasingly used for streetlights, for automobile headlamps, and in illuminating buildings.

IODINE

Iodine, the fourth member of the halogen family, was the second to be discovered (after chlorine) in the early 19th century. French chemist Bernard Courtois happened upon iodine vapor in 1811 while separating niter from seaweed. A violet-colored vapor arose and was collected. After analysis, it turned out to be a wholly new element. Davy suggested that the new element be named iodine, echoing the Greek word for the color violet. At room temperature, iodine takes the form of grayish-black flakes. When heated, it passes directly from a solid to a vapor, without taking a liquid form, in a process known as sublimation.

There is no elemental iodine in nature, but compounds of iodine and chlorine are found, and they are especially concentrated in seaweed and kelp (although chlorine is present in much greater amounts than iodine). Iodine is less reactive than bromine, chlorine, and fluorine, owing to its much greater atomic weight. Its electron configuration consists of five shells holding 2, 8, 18, 18, and 7 electrons, respectively.

Iodine has been used as a mild antiseptic. Tincture of iodine, a diluted solution of the element, was often swabbed on scrapped elbows and cut knees, although today other antiseptics are more commonly employed.

The human body requires a minute amount of iodine, which is used to produce thyroid hormones essential to physical and mental development. Normally a small but sufficient amount of iodine is ingested in the food we eat, but there are some regions, such as parts of the midwestern United States and certain Alpine areas of Europe, that are devoid of this element. Lack of iodine can lead to goiter, an enlargement of the thyroid gland and neck. To prevent iodine deficiency, table salt is routinely sold as a combination of sodium chloride (NaCl) and sodium iodide (NaI).

Iodine is essential for the proper functioning of the thyroid gland. Although most Americans obtain their daily requirement of iodine through the food they eat, the element is still routinely added to table salt as a precaution.

Little is known about the halogen astatine—a short-lived, radioactive element with properties similar to those of iodine. Astatine was first synthesized in 1940 by researchers using a cyclotron (above) at the University of California, Berkeley.

ASTATINE

The last of the halogens is also the rarest. The name of this element, astatine, comes from a Greek word meaning "unstable," and astatine is nothing if not unstable. Very small amounts of this radioactive element occur in nature in combination with other radioactive elements. For all practical purposes, however, it must be synthesized artificially in order to study its properties. This was done for the first time in 1940 by Dale R. Corson, K. R. MacKenzie, and Emilio Segrè, using the cyclotron at the University of California, Berkeley. The trio used the accelerator to bombard bismuth with alpha particles in order to produce astatine. Astatine has a half-life of only eight hours, and investigators have been able to form only a few compounds with astatine.

Astatine is the heaviest halogen. It has a total of six electron shells, with 2, 8, 18, 32, 18, and 7 electrons, as one moves from the innermost to the outermost orbit. Although astatine is little-known compared with the other halogens, it seems to resemble iodine, its close cousin. There are, of course, no real industrial applications for this fleeting, hard-to-handle element.

HYDROGEN: A HALOGEN WANNA-BE?

If you pick up an older chemistry textbook, you might find the element hydrogen grouped with the halogen family. In some versions of the periodic table, hydrogen appears above fluorine at the top of column VIIA. Other books, meanwhile, show a periodic table with hydrogen placed at the top of column IA, all the way over on the left. Still other books show hydrogen twice, once in column IA and again in column VIIA.

This confusion stems from the nature of hydrogen, which has properties of both column IA and VIIA elements. Hydrogen has only one electron shell and only one electron in orbit. The stable arrangement for an element with only one shell is two electrons (rather than eight), so hydrogen attempts to gain an extra electron, just like the halogens. On the other hand, hydrogen combines with atoms of other elements in the same ratio as lighter elements in column IA, such as lithium, sodium, and potassium. These elements, known as the alkali metals, all have one electron in their outermost electron shell—but none have only one shell. Some periodic tables set hydrogen apart entirely, recognizing that the element is unique. The ambiguity of hydrogen was recognized early on: in 1869, Dimitri Mendeleyev, the father of the periodic table, placed hydrogen on its own in his outline of relationships among the elements.

The Ties That  ind

by P. J. Skerrett

Boy Scouts fumbling their way through a big square knot don't imagine it exists. Nor do surgeons tying off a tiny stitch on a blood vessel. Even old salts whipping up a Round Turn Spilled-Hitch Bowline are unlikely to suspect they're also exploring a once-obscure but increasingly important branch of mathematics. Lurking inside the crisscross pattern that forms a knot is a complex theory that has puzzled and challenged mathematicians for more than 100 years.

TIP OF THE "KNOT-BERG"

Thanks to several unexpected connections, knot theory is now emerging as a powerful tool for solving a broad array of practical problems. It explains how tightly coiled DNA manages to replicate inside cells. And it's helping to define the very structure of space. Knot theory is aiding the search for effective antibacterial and anticancer drugs, and it may make computer networks more reliable and efficient.

These applications represent just the tip of the "knot-berg." As more scientists struggle to understand this intricate theory and knot theorists turn their attention to real-world problems, practical applications will likely mushroom. That's not a bad turnabout for a branch of mathematics once derided as recreational doodling for terminally bored topologists.

Weavers, fishermen, and sailors have depended on knots for thousands of years; mountain climbers and surgical patients stake their lives on them. Knots appear in artwork and religious ceremonies around the world. Hundreds of different knots have evolved, from the simple overhand to the showy combinations used by macramé artists. The *theory* of knots, by comparison, is a relative newcomer, originating in the 1860s as a perfectly practical offshoot of chemistry.

Dissatisfied with the then-current theory of atoms as hard spheres held together by mysterious forces, William Thomson (who became Lord Kelvin) guessed that atoms might be "knotted vortices in the ether." He imagined these vortices, or elongated whirlpools, bonding together by forming tiny knots. Scottish chemist Peter Tait started cataloging knots, and ultimately created a crude periodic table, classifying them by the number of times their strands crossed. Tait and assorted colleagues spent years on this project, and the mathematical relationships they discovered gave birth to a new field.

WHAT'S A KNOT?

In the real world of neckties and bakery boxes, knots are simple devices for securing a rope to itself or to something else. In the writings

The theory of knots—once the exclusive province of sailors, weavers, and Boy Scouts—is now a hot topic in the halls of science, with important implications for medicine, chemistry, mathematics, and other disciplines.

Mountain climbers often stake their lives on the quality of their knots. More advanced applications of knot theory may also save lives—and help scientists decipher the complex nature of the universe.

of the scientist-futurist Buckminster Fuller, knots physically store information by capturing (or tracing) the trajectory of two rope-holding hands. Mathematicians, as is their habit, see knots more formally: one-dimensional curves sitting in three-dimensional space that begin and end at the same point and never intersect themselves. That means that linked rings (in fact, any rings), such as those in the Olympic insignia, are knots. It also means that the bows we tie on our shoes, or the hopelessly snarled ball of fishing line in the bottom of the boat, aren't really knots.

"If a knotted string has loose ends, it's really not a knot, since you can always slide a free end around and eventually, if you have the time and patience, get back to a nice untangled line," explains De Witt Sumners, a mathematician with Florida State University in Tallahassee. To make a knot that would satisfy Sumners and other mathematicians, take an electrical extension cord—or string of pearls if you're feeling extravagant—tie a simple overhand knot, then plug or clasp the free ends together.

Given the no-free-ends rule, the simplest knot is a circle, sometimes called the "unknot" or trivial knot. A trefoil has three crossings of the rope, pearls, or extension cord. The trefoil comes in two "flavors,"

right-handed and left-handed. No amount of twisting or sliding can transform one into the other. Only one knot has four crossings, the familiar square knot and its mirror image, the granny knot. From there, the number of knots in a group grows exponentially—there are seven knots with seven crossings, 21 with eight crossings, 49 with nine crossings. The most complete table to date contains 12,965 knots with 13 or fewer crossings, not counting mirror images.

Mathematicians, following their instincts to ferret out patterns that occur in nature, look for some common rules that will let them label a knot, determine whether something is really knotted, or tell whether two dissimilar-looking knots are in reality the same. Trivial problems? Think again. It took almost 100 years to prove that two different-looking knots with 10 crossings listed in Tait's periodic table were, in fact, the same. This difficulty arises because a single knot can be twisted and rearranged into what looks like different shapes, yet by the rules of topology, it remains the same as long as it isn't cut.

The Same Knot

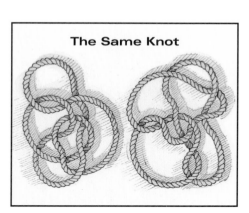

The rules for classifying knots can be tricky. Scientists labored almost 100 years to prove that two dissimilar-looking knots (above) are the same.

The Periodic Table of Knots

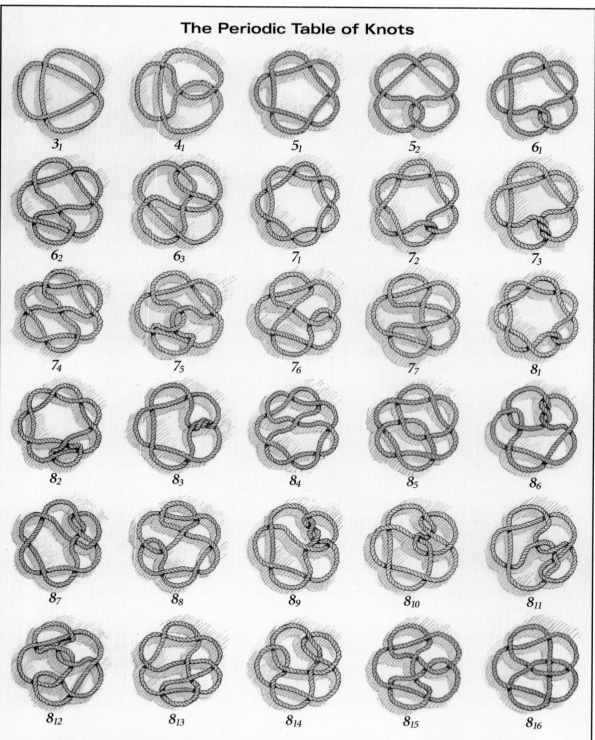

Knots are identified by the number of crossings they contain. For each knot above, the top number denotes the number of crossings, while the subscript designates which knot it is in that series. The table contains all possible knots from three to seven crossings and 16 of the 21 knots with eight crossings.

STOP-AND-GO SIGNALS

For several years, mathematicians searched for a universal number or formula that could uniquely define different knots. A breakthrough came in 1984. New Zealand-born mathematician Vaughan Jones discovered a powerful method for labeling knots. Much to everyone's surprise, his startling new approach shared equations with quantum physics and statistical mechanics, the study of systems with a massive number of components.

"The discovery that Jones made linking statistical mechanics and knot invariants [formulas that describe knots] immediately got people wondering how close this relationship was, and where else it might lead," says mathematician Louis Kauffman of the University of Illinois at Chicago. Kauffman is widely credited with exploring this connection and stimulating others to investigate the link between knot theory and the physical sciences. By the time Jones was awarded a Fields Medal—the mathematics equivalent of a Nobel Prize—for his work in 1990, knot theory had become a vital tool in biology, and its applications were rippling through physics, chemistry, and engineering.

Perhaps knot theory's most dazzling, or at least its most practical, application to date is in molecular biology. The DNA inside cells, it turns out, naturally kinks up into knots, loops, and links. These pose serious problems for the enzymes that copy DNA or translate its genetic information, because they work only on flat, untwisted sections.

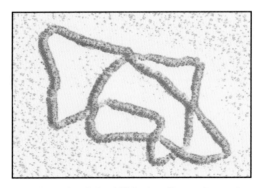

Knot theory has helped biologists discern the mechanisms of DNA. The study of enzymes that twist and knot DNA has yielded anticancer drugs that disrupt the propagation of tumor cells.

On the other hand, knots and kinks may provide crucial topological stop-and-go signals for these enzymes.

"Knot theory is really the next chapter of the DNA story," now that DNA's structure and chemistry are fairly well understood, suggests mathematician Avner Friedman at the

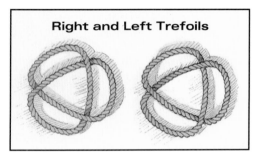

Right and Left Trefoils

All knots, like people, are either right- or left-handed. In chemistry, such handedness, called chirality, can give otherwise-identical compounds different properties.

University of Minnesota in Minneapolis. DNA, or deoxyribonucleic acid, is an extraordinarily long, ladder-shaped molecule that carries the entire genetic code for making and operating a bacterium, a beech tree, or a baby.

Actually, *long* is an understatement. If a muscle cell's nucleus were the size of a basketball, then the DNA packed inside would be as thin as a fisherman's monofilament line, and would stretch about 125 miles (200 kilometers). Cramming that much DNA into a tiny space requires some regular method of compression, and living organisms have adopted supercoiling. This is what happens when you repeatedly twist the ends of a rubber band in opposite directions. Cells also wrap sections of DNA around tiny globular proteins. In addition to making DNA more compact, this wrapping also knots it up, just as wrapping a perfectly untangled garden hose around a circular storage rim causes kinks and twists to form in the hose still lying on the grass.

POETIC SUPERCOILS

Biologists have discovered several proteins whose job in life is twisting, knotting, and unknotting DNA. Called topoisomerases, these enzymes act like molecular fingers that tie and untie strands of genetic material. Knot theory has been invaluable in helping unravel the mechanism by which topoisomerases work. It's impossible to watch them in action inside a cell or in a test tube. But when you know the DNA's starting configuration and what it looks like after a topoisomerase does its job, then basic knot theory "lets you deduce the enzyme's reaction mechanism," says De Witt Sumners of Florida State.

Gyrase, a poetically named topoisomerase, helps twist the DNA double helix into a supercoil. Another class untwists supercoiled DNA, opening the way for yet other enzymes to read or copy the genetic message stored in a particular stretch of the molecule. Still other topoisomerases knot and unknot DNA by snipping open a section of double helix, sliding a nearby section through the break, and resealing the cut. University of California, Berkeley, biologist Nicholas Cozzarelli calls this "incorporealizing the DNA"—making it act for an instant as if it had no body and, like a ghost, could pass through solid DNA strands.

Computer simulations carried out at the Courant Institute of Mathematical Sciences in New York City show that small pieces of DNA probably coil up and form simple knots like the two-ringed figure eight even in the absence of any proteins. This writhing, slithering, and twisting—all precisely defined mathematical terms—may create knots or bulges that act as road maps for proteins.

This new picture of DNA has led to the discovery of powerful drugs that stop bacteria from multiplying inside our bodies, and kill cancer cells before they divide out of control. Basically, these new drugs turn a cell's unknotting enzymes against its own DNA. Ciprofloxacin, one of the most effective and widely prescribed antibacterial drugs, allows

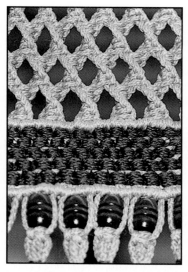

Knots have appeared in the arts since medieval times. Macramé, an art form developed in the Middle East, is made of cords tied into various knots. The medium has enjoyed a modest revival.

one kind of topoisomerase in the invading bacteria to untwist DNA and snip it open. But then the drug blocks the enzyme from resealing these breaks. When the bacterial cells divide, they split into daughter cells with deadly, nonfunctioning DNA. And since the drug doesn't target human topoisomerases, only the bacterial cells are affected. Several anticancer drugs use essentially the same strategy, acting only on cells that divide rapidly, such as tumor cells.

QUANTUM KNOTS

Biology isn't the only field enriched by knot theory. Physicists are using it to develop a long-sought theory of gravity that works on both the galactic and subatomic scales. Einstein's general theory of relativity explains gravity in the visible world—the attraction between a boulder and Earth, or how stars influence the movement of planets. But his equations don't work at the tiny, unseen distances between atoms and the basic building blocks of matter. Here the mathematics of quantum mechanics must be used to explain particle interactions.

A team of scientists thinks that knot theory may help tie general relativity and quantum mechanics into a unified theory of quantum gravity. Their work also gives new meaning to the term "fabric of space." In 1988, physicists Carlo Rovelli and Lee Smolin noticed that a new translation of Einstein's equations by physicist Abhay Ashtekar bore an uncanny resemblance to equations from knot theory. Rovelli suggested melding Ashtekar's equations with different knot polynomials—equations that describe various knots. The combination clicked, especially for the class of knots called links, open circles connected to each other.

These hybrid-knot equations appear to explain gravity at all distances. They also point to a physical model of space that could resemble The Weave, something Rovelli built using hundreds of key rings, each attached to several neighboring rings. If Rovelli and his associates are right, space looks like three-dimensional chain mail.

The loop model even describes gravity graphically. When two bodies approach each other, they may increase the number of links in space, or the loops may link up with a greater number of neighbors, says Rovelli.

KNOT CHEMISTRY

Chemistry also has its knot theorists. In 1989, French chemists synthesized the first knotted compound ever made, a 124-atom molecule shaped like a trefoil. More knotted molecules are in the works. Chemist David Walba of the University of Colorado in Boulder uses a Möbius-strip molecule—a circle with one or more half twists—made from carbon and oxygen as the starting point for pretzel-shaped trefoils, square knots, and more-complex chemical arrangements. Why bother? Partly because of the challenge, explains Walba. "Bucky-balls were first made just because of their cool geometry. Now they're appearing in all sorts of useful applications. By tackling targets that are impossible to make, we develop new synthetic pathways and elements."

The rope hitches that for centuries were used to rig sailing ships did much to inspire modern knot theory. Researchers in this fast-growing field are applying advanced mathematical tools to unravel a new generation of scientific mysteries.

Knots also share the property of chirality, or handedness, with many natural and artificial compounds. Handedness plays a crucial role in chemical activity. Right- and left-handed thalidomide, for example, share identical chemical formulas and structures. But left-handed thalidomide acts as a powerful tranquilizer, while its right-handed twin severely disrupts fetal development. This sinister difference wasn't discovered until long after pregnant women who took thalidomide in the 1950s bore children with severe birth defects. Elements

of knot theory used to distinguish mirror-image knots may someday help chemists do the same with newly synthesized molecules, says mathematician Kenneth Millett at the University of California, Santa Barbara.

Even computer science is benefiting from a dash of knot theory. Until recently, programmers found it nearly impossible to predict how fast, or even if, a computer could solve a particularly complex problem. U.C., Berkeley, mathematician and Fields Medal winner Steve Smale borrowed a page from braid theory, one of knot theory's close cousins, to devise a solution. Essentially, he found that the more "if-then" statements a program requires, the more tangled its braids, and the longer the computations must run.

EVOLVING FIELD

Even as it is applied to an ever-expanding number of problems, knot theory is evolving at a rapid clip. This is partly due to the field's reinvigoration by Vaughan Jones and those he has inspired. It is also due to mathematical tools imported from the very fields where knot theory is now being applied. The new polynomials and elegant solutions for knot, braid, and tangle problems may be put to work in as-yet-undreamed applications.

That's not to imply that knot theorists always keep an eye on practical problems. In fact, perhaps the bulk of knot-theory research is performed with no real application in mind. John Sullivan at the University of Minnesota's Geometry Center, for example, wants to know what happens when you distribute a negative charge evenly around a computer-drawn knot. "I can't imagine what practical use this might have," he says. "But mathematicians have great faith that if you find something that exhibits really interesting patterns, it will eventually have some application."

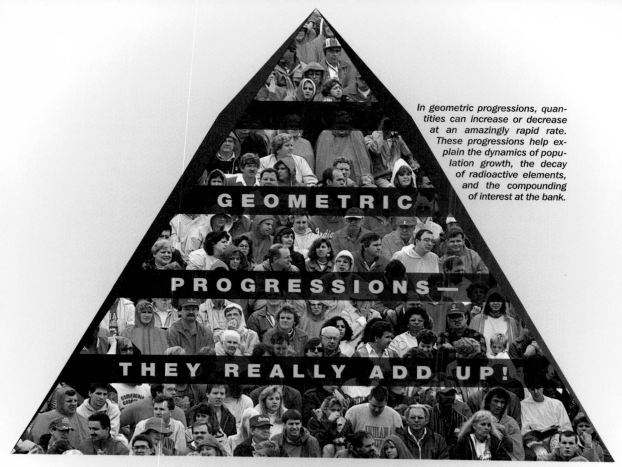

In geometric progressions, quantities can increase or decrease at an amazingly rapid rate. These progressions help explain the dynamics of population growth, the decay of radioactive elements, and the compounding of interest at the bank.

by David A. Pendlebury

Growth can be fast or growth can be slow, but there is one type of growth so powerful that it seems like magic. Mathematicians call this kind of growth geometric progression. The mathematician John Allen Paulos recently described a vivid example of geometric progression: "If 2 cents are placed on the first square of a checkerboard, 4 cents on the second, 8 cents on the third, and so on, the last square will have almost $200 million billion on it." He contrasts this accumulation of wealth with a type of growth called arithmetic progression. In this series, 2 cents are placed on the first square, 4 cents on the second, 6 cents on the third, and so on until one reaches the last square—on which sits a mere $1.28.

An arithmetic, or linear, progression adds a set amount to the preceding sum in the series. In the latter example above, a constant amount—2 cents—is added to the amount in the previous square (2, 2+2=4, 4+2=6, 6+2=8, 8+2=10, 10+2=12, …). In a geometric,

or exponential, progression, on the other hand, each number in the series is multiplied by a constant factor. To obtain the next number in the checkerboard series, the preceding amount is multiplied by 2 (2, 2x2=4, 4x2=8, 8x2=16, 16x2=32, 32x2=64, …). The difference between geometric and arithmetic progressions is amazing, and the longer the series, the more astounding the difference becomes.

AN INTERESTING EXAMPLE

The most common encounter that most of us will have with a geometric progression is at the bank. Nowadays banks and other financial institutions pay compound interest for the use of money. In the past, some banks paid what was called simple interest. The relationship between simple and compound interest mirrors the differences between an arithmetic and a geometric progression.

Over time, these differences become more dramatic. If, for example, you deposited $1,000 at a bank and received simple interest, the bank would pay you a set percent, say 6 percent each year, on your money. That would translate into $60 in interest payments each year, and, after 10 years, you would have earned $600. If, however, you were paid compound interest at the same rate, your interest payments would grow larger every year. You would receive $60 at the end of the first year, $63.60 at the end of the second year, $67.42 at the end of the third year, and so on. After 10 years, you would have received $790.85—nearly $200 more than in the simple-interest method. In the second case, the last amount in the series is *multiplied* by a certain factor (6 percent), whereas in the first case, a set amount (6 percent of the initial deposit) is *added* to the last amount in the series.

COMPOUNDING WEALTH

Compounding has played a key role in the financial career of superstar investor Warren Buffett of Omaha, Nebraska. Buffett, one of the richest people in the United States, amassed a fortune of several billion dollars over a 40-year period. Buffett takes advantage of the magic of compounding by attempting to buy and then hold stocks for long periods, rather than frequently buying and selling shares. This method can be superior to frequent trading, since Buffett avoids paying tax on the profits, or capital gains, realized on his investment. Robert G. Hagstrom, Jr., who has written about Buffett's career, sums up the reasoning behind Buffett's approach. "Because of the tax on capital gains, Buffett figures that his buy-and-hold strategy has a financial advantage over investment approaches that emphasize short-term trading." To explain, he asks us to imagine what happens if we buy a $1 investment that doubles in price each year. If we sell the investment at the end of the first year, we would have a net gain of 66 cents (assuming we are in a 34 percent tax bracket). If the investment continues to double each year, we continue to sell, pay the tax, and reinvest the proceeds. At the end of 20 years, we would gain $25,200 after paying taxes of $13,000. If, on the other hand, we purchased a $1 investment that doubled each year and was not sold until the end of 20 years, we would gain $692,000 after paying taxes of approximately $356,000.

Warren Buffett is universally acknowledged to be a financial genius, but this sophisticated investor enjoys illustrating the power of numbers. Some 30 years ago, Buffett described to investors the miracle of compound interest. He recalled the Native American sale of the island of Manhattan in 1626 to Dutch settler Peter Minuit for the equivalent of $24. Buffett figured that the island contained about 620 million square feet (58 million square meters). He then assumed that the land value (in 1965) would bring the current value of the land, when fully rented, to about $12.5 billion. "To the novice," Buffett noted, "perhaps this seems like a decent deal. However, the Indians have only had to achieve a 6.5 percent return . . . to obtain the last laugh on Minuit. At 6.5 percent, $24 becomes more than $42 billion in 338 years, and if they just managed to squeeze out an extra half point to get to 7 percent, the present value becomes $205 billion."

SCIENTIFIC GROWTH

There are many other real-world examples of geometric growth. The field of science, for example, has exponentially grown during the past few centuries. Science historian Derek J. de Solla Price observed in 1963 that "many numerical indicators of various fields and aspects of science [show that the] normal mode of growth is exponential. That is to say, science grows at compound interest, multiplying by some fixed amount in equal periods of time."

If the Native Americans who sold Manhattan for $24 in 1626 had parlayed that sum into investments earning 7 percent compound interest, they could have made $200 billion by now.

Price showed that the number of scientists and scientific publications has doubled every 10 to 15 years since the early 1700s. He went on to observe how this rate of expansion "agrees with the common natural law of growth governing the number of human beings in the population of the world of a particular country, the number of fruit flies growing in a colony in a bottle, or the number of miles of railroad built in the early industrial revolution." Price knew, however, that the geometric growth in the number of scientists could not continue, noting that if such growth were to continue, "we should have two scientists for every man, woman, and dog in the population."

A GROWING PROBLEM?

Price mentions that populations—whether human or insect—tend to grow geometrically. This is an observation that British economist and cleric Thomas Malthus brought to the attention of the general public in 1798 in his famous *Essay on the Principle of Population, As It Affects the Future Improvement of Society*. Pointing out that the human population grows geometrically, whereas the production of food increases only arithmetically, he described a potentially calamitous condition.

Studies show that the length of quotations from politicians seen on television is decreasing exponentially. While these quotes may continue shrinking, the laws of geometric decline dictate that they will never disappear altogether.

Malthus saw famine, poverty, disease, and war as inevitable consequences of the increase in population outpacing the increase in the food supply. Several developments not foreseen by Malthus—such as improved food-production technology—have fortunately allowed us to avoid the dire "worst-case" circumstances he envisioned. The incomplete fulfillment of Malthus' predictions also illustrates a common characteristic of most geometric progressions: they cannot go on forever.

The common chain letter is a case in point. Suppose that someone begins a chain letter and sends it to 10 friends. Each of these friends must mail it to 10 of their friends to keep the letter going and to avoid breaking the chain. Each of the recipients must in turn send the letter to 10 of their friends, who must continue the cycle themselves. Let us also suppose that no one can participate more than once. After the eighth step in this progression, more than one of every three people in the United States would have already played the game. The 10th sequence in the chain would break down for lack of anyone left on Earth to play the game.

SOME THINGS DON'T ADD UP

Not all geometric progressions increase: some series exhibit an exponential decline. Radioactive decay, for example, illustrates a negative geometric progression. (A radioactive element's half-life measures how long it takes for one-half of its radioactivity to dissipate.) Similarly, the cost of computing power, measured in dollars per unit of performance, has declined exponentially over the past two decades.

One amusing case of exponential decline, noted by *The Economist* magazine in 1992, concerns the length of quotations, or sound bites, from U.S. presidential candidates broadcast by television and radio stations. In 1968, the average sound bite of a candidate's speech lasted 45 seconds. In 1984, it was down to 15 seconds. And in 1988, the quotes averaged just 9.8 seconds. With these data in hand, the magazine fancifully predicted that "at that rate they will have disappeared altogether before the election in 2000." But with all decreasing exponential progressions, a zero value—a place where radioactive elements disappear altogether, and sound bites do not exist—can never be reached.

PHYSICS

ON THE FAIRWAY

by Donna Hood Crecca

Frank Thomas has a way of teeing off the world of golf. As the technical director of the United States Golf Association (USGA), Thomas helps set the standards for golf clubs and balls. His work has earned him more than one instance of character assassination, and he has been named in multi-million-dollar lawsuits by manufacturers enraged at his rejection of new club designs.

Undaunted, Thomas once again raised the ire of manufacturers when he told the attendees of the Second World Scientific Congress of Golf at St. Andrews, Scotland, during the summer of 1994 that the billions spent each year on research and development are all for naught: golfers have improved very little over the past 25 years. In fact, Thomas told the throng of academics and golf-industry representatives, the driving distances of the best professional players have increased only 12 yards (11 meters) since 1968, and the average winning score has fallen one stroke per round per 21 years. Apparently, the marketing hype about improved swings and lower scores has little basis in fact.

But, as the soft-spoken South African native is wont to do, Thomas followed this embarrassing proclamation with an olive branch of sorts. During the course of the congress, a team of researchers from the USGA presented six technical papers, the results of the first phase of an ongoing research project

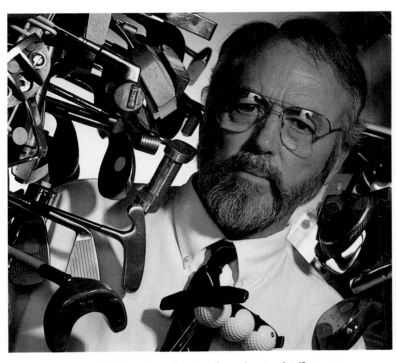

Modern science has transformed pastoral golf courses into decidedly high-tech proving grounds. At the fore of such work, Frank Thomas (above) and colleagues at the U.S. Golf Association (USGA) are applying rigorous scientific methods to analyze the 400-year-old game.

to explain in scientific terms what happens from the moment the golfer picks up the club until the ball drops into the cup, hopefully in par or less. Any anger at Thomas' keynote address faded as equipment designers seized upon the mathematical models and biomechanics research presented by the USGA team. For within these initial findings lies the future of a 400-year-old game played by millions and yet understood by few.

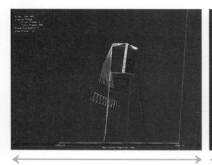 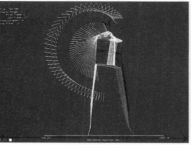 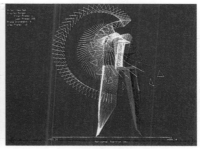

"There's been a tremendous amount of trial and error in product development, but science has not really entered the game yet," says Thomas. "Yes, golf-ball design has become highly sophisticated, and scientific principles have been applied, but not so much to the golf club," he adds.

Thomas was among the coordinators of the First World Scientific Congress of Golf, held in 1991 to examine the applications of science and technology to the game. "There's been a lot of educated guesses based on historical performance data," explains Thomas, "but no one really knew what was happening when a club struck a ball. At the USGA, we had been fidgeting on the edge of real scientific research for years, and we finally applied everything we could to understanding the game."

SCIENCE IN THE NAME OF FUN

Since 1993, the USGA's scientists have worked furiously at the organization's headquarters in sleepy Far Hills, New Jersey, using state-of-the-art technology to understand the forces involved when a golf club collides with a golf ball, an event that takes 500 millionths of a second and is the definitive point of the entire game. The USGA team's findings may serve to alleviate at least some of the frustration of the more than 26 million duffers who spend hours on golf courses each weekend, whacking dimpled spheroids, all in the name of fun and relaxation.

The research program is Thomas' pet project, and it satisfies his scientific curiosity about the game he has devoted his life to playing and preserving. A mechanical engineer specializing in composites and structures, Thomas joined the USGA in 1974,

having already revolutionized the game by designing golf clubs with shafts that took advantage of the lightweight, durable graphite that the aerospace industry was also putting to extensive use.

As technical director of the USGA, Thomas runs thousands of golf balls through a series of exhaustive tests, and examines as many new club designs each year, to determine if they conform to the USGA's standards. Thomas is charged, as he puts it, "with preserving the challenge of the game by preventing manufacturers from introducing clubs and balls that reduce the skill required to play."

While he has certainly succeeded in that endeavor, to the chagrin of some manufacturers, he has also transformed the USGA into the leading golf-research facility.

Thomas secured $2 million in funding from the USGA in 1991 to expand its Research and Test Center to include new lab space, equipment, and personnel. In his large corner office overlooking the bucolic grounds of the USGA headquarters, the otherwise reserved 55-year-old Thomas shifts into high gear when asked about the research program. "I've divided the game into five areas," he says, springing up from his chair and moving to a blackboard, on which he begins sketching crude figures.

The first is a stick figure. "There's the human factor—we're looking into biomechanics and trying to define this guy, even consider his emotions. Next is the golf-club shaft, and trying to determine the forces on it, the vibrations, the energy involved, and how that energy is transferred," he says, sketching a shaft. Next to it, he draws a club head. "What's its mass? What are the inertial properties at the

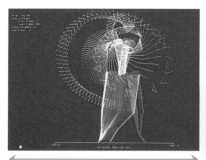

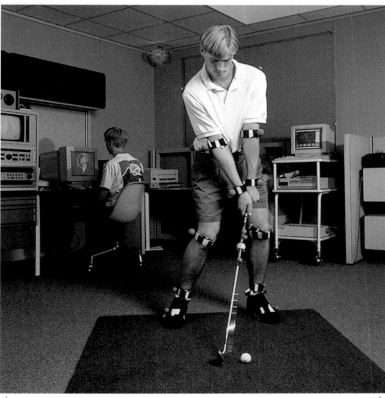

In the USGA's biomechanics laboratory, researchers are beginning to unravel the complicated physical forces involved in swinging a golf club. The lab is equipped with infrared cameras that track markers attached to a volunteer's body, clothing, and club (below). Information regarding the golfer's movements are then fed into a computer that can display and analyze every facet of the subject's swing (sequence beginning at far left).

point of impact with the ball? No one has really been able to explain that."

Sketching a club as it meets a golf ball, Thomas reaches a fevered pitch in his delivery. "What's the twist of the club head at impact? What effect does changing the location of the club's mass have on the moment of inertia? Where is the center of gravity?" Moving on, he draws a sphere with lines behind it to indicate movement—a golf ball in flight. "We wanted to measure the ball's lift, drag, and other properties and their contribution to distance. We wanted to look at all of this and try to explain it."

But hasn't this all been explained? Haven't equipment manufacturers poured billions into the research and development of clubs that hit longer and straighter, and balls that fly longer and straighter? Well, yes and no, according to the ever-diplomatic Thomas. "It has not been pure research as much as product development, and that has not explained the entire process of the swing and all the forces involved." At least, not to Thomas' satisfaction.

ENGINEERING A BETTER SWING

To do that, he assembled a group of accomplished scientists and eager graduate students and commissioned them to explain his favorite pastime. Among them is Stanley Johnson, professor of mechanical engineering and mechanics at Lehigh University, Bethlehem, Pennsylvania, who, along with Lehigh graduate student Alexia Brylawski, investigated the effect of shaft flexibility on club-face positioning at the moment of impact. Johnson joined with longtime USGA consultant Burton Lieberman of Brooklyn Polytechnic University in New York to develop a mathematical model of the moment of impact, and of the ball's trajectory, or flight path.

Through those models, they were able to describe why a golf ball flies as it does. While a golf swing may seem like a simple movement, it is actually quite complex, and the smallest variable can send a ball into a sand trap, or worse. As a golfer swings, the club

A Triumph of Design

According to the laws of aerodynamics, a smooth surface provides the least wind resistance. It stands to reason, then, that a smooth-surfaced ball would fly faster and farther through the air than one with a rough surface. If that were true, golf balls would cost a dime a dozen.

But with aerodynamic properties similar to those of the wing of an airplane, golf balls are perhaps the most complex spheroids in sports today. A golf ball's performance is largely determined by its dimple pattern, a feature that was developed through astute observation and has evolved over time.

Early golf balls were made of wood. Seeking a softer feel, the Scottish founders of the game stuffed leather pouches with boiled feathers. Hard rubber balls came into the game about 1848. When players noticed that nicks on the surface of the smooth balls caused them to fly farther, ball makers began to mold them with indented or raised surface patterns.

IT'S THE DIMPLES

With the introduction of the wound ball at the turn of the century, dimples became a part of the construction. In the 1950s, the average number of dimples was 336. Today balls can have as many as 500 dimples covering more than 70 percent of the surface.

Dimple patterns work with the ball's spin to move the ball through the air. The backspin on the ball is determined by its construction and the club-head angle—its degree of loft—and is a crucial contributing factor to the ball's trajectory, or flight pattern. As the ball is spinning backward, the dimples create a turbulence pattern in front of the ball, and a drag tail that generates an airflow much like that of an airplane wing. The air pressure is higher on

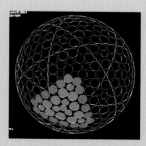

Designers maximize a golf ball's flight performance by geometrically arranging as many as 500 tiny dimples on the ball's surface.

the bottom of the ball and lower on the top, thus creating an upward lifting force.

Dimples are, in essence, one of humanity's attempts to manage air. A ball with no dimples will travel 130 yards (119 meters) and behave much like a bullet, with a straight trajectory. A dimpled ball, on the other hand, can travel 280 yards (256 meters), rising through the air because of its lift.

BUILDING A BIGGER BALL

Designers have become obsessed with fitting more and more of these impressions on the spheroids. Ball designers at Spalding in Chicopee, Massachusetts, found that one way to fit more dimples was to increase the surface area. Because the USGA has a standard that balls can be no smaller than 1.68 inches (4.27 centimeters) in diameter, but no restriction on how large a ball can be, the solution was obvious: make a bigger ball.

Most oversize balls measure 1.72 or 1.74 inches (4.37 to 4.41 centimeters) in diameter, but that minute expansion presents yet another contradiction to the accepted laws of aerodynamics—a larger mass moves through the air more slowly—and a debate has ensued over claims of increased distance made by manufacturers of oversize balls. Terry Melvin, vice president of research at Spalding, contends that the increased drag created by the larger ball is compensated for by the increased number of dimples on its surface. On the other hand, Wilson's Carl Scheie says that larger balls provide no advantage, but rather, have greater air resistance.

Frank Thomas, technical director of the USGA, says only that hard-hitting hackers may get more distance from an oversize ball. Marketing claims aside, he considers it a breakthrough in design that manufacturers have created a larger golf ball that performs much like a traditional one.

twists and gains speed during the down-swing, so the face of the club is angled as it strikes the ball. That angle gives the ball its lift and, along with the ball's aerodynamic properties, helps determine its trajectory.

The other determining factor is whether the weight center, or the "sweet spot," of the club strikes the ball, or if the hit is off-center. Also, because the club shaft is not perfectly perpendicular to the head, the head twists further as it strikes the ball, thus diminishing the probability that the sweet spot will be the point of impact.

Manufacturers have experiment-ed with club design, enlarging the sweet spot and introducing perime-ter weighting designed to lessen the twist at impact and give the golfer more opportunity to hit from the center. For the most part, says Thomas, these innovations have been reached through trial and error, using computer-aided design (CAD) systems. Johnson, however, has developed a model of an inertia ellipsoid—a dimensional diagram of ellipses that describes exactly how the club head rotates at impact and where the center of gravity is as the ball and club collide.

"We can create a mathematical simulation of the downswing and impact, and understand how the club twists and why one club per-forms differently from another," says Johnson. "From that, we create a computerized ellipsoid represen-tation of the club as it twists. What's next is for us to determine what is a good ellipsoid—one that results in a square hit—and what is a bad ellipsoid."

"Designers have been on the outskirts of this for some time," adds Thomas. "Now they can plug the inertia measurement into a CAD system and use it to design a new club head."

Lieberman developed a computer model of a golf ball's trajectory, taking into consid-eration a variety of launch conditions, some of which may seem like petty issues, but which are of concern to the devoted golfer. For instance, grass was traditionally thought to interfere with a ball's launch and slow its release from the club head. Lieberman found, however, that when grass comes between the ball and club face, it is actually slippery enough to assist the ball's launch. "This is something that was not part of the rules of aerodynamics," he says.

Golf-equipment manufacturers have spent billions of dollars trying to develop and market improved clubs and balls. Amazingly, studies indicate that scores have changed very little during the past 25 years.

FREQUENT FLIERS

But the downswing and moment of impact were only part of the picture. Lex Smits of Princeton University in New Jersey worked with Princeton Ph.D. candidate Mark Zagaro-la to further define the aerodynamic proper-ties of a golf ball in flight, using a new testing system. "In the past, wind tunnels had been used, which require that the ball be held in a laminar, or smooth, airflow, which is very dif-ficult to do, and the measurements are only 5 or 6 percent accurate," Thomas explains. Smits and Zagarola designed an Indoor Testing

Range (ITR), the first of its kind, at the USGA. Thomas predicts the range will make wind tunnels obsolete. "With the ITR, we can actually shoot the ball and control everything, so the measurements of spin rate and velocity are much more accurate," he says. Those properties are practically an obsession with golf-ball designers, so access to the ITR is being sought by several ball manufacturers.

Located in the bowels of the Research and Test Center, the ITR is a sprawling contraption taking up the length of a room, and is surrounded by safety nets. At one end is the launching machine, which includes four 25-inch (64-centimeter) wheels arranged in a square. The upper and lower pair each share a belt and are driven in opposite directions. At Thomas' request, Zagarola shouts "clear," and shoots a marked golf ball out of a pressure-driven air gun. The belts grip the ball as it passes through them, imparting its spin as well as its velocity: 238 feet (73 meters) per second. The ball travels 70 feet (21 meters), passing through three stations, at which it breaks light screens similar to the ballistic screens used to measure a bullet's velocity and position. The markings are read by the light screens, and the ball's positioning at each station is fed immediately into a computer that models its performance under a variety of circumstances.

"We can determine the lift and drag properties, and predict how far this ball will go on the fairway," says Thomas. "By taking these measurements once, we can predict how the ball will fly under any variety of launch conditions. No one in the industry can do that."

When Zagarola presented a paper on the ITR at the World Scientific Congress of Golf, ball designers were ecstatic. "Everyone has been trying to model a golf ball's flight," says Terry Melvin, vice president of research at Spalding, the Massachusetts-based maker of the Top Flite line of golf balls. "What they're doing is so important in terms of understanding what's going on."

THE ANDROID GOLFER

But the paper that galvanized the meeting in Scotland was presented by Steve Nesbit, a mechanical engineer who specializes in robotics at Lafayette College in Easton, Pennsylvania. Nesbit has spent two years in the USGA's biomechanics lab, inviting volunteers in to swing a club for the betterment of the game. Entering the lab, Thomas can hardly contain himself, and he beams as Nesbit explains his project.

"What we're studying here is kinematics, specifically the kinematics of the golfer as he swings," says Nesbit, referring to the dynamic study of motion. Subjects in Nesbit's project are fitted with 28 markers attached by Velcro to their clothing. Markers are also attached to the club shaft and head. The golfer stands on a patch of indoor turf, addresses a ball on a tee, and swings, driving the ball into a curtain against the back wall. Four infrared cameras mounted in the corners of the room record every movement by tracking the 28 markers, and they feed that information to a computer that develops a model of the golfer's swing in motion.

While biomechanical studies of athletes are nothing new—skiers, swimmers, runners, and golfers have long been the subjects of such analysis—the USGA has taken it to a new level by creating an android golfer. Nesbit uses the model to drive the android, which replicates a golfer's motions on the computer screen, revealing every twist of the golfer's body and the club throughout the swing. Nesbit's work brings together the research undertaken by the rest of the USGA team by attempting to define the most mysterious factor of all: the human.

"We can stop the computer android at any point and see where the golfer's body is and where the club is," he explains. Drawing on Johnson and Lieberman's models, Nesbit can analyze a golfer's swing and various aspects of the club. "This helps us understand the forces involved: How fast does the club accelerate? What's the torque on the club as the swing comes down? We then can determine what will happen if we change these things, and work with the golfer to see how the alterations feel."

THE PROMISE OF PERFORMANCE?

While the implications of the biomechanics study are obvious—the Professional Golfers' Association (PGA) and several other golf-instructor organizations have already inquired about using this technology to demonstrate to golfers exactly where in that six- or seven-second motion they're going wrong—Thomas is quick to point out that correcting golfers' swings is not his intention, nor that of the USGA. "What business is it of the USGA to teach people how to swing? None!" he says. "This will help those in the field of sports medicine and injuries understand what the body goes through in various activities, what the forces are on the joints. They can then determine what parts of the body need to be exercised to avoid undue strain on the joints, or what should be done differently to prevent injury."

Great news for sports medicine, but there's got to be some value to the designers struggling to fulfill the demands of weekend duffers. "What this will lead to is customizing clubs for particular types of people and particular levels of golfers," says Thomas. In his vision, designers will use the android golfer and mathematical models to design clubs for a specific type of player—incorporating factors such as the player's body type and movement—and golfers will be able to quickly match themselves to a set of clubs.

But wait a minute. Customized equipment could help a golfer play better, and doesn't that fly in the face of Thomas' mandate as technical director? He responds with a chuckle. "No, nothing is going to increase your distance, your club-head velocity, or anything else—that requires skill and confidence," he says.

Manufacturers admit that, for all their efforts, they are really in the business of selling hope. "We sell the promise of performance," says Carl Scheie, a veteran designer at Wilson Sporting Goods in River Grove, Illinois. "If something we bring out instills more confidence, then it's worth the price."

Nevertheless, in the wake of the World Scientific Congress of Golf, the USGA has been inundated with requests for information from designers, and the new understanding of the club, the ball, and the golfer will eventually make its way onto the fairways. But the work is far from over. Thomas' research continues, and new projects, such as assistant technical director Bernard Soriano's study on putting, have begun. However, Thomas warns about becoming too excited about the new role of science in the world of golf. "This game has been played for hundreds of years, and, for hundreds of years, golfers have sought out the perfect ball and the perfect club," he says. "Frankly, if we haven't discovered it yet, I don't think it's out there."

But Thomas also confesses to being a maniacal golfer, and as such, he believes in something to which most scientists do not

The traditional trial-and-error approach to golf-club design may soon be supplanted by computer-generated analyses (below) that compare and quantify the performance characteristics of different club heads.

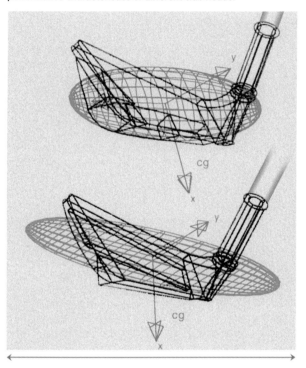

give much credence: magic. "What it comes down to is the confidence level. If I get a new club—and this has happened to me—I think it's going to help me hit better, [and] then I'm feeling confident. I'm thinking about this great new club, so my brain is not interfering with what my body is doing, and I swing and hit beautifully. It's magic, absolute magic. Developing this equipment is like searching for the Holy Grail—the right club or the perfect ball is just around the corner, and the anticipation is so exciting."

ASK THE SCIENTIST

> *In my mathematics class, we often plot points on a graph that has an x-axis and a y-axis. What is the meaning of these axes? Is it true that there is also a z-axis?*

A graph using an x-axis and a y-axis is a two-dimensional framework for plotting and displaying data. Generally, the x-axis is a horizontal line, and the y-axis is a vertical line that intersects the x-axis at a right angle. The area defined by these axes is called a Cartesian plane, in honor of the French mathematician and philosopher René Descartes, who pioneered the use of such graphs in analytic geometry.

Each data point within a Cartesian plane can be plotted or located by reference to its x and y coordinates, which are two related values. For example, suppose that one is exploring the relationship between the weight of a shot-put thrower and the average distance of the individual's throws. In this case, the weight of each individual measured might be plotted along the x-axis, while the average distance achieved for that individual is plotted along the y-axis. After plotting these numbers—called an ordered pair (x,y)—for a large group of shot-putters, a relationship between weight and length of throw might be discovered. One might even see in the graphical representation an optimal weight for achieving the longest throw.

When the x-value is positive, it will be plotted to the right of the y-axis, and when it is negative, it will appear to the left of the y-axis. Likewise, when the y-value is positive, it will appear above the x-axis, but when it is negative, it will be plotted below the x-axis. The point where the x-axis and the y-axis meet is called the origin (0,0).

Euclidean geometry requires only a two-dimensional plane. The field of solid, or spatial, geometry, however, requires some method for indicating a third dimension, so a third axis, called z, is employed. The z-axis is defined by a line that intersects the origin at right angles to both the x-axis and the y-axis. Data can then be plotted in three-dimensional space, and each data point would have three values to define its position (x,y,z).

> *Is zirconium a common element? Who discovered it? What are the major sources of the element? Are there everyday applications for zirconium?*

Zirconium (symbol Zr, atomic number 40) is relatively abundant. It is the ninth-most-frequently occurring element in Earth's crust. Since it is highly reactive—meaning that it tends to form compounds with other elements—it is found only in combined form. Zirconium prefers to bond with oxygen, and it is most commonly found as the minerals zircon ($ZrSiO_4$) and baddeleyite (ZrO_2). In its elemental form, zirconium is a white, soft metallic substance. German chemist Martin Heinrich Klaproth discovered zirconium in 1789 while studying zircon stones from the island of Ceylon (now Sri Lanka).

Zirconium is obtained for commercial purposes by separating it from zircon, which is found on beaches and in dune sands in Florida, North Carolina, Australia, Brazil, and India, among other places. The colorless varieties of zircon, the chief source of zirconium, are also used as brilliant gemstones.

Some compounds of zirconium are heat-resistant, and so are frequently used as thermal and electrical insulators. Foundry molds, for example, are often made with zirconium compounds. The compound can also be used as a heat shield for rocket engines. Because zirconium does not absorb neutrons, it is employed in constructing nuclear reactors (as an alloy in steel). Among everyday uses, zirconium is found in flash-bulbs, in water-repellent coatings on textiles, in topical remedies for poison ivy, and in body deodorants.

▶ *What is the principle behind the way a prism creates rainbowlike colors? Does it have any relationship to the cause of rainbows?*

A prism, a triangular block of glass or plastic, is designed to bend or disperse light into its component parts. Although we see light as white or yellow, it is actually a mixture of colors, each determined by specific vibrational patterns or frequencies known as wavelengths. The prism deflects, or refracts, white light into a continuous spectrum of colors—red, orange, yellow, green, blue, indigo, and violet—each having a specific wavelength. Red has the longest wavelength, and violet has the shortest. The wavelength or frequency, v, of each, when multiplied by Planck's constant, h, produces the energy value, E, of a particular color of light.

A rainbow is produced in a similar manner, but, rather than a prism, it is raindrops that act as the medium through which light is dispersed. When we see a rainbow, red appears at the top of the arc, and violet appears on the bottom. Sometimes a larger secondary rainbow is visible, and the order of the colors is reversed. This reversal results from light within the raindrops experiencing two, rather than one, internal reflections before exiting the raindrop. The French mathematician René Descartes was the first to calculate the angle from the Sun's rays at which a viewer can see a rainbow: 43 degrees.

Every rainbow is a full circle. Although the full circle of a rainbow cannot be observed from the ground, it can be seen from an airplane.

▶ *When I was a child, it seemed as though a sonic boom was a somewhat regular phenomenon. Why don't I hear them anymore?*

A sonic boom is an explosive noise (or multiple noises) caused by an aircraft or projectile that is traveling faster than the speed of sound (1,100 feet—336 meters—per second). As the aircraft moves at supersonic speed, it creates a pressure, or shock wave, of sound that, when it hits the ground, is heard as a boom. The sound wave travels along with the aircraft, although, to the observer on the ground, the sound wave seems to occur at a specific moment. The speed and trajectory of the aircraft, weather conditions, and local topography can all influence how big a boom is generated. Aeronautical engineers have not yet been able to design a type of aircraft that avoids creating a sonic boom.

In fact, there *were* more sonic booms heard in the United States in the years between the end of World War II and the late 1970s than are heard today. Sonic booms can break windows, rattle glass and china, and crack plaster and masonry. They can also produce a significant psychological strain on humans and animals. For this reason, civilian and military authorities have instituted flight controls to prevent sonic booms from occurring over inhabited areas of the United States. Military aircraft, for example, are prohibited from supersonic flight under 30,000 feet (9,150 meters). The only civilian aircraft capable of supersonic flight is the Concorde, operated by British Airways and Air France. These aircraft fly regularly between New York City or Washington, D.C., and Europe, but they are prohibited from traveling at supersonic speeds over land or over water close to the continental United States.

TECHNOLOGY

■ COMPUTER DISKS AND ELECTRONIC COMPONENTS ARE OFTEN MANUFACTURED IN "CLEAN ROOMS." IN SUCH WORKPLACES, EMPLOYEES MUST WEAR MASKS, GLOVES, AND OTHER GEAR; THE AIR IS CONSTANTLY FILTERED BY SPECIAL VENTILATION SYSTEMS. THE SENSITIVE PRODUCTS ARE THUS PROTECTED FROM CONTAMINATION ACQUIRED THROUGH HUMAN CONTACT OR AIRBORNE DUST PARTICLES.

CONTENTS

MAKING MONEY

by Judith Anne Gunther

It seemed like a quick and easy way to double the value of his Christmas fund. But when the 14-year-old boy slipped a crisp $50 bill onto his school's new computer scanner, it eventually earned him a stern lecture from the Secret Service.

Nabbing a dollar-duping teenager at a Scottsdale, Arizona, middle school in April 1993 might seem excessive. But the incident highlights the skyrocketing number of individuals across the nation who are using high-resolution copiers and printers to make bogus bucks. In fact, the output of forged bills by these "casual counterfeiters" has doubled every year since 1989. In 1992 alone, according to the National Research Council (NRC), as much as $8 million worth of phony money made on printers and copiers wormed its way into circulation.

If the problem is becoming apparent within the United States, it is becoming obvious abroad. The dollar has become, says one government official, "a de facto world currency" because of its stability. In fact, roughly two-thirds of the 350 billion U.S. dollars in circulation are held in foreign countries, according to the Treasury. The combination of unfamiliarity and acceptance abroad makes the dollar an easy target. According to officials at the Secret Service, more than $120 million in counterfeit U.S. dollars was seized in foreign countries in 1993; in comparison, $44 million in fake dollars was discovered domestically.

FAKE MONEY FREE-FOR-ALL

Alarmed by the burgeoning fake-bill free-for-all, the Treasury Department announced during the summer of 1994 the most radical redesign of U.S. currency since 1929. The new bills, which will soon have finalized designs and should be rolling from the Treasury's printers in 1996, may incorporate such innovative counterfeit-deterrence features as color-changing inks, tiny iridescent disks, and intricate patterns that become distorted when digitally scanned. Covert changes will likely be made as well.

These difficult-to-duplicate features won't arrive a minute too soon. In 1995, approximately 4.9 million color printers were linked to personal computers in the United States, each of them capable of making a realistic-looking piece of "currency." That, coupled with the availability of color copiers, may present too much temptation for, say, white-collar employees looking for quick pocket money, bored teenagers passing time at a mall's copy center, or computer hackers looking for a new antisocial technological triumph.

Ever since the end of the Civil War, when President Abraham Lincoln established the Secret Service to hunt down forgery operations, the Treasury has relied on a handful of strategies to keep counterfeiters at bay. One of the most effective has been the substrate—the paper—which is made of cotton and linen, giving it a distinctive "feel." Tiny red and blue fibers, scattered randomly like lint on a jacket, further authenticate paper money.

The black design on the front and the green image on the back are intaglio printed—a form of embossing combined with a viscous ink. "The intaglio process provides a very clear,

BOGUS BILLS
Counterfeiting of U.S. currency in foreign nations is increasing at a dramatic rate.

COUNTERFEIT DOLLARS SEIZED ABROAD

$120.0 mil.

$32.7 mil.

sharp image," says Thomas Ferguson, assistant director of research and development at the Treasury's Bureau of Engraving and Printing. "Whatever the engraver designs, it reproduces exactly." (By comparison, conventional commercial printing via lithography creates a close approximation of images using dots.)

Intaglio printing begins with an engraver, who carves the design in a soft steel plate; then thick ink is smeared on. Next the plate is wiped to remove all ink except that which lies in the grooves. Then, at pressures reaching 15,000 pounds per square inch (1,055 kilograms per square centimeter), the plate is pressed against paper. The process leaves an image raised about 20 microns (1 micron equals 0.00004 inch) off the paper substrate.

By making the etched lines wider or deeper, the engraver can precisely control the lightness or darkness of each shade of ink. The result, with a master engraver's work, has a three-dimensional effect that other printing techniques cannot duplicate.

SECURITY THREADS

The July 1994 announcement wasn't the first time the Treasury has tried to stay ahead of imaging technology. In 1983, the Treasury began sponsoring studies to combat the mounting threat of reprographic machines. The outcome was the security thread, embedded in $100, $50, and $20 bills beginning with the 1990 series. This metallized polyester strip, just 0.04 inch (0.1 centimeter) wide and 10 to 15 microns thick, bears the letters "USA" and the denomination of the bill.

The 1990 series bills also wear the phrase "The United States of America" in microprint in a loop around the portrait. Barely readable without a magnifying glass, the letters are 0.006 to 0.007 inch (0.015 to 0.017 centimeter) wide—the smallest type the government's intaglio printers can handle.

These two measures, then Treasury Secretary Lloyd Bentsen told the House Banking

American currency has long enjoyed a virtual immunity from quality counterfeiting, thanks in part to the complicated engraving process used to produce it. High-tech counterfeiters have changed all that, prompting the Treasury to initiate a sweeping redesign of U.S. money.

Committee on July 13, 1994, "have been very effective. But we would risk eventual diminishment of confidence in the integrity of our currency if we did not change it to meet the challenges of a new generation of technology." Indeed, the measures may be on the verge of being outdated: already the Secret

COMBATTING COUNTERFEITING

To prevent counterfeiting, the government has included a number of security features in U.S. currency.

CURRENT SECURITY FEATURES

Federal Reserve seal
The code letter is the same as the first letter in the serial number.

Microprinting
"The United States of America" is printed repeatedly on the sides of the portrait. The letters are too small to read without a magnifier or for distinct copier reproduction.

Serial numbers
The serial number appears in two places and is distinctively styled and evenly spaced, with ink the same color as the Treasury seal. No two notes of the same series and denomination have the same serial number.

Security thread
Polyester strips, which cannot be reproduced in the reflected light of copiers, have been embedded in $20, $50, and $100 notes.

Treasury seal
The sawtooth points are sharp, distinct, and unbroken. The seal's color is the same as that of the two serial numbers.

Border
The border's fine lines and lacy, weblike design are distinct and unbroken.

Paper and fibers
Cotton and linen rag paper has a strong, pliable feel with no watermarks; tiny red and blue fibers are embedded in the paper.

Portrait
The portrait is distinct from the screenlike background.

FEATURES UNDER CONSIDERATION

Larger, off-center portrait

Color-shifting inks
These inks change color when viewed from different angles. An ink that may appear gold when viewed directly, for example, may change to green when viewed obliquely.

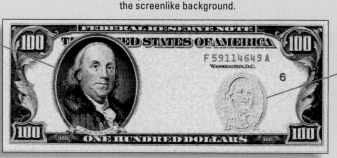

Localized, portrait watermark
This image is visible when held against a light source. It does not copy on color printers.

Service reportedly has found fake bills sporting jury-rigged security threads. And, warns an NRC report, copiers and printers are rapidly reaching levels of resolution at which they will be able to reproduce images as tiny as microprint.

REDESIGNED CURRENCY

When it comes to selecting the most effective deterrents, Bentsen told the House Banking Committee, "No single feature alone is sufficient, and no single currency design can be absolutely counterfeit-proof over time." Indeed, nearly every new proposed feature can be simulated to some extent. Instead, the Treasury is betting the strategic combination of features will, one way or another, thwart forgers.

One of the most noticeable new changes planned is to enlarge the bill's portrait and shift it to the left. The extra space gained on the right will probably bear a watermark, in an age-old technique that leaves a ghostly image in the paper. Visible only when the bill is illuminated from behind, these pictures are created by variations in the paper's density. Although forgers can't use copiers to reproduce watermarks, they can draw passable imitations by using fatty substances that leave transparent stains on the paper.

Like the 1990 series bills, the redesigned currency will use a security thread, although it may now be positioned at different places on the bill depending upon its denomination. This should help discourage forgers from converting $5s into $50s.

Planchets, tiny confetti-like flakes made of paper or plastic, may be sprinkled across the entire bill. These will probably have an iridescent sheen, making them easy to spot under a light, but impossible to photocopy. In addition, microprinted words could be stamped on each. However, the NRC reports, while nearly impossible to duplicate, iridescent planchets could be roughly simulated with ease, using widely available light-reflecting inks.

Perhaps the most effective authentication aid in the Treasury's arsenal is color-shifting ink, used by France, Germany, and Thailand, among other countries. "The effect is similar to the color shifts you see with oil on water," explains Michael Morris, an expert in optics at the University of Rochester in New York and a member of the NRC panel. When the bill is held to the light at one angle, the ink appears shimmery green. Shift the angle, and the ink looks blue.

This spectral switch is created with millions of tiny flakes—each just 1 micron thick—made of materials arranged in layers,

Domestic counterfeiters are stymied as much by the methods of the U.S. Treasury (above) as they are by the uncanny ability of most Americans to spot a bogus bill. Counterfeit versions of U.S. money produced abroad face neither Treasury inspection nor citizen scrutiny, making them easier to pass undetected.

like a sandwich. Flakes that produce a green-to-blue color shift, for instance, are made of two layers of chromium separated by an inner core of aluminum. When light strikes the ink, some light waves reflect off the chromium, while others penetrate through to, then reflect off, the aluminum below.

The visual effect depends upon the position of the observer's eye. At close to a right

The Changing
Faces on Money

If you can judge a country by its currency, what does the rash of freshly printed money say about the new governments sprouting all over?

A political roller coaster over the past few decades, Cambodia has gone from picturing ancient religious sculptures and rituals on its currency during its pre-Vietnam War days to having machine gunners and rocket launchers on the scarce riel while the country was called Kampuchea in the mid-1970s and under the rule of the murderous Khmer Rouge. Under the subsequent Communist regime, water buffalo, tractors, and workers in fields appeared on the currency.

Now that Norodom Sihanouk is once again the head of state, Cambodia's long-suffering people began using banknotes bearing the cheerful visage of their mercurial monarch in early 1995.

Rwanda—with a desperately poor and mostly illiterate population—has seen one of the most horrific civil wars in recent times, with the Hutu slaughtering at least 500,000 Tutsi in the space of two months during 1994. The Tutsi are now in control, and, in January 1995, the gorillas, zebras, and men in canoes on the old francs were replaced by lions, waterbuck, banana trees, and mountains.

According to Joseph Mutaboba, the Rwandan chargé d'affaires in Washington, D.C., the images on the new currency carry no specific symbolism. They represent a clear visual change so that Rwandans will recognize the notes under the new government by the images on them. This is particularly important, says Mutaboba, so that Rwandans won't be fooled into accepting the now-worthless old notes

angle, the reflected light waves from the two layers reinforce one another, and the ink looks green. At other angles, some of the light waves cancel, and the ink appears blue.

INVISIBLE DETERRENTS

Some of the deterrents under consideration won't be visible—at least until they are run through digital machinery. The Treasury seems to be favoring one such technique, called moiré-inducing lines. A simple way to create a moiré pattern yourself is to place one piece of window screening over another. Move one screen, and dancing lines appear.

In the same way, designers can create closely spaced line patterns that, when electronically scanned, trigger the same effect. Essentially, the line-resolution capabilities of the imaging device cannot match that of the original image, and distortions are induced.

"Moiré-inducing patterns are hard to get rid of, even with high-frequency scanning," says Morris. "Even if you can manipulate the image and fix the distortions, they can come back when the printer produces the image."

Alternatively, the Treasury could employ a pattern of dots in two different sizes, one

that the refugees in the camps outside the borders might try to smuggle in.

In a Russia where people can be openly proud of their prerevolutionary cultural heritage minus an overlay of Communism, the new rubles—first released in 1993—no longer carry Lenin's portrait. Instead, historically important architectural monuments like the Kremlin, Spassky Tower, and Red Square grace the bills. (Red Square was so named in the Middle Ages, when *krasnaya* implied "beautiful," not "Communist.")

These days, the old Lenin-faced ruble is in use only in the small Russian-occupied region of Moldova called Trans-Dniester, but this ruble has a stamp pasted on it showing the 18th-century Russian military hero Aleksandr Vasilyevich Suvorov.

From the plains of Uzbekistan to the town squares of Slovakia, from the markets of Mongolia to the hills of Slovenia, images of mosques, Madonnas, and musicians are replacing workers, soldiers, and farmers.

"Money is history in your hands," says Robert J. Leuver, executive director of the American Numismatic Association and former director of the U.S. Bureau of Engraving and Printing. "New governments want to represent the history of their country and show that they have had a significant change of administration."

According to David Harper, editor of the monthly magazine *Bank Note Reporter*, "Most nations pick the images that reflect their cultural or political interests."

For instance, Islamic countries generally do not have images of people on their currency because Islam proscribes the use of human figures. You can trace the evolution of the religion's influence on the cul-

above the resolution of most copiers, the other below. "To your eye," says Morris, "the area looks uniformly one color. But when a copier tries to duplicate it, it only 'sees' the larger dots." The smaller ones disappear on the copied image. If the remaining dots spell out a warning, such as "void," it's unlikely someone will accept the forged note.

But Morris says this won't be an effective deterrent for long. "If you have a high-resolution scanner, and a pretty good computer, you have the ability to change that image pixel by pixel," he says—so you could electronically wipe away the warning sign.

Of all the technologies under review, the most intriguing may be the covert features—detectable only by machines—that verify a bill's authenticity. One example, already in use (albeit not widely known), is the presence of magnetic ink on each bill. Many automatic money-changing and vending machines rely on this subtle feature to distinguish real money from counterfeit bills.

In the same way, the Treasury could add fibers or microcapsules with unique properties, such as microprinting, magnetism, iridescence, or reactivity to ultraviolet or

ture by whether or not there are people pictured on the banknotes.

The breakup of the Soviet Union in 1991 is responsible for the birth of more new countries than at any other time since the decolonization of Africa in the 1960s and 1970s. Bearing few hints of past Soviet relations, the banknotes of these countries reveal long-repressed interests.

In Belarus, interim banknotes—which have yet to be replaced by hard currency backed by financial institutions—bear images of animals like wolves, lions, and beavers. "People complain our money is a zoo!" says Clara Rukshina, a former resident of Minsk. "The government answers, 'When we have real money, we will depict something real.'"

Churches and saints appear on Ukraine's interim notes, some of which highlight the nation's age-old Christian heritage, which had been suppressed under the Soviets.

Kazakhstan in 1993 introduced its currency—the tenge—showing national poets, heroes, and scholars like al-Farabi, the 10th-century Muslim philosopher and compiler of an encyclopedia.

The 100-koruna (crown) bill from Slovakia depicts a Madonna by the 15th-century master wood-carver Pavel of Levoce. "There was no way you would have Madonnas in the '70s and '80s on the banknotes while Slovakia was still part of Czechoslovakia and under Soviet influence," says Jan Orlovsky, a spokesman in the Slovak Embassy in Washington.

In the Republic of Mongolia, the old tugrik featured Damdiny Sukhbaatar, a national hero who fought for independence in 1920, wearing a Russian-style

infrared light. In fact, the red and blue fibers in today's bills may already carry some kind of hidden characteristic.

A more complicated covert method would be to give each bill a unique fingerprint of sorts, then encode that as information elsewhere on the bill. For example, very fine optical fibers could be mixed into the paper slurry. "Then, if you illuminate the bill from a certain angle, you'd see the reflection of the fiber ends," says Morris. "Like a snowflake, it would be a random pattern—no other bill would have fibers in the exact same place." The position of those optical fibers could be converted to a number or symbol that is printed somewhere else on the bill. Later, to authenticate a bill, a machine would scan the fibers, then compare the result to the printed information.

Yet experts acknowledge that even such complex methods are not foolproof. "What happens if the fibers break?" Morris asks. Wear could alter a bill's fingerprint.

AN ONGOING PROCESS

No matter which deterrent features the Treasury chooses, the problem of keeping ahead

uniform. For the new tugrik, designers reached way into the past—to the 13th-century Mongol conqueror Genghis Khan. Sukhbaatar still appears on a few of the smaller notes, but he now sports a traditional hat and robe.

China has been in the hands of the Communists since 1949, but shifts in leadership and economic policies have been responsible for four major sets of circulating bills. The notes now in use were designed after Deng Xiaoping came to power in 1979. The earlier series, designed in 1958 and depicting proletariat themes like lathe- and steel-workers, gave way to bills showing ethnic groups in their various costumes. Then, in the mid-1980s, when the Chinese economy took off, the 50- and 100-yuan (dollar) notes made their debut. For the 50-yuan note, a scholar—a reviled figure during the

Cultural Revolution—replaced the soldier in the once-sacrosanct revolutionary grouping of worker, farmer, and soldier.

If nothing drastic happens to the direction of the country's economy once Deng dies, the present currency will probably remain unchanged. And if the economy continues to expand as it has (inflation was 23 percent last year), a new 500-yuan bill will undoubtedly make its appearance. Few people have credit cards or bank accounts, and most purchases and even telephone bills must be paid for with cash.

And what image will the designers put on the 500-yuan bill?

"If we continue to follow political policies," says Zhou Lingzhao, a currency designer in China, laughing, "we should show an entrepreneur."

Nancy Berliner

of reprographic technologies will remain. With that should come a host of new techniques. Experts predict, for example, that holographic images, now a staple on credit cards, may appear on future bills. Only problems of durability prevent use of holograms now.

Technology can be used to stop forgers in other ways as well. For example, Canon, a business-machine manufacturer based in Japan, recently unveiled a color copier that identifies—and refuses to duplicate—currency. It does this by comparing the item to be copied with patterns stored in its memory.

More-covert technology in development by some copier manufacturers encodes a hidden pattern on each copy made. This concealed pattern, such as a series of tiny yellow dots, can later be decoded by a machine to identify the serial number of that copier. Such information could enable Secret Service agents to trace—and nail—a photocopying forger.

"We recognize that technology isn't standing still," says Ferguson, "and we can't wait another 60 years to change the bills again. When this design moves into production, we will probably start this process all over." ◪

Manufacturing for Reuse

by Gene Bylinsky

In a big gray-brick building in Highland Park, Michigan, half a dozen technicians and engineers in shirtsleeves are hard at work killing American ingenuity. Armed with air-powered socket tools, screwdrivers, and hammers, they are tearing apart showroom-new cars—a red Ford Aspire here, a blue Chrysler Neon over there. They dissect subassemblies, weigh each component, and videotape and time the procedures. Black-wire electrical harnesses are removed and hung on tall white boards as if they were the innards of cats on display for a freshman anatomy class.

This most unusual lab is the Vehicle Recycling Development Center, the automakers' joint effort that went into full operation in 1994. Specialists from collaborating recycling associations do most of the demolition, but engineers from the Big Three automakers—Chrysler, General Motors (GM), and Ford—visit frequently to observe, often to participate. The aim is to teach the Big Three to better design cars for easier dismantling—for instance, by improving access to key parts for future removal.

Draining fluids (below) is the first of many steps in disassembling a car. Engineers can simplify this complex process—and trim environmental waste—by knowing how parts, such as those in an automotive wiring system (left), interconnect.

CLOSING THE LOOP

The men and women at the new center are riding the hottest new production trend in the world: design for disassembly (DFD). The goal is to close the production loop: to conceive, develop, and build a product with a long-term view of how its components can be refurbished and reused—or disposed of safely—at the end of the product's life. In a world where the costs of disposal are rising, ease of destruction becomes as important as ease of construction.

The idea has fired the imaginations of manufacturers from around the world. Siemens coffeepots and Caterpillar tractors, Xerox photocopiers and Eastman Kodak cameras, American personal computers (PCs) and Japanese laser printers, German locomotive engines and Canadian telephones—plus many other products—are beginning to be built to be taken apart.

The forces behind this newfound environmentalism have more to do with return on capital than with a return to nature. Unlike prior environmental schemes, green manufacturing holds out the promise for companies to do well as they do good. Some U.S. companies, including Xerox and Kodak,

Companies have placed new emphasis on making products that can be efficiently disassembled into reusable or recyclable parts. Besides making environmental sense, manufacturing for reuse has also helped the bottom line.

are already coining money by designing for disassembly and component reuse.

Green machines, with their emphasis on reducing parts, rationalizing materials, and reusing components, are proving more efficient to build and distribute than conventional ones. Such gains are possible because green production meshes with today's favored manufacturing strategies: global sourcing, design for manufacture, concurrent engineering, and total quality.

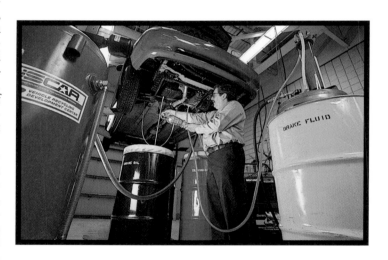

NEW LAWS, NEW DESIGNS

If that is not enough, new laws across Europe will soon compel manufacturers of everything from autos to telephones to take back used products. In Germany, the root of the green movement, manufacturers are already responsible for the final fate of their products' packaging.

This green wave of German legislation is rolling across the Atlantic Ocean. The Germans have established a de facto global manufacturing standard. U.S. companies wishing to compete globally must start making products that will comply with the green dictates

Thanks to research at the Vehicle Recycling Development Center (above), U.S. automakers will soon be building cars that can be easily taken apart and recycled.

of the huge European market. "Things are moving too fast, with 12 countries already participating in green manufacturing," says Joanna D. Underwood, president of Inform, a New York City-based company that advises corporations on environmental matters.

So-called green product design could also be the antidote to the astonishing depletion of the Earth's mineral riches. And it might cut the amount of junk that threatens to flood landfills in the industrial world. Design dictates a whole chain of events, both pre- and postmanufacturing, that governs the use, or misuse, of natural resources. Take raw-materials extraction, for instance. Judicious use of finished materials like steel could reduce mining demand that totals 20,000 pounds (9,000 kilograms) annually for each U.S. citizen. The consequences of this are enormous. According to the National Academy of Sciences (NAS), 94 percent of the stuff that is pulled out of the earth enters the waste stream within months.

European lawmakers are encouraged by the fact that Germany's packaging-takeback legislation is working. It has worked so well that the private company organized by manufacturers to collect and dispose of packaging materials has been gathering too much trash—almost going broke in the process because sufficient facilities to remold plastics, for instance, are not in place. But the takeback law reduced the amount of packaging waste by 600 million tons, or 4 percent, during its first two years of operation.

BUILDING GREEN MACHINES

Although corporations often fight such regulations, the green laws in Germany have stimulated companies to develop imaginative ways to market goods with less packaging. Colgate-Palmolive, for instance, designed a toothpaste tube that stands on its head, sans box; it now sells some products that way in the United States, too.

Hewlett-Packard's (H-P's) workstation designers in Germany literally moved the packaging inside, substituting plastic foam for the metal skeleton that holds interior parts, thus reducing the need for metal inside and for wrapping outside. A polypropylene-foam chassis has cutouts for each component so that all nestle snugly. The new chassis reduces transport packaging by 30 percent, while disassembly time has been cut 90 percent. This idea will be applied to H-P personal computers as well.

Theoretically, anything from a coffeemaking machine to a Caterpillar tractor can be designed for disassembly. The more value in an item, of course, the more sense it makes to reuse its parts.

Some examples follow of how valuable products are being redesigned in the United States and in Germany to fit what the Germans call the new closed-loop economy.

Automobiles. Almost everywhere cars are built, efforts are in high gear to make them more suitable for disassembly and to reuse component parts. Obviously, no one wants to make a car fall apart. Cost, customer appeal, and performance still come first. But car companies are changing some of the ways of automaking in order to enhance "autobreaking." BMW estimates that by the end of this decade, 20 million cars per year in Europe will make return trips, 250,000 of them BMWs. To put this many cars into reverse, BMW and other German automakers have been setting up experimental disassembly plants and even destroying new-car models in order to learn more about how to take them apart.

BMW's 1991 Z1 Roadster, whose plastic side panels come apart like the halves of a walnut shell, is an example of a car designed for disassembly. One of the lessons learned, says spokesman Rudolf Probst, is that glue or solder in bumpers should be replaced with fasteners so that the bumpers can come apart more easily and the materials can be recycled. BMW has pushed the recycled portion of a car to 80 percent by weight, and is aiming for 95 percent. François Castaing, Chrysler's vice president for vehicle engineering, says the United States will be in that range by the end of the decade. Volkswagen, too, is on the bandwagon and is planning recycling centers throughout Germany.

The Germans could take a lesson from the United States and its robust, market-based auto-recycling industry. Arguably the world's most efficient auto recycler, the United States already reuses a remarkable 75 percent by weight of nearly every American car. Cars are first stripped of valuable parts such as engines, generators, alternators, and other components that can be refurbished and resold by some 12,000 auto-parts recyclers. Next the metal carcasses wind up in the gaping maws of some 200 shredders that reduce the metal skeletons to steel fragments, which are shipped to steelmakers to make more new-car bodies. This is already a profitable, multi-billion-dollar-a-year business in the United States. But it is also fraught with problems, such as disposing of tires, glass, and plastic. Green manufacturing—thinking these problems through beforehand—can lower recycling costs dramatically and reduce environmental hazards.

Computers. There are probably insect species with longer life cycles than a PC—now obsolete less than 12 months after it leaves the factory, according to scientists at Carnegie-Mellon University in Pittsburgh, Pennsylvania. "Seventy million obsolete computers are sitting in the basements of various organizations and will eventually end up in landfills if they are not recycled," says the university's D. Navin-Chandra. "Today two computers become obsolete for every three purchased. By 2005, the ratio will be 1 to 1, which means we should be able to recycle computers as fast as we make them.

New models from German automaker BMW use recycled components (blue) and parts that can be reused (green). Such construction will soon be mandated throughout Europe.

For this reason, recycling must be treated like any regular manufacturing task."

In the United States, laws concerning toxic wastes are scaring computer makers and other manufacturers out of their wits. If their old machines wind up in landfills and commence polluting the ground, the makers are held

Some computer makers have already adopted green design methods. IBM's PS/2 E (below), for example, contains recycled plastic and is built for simple disassembly.

responsible. So most U.S. computer companies have begun so-called reverse distribution for old machines, especially from big customers.

Disassembling old computers is not new. It began in the early 1990s, mainly to retrieve precious metals like gold and platinum. These metals were used in larger quantities in the older machines, deposited as paths to

By weight, about 75 percent of the typical American car is reused or recycled. Unfortunately, many glass, plastic, and rubber components still wind up in the scrap heap.

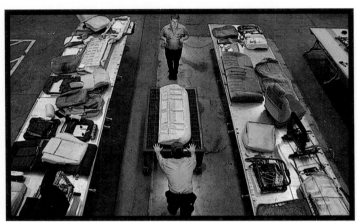

connect chips on a board. The boards were then sold to chip retrievers, which resold the chips to such users as toy manufacturers.

Computer makers that can reduce the number of parts and the time it takes to disassemble a PC will profit when the product, like a sort of silicon salmon, returns to its place of

Germany has long been a global leader in the recycling movement. The German firm pictured below extracts and reuses electronic parts from old television sets.

origin. IBM, H-P, Digital Equipment Corporation (DEC), and other makers are rapidly introducing DFD technology across the board. As early as 1991, IBM designed two personal-computer models both for easier disassembly and lower energy consumption. Now all IBM designers are being urged to switch to green schemes. For more than a year, H-P has used a DFD approach to build all 12 models of its Vectra PC. Each Vectra now contains only three screws, a construction that also allows easy upgrade by users.

For more than three years, in Research Triangle, North Carolina, IBM has been practicing takeback and disassembly at a facility called the Engineering Center for Environmentally Conscious Products. (It might think about disassembling that name.) The computer colossus is evaluating how such collection could be done at minimal cost, or even at a profit, says center director J. Ray Kirby. IBM takes back its old machines in eight European countries for a small fee, as do most other computer manufacturers.

H-P, which has been in the disassembly business longer than IBM, already runs a profitable operation, according to executives there. DEC says its Resource Recovery Center in Contoocook, New Hampshire, is "cost-effective." Germany's Siemens Nixdorf, on the other hand, says its recycling is not yet profitable, because not enough old machines are being processed.

Telephones. When monopoly prevailed in telephony, manufacturers leased telephones and then refurbished and rebuilt them to lease anew. The breakup of the Bell System disrupted this process, since most phones are now purchased rather than leased. But profitable leasing continues in Canada. In a big plant outside Toronto, Ontario, Northern Telecom breaks down old telephones, puts their innards into new plastic housings, and sends them out again.

Beyond that traditional activity, Northern Telecom is switching to companywide DFD. "We're on the threshold of moving to a new platform that will truly change the philosophy behind our entire product strategy," says Margaret Kerr, senior vice president for environment and ethics at Northern Telecom in Toronto.

AT&T, moving a bit more deliberately, is in the midst of a demonstration project called "green product realization" to generate guidelines for green product design.

Engines. Sometimes DFD occurs naturally. In a bustling plant in the quaint Bavarian village of Uebersee at the edge of the Alps, the German engine manufacturer Deutz Service International, a subsidiary of Klöckner Humboldt Deutz, rebuilds thousands of Deutz engines a year. They are used in machines ranging from tractors to locomotives. "We noticed that a market had developed for replacement Deutz engines," says Bruno Baum, the plant manager. "Our engines are built in such a way that they are extremely easy to take apart and put back together."

This DFD occurred by happy circumstance. Explains Baum: "a popular trend in the 1970s called for a lot of the metal pieces to be soldered together, pieces that used to be held together with screws. It makes production cheaper, but also makes it hard to recover many of the parts. Fortunately, we didn't go along."

Deutz-engine users around the world noticed the ease of disassembly, and small companies sprang up specializing in rebuilds. Deutz decided it wanted that business for itself. It now buys more than 5,000 old engines per year, and last year turned them into 3,500 remanufactured versions—"as good as new," says Baum—that sell for up to 25 percent less than new engines. Adds Baum: "A product-takeback law would only be to our advantage because we already fulfill its requirements. Our competitors don't." The company also plans to rebuild in the United States.

KNOWING WHEN TO REUSE

Large U.S. companies such as IBM, Ford, and Digital Equipment have joined consor-

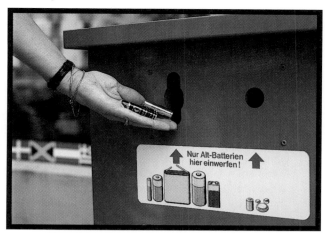

German stores collect cardboard, Styrofoam, and even used batteries (above). Such efforts have cut the nation's packaging waste by 600 million tons in two years.

tia at universities such as Carnegie-Mellon, the University of California at Berkeley, and Tufts University in Medford, Massachusetts, to learn more about green product design. The U.S. Department of Commerce plans to help small companies master the techniques at the Great Lakes Manufacturing Technology Center in Cleveland, Ohio.

Also coming to manufacturers' aid today are sophisticated software programs such as the pioneering ReStar from Green Engineering Corporation of Pittsburgh. A brainchild of Carnegie-Mellon's D. Navin-Chandra and his associates, who founded the company less than a year ago, ReStar carries a hefty price tag: $19,600. But the user gets a remarkable amount of help. First and foremost, ReStar answers the key question about disassembly: Exactly where and when do you stop it before you start losing money? Navin-Chandra calls this "the crux of successful disassembly."

A ReStar user can also determine what materials to employ most profitably and whether the retired product should be bought back or sold to a third-party recycler. To make ReStar do its magic, the user enters data on each part that goes into the design, including the part's weight and material content. Each point at which parts connect is also described and identified from a roster in ReStar's database. If the database lacks that information, the user can add new joint- and material-type descriptions to the database. The assembly is described in terms of geometric relationships between the parts. For each direction from which a target part can be removed, for instance, the user lists the other parts that have to be removed before the target part comes off.

From the geometric relationships entered into the database, ReStar creates a three-dimensional model of the entire assembly. With that information, the program can identify all possible stages of disassembly of the product, from partial to complete. ReStar selects the best strategy by calculating the economic consequences of moving to each stage.

The user can have ReStar generate disassembly plans with full cost and timing information. Navin-Chandra calls ReStar's "what-if" capability the program's "biggest feature." The model also keeps track of such questions as: How much has been spent on disassembly until now? Are separated parts composed of compatible materials? If not, how much will it cost to get rid of them?

Two Successful Pioneers

Valuable lessons come from two successful green manufacturers. Kodak and Xerox have moved well beyond the what-if stage, though each took a different path.

Kodak learned the hard way. In the late 1980s, a group of engineers came up with a disposable 35-millimeter camera called Fling. The project got lukewarm support from top management because the idea ran counter to Kodak philosophy. Alan Vandemoere, who participated in the project, says Kodak's belief was "that God intended people to buy a roll of film and a camera, and use the film to load the camera."

Indeed, Fling went bust. It sold poorly, and its name enraged environmentalists. Vandemoere's group did not give up. One engineer devised a double lens that enabled the camera to take wide-angle shots. Creating a panoramic view with a $10 camera was novel. They also developed an underwater version and renamed the camera FunSaver 35. The new model soared—but it still ticked off environmentalists. And for good reason: hundreds of thousands of returned cameras ended up in landfills.

Eager to recycle the camera, the engineers proposed DFD and component reuse. Kodak management yawned. It woke up

when a U.S. congressman gave the company his Wastemaker of the Year Award for the disposables.

By the end of 1990, Kodak had converted the disposable cameras to recyclable ones. The previously ultrasonically welded camera case was redesigned to snap apart easily. The customer would deliver it to a photofinisher, who would return it to Kodak for a small fee. Kodak hired OutSource, a New York State-sponsored organization that employs disabled people, to break down the cameras.

In the recycling center, the covers and the lenses are removed. Plastic parts are ground into pellets and molded into new camera parts. The camera's interior—its moving parts and electronics—are tested and reused up to 10 times. By weight, 87 percent of a camera is reused or recycled. Kodak sold about 30 million disposable cameras worldwide in 1993. The flash version of the FunSaver is the company's fastest-growing and most profitable product.

Xerox launched its green manufacturing program four years ago under the banner of cost savings. Says Jack C. Azar, corporate manager for environmental design and resources conservation: "We demonstrated to our senior management that we could probably do it very cost-effectively and increase our productivity in the process."

At first, Xerox disassembled without having designed for it. The cartridge assembly, for instance, was welded together ultrasonically and had to be torn apart by hand. Xerox replaced that demolition disassembly with a design that anticipates recycling. Potentially reusable parts were put in easily accessible places; snaps replaced screws. Common parts, such as plastic panels, were standardized for use in different products. Engineers were taught the elements of disassembly. A 35-person team called Asset Recycle Management Organization helped master the new discipline.

Widening Horizons

As Kodak, Xerox, and other companies have learned, the topsy-turvy world of DFD suddenly turns the gang in the lab into corporate strategists. It challenges them to take a much wider view of design than they have been

The Kodak FunSaver camera (shown disassembled at top) is a textbook testimonial for environmentally aware product design. Photofinishers return used FunSavers to a recycling center, where workers sort, disassemble, test, refurbish, and repackage the cameras (sequence above). Kodak claims that vital parts can be reused up to 10 times, and that recycled or reused materials comprise nearly 90 percent of each camera. The growing corporate interest in such a landfill-friendly strategy has as much to do with return on investment as with a return to nature; indeed, some FunSaver models are among Kodak's best-selling products.

taught. The most important lesson learned, says Donald Bloyer, an H-P senior product-design engineer with 27 years' experience, is not to be rigid. Coping with sometimes-contradictory notions and demands, a designer must juggle quality and reliability with green engineering.

Recycling has brought another interesting fact to light: used or refurbished parts sometimes work better than new ones. This is particularly true in digital electronics. A memory chip or a microprocessor, unless it has suffered repeated thermal insults or physical damage, is virtually immortal, since the only moving parts are electrons. So Fox Electronics, a fast-growing San Jose, California, reclaimer and reseller of chips, does not even bother to test old chips it resells. The reason: what the trade calls "infant mortality" of new chips during initial tests is 5 percent, but Fox discovered that old chips are more reliable—only 2 percent die.

But old beliefs die even harder. Cheap cameras notwithstanding, getting Americans to buy retread products as new will be a tough sell. Xerox is meeting some resistance to selling or leasing refurbished photocopiers as new, even though they carry the same warranty as machines with all new parts. Car buyers will likely balk at a new car with a refurbished alternator. It's one thing to buy a new Ford with 50 reground plastic soda bottles making up its grille liner. But it's another to accept a used part—refurbished or not—that moves or rotates and wears down with use.

"We still have some educating to do," concedes Xerox's Azar. "There are pockets in the consumer base—and that includes government agencies—that keep saying, 'We only want 100 percent new products.'" Azar is pleased that late in 1993, the Clinton administration, in an end run around Congress, issued an executive order that urges (but does not require) federal agencies to buy green products like refurbished photocopiers.

No one knows how many of today's products are green. Maybe 5 percent, maybe 10 percent. But in 10 years, predicts IBM's Kirby, all products will be made for disassembly and refurbishing—turning both the Earth and some companies a greener shade. ◢

In 1987, C. W. (Paul) Chu of the University of Houston, in Texas, was racing against scientists from Moscow to Long Island, New York, for a breakthrough in high-temperature superconductivity. On a hunch, he prepared a bit of copper, barium, lanthanum, and oxygen smaller than a BB pellet. Then he worked high-pressure alchemy, squeezing the mixture under pressure 18,000 times as great as that at sea level.

Bingo: when electrodes were plugged into the blend, it conducted electricity with zero resistance. Chu then guessed he could achieve the same effect at ordinary pressure by substituting yttrium for lanthanum. The substitution worked—and earned Chu worldwide fame for a material that superconducted at a record high temperature: -292° F (-180° C).

SQUEEZING OUT NEW SECRETS

Chu's work highlighted how extraordinarily high pressures can strong-arm elements into yielding their secrets. The high-pressure manufacture of synthetic diamond (by squeezing carbon) is already a near-billion-dollar industry. Today researchers are using pressures exceeding those at the center of the Earth to break and re-form chemical bonds in everything from hydrogen to beach sand. "Even by a conservative estimate, we could triple the range of materials we now know just by squeezing them," says Robert M. Hazen, a research scientist with the Carnegie Institution's Geophysical Laboratory in Washington, D.C., and author of a 1993 book on the topic, *The New Alchemists*.

If gases can be compressed into stable metallic crystals, they might superconduct even at room temperatures. Superhard glass made from silicon dioxide—or quartz—

PRESSING MATTERS

Opposing diamond anvils (above) are at the center of high-pressure research. The anvils are used to achieve the extreme compression required to squeeze molecules together to produce such exotic materials as high-temperature superconductors.

by Ruth Coxeter and Peter Coy

could serve as windshields for rockets. A metallic form of hydrogen could be an incredibly dense form of stored chemical energy. "It would be something like 30 times more efficient than any existing rocket fuel," Hazen says.

Oxygen, which in its normal state exists as a transparent, colorless gas, is transformed into colorful red, yellow, and blue crystals (below) when subjected to extraordinarily high pressure.

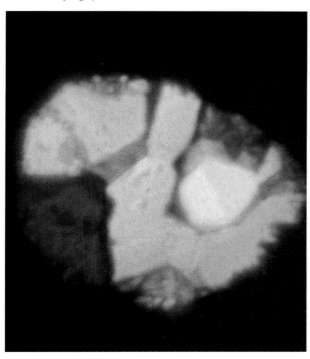

HIGH-PRESSURE ALCHEMY

MATERIALS	POTENTIAL USES
Hydrogen, Oxygen	Fuel cells, superconductors
Carbon 60, or Buckyballs	Coatings for computer disks, abrasives
Silicon dioxide	Superhard glass, lightweight car components
Ikaite	Indicator of how mineral deposits form
Helium nitride	Aid to research on inert gases

Data: Carnegie Institution, *Business Week*

The laboratory equipment required to achieve these awesome pressures, a diamond anvil, is no more than 8 inches (20 centimeters) tall and can be screwed tight by hand. It works by amplifying arm power through gears, and concentrating all of that power into an extremely small area. That is done by placing a tiny sample between the tips of two cut diamonds. A plate with a hole in it corrals the sample.

Research on such a small scale has big drawbacks. The products are too tiny—about 0.000001 ounce (0.000031 gram)—to be useful for anything except research. Many materials revert to normal once the pressure is off. And high-pressure science can be hazardous. Having witnessed one explosion, David Mao and Russell Hemley of the Carnegie Institution now operate experiments from behind a steel wall.

With real money probably years off, most work on exotic high-pressure materials is going on in universities, not companies. Cornell University, Harvard University, and the University of California, Berkeley, have substantial programs. In 1992, the National Science Foundation (NSF) established a Center for High-Pressure Research, pooling efforts at the Carnegie Institution, Princeton, and the State University of New York at Stony Brook.

HARD LUCK

High-pressure research got a jolt in May 1994, when 11 Russian and French researchers claimed in the journal *Physics Letters* that they had created a material harder than diamond from "buckyballs," or carbon 60. But similar claims have arisen before, and some scientists argue that the samples were too small to be reliably tested.

Squeezing materials does more than harden them. Compressing gases such as hydrogen liberates

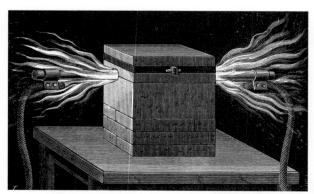

atmospheres, or megabars, at which point its molecules line up like watermelons. Carnegie brags it was the first to reach 2.5 megabars. No one has surpassed 3 megabars, where, scientists speculate, hydrogen becomes fully metallic and super-conducting. The big question: will metallic hydrogen remain metallic once the pressure is off?

MICROPOPS

Commercialization is just one goal. High-pressure researchers also seek to understand the composition of stars and planets and the sources of earthquakes. UCLA's Nicol has even re-created conditions of the early Earth to form chains of hydrogen cyanide, which he believes are precursors to DNA. One favorite for research is ikaite, a watery calcium compound. Its behavior under high temperature and pressure sheds light on how veins of gold, silver, and other ores are formed. Raymond Jeanloz, a physicist at the University of California, Berkeley, and graduate student Charles Meade proposed a new seismic theory after pressurizing serpentine, a greenish, waxy mineral. A microphone attached to a diamond anvil picked up a popping sound—perhaps a miniature version of a quake that occurs when water is forced out of serpentine deep underground.

In 1893, chemist Henri Moissan used an electric furnace (above) to synthesize diamond from graphite. Although he believed the experiment a success, his claim is now disputed.

Alvin Van Valkenburg (right) invented an early model of a diamond anvil that operated with the turn of a screw. A microscope was used to observe changes in the sample as it was squeezed by the anvil.

their electrons, turning them into excellent electrical conductors. Helium, ordinarily inert, will bond with nitrogen when sufficiently compressed. Oxygen is ordinarily colorless—but under extreme pressure, it forms crystals with facets of red, yellow, and blue. Malcolm F. Nicol, a professor of physical chemistry at the University of California, Los Angeles (UCLA), speculates that sulfur crystals could store information, with different colors of light serving to write, erase, and read data.

The quest for a superconducting metallic hydrogen is taking scientists into realms of pressure never experienced on Earth—and into heated rivalries as well. Researchers at Harvard University in Cambridge, Massachusetts, and at the Carnegie Institution disagree over what happens to hydrogen at 1.5 million

Doubts about the commercial value of exotic high-pressure materials have kept away mainstream producers of synthetic diamonds, such as General Electric (GE), Sumitomo, and De Beers. "We're a materials supplier. Just creating high-pressure phases doesn't make you any money," says William F. Banholzer, manager of engineering for GE Superabrasives in Worthington, Ohio. But in labs like Paul Chu's, the big squeeze is paying off. Chu recently found a superconductor that he hopes could be produced in industrial quantities by depositing the materials in vapor form. That discovery is the kind of advance that keeps the pressure on.

DOTS OF ILLUSION

by M. Alexandra Nelson

Toddlers have been enchanted by pop-up books for years. But now everyone from kindergartners to grannies is getting in the picture, so to speak, with a mysterious new variety of three-dimensional (3-D) posters, cards, and books. Looked at in a certain way, these so-called autostereograms defy the old adage that "what you see is what you get." For what you get with these illustrations are three-dimensional images hidden within the wallpaper-like designs.

Called the Magic Eye, the technique has been popularized by N.E. Thing Enterprises, a company based in Bedford, Massachusetts, that first marketed posters with computer-generated art that contained hidden 3-D images.

In the six months following November 1994, more than 1 million copies of Magic Eye books were sold in the United States. Several companies have been selling such books, cards, and posters. Enthusiasts can even print their own stereograms with one of several computer programs, such as I/O Software's Stereolusions for Windows, a hidden-image creator.

Within the illusory picture, or autostereogram, below, a trained eye can find a hidden three-dimensional image.

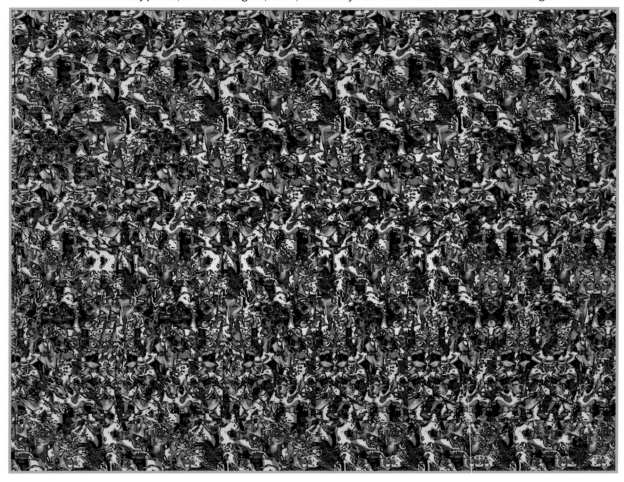

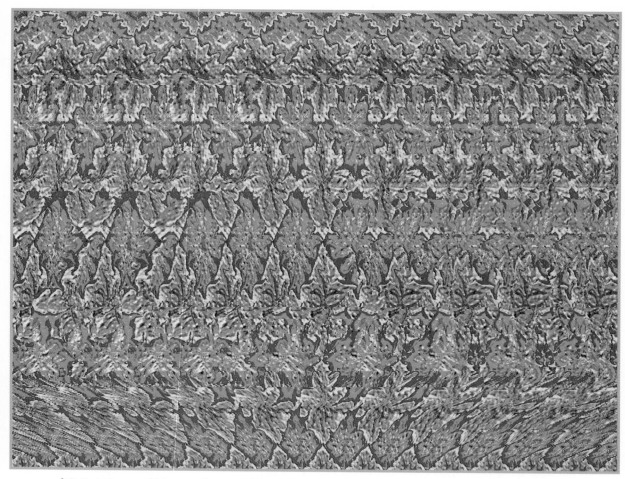

Autostereograms—which appear in scores of books, cards, and posters—have revived public interest in 3-D images.

How to See in 3-D

Each illustration contains a repeating pattern. Tucked within is a slight variance or distortion that hides the three-dimensional (3-D) image. To grasp the image, you must make each eye look at similar points in different repetitions of the pattern long enough for the brain to make a connection between the two. Getting the gist of the process is easier if you are relaxed, almost meditative. By concentrating on looking through the picture, that is, by throwing your focus into the distance, your eyes find their way outward to a "walleyed," or wide-eyed, position that's the opposite of crossed.

Hold the picture against your face, and think about looking through the image. Pretend you are languidly staring off into the distance. Slowly begin moving the picture away from your face, pausing at every inch or two for a few seconds to let your mind adjust to the new position. Continue until the picture is 1 foot (30 centimeters) or so away, where you would normally hold a book or a magazine to read it. The hard part is maintaining the gaze during the pauses, not allowing the brain's curiosity about the image at hand to tease the eyes into refocusing, peering closer. Deciphering the 3-D in stereograms is a learned skill.

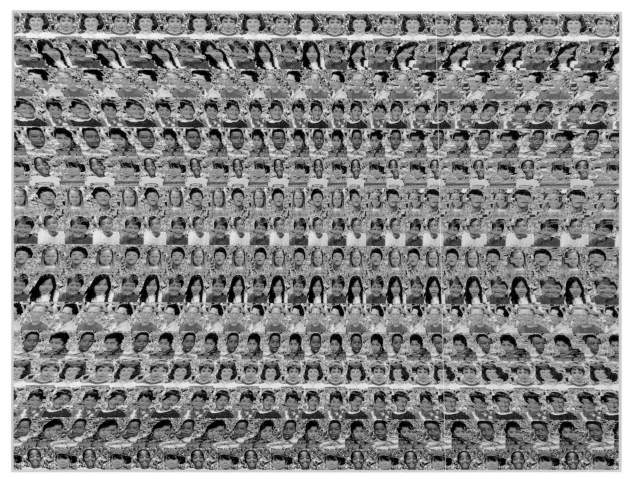

The human brain perceives depth in autostereograms by fusing separate images from the left and right eyes.

TWO IMAGES IN ONE

The Magic Eye capitalizes on the novelty we find when we see three dimensions on two-dimensional surfaces. Look at any of the illustrations, and you will see psychedelic colors splashed across the page in a pattern of butterflies or swirls or blobs; or, alternately, they depict a scene in vivid college-dorm-poster style. Then stare again, allowing your vision to diverge, and another image—say that of a forest or a winged horse, each with a clear illusion of depth—will pop out and float in space as if by magic.

Our ability to discover these images derives from our binocular vision and the brain's skill at merging the slightly different views perceived by each eye into a single picture, one that includes a perception of the relative distances between objects. Our natural stereoscopic vision enables us to navigate easily through a crowded world . . . and have fun with 3-D fads.

No one knows exactly how the brain interprets images as three-dimensional. In fact, for a long time, no one suspected the brain was even involved in the process. It was thought to be purely an ocular ability, solely the concern of the body's two miniature cameras—the eyes.

MASTERING THE THIRD DIMENSION

The attempt to visualize three dimensions on a flat or two-dimensional plane has intrigued humans since the dawn of leisure time. Stereo visuals have been attempted in one form or another at least since the cave painters of Lascaux (located in modern-day France) placed their drawings on rough rock in such a way that flickering firelight gave depth to the images. Philosophers, scientists, and artists have all struggled with the problem of three-dimensionality. How do we see depth? How can we re-create the depth of the world around us on a flat plane?

One way to do this is to take advantage of the fact that we have two eyes, and thus fabricate, sometimes with the aid of some device, two pictures that can be fused immediately by the mind into a single image containing depth. In the 1950s, two such devices became fads. In one such craze, 3-D movies like *Bwana Devil* demanded that audiences wear glasses with red and green filters. About the same time, handheld stereoscopes like Viewmaster, into which revolving slides were inserted, showed storybook scenes that became as much a part of the average kid's toy box as roller skates.

Both of these devices employed principles outlined by Charles Wheatstone in 1838 when he invented the stereo viewer, with its paired images. When photography was born a year later, the equipment was in place for 3-D slides or moving pictures.

By inventing the random-dot stereogram while at Bell Labs in 1959, a cognitive psychologist named Dr. Bela Julesz created a diagnostic tool for illustrating the brain's

How the 3-D Image Is Made

1 Using off-the-shelf software, the artist creates a wire-frame drawing of the image (the Statue of Liberty) that will be hidden. Shadings from 256 gray levels are used to fill in the frame, based on the rule that the darker the area, the farther away it will appear.

2 A starter strip (the colorful pattern) is designed, which will serve as the two-dimensional overlay you'll see at first glance. Colors in the strips will be used to replace the gray-scale image.

3 Strips are produced as a stereo pair for the right eye's (top) and left eye's (bottom) points of view. (The unpaired strips at the ends of the picture do not exhibit depth.) Each pair shows the same slice of the picture, but pixels in the second part of the pair

are shifted slightly. The amount of this displacement (by up to about 256 dots) is based on the shade of gray contained in the hidden image. Since darker areas are shifted the most, they are perceived by viewers as revealing the most depth in the picture. The colors seem to wrap around three-dimensional objects in the completed picture.

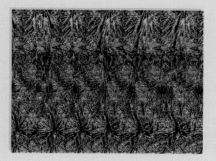

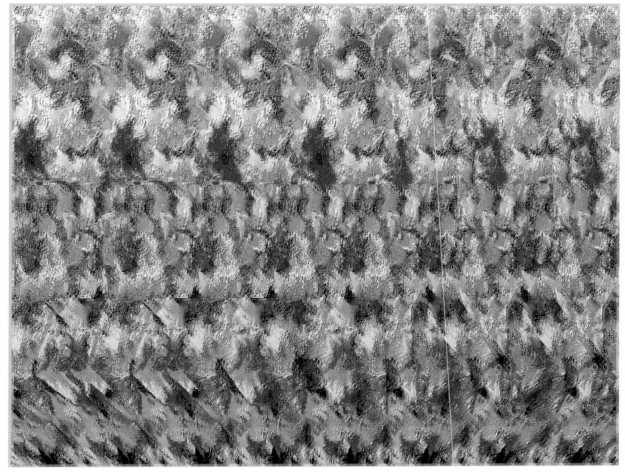

New software programs enable enthusiasts to generate their own 3-D illusions on a personal computer.

involvement in fusing information received from two eyes viewing an image from two slightly different positions. The random-dot stereogram is exactly what it sounds like: a pattern of random dots that hides an image that can be seen while wearing special glasses. Like the 3-D movies of the 1950s, both of these systems depend on separate images for the right and left eyes that are then fused by the brain in such a way as to give the appearance of depth.

ILLUSIONS FOR THE NAKED EYE

Dr. Christopher Tyler, who worked with Julesz, took the process one step further in 1979 by developing what he called the autostereogram, a picture in which the illusion of depth could be seen by a pair of naked eyes. He did this by calling to mind the wallpaper effect noted by Sir David Brewster in 1844. Brewster observed that if he stared cross-eyed at wallpaper with its repeating patterns of, say, twining ivy and cherubs, he would get an impression of depth. The impression arose because each eye focused on the same piece of pattern but on a different repetition.

Tyler's invention combined the wallpaper effect with the random-dot stereogram. It was programmed on an Apple II computer in the BASIC programming language, and became the basis of today's mass-marketed 3-D images. By shifting parts of the pattern, the computer could make them appear close up or farther away.

To understand how these images are formed, think of doodling a pattern over and over. On each repetition, you must distort the pattern almost imperceptibly. This will create a "ghost image" that corresponds to the three-dimensional image that is to be hidden within the picture immediately in view.

Someone could make their own auto-stereograms by hand, but the amount of precise cutting and pasting would be prohibitive. Desktop publishing automates this process.

Commercially available paint software enables a graphics artist to create a gray-shaded image and then have a program convert it into a 3-D depth image. The gray-scale information, a measure of how dark the shade looks—from almost white to jet black—is used to compute how far to shift the dots in the repeat pattern to create the required distortion. Depending on the resolution of the equipment, an image can have anywhere from 16 to 256 levels of gray.

The basic principle in generating the 3-D effect is that depth comes forward where the gray-tone image is light, and it recedes where the gray is dark. The artist decides where to apply various levels of depth by brightening or darkening areas of the image.

The artist designs a colorful pattern to serve as the two-dimensional overlay that one sees on first glance. This strip is repeated, and information from the original gray-scale image is hidden within these strips.

Strips are paired up for the right and left eyes' points of view. Each pair shows the same slice of the picture, but pixels in the second part of the pair are shifted slightly. The amount of this displacement is computed according to the gray levels contained in the hidden image. Darker areas are shifted the most; a distance is measured in pixels, and directly correlates to the gray-scale number. The colors seem to wrap around 3-D objects in the completed picture.

INSPIRATION FOR A FAD

In 1990, Tom Baccei started N.E. Thing Enterprises, after he came across the idea for such 3-D books while reading an article on a technique developed by a cognitive psychologist for studying vision.

"I was smote on the spot," he says, and promptly used the technique in an ad for a magazine with a circulation of 30,000. When the ad drew 2,000 responses in the first month, he knew he was onto something. When Baccei published his first book of images in Japan, it set off a craze. The Japanese began stamping these 3-D illusions on everything from neckties to bathroom tiles. Within about 16 months, though, the fad died off almost as rapidly as it had begun.

Whether the rage lasts any longer in Europe and the English-speaking world remains to be seen. For the moment, consumers can find 3-D hot dogs or race cars on Pepsi cans in England, and bees or dinosaurs on some varieties of Cheerios boxes in the United States. Such images will show up in animated videos produced by Cascom, a firm based in Nashville, Tennessee, and as syndicated puzzles on the comic pages of 150 newspapers.

Baccei refuses to see philosophical or New Age consequences in the "oh, wow" enthusiasm that often accompanies discovering the 3-D images. He believes the value of the pictures will continue to be one of entertainment. "It's clever how we see these images, isn't it?" Baccei comments. "I can say that because I didn't invent them. I saw an opportunity and seized it."

THE IMAGES UNVEILED

The four pictures below depict the surprising images that lurk within the autostereograms on the preceding pages.

PAGE 269

PAGE 270

PAGE 271

PAGE 273

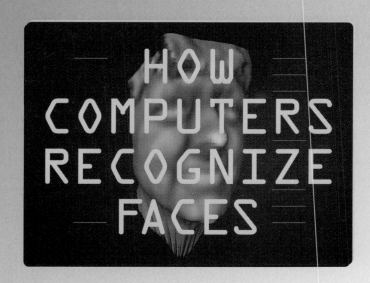

HOW COMPUTERS RECOGNIZE FACES

by Richard Lipkin

Between each and every pair of ears lies a unique world: a face. How well we know our own faces—even more the faces of those we love. But how do we distinguish one face from another, quickly finding a familiar one in a crowd? How does a mother find her daughter instantly in a nursery, or a man know his brother after 20 years' passage? The human brain has mastered this feat through evolution. And yet, we can be fooled. Color someone's hair, add a beard, and even a spouse may pass as a stranger.

The mystery of face recognition poses a by no means trivial problem. Using the latest techniques, psychologists and neuroscientists are only now getting a hint of how the brain recognizes images. Incrementally, they are finding that the secret lies, not in one neurological process, but in many. A battery of neurons must fire before one person can recognize another. Some combination of fuzzy, holistic neuronal matchings captures the overall picture, and thousands of detail-monitoring nerve cells note a subtle skin tone or a mouth's distinct angle.

Many scientists presume that if the human brain can recognize a face in a split second, a computer can be programmed to do the same thing. The question, though, is how. What must a computer do to identify and verify a particular face? Answering this complex question will yield strong returns in better security systems and perhaps even marvelous new animation techniques.

DECODING A MUG SHOT

Within the gadget-filled offices of the Media Laboratory at the Massachusetts Institute of Technology (MIT) in Cambridge, Massachusetts, Alex Pentland tinkers with a computer system that can single out one face among thousands with surprising accuracy. Given a database of 7,562 images (variations of the faces of 3,000 people), Pentland's system can ferret out an individual purely by decoding the person's "mug shot"—a flat, head-on snapshot.

Even when people shift position or expression, don new hairstyles or sunglasses, the program succeeds. In one test of 200 random faces, the computer topped 95 percent accuracy when asked to find the most similar face in the image database.

Pentland, a mathematically inclined computer scientist, has designed this system, called Photobook, to treat mug shots not as images per se, but as visual information. Thus, the computer never really "sees" someone's face. Instead, it interprets each picture as a grid of information, as defined by a

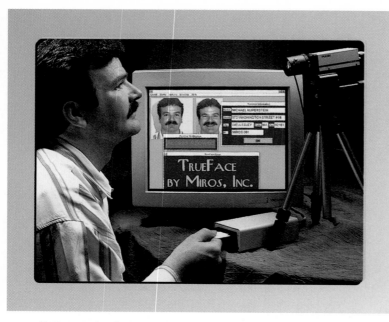

First-generation face-recognition systems are already commercially available. One such product called True-Face uses a video camera and a personal computer to match a subject's face with a previously taken and stored picture.

facial images and treating them as one huge matrix of information, the computer finds the main features of the faces in its database and combines them to form one face.

In essence, the computer takes all the stored faces and averages them, generating a single, ghostly-looking eigenface—a sort of fuzzy everyface. Photobook then ranks an individual face as a unique variation of the eigenface. Thus, each face becomes a unique version of a known type of object.

Though this analysis carries the cool edge of digital processing, it may not operate too far afield from the human brain. When a woman gazes at her lover's face, that image occurs first as mere scattered light on her retinas. Of course, random retinal pulses mean nothing until they become linked, through some subconscious route, to the implicit notion that faces exist. Once her brain has registered that it sees a face, and not something else, it can begin to appreciate the uniqueness of that face.

Underlying this fleeting cognitive process is the tacit knowledge that human beings wear faces on the front of their heads; that faces serve well for identifying people; and that faces have features to look for—eyes, ears, nose, and mouth. Such knowledge refines the plethora of possibilities that any image presents, narrowing the field for a human brain to interpret.

A computer face-recognition system does this, too.

FINDING FACES IN A CROWD

One of the biggest problems in digital recognition is finding the face in an image, Pentland says. "Once the computer finds the face, you're halfway home." Photobook has become fairly nimble at finding faces in pictures. But then, it looks at ordinary mug shots.

What happens when a live video camera monitors a scene, looking for someone

branch of mathematics called information theory. An image of a face—as of a house or a tree—imparts a unique set of information to a viewer. This computer program analyzes the content of that information and compares it with the image database.

Photobook uses a two-tiered method to recognize faces—a holistic view and feature analysis. On the holistic side, the computer gives a facial image a quick overview, ascertaining how the face fits together as a whole. Then, by treating the image as a matrix of information, it searches for eigenvectors, or mathematical patterns, characteristic of that particular face.

These eigenvectors (the German prefix *eigen* means "own" or "individual") describe precisely how that face differs from other stored facial images. "A face's key features, in terms of eigeninformation, may or may not relate to what we call facial features, like eyes, nose, lips, and hair," Pentland says. "But they are markers that denote unique characteristics of that face."

Pentland calls this approach "eigenface," based on mathematical eigenvalues in "face space," the computer's three-dimensional storage space. By working with a fixed set of

randomly entering a room? "This is a much bigger problem," says Baback Moghaddam, an MIT computer scientist. "The computer doesn't even know where to look. So we must build into it mechanisms for detecting heads and facial features, so it knows where to look. For instance, you don't generally look for a head on the floor."

Finding a face in a crowd would pose a problem for a hidden airport security system automatically scanning passersby for known terrorists, or for an office clearance system that admits only key employees. Working on an experimental system called Face-Rec, Moghaddam is tackling the problem that arises when someone randomly walks up to the video eye of a computer identification system—how to find that person's face among the visual clutter.

Once the computer finds and sizes up a face, it must determine who's there—that is, identify the face. In a test using 2,500 mug shots, Pentland and his colleagues varied the lighting, size, and head orientation of 16

male graduate students. Photobook correctly identified 96 percent of them despite changes in lighting, 85 percent despite a turned head, and 64 percent despite adjustments in size. Overall, the test bore out the system's strength and accuracy.

MIT's Media Laboratory is not the only prominent research organization studying face recognition. Another leading player in the field is The Analytic Science Corporation (TASC), located in Reading, Massachusetts. This firm has developed a computer system called FacePrint that uses three-dimensional modeling to describe and identify faces.

CONFIRMING AN IDENTITY

Once a person has been identified, there's a final problem: verification. In this process, the computer must ask and accurately answer the question, "Are you really who you say you are?"

"Most security systems these days rely on verification, which is an inherently easier problem than identification," says Pentland. "You're dealing with a much smaller set of possibilities. The person says who [he or she is], and then the system decides if that's true."

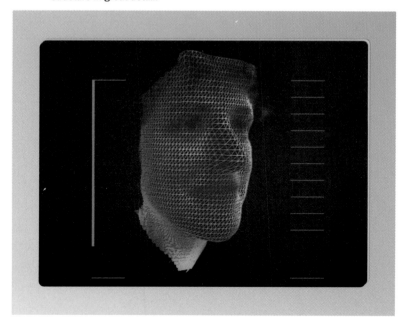

FacePrint, a face-recognition product developed by The Analytic Science Corporation (TASC), can generate an accurate model that depicts facial contour and structure in great detail.

Bank cash machines do this, asking for a personal identification number before doling out dollars. A more complex setting, such as a courtroom, may require fingerprints as an identifier. Yet fingerprints generally prove more useful for verifying than for identifying a person.

To shore up Photobook's accuracy in verification, Moghaddam is adding eigenfeature templates to it—things like eigeneyes, eigennoses, and eigenmouths. These help keep the system from getting fooled when someone sports a new hairdo, grows a beard, puts on glasses, or just alters facial expression. With eigenfeatures added to eigenfaces, recognition accuracy hovers around 98 percent.

TEACHING A SYSTEM TO YAWN

Both the Photobook and Face-Rec systems can learn new faces on their own. When presented with a new face, the computer checks it out repeatedly in face space, then decides whether the person is unrecognizable or bears a new face. If the latter, these systems enter the new face and average it into the eigenface.

Pentland believes that with this degree of accuracy, real-world applications become feasible, as in police stations, which must maintain huge files of mug shots for quick suspect identification. Or a customs center, which must screen for outlaws passing the border. Or voter registration. The Mexican government, for example, wants to assemble a cache of 50 million facial images to stem the problem of double balloting.

Yet, to achieve such power, a computer must be able to handle many views of someone's head, such as a profile or three-quarter view. This requires facial modeling and, at some level, an understanding of a variety of facial expressions.

"When you look at a photo, you can tell if someone's happy, sad, contemptuous, or angry," says Irfan A. Essa, a research assistant at MIT. "We want to make computers that can detect known facial patterns, like a smile or frown. Or the difference between a real or fake smile."

The search for such subtlety has taken Essa into new territory, using computer vision to model and animate people's expressions. By watching and imitating people, a prototype computer learns how faces express themselves. The computer sees how eyes and lips move, which features move together, and how fast each goes.

"Some muscles actuate faster, some slower," Essa says. "For an expression to look real, timing is critical."

From this interactive system, the list of options begins to mushroom. As the system practices imitating smiles and frowns, Essa sees the potential for realistic animation—the possibility of generating three-dimensional images that convey emotional depth. "We taught the system to yawn and sneeze," Essa says. "It took two minutes. Conventional animation techniques take a whole day."

Thus, a real-time facial-animation system, which maps live movement patterns onto a facial model that understands muscle control, has arrived under the combined touch of Essa and Trevor Darrell, an MIT computer scientist. While Essa concentrates on details of facial models and muscle control, Darrell forges ahead with real-time facial animation.

Taking its cues from pixel-by-pixel motion detectors, the facial-animation system marries this input to a simulated face mask rooted in human anatomy. Among this system's many

These color-enhanced images, captured on TASC's FacePrint system, illustrate the three-dimensional shape (top row) and curvature (bottom row) of a face.

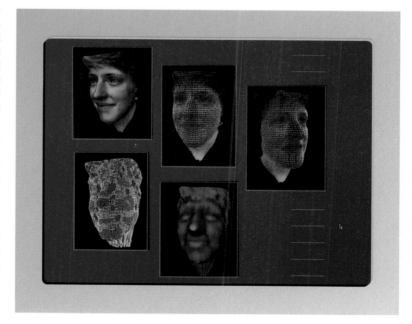

virtues is its ability to portray an authentic smile by mimicking the raising of eye corners that accompanies the upturning of lips. With a built-in understanding of typical facial gestures, the computer tailors the animated image to an individual's face within a fraction of a second. For pure animation, it will generate facial movements.

VIRTUAL PLAYMATES

But why stop at faces? Why not simulate, even automate, whole-body animation? Why not train a computer to watch athletes, dancers, or movie stars and learn their special, subtle moves—a Larry Bird layup, a Charlie Chaplin waddle, or perhaps a Judy Garland croon? Envision a computer system that could take in a great ballet, and from the dancers' movements, narrate the story.

At the Media Lab, such ambitious visions not only raise no eyebrows, they live as bona fide project goals. In a new system called ALIVE, a person wandering before the computer's gaze can watch an accurate replica of him- or herself moving in a virtual world. Within the confines of a virtual 16-foot by 16-foot (5-meter by 5-meter) room, animated autonomous agents can roam free in a land of illusion, interacting with other virtual beings.

This project aims, according to Pattie Maes, an MIT computer researcher, to create an artificial environment in which a person can interact, in natural and believable ways, with autonomous, semi-intelligent replicas whose behavior appears equally natural and believable.

In other words, an automated animation system with no cumbersome strings—such as headgear or wire-laden data gloves—attached. A system in which a live person's video image unobtrusively feeds a "magic mirror" that interprets that person's silhouette, movements, and gestures in real-time, three-dimensional space.

FacePrint developer Gaile G. Gordon analyzes a computer-generated model of a familiar face—her own.

Meanwhile, the user's virtual playmates wander independently in a world they appear to sense, acting on self-generated goals and taking cues from the user's gestures.

In one virtual world, for example, an animated puppet comes over to play, taking the user's virtual hand. When motioned away, the puppet pouts and leaves. When waved back over, the puppet returns, giggling. Another virtual setting brings a hamster begging for a meal. Food from a virtual table curbs its appetite, followed by a virtual rub of its virtual tummy. When a predator enters the scene, the hamster scampers away.

In the real world, where most communication occurs without words, such humanized computers represent invaluable learning tools. Since bodies and faces hold such expressive power, one can often glean more about a person's actual moods, intentions, or beliefs from gestures and expressions than from words.

"If a computer has a more human face and is less [emotionally] cool to work with, people can interact with it more naturally," Maes says. "Humanlike agents could train, educate, and motivate people, give personalized feedback, or do tasks for you. But for that to happen, computers must understand facial expressions and gestures as a way of communicating."

NAVIGATING THROUGH BLINDNESS

by Daniel Goleman

The other day, Reginald Golledge, Ph.D., who is blind, took a remarkable stroll through the campus of the University of California at Santa Barbara. As Dr. Golledge walked along, places and impediments in his path seemed to call out their names to him—"library here, library here," "bench here, bench here"—guiding him through a Disneyesque landscape of talking objects.

A PROTOTYPE WITH POTENTIAL

Dr. Golledge, a geographer at the university, was testing a prototype navigation system for the blind that announced the whereabouts of the objects through stereo headphones mounted to a computer in his backpack, creating a virtual-reality landscape. The information came, not from some miniature radar, but from the signals broadcast by the military's network of Global Positioning System (GPS) satellites. One day, its developers hope, miniaturized versions of this navigation device, which now weighs 28 pounds (13 kilograms), will help the blind navigate unfamiliar neighborhoods.

"With this system, you don't need to know a thing in advance about where you're going," says Roberta Klatzky, Ph.D., a psychologist at Carnegie-Mellon University in Pittsburgh, Pennsylvania, who is working with Dr. Golledge to develop the navigating device, which is used in conjunction with either a cane or a guide dog. "Blind people can find their way through totally unfamiliar terrain."

The "personal navigation system," as it is being called, promises to expand blind people's horizons to unfamiliar streets and neighborhoods. Seeing Eye dogs, by contrast, rely on their owners for cues to tell them where to go.

"This system will potentially improve tremendously the freedom of movement blind people have," says Michael Oberdorfer, M.D., branch chief of the Visual Processing Program at the National Eye Institute in Bethesda, Maryland, which is financing the research. "A blind person could walk down the street and know, not just that he was at 80th and Broadway, but what stores are around, and that Zabar's delicatessen was up ahead."

The "personal navigation system" worn by Reginald Golledge (below) creates a "virtual acoustic display" whereby objects (such as buildings) announce their presence to the blind user.

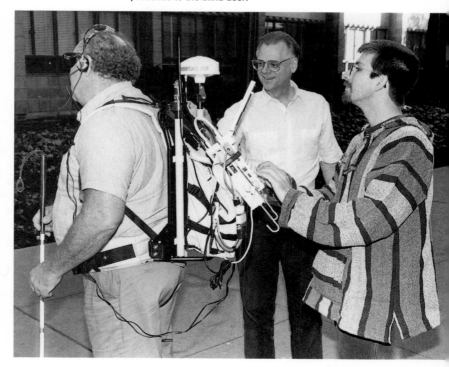

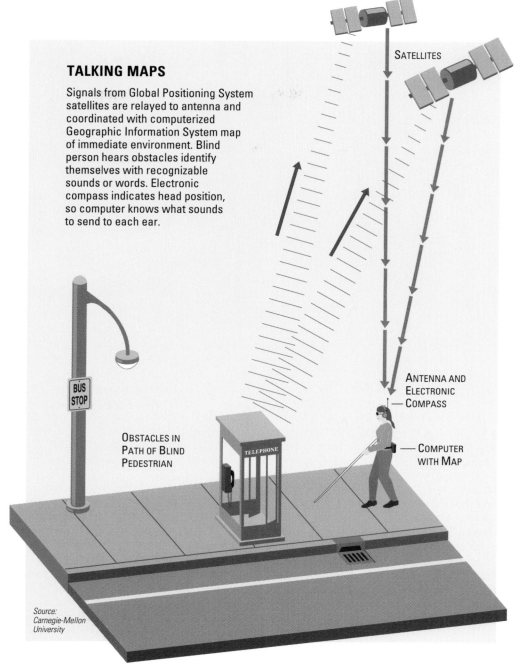

TALKING MAPS

Signals from Global Positioning System satellites are relayed to antenna and coordinated with computerized Geographic Information System map of immediate environment. Blind person hears obstacles identify themselves with recognizable sounds or words. Electronic compass indicates head position, so computer knows what sounds to send to each ear.

SATELLITES

ANTENNA AND ELECTRONIC COMPASS

COMPUTER WITH MAP

BUS STOP

TELEPHONE

OBSTACLES IN PATH OF BLIND PEDESTRIAN

Source: Carnegie-Mellon University

The developers estimate that everyday use of such devices is at least a decade away, but as other technologies have shown, advances can come much more quickly. Simpler devices, like eyeglasses using sonar signals to warn of looming obstacles, are much closer to market.

"But this navigation system tells you, not just where there are obstacles, but your overall location geographically," says Dr. Oberdorfer, because it lets blind users construct a mental map of new surroundings and learn their way around.

A TALKING MAP

The navigation system uses signals from a satellite-linked positioning device and a computerized map to create a "virtual acoustic display," a kind of talking map in

which large objects seem to announce themselves in the headphones with the precise timing and loudness that would be the case if the objects were actually making a sound. This allows the blind person to sense immediately their distance and direction, and use that information for guidance. While no one knows whether it is because blind people tend to develop a sharper sense of hearing, those who have tried the system say they quickly adapt to locating an object through the sounds.

"One of the crucial features of this system is that it takes advantage of sensory psychophysics—how the brain interprets signals from outside to make a map of your surroundings so you can navigate," Dr. Oberdorfer says.

The device relies on a triangulation of signals from four to eight GPS satellites to find the person's precise location. That information is transmitted to the computer, which contains the map. An electronic compass on the person's head tells the computer the exact position of the ears, so that the computer can then send messages calibrated to mimic a voice from the location of the object.

On a walk through the campus at the University of California at Santa Barbara, for instance, a simple version of the system might simulate a steady sound that would get louder as Dr. Golledge approached. As he reached the beacon at a turn in a path, the sound would stop, and a fresh sound from the new direction would guide him in that way.

The developers are testing different messages, like "library is 30 feet ahead, 20 feet ahead, 10 feet ahead," or compass readings, like "library is at 30 degrees," to see which work best. A more sophisticated version narrates a journey down the street in terms of the main landmarks being passed. "You'd hear 'I'm the library, I'm the library,' coming from the direction of the library, and it would alternate with other landmarks calling their name, like 'art museum here, art museum here,' to orient you," Dr. Klatzky says. "Then, as you reached the building you're going to, it would tell you, 'entrance here, entrance here,' coming from the right direction."

One advantage of the computerized system is that a blind person can preview a walk to be taken. "You can sit in a chair at home and play the auditory beacons you'll be using so you can rehearse the walk," Dr. Klatzky says.

FIRST VIRTUAL-REALITY DISPLAY

While several teams of researchers around the world are trying to develop similar navigational systems for the blind, the team that includes Dr. Klatzky and Dr. Golledge is the first to use a virtual-reality display that simulates sounds coming from the various locations a blind person passes.

"The computer knows the direction the wearer faces and has a local map," Dr. Klatzky says. "From the satellite, it knows where you are on Earth to an accuracy of 1 meter [3.3 feet]. Once it puts you on the map, the computer determines your exact angle from a location, and then sends a sound that arrives at each ear at slightly different times and intensities, so that the brain will register it in a way that tells you its direction and distance."

Although the military signal is periodically degraded to prevent unauthorized uses, the research team devised a way to get continued accuracy by comparing the satellite signals with a stationary land-based signal. Whenever the distances between the two readings differ, the researchers correct the satellite signal accordingly.

The virtual display is based on the work of Dr. Klatzky's main collaborator, Jack Loomis, Ph.D., a perceptual psychologist at the University of California at Santa Barbara. Dr. Loomis has studied the auditory cues the brain uses to compute the location of the source of a sound. Since the distance between a distant point and each of the ears is slightly different, the brain uses the difference in time that it takes a sound to arrive at each of the ears to calibrate how far away the sound is and from which direction it is coming.

Dr. Klatzky's research has focused on the ability of blind people to navigate. Earlier studies had cast doubt on the ability of blind people to orient themselves in a room unaided when given minimal cues about the location of things. But in a series of tests—like having a person walk two lengths of a triangle, then asking him or her to take the short-est path back to the beginning—Dr. Klatzky found that blind people fared about as well as sighted people who were blindfolded.

These tests "gave us confidence our navigation system would not be useless because of some deficiency of the blind in finding their way around," Dr. Klatzky says.

The research also draws on the expertise of Dr. Golledge, a geographer with a research specialty in psychological issues, such as how people construct mental maps of their surroundings. Dr. Golledge became blind about 10 years ago from a degenerative disease of the optic nerve, but continues to teach and do research.

LOOKING FOR THE RIGHT MIX

One goal of the research team is to miniaturize the navigation system's components so they will be lighter and less conspicuous, worn in a waistpack with wires to earphones.

Another goal is to find the optimal mix of spoken markers to give to the person using the system. "The question is, How many objects should talk to you at a given time?" Dr. Klatzky says. "If you walk down a street, dozens of objects may call to you, but too many will overwhelm your memory and attention capacity. Learning a new layout may demand a more general level, while just getting down the street might require a more detailed chorus of voices."

Other questions under investigation include details like the point at which a landmark down the road should start announcing itself, and the most useful phrases to use.

In a report published in the proceedings of the first annual Conference on Assistive Technologies, which was held in Marina del Rey, California, in October 1994, the Santa Barbara researchers say they hope one day their navigation aid will instill in those who use it "feelings of independence and confidence that are lacking in all but the most adventurous of blind travelers."

Even so, Dr. Golledge also uses his cane on test voyages, just to be sure no surprises block his path. Dr. Klatzky says, "We don't envision this system as entirely relieving the need for a Seeing Eye dog or cane. They'll still be needed to be sure about obstacles like moving cars that aren't on the computer's map."

Ask the Scientist

▶ *It seems as though every time I open the paper or watch the news, I see or hear the word "cyberspace." Exactly what does cyberspace mean? What about cybernetics?*

Because computer modems can now access transcontinental telephone lines, a vast computerized landscape has been created, often referred to as the Information Highway, or, more generally, "cyberspace." This electronic frontier consists of vast networks such as the Internet, commercial and institutional databases, and privately run computer bulletin boards, as well as multisensorial interactional experiences falling under the heading of "virtual reality." It is expected that an expanded accessibility of information will continue, especially as fiber-optic networks grow more sophisticated.

Author Norbert Wiener coined the term "cybernetics" in his 1948 book of the same name. He derived the term from a Greek word meaning "steersman," defining his neologism as "the science of controls of both human and machine systems," giving the automatic-pilot system on an airplane as an example of a cybernetic system. Over the intervening years, cybernetics has evolved into something slightly different, and now means the science of control and communication systems in animals and machines. A variant of the term is the related word "cyborg," which itself is an abbreviated version of "cybernetic organism."

▶ *Do people who use satellite dishes gain access to more television channels than I do through my cable television?*

Community antenna television, also known as CATV or "cable TV," an arrangement in which homes are linked via coaxial cable to a program-distributing source—does offer a greater program range than does conventional broadcast TV. In fact, most local cable companies pick up a partial programming feed within the "footprint" (regional range) of a single orbiting television satellite. A satellite dish, however, usually is able to access several complete satellite "footprints"—although, because of hilly terrain, buildings, trees, or the direction the "dish" is pointing, not all dishes have a clear "view" to all satellites. That little disclaimer aside, a satellite dish can usually receive broadcast signals directly from several geostationary (relatively fixed-position) space satellites locked into geosynchronous orbital slots.

"People who use a satellite dish can access up to 300 channels worldwide, while local cable companies deliver a fraction of what's available," says Lorna Merrill, a spokesperson for NWS Communications Corporation, based in Westfield, Massachusetts.

▶ *How does a suspension bridge work? During a hurricane a few years ago, officials closed down a suspension bridge near me. Why?*

Suspension bridges usually are constructed of two main cables up to 3 feet (0.9 meter) thick. The cables are secured to the bridge abutment on one bank of a watercourse, and run over two towers to an anchoring point on the other side. Smaller cables, called suspenders, run down from the main cable to a steel truss. The deck is then laid over the truss.

Only occasional mishaps have occurred with suspension bridges, the most famous being the collapse of the Tacoma Narrows Bridge on November 7, 1940. Unfortunately, the stiffening trusses or girders of this bridge were only 8 feet (2.4 meters) deep in a span of 2,800 feet (853 meters)—giving it extreme vertical flexibility. On the day it collapsed, a steady horizontal wind no greater than 42 miles (67.6 kilometers) per hour caused oscillations of the bridge to reach destructive amplitudes—until the main span broke up and ripped loose from the cable stays, sending the bridge crashing into Washington's Puget Sound.

As for the suspension bridge near you, assuming it was constructed correctly, the bridge was probably closed as a precaution to motorists rather than from any fear of the span's collapsing. Hurricane-force winds could conceivably blow cars and especially high-profile vehicles off the bridge into the storm-tossed waters below.

Is cargo still moved across the Atlantic Ocean primarily by boat? Do airplanes carry a significant amount of cargo?

Acting director C. William Johnson at the transport-services division within the U.S. Department of Commerce estimates that fully 99 percent of the world's bulk goods in terms of tonnage is still transported by ocean vessels, although transatlantic-boat-cargo figures are probably a percent or two lower. In 1994, the actual tonnage of ship-sent cargo exported from the United States amounted to some 368 million tons versus 2.2 million tons for transoceanic air shipments. The most-recent (also 1994) figures for imports were even more disproportionate: 647 million tons versus 2.4 million tons.

In terms of value, however, the cargo holds of airplanes transport far more than their share. In fact, despite the much greater volume of bulk goods traveling by

boat, the 1994 dollar values for U.S. imports were comparable—$143 billion received via air versus $339 billion via ship—and for the year's exports, nearly equal: $150 billion sent via airplane versus $177 billion via ocean vessels.

In the past few years, it seems as though many new area codes for telephones have been created in the United States. Why is that? Can any sequence of three numbers constitute an area code? Also, is there any relationship between area codes and ZIP codes?

Since 1980, "there's been an explosion in the demand for telephone numbers," says Ron Conners, director of the North American Numbering Plan administration for Bell Communications Research (BELLCORE)—the people who bring us all phone numbers, including area codes. Conners theorizes that the area-code "boom" has something to do with a change in how society has come to regard telephones. "It used to be that the average residential household had one phone. Now most people have several phone lines in their home, each with different numbers. The rest is simple: as you use up the telephone numbers, you need new area codes," he says.

There is a limit to the number of possible phone-number combinations. The North American Numbering Plan serves the United States and Canada, as well as Bermuda and some 15 Caribbean islands. (Mexico has its own distinct numbering system.) Within the North American region, an estimated 10,000 line numbers theoretically exist, but most of these are four-digit suffixes (a party's identifier code). Prefix numbers must begin with those digits between 2 and 9. A few other obscure numerical exceptions also exist, leaving a total of 792 possible area codes (many which have yet to be used). Codes that end in "00" are used for special purposes. These include 900 numbers (expensive services such as "psychic hot lines"), 800 numbers (usually free calls), 700 (presidential and governmental "secret" numbers), 600 (used exclusively in Canada and on a "reserved" basis in the United States), and 500 (personal communications, the so-called "follow-me" numbers). The next three-digit code is the local area code, followed by the four-digit suffix.

There is absolutely no relationship between area codes and ZIP codes.

▶ *I would like to become an architect. To study architecture, would I need to attend a four-year college, or could I go to a trade school? What sort of courses would I be expected to take?*

According to professional architect Bob Stillings of the firm Architectural Resources, Incorporated, in Providence, Rhode Island, "You basically have two options: the 'four-plus-three' and the 'five year' programs." Architectural schools sponsored by some universities (including Harvard, Dartmouth, and Columbia) now favor four years of prearchitectural training (similar to the premed and prelaw cumulative courses), followed by a three-year intensive architectural program.

Most U.S. schools, however, still favor the traditional five-year plan; candidates who qualify enter architectural school directly from high school and eventually obtain a Bachelor of Architecture degree. In either case, architects-to-be must apprentice for three years under a "master architect" in an architectural firm, and then must pass a rigorous architectural-board exam in order to qualify as a "registered architect."

Although many U.S. trade schools do offer a two-year certificate in architecture, such trade schools provide only enough education to qualify their graduates to do drafting or computer-aided design (CAD). "A registered architect might give a draftsman a sketch to draw up. Such a person doesn't have the complete knowledge that an architect has," Stillings says.

Architectural courses are multifaceted. Besides the standard liberal-arts classes and electives, a sound architectural program should include structural courses, design courses (similar to art courses), history-of-architecture overviews, materials courses, and construction courses.

▶ *What is the difference between an atom bomb and a hydrogen bomb? Also, several years ago, there was quite a bit of discussion about a neutron bomb that killed people, but left buildings intact. How would such a bomb have worked?*

Christopher Campbell states in the *Nuclear Weapons Fact Book* that "the atomic bomb relied on fission for its power, whereas thermonuclear devices (hydrogen or H-bombs) work by fusion."

Nuclear *fission* is the splitting of the nuclei of heavy atoms such as uranium or plutonium. Nuclear *fusion* is the combination of light atoms such as hydrogen isotopes. In both processes, part of the mass of these elements is converted into energy, and, if this can be made to happen fast enough, a nuclear explosion is the result. Of the two, fusion is much more potent. The thermonuclear weapons called H-bombs, developed in the 1950s, held far greater explosive power than the atom bombs dropped on Japan in 1945. The biggest ever known to be tested, by the Soviet Union in 1962, exploded with a force of 3,000 Hiroshima bombs.

The neutron bomb, developed around 1970, is a smaller, enhanced-radiation (ER) weapon calculated to throw out neutrons, which are deadlier to humans than are other forms of radiation. ER weapons, which can be delivered by artillery shells or battlefield-range missiles, are atomic explosives designed to minimize the blast but "enhance" the deadly radiation effects. Stopping tanks was the original reasoning behind ER weapons, which would destroy an armored attack by incapacitating the crew rather than the tanks.

REVIEWS

Agriculture

Production and Income

In a marked departure from the norm, the United States, long among the world's largest exporters of grains, imported several million tons of grain—primarily feed wheat, durum wheat (used for making pasta), oats, and barley—in the first six months of 1994. Most of these imports came from Canada and reflected a weak Canadian dollar, differences between U.S. and Canadian agricultural price-support policies, and U.S. grain supplies that were severely reduced by disastrous flooding in the U.S. Midwest in 1993. Large harvests of fruits, vegetables, and grains increased income for U.S. crop producers in the last half of 1994, though the abundance depressed market prices.

In California, the nation's top agricultural producer, officials continued a controversial battle against the fruit fly. A Mediterranean fruit fly (Medfly)-eradication program was activated in Ventura and Riverside counties to eliminate the pest from the area. Agriculture specialists also found a small number of

California continues to use controversial insecticides to eradicate the Mediterranean fruit flies that threaten to destroy the state's fruit industry.

guava fruit flies, an unusual but serious pest that also could threaten the state's fruit crops.

U.S. farmers produced a record supply of meat in 1994, depressing the prices of beef, pork, and poultry to their lowest levels in more than a decade. Livestock producers thus experienced great financial loss.

The pork industry continued to rapidly move toward large integrated-production systems. North Carolina, benefiting from rapid growth of large-scale production systems, moved from the sixth-ranking state in pork production in 1990 to second place in 1994, with the state's total production of pork nearly doubling in that period. Other states with growth in large-scale producing units include Iowa, Missouri, Oklahoma, and Utah. The rapid growth of integrated-pork-production systems sparked controversy in areas where smaller hog farms were common. Critics voiced concerns about odors, water pollution, and other environmental problems from large hog-production units.

Abundant supplies of milk, other dairy products, and eggs were produced, despite feed-supply problems in the upper Midwest. For the first time, Wisconsin slipped to second place, behind California, in U.S. milk production. The reduced production in Wisconsin reflected a poor harvest of feed crops in 1993, the higher costs associated with purchasing feed (rather than raising it on the dairy farms themselves), and heavier-than-normal culling of dairy herds due to the limited feed supplies.

Western Water Supplies

Despite rising milk production in California, several of its large dairy farms moved out of state to avoid population pressures, high land values, rising taxes, and reduced availability of water for agricultural uses. Growing urban demand for water in California and lingering drought conditions led to increased restrictions on water use for agriculture. Some farms sold part of their water rights to urban users and concentrated the use of remaining water supplies on the irrigation of high-value crops.

In neighboring Nevada, growing water demands in Las Vegas raised concerns throughout the West. Las Vegas, the fastest-growing urban center in the United States, was considering ways of obtaining additional water from the Colorado River, which provides water to seven states. Farmers and ranchers were concerned that the city's plans would reduce water availability to agriculture in neighboring states. Opponents also noted that Las Vegas had an extremely high per-capita water consumption.

POLICY AND PROGRAMS

In late 1994, the U.S. Department of Agriculture (USDA), Congress, and agricultural groups developed initial plans for 1995 agricultural legislation. The 1990 U.S. agricultural legislation expires late in 1996, and will require replacement before that time so farms and agricultural businesses can make production and marketing plans. Proposals ranged from fine-tuning existing policies to replacing long-standing support programs with an income-assurance program.

The proposed income-assurance program would provide a type of insurance protection to farmers, giving support payments in years when farm incomes fell below a certain percentage of the long-term average. Unlike the case in most other industries, farmers are unable to precisely control production, due to fluctuations in weather, diseases, insects, and other biological hazards. As a step toward assessing an income-assurance program, the USDA initiated a new crop-insurance program in several pilot counties. Loss payments to farmers were triggered when their county's average yield fell below a predetermined level.

In return for agriculture's support for legislation to ratify the General Agreement on Tariffs and Trade (GATT), the Clinton administration agreed to request funding for the Conservation Reserve Program (CRP) for at least two more years in future budgets. The CRP has been in effect since 1985, removing about 37 million acres (14.9 million hectares) of fragile cropland from production under 10-year contracts. The first of these contracts was scheduled to expire in late 1995. The CRP has helped control soil erosion, improve water quality, and increase wildlife habitats. It also has helped to curtail surplus agricultural production and has reduced the need for expensive programs to store surplus crops.

U.S. corn and soybean exports to Mexico increased substantially in 1994, in response to the North American Free Trade Agreement (NAFTA) and to strong growth in the Mexican economy. The United States and Canada negotiated new restrictions on imports of wheat into the United States. The agreement should reduce negative economic impacts on U.S. wheat farmers from Canadian imports and should counter distortions stemming from NAFTA.

ENERGY FROM AGRICULTURE

In mid-1994, the U.S. Environmental Protection Agency (EPA) issued rules for reformulated fuels for the nation's most heavily polluted cities. The new rules required that 15 percent of the raw material for increased oxygenation of gasoline must come from renewable feedstocks in 1995, with 30 percent from renewable feedstocks mandated for 1996 and later years. This rule was challenged in court by the petroleum industry and was scheduled to be reviewed again in 1995.

Although most of the agriculturally based fuels come from corn processed into ethanol and its derivatives, the American Soybean Association was working with the transportation industry to find cost-effective ways of using soybean-oil/diesel-fuel blends to reduce urban pollution from diesel engines.

THE EURODUNG CONTROVERSY

In the Netherlands, a private firm announced plans to help with a livestock-manure crisis by exporting large quantities to developing countries. With very high livestock densities in the Netherlands and neighboring countries, air- and water-pollution problems have grown more serious. As a result, restrictions have been placed on the amount of manure that can be applied locally to farm fields. The Dutch firm plans to supply developing nations with manure for use as fertilizer and to help replace topsoil that has been lost through decades of intensive farming. Developing countries showed mixed reactions to the proposal, known as Eurodung, expressing concern that excess supplies could increase pollution in their rivers and other water supplies.

Robert Wisner

ANTHROPOLOGY

EARLY PRIMATES IN CHINA

Investigations at a limestone quarry near Shanghuang in eastern China reveal fossil bones of at least five new types of early primates that date back some 45 million years. Scientists are surprised by the variety of primates represented at the site. The finds include teeth, jaw fragments, and limb bones of a small, mouse-sized monkey. These discoveries suggest that East Asia may have been an important region in the early development of primates, including the ancestors of humans. Because of difficulties with the dating techniques, it is not yet clear whether the oldest known fossil primates are these newly discovered ones from China, or fossils of African origin.

CLIMATE CHANGE AND HUMAN EVOLUTION

Scientists have argued that an important factor in human evolution occurred about 5 million years ago, when our primate ancestors moved from a life in the trees to one on the open grasslands of East Africa. This shift has been linked to the development of the bipedal gait—walking upright on two legs. Some researchers believe that a major climatic change brought about this shift from an arboreal to a terrestrial environment, as forests declined and grasslands spread.

New studies of soil samples from sites in East Africa, involving tests on traces of carbon in the soil, suggest that no substantial climatic change occurred 5 million years ago. If future analyses support these results, then a new model will be needed to explain why the ancestors of humans developed the practice of walking upright. Some approaches view the question in terms of the varied opportunities offered to the evolving hominids around 5 million years ago, leading them to adapt to new environments and new forms of locomotion.

FOSSILS OF THE EARLIEST HUMANS

Fossil jaws, teeth, and fragments of skulls and limb bones belonging to 18 individuals have been discovered at Aramis in Ethiopia. These fossils date back about 4.4 million years to a period when scientists think that the ancestors of modern humans branched off from the ancestors of modern apes. The fossils are attributed to a newly identified species, named *Australopithecus ramidus*. Physical anthropologists consider the new finds more apelike than other known early hominid fossils, but nonetheless believe that *A. ramidus* belongs to the hominid, or human, line of evolution. The shape of the teeth is a particularly important contributing factor in drawing this conclusion.

Environmental evidence recovered in association with the fossil bones suggests a wooded landscape at the time that the bones were deposited. The fossil evidence does not indicate clearly whether the individuals walked upright, but the shape of the skull bases suggests that these hominids may have been bipedal. The skulls are believed to have been broken, perhaps by predators, before the bones were deposited on the ground.

THE HUMAN THUMB AND TOOLMAKING

Studies of the first metacarpal, a bone that links the thumb to the hand in modern humans and in fossil hominids, are yielding important information about the toolmaking capability of early humans. The presence and shape of this bone allow for humans to grip objects between the thumb and fingers and to apply both delicate motion and force.

Study of the fossil bones, which were dated to around 3.5 million years ago, indicates that *Australopithecus afarensis*—the group to which the fossil known as "Lucy" belongs—did not have a metacarpal of the same shape as that of modern humans. Perhaps, therefore, this early hominid would not have been able to physically make and use tools in the same way that later hominids could. Specimens of fossil bones of *Australopithecus robustus* (1 million to 2.5 million years old), *Homo erectus* (200,000 to 1.8 million years old), and *Homo sapiens neanderthalensis* (40,000 to 150,000 years old) show that these later hominids had thumbs similar to those of modern humans, making them physically capable of fashioning and using tools. In fact, abundant stone tools are found associated with fossils of these early humans. The earliest known stone tools date to about 2.5 million years ago. This evidence suggests a close link between the development of the modern-shaped metacarpal bone and the beginning of toolmaking.

According to current dating evidence, *Australopithecus robustus* and *Homo erectus* overlapped for some 800,000 years. Thus, two different types of toolmaking early humans appear to have lived at the same time.

MIGRATORY REINDEER HERDERS

Scientists exploring northern Siberia met a group of people that maintain traditions linking them with peoples who lived in the region thousands of years ago. Some 5,000 of these people, known as Nenets, keep their traditional lifestyle, living primarily on reindeer meat and fish and practicing reindeer sacrifice. They are nomadic and drive their reindeer herds some 1,000 miles (1,600 kilometers) annually. Their dwellings include tepees made of reindeer skin. The Nenets make most of their own tools, some of which resemble those used by their predecessors thousands of years ago. Scientists hope that further study of these people will provide a better understanding of the ways of life of the inhabitants of this region over the past 8,000 years.

The existence of the Nenets, a group of so-called "reindeer people," has only recently come to the attention of Western scientists. The people, who live in a remote region of northern Siberia (see map), maintain a traditional lifestyle that some scientists believe has changed very little in 8,000 years.

EARLIEST HUMAN IN THE BRITISH ISLES

A fossilized human tibia, or shinbone, recovered in a quarry at Boxgrove in West Sussex in the United Kingdom was dated using associated animal bones to about 500,000 years ago. The new fossil is directly associated with stone tools, providing a valuable link between the physical character of the humans and the tools they made and used a half million years ago. The size of the shinbone suggests that the individual, probably a man, stood about 6 feet (1.8 meters) tall.

Although substantial archaeological traces of humans have been recovered in Europe that date back as long as 1 million years, the physical remains of early humans are nonetheless much less common in Europe than in Africa. The only possibly earlier human fossil known from Europe is the mandible (jaw) found in a quarry at Mauer in Germany. The Mauer fossil is believed to be about 600,000 years old.

NEW FINDINGS FROM THE ICE MAN

Extensive physical studies are being conducted on the body of the Ice Man, the mummified remains of a prehistoric human found in 1991 by mountain climbers in the Alps. Test results are revealing important information that is enhancing our understanding of the health of humans 5,000 years ago. While thousands of human skeletons from that time and before have been obtained for study from cemeteries all over the world, the Ice Man is unique in providing scientists with surviving human skin and internal organs from that long ago. Analyses of his bones show that this man, who was between 25 and 40 years old at the time of his death, suffered from severe osteoarthritis. Investigation of blood vessels indicates that he had the heart disease known as arteriosclerosis, or hardening of the arteries. Since only this one individual is so well preserved, scientists do not know whether his poor health was typical of men of his age in that period. Investigators also observed that some of his ribs were broken, but it is not yet clear whether they were broken during his lifetime or during the recovery of the body in 1991.

SIBERIAN ICE WOMAN

The body of a woman 18 to 20 years old was recovered from frozen ground at Ukok in the Altai Mountains of southern Siberia. As in the case of the Ice Man, the constant frozen condition of the corpse resulted in excellent preservation of this 2,000-year-old individual. The woman, who stood about 64 inches (1.6 meters), was buried in a shirt of white silk, a red dress, and stockings. She had tattoos on her left arm. The internal organs had been removed before burial, and the spaces packed with peat. The coffin in which she was buried was made from a tree trunk, and she was accompanied in the grave by vessels, equipment from a horse's harness, and a mirror. She was a member of the people known as Scythians, described by the Greek writer Herodotus in the 5th century B.C. Her fine clothing and lavish grave goods suggest that she was a member of an elite social group within the society.

Peter S. Wells

ARCHAEOLOGY

PALEOLITHIC CAVE PAINTINGS

In December 1994, explorers in the Ardèche region of south-central France came upon a partially hidden entrance to a limestone cave that contains more than 300 paintings of animals and of human hands. Among the animals represented, woolly rhinoceroses and bears are especially abundant; other animals depicted include mammoths, wild cattle, horses, lions, hyenas, panthers, and owls. Preliminary estimates suggest that the paintings are about 20,000 years old.

The newly discovered cave, located near Vallon-Pont-d'Arc, may be larger and contain a richer assemblage of art than the renowned caves at Lascaux in southwestern France and Altamira in northern Spain. This newly found cave appears to have been undisturbed by later intrusions. Along with the painted walls, the cave contains ancient fireplaces, stone tools, and footprints of humans and of bears. A bear skull was found on a rock close to paintings of bears on the walls. By studying the archaeological remains on the floor of the cave, scientists hope to gather new information about the uses of these painted caves.

CENTRAL AMERICAN CAVE BURIALS

In Cueva de Rio Talgua, a complex cave system in Honduras, scientists have found human remains that indicate systematic placement of the dead deep in a gallery. Long bones were arranged in piles, and the skulls of some 150 individuals were arranged in the gallery, apparently after the flesh had decayed. Some of the bones were coated with a red coloring substance. Associated objects include ceramic bowls, vessels carved of stone, and fragments of jade ornaments. Radiocarbon tests date the artifacts to around 900 B.C. Remains of a nearby settlement can be linked with the graves through similar pottery found at the two locations. These cave burials provide important new information about little-known peoples of this region east and south of the Maya heartland. This discovery also affords scientists a valuable glimpse of an early stage in the development of Meso-american civilization.

ARCHAEOLOGICAL SKEPTICISM

A team of experts on the archaeology of the earliest peoples in the New World examined 45,000-year-old objects from Pedra Furada, believed to be a site of human habitation in the Americas, but the experts are not convinced that the materials from this Brazilian location are the products of human efforts. For example, the alleged stone tools the archaeologists examined were judged to be stones broken by natural processes rather than implements fashioned by human hands. Nor did the scientists accept evidence for the presence of human-built fireplaces from which charcoal was extracted for radiocarbon dating. The charcoal could have resulted from natural fires, they contend. Thus, despite ongoing research for earlier indications of humanity, currently the earliest dates generally accepted by scientists for clear evidence of human activity in the Americas range from 12,000 to 15,000 years ago.

MASTODON BUTCHERING IN FLORIDA

A mastodon tusk measuring about 7 feet (2 meters) long, with butchering marks made with stone knives, was found near Tallahassee, Florida. A flake of stone that may have been part of a cutting implement was recovered nearby, along with tools made of ivory. Radiocarbon dates obtained from seeds found in association with the tusk indicate a time around 12,200 years ago. This discovery is the earliest evidence found in North America that confirms butchering by human hunters. The find also indicates the presence of humans in Florida by 12,000 years ago, and contributes to the ongoing discussion about the role of humans in the extinction of big mammals at the end of the Ice Age. As world climate warmed and the great ice sheets retreated at the end of the last glaciation, large mammals such as mammoths, mastodons, and woolly rhinoceroses became extinct. It is not clear whether the extinctions were caused primarily by climatic change and resulting changes in vegetation, or whether human hunting played a major role.

EARLY DOMESTICATION OF PIGS

Evidence for the very early domestication of pigs was discovered during excavations

Hadrian Survives

A marble statue of the emperor Hadrian was discovered during the restoration of a Roman odeum, or theater, at Ilion, the site of ancient Troy. The larger-than-life-sized statue, which dates to the 2nd century A.D., is considered by archaeologists to be especially valuable because its head is perfectly preserved. Evidence suggests that the

statue had been the focal point of the stage, and that the odeum itself was either built by or dedicated to Hadrian. Based on coins found in the excavation site, experts believe that an earthquake destroyed the odeum and the nearby public buildings sometime around A.D. 475. Miraculously, the statue of Hadrian survived the catastrophe nearly intact.

conducted at Hallan Cemi in southeastern Turkey, a site that will soon be inundated by waters that will build up behind a new dam. One factor that implies domestication is the nature of the porcine teeth—the molars are smaller than those of wild pigs, suggesting a changed relationship between humans and pigs. Another is the age distribution of the bones: the remains of large numbers of male pigs less than one year old are represented, more remains than would be expected from a wild, hunted population. Through radiocarbon dating, the artifacts were determined to be about 10,200 years old.

The pattern observed at Hallan Cemi suggests systematic breeding of pigs by the occupants. Houses on the site were built of stone, implying permanent occupation of the settlement, and growth rings on mollusk shells also point to year-round habitation. Besides raising pigs, the people collected seeds and nuts, and they hunted deer and wild sheep. The evidence from Hallan Cemi suggests a very different pattern of early domestication and permanent settlement from that in the Levant region to the south and in the foothills of the Zagros Mountains to the southeast. In those areas, the first villagers of the Neolithic period based their economies on wheat and barley cultivation, and on domestication of sheep and goats. The excavation results indicate that domestication of plants and animals seems to have occurred in different ways in different places.

OLDEST PAVED ROAD

The oldest known paved road has been discovered in Egypt. The road, about 7 miles (11.3 kilometers) long and 6 feet (1.8 meters) wide, and paved with limestone and sandstone, is located southwest of Giza, where the great pyramids are situated. The road ran from a basalt quarry to the edge of former Lake Moeris (modern-day Lake Karun). The basalt, a black or gray volcanic rock, was likely quarried for use in burial monuments in Giza. Scientists think that the quarried stone was then hauled along the road, perhaps with the aid of log rollers, loaded onto barges, and brought across the lake in the direction of the Nile for shipment to the site of Giza. Pottery found associated with the road, with the quarry, and with a nearby settlement indicates a time during the Old Kingdom, around 2600 to 2200 B.C.

SUBWAY ARCHAEOLOGY IN ATHENS

Large-scale archaeological rescue excavations are being carried out in Athens, Greece, as construction crews build stations and tunnels for an extensive new subway system. Although much of ancient Athens is known to archaeologists and architectural historians from standing remains and from historical texts, many new discoveries are being made as the ground is opened and cleared for the modern construction. So far, an aqueduct dating from the 5th century B.C. has been unearthed, as well as a Roman aqueduct. Besides bronze-casting shops and a Roman bath complex, graves from early Christian times and storage buildings from the Byzantine period have also been identified. Although many archaeologists would like to see these structures preserved, all of the remains must be removed for the building of the subway system, designed to alleviate the city's growing traffic congestion. Archaeologists must work quickly to record all of the information before the ancient features are destroyed.

ANCIENT ATMOSPHERIC POLLUTION

Studies being conducted in different parts of the Northern Hemisphere are finding evidence of extensive lead pollution dating from ancient Greek and Roman times. In the production of silver from its ore, sizable amounts of lead are released into the atmosphere. Scientists know that the ancient Greeks and Romans made extensive use of silver—in coins, ornate vessels, and decorations of various kinds. Scientists studying world climate and air quality are examining long cores drilled from the glacial ice in Greenland. Analyses of layers of ice laid down millennia ago indicate a huge increase in atmospheric lead around 500 B.C. This level of atmospheric lead was maintained for some 800 years until about A.D. 300, when a decrease began. The same pattern is apparent in lake beds in Sweden. The cause of this atmospheric lead is believed to have been metalworking activity by Greek and Roman silver smelters.

Peter S. Wells

ASTRONOMY

THE SOLAR SYSTEM

The impacts of fractured Comet Shoemaker-Levy 9 with Jupiter provided astronomers an unprecedented opportunity to observe this powerful collision. Altogether, at least 21 fragments of the comet struck Jupiter, the largest being about 2 to 3 miles (3.2 to 4.8 kilometers) in diameter. (A complete review of this event begins on page 64.)

In response to a congressional directive, the National Aeronautical and Space Administration (NASA) announced in August 1994 the establishment of a committee to develop a plan to identify and catalog within 10 years comets and asteroids larger than about 0.6 mile (1 kilometer) across that cross Earth's orbit and may threaten the planet. Appointed as chairman of the eight-member Near-Earth Object Search Committee was Eugene Shoemaker, Ph.D., an astrogeologist with the Lowell Observatory and codiscoverer of Comet Shoemaker-Levy 9.

Spectacular images taken in December by the Wide-Field/Planetary Camera 2 (WF/PC-2) of the Hubble Space Telescope (HST) showed a storm—as large as Earth—whipping through the atmosphere of the planet Saturn.

Three spectacular images of the planet Uranus, taken on August 14 by the Hubble Telescope's WF/PC-2, revealed the planet's rings, at least five of the inner moons, and bright clouds and a high-altitude haze above the planet's south pole.

EXTRASOLAR PLANETS

French astronomers at the European Southern Observatory's 11.8-foot (3.6-meter) telescope in La Silla, Chile, took high-resolution infrared photos of the dusty disk around the star Beta Pictoris, and found that the inner part of the disk may be swept free of dust by planets larger than Earth.

In June 1994, NASA announced Hubble Telescope findings that the process that may form planets is common in the Milky Way galaxy. C. Robert O'Dell, Ph.D., of Rice University in Houston, Texas, and a colleague,

Zheng Wen, formerly of Rice and now at the University of Kentucky in Lexington, surveyed 110 stars and found protoplanetary disks around 56 of them.

After two years of study, radio astronomer Alexander Wolszczan of Pennsylvania State University in State College reports "irrefutable" evidence confirming the existence of at least two planets orbiting a pulsar in the direction of the constellation Virgo. Estimated at about three times the mass of Earth, these planets have become the first ever identified outside the solar system.

LIFE CYCLES OF THE STARS

In February 1994, the Hubble Telescope obtained the best images yet of a mysterious mirror-imaged pair of rings of glowing gas that surround the site of the stellar explosion Supernova 1987-A. One explanation for the strange sight is that the two rings might be "painted" by a high-energy beam of radia-

Within a week of its discovery, Supernova 1994-I (above) dramatically brightened, ultimately reaching a light intensity equivalent to 100 million Suns.

tion or particles, like a spinning light-show laser beam tracing circles on a screen. The source of the radiation might be a previously unknown stellar remnant that is a binary companion to the star that exploded in 1987.

On April 2, amateur astronomers discovered Supernova 1994-I in the inner regions of the "Whirlpool Galaxy," M51, located 20 million light-years away in the constellation Canes Venatici. The exploding star reached a peak brightness of 100 million times that of the Sun a week later, and quickly became the target of investigations by astronomers using ground-based optical and radio telescopes, and the Hubble Telescope.

An unusually bright X-ray source—one of the three brightest in the sky—was discovered in the southern constellation Scorpius by an instrument aboard NASA's Compton Gamma Ray Observatory (GRO) on July 27, 1994. Named X-ray Nova Scorpii, or GRO J1655-40, it might be caused by matter spilling from a normal star into a black hole.

SEEKING DARK MATTER

Two teams of astronomers, working independently with the Hubble Telescope, showed in November 1994 that faint red-dwarf stars rarely form and are sparse in the Milky Way galaxy. The astronomers also ruled out the possibility that these red dwarfs constitute the invisible matter, called "dark matter," believed to account for more than 90 percent of the mass of the universe.

Astronomers have also uncovered indirect evidence for a dark-matter candidate called a MACHO (Massive Compact Halo Object). Observations detected several instances of an invisible object that happens to lie along the line of sight to an extragalactic star, where it amplifies—or gravitationally lenses—the light from the distant star.

BEYOND THE MILKY WAY

In October 1994, astronomers announced that they had accurately measured the distance to the galaxy M100 in the Virgo galaxy cluster using observations of Cepheid variable stars by the Hubble Telescope. The distance was measured as 56 million light-years, meaning that the universe is between 8 billion and 12 billion years old, far younger than previous estimates of up to 20 billion years.

Hubble also found seemingly conclusive evidence for a massive black hole in the center of the giant elliptical galaxy M87, located 50 million light-years away in the constellation Virgo. The object weighs as much as 3 billion Suns, but is concentrated into a space no larger than our solar system.

In September, Hubble astronomers found a new quasar—not billions of light-years away like most, but a mere 600 million light-years away. Quasars emit hundreds of times more energy than an entire galaxy with more than 100 billion stars; finding a quasar at such a nearby distance is unusual.

The Compton Gamma Ray Observatory uncovered evidence that gamma-ray bursts occur in the far reaches of the universe, bear an imprint of the universe's expansion, and occur so far away that they show relative "time dilation." The result provided additional evidence that gamma-ray bursts are not limited to the Milky Way galaxy.

A series of remarkable pictures taken with the Hubble Telescope suggests that elliptical galaxies developed quickly into their present shapes, while spiral galaxies in large clusters evolved over a much longer period—the majority being built and then torn apart by dynamic processes in a restless universe.

An international team of Hubble astronomers announced in July 1994 the presence of helium in the early universe. The element was detected in the light of a remote celestial body, a quasar, located in the constellation of Cetus at a distance so great that its light has taken approximately 90 percent of the age of the universe to reach us. This may mark the discovery of a tenuous plasma that fills the vast volumes of space between the galaxies.

NEW-GENERATION TELESCOPES

A 21-foot (6.5-meter) replacement mirror for the Multiple Mirror Telescope of Southern Arizona was ground and polished at the University of Arizona's Steward Observatory Mirror Laboratory. Meanwhile, a second 6.5-meter blank was successfully cast using the lab's "spin-cast" technology.

In May, the 27-foot (8.3-meter) blank for the Japan National Large Telescope, named Subaru, was heated to make it sag to the desired curvature, before being shipped to Pittsburgh, Pennsylvania, for further work.

The Very Large Telescope (VLT) has suffered budget problems, causing major optical innovations to be eliminated temporarily. And in spring 1994, a judge ordered construction work at its site on Cerro Paranal halted after an ownership dispute over the mountain, before his decision was overturned.

Dennis L. Mammana

Automotive Technology

New Cars

Ford Motor Company, a leader in incorporating aluminum into cars, produced a small number of test cars (Mercury Sables) made with aluminum frames and bodies. Aluminum is lighter than steel, the traditional structural material, a fact that argues for aluminum's use in fuel-efficient cars of the future. Aluminum already is used in today's cars for radiators, wheels, and hoods, but not for main structural components.

Using aluminum in fitted structural parts presents processing problems. Stamping or pressing aluminum parts creates imperfections in the metal surface, and welding aluminum is more problematic than welding steel. Aluminum components must therefore be glued together.

Two overseas companies, Honda (Japan) and Audi (Germany), already produce aluminum cars, but they are expensive high-performance vehicles not appropriate for mass marketing. Ford is gambling that gains in processing eventually will yield a modestly priced aluminum car. They hope eventually to produce 300,000 to 400,000 aluminum cars annually.

Automobile frames made from aluminum are considerably lighter than their steel counterparts, a property clearly demonstrated by the two Ford Motor Company technicians below.

The German car company Mercedes-Benz and the Swiss company Ste. Suisse Microélectronique et d'Horlogerie, which is best known for making Swatch watches, have developed a "microcompact" car. The new egg-shaped car, nicknamed the "Swatchmobile," is about 8 feet (2.4 meters) long and 4.5 to 5 feet (1.4 to 1.5 meters) wide. Two versions of the car—basic and sporty—were displayed by Mercedes-Benz in March 1994. Each seats two adults, and targets urban travelers who might benefit from the extreme maneuverability of such a small automobile. Although slow to accelerate, the cars are inexpensive and stylish. The developers plan to begin selling the cars in 1997.

New Safety Devices

Small manufacturers and the Big Three U.S. car companies are developing collision-warning systems for cars and trucks. The systems, which use a variety of mounting sites and different wavelengths of light, detect objects in the blind spots on each side of the rear of a vehicle. The systems include side-mounted devices that send out light waves into the blind spots. If the waves meet and reflect from an object, a sensor informs a computer, which causes small lights on the driver's side-view mirror to flash. Some systems also trigger an audio alarm.

The system developed by General Motors (GM), which uses microwaves as "feelers," provides a visual signal whenever an object enters the blind spot, and sounds an audio alarm if the turn signal is engaged. The

The so-called "Swatchmobile" represents the latest European thinking in compact-car design. The inexpensive two-passenger vehicle is expected to hit the market in 1997.

company already installs the system in some buses, and plans to offer it in passenger cars within the next few years.

A similar system offered by Amerigon Incorporated of Monrovia, California, uses radio-wave pulses as feelers, which requires less computer processing. AutoSense of Denver, Colorado, offers still another system, this one using infrared light. Wave emitters and receivers are installed in the housings of the car's taillights. The AutoSense alarm, which is visual only, operates when the turn signal is engaged.

Volvo of Sweden became the first car company to offer side-impact air bags on some of its models. The bags are mounted in the outer edges of the front seats, near the driver's and passenger's outer arms. In the event of a side collision, sensors in the door set off a small explosive charge, which inflates a bag pushing out from the seat edge along the side of the occupant. Twelve milliseconds elapse between impact and full extension of the bag. The inflated bag has a length of about 1 foot (30.5 centimeters) and a width of about 5 inches (12.7 centimeters). Most automobile companies are developing side air bags, many of which are mounted in the doors rather than in the seats.

Auto companies proceeded with plans to introduce high-intensity discharge (HID) lights into future models. These lights are currently available only on some BMWs. An HID light is more than twice as bright as a low-beam halogen lamp, burns 10 times as long, uses less electricity, and can be formed into a wide range of small shapes. HID lights are composed of a quartz capsule filled with xenon gas and two electrodes. A charger delivers large, momentary surges of electricity to the electrodes, producing an arc of light through the gas.

The brightness and adaptability of HID lights can expand both forward- and peripheral-lighted regions at the front of a vehicle. In addition, HID light can be transmitted throughout a car by fiber optics, bringing accessory lighting to wherever it is needed without requiring additional bulbs. American car companies plan to offer HID lighting in their models by the end of the decade.

NEW CONVENIENCES

If you have a problem with unexpected rain passing through your car's open sunroof while you are shopping, help is on the way. Kenneth West, an inventor from Garland, Texas, patented an electronic device that senses moisture and instructs a car to close its windows, sunroof, and convertible top. The car's own electronics and mechanics do the actual closing. West's sensor, which attaches at a low point on the windshield, can be adjusted to account for humid environments. It will activate only when the car is turned off (so people who wish to can still drive in the rain with the top down).

A number of Ford models now offer an innovative sonic-technology feature—a digital-signal-processing (DSP) chip to analyze the acoustic properties of a car's interior. The DSP chip then adjusts the stereo system to produce music with the sonic ambience of an opera house, cathedral, nightclub, or other stirring environments. The effect is aided by a system of at least eight speakers.

Donald W. Cunningham

AVIATION

HEAVY TRAFFIC, SMALL PROFITS

U.S. airlines flew more passengers than ever, but they showed a small profit in 1994, according to the Air Transport Association (ATA), an industry group. By the third quarter of 1994, the airlines reported a net income of $540 million. However, since price wars in the fourth quarter usually drive profits down, the total profit for the year will probably be $200 million to $500 million.

The profit is good news, given that in the past four years, the industry has suffered approximately $12.8 billion in losses. Still, with airline competition increasing, and fare wars making prices drop, analysts warn that carriers may take a long time to recover from the losses of previous years.

For example, in 1994, airlines flew a record 517 million people on scheduled flights, a 6 percent increase from 1993. However, price wars decreased ticket costs in the same period, cutting into profits.

Other factors also cut into airline profits. For example, delays due to air-traffic-control problems resulted in approximately $2.3 billion in fuel, labor, and other costs, according to the ATA. The ATA reports that in 1994, there were an average of 688 air-traffic-control delays of 15 minutes or more each day, a figure that is actually 11 percent lower than the delays experienced in 1993.

COMMUTER-PLANE ISSUES

After an American Eagle commuter plane crashed in bad weather, killing 68 people, the Federal Aviation Administration (FAA) in November 1994 restricted the use of some commuter planes in icy conditions. By January, however, the FAA lifted the restriction and imposed new procedures for using the planes in bad weather.

In November, the agency restricted the use of the autopilot in icy weather on all ATR-72s, turboprop planes that make up 7 percent of the country's commuter-airline fleet. The ban came after American Eagle flight 4184

crashed in Indiana on October 31. Experts speculate that the crash may have been due to a buildup of ice on the wings, and that the pilot did not notice the ice because the plane was on autopilot. The autopilot may have automatically compensated for the ice, hiding the problem until it was too late to correct. By not using the autopilot, aviation experts suggested, a pilot would notice the gradual loss of control.

The order also instructs airlines to develop procedures that would "minimize" the chance of sending ATRs into icy conditions during their flights or in holding patterns. The FAA stopped short of completely grounding the planes.

The agency's action resulted in a reshuffling of the fleets of many commuter airlines, with ATRs being sent to warmer climates where they would be unlikely to encounter icy weather.

However, in January, after an extensive review of the performance of ATRs in icy conditions, the FAA lifted some of the restrictions and imposed others. ATRs are now banned from flying into known or forecast areas of freezing drizzle and rain, for instance. Moreover, pilots must turn off the autopilot if they encounter such weather, and they must immediately fly the airplane out of an area of freezing rain and drizzle. Finally, air-traffic controllers

After questions arose about the performance of its French-built ATR aircraft (above) in icy weather, American Eagle, a commuter airline, reassigned its fleet to warm climates during the winter months.

will now give priority to ATRs that have unexpectedly flown into an area of icy weather.

Other aspects of commuter airlines also raised concerns about safety in 1994. In November, the National Transportation Safety Board (NTSB) issued a report critical of commuter airlines.

In the report, the NTSB says that pilots of commuter airlines are allowed less time to rest between flights than are pilots of major airlines. In addition, because commuter airlines often do not have flight simulators in which pilots train, pilots must instead fly training flights at the end of the workday—when they are tired. Because of this, according to the NTSB, the pilots receive less training than do pilots of major airlines.

In addition, the board notes that although commuter airlines are often operated by a separate company under contract with the main airline, the public may be deceived into thinking that major airlines operate the commuter planes. Commuter planes are often painted with the colors of a main airline, for instance.

Overall, the NTSB report called for the Federal Aviation Administration to place commuter airlines under the same rules as major airlines. As of November 1994, the FAA said that it will issue new regulations to follow that recommendation.

CRASHES PLAGUE USAIR

Two USAir flights crashed in 1994. The two accidents make five crashes in five years for the airline, which is the sixth-largest domestic carrier in the United States.

On July 2, 1994, USAir flight 1016 crashed in Charlotte, North Carolina, killing 37 people. Investigators blamed bad weather for the tragedy: the plane went down in a thunderstorm, after the pilot aborted a landing. According to at least one witness at the NTSB hearing, the crash could have been avoided if the pilots had used the correct landing procedures for violent wind conditions.

A second USAir plane crashed on September 8, when flight 427, making a Chicago, Illinois, to Pittsburgh, Pennsylvania, run, went down outside of Pittsburgh, killing all 132 people on board. As of January 1995, the cause of the disaster had yet to be determined. Before crashing, the Boeing 737 had

made a left turn and possibly encountered turbulence from the wake of a 747. The plane then rolled sharply to the left, flipped over, and finally plunged nosefirst into the ground. The force of the impact and the fuel on the plane caused the jet to explode.

So far, experts speculate that the crash may have been the result of a failure of an element in the control system of the plane, perhaps with the hydraulic system that controls the rudder and elevators. The NTSB is expected to issue its final report on the accident in the summer of 1995. The crash was the deadliest in the United States in seven years.

TRAVEL-AGENT WOES

In late 1994, Delta Air Lines announced that it would begin cutting commissions to travel agents. Delta's decision, which the airline said it undertook to help cut costs, brought an angry reaction from travel agents.

Before the change, Delta paid travel agents a commission of 10 percent of the price of the ticket. Effective in December 1994, on round-trip domestic tickets of more than $500, Delta began paying travel agents no more than $50 commission. For one-way domestic flights of more than $250, the airline now pays a maximum commission of $25. According to a spokesperson for Delta, commissions are the airline's third-largest expense, behind payroll and fuel, costing some $1.3 billion a year.

Other airlines have not yet followed Delta's example, although United Airlines said it was studying Delta's decision.

In addition to reduced commissions from tickets, travel agents are now faced with the loss of business from new ticketless systems. Instead of tickets, passengers who book a flight with a credit card now receive a confirmation number. On arrival at the airport for their flight, passengers then present their confirmation code to receive a boarding pass and seat assignment.

With tickets costing anywhere from $15 to $30 for airlines to produce, industry analysts expect that the ticketless system will save approximately $1 billion a year. However, airline passengers who used to receive their boarding passes from travel agents will now have to wait on potentially long lines at airports to receive these documents.

Devera Pine

BEHAVIORAL SCIENCES

STRESS-INDUCED MEMORY BOOST

Scientists report that memory improves markedly for emotionally arousing events, thanks largely to the release of certain stress hormones that help to store information linked to intense feelings.

Drugs widely prescribed for the treatment of high blood pressure and heart disease, known collectively as beta-blockers, interfere with the action of memory-enhancing stress hormones and may worsen recall for vivid and emotional experiences, asserts study director James L. McGaugh, Ph.D., a psychologist at the University of California, Irvine.

McGaugh and his coworkers had 19 women and 17 men listen to one of two recorded stories, each accompanied by a series of 12 slides that showed various scenes in the story. An emotionally neutral story described a boy's visit to a hospital, where he watched members of a surgical team carry out a disaster drill and practice emergency medical care. An emotionally arousing story told of a boy who was critically injured by a car and rushed to a hospital, where he received emergency surgery.

One hour before these trials, volunteers took either a placebo pill (which has no active ingredients) or propranolol, a medication that lowers blood pressure by stifling the activity of beta-adrenergic stress hormones.

Participants took a memory test one week after exposure to the story. They told experimenters everything they could remember about the story, and also answered multiple-choice questions about what took place in the narrative.

Those given placebos had much better memories for the arousing story, and particularly for its most emotional segments, than for the neutral story. Volunteers who received propranolol remembered much less about the arousing story than the placebo group

did, but the active drug did not interfere with memory for the neutral story.

Adrenergic hormones, which surge in response to emotional experiences, may strengthen memories of those events, according to McGaugh. This biological process may promote the intrusive, disturbing memories that often plague people who have survived life-threatening or otherwise traumatic incidents.

ADOPTED TEENS ADJUST WELL

According to a recent survey, teenagers adopted as infants generally have a positive view of themselves, get along well with their parents, and display psychological health comparable to that of teenagers raised by their biological parents. The survey results challenge the opinion of some mental-health workers that adopted adolescents routinely encounter difficulties in forming a stable identity and, as a result, often develop emotional problems.

The new survey was conducted by scientists at the Search Institute, a Minneapolis, Minnesota, organization that studies children and teenagers. The researchers' inquiries at public and private adoption agencies in

Interracial adoptees show the same level of mental health and psychological adjustment as do children adopted into families of the same race.

Colorado, Illinois, Minnesota, and Wisconsin yielded 715 families with teenagers who had been adopted as infants. A total of 1,262 parents, 881 adopted adolescents, and 78 non-adopted siblings filled out surveys on their psychological and family lives.

Nearly three out of four adopted teens cited good mental health, as measured by the absence of cigarette, alcohol, and illicit-drug use; sexual activity; depression; suicide attempts; delinquency; school problems; and eating disorders. Adopted adolescents fare about as well on these indicators as two large groups of mainly nonadopted teenagers recruited from public school, asserts Anu Sharma, Ph.D., Search Institute psychologist. Also, the 289 interracial adoptees in the survey—most of whom were born in Korea—reported the same levels of psychological adjustment as adoptees in same-race families.

Adoptees cited much more involvement in churches and in volunteer and community organizations than did other youngsters, a finding that may reflect an emphasis on such activities by adoptive parents.

Several aspects of the new survey make it difficult to interpret, according to some clinicians who work with adoptees. For instance, half the adopted families first contacted by researchers declined to complete surveys, and their responses might have changed the overall results. In addition, investigators did not estimate the amount of security teenagers derived from their reported sense of emotional attachment to adoptive parents. More-

over, it remains unclear whether the findings apply to children adopted through independent non-agency means.

CROWDING OUT AGGRESSION

Rhesus monkeys studied in locations ranging from small pens to an entire island exhibited stable amounts of aggressive behavior regardless of how crowded their living quarters became. The monkeys kept such behavior in check by using behavioral strategies to avoid confrontations, thus challenging an influential theory that crowding makes people and other primates more likely to threaten and attack one another.

Although generally considered the most fight-prone of monkeys, rhesus individuals took a number of steps to defuse hostility in crowded situations, contend psychologist Peter G. Judge, Ph.D., and ethologist Frans B. M. de Waal, Ph.D., both of the Yerkes Regional Primate Research Center in Atlanta, Georgia. They argue that the ability to adapt to crowding probably evolved in a similar way in all primates, including humans. In contrast, previous studies had found that rats and mice respond to overcrowding by violently preying on one another.

The researchers studied 413 rhesus monkeys who had lived for at least several years in either small indoor pens, medium-sized cages with indoor and outdoor sections, large outdoor corrals, or on a small island. Detailed observations of the monkeys' social interactions were gathered.

Open acts of hostility rose slightly as living situations became more crowded. But these differences in aggressive behavior were extremely small considering that island monkeys had 6,000 times more available space than those kept in pens, the researchers assert.

Congested conditions elicited large increases in what Judge and de Waal call "coping behaviors." For instance, monkeys made efforts to defuse potential fights more than twice as often in indoor pens as in any other location. They also tended to huddle together with relatives and stay still—a tactic the scientists compared to the tendency of people to avoid eye contact and talking on a crowded elevator or subway.

Bruce Bower

People on a crowded train often exhibit such typical primate "coping behaviors" as avoiding eye contact and not interacting with others.

BIOLOGY

CELL "CAVES"

In addition to its membrane and nucleus, each cell (except for bacteria and bacteria-like organisms) contains a number of other specialized structures called organelles ("little organs"). Each organelle has a specific function. For example, mitochondria obtain energy from food molecules; lysosomes destroy infecting organisms.

In the spring of 1994, Michael Lisanti, Ph.D., and his colleagues at the Whitehead Institute in Cambridge, Massachusetts, announced their discovery of two hitherto-unknown functions of the organelles called caveolae ("little caves"), which are located on the outer surface of a cell's membrane. These cavelike structures contain many different types of proteins.

One such protein, called CD36, is found in large numbers in the cells lining the inner surface of blood vessels. The CD36 proteins serve as attachment sites for cholesterol-containing low-density lipoproteins (LDLs). Lisanti suggests that CD36 proteins pick up LDLs from the bloodstream. Whenever LDL-CD36 complexes are formed, the caveolae close around them, forming closed vesicles that travel to the outer wall of the blood vessel. There the vesicles open, and the cholesterol is deposited deeper within the blood-vessel wall. With time, the cholesterol builds up into a fatty plaque. Eventually this will reduce the diameter of the vessel—restricting the flow of blood, and possibly leading to a heart attack or stroke. Many cell biologists suspect that caveolae also play a role in other human diseases such as diabetes and cancer.

A second protein that Lisanti's team discovered in the caveolae is called a "porin." Shaped like a piece of pipe with doors at both ends, the porin protein is fixed in position. The outer door opens to admit various molecules needed by the cell. Then the outer door closes, and the porin transports these molecules from outside the cell

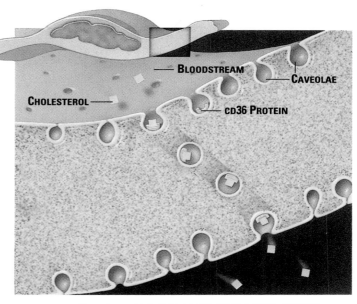

Caveolae, which form on the inner surface of blood vessels, contain proteins that pluck cholesterol from the bloodstream. The caveolae then deposit the cholesterol deeper within the vessel wall, gradually causing the vessel to narrow.

across the cell's membrane. The inner door opens, and the porin discharges the molecules into the cell as needed. With further research, additional functions of the caveolae will undoubtedly be discovered.

PROCESSING THE IMMUNE RESPONSE

When bacteria or other foreign organisms invade a person's bloodstream, their presence stimulates an immune response. The process begins when a type of white blood cell called a macrophage engulfs one of the infective agents. In the macrophage, a portion of one of the pathogen's surface proteins is attached to a protein that is the product of one of the genes of the person's HLA (human leukocyte antigen) locus. This fused foreign- and human-protein complex is then brought to the cell surface, and the foreign-protein portion is exposed to the bloodstream around the cell. The foreign protein attracts to itself a different type of white blood cell called T helper cells (lymphocytes), and stimulates them to secrete chemical messengers called lymphokines. These, in turn, activate B-type lymphocytes to secrete antibodies against the infective agents in the bloodstream. In addition, lymphokines stimulate T-type lymphocytes to attack and destroy any cell already infected with the pathogen.

Researchers have known that foreign organisms are digested in the cell organelles called lysosomes, and that the HLA proteins are produced in the cell organelle called the Golgi body. But, until recently, the site in the macrophage cell where the fusion of foreign and HLA proteins occurred remained a mystery. Using biochemical probes to trace the paths of foreign and HLA proteins, cell biologists have discovered that the fusion of these proteins occurs in yet another hitherto-unknown organelle. Sandra L.

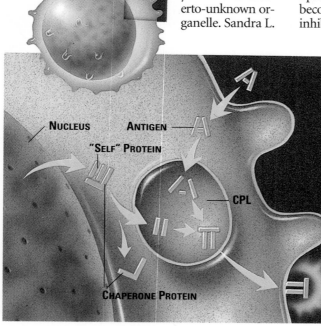

NUCLEUS   ANTIGEN

"SELF" PROTEIN

CPL

CHAPERONE PROTEIN

The CPL plays a key role in the immune system's defense of the body. Within the CPL, bits of invading antigen are joined with "self" protein. The newly formed complex signals the immune system cells to attack the foreign invader.

Schmid, Ph.D., at the Scripps Research Institute in La Jolla, California, has called the new organelle the "compartment for peptide loading" (CPL). Immunologists believe that continued research on CPLs will provide valuable additional information about the immune-response process.

CELL-CYCLE INHIBITORS

Early embryonic development of an organism is characterized by the rapid division of its cells. Later the cells become specialized (muscle, brain, liver, etc.), and, in doing so, a large number of them stop dividing. Many genes are involved in determining whether a cell will divide. Some genes control the production of proteins that stimulate a cell to divide; others produce proteins that prevent cell division.

Recently, Andrew B. Lassar, M.D., of Harvard Medical School in Boston, Massachusetts, and others at various institutions reported on the mechanism by which developing muscle cells stop dividing as they become specialized. The main cell-cycle-inhibiting protein is produced by the retinoblastoma (Rb) tumor-suppressor gene. (The absence of the Rb gene product results in the development of a number of human cancers.) However, the activity of the Rb protein is controlled by the cell-cycle-promoting enzymes called cyclin-dependent kinases (cdks). The cdks attach phosphate groups to the Rb protein, preventing it from functioning and, as a consequence, allowing cell division to continue.

As potential muscle cells begin to differentiate, other genes within the cell are activated to produce one protein called p21 and another called p16. Both of these proteins interfere with the activity of cdks, thereby permitting the Rb protein to inhibit cell division and allow the muscle cells to develop normally.

In a related line of research, Tsutomu Nobori, M.D., and his colleagues at the University of California, San Diego, examined laboratory cell cultures derived from various types of cancers for abnormalities in the region of chromosome 9, where the p16 gene is located. They found that about 61 percent of melanoma (skin) cell lines, 87 percent of glioma (nerve) cell lines, 64 percent of leukemia (blood) cell lines, and 36 percent of non-small-cell lung-cancer cell lines lacked p16 genes. The accompanying lack of p16 protein in these cancer cells permitted the cdks to stimulate continued cell division. What other genetic factors caused the other cells in the various lines to be cancerous are as yet unknown.

POLLUTION AND REPRODUCTIVE DEVELOPMENT

Whether an organism will develop into a female or male is usually determined by the genetic constitution (XX or XY) of the fertilized egg. However, sexual determination in some species also may be affected by other factors, such as temperature and chemical exposure. For example, it is known that the application of the female hormone estrogen to the eggs of turtles will produce all females. Recently, Judith M. Bergeron, Ph.D., at the University of Texas in Austin demonstrated that if polychlorinated biphenyl (PCB), an industrial waste product, is painted on turtle eggs, its effect is similar to that of estrogen. Other industrial environmental pollutants that mimic estrogen include DDT and dioxin.

In long-term studies of wildlife in various lakes where high levels of PCB, DDT, and dioxin have been recorded, it has been found that, over time, there has been a general decrease in size of the wildlife populations, accompanying, in many cases, a feminizing of the males of various species of birds and reptiles.

Jacques Auger, Ph.D., and his colleagues at the University of Paris in France reported the results of a 20-year study of sperm production in human males. They found a steady drop in concentration, motility, and percent of normal-shaped sperm among the 1,351 fertile men they studied. Of interest, in connection with these findings, is the generally noted two- to fourfold increase in testicular cancer in industrialized countries over the past 50 years. Testicular cancer now strikes 1 in 20,000 men, most of whom are in their 20s and 30s. A number of scientists fear that these phenomena have been caused by the estrogen-like action of industrial waste products that have increasingly polluted our environment.

Louis Levine

BIOTECHNOLOGY

FAMILIAL HYPERCHOLESTEROLEMIA

When the blood level of low-density lipoprotein (LDL) rises above normal, the cholesterol it contains is deposited in the walls of arteries, building up over time and eventually causing hypertension and heart attacks. Maintenance of a safe blood-cholesterol level requires the removal of any excess LDL by the liver cells. However, the cells must possess low-density lipoprotein receptors (LDLRs), to which the LDL molecules bind before being brought into the cells.

Unfortunately, in the inherited condition called familial hypercholesterolemia, which is caused by a dominant mutation on chromosome 19, there is a reduction in the number of LDLRs. Should an individual have this dominant mutation on both #19 chromosomes, the liver cells are almost completely devoid of LDLRs. One such afflicted female, whose two brothers died of heart attacks in their early 20s, underwent a gene-therapy procedure in which 10 percent of her liver cells were removed and cultured in the laboratory. A gene for LDLRs was inserted into each of the liver cells. These were then injected into the patient's hepatic-portal vein. This vein goes to the liver, where the gene-altered liver cells reestablished themselves. J. M. Wilson, M.D., and colleagues at the Michigan Medical Center in Ann Arbor recently reported that the female patient who had undergone this procedure about three years ago was doing well. Her blood-cholesterol level was reduced by one-third (still above normal), and X rays of her coronary arteries showed no further deposition of cholesterol. It also was reported that four other such individuals have undergone the procedure, the youngest of them a seven-year-old.

FOOD PRODUCTION

Before any food that has been genetically altered can be marketed in the United States, it must be approved by both the Food and Drug Administration (FDA) and the Department of Agriculture. The first two such foods that have been approved are a strain of tomato and a strain of squash.

Most store-bought tomatoes are picked green, refrigerated while shipped, and then treated to bring on the red color. Vine-ripened tomatoes are found to be too soft for shipping. By inserting a gene that drastically reduces the softening process, Calgene, a biotechnology company in Davis, California, was able to produce a strain of tomato that could be left to ripen on the vine, allowing its flavor to develop fully before it is shipped— without refrigeration. The bioengineered tomatoes have been labeled Flavr Savr.

One of the greatest threats to food production is the destruction of crops by one or more plant viruses. However, it has been found that if a gene for one of the coat proteins of an infective virus is transferred to the cells of a plant, the virus will not be able to attack the plant. A biotechnology company, Asgrow Seed Company of Kalamazoo, Michigan, has inserted protein-coat genes from the watermelon mosaic virus-2 and the zucchini yellow mosaic virus into a strain of squash. The genetically altered plants are resistant to invasion by these viruses that, in the past, have caused great destruction to squash crops.

ORAL TOLERIZATION

There are various medical conditions, known collectively as *autoimmune diseases* (insulin-dependent diabetes, multiple sclerosis, rheumatoid arthritis, and others), in which the body's immune response, which normally reacts only to infective organisms, is instead directed against the individual's own tissues. In a novel approach to the cure of these diseases, H. Weiner, M.D., of Harvard Medical School in Boston, Massachusetts, and colleagues elsewhere have turned to a procedure called *oral tolerization*. Patients are fed small amounts of the particular tissue protein that is the target of the body's immune response. By gradually building up the body's level of the target protein, researchers hope to overwhelm the immune response, thereby leading to its shutdown.

A number of programs of oral tolerization have been instituted. Children who are at risk for insulin-dependent diabetes are fed small amounts of insulin to see if the onset of the disease can be delayed and for how long.

Individuals suffering from multiple sclerosis are given a protein that is present in the myelin sheath, which surrounds nerves in the brain and spinal cord. Lastly, patients with rheumatoid arthritis are fed the protein collagen, in the hope of reducing the tenderness and swelling of the joints of these individuals. The results obtained will be most important in determining the future treatment of these and other autoimmune diseases.

PLASTICS FROM PLANTS

The chemical structure of plastics consists of long chains of carbon atoms, a configuration much like that of petroleum, from which plastics are derived. Based on small but significant differences in the kinds of atoms attached to the carbon chain, scientists can obtain such products as celluloid, Bakelite, Teflon, Lucite, nylon, and many others. Unfortunately, most plastics are not biodegradable. After being used and discarded, plastic waste ultimately contributes to the pollution of the environment.

Some plastics are biodegradable, however. One of these, polyhydroxybutyrate (PHB), consists of chains of butyric acid molecules. It is made by a bacterium, but not in commercially usable amounts. Chris Somerville, Ph.D., and his colleagues at the Carnegie Institution of Washington at Stanford University in California have inserted the bacterial genes involved in PHB formation into the mustard plant *Arabidopsis thaliana*. They have found that 20 percent of the dried plant consists of PHB. In five to six years, several companies hope to begin selling plastics that use PHB.

Another approach to the development of biodegradable plastics has been pursued by Cargill, Incorporated in Minneapolis, Minnesota. Cargill has taken the stalks of corn plants and subjected them to fermentation. One of the end products of this process is lactic acid. The individual lactic acid molecules are then chemically joined to form polylactic acid chains, which have the properties of plastic with the added advantage of degrading completely when discarded. Plastic products made of polylactic acid chains may be available by 1997.

Louis Levine

Book Reviews

Animals and Plants

• Hölldobler, Bert, and Edward O. Wilson. *Journey to the Ants: A Story of Scientific Exploration.* Cambridge, Massachusetts: Belknap/Harvard University Press, 1994; 225 pp., illus.—A fascinating sequel to *The Ants,* the authors' 1990 Pulitzer Prize-winning book.

• Lopez, Barry. *Field Notes: The Grace Note of the Canyon Wren.* New York: Knopf, 1994; 176 pp.—A collection of short stories about observing animals, birds, and fish by the award-winning naturalist.

• Moffett, Mark W. *The High Frontier: Exploring the Tropical Rainforest Canopy.* Cambridge, Massachusetts: Harvard University Press, 1994; 189 pp., illus.—A wonderful cross between an adventure story and poetic biology.

• Weiner, Jonathan. *The Beak of the Finch: A Story of Evolution in Our Time.* New York: Knopf, 1994; 336 pp., illus.— The fascinating story of Peter and Rosemary Grant, whose observations of natural selection among the finches of the Galápagos Islands showed that Darwin was right.

• Wilson, Edward O. *Naturalist.* Washington, D.C.: Shearwater Books/Island Press, 1994; 352 pp., illus.—An anecdotal autobiography by a controversial pioneer of sociobiology.

Astronomy and Space Science

• Barrow, John D. *The Origin of the Universe.* New York: Basic Books, 1995; 176 pp., illus.—A short account of the beginning of the universe, including the latest scientific discoveries and speculative theories.

• Chaikin, Andrew. *A Man on the Moon: The Voyages of the Apollo Astronauts.* New York: Viking, 1994; 688 pp., illus.—A lively and readable retracing of the history of the 1969 Moon landing.

• Dressler, Alan. *Voyage to the Great Attractor: Exploring Intergalactic Space.* New York: Knopf, 1994; 355 pp., illus.—An insider's account of the discovery that the universe was expanding in a lopsided manner, and its subsequent impact on the science and lives of the astronomers involved.

• Lovell, Jim, and Jeffrey Kluger. *Lost Moon: The Perilous Voyage of Apollo 13.* Boston: Houghton Mifflin, 1995; 384 pp., illus.—A riveting account of one of the most suspenseful missions in the history of space exploration.

• Neal, Valerie, ed. *Where Next, Columbus?: The Future of Space Exploration.* New York: Oxford University Press, 1994; 256 pp., illus.—An engaging look at the past and future of our voyage across the last frontier.

• Sagan, Carl. *Pale Blue Dot: A Vision of the Human Future in Space.* New York: Random

House, 1995; 448 pp., illus.—The noted popularizer of space exploration struggles to define a future for the human species after the destruction of the solar system.

Earth and the Environment

• Harte, John. *The Green Fuse: An Ecological Odyssey.* Berkeley: University of California Press, 1994; 168 pp.—An introduction to the practices and principles of ecology, with warnings about the long-term environmental consequences of industrial society.

• Keene, Ann T. *Earthkeepers: Observers and Protectors of Nature.* New York: Oxford University Press, 1994; 224 pp., illus.—Stories of more than 100 naturalists and environmentalists from ancient times to the present day.

- Mann, Charles C., and Mark L. Plummer. *Noah's Choice: The Future of Endangered Species.* New York: Knopf, 1995; 336 pp.—A writer and an economist examine the Endangered Species Act of 1973 and look at the broader question of balancing the needs of humans and endangered species.
- Wade, Nicholas, Cornelia Dean, and William A. Dicke, eds. *The Environment from Your Backyard to the Ocean Floor: The New York Times Book of Science Literacy, Volume 2.* New York: Times Books/Random House, 1994—Based on articles that appeared in *The New York Times* between 1990 and 1993, this book aims to provide a basic understanding of environmental issues.

- Hobson, J. Allan. *The Chemistry of Conscious States: How the Brain Changes Its Mind.* Boston: Little, Brown, 1994; 336 pp., illus.—The author sums up in layman's terms what he has learned in a lifetime of studying sleep, dreaming, and the brain.
- Rutkow, Ira. *Surgery: An Illustrated History.* St. Louis: Mosby-Year Book/Norman, 1994; 550 pp., illus.—An attractive volume chronicling the art of wounding to heal from prehistory to the present.
- Terr, Lenore. *Unchained Memories: True Stories of Traumatic Memories, Lost and Found.* New York: Basic Books, 1995; 304 pp.—A leading expert on trauma and memory explains traumatic memory loss and shows how false memories can be planted.

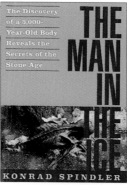

HUMAN SCIENCES

- Calvin, William H., and George A. Ojemann. *Conversations with Neil's Brain: The Neural Nature of Thought and Language.* Reading, Massachusetts: Addison-Wesley, 1994; 352 pp., illus.—A patient suffering from epilepsy after an auto accident has his doctors explain the workings of his brain and how surgery affects it.
- Cohen, Leah Hager. *Train Go Sorry: Inside a Deaf World.* Boston: Houghton Mifflin, 1994; 296 pp., illus.—An insightful journey through the culture and conflicts of the deaf.
- Garrett, Laurie. *The Coming Plague: Newly Emerging Diseases in a World Out of Balance.* New York: Farrar, Straus & Giroux, 1994; 750 pp., illus.—A sobering look at newly emerging diseases in the modern world.

PAST, PRESENT, AND FUTURE

- Davies, Paul. *The Last Three Minutes: Conjectures about the Ultimate Fate of the Universe.* New York: Basic Books, 1994; 176 pp.—A dramatic look at the way the world might end.
- Fagan, Brian. *Time Detectives: How Archaeologists Use Technology to Recapture the Past.* New York: Simon & Schuster, 1995; 288 pp., illus.—A fascinating and anecdotal look at how archaeologists use technology to study the past.
- Johanson, Donald, Lenora Johanson, and Blake Edgar. *Ancestors: The Search for Our Human Origins.* New York: Random House, 1994; 240 pp., illus.—A profusely illustrated survey of scientific discoveries in the field of human evolution.
- Spindler, Konrad. *The Man in the Ice.* New York: Random House, 1995; 320 pp., illus.—An archaeologist tells the story of the astounding 1991 discovery of a 5,300-year-old man

that gave scientists their clearest knowledge to date about life during the late Neolithic age.

- Wallace, Joseph. *The American Museum of Natural History's Book of Dinosaurs and Other Ancient Creatures.* New York: Simon & Schuster, 1994; 144 pp., illus.—A profusely illustrated survey commemorating the opening of the museum's rebuilt exhibits of prehistoric fossils and animals.

PHYSICAL SCIENCES

- Adair, Robert Kemp. *The Physics of Baseball,* 2d rev. ed. New York: Harper Perennial, 1994; 160 pp., illus.—Uses the laws of physics to explain how knuckleballs work or why some swings of the bat are more effective than others.

illus.—Another look at the far reaches of theoretical physics from a scientist who, as a teenager, built a working particle accelerator in his family's garage.

- Van der Meer, Ron, and Bob Gardner. *The Math Kit: A Three-Dimensional Tour Through Mathematics.* New York: Scribners, 1994; 13 pp., illus.—An instructional pop-up book for adults that represents abstract ideas graphically.

TECHNOLOGY

- Brand, Stewart. *How Buildings Learn: What Happens After They're Built.* New York: Viking Penguin, 1994; repr. 1995; 256 pp., illus.—A beautifully illustrated and inno-

- Dunham, William. *The Mathematical Universe: An Alphabetical Journey Through the Great Proofs, Problems, and Personalities.* New York: John Wiley, 1994; 320 pp., illus.—A guide to mathematics and its personalities.
- Field, Michael, and Martin Golubitsky. *Symmetry in Chaos: A Search for Pattern in Mathematics, Art, and Nature.* New York: Oxford University Press, 1994; 232 pp., illus.—A profusely illustrated look at new mathematics in the making.
- Fritzch, Harald. *An Equation That Changed the World: Newton, Einstein, and the Theory of Relativity.* Chicago: University of Chicago Press, 1995—Uses an imaginary dialogue between Einstein and Newton to explain the special theory of relativity.
- Kaku, Michio. *Hyperspace: A Scientific Odyssey Through Parallel Universes, Time Warps, and the Tenth Dimension.* New York: Oxford University Press, 1994; 359 pp.,

vative look at architecture, proposing that buildings are being constantly reshaped and redefined by a host of forces.

- Collin, Simon. *The Way Multimedia Works.* Redmond, Washington: Microsoft Press, 1994—An engaging introduction to multimedia technology and its uses.
- Freedman, David. *Brainmakers.* New York: Simon & Schuster, 1995; 256 pp.—The progress and limits of artificial intelligence.
- Kinkoph, Sherry. *Computers: A Visual Encyclopedia.* Carmel, Indiana: Alpha Books, 1994; 1,100 pp., illus.—A colorful primer explains more than 1,000 computer terms.
- Levine, John. *The Internet for Dummies,* 2d ed. San Mateo, California: IDG Books, 1994—An updated guide for new and experienced Internet users.

Jo Ann White

BOTANY

Even Better Garlic

Close your eyes for a few seconds and think about garlic. Imagine how its aroma fills a kitchen, how its taste fills your mouth, how it elevates many a meal from simple sustenance to gastronomic glory. Now try to imagine—if you can—that garlic could someday become a more heavenly substance than it already is.

That leap into a nearly inconceivable realm may be near. Geneticists have discovered how to make garlic, which is normally sexually sterile, produce fertile seed. In doing so, they've cleared the way for plant breeders to do the genetic mixing-up that makes improvement possible.

At one time in its history, garlic reproduced sexually—that's how we got the couple of hundred different strains of garlic that are around today. But somewhere along the way, garlic flowers stopped making fertile seed. No one is sure why; it could be that a structural abnormality made the flowers sterile, or that the small bulblets that are produced asexually beside the flower buds in the aboveground flower head are competing too well. Or it might be that long ago, two fertile species crossed and created a sterile offspring, much in the way that crossing a horse and a donkey produces a sterile mule.

Mercifully, garlic didn't cease to exist when it stopped making fertile seed. Because garlic can reproduce asexually, it can clone itself. The clones come from the garlic cloves, the very same ones that you pull off the head of garlic, rap with a knife handle to loosen the skin, and toss into a hot skillet with some olive oil. Each clove, if planted, can form a new head of garlic full of cloves identical to the original. Garlic also reproduces itself by growing smaller bulblets—called top sets—in the aboveground flower head that grows out of the underground head. The top sets can also form heads, but only after they fall to the ground.

To encourage garlic to produce fertile seed, U.S. Department of Agriculture geneticist Phillip Simon and coworkers at the University of Wisconsin at Madison planted about 175 types of common garlic (*Allium sativum*) and a wild ancestor, *A. longicuspis*, over a four-year period. They removed the top sets from the flowerheads, leaving the flower buds. Then they cut about 90 percent of the flower stalks from the plants, placing the stalks in jars of water to keep them alive. The researchers left the rest growing on the plants. Some of the flower buds were pollinated by insects, others by hand. Of the 175 clones Simon started with, 11 produced a total of 63 viable seeds. Five of those seeds matured and produced bulbs.

Clearly, this is not a lot of garlic—about enough to flavor a week's worth of pizza. Still, even though the research did not result in loads of seed, it gives researchers a starting point in finding ways to cross different strains of garlic. Such a breeding program could create new types of garlic that are more resistant to disease, are more productive, mature faster, and have other desirable traits.

Even if only small amounts of seed from improved strains can be produced, the strains could then be reproduced asexually on a larger scale. But researchers hope that the garlic seed itself can be produced in large numbers. Because it's easier to ship and handle lightweight seed than the cloves, seed-grown garlic would be considerably less expensive to produce.

Plastic-producing Plants

Thirty years ago, when a centerpiece of plastic flowers was considered cutting-edge technology, who could have foreseen that living plants would one day produce plastic in their cells?

A research team led by botanist Christopher Somerville of the Carnegie Institution, Stanford, California, has spliced genes into mouse-ear cress (*Arabidopsis thaliana*), a member of the mustard family, to make it produce a biodegradable plastic called polyhydroxybutyrate (PHB) in its cells. PHB is similar to petroleum-based polypropylene, which is widely used in milk jugs, plastic containers, household items, and tools. Besides being easy for bacteria to biodegrade—a difficult characteristic to add to synthetic plastics—PHB has the advantage of coming from a nonpolluting source.

In Somerville's initial experiments in 1992, the mouse-ear cress churned out only minute amounts of PHB in the cytoplasm and nucleus of the cells. The effort so taxed the plants that their growth was severely stunted. Fortunately, Somerville found a way to increase the yield of plastic 100-fold without compromising the health of the plant: he moved the site of production to the chloroplasts, the specialized chlorophyll-producing organelles within plant cells, so that the plastic-making process did not steal energy needed for cell reproduction.

There are still several obstacles to overcome before plant plastics have commercial value. For one, pure PHB is not a good plastic—it is brittle, and about half of it breaks down upon melting. But Somerville's work proves that plants can be engineered to make plastics in useful quantities, and provides techniques that can be used to produce related plastics that have better characteristics.

The goal now is to engineer crop plants that are grown on a large scale, such as corn and soybeans, to produce PHB and related plastics in their seeds. When that happens, the plastics can be extracted from the seeds, much as corn oil and soybean oil are extracted today.

Eventually plastic production may be directed to other parts of commercially grown crops, such as the tuber (the edible part) of potatoes or the roots of sugar beets. It may even be incorporated into cotton to change the nature of cotton fibers.

SOLVING AN OLD MYSTERY

More than 100 years ago, Charles Darwin noticed that some plants do not pollinate themselves. Since then, botanists have tried to deduce how self-infertility works. Now biologists at Pennsylvania State University in University Park have found a big clue: they have isolated a gene that, when active, produces a protein in the female part of the flower—the pistil—that rejects pollen from the same plant.

Teh-hui Kao and coworkers made their discovery by working backward: they started with a self-infertile petunia, inserted DNA that blocked formation of the protein, then fertilized the flower with its own pollen. When the flower produced seed, the researchers knew they had turned off the right mechanism.

Self-infertility is a valuable adaptation because it promotes the genetic diversity that increases a species's chance of surviving. Not all plants are self-infertile, but among those that are, more than half use the mechanism that Kao is studying. Other species avoid

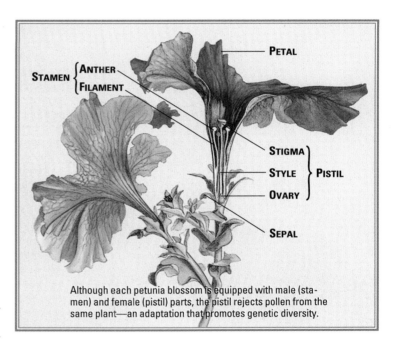

Although each petunia blossom is equipped with male (stamen) and female (pistil) parts, the pistil rejects pollen from the same plant—an adaptation that promotes genetic diversity.

self-fertilization by producing male and female flowers at separate times. Some plants produce only male or female flowers, not both.

Although identifying the gene that causes self-infertility is a big step, researchers still don't know exactly how the protein rejects the pollen. But even at this stage, their work may have commercial applications. If self-infertility can be turned on in plants that now pollinate themselves, it will be easier to breed hybrids of valuable crops, creating new varieties that are more productive or that better resist pests and environmental stresses.

Over the millennia, two hardy desert denizens—the yucca plant and the yucca moth—have worked out an unusual, life-sustaining symbiotic relationship. After nightfall, the bell-shaped flowers of the yucca plant unfold and emit an aroma that attracts moths. As female yucca moths flutter among the white and violet blooms, they deposit pollen and lay a single egg inside each flower. When an egg hatches, the newborn larva feeds on the plentiful seeds inside the green fruit of the yucca plant. Scientists had long wondered how the yucca plant—which depends upon

The yucca plant and the yucca moth (above) have a mutually beneficial relationship. The plant depends on the moth for pollination, and the moth larvae rely on the plant's seeds for food.

the moth to pollinate all of its flowers—discourages moths from depositing all of their eggs inside only one or two flowers.

During 1994, ecologists with the U.S. Environmental Protection Agency discovered that the yucca plant aborts about 90 percent of its flowers before they produce fruit. Researchers now believe that centuries of evolution have programmed the moths to spread their eggs in many flowers, all in the hope that some of their offspring will have the good fortune to subsist on the pulpy mature fruit of the yucca.

Erin Hynes

CHEMISTRY

THE PERIODIC TABLE

It may soon be time to replace the old periodic table: scientists discovered two brand-new elements, and the International Union of Pure and Applied Chemistry (IUPAC) proposed names for nine existing transfermium elements (elements 101–109).

New Elements. In a brief span of time, a team of researchers led by physicist Peter Armbruster at GSI, the center for heavy-ion research in Darmstadt, Germany, announced the discovery of two new elements. First, in November 1994, they reported detecting an isotope of element 110 with an atomic mass of 269 that was produced when a lead isotope was bombarded with nickel atoms. A month later, the German scientists discovered yet another element, the heaviest known so far: element 111—three atoms of which were created by fusing nickel and bismuth. The new atoms have a half-life of approximately 1.5 milliseconds, and an atomic mass of 272.

Elements 110 and 111 have not yet been assigned names. Also, no immediate applications of the new elements are clear at this time.

IUPAC Rejects "Seaborgium." When the IUPAC Commission on Nomenclature of Inorganic Chemistry (CNIC) recommended new names for the transfermium elements 101–109, it rejected the name "seaborgium" for element 106. The name had been suggested by a team of scientists at the Lawrence Berkeley National Laboratory (LBL), Berkeley, California, who are credited with the discovery of the element. In refusing to go along with the Berkeley suggestion, the CNIC argued that an element should not be named after a living person.

The CNIC instead proposed the following names for the elements 101–109 (their atomic numbers are given in parentheses): mendelevium (101), nobelium (102), lawrencium (103), dubnium (104), joliotium (105), rutherfordium (106), bohrium (107), hahnium (108), and meitnerium (109). The recommendations were accepted unanimously by the IUPAC's Bureau (executive body), but are subject to final ratification by the IUPAC Council at its August 1995 meeting.

A new energy-efficient sulfur lamp (at left, in inset) produces the same amount of light as 120 of the larger high-intensity mercury bulbs (at right, in inset). Just two sulfur bulbs, one placed at each end of a long light pipe, brighten the enormous area above.

As expected, the rejection of "seaborgium" generated considerable controversy (and some anger) in the United States. The announcement disappointed the LBL scientists, who had named element 106 to honor Glenn T. Seaborg, associate director of the LBL and 1951 Nobel prizewinner for the discovery of plutonium and nine other transuranium elements. Seaborg himself was quoted as saying that "this would be the first time in history that the acknowledged and uncontested discoverers of an element are denied the privilege of naming it."

In addition, the American Chemical Society (ACS) got into the fray and issued a statement indicating that the society is "very disappointed that element 106 has not been named after America's preeminent nuclear chemist, Dr. Glenn Seaborg, as had been specifically recommended by his colleagues."

NEW DISCOVERIES

New Sulfur Lightbulb. A new lightbulb was unveiled by the Department of Energy (DOE), which called it a "revolutionary 21st-century lighting system." Invented by Fusion Lighting of Rockville, Maryland, the bulb consists of a closed quartz sphere filled with an inert gas (argon) and a tiny amount of sulfur. It reportedly produces as much light as hundreds of high-intensity mercury-vapor lamps.

When the golf-ball-sized bulb containing sulfur and argon gas is bombarded by micro-

waves, it produces bright illumination. Unlike most other high-intensity lighting sources, the sulfur lamp is electrodeless. This is regarded as a major plus because experts consider electrodes to be the principal limitation to achieving long life in conventional bulbs.

The new energy-efficient bulb is used in combination with "light pipes," which are long plastic tubes lined with a semireflective film. A sulfur bulb is placed at one end of the light pipe, and a mirror or second sulfur bulb is positioned at the other end. Light from the bulb is reflected back and forth along the length of the light pipe. Some light rays escape through the semireflective film and illuminate the surrounding area.

In two test installations, light pipes equipped with sulfur bulbs used one-third as much electricity, gave off four times as much light, and cost significantly less than the conventional bulbs that they replaced.

Commercial production of the new lightbulbs is not expected until later this year. The first applications of the bulbs are expected for lighting such large outdoor and indoor spaces as aircraft hangars and factories.

"Immortality" Enzyme. Scientists at the University of Texas Southwestern Medical Center in Dallas, and Geron Corporation, Menlo Park, California, discovered that the enzyme telomerase allows cells to reproduce without limits in many types of cancers.

In an earlier study, scientists observed that in humans and other multicellular organisms, molecules called telomeres, which are attached to the tips of chromosomes, become whittled away with each cell division. As the telomere shortens, the cell divides more slowly. Eventually the cell stops dividing, the chromosomes disintegrate, and the cell dies. Normally a cell divides 50 to 100 times before it ages and dies.

In related work on the enzyme telomerase, Calvin Harley, Ph.D., and his associates at McMaster University in Hamilton, Ontario, discovered that if the gene for telomerase is activated, a normal cell behaves like a cancer cell, continually dividing without restriction.

Most recently, researchers using a new, highly sensitive assay detected telomerase in nearly all of the 12 different types of human-cancer specimens tested, but telomerase was not seen in other types of cells that age and die. Scientists believe that a test that could quickly detect telomerase could aid doctors in their diagnosis and treatment of cancer patients. The development of a drug that blocks telomerase activity could potentially lead to a cure for cancer.

Flexible Plastics. Francis Garnier, a materials scientist at the Laboratoire des Matériaux Moléculaires in Thiais, France, and his colleagues developed "flexible" plastic electronic circuits. The circuits made from flexible plastic keep on working, even after they are bent by as much as 90 degrees. In contrast, most of the electronic circuits currently used in radios, telephones, and televisions have rigid components, and are made of metallic, silicon, and ceramic materials. These circuits normally stop functioning when they are bent by 90 degrees.

From such organic-polymer electronics, Garnier foresees the development of "pocket-sized 'smart' cards with plastic logic circuits." He also sees car and airplane windshields that can display information, as well as "a large flat-panel display, like a television, that you could roll up."

Molecular-Scale Wire. Information processing at the "molecular" scale—as opposed to processing in "bulk," silicon-based semiconducting materials (the basis of existing electronic devices)—has been touted as the key to developing computer circuitry for a new generation of miniature, high-power, high-speed computers and other optoelectronic devices. Scientists at Carnegie-Mellon University, Pittsburgh, Pennsylvania, took an important step toward building molecular systems when they announced development of a "molecular-scale wire."

Linus Pauling gained renown for his groundbreaking research in molecular chemistry, his efforts to advance world peace, and his controversial advocacy of Vitamin C therapy.

The molecular wire transmits signals by receiving an input—that of a light photon—at one end, and delivering the signal at the other end by producing another photon. This molecular wire, made of an array of light-absorbing pigments (similar to the chlorophyll molecules that are involved in photosynthesis), is 100 times smoother than existing computer circuitry. Potential technological spin-offs of molecular-scale optoelectronics might include molecular-scale circuitry, artificial retinas, ultrasensitive photoreceptors, and nanoscopic light sources.

LINUS PAULING DIES

Linus C. Pauling, twice a Nobel prizewinner and considered a giant of modern chemistry, died on August 19, 1994, at age 93. Pauling spent his most productive years as a chemistry professor at the California Institute of Technology (Caltech) in Pasadena.

Pauling is known for his seminal work on the nature of chemical bonds—including the concepts of resonance and hybridization. For these contributions, he was awarded the 1954 Nobel Prize in Chemistry. In the 1950s, he worked to achieve a total ban on all nuclear-weapons tests. For this and other efforts, he received the 1962 Nobel Peace Prize. Pauling thus became the only person ever to receive two unshared Nobel prizes. Over the years, he was also known for his controversial advocacy of Vitamin C, which he believed wards off common colds and prevents cancer.

Vinod Jain

CIVIL
ENGINEERING

NEW CONSTRUCTION MATERIALS

The creation of more-durable, cost-efficient construction materials continues to be of major interest to civil engineers. Researchers for the French construction firm Bouygues Corporation created a concrete with compressive strengths of 29,000 pounds per square inch (psi), and an ultrahigh-performance material with compressive strengths of up to 116,000 psi. Such materials could possess the weight of concrete, the compressive strength and dimensional stability of the strongest rock, the tensile strength of many metals, and a high degree of ductility.

Now, in cooperation with the U.S. Army Corps of Engineers' Construction Productivity Advancement Research Program (CPAR), Bouygues and its U.S. affiliate, HDR Engineering, Omaha, Nebraska, are further developing both materials. CPAR researchers will test the high-strength concrete for use in culvert and sewer piping and in concrete piling at the Corps' Waterways Experiment Station in Vicksburg, Mississippi. Bouygues researchers improved the homogeneity of the concrete by using a powder concrete in which aggregates and traditional sand are replaced by ground quartz less than 0.012 inch (300 microns) in size. A high level of ductility was achieved by adding steel microfibers.

Eventually, say researchers, the 116,000-psi concrete may be used as a substitute for steel. Since protective panels made from the material performed well in the lab against impacts from projectiles, the new concrete also may have military applications.

In a separate project, the U.S. Army Corps of Engineers is testing experimental antifreeze admixtures that make it possible to place concrete at temperatures as low as 23° F (-5° C). According to Charles J. Korhonen, research engineer at the U.S. Army Corps of Engineers' Cold Regions Research and Engineering Laboratory (CRREL), Hanover, New Hampshire, lowering the allowable concrete-curing temperature from 41° F (5° C) to 23° F can add two months to the construction season for many colder areas of the United States. Various studies have shown that the construction industry spends $800 million a year to keep concrete from freezing as it cures. In some cases, heating costs can double construction costs.

Once ice forms, concrete can lose up to half its potential strength. The new antifreeze admixtures depress the freezing point of water and accelerate the hydration of portland cement at low temperatures. This allows concrete placed in subfreezing temperatures to gain strength at the same rate as normal winter concreting. The current research builds on existing proprietary formulations developed by W. R. Grace, New York City, and Master Builders, Cleveland, Ohio.

MAINTAINING MATERIALS RELIABILITY

Maintaining the integrity of materials and the structures that they form are major concerns among civil engineers. Researchers at Westinghouse Science and Technology Center (STC), Pittsburgh, Pennsylvania, have developed a process called magnetic tagging that could monitor the reliability of most of the popular construction materials—concrete, asphalt, polymers, and geotextiles—for which conventional nondestructive techniques do

The federal building in Oklahoma City was built with exposed support columns and other structural elements not designed to withstand an explosion like the April 1995 bomb blast that wrecked the building.

not apply. Unless the structure is made of steel, which can be tested through several methods, visual inspections have been the only cost-effective option.

The magnetic-tagging process involves adding a small amount of magnetic ceramic particles to construction materials during the manufacturing process. Magnetic tagging provides a "bar code" that can be read with an electromagnetic device, according to Bill Clark, STC manager of materials reliability. STC developed the technology, patented as Westag, so the U.S. Department of Energy could ensure the integrity of new concrete radioactive-waste containers. Now that this project has been put on hold, Westinghouse is planning to join with other companies or government agencies to continue to develop the tagging process.

There are several ways to check the integrity of a geomembrane-surface impoundment liner, used in holding ponds and landfills, but no economical or efficient method to repair a leak. Now clay particles, drawn by an electric force, can seal a leak while liquid wastes remain in the impoundment. Researchers at Leak Location Services, Incorporated, and the Southwest Research Institute, both in San Antonio, Texas, tested the process in 1995 with a full-scale demonstration in a lined test pond.

Normally, if repairs are attempted at all, crews drain an impoundment to apply a thick layer of grout or sealant clay, or they retrofit the impoundment with a new liner. The new technology takes advantage of electrophoresis, in which suspended particles move through a fluid or gel under the action of an electromotive force applied to electrodes in contact with the suspension. In this application, direct-current electrodes are placed above and below a liner, and a small amount of clay slurry, which is made of fine particles capable of carrying an electrical charge, is introduced into the water. The liner in effect acts as an electrical insulator. A leak breaks the insulation and permits a flow of electrical current. Because of electrophoresis, the electrically charged particles in the clay slurry gravitate toward the leak. The resulting accumulation of clay creates the seal.

Teresa Austin

COMMUNICATION TECHNOLOGY

THE YEAR OF THE INTERNET

Experts continue to debate who will control the flow of information in the future. As computer and television technologies battle it out to be the premier provider of information, entertainment, and news, the focus during 1994 shifted from the ambitious fiber-optic information superhighway to the vast computer network known as the Internet.

Have you ever wanted to take a stroll through the Louvre Museum in Paris, visit a shopping mall, attend a concert put on by an alternative rock band, or chat with a movie star—without leaving your room? To do all of these things, you would ordinarily have to take a flight to France; drive a car to the stores; buy tickets to attend a show; and have a celebrity for a friend. Now you can do all of these things—and more—right at your computer, thanks to a worldwide computer network that makes up the Internet.

• **Development.** It is hard to imagine—but true—that the Internet was developed to minimize the chaos of a natural disaster or nuclear war. More than 25 years ago, the Defense Advanced Research Projects Agency (DARPA) of the U.S. Department of Defense set up a system that allowed government-related computers to talk to each other in the event of a national crisis. DARPA found a way to install a minicomputer at each location to ensure communications between the host computer and the other computers on the network. This network—dubbed ARPAnet—depended on a technology called packet switching. In such a system, chunks, or packets, of information are encoded with an address in order to reach a destination. If any part of the computer network shuts down, the packets can be rerouted because other computers in the network can read the address and send the information on its way.

Nonmilitary organizations, such as educational institutions, soon followed ARPAnet's design and created their own networks. The major networks were then merged, or internetworked, to form the Internet. As the so-called

Net grew, it became necessary to create a protocol, or common language, so all the computers could talk to each other. This language—Transmission Control Protocol/Internet Protocol (TCP/IP)—was introduced in 1982.

As use of the Internet for research and exchanging information grew, some institutions, and even foreign countries, took it upon themselves to organize the reams of information available over the Net. The Internet's basic browsing tool for these searches, called Gopher, was developed by computer scientists at the University of Minnesota in Minneapolis. The Gopher was named after the school's mascot—a name that also denotes a system that can "go for" the files you need. Gopher systems help a user carry out a search by displaying menus of topics available from a given institution.

As information became easier to access, Internet users at government agencies, private universities, and research institutions were joined by millions in the general public. Today upwards of 15 million users, on tens of thousands of host computers around the world, have access to the Internet. That number is expected to keep growing, with potential worldwide access estimated at 30 million.

• *Communications Capabilities.* Two major innovations helped prompt the recent explosion in Internet usage. The first was the creation in 1989 of the World Wide Web, a user-friendly system for maintaining and distributing multimedia documents, which incorporate text, pictures, audio, and video. The second was the creation of the National Center for SuperComputing Applications (NCSA) Mosaic, the first graphical user interface (GUI), or Web browser, for accessing this Web of worldwide information. These two creations allowed personal-computer (PC) users to more easily "surf the Net" without knowing the complexities of UNIX computer language.

Hypertext is the link to additional information on the World Wide Web. By simply highlighting an underlined or boldfaced passage with a click of the mouse, the user can be connected to more information related to the highlighted text.

One powerful capability of the Internet allows users to interact with each other. The Internet's USENET is a collection of bulletin boards on the Net where users can exchange information on thousands of topics. Net users often leave messages with questions, requests, or advice, and can read everyone else's messages on a board.

Real-time chat, on the other hand, allows a user to "speak" to another user, who can read the message he or she is receiving as it is being typed by the sender.

SATELLITE TELEVISION

Direct-broadcast-satellite, or DBS, companies have been thinking small, especially now that they offer satellite dishes that measure only 18 inches (45 centimeters) to 4 feet (1.2 meters) across. These companies hope to entice customers to switch from premium cable or strictly antenna services to satellite television.

Touting a lower cost than the much larger, motorized dishes of the past, DBS services are providing upwards of 100 channels, primarily to rural viewers who cannot get cable television, and to people who are partial to satellite services because they are already using a big dish. Like cable, DBS also offers pay-per-view movies and sporting events. What's more, advanced technology allows these services to be transmitted with a CD-quality sound and laser-disc-quality pictures. DBS companies even claim that transmissions will not be marred by bad weather.

Consumers who want to think small must decide whether to buy or lease their satellite equipment. For those looking to buy, the RCA Digital Satellite System (DSS)—consisting of an 18-inch dish, set-top box, and remote control—is sold in retail and electronic outlets. The set-top box, which descrambles the satellite signal, can also store and request pay-per-view orders made from an on-screen menu. The basic kit costs about $700. A deluxe package includes an antenna with dual outputs to independently serve two TVs. DSS customers can order programming through two companies: DirecTV and United States Satellite Broadcasting, at a monthly cost comparable to cable television.

Primestar Partners, a DBS company created by the cable-television industry to service non-cable areas, charges a monthly lease fee for both its programming and equipment. The dish measures about 3 feet (90 centimeters) in diameter. Both Primestar and DSS charge an initial installation fee of approximately $100 to $200.

Both systems receive signals from high-powered satellites located more than 22,000 miles (35,000 kilometers) above the Earth's surface. These satellites broadcast signals to a set-top receiver, which unscrambles the signal. A credit-card-sized cartridge in the receiver tells the box which channels to

The small, unobtrusive dish antenna above can receive signals for 175 TV channels from a direct broadcast satellite (DBS). The system delivers laser-disc-quality pictures with CD-quality sound.

unscramble, depending upon the level of service. The cartridge, which is programmable, can upgrade a customer's service through the remote control. Parents can also use the remote to block programs and channels or to limit pay-per-view events.

For billing purposes, the receiver is hooked into a telephone jack. Through a toll-free call, the set-top box can then report to the satellite company about which pay-per-view events were watched. One downside to this satellite service is that in order to receive local or network programming, a basic-cable subscription is still necessary, or an aerial antenna or "rabbit ears" must be used.

Susan Nielsen

COMPUTERS

THE PENTIUM DEBACLE

In 1993, Intel Corporation of Santa Clara, California—the world's largest producer of microprocessor chips—introduced its Pentium chip, said to be among the fastest microprocessors ever mass-produced. Approximately 4 million personal computers (PCs) sold in 1994 contained the 32-bit Pentium chip, which cost an estimated $1.35 billion to develop. In November 1994, however, Intel acknowledged that a flaw in the chip could cause computers to give inaccurate answers to some complex mathematical calculations. The company had known about a defect in the chip's so-called floating-point unit for several months, but had not announced it publicly. Intel claimed that the flaw would cause a problem only once in every 37 billion calculations, and that the average user would encounter an error only once every 27,000 years. The error was fixed, and all new chips are unflawed.

When the problem first was made public, Intel offered free replacement chips only to customers who could prove they needed such absolute accuracy. This policy confused and angered many Pentium owners. The Pentium controversy grew even louder after IBM, the world's largest computer maker, took the unusual step of suspending sales of all of its computers containing the Pentium. According to IBM, the chip made far-more-frequent mistakes than acknowledged by Intel. Some industry observers, however, questioned the motives of IBM—a firm that is both a sizable purchaser of Pentium chips and a competitor in the microprocessor market. After IBM's action, Intel agreed to supply corrected replacement chips free of charge to anyone requesting them, and offered a free program to test a PC in order to find out whether it had a flawed Pentium or a corrected chip.

ENCRYPTION AND SECURITY

Debate intensified in 1994 over the U.S. government's proposal to install encryption devices called Clipper chips in telecommunications products. The Clipper microprocessor, developed by the National Security

Agency (NSA), encodes digitized voice, fax, and computer data traveling over phone lines, making such data secure from interception. However, the government would hold a "key" enabling it to decode transmissions and monitor them. The government claims this is necessary to help it conduct electronic surveillance and capture criminals in the digital age. Privacy advocates, however, object strenuously to the Clipper-chip plan—as do major companies such as Microsoft, Apple, IBM, and Sun Microsystems, which argue that products containing Clipper chips would face consumer resistance. Many customers—both in the United States and abroad—might choose to purchase foreign-made computers and telephone equipment, owing to customer discomfort with the possibility that the U.S. government could monitor their communications.

Encryption programs already are used widely. Many banks, for example, use a government-sponsored standard called Data Encryption Standard (DES) to safely transfer funds electronically all over the world. The encryption system of the Clipper chip is said to be much more powerful than DES, and therefore much more secure. However, the fact that the U.S. government could intercept data with the Clipper chip has people worried. In 1994, the government clarified its stand on Clipper: it would be a voluntary system, no other currently available encryption system would be outlawed, and it would pertain only to information transferred over telephone lines. However, federal agencies are strongly encouraged to use Clipper as their encryption standard. Many observers believe that such a policy would force companies and individuals doing business with many government agencies to use the system as well.

An additional concern cropped up in mid-1994 when a computer scientist at AT&T Bell Laboratories found a reasonably simple way to fool the Clipper chip. By generating and transmitting a code that falsely identifies which "key" should be used to decode a message (a process taking only about 30 minutes), a user can fool the system and make the message indecipherable when decoded by Clipper. Although this flaw in the chip would not apply to voice and fax transmissions, it would affect computer-to-computer transmissions such as electronic mail (E-mail).

In preparation for the acceptance of the Clipper chip, the U.S. Congress late in 1994 passed the Digital Telephony and Communications Privacy Improvement Act of 1994, which requires future telecommunications systems to be accessible to wiretaps by the Federal Bureau of Investigation (FBI) and other law-enforcement agencies. Congress, however, had yet to debate the Clipper plan itself.

Encryption systems and other security measures are receiving growing attention among computer users. (More than 800 cryptographic products are available commercially in more than 30 countries.) As more and more individuals and businesses take to cyberspace, electronic crime is becoming an ever-increasing problem. Various types of lawbreaking—the illegal electronic transfer of money from one bank account to another, the obtaining and reselling of long-distance calling codes and credit-card numbers, the on-line transmission of child pornography, and the huge software-piracy market (which costs the software industry as much as $9 billion per year)—have grown to alarming levels.

Another major concern among Internet denizens is the unauthorized examination of an individual's personal information—such as health and financial records. Stolen passwords can give unauthorized users access into many private electronic files. The information in these databases can be tainted by a malicious hacker, potentially damaging someone's credit rating or insurance eligibility, for example. And then there are individuals who crash systems and steal information apparently just for the thrill or challenge of it—most notably Kevin Mitnick, who eluded authorities for three years during his most recent electronic crime spree. Mitnick, arrested early in 1995, allegedly stole as much as $1 million worth of data from computers worldwide. His success and the inability of authorities to track him down for so long demonstrated the vulnerability of the Internet to sabotage. Passwords and security measures often are useless against talented hackers who use various methods to steal passwords, gain top-level access to computer systems, and then wreak havoc.

Although debate over the civil-liberties issues involved with the government's Clipper-chip plan will undoubtedly continue, the need for secure transmission and encryption standards will grow as business activities are increasingly performed on-line.

NEWS IN CD-ROMs

A virtual explosion has occurred in the variety of programs, games, and other material available for personal computers in the compact-disc, read-only-memory (CD-ROM) format. Thousands of quality titles were introduced during 1994. This growth was fueled by a huge jump in the number of multimedia PCs sold (80 percent of PCs bound for the consumer market featured CD-ROM drives by late 1994), and by improvements in the technology and cost of CD hardware. In turn, the sales of CD software increased even more as multimedia technology became more affordable, powerful, and easy to obtain.

Double-speed CD-ROM drives—units that can spin discs at twice the rate of first-generation drives—were introduced in early 1992; by mid-1994, "quad-speed" CD drives had become the choice for many savvy PC buyers. The increase in speed means that features of CD programs work noticeably better—graphics are crisper, searches are faster, motion video is more fluid and lifelike. The introduction of fast microprocessors like Intel's Pentium also helped multimedia programs grow in popularity.

As CD technology continues to advance, allowing programmers to create ever-more-complex and realistic games, CDs are expected to give game systems such as Nintendo and Sega a run for their money. Many computer firms argue that consumers would prefer to have one machine on which they can perform many tasks—from accounting to game playing to helping children learn to read—over a machine that performs only one task (such as game playing). Educational software to familiarize very young children with computers and help them prepare for school, as well as programs to tutor older children in specific areas or encourage artistic interests, also are popular. Several corporations even released their annual reports on CD-ROM—including Oracle Corporation, a database-software company in Redwood City, California, and software producer Adobe Systems Incorporated, based in Mountain View, California.

Meanwhile, the next generation of CD technology waited—and competed—in the wings. Two technologies were battling to become the standard for so-called digital videodiscs, which were expected to enter the market late in 1995. These discs would be compatible with computers, audio CD players, video-playback machines, and video-game players. They could contain up to 15 times the information held by current CDs, and eventually could be rerecordable (CD-ROMs—with their "read-only memory"—are by definition unalterable).

Sony and Philips Electronics were working together on one version of the new disc, derived from existing CD-ROM technology; Time Warner and Toshiba teamed up on the other version, derived from laser-disc technology. The Sony/Philips version will store 3.7 gigabytes of information (1 gigabyte equals 1 billion bytes, or characters)—enough to contain a two-hour, high-resolution video with an enhanced sound track. By comparison, current CDs can hold 640 megabytes (640 million bytes). The double-sided videodisc envisioned by Time Warner and Toshiba would hold 4.8 gigabytes of information per side. The players for both versions would work with existing CDs, and the new discs should be no more expensive to produce than current CDs.

Meghan O'Reilly

CONSUMER TECHNOLOGY

It seems that no matter where you go today, or what you are doing, a new or enhanced technology is there. And in many cases, digital applications are making possible what would have been impossible only a few years ago. Yet, as a revolution is taking place in multimedia and other electronic technologies, manufacturers appear dedicated to an unchanging condition: the consumer's desire for innovative products that make life easier or more fun.

HOME ELECTRONICS

- *Toshiba Integrated Multimedia Monitor.* Write about a television show and then watch one—all on the same screen. Called TIMM, this 20-inch (50-centimeter) video display works as both a personal computer (PC) monitor and a TV. This multimedia monitor comes complete with all of the necessary connectors for video accessories and IBM-compatible PCs (an optional adapter is available for Apple Macintosh computers); its built-in speakers feature a 10-watt audio amplifier and bass-enhancement circuitry.
- *StarSight TV Listings.* With so many channels available on cable TV nowadays, it can be a daunting challenge to find out what you are watching as you flip from station to station with the remote control. StarSight Telecast Incorporated's interactive TV listings tell you—with just a glance at the TV screen—what you are watching, how much program time is left, and more. Viewers can scroll through a synopsis or program grid in order to study the programming for a week. And by highlighting a show with your remote, you can tune into the program or set your VCR to tape it with the press of a single button. Listings can also be sorted by such themes as comedy, drama, and sports.

StarSight is available with some new Zenith and Mitsubishi television models, and with Zenith, Goldstar, and Samsung VCRs. A factory-installed chip decodes the data from the StarSight signal and downloads the information into the TV's or VCR's memory.

For older TVs that do not incorporate this technology, Magnavox now offers a dedicated StarSight set-top unit. No matter how StarSight is received, consumers must pay a monthly subscription fee of about $4. StarSight Telecast is located in Fremont, California.
- *Sony's MiniDisc Data System.* The computer hard drive may someday become obsolete with advances in magneto-optic, or MO, storage technology. MO disks and drives can store, read, and write hundreds of megabytes (MB) of data to a special 3.5-inch (8.9-centimeter) or smaller disk. Sony's MD Data System holds up to 140 MB on a 2.5-inch (6.4-centimeter) disk. The drive can be used with DOS, Windows, or Macintosh PCs.
- *MovieWave CD Station.* This multidisc player with remote accepts any type of compact disc, including video CD, audio CD, interactive CD (CD-i), Karaoke CD, and Kodak Photo CD. Made by MultiWave Innovation of Campbell, California, the unit features surround-sound audio capability and video-output jacks so you can hook the player up to your TV for a realistic home-theater experience.
- *Wireless Speaker System.* In June 1989, the U.S. Federal Communications Commission (FCC) allocated a band of radio frequencies for wireless in-home use. The new Recotan wireless speaker system uses this band to transmit stereo signals up to 150 feet (45 meters), through walls, ceilings, and floors, no matter which room a stereo is based in. This sound system is manufactured by Comtrad Industries of Midlothian, Virginia.
- *Pre-Fone Filter.* Never again waste time talking to telephone salespeople or other unwelcome callers. This blocking device, available in three models, intercepts calls from telemarketers before your phone rings. It then plays a message that instructs them to place your name and phone number on their do-not-call list, which they are obligated to do by law. Nonsales callers press "5" to make your phone ring. The standard model allows you to record your own message; the deluxe device can be programmed so a distinctive ring will alert you to who's calling or for whom. The Pre-Fone Filter, from the Pre-Fone Filter Company of Troy, Ohio, plugs into both your telephone and a wall jack.

- **Solar Mower.** Concerned about the air pollution that your gas-powered mower is creating? Let the sunshine in! The Solar Mower can run for 90 minutes on a day's worth of direct sunlight. In fact, the Solar Mower's mulching blade spins at 3,200 revolutions per minute (rpm)—30 percent faster than gasoline-powered mowers. Sunlight absorbed by the mower's solar panels charges the 12-volt direct-current (DC) battery that runs the motor. On cloudy days, the mower can be charged in about three hours with an optional alternating-current (AC) adapter. The Solar Mower is made by Solar Power International of Bloomfield Hills, Michigan.

A recently introduced solar-powered lawn mower cuts out the noise, mess, and pollution associated with the traditional gasoline-powered mower.

- **Miraflex Insulation.** Researchers at the Owens-Corning Fiberglas Corporation in Toledo, Ohio, have created the first new form of fiberglass to be developed in nearly 60 years. Miraflex consists of two types of glass fiber, fused into long strands. These strands have random curls that keep the fiber from irritating the skin. (In contrast, traditional fiberglass fibers are short and straight.) The Miraflex curls, which look and feel like soft cotton fibers, also create a natural loft for a high energy-conservation value in such applications as insulation.

AT WORK

- **Business-Card Reader.** Confused about what to do with all those business cards? Often they end up in a cluttered desk drawer or tucked into a crowded Rolodex file. Panasonic has designed an electronic filing system that may simplify this often-disorganized process. The CF-CR100 Neofile scans in up to 500 business cards for storage and retrieval. Plus, you can add information to each of the entries, as well as sort them by company name or phone number, for instance. The unit weighs in at less than 1 pound (0.5 kilogram), and runs on six AAA batteries.
- **PocketJet Printer.** Measuring less than 1 foot (30 centimeters) long and 3 inches (8 centimeters) wide, and weighing a little more than 1 pound (0.5 kilogram), the PocketJet from Pentax Technologies is one of the smallest printers ever developed. This LaserJet-compatible unit runs on a battery, and prints text and graphics at 300 dots per inch (dpi) on thermal paper.

ON THE ROAD

- **Autostick.** Car buyers have long had to choose between an automatic and a manual transmission. Now consumers can have both in one car. Chrysler's Autostick, set to debut in the 1996 Eagle Vision TSI sedan, is an automatic transmission that uses an electronic system to shift manually. The system relies on sensors that adjust the internal gearing to make upshifts and downshifts. In place of a clutch, a computer signal disengages one gear and goes to the next. For a manual-mode override, the shift lever is placed in the bottom shift position, and upshifts and downshifts are made by moving the lever left and right. The transmission also operates in a fully automatic mode.
- **Next Generation DieHard.** Sears, Roebuck, and Company has come out with a new

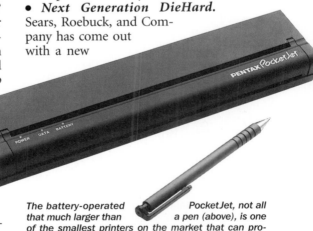

The battery-operated that much larger than of the smallest printers duce text and graphics.

PocketJet, not all a pen (above), is one on the market that can pro-

battery in its popular DieHard series. This latest product has a corrosion-resistant lead-calcium alloy and a shield that traps evaporating battery acid. These features are said to give the Next Generation DieHard more reliability in hot weather and extra starting power in cold weather.

- *Automotive Theft-Deterrence System.* Unlike other car-security devices—such as The Club—which lock the wheel, this British-made theft deterrent unlocks the wheel from the steering column, rendering the car unmaneuverable. The system is deactivated when the car key is inserted in the ignition. Made by Malvy Technology Limited of London, England, the system can be installed in new cars as a dealer option.

- *DesertOx Safety Front-Effect Bar.* This aftermarket impact bar for sport-utility vehicles brings a softer touch to front-end protection. The grille is designed to absorb the force of impact in a crash and return to its original shape. The steel frame of the DesertOx is crimped and slit and covered in thick polyurethane padding. This bar, manufactured in the Netherlands, is distributed in the United States by DesertOx of Denver, Colorado.

AT PLAY

- *Electra Globe.* Made by Specialized Bicycle Components of Morgan Hill, California, this power-assisted electric-motor bike is ideal for commuters. Its electric motor helps a bicyclist climb hills, fight headwinds, or simply speed along at up to 18 miles (29 kilometers) per hour. The prototype Globe also includes a shock-absorbing seat, a windshield, a rechargeable battery, and enclosed chain and gears to keep clothes grease-free.

- *Batter Up/TeeV Golf Video-Game Accessories.* Forget the standard joystick or button controller that comes with a sport video game. Enjoy a more realistic game of baseball or golf with the high-tech controller accessories from Sports Science Incorporated of Twinsburg, Ohio. Batter Up is an electronic bat that advances the video-game action every time you swing at the game's pitcher. TeeV Golf is a 2-foot (60-centimeter)-long electronic golf club that is weighted at the end so that it simulates the feel of a real club.

Instead of hitting a golf ball, however, an infrared beam passes over a sensor pad on the floor. The flight of the ball in the video game is determined by how accurately and strongly you swing the club over the sensor pad.

PORTABLE WONDERS

- *Infraceptor Watch.* Dick Tracy would be impressed. Casio's Infraceptor watch is also a phone book, game system, stopwatch, and an infrared message sender. The watch allows users to input data on up to 10 people in the phone book. More-ambitious consumers can record messages on a Casio JD-6000 Digital Diary and then store them in the watch. The watch's infrared beam allows you to play a fantasy adventure game against other Infraceptor users.

- *Tango Pager.* In order to answer a message on a conventional pager, you have to respond by telephone. Motorola's new Tango, however, answers for you. This two-way alphanumeric pager uses a built-in radio transmitter to return a preprogrammed response or a message selected from a customized menu sent by your service provider.

The prototype Electra Globe is a power-assisted bike that offers the rider a practically maintenance-free form of alternative transportation.

- *Multimedia Notebook PCs.* CD-ROMs are on the run! CD-ROM drives, speakers, and other multimedia features have made their way into some notebook PCs. IBM's

ThinkPad 755 CD, for instance, has the drive on a slide-out tray, similar to the setup on an audio CD player. Panasonic's V41 notebook has a keyboard that lifts up to reveal the CD drive and a space to store an additional compact disc.

• *Steiner Mini-Scope.* When it comes to field glasses, think small. This minimonocular measures only 3 inches (7.6 centimeters) long and weighs only 3 ounces (85 grams). Despite the Mini-Scope's small size, its field of view is respectable. The eight-power lens provides a 360-foot (110-meter) field of view at 1,000 yards (915 meters). The Mini-Scope is available from Pioneer Research of Westmont, New Jersey.

BeeperKid, a device worn by a child and a caregiver, emits a warning signal that alerts the adult if the youngster strays more than 15 feet away.

• *BeeperKid Child Tracker.* Losing a child is every parent's worst nightmare. A new device from A + H International Products of Long Beach, California, helps ease this worry by using technology developed for military communications. BeeperKid consists of two small, round units: one is worn by the parent, the other by the child. If the child should wander beyond a 15-foot (4.6-meter) radius, the parent's unit beeps. The digital signal transmitted between the units is of a nonradio frequency that can even travel through walls and metal objects. The units are individually coded so other BeeperKids in the area will not interfere with a parent's unit.

Susan Nielsen

ELECTRONICS

SOLAR CELLS ON A ROLL

No energy technology offers greater promise than solar power. But silicon solar cells, which convert sunlight into electric current, are difficult and expensive to make. Now scientists at United Solar Systems Corporation in Troy, Michigan, report a way to mass-produce flexible, inexpensive solar cells that generate power with unprecedented efficiency—converting into electricity more than 10 percent of the light energy they receive.

To make the thin-film, silicon-alloy solar cells, researchers use a process called roll-to-roll deposition. A roll of stainless steel—measuring 0.2 inch (5 millimeters) thick, 14 inches (36 centimeters) wide, and 0.5 mile (0.8 kilometer) long—is run through a machine that deposits layers of amorphous silicon material onto the metal backing. The procedure yields a waferlike, multilayered sandwich of silicon alloy and germanium.

The thin-film silicon solar cells are then cut into squares. The scientists estimate that roughly 1.2 square yards (1 square meter) of the material would be needed to power a 100-watt lightbulb. The researchers are developing a manufacturing system to produce these solar cells at low cost for large-scale use.

SOFT PLASTIC TRANSISTORS

Electronic circuits for portable radios, car phones, and other consumer devices may soon become flexible enough to bend without breaking. Today such circuits are made mostly of brittle metals and silicon. However, materials scientists in Thiais, France, recently reported the development of a field-effect transistor (FET) made entirely of an organic polymer.

To make the transistors, the scientists developed a special printing technique that enables them to stamp out circuits on a soft, organic material in a manner similar to printing a magazine page on a roll of paper. Producing rigid transistors ordinarily requires high temperatures and vacuums—difficult, energy-consuming processes that can easily go awry because of contamination or system failures. The new procedure, the researchers maintain, bypasses many of these complications. In a battery of tests, the researchers rolled, twisted, and bent the new electronic devices out of shape. The transistors continued to work, despite extreme physical deformations.

The researchers believe that the flexible transistors may open the way to large-scale, low-cost plastic electronics. For example, they envision such futuristic applications as pocket-sized "smart" cards, large flat-screen televisions, and windshields that display information.

CONDUCTIVE CERAMICS GROW IN A BEAKER

Making a highly conductive ceramic such as superconducting copper oxide is nor-

A new, highly conductive ceramic material can be grown in a beaker at room temperature, a method far simpler than other means used to synthesize comparable superconductors.

mally a tall order. Scientists need high-temperature kilns and powerful vacuums in order to fashion the delicate structures.

In their efforts to develop an easier approach, scientists at the University of Missouri at Rolla report growing a highly conductive ceramic in a room-temperature solution in a beaker. The new material, called a defect chemistry superlattice, is made of many sandwichlike layers of thallium (III) oxide. Using electrochemical techniques, the researchers deposit the layers—each only 6.7 nanometers (0.000026 inch) thick—one at a time by pulsing an electric current through a solution. The layers accumulate parallel to the electrodes.

Scientists report that the new ceramic has both strong optical and electrical qualities. It also transmits light efficiently at near-infrared wavelengths, making it potentially useful for optical switches in high-speed computers and for long-distance communication.

OPTICAL COMPUTING WITH ATOMIC VAPOR

Many scientists believe that faster and more-powerful computers of the future will transfer light signals rather than electric charges to perform computations. Researchers suspect that these optical computers will be able to process many pieces of information simultaneously—a substantial leap from conventional computers, which process bits of data one at a time. But in order to make computing with light possible, engineers need suitable "nonlinear" materials for comparing information by optical means.

Searching for such a material, scientists at the University of Southern California (USC) in Los Angeles report developing an optical correlator, a device that uses a vapor of cesium to look for similarities and differences between two images presented on laser beams. The laser beams pass through a glass cell filled with a cesium vapor that emits a signal indicating whether the two images directly overlap.

The researchers chose cesium because of its high sensitivity, which exceeds that of most semiconductors. As a nonlinear optical material, cesium vapor also emits more light than it receives, reacting strongly to certain wavelengths.

In order to test the cesium optical correlator, the scientists compared tiny images of the first three letters of the alphabet. Each character stood only 0.009 inch (230 micrometers) high. Optical comparisons took only 30 nanoseconds (0.00000003 second). The researchers believe that cesium-based optical correlators could lead to better computerized vision- or pattern-recognition systems, such as those used by pharmaceutical companies for inspecting pills on an assembly line.

QUANTUM-CASCADE LASER

Lasers—light-emitting devices that have greatly advanced delicate surgical techniques, long-distance communication, and audio equipment—may soon come in another form. Scientists at AT&T Bell Laboratories in Murray Hill, New Jersey, recently reported a new type of semiconductor injection laser that they call a quantum-cascade laser.

A laser creates a focused beam of uniform-wavelength light by driving charged particles such as electrons into highly energetic states. The process generates particles of light called photons at specific energy levels. In the new laser, electrons are driven up several energy levels, then allowed to drop down step-by-step, emitting a photon at each plateau.

The researchers assert that the quantum-cascade laser offers several advantages over diode and gas lasers, including its more compact size, greater flexibility, and lower manufacturing cost. Scientists can tune the new laser to emit light with a relatively wide range of wavelengths by changing the thickness of layers in the laser's sandwichlike semiconductor. The laser will prove useful for remote applications, such as air-quality monitoring, collision-avoidance radar, and point-to-point communication.

MATERIAL MOVED BY LIGHT

Materials that change shape when exposed to specific wavelengths of light could lead to new communication devices. Such so-called photostrictive materials in effect convert photo energy directly into mechanical energy.

Scientists at Pennsylvania State University in State College reported advances in a material called PLZT, which forms a crystalline array of lead, lanthanum, zirconium, and titanium. The material takes advantage of two phenomena—the photoelectric and piezoelectric effects—that create an electric field in the array that causes it to flex. Photostrictive materials respond mostly to wavelengths of light in the purple band of the spectrum.

Based on the properties of this material, researchers envision making photo-driven electronic relays and switches, robots, and acoustic devices such as photophones, which would convert laser signals into sound.

Richard Lipkin

ENDANGERED SPECIES

THE RETURN OF THE WOLF

For most of the 19th and 20th centuries, the gray wolf (or timber wolf) was so ruthlessly poisoned, shot, and trapped that it is now all but extinct in many parts of North America. By 1960, the wolf had disappeared from all of the lower 48 states except northern Minnesota and Michigan's Isle Royale in Lake Superior.

But following the passage of the Endangered Species Act in 1973, the wolf began returning to some portions of its original range in the United States. Gradually, and in small numbers, wolves ventured south from Canada (where they continue to be plentiful) into Washington, Montana, Wisconsin, and the Upper Peninsula of Michigan. With their gradual return has come a gradual change in attitudes toward the predator. Many hunters and ranchers who once might have shot a wolf on sight now recognize that the animal plays an integral role in the ecosystem. Even many people in the livestock and ranching business accept the presence of wolves. In Minnesota, for instance, U.S. Fish and Wildlife Service researchers discovered that about 1,700 wolves live near 7,000 farms, and that each year an average of only 29 of those farms suffer any loss of their livestock to wolf predation. The wolf's reputation as a man killer has also been disproved: there has never been a documented case in North America of healthy wild wolves attacking and killing a human. It is becoming increasingly clear that wolves and people can coexist.

That attitude is not universal, however. When the U.S. Fish and Wildlife Service announced in the summer of 1994 that it planned to release 30 gray wolves each year for three to five years in Yellowstone National Park and the wilderness of central Idaho, there was a strong upswell of opinions. On one side were wildlife managers and environmentalists who wish to see wolves returned to some of their original range in the Rocky Mountains. On another side were environmentalists who want the wolves to return, but prefer to have them return naturally, without the interference of humans. On a third front were livestock producers and ranchers who fear the wolves will prey on their domestic stock or even hunt humans. The controversy had not abated by early 1995, when 15 wolves were released in Yellowstone, and another 15 were released in Idaho. Early indications for their survival were not encouraging. Less than two weeks after the release of the wolves in Idaho, one was found shot dead near a dead calf. The stomach of the calf had been torn open, leading to initial reports that the wolf had been justifiably killed. But an autopsy revealed the wolf did not kill the calf. The calf had died of natural causes, and the wolf had been at the wrong place at the wrong time. (See also the article beginning on page 29.)

THE STATUS OF BIG CATS

The economic crisis in the former Soviet Union has had immediate and dire consequences for wildlife. Siberian tigers, while never abundant in modern times, have dwindled to an estimated 300 animals as poachers hunt them for their fur and body parts, and loggers decimate the forests that are their last refuge.

Even more imperiled by Russian economics is the Amur leopard, a 90- to 140-pound (40- to 63-kilogram) subspecies of leopard that is considered the most endangered of the world's big cats. While efforts are under way to establish a nature reserve on the border of Russia and China, in the heart of leopard habitat, poachers are targeting the leopard and openly selling its coat, which is reportedly worth several thousand dollars. Only 30 to 50 of the cats still live in Siberia, northern China, and North Korea. And with trees in the region falling rapidly to logger's chain saws, it has become urgent that a portion of the forest be set aside to protect the leopard.

Cats elsewhere are also having a difficult time. There are now probably fewer than 5,000 wild tigers in Asia, and the number is going down at an appalling rate as poachers supply a lucrative market in body parts used in traditional Chinese medicine. Until recently, officials in India, home to two-thirds of the world's tigers, insisted that their nation's 20 tiger reserves supported stable, even growing, populations of Bengal tigers. But poaching has become epidemic on the reserves, and the tigers of India are in danger of being eradicated. In March 1994, India's environmental minister, Kamal Nath, organized a meeting of nine Asian nations and established the Global Tiger Forum with the intention of preserving habitat and combating poaching. But following the refusal of China to participate, and the less-than-enthusiastic support of several other "tiger-range" countries, Nath voiced fear that the forum might be doomed to failure. "If there are no new efforts made now," he said, "it will not take more than a decade to see the tiger go."

An underground trade system transports the carcasses of tigers to apothecaries in China, Taiwan, Hong Kong, and Chinatowns in Europe and North America. There eager customers line up to buy an array of pills, balms, and libations made from the skulls, bones, blood, whiskers, and organs of tigers. In traditional Chinese medicine, the potions are prescribed to treat various ailments and injuries and to enhance sexual potency and restore vigor. The demand for the medicine is high, and the prices reflect it: powdered tiger bone sells for as much as $500 per gram in Taiwan.

The survival of elephants, tigers, leopards, and other seriously endangered species is further jeopardized by poachers, who trade in furs and in body parts used in traditional medicine.

In Africa, the lions of Tanzania's Serengeti are facing a foe of a different kind. In 1994, at least 100 of the cats died from canine distemper, a virus better known for killing wolves, coyotes, foxes, and domestic dogs. A few cases of the virus have been found in hyenas and foxes, and there is concern that it might spread to jackals, wild dogs, and leopards. The immediate threat is to the 3,000 lions that live in the vicinity of Serengeti National Park. The 100 fatalities represent an extremely high mortality for the lions, and veterinarians worry that the virus has spread to remote parts of the park, where the number of lions killed could be even higher.

BALD EAGLE RECOVERY

When the bald eagle was listed as an endangered species in 1978, there were only a few hundred breeding pairs in the lower 48 states. By 1994, the population had increased to more than 4,000 pairs, inspiring the U.S. Fish and Wildlife Service to propose lowering the bird's status from endangered to threatened. The new designation should make little difference in defending eagles in the wild. The birds are still protected against hunting and harassment, and their nests and eggs cannot be legally disturbed. The new status relaxes some of the protection afforded the places where eagles live and nest, though logging, road construction, and other development will remain subject to review on a case-by-case basis.

Nonetheless, some conservationists are concerned about the future of the national bird. Specifically, biologists are worried about the unexplained deaths of a number of eagles in Wisconsin and Arkansas. In late 1994 and early 1995, at least 27 of the birds were found dead in Arkansas, victims of an unidentified toxin that caused brain damage. In early 1995, nine eagles were found dead in southern Wisconsin, apparently killed by a toxin that attacked their livers. Recalling the decimation of eagles before the insecticide DDT was banned in 1972, some biologists worry that the eagles in Arkansas and Wisconsin might be victims of an unknown environmental hazard, and that their deaths might be a warning of more-serious consequences to come. (See also the article beginning on page 16.)

Jerry Dennis

ENERGY

More than enough energy was available in the United States in 1994, leading to increased consumption and stable or lower prices. Debate continued on the issue of nuclear-waste disposal during 1994. One proposal by the Mescalero Apache to store highly radioactive waste on their tribal lands in New Mexico gained steam, although the U.S. Department of Energy (DOE) was under increasing pressure to meet its legislated obligations in taking possession of this waste. Meanwhile, controversy continued to swirl around the future of electric automobiles in the United States.

FOSSIL FUELS

● *Oil.* Oil was used to produce 3.1 percent of the country's electricity in 1994, down from 3.3 percent in 1993. Oil was the largest contributor to the nation's overall energy consumption: 40.6 percent, up from 40.3 percent. This continued a trend of many years as utilities relied less on oil for producing electricity, and U.S. consumers increased their consumption by driving more and using more petroleum-based products.

The year started with oil prices in a slide, eventually hitting $13 per barrel in February 1994, the lowest price this decade. Prices slowly rebounded, ending the year at an average composite of $15.59. The Organization of Petroleum Exporting Countries (OPEC) tried to reestablish its former control of worldwide prices and supply. Prices did rally after a March OPEC agreement to hold to production quotas, but then held steady through the rest of the year. In November, OPEC agreed to hold quotas steady through the end of 1995. As a result, many observers forecast that prices would head upward—probably into the $20 range. Imports increased during 1994, at times providing more than half of the oil consumed in the United States.

In April, Texaco and Exxon announced plans to explore and begin tapping into crude-oil reserves inside the Arctic Circle. They estimate that 2 billion to 5 billion barrels of oil could be recovered from the area as part of a project that could cost $60 billion over 50 years.

Domestic production of oil continued dropping in 1994, averaging 6.6 million barrels per day, down from 1993's 6.8 million barrels, and far below the record 9.2 million barrels in the early 1970s. With worldwide prices remaining relatively low and supplies plentiful, and with increasing environmental concerns and domestic regulations, there was little incentive for U.S. oil companies to undertake new, costly exploration projects. In fact, oil companies had been undergoing major restructuring for over a decade, with an estimated 500,000 jobs eliminated and losses of some $300 billion.

Gasoline prices fluctuated during 1994, peaking in the summer, but ending at an average $1.11 per gallon for unleaded regular. The Clean Air Act required that, by January 1, 1995, nine cities where pollution levels have historically been high start using a lower-emission gasoline. This gasoline is formulated with oxygen-rich compounds so it burns more cleanly. This move increased prices and also led to consumer complaints about reduced performance. Some consumers also reported problems when using the new gasoline in some lawn-mower and other small engines in which oil is mixed directly with gasoline.

The litigation surrounding the 1989 *Exxon Valdez* oil spill in Alaska reached another milestone in 1994 as juries assessed the company nearly $15 million in damages.

- **Natural Gas.** Demand for natural gas increased in 1994; it supplied 24.8 percent of the energy consumed in the United States, up from 24.3 percent in 1993. Natural gas also was used to produce 10 percent of the nation's electricity, up from 9.2 percent the year before. Prices to producers—the wellhead price—dropped to $1.83 per 1,000 cubic feet from $2.06 in 1993. Prices to consumers, however, continued to rise, averaging $6.40 per 1,000 cubic feet (28 cubic meters), up from 1993's $6.16.
- **Coal.** Domestic coal production increased nearly 9 percent in 1994, to 1.03 billion tons from 1993's 947 million. Coal supplied 56.2 percent of the country's electricity, an increase over the 55.2 percent supplied the year before. Coal also provided 22.9 percent of the nation's overall energy use in 1994, down from 1993's 23.5 percent.

NUCLEAR POWER

The country's 108 nuclear-power plants supplied 22 percent of U.S. electricity in 1994, up from 21.5 percent in 1993. With plant operation improving, and with no new nuclear plants having been ordered in the United States for 25 years, many observers assert that this source of energy may be nearing its peak. While research continues on new, safer designs, it appears the most likely market for new plants is outside of the United States.

Economics continued to be the major issue in nuclear power, with regulators and utilities alike working on ways to reduce costs without compromising safety. The controversial issue of spent-fuel disposal heated up as utilities and consumers became increasingly frustrated with the apparent lack of action by the Department of Energy in meeting its schedule for taking this highly radioactive waste out of the pools where it currently is stored. The DOE announced in 1994 that according to its interpretation of legislation, it was not required to

Cars powered by natural gas, an abundant fuel touted for its low cost and clean emissions, have generated little enthusiasm among U.S. consumers and automakers.

take possession of this waste until 1998. After this announcement, several states and utilities filed suit against the department. With billions of dollars already collected from consumers, the issue began to hit home as the specter of escalating payments loomed.

The Mescalero Apache of New Mexico began work with a consortium of utilities, hoping to establish a temporary storage site on Mescalero tribal lands. This proposal was at first defeated, then approved, by a vote of tribe members. At year's end, the project was alive, but there were questions about its future—regarding both its costs and its long-term plans with the DOE.

ELECTRIC CARS

Hopeful signs of progress began to fade in 1994 as Detroit's Big Three automakers—Ford, General Motors (GM), and Chrysler—said they would be unlikely to meet California's demand that 2 percent of the cars sold there in 1998 be electric—rising to 5 percent in 2002, and 10 percent by 2003. High cost and limited range are the main hurdles to overcome, with current vehicles costing over $100,000 and limited to drives of less than 100 miles (160 kilometers)—usually followed by an eight-hour recharge. With the wave of antiregulatory sentiment growing throughout the country, automakers increasingly concentrated on lobbying and developing grassroots support to change California's legislation. Multimillion-dollar advertising campaigns were being developed around several messages, including the argument that California's legislation is an intrusion of government into the marketplace.

Automakers launched similar efforts in other parts of the country to remove mandates requiring the production of electric cars. In the place of such mandates, the manufacturers promised to build cleaner-operating gasoline-powered cars. In the Northeast, for example, automakers tried to lobby a 12-state consortium to adopt a plan calling for lower-emission vehicles, but not electric cars. The consortium opted, however, to leave that decision up to the individual states. New York and Massachusetts passed legislation requiring electric vehicles.

Anthony J. Castagno

ENVIRONMENT

THE CALIFORNIA DESERT PROTECTION ACT

In November 1994, the California Desert Protection Act—the largest U.S. land-conservation measure since the Alaska Lands Bill in 1980—was passed by Congress and signed into law by President Clinton. The measure, whose proponents had fought for its passage for nearly 10 years, protects almost 8 million acres (3.2 million hectares) of California's ecologically fragile desert area. The Joshua Tree and Death Valley national monuments are to become national parks, thus affording them greater environmental protection; their boundaries also are to be expanded. The area of the state covered by the act extends from the Sierra Nevada to the Mexican border; included in this region are some 2,000 species of plants and wildlife.

Environmentalists objected, however, to an amendment to the bill ensuring that property owners will be compensated for their land if it is designated as an endangered-species habitat. Also criticized were concessions made to satisfy various special-interest groups and reluctant members of Congress. The Mojave area, for example, was turned into a national preserve—a designation that allows hunting. Other parcels of land were opened up to ranching, mining, and off-road-vehicle use, as well as for U.S.-Mexican border-control activities. Critics noted that these uses could threaten endangered species and permanently damage fragile land. (See also the article beginning on page 102.)

OIL SPILLS

In the fall of 1994, a major oil spill occurred in the Russian Arctic, near the city of Usinsk. Apparently, oil had been leaking for months from a pipeline in bad repair, and several dikes had been constructed to contain the spilling oil. In October, however, one of these dams burst after heavy rains, and a river of oil more than 3 feet (1 meter) deep and 14 yards (12.8 meters) wide flowed toward the Pechora River, which empties into the Arctic Ocean. A huge amount of oil thus was released into the tundra, harming native plant and animal life. U.S. and Greenpeace officials estimated the size of the release at 2 million barrels (84 million gallons, or 318 million liters)—making it one of the largest oil spills in history, eight times larger than the 1989 *Exxon Valdez* disaster in Alaska. Russian officials claim that the release constituted only 100,000 barrels (4,200,000 gallons, or 16 million liters).

The Russian spill was an environmental catastrophe, regardless of its exact size. Cleanup crews worked into December to clear the mess, but the Arctic winter put further efforts on hold until spring. Russian cleanup workers claimed that 80 percent of the oil had been removed—an estimate disputed by U.S. observers.

Also in October, torrential rains caused severe flooding in Houston, Texas, washing away the support for several oil pipelines. At first, two pipelines were reported to have burst; a total of seven were damaged by the time flooding receded. Officials estimated that about 60,000 barrels (2.5 million gallons, or 9.46 million liters) of gasoline and diesel fuel escaped from the first two broken pipelines, and that some 5,000 barrels (200,000 gallons, or 757,000 liters) of crude oil flowed into the San Jacinto River from other pipelines. The oil

was reportedly light-grade crude, which evaporates quickly. This, coupled with the fast-flowing nature of the river, helped ease cleanup of the disaster. Fires broke out at the site of the pipeline breaks, however, polluting the air and causing many injuries.

The 1989 *Exxon Valdez* oil spill continued to be in the news. In September 1994, a federal jury ordered Exxon to pay $5 billion in punitive damages to Alaskan plaintiffs in the spill, including fishermen and property owners. The verdict was upheld in January 1995 despite Exxon's filing of 11 requests for relief. It was the largest pollution settlement in history.

THE OZONE HOLE

It was reported in October 1994 that the ozone hole over the Antarctic was no larger than in 1993. The hole, about the size of North America—9.4 million square miles (24.35 million square kilometers)—was, in fact, slightly smaller than in 1992, when the amount of ozone thinning set a record. Also, the ozone layer over North America was thicker than during previous winters. This seemed to end a pattern in which the hole grew steadily larger each year.

Scientists for the National Aeronautics and Space Administration (NASA) provided new evidence that ozone thinning is largely caused, as suspected, by human activity—specifically, the production of chlorofluorocarbons (CFCs). Data returned to Earth since 1991 by the Upper Atmosphere Research Satellite (UARS) indicated that this is the case. Most industrialized nations, under the Montreal Protocol, have agreed to phase out their production of CFCs—long used in refrigerants and

The San Jacinto River in southeast Texas caught fire when floodwaters caused gasoline pipelines beneath the riverbed to rupture. The thick smoke could be seen from miles away.

insulation—over a period of several years. Although the slight reduction in size of 1994's ozone hole was encouraging, indicating that human-made environmental damage to the ozone layer can be reversed, it will be approximately 50 years, scientists estimate, before the size of the Antarctic ozone hole drops appreciably. CFCs will take many years to dissipate from the atmosphere, even when production is halted completely.

Thousands of environmentally minded people gathered on the National Mall in Washington, D.C., to celebrate the 25th anniversary of the first Earth Day—April 22, 1970.

DESERTIFICATION

In October 1994, 87 of the world's nations signed a pact pledging to help prevent desertification. Desertification was defined at the 1992 Earth Summit in Rio de Janeiro, Brazil, as "land degradation in arid, semiarid, and dry subhumid areas resulting from various factors, including climatic variations and human activities." About one-quarter of Earth's landmass is made up of arid land prone to desertification; this land supports some 900 million people. Almost 75 percent of Africa's land already is considered to be degraded.

The Convention on Desertification will become an international treaty when it is ratified by at least 50 of the signing countries. The United Nations Environment Program (UNEP) estimates that it will cost between $10 billion and $22 billion annually for 20 years to fight desertification successfully. Less than $1 billion per year is being spent currently on this cause. The wealthier nations pledged little money outright, but a "Global Mechanism" was established by the convention to coordinate projects and to find money to finance them. Some less developed nations were critical of the lack of funds promised.

Among the causes of land degradation are changing weather conditions and various human activities such as overgrazing, overcultivation, and erosion due to deforestation. Deforestation from indiscriminate logging was singled out for special international attention during the year. Early in 1994, an agreement was drafted by 23 tropical timber-producing countries and 27 consumer nations to make forest preservation a high priority in the international timber industry. Northern timber-producing nations such as the United States also agreed to adopt guidelines to manage their own forests. The pact's resolutions were vague, however, and compromises were made by both sides. Environmentalists were critical of the agreement, calling it a public-relations facade. United Nations (U.N.) studies indicate that human activity has caused the destruction of as much forest in the past 20 years as was destroyed in all of Earth's previous history.

Meanwhile, scientists studying the Sahara and its immediate surrounding area found that, by contrast, permanent desertification may not really be occurring, and that land degradation is caused as much by natural factors as by human activities. Scientists from NASA and from the University of Lund in Sweden failed to find any trends that could not be explained by annual variations in rainfall. Their findings, based largely on satellite measurements and ground observations made by aircraft, indicate that the pattern is for the desert's borders to expand in dry years and to retreat in wetter years. However, scientists agree that more-extended observations (perhaps for 40 to 50 years) are needed before it can be determined whether there indeed is a long-term trend toward desertification. They concur that, even if it is confirmed that the world's deserts are not growing, arid lands are suffering increasing degradation and damage from human activity.

CONCERNS ABOUT CHLORINE

Human-made chemical compounds, especially chlorine-based ones, received much negative attention during 1994. Environmentalists pointed to several research experiments showing that these compounds have a wide range of negative effects on animals, humans, and the environment, from causing thinning of the ozone layer to triggering cancer and birth defects. Concern is especially great because chlorine compounds are particularly stable, making them persistent and bioaccumulative. Newer research suggests a link between reproductive irregularities and some chlorine-based compounds such as dioxin. In January 1994, scientists from the United States and Europe revealed data that seem to imply that males of certain species in the wild—alligators, turtles, and trout among them—are being feminized through exposure to these pollutants, causing a drop in successful reproduction. Although there is as yet no hard evidence that reproductive disturbances are taking place, such an effect could account for several recent trends in humans living in industrialized countries: unexplained increases in breast-cancer and testicular-cancer rates, and falling sperm counts and semen production.

Although environmentalists seek to persuade the government to ban all chlorine production completely, industry representatives and some scientists point out the beneficial aspects of many chlorine-based compounds (such as the chlorination of water and the use of chlorine compounds in pharmaceutical production), as well as the fact that polyvinyl chloride (PVC) plastics are used to make an extremely wide range of useful modern products. In fact, some 15,000 products use chlorine. Critics also pointed out that many potentially dangerous chlorine compounds are found in nature, and that many nonchlorine chemicals are also thought to be harmful.

In February 1995, Environmental Protection Agency (EPA) administrator Carol Browner stated that the EPA "will develop a national strategy for substituting, reducing, or prohibiting the use of chlorine and chlorinated compounds," indicating an intention to investigate the feasibility of substituting other substances for chlorine or reducing its use in applications where it seems possible. Predictably, this satisfied neither industry members nor environmentalists.

One particular chlorine-based compound, dioxin, was strongly criticized by the EPA. In September 1994, the agency released a draft of a study concluding that dioxin is a probable cause of cancer in humans, although it does not constitute as strong a risk as does smoking. (In 1985, the U.S. government had come to a similar conclusion.) This draft was the result of a three-year study by scientists both in and out of the government; it also stated that dioxin can cause a range of less obvious effects like developmental disorders. In general, the study stated that levels of environmental dioxin have been falling since the United States established stricter pollution controls. In the United States, the main source of human exposure is through the consumption of meat and poultry products. The EPA, the Department of Agriculture, and the Food and Drug Administration (FDA) currently are participating jointly in a study of dioxin levels in beef, pork, and poultry. The EPA stated that, early in 1995, it would propose guidelines to reduce human exposure to the chemical.

Environmentalists characterized the findings as evidence that dioxin exposure is a "public health emergency," and again urged the complete banning of all chlorine-based chemicals.

Meghan O'Reilly

FOOD AND POPULATION

The Food and Agriculture Organization (FAO) of the United Nations (UN) reports that the total output of cereal grains for 1994 was a possibly record-breaking 1.951 billion metric tons. An increase of nearly one-third in the North American harvest made up for sharp drops in output in Australia and the former Soviet Union. The result was a very mixed pattern of food production and distribution throughout the world.

FOOD DISTRIBUTION

The basic food staples for human and animal consumption are cereal grains (mainly wheat, corn, and rice). Of the nearly 2 billion metric tons of grains produced in 1994, 90 percent was consumed in the country in which the grains were grown; the rest was traded (178 million tons) or provided as food aid (13 million tons). Most of the grain (wheat and corn, not rice) that was traded was grown in the industrialized countries, and one-third of it was exchanged among these developed countries. The sharpest increase in grain trade was in coarse grains, like corn, most of which is fed to animals; this reflects a comparable increase in meat consumption.

People's access to food depends on how well the growers, suppliers, processors, marketers, and regulators manage the international food system. Unfortunately, nearly 800 million people suffer from chronic hunger and malnutrition because they lack access to food; either they cannot afford to grow or buy it, or their numbers overwhelm the portion of the food produced that is actually available to them through subsidies or donations.

FOOD PRODUCTION

On the production side, too, there are serious constraints. The most obvious are shortages of land, water, and energy; lack of adequate equipment and appropriate technology; environmental stress; often unfavorable weather conditions; and the lack of research directed toward sustainable and subsistence agriculture.

At the same time, overconsumption by the majority of people in the industrialized countries and affluent minorities in the developing countries adds pressures on the food supply. This combination of supply- and demand-side constraints deepens the continuing food insecurity of one-seventh of the world's people, mainly in the developing countries, who are hungry and whom the FAO has described as at risk.

In most sub-Saharan African countries, per-capita food production has generally not been keeping pace with consumption. In 1994, however, output improved, except in countries affected by conflict—Angola, Burundi, Liberia, Rwanda, and Sudan. Northern Africa and the Sahelian region of West Africa had good harvests and show promising crop futures, but the prospects in Southern Africa remain uncertain. Population growth continues to exert pressure on the food supply, and malnutrition is particularly high in the camps where millions of refugees and displaced persons live under miserable conditions.

Weather conditions seriously affected harvests in Asia. Although, on the whole, the situation was favorable, there was some concern about such populous countries as Bangladesh, China, and Indonesia. Australia had its worst cereal harvest since 1972 (50 percent less than a year earlier). A cereal-production drop in Central America was balanced by increased harvests in South America. Crops in Eastern Europe, the former Soviet Union, and the European Community (EC) declined across the board.

The total production of nearly 2 billion tons, combined with the global carryover of more than 300 million tons, once again was adequate to feed all the world's people, even with a yearly overall population growth of about 95 million. The rate of population growth has begun to decline, but the increased numbers are expected to continue well into the 21st century. With food production also expected to climb under the influence of biotechnology and other research, the 2-billion-ton mark may be reached by the year 2000.

The brutal civil war in Rwanda created a refugee problem of epic proportions. Malnutrition became a major problem among the displaced people, despite frequent shipments of food from the Red Cross (above) and other donors.

INTERNATIONAL ATTENTION

Officials of the Consultative Group on International Agricultural Research (CGIAR), meeting in Switzerland in early February 1995, expressed great concern for the adequacy of food production in the future, noting that, in 1994, production did not meet demand for any of CGIAR's 12 listed crops.

The major food and agriculture problem, however, continues to be integral to the system, that is, to the production-distribution-consumption cycle. Production gains have taken place mainly in the industrialized food-exporting countries where capital-intensive agriculture is the norm. Production for domestic consumption in the food-deficit countries, however, has not improved; nor has the access of poor people to food. The FAO's estimate of 800 million people facing starvation worldwide, published last year in *Agriculture Toward 2010*, still applies.

A little over 20 years ago, the UN's World Food Conference discussed all these problems in considerable detail. There was a general agreement among the conferees that the basic solution to the problem of world hunger was to grow more food in the food-deficit countries. Two decades later, although there has been some small movement in the direction of sustainable agriculture in the developing countries, little improvement has been noted in the overall picture.

What may have seemed a fairly hopeful prospect a year or so ago, even though difficult and painful, has clearly soured. Hunger is on the rise, not only in the poor countries of what used to be called the Third World, but in the industrialized nations as well—even in the United States.

In late 1993, the issue of hunger reappeared on the world's agenda: the World Bank held a conference about it; the Rio Earth Summit's goals with respect to it were reaffirmed; and there was agreement that helping poor farmers in food-deficit countries grow more food and distribute it fairly was an urgent and viable goal. But the figures are still stark, the problem is still with us, and the prospects are not encouraging.

Martin M. McLaughlin

GENETICS

During an unusually productive year, researchers identified a long-sought gene that causes the majority of inherited cases of breast cancer, two genes linked to inherited colon cancer, a major new tumor-suppression gene, and the genes that cause two of the three major forms of dwarfism. Researchers also showed that Type I diabetes is caused by a group of as many as 18 genes.

BREAST CANCER

The elusive breast-cancer gene, called BRCA-1, is carried by about 600,000 American women. These women have an 85 percent risk of developing breast cancer by the age of 65, as well as an unusually high risk of developing ovarian cancer. The gene is responsible for about half of all cases of inherited breast cancer, which in turn accounts for about 5 percent of the 182,000 cases of the disease that occur in the United States each year. About 46,000 women die from the disease each year, making it second only to lung cancer as a cause of death among women. Identification of the gene among these women could allow close monitoring of their health, allowing identification of a tumor at an early, still-curable stage. Equally important, identification of women in families with a history of breast cancer who do not have the gene can relieve anxiety and allow them to forgo unnecessary testing.

The discovery of BRCA-1 was announced in September 1994 by a team headed by Mark H. Skolnick, Ph.D., a geneticist at the University of Utah, and Myriad Genetics Inc., both in Salt Lake City. The team located the gene on chromosome 17, one of the 23 pairs of chromosomes that make up the human genetic blueprint. Researchers are not yet sure of the gene's function, but preliminary results suggest that it is a tumor-suppressor gene—that is, its normal function is to keep cells from proliferating.

Also in September, a second team, headed by molecular biologist Douglas F. Easton, Ph.D., of the Institute of Cancer Research in London, England, reported that it had identified the approximate location of a second gene, called BRCA-2, that is thought to be responsible for most of the cases of familial breast cancer not caused by BRCA-1. Some independent evidence suggests that this gene might be related to many sporadic cases of breast cancer, although such a determination awaits isolation of the gene.

DWARFISM

In July 1994, a team headed by John J. Wasmuth, Ph.D., a molecular biologist at the University of California, Irvine, reported the discovery of the gene that causes achondroplasia, the most common form of dwarfism. The disorder, which affects about 1 in 20,000 people, causes alterations in bone growth and development, resulting in an enlarged head, normal-sized trunk, and short limbs. The gene, which is found on chromosome 4 and is called fibroblast growth-factor receptor-3 (FGFR-3), was initially identified three years earlier during the search for the gene that causes Huntington's disease; its link to dwarfism was uncovered only recently. FGFR-3 serves as the blueprint for a growth-factor receptor on bone cells. When it is defective, bones in the limbs are not able to elongate normally.

Although the Irvine researchers developed a test for the gene, they emphasized that it should be used only for prenatal screening of pregnancies at risk for having two copies of the abnormal gene. Even though dwarfs with one abnormal copy of the achondroplasia gene are generally quite healthy, couples in which both parents manifest this form of dwarfism have a 25 percent chance of giving birth to a child with two defective copies of the gene, which is invariably fatal shortly after birth.

In September, a team headed by molecular biologists Eric Lander, Ph.D., of the Massachusetts Institute of Technology (MIT) in Cambridge and Albert de la Chapelle, Ph.D., of the University of Helsinki in Finland reported the discovery of the gene for diastrophic dysplasia, the most common form of dwarfism in Finland, and the third-most-common form in the U.S. In Finland, where the disease affects 1 in every 30,000 births, an estimated 2 percent of the population carries the defective gene.

This form of dwarfism is associated with misshapen bones and painful, early-onset arthritis.

Researchers normally search for such genes by studying members of affected families. In this case, they were able to treat the entire Finnish population of 5 million as one big family because virtually all are descended from a small group of "founders" who settled in the area 2,000 years ago. Geneticists believe one of those founders carried the original gene, which the researchers discovered on chromosome 5. Unlike the achondroplasia gene, this one is harmless when the subject carries only one copy. The gene causes disease only when two copies are present. Studies show that the gene is the blueprint for a protein called a sulfate transporter, which researchers had not suspected was involved in the biology of diastrophic dysplasia. Sulfate is an inorganic ion essential to a healthy metabolism. Laboratory studies on cells from patients confirmed that the cells could not, in fact, transport sulfates properly. The discovery thus opens up new possibilities for therapy.

OBESITY GENE

In November 1994, researchers at Rockefeller University in New York City culminated a 40-year search by identifying the gene that causes obesity. The gene is the blueprint for a protein that tells the brain to stop eating once a sufficient amount of body fat is stored. When the gene is defective, the individual keeps eating, even though his or her stomach is full, and thus gains weight. The researchers hope that it will eventually be possible to administer the healthy form of the protein—just like insulin is given to diabetics—to control appetite. Identification of the gene in young children could also enable parents to help the children learn how to control their eating behavior at an early age.

COLON CANCER

Two teams of researchers have independently found two colon-cancer genes that account for 90 percent of inherited cases of colon cancer. Between them, the two genes are the cause of one in every six of the 156,000 new

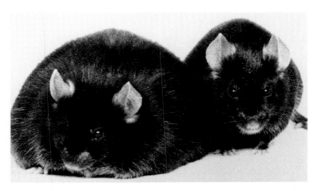

Researchers have identified the gene in mice that, when defective, inhibits a protein signal that tells the brain when to stop eating.

cases of colon cancer each year. The genes may also be the cause of about 30 percent of the remaining cases of sporadic colon cancer. Sometime in 1995, the researchers hope to have available diagnostic tests for the presence of the genes. Such tests would allow close monitoring of people carrying the genes, enabling the tumor's detection while it is still curable by surgery. The development of such a test is difficult, however, because at least a dozen different mutations in the genes have been observed, and each must be accounted for in any test.

The two teams are headed by researchers from Johns Hopkins University and the University of Vermont, Burlington. The discoveries were announced in December 1993 and March 1994. The two groups have also tentatively identified a third gene that they believe is responsible for most of the remaining inherited cases of colon cancer.

The functions of the two genes, which occur on different chromosomes, are fairly well known because researchers at Vermont and the Dana-Farber Cancer Institute in Boston, Massachusetts, have been studying the function of identical genes in yeast and bacteria for nearly 20 years. The proteins act much like the spell-check function of a word-processing program on a computer, monitoring the replication of DNA to correct mistakes. The first protein scans newly synthesized DNA to check for errors that have occurred during synthesis. If an error is found, the second protein binds to the first and repairs the error. If the first gene is defective, mistakes in DNA formation are not recognized. If the second gene is defective, mistakes are not repaired. Either way, mistakes accumulate until a cancer cell is formed.

DYSLEXIA

Researchers have discovered the approximate location of a gene that causes the reading disorder dyslexia, a finding that definitively establishes that the disorder is genetic in origin, and that promises early detection of the disorder so that corrective measures can be taken. In dyslexia, a person's ability to perceive and process words, numbers, and other symbols is impaired. Often, for example, letters and numbers may appear reversed, making it difficult for a person to absorb the information on a page. An estimated 5 to 10 percent of the population is affected by dyslexia. New interventions can make significant improvements in the reading ability of perhaps half the children treated if the intervention is accomplished at ages 5 or 6. Most children with the disorder are not diagnosed until about the age of 8, by which time no more than 25 percent can be helped. If the disorder is diagnosed much earlier, experts hope an even higher percentage may benefit from the interventions.

In August, New Jersey researchers reported that a particular region in the temporal-lobe

When diagnosed and treated at an early age, children with dyslexia—a genetically caused reading disorder— have an improved chance of progress.

area of the brain contains a deficiency in cells that specialize in comprehending rapid sounds. This lack of comprehension, experts say, may be a major factor in the later difficulty in learning to read. In October, a team headed by researchers at the University of Colorado in Boulder reported that this deficiency of cells might be caused by a defective gene located in a small region of chromosome 6. The region, they say, could contain anywhere from 6 to 200 genes; researchers are now racing to discover which one is responsible for the disorder.

DIABETES

British researchers reported in September 1994 that they have identified as many as 18 genes that participate in causing Type I (insulin-dependent) diabetes, the most serious form of the disease. Type I diabetes results when insulin-secreting cells of the pancreas are destroyed by the body's immune system. Insulin helps cells use and store sugars from the diet; without insulin, an individual can quickly fall into a coma and die. Short-term symptoms can be controlled by regular injections of insulin, but complications develop because of the wide swings of sugar concentration in the blood. Complications of diabetes include blindness, kidney disease, heart problems, strokes, and peripheral-nerve damage.

Most genetic diseases are caused by a single defective gene. But diabetes, like heart disease, cancer, and many other disorders, is polygenic, meaning that several genes must be altered for the disease to occur. In many cases, including diabetes and cancer, the victim must be exposed to an environmental trigger, such as a virus or a chemical, for the disease to occur. In the new study, researchers at Oxford University in Cambridge, England, identified 18 separate locations of genes that play a role in the disorder. The immediate task is to identify each of the genes and determine what role it plays in the development of the disease. But even before then, researchers are confident it will be possible to identify individuals whose genetic makeup renders them vulnerable to diabetes, and to intervene to prevent the disease.

Thomas H. Maugh II

Geology

Earth's Lopsided Heart

By studying the recordings of 15,722 earthquakes, seismologists Wei-jia Su and Adam Dziewonski of Harvard University in Cambridge, Massachusetts, discovered that Earth's solid iron core is tilted. The scientists made their find by examining how long it took seismic waves from different earthquakes to pass through the core and return to Earth's surface. They noticed that the waves did not all travel at the same speed; quake vibrations traveled fastest when they followed a path inclined 12.5 degrees from Earth's spin axis. The direction corresponded to a route either toward or away from Siberia.

To explain the speed differences, the seismologists suggested that iron crystals within the core may point in the direction of Siberia. Such a pattern may have developed because of the orientation of Earth's magnetic field. The field would arrange the crystals as they dropped out of the liquid outer core and solidified on the surface of the inner core. Previously, scientists had thought that the crystals pointed in line with Earth's spin axis.

If the crystals do indeed have a tilted orientation, they could reveal important new insights into the history of Earth's magnetic field. Scientists still have many unanswered questions about what forces create the magnetic field, and how it has evolved through the planet's history.

Shuttle Radar Spies on Globe

Astronauts on the space shuttle *Endeavour* gathered highly detailed images of Earth's surface during the Spaceborne Imaging Radar experiment in April and October of 1994. Two radars bounced microwave radiation off the ground and measured the waves that reflected back to the shuttle. These were the first spaceborne radars to observe Earth using several wavelengths of light at the same time. By flying the instrument on two separate flights, scientists could compare images taken six months apart and identify changes in the land surface.

The radar observed hundreds of sites—capturing images of volcanoes, forests, cities, deserts, and other types of geologic features. Scientists also monitored unexpected events

Shuttle-based radar captured images of the eruption of the Klyuchevskaya volcano in Russia. Lava flows appear as yellow-green streams on the volcano's slopes.

such as flooding in Germany and in the midwestern United States, a tropical cyclone, and a volcanic eruption on Russia's Kamchatka Peninsula.

A Runaway Glacier

The Bering Glacier is the largest and longest glacier in North America. This huge body of ice, which creeps slowly down the slopes and valleys of southeast Alaska, is 125 miles (201 kilometers) long and covers 2,300 square miles (5,957 square kilometers)—an area larger than the state of Rhode Island. In 1993 and 1994, the glacier captured the attention of scientists when it sped up dramatically, at certain times moving at 100 times its normal speed.

Glaciologists noticed that the glacier began to surge in August 1993, when ice ridges were seen advancing as much as 328 feet (100 meters) a day. Within nine months, the end of the glacier advanced 5.6 miles (9 kilometers), covering part of the lake at the glacier's foot. By late 1994, the ice surge had

Shortly before the Bering Glacier began a 6-mile surge southward, geologists examined a large melted depression wider than a football field that had formed within the margin of the glacier.

slowed dramatically, returning to a more normal pace. Overall, the glacier moved more than 6 miles (9.6 kilometers) south toward the Pacific Ocean, stopping just 5 miles (8 kilometers) from the open sea.

Glacial surges are not uncommon, and the Bering Glacier displays such activity every 20 to 30 years. The Bering's last surge

ended in 1967. According to Dennis Trabant, a scientist with the U.S. Geological Survey (USGS) in Fairbanks, Alaska, this event was "the most aggressive surge that's occurred since 1960." He adds, "What has happened at Bering is world-class speed. Very few people will live to see the next one."

Last year's surge was unusual because scientists managed to observe it closely from beginning to end, enabling them to learn more about what causes such events. Water accumulations beneath the glacier played a role in allowing the ice to advance so quickly downslope, according to Bruce Molnia, deputy chief of the USGS office in Reston, Virginia. "A carpet of water separates the bottom of the ice from an earth bed, and it [the glacier] almost hydroplanes," he says. Eventually the water escapes, and friction between the ice mass and the ground causes the glacier to stop.

ROBOT EXPLORES VOLCANO

Venturing into territory too dangerous for human geologists, a spiderlike robot descended into an Alaskan volcano. Named Dante II, the 9.8-foot (3-meter)-tall robot captured worldwide attention when it crawled down the steep walls of Mount Spurr, an active volcano that last erupted in 1993.

Designed by engineers from Carnegie-Mellon University in Pittsburgh, Pennsylvania, the eight-legged walker climbed 656 feet (200 meters) into the crater, negotiating patches of deep snow, big boulders, and unstable slopes. Human pilots in California steered Dante II for part of the trip via a satellite link; for other segments, the robot directed itself using onboard computers. When it reached the crater floor, the machine analyzed volcanic gases rising out of fumaroles. It also snapped pictures of the crater's interior for use in future mapping.

In 1992, Carnegie-Mellon engineers had tested an earlier version of the robot by trying to explore a volcano in Antarctica. But the original Dante advanced only a few steps before its communication cable broke.

The newer robot also suffered a mishap. On the climb out of Mount Spurr's crater, Dante II fell over on a steep slope and could not regain its footing. The helpless robot lay on its back for several days until two climbers risked the dangers of the crater to rescue the machine. They attached a line to Dante II, and a helicopter carried the 1,694-pound (770-kilogram) mechanical spider out of the crater.

CHESAPEAKE BAY CRATER

Geologists discovered evidence that a meteorite may have punched a large crater in what is now the southern portion of Chesapeake Bay. According to this theory, the crash 35 million years ago would have helped form the bay by causing rivers to drain toward the crater.

The scientists raised the meteorite theory after finding a pattern of buried faults arranged in concentric circles beneath the bay. Such fault rings resemble structures seen at well-known meteorite craters. The meteorite theory also would explain the presence of unusual rock layers discovered while drilling in southern Virginia. The buried deposits of jumbled rocks look like debris created by giant waves, which would have sloshed through the Atlantic Ocean after an impact. If geologists can confirm the theory, this crater would rank as the largest known in the United States.

GERMANS DRILL DEEP HOLE

A German drilling team completed one of the world's deepest research boreholes in October 1994. The hole reached 5.7 miles (9.1 kilometers) into Earth's crust, providing geologists with a window into a realm they rarely can explore.

The Germans chose to drill the $300 million hole near Windischeschenbach in Bavaria. In this spot, two tectonic plates collided 320 million years ago to form the Eurasian plate. By drilling through the ancient suture, scientists could study the process of plate-tectonic collisions.

The drill team had planned on reaching a depth of 6.2 miles (10 kilometers). But they had to stop short of the goal because the rock at 5.6 miles (9 kilometers) was soft enough to flow, making further drilling impossible.

Richard Monastersky

HEALTH AND DISEASE

During 1994 and into 1995, political and economic aspects of health care dominated headlines. Particularly worrisome to the medical community were cutbacks—both actual and threatened—in budgets for research, hospitals, education, nutrition programs, and other critical elements of the nation's health-care system.

MALADIES OF AN AGING POPULATION

As America's population ages, the number of people with disorders such as Alzheimer's disease and arthritis is projected to grow dramatically. Alzheimer's, an incurable ailment that causes progressive mental deterioration, afflicts an estimated 4 million, mostly elderly, Americans. The Centers for Disease Control and Prevention (CDC) estimates that nearly 40 million Americans have arthritis, an inflammation of joints that causes pain, swelling, and limited movement. Because of the aging of the U.S. population, particularly the baby-boom generation, this figure could grow to 59.4 million by the year 2020.

Researchers at Harvard Medical School in Cambridge, Massachusetts, found a simple eyedrop test that appears to identify people with Alzheimer's disease months before they have obvious symptoms of the disease. The test uses a very dilute solution of atropine. The pupils of the eyes of people with Alzheimer's dilate in response to the drops; pupils of other people do not react.

A study led by John Breitner, M.D., of Duke University, Durham, North Carolina, reports that anti-inflammatory drugs used to treat arthritis (ibuprofen, naproxen, and piroxicam) may delay the onset of Alzheimer's. Dr. Breitner and his colleagues compared the medical histories of 50 pairs of elderly twins. They found that the twins who had used anti-inflammatory drugs were four times more likely to not have Alzheimer's, or to develop it later in life, than the twins who had not used anti-inflammatory drugs. Among identical twins, there was a 10-to-1 difference.

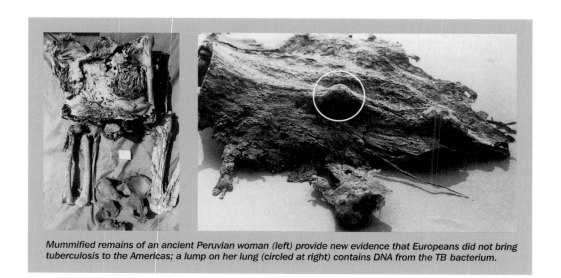
Mummified remains of an ancient Peruvian woman (left) provide new evidence that Europeans did not bring tuberculosis to the Americas; a lump on her lung (circled at right) contains DNA from the TB bacterium.

Other work suggests that estrogen, which appears to play an important role in maintaining brain-cell connections, may help prevent Alzheimer's. Women, who have a higher incidence of Alzheimer's than men, produce declining amounts of estrogen as they enter and go through menopause. Men do not produce estrogen; instead, their glands produce the hormone testosterone, at levels that often remain high until late in life. The testosterone, which is converted to estrogen in the brain, may be providing men with protection against Alzheimer's.

In late 1994, it was reported that an experimental drug, a type of monoclonal antibody, shows promise in treating people with rheumatoid arthritis, one of the most prevalent of the more than 100 forms of arthritis. The drug blocks the action of tumor necrosis factor alpha (TNF-alpha), an inflammatory protein commonly associated with rheumatoid arthritis. The Arthritis Foundation has expressed cautious optimism about the new immune therapy, and has called for longer-term and larger-scale studies to assess the drug's safety and effectiveness.

BACTERIAL DISEASES

In India, 54 deaths were attributed to an outbreak of pneumonic plague, a bacterial disease last reported in India 30 years ago. Most of the deaths occurred in the western city of Surat, especially in crowded neighborhoods with inadequate sanitation and drinking water.

New evidence refuted two widely held beliefs about tuberculosis. The first example involved the remains of a mummified woman in southern Peru who died about 1,000 years ago. Tests revealed that she had lesions typical of tuberculosis. This indicates that the disease was not introduced into the New World by European explorers of the 15th and 16th centuries. In the second case, two studies showed that more than 30 percent of the increase of tuberculosis in New York City and San Francisco, California, has been caused by recent transmission of the bacteria. Previously, reactivation of latent infections had been thought to be responsible for 90 percent of all tuberculosis cases.

Research at Johns Hopkins University, Baltimore, Maryland, and the University of Louisville in Kentucky suggests that *Chlamydia pneumoniae*, common bacteria known to cause pneumonia and bronchitis, may contribute to heart disease. The scientists showed in laboratory experiments that the bacteria can infect and multiply inside smooth muscle cells like those found in coronary arteries. Such infection might be involved in the formation of plaques—clumps of tissue and debris—that block the coronary arteries and cause cardiac disease, including heart attacks.

New Vaccines on the Horizon

Malaria, one of the world's deadliest scourges, may finally have met its match. The disease, caused by a protozoan spread by mosquitoes, kills some 2 million people annually, 90 percent of them in tropical Africa. A vaccine developed by Manuel Patarroyo, a Colombian biochemist, appears to offer significant protection against infection. In one trial involving 586 young children in Tanzania, the vaccine reduced malarial cases by 31 percent.

There are about 4 million cases of chicken pox a year in the United States. Not simply a harmless childhood disease, chicken pox is responsible for some 9,000 hospitalizations and 90 deaths—many among very young children—each year. A vaccine made by Merck & Company in West Point, Pennsylvania, was found to be safe and effective for use by children. Of 11,000 people who received the vaccine, only a few later contracted the disease, and their cases were much milder than normal.

Vaccines—usually administered by injection—provide protection against certain diseases. Scientists are continually working to develop new vaccines: a malaria vaccine trial is currently under way, and a vaccine for chicken pox is now available.

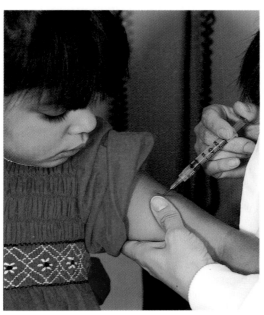

The U.S. Food and Drug Administration (FDA) approved the vaccine, known as Varivax, in March 1995 for children age one or older.

The World Health Organization (WHO) announced the first large-scale trials of two experimental vaccines against HIV, the virus that causes AIDS. Both vaccines have successfully gone through the first two stages of a three-stage testing system, indicating that they are safe and trigger immunologic responses. The third phase will test the vaccines' ability to protect against the disease. It was hoped that the trials would begin by mid-1996, probably in Brazil and Thailand. WHO estimates that 17 million people have been infected with HIV worldwide, with 90 percent of the infections occurring in developing countries. In the United States, AIDS had claimed more than 250,000 lives by the end of 1994; it is now the leading cause of death among Americans aged 25 to 44.

A Drink a Day?

Over the past two decades, many studies have found that moderate consumption of alcohol can reduce the risk of heart disease. Work by researchers at Brigham and Women's Hospital in Boston, Massachusetts, may explain why. They found that people who drank alcohol daily had the highest levels of endogenous tissue-type plasminogen activator (t-PA); nondrinkers had the lowest levels. t-PA is an enzyme that helps protect against the formation of blood clots that lead to heart attacks.

Although moderate alcohol consumption may benefit the heart, it also can increase the risk of cancer and other health problems. An 11-year study at Harvard University Medical School concludes that men who had two to four drinks a week had the lowest death rate from all causes—about 22 percent lower than men who were nondrinkers. But men who averaged a drink a day had the same death rate as nondrinkers. Those who drank more increased their risks. For example, men who averaged two or more drinks a day had a death rate 63 percent higher than that of nondrinkers.

Debate continues over the possible health risks associated with exposure to electromagnetic radiation (EMR). In a recent study, electric-utility workers exposed to high levels of EMR had a 2.5 times greater risk of dying from brain cancer than did other workers.

ENVIRONMENTAL DANGERS

A draft report of a three-year study at the Environmental Protection Agency (EPA) reaffirms that dioxins are "probable" causes of cancer in humans. The report indicates for the first time that even trace amounts of dioxins in foods may be health hazards, increasing the risk of immune, reproductive, and developmental damage. Dioxins are highly toxic chemicals released into the environment as by-products of garbage incinerators and industrial processes that use chlorine and chlorinated compounds. They also occur in meat and dairy products. The report says that most Americans are exposed to several trillionths of a gram daily.

Efforts to determine whether exposure to electromagnetic fields can cause cancer continue to produce inconclusive results. An epidemiological study of 138,905 electric-utility workers conducted at the University of North Carolina at Chapel Hill finds that the risk of dying from brain cancer is 2.5 times greater in workers exposed to the highest levels of magnetic radiation than in workers with the lowest

To protect themselves from toxic biological and chemical agents during the Persian Gulf War, U.S. soldiers wore gas masks and protective clothing (left) and took preventive medications. Some veterans now suffer from debilitating conditions possibly caused by these drugs.

exposure. However, no significant difference in death rates from leukemia was found. Other recent studies found a correlation between magnetic radiation and leukemia deaths, but little or no association between exposure to the radiation and brain cancer.

At least 20,000 American troops who participated in the Persian Gulf War have experienced a variety of debilitating symptoms. A panel organized by the National Institutes of Health (NIH) reported in 1994 that "there is no single disease or syndrome apparent, but rather multiple illnesses with overlapping symptoms and causes." A Senate committee investigation suggests that some of the unexplained illnesses may have been caused by drugs given to the troops to protect them against chemical and biological warfare. Symptoms such as skin rashes, short-term memory loss, breathing difficulty, and nausea are similar to side effects of some of the drugs.

Jenny Tesar

MATHEMATICS

If Hollywood were to make a movie about a mathematician, it would probably script a true loner, the type of person who is more comfortable in front of a computer than in the company of people. This mathematician would probably spend lots of time indoors working on equations, and would finally emerge with a brilliant (if very difficult) insight into a far-out problem. This stereotype has been reinforced recently with the reports in newspapers around the world about Andrew Wiles and his solution to Fermat's last theorem. Wiles spent seven years working alone in his attic on this mathematics problem, and he finally announced a solution. This stereotype, like many Hollywood creations, is not very close to the truth of how most mathematics research is done today.

THE BUILDING BLOCKS OF SYMMETRY

The Classification of Finite Simple Groups is a recently solved problem, and it provides a counterexample to the popular notion of how mathematics is done. This problem involved mathematicians from around the world, working together in what one of the participants called "the 30 years' war." (The war was against the problem, not the other mathematicians!)

In order to understand the Classification of Finite Simple Groups, it is helpful to have an understanding of what types of questions mathematicians ask. Most mathematical questions involve trying to figure out the easiest and most basic explanation for some phenomenon. For example, when early humans began counting objects, it became immediately apparent that the integers—such as 1, 2, and 3—were useful in describing the world.

As the different civilizations became more sophisticated, they began doing more-clever operations with the integers: first was probably addition, followed naturally by subtraction. Eventually multiplication would have to be discovered in order to make commerce flow easily: 7 sheep at 5 gold coins apiece would cost 35 gold coins. As these new discoveries were being used, many properties of

multiplication were being discovered. For example, people noticed that some numbers—such as 9, 12, 16, and 35—could be obtained by more than just one multiplication combination ($16 = 8 \times 2 = 4 \times 4 = 1 \times 16$). Other numbers—such as 2, 3, 5, and 7—did not have any combinations that multiplied to them other than 1 and themselves ($7 = 7 \times 1$). These "special" numbers are now called *prime* numbers. The ancient Greeks were fascinated with prime numbers. The Greeks were the first to observe that there had to be an infinite number of primes. They also observed that all of the numbers that were not prime were somehow built out of primes. For example, $9 = 3 \times 3$, $12 = 3 \times 2 \times 2$, $16 = 2 \times 2 \times 2 \times 2$, and $35 = 5 \times 7$. Every number that the ancient Greeks could think of could be written as a product of primes.

Thus, starting from a very natural concept (counting), a very sophisticated mathematical result was achieved, namely, that every integer has a unique prime factorization. In an effort to further understand the integers, mathematicians have discovered numerous generalizations of this result. All of the effort is aimed at finding a simple, elegant way to work with a simple system.

SIMPLE GROUP THEORY

Group theory has a slightly more complicated beginning, but it can be described as coming from the natural world. When drawn, a five-pointed star can be rotated in such a way that it looks exactly like the original. For example, if the top point is labeled 1, and the other points are numbered 2 through 5 going clockwise, point 1 could be rotated to where point 2 was, point 2 to where point 3 was, and so on. This is called a symmetry, because moving the object does not change its appearance. Another symmetry is to leave point 1 fixed, but to flip the whole star so that point 2 switches with point 5, and point 3 switches with point 4. Again the star will look exactly as it did before. Such a collection of symmetries is what mathematicians call a group.

Groups provide mathematicians with some good questions to work on. What are the basic building blocks for these groups (if any)? Is there any analogy to the prime numbers/integers relationship?

In the late 1800s, mathematicians realized that every group is somehow built out of combinations of *simple groups*. Simple groups were simple in the sense that there was no further way of breaking them down, just as primes cannot be factored any further. Thus, the search was on for finding these basic building blocks of groups.

Fairly early on, several infinite families of simple groups were discovered. A curiosity appeared when Émile Mathieu discovered a collection of five simple groups that were not part of one of the infinite families, and they seemed to be oddities. They were nicknamed *sporadic* because they seemed so strange. For a long time, these were the only ones known. Many other techniques were being developed for understanding groups, but no one knew if there would be other basic building blocks for groups.

In the early 1950s, Richard Brauer started making some progress in understanding what simple groups were all about. His questions and approaches led to a groundbreaking analysis by Walter Feit and John Thompson in the early 1960s. Their work provided hope that the problem of finding all simple groups could be done.

THE 30 YEARS' WAR

In the late 1960s, one mathematician, Dan Gorenstein, started formulating an approach; in 1972, he published a 16-step plan for attacking the problem. Over the next few years, the steps were knocked off one by one. One interesting part of the work involved a group called the Monster. For many years, mathematicians knew of the possibility of a simple group with roughly 8×10^{53} elements in it. In 1980, Robert Griess was able to construct this group by hand.

With that result and other subsequent results, Gorenstein announced that the job was complete. The task had taken an army of mathematicians roughly 30 years and approximately 10,000 journal pages. Thus, if Hollywood is going to get its movie character accurate and realistic, it had better make sure its mathematician is actively involved in communicating ideas to other mathematicians.

James A. Davis

METEOROLOGY

Within both the government and private sectors, research is under way to provide the public with more-valuable meteorological information. In particular, scientists and government officials are seeking to modernize the systems that forecast the weather and then disseminate the data. These efforts range from designing better weather models to building faster computers to run them on.

SAFER SKIES

One area undergoing tremendous scrutiny concerns how the weather affects aviation. Weather, of course, plays a major role in the airline industry. In fact, it results in 65 percent of all system delays and 30 percent of all aircraft accidents and mishaps. Of the $4.1 billion per year that weather-related accidents and delays cost the airlines, experts estimate that $1.7 billion is avoidable. In the past, weather phenomena that have had the most-adverse effect on the airlines include: abnormal winds (including microbursts); low cloud ceiling and poor visibility; icing; severe atmospheric turbulence; snowfall; thunderstorms; and tornadoes.

In an effort to diminish the effects of such adverse weather conditions, the Federal Aviation Administration's (FAA's) Aviation Weather Development Program (AWDP) is conducting research in order to provide better weather information to the National Airspace System (NAS), the organizational structure through which weather forecasts and meteorological data are disseminated to aviators. Underlying this research is a simultaneous effort by the National Weather Service (NWS) to modernize its systems. Both tasks will continue into the next century.

The goal is to reduce the number of weather-related accidents by 20 percent by the year 2000 and, by 2005, to decrease weather-related delays by 15 percent. NAS officials hope to reach these goals by improving the timeliness and accuracy of the forecast for both the terminal area as well as the en-route airspace.

Under the existing NAS system, pilots, air-traffic controllers, and others involved in

New computer models will soon improve the accuracy with which meteorologists predict thunderstorm development and other weather phenomena that form suddenly.

aviation receive meteorological observations and forecasts through a complex system that includes the NWS, the FAA, the U.S. Department of Defense, and private industry. The NWS is primarily responsible for forecasting the weather, while the FAA is in charge of communicating this information—along with data from the military, private forecasters, airline meteorologists, and pilots—to air-traffic personnel. This system has been in place for decades, and has not grown and changed as rapidly as the airline industry. NWS and FAA officials intend to reverse this trend.

INTO THE YEAR 2000

Teams of researchers and commercial vendors are working in conjunction with the NWS and FAA to build a prototype system to process weather data and to display it to users. This system will integrate data from terminal weather sensors located around an airport, and will provide both forecasts and so-called "nowcasts" in easily understood graphic and textual forms. This technology is expected to predict a number of variables—including wind shear and microbursts, high-level lightning and storm-cell formation, winds, and ceiling and snowfall data—for the immediate 30 minutes ahead. This data could affect decisions from takeoff times to deicing procedures.

In this new system, many different types of technology will work in conjunction to provide the best possible information for pilots and other airline-support personnel. For example, the Low Level Wind Shear Alert System (LLWAS) will provide, along with Doppler weather-surveillance radar, an integrated wind-shear-alert product for air-traffic controllers. LLWAS will alert both air-traffic controllers and pilots to areas of wind shear. Such advance warning will allow pilots to take off from different runways or to change their landing procedures accordingly.

Pilots will also benefit from a new generation of Digital Altimeter Setting Indicators (DASIs), which allow pilots to adjust their aircraft to correspond to the elevation of the airport from which they are taking off or at which they are landing. This correction enables pilots to maintain the correct vertical distance between their plane and the ground or buildings below. The new DASIs will employ state-of-the-art technology in conjunction with automated weather stations on the ground.

Several additional software products are slated for 1996. These systems will provide both hourly analysis and 6- to 12-hour forecasts to aid in an airline's decision-making process. These products will track a number of meteorological variables—including winds, temperature, icing, precipitation type, ceiling, and visibility data.

Other changes will not be fully implemented until early in the next century. When improved data-link capabilities and direct dissemination of meteorological data to the cockpit are initiated, air-traffic controllers and flight-service specialists will no longer be the conduit for routine weather information. Meteorologists will still support the controllers and traffic-management personnel by forecasting weather conditions and issuing significant weather alerts and warnings. However, much of the more-routine forecasting will be automated.

The FAA is also considering the possibility of allowing private-sector firms to provide a major portion of preflight weather information to pilots. Companies such as Weather Services International already provide pilot-briefing systems to selected airlines. In the future, it may be the FAA's responsibility to disseminate one portion of the weather while the private sector handles another.

OTHER IMPROVEMENTS

The National Weather Service is also beginning to modernize its systems. This modernization spans everything from faster, more-accurate long-range forecasting to an improved ability to predict thunderstorm development. Advances like these will tie into the FAA's modernization effort to make the airways safer. A great deal of the research on severe weather is undertaken at the NWS facility in Norman, Oklahoma. As workstation computers become increasingly powerful, computer-generated models may be able to predict how the atmosphere will behave over the next few hours.

One of the newest NWS models being tested is the Advanced Regional Prediction System (ARPS). The horizontal resolution of this thunderstorm-predicting model is only 0.6 mile (1 kilometer). This system, however, is only in the initial stages of development. Some positive results already have been seen when predicting the formation of thunderstorms over a small experimental area, but this model has yet to be tested over more-complex and -varied terrain. In addition, the time needed to feed the initial data into the computers and to calculate a forecast leaves little

lead time before an actual weather event occurs. One such event recently occurred in Midland, Texas, where the ARPS successfully predicted a storm's development right down to the shape of the echoes on the radar. Unfortunately, the output was not available until after the storm had already formed. When these forecasts are improved and released in a more-timely manner, they will be useful to everyone from pilots to backyard barbecuers.

In the future, these new advances should provide the airline industry and the general public with faster and more-accurate forecasts. However, even with all these breakthroughs, the weather will still hold many surprises in store for all of us. One need only look back at the past year to see how unpredictable the weather is.

WEATHER HIGHLIGHTS

Severe storms pounded much of the United States during the spring of 1994. An outbreak of tornado activity in the Southeast in late March left 40 people dead, including 20 who died in a single church in Piedmont, Alabama. Heavy rains also fell in the Midwest, raising fears that the record flooding of the previous year might return.

Early summer brought record heat to the Southwest and the Northeast. Temperatures in the southern deserts of California, Arizona,

On June 1, 1995, the first day of the new hurricane season, the National Hurricane Center moved into a new headquarters facility at Florida International University in Miami.

and Nevada topped 120° F (49° C) for several weeks in June and July, while Washington, D.C., notched 14 straight days above 90° F (32° C), and Albuquerque, New Mexico, hit an all-time high of 107° F (42° C). Much of the West endured the hottest and driest summer since 1895, conditions that contributed to a season of widespread forest fires throughout the region.

The South experienced a very wet summer. In early July, Tropical Storm Alberto caused severe flooding in Georgia, Alabama, and the Florida panhandle. The town of Plains, Georgia, recorded more than 24 inches (61 centimeters) of rainfall in July alone. Hundreds of bridges and dams in Georgia were destroyed by the record floodwaters. In August, this area absorbed more heavy rain and tornadoes with the passing of the weak but wet Tropical Storm Beryl.

Destructive weather continued into the fall. Southern Texas and Louisiana endured heavy October rainfall and flooding. Some areas near Houston, Texas, recorded as much as 30 inches (76 centimeters) of precipitation in just four days. At least 19 deaths were blamed on the resulting flooding. The following month, the unusually late and erratic Tropical Storm Gordon hit Florida—leaving eight dead and destroying valuable crops—and threatened the Carolinas before weakening at sea. Meanwhile, the West received a steady barrage of early storms, bringing rain to coastal areas, and heavy snow to the Sierra Nevada and the Wasatch Range. Some locales near Salt Lake City, Utah, had more than 6 feet (1.8 meters) of snowfall during Thanksgiving weekend.

In the western half of the nation, the winter of 1994-95 was a mirror image of the previous year, with the area subjected to much bad weather. In particular, California—a state already ravaged by wildfires and earthquakes—hosted a steady cycle of destructive storms. Ski areas in Colorado's Rocky Mountains enjoyed prodigious precipitation, with snowfall continuing well into May 1995. By contrast, the Northeast, which suffered through a bitterly cold and snowy winter a year earlier, had a season that was uncommonly dry and warm.

David S. Epstein

NOBEL PRIZE: CHEMISTRY

The 1994 Nobel Prize in Chemistry honored organic chemist George A. Olah, Ph.D., of the University of Southern California in Los Angeles for his contributions to the understanding of chemical compounds known as hydrocarbons. Composed of hydrogen and carbon, hydrocarbons make up a large group of organic compounds that include oil and natural gas. Dr. Olah's work in the 1960s made it possible for these compounds to be studied in detail for the first time. Thanks to Dr. Olah's advances, chemists have been able to synthesize new forms of hydrocarbons for use in a variety of industrial and pharmaceutical applications.

George A. Olah, Ph.D., was awarded the Nobel Prize in Chemistry for his work on carbocations and "superacids."

REACTIVE INTERMEDIATES

Dr. Olah concentrated his efforts on hydrocarbon fragments known as "carbocations" (car-bo-CAT-eye-ons). During certain organic-chemical reactions, these positively charged carbocations serve as *reactive intermediates*, coming into existence fleetingly during the interactions of atoms and molecules and the creation of new chemical products—and then disappearing. Since early in the 1900s, chemists had theorized about the structure and function of these reactive intermediates. However, their existence was so brief—lasting just millionths of a second—that chemists were unable to study them. In fact, when Dr. Olah took up the problem, some chemists even believed that carbocations existed only in theory. The challenge was to slow down the chemical reactions and prolong the life of the elusive carbocations.

Dr. Olah found the answer. He began experimenting with so-called "superacids"—compounds that are thousands of times stronger than such traditional acids as sulfuric or hydrochloric acid. Olah and his colleagues used superacids prepared from such compounds as hydrogen fluoride and antimony pentafluoride. When these solvents interacted chemically with carbocations, they thwarted the hydrocarbon fragments, preventing them from following their normal course of action. Instead of reacting instantaneously with almost anything they came into contact with, the carbocations became stable. And instead of vanishing in millionths of a second, they could be kept on hand for months on end. This gave chemists time to explore their structures.

Early investigation into the structure of carbocations yielded surprises. Dr. Olah observed that some of the carbocations possessed highly unusual shapes: five- or even six-sided structures, in contrast to the usual four-sided shape. "Olah's discovery," as the Nobel committee observed in its announcement, "completely transformed the scientific study of the elusive carbocations."

Since Dr. Olah's initial discoveries, he and other chemists have developed numerous superacid compounds for the preparation and study of a large number of carbocations. The knowledge that he made possible has been applied in the synthesis of many organic compounds. This has resulted in the development of new fuels based on petroleum, coal, methane, and other carbon-based substances. Similarly, plastics and other petroleum-based products can now be produced with less damage to the environment.

George A. Olah was born in Budapest, Hungary, in 1927. He obtained his doctoral degree at the Technical University of Budapest in 1949, and held various teaching positions there until 1954, when he moved to the Central Research Institute of the Hungarian Academy of Sciences, also in Budapest. In 1957, Olah emigrated to North America, working as a research chemist at the Dow Chemical Company in Canada and in the United States. He is now a U.S. citizen. Olah was a professor at Case Western Reserve University, Ohio, between 1965 and 1977. In 1977, he joined the faculty of the University of Southern California, where, in 1991, he became director of the Loker Hydrocarbon Research Institute.

Christopher King

NOBEL PRIZE: PHYSICS

Two physicists—one Canadian, the other American—shared the 1994 Nobel Prize in Physics for their development of neutron scattering, a method of studying condensed matter. Working separately during the 1940s and 1950s, the two scientists—Bertram N. Brockhouse, Ph.D., and Clifford G. Shull, Ph.D.—devised methods and equipment for using uncharged subatomic particles known as neutrons to see inside materials at virtually the tiniest level—that of individual atoms. More powerful than X-ray technology, neutron scattering has provided key insights into how atoms are arranged within matter and how they behave. As the Nobel committee noted in its announcement, Dr. Shull "has helped answer the question of where atoms 'are,' Dr. Brockhouse the question of what atoms 'do.'"

WORKING WITH NEUTRONS

In the 1940s, shortly after the end of World War II, Dr. Shull went to work at the Oak Ridge National Laboratory in Tennessee, the site of one of the first nuclear reactors. The reactor, and others like it, produced neutrons, and scientists were investigating the possibility of using these particles to see inside matter at the atomic level. Atoms consist of positively charged protons; negatively charged electrons; and neutrons, which carry no charge. This lack of charge makes neutrons an ideal particle with which to probe the atomic structure of a given material, since they will not interact with the electrons within the sample, and will therefore penetrate completely. A decade or so previously, scientists had begun to discuss the idea of shooting beams of neutrons into prepared samples of matter. The atoms within the sample would cause the neutrons to be diffracted. By studying the patterns in which the neutrons were diffracted, scientists could construct a picture of the material's atomic structure.

However, for Dr. Shull and other researchers, there were many obstacles to overcome. One problem was that the patterns in which the neutrons would leave the sample—the "scattering waves"—depended on the wavelength, or speed, of the neutrons as they entered the sample. And neutrons do not all travel at the same speed. Dr. Shull and his colleagues developed special crystals that deflected the neutrons into uniform wavelengths. The neutrons, once they had been "monochromatized," were then passed into the sample. Using a detector that could be rotated around the outside of the sample, Dr. Shull and his collaborators were able to study the patterns made by the diffracted neutrons as they left the test material. The scientists could thereby learn the relative positions of the atoms within.

VIBRATIONAL ENERGY

Dr. Brockhouse began his key work in the 1950s at a research reactor run by Atomic Energy of Canada, Ltd., at Chalk River, Ontario. Unlike Dr. Shull, who primarily explored the position of atoms in materials, Dr. Brockhouse was more interested in the movement of atoms. Neutron beams that are passed through a sample cause the atoms within to vibrate, creating energy measured in units called "phonons." By tracking neutrons as they were scattered through the sample, and by measuring how fast they emerged, Dr. Brockhouse could gauge how much energy the neutrons had lost within the sample. This allowed him to make calculations about the vibrational energy of the material's atoms. A material's vibrational energy determines its properties, such as how well it conducts heat or electricity.

Clifford G. Shull, Ph.D. (above), and Bertram N. Brockhouse, Ph.D. (below), shared the Nobel Prize in Physics for the development of neutron-scattering techniques, which allow physicists to explore the structure, position, and behavior of atoms.

The methods developed by Drs. Shull and Brockhouse permitted new explorations of the structure and dynamics of atoms in crystals and other solids, as well as in liquids. Neutron diffraction also made it possible, for the first time, to study magnetic materials at the atomic level.

Today the technology devised by Drs. Shull and Brockhouse continues to keep scientists very busy. For example, neutron-scattering techniques are used to study superconductors—experimental materials that conduct electricity with no resistance. Neutron scattering has also allowed scientists to study the structure of viruses in order to see, for example, how they defend themselves against dehydration.

Clifford G. Shull was born in 1915 in Pittsburgh, Pennsylvania. He earned his bachelor's degree at the Carnegie Institute of Technology in 1937, and his doctoral degree in 1941 from New York University. In 1956, he joined the faculty at Massachusetts Institute of Technology (MIT), Cambridge, Massachusetts, where he is now professor emeritus in the department of physics.

Bertram N. Brockhouse was born in 1918 in Lethbridge, Alberta, Canada. He earned his bachelor of science degree from the University of British Columbia in Vancouver in 1947, and did his graduate work at the University of Toronto, Canada, earning his Ph.D. in 1950. In 1956, he joined the faculty in the department of physics at McMaster University in Hamilton, Ontario. Having retired in 1984, Dr. Brockhouse is now professor emeritus.

Christopher King

NOBEL PRIZE: PHYSIOLOGY OR MEDICINE

Two Americans, biochemist Martin Rodbell, Ph.D., and pharmacologist Alfred G. Gilman, M.D., Ph.D., received the 1994 Nobel Prize in Physiology or Medicine for their discovery of "G-proteins." These molecules play a crucial role in cellular action, converting inbound signals from outside the cell into the biochemical chain reaction by which cells grow, differentiate, and perform other essential life processes. For example, G-proteins help the eyes sense light, and the nose sense odors. Malfunctions in the action of G-proteins underlie many human diseases, such as cholera and whooping cough. Scientists suspect that G-protein malfunction may also play a role in the development of alcoholism, and perhaps even in cancer. The advances made during the 1960s and 1970s by Drs. Rodbell and Gilman, who worked independently of one another, "have opened up a new and rapidly expanding area of knowledge," noted the Nobel committee in its announcement.

CELLULAR SIGNALING

The human body contains several trillion cells. For decades, scientists have studied how cells interact with each other and how they respond to signals from their external environment. Each cell is surrounded by a membrane—a barrier that separates the interior of the cell from the world outside. The surface membrane contains groups of proteins known as receptors—molecules that specialize in receiving chemical signals from hormones, neurotransmitters, and other sources. During the 1950s, American scientist Earl Sutherland clarified the mechanism by which cells process and act on signals from the outside. In a constant series of split-second reactions, hormones and other chemical signals bind to receptors on the cellular membrane, acting as a first messenger. In many cases, this signal is converted inside the cell to form a second messenger, a substance that starts a cascade of molecular events, triggering biochemical responses within the cell. For discovering the second-messenger compound known as cyclic AMP—the first such compound to be identified—Sutherland received the Nobel Prize in Physiology or Medicine in 1971.

While working at the National Institutes of Health (NIH) in Bethesda, Maryland, during the late 1960s and early 1970s, Dr. Rodbell followed up on Dr. Sutherland's work. He studied how cells form second messengers such as cyclic AMP. At the time, scientists believed that the transmission of signals from the exterior to the interior of cells involved only two substances, an enzyme and a receptor. Rodbell concluded that there must be a third biochemical step involving another molecule in the cell membrane. He called this molecule a "transducer." The transducer, Rodbell theorized, acts as an intermediary, or "middleman," receiving messages from receptors, modifying the signal, and sending the signal on to an amplifier protein, which in turn initiates the formation of cyclic AMP and other second messengers.

Like many groundbreaking scientific ideas, Rodbell's theory of a signal-transducing molecule met with considerable resistance from the research community. Eventually, however, Rodbell and his collaborators were able to demonstrate that the presence of a transducer is essential to the process of cell signaling. Rodbell determined that there are several different transducing molecules. Rodbell observed that these molecules, in modifying and transmitting signals within the cell, react with an energy-rich compound known as guanosine triphosphate, or GTP.

FINDING THE PROTEIN

Thanks to the work of Dr. Rodbell, the existence of transducing protein molecules had been established. However, isolating the proteins and determining their exact chemical nature was another story. That was the task that Dr. Gilman, then working at the University of Virginia School of Medicine in Charlottesville, set for himself and his colleagues in a series of experiments during the late 1970s.

Using leukemia cells whose genetic make-up had been altered through mutation, Gilman and his team studied the formation of cyclic AMP in these cells. They found that one type of mutated leukemia cell possessed a normal receptor and a normal amplifier protein that generated cyclic AMP as a second messenger. However, nothing happened when the cell was challenged with an outside signal—the cell failed to respond in the usual way. The reason, Gilman determined, was that these mutated cells lacked the transducing protein. When extracts from other, normal cells were added to these mutated cells, they regained the ability to synthesize cyclic AMP in response to external signals.

In 1980, members of Gilman's team were able to isolate and purify the first transducing protein. Because they had observed that the proteins cannot act without the energy supplied by GTP, the researchers gave them the name by which they are now known: G-proteins.

Since the isolation of the first G-protein, researchers have discovered several different kinds of the transducing, intermediary molecules. These proteins are composed of three separate peptide chains, which are designated alpha, beta, and gamma. Because these peptides can be combined in numerous configurations, it is possible that as many as several hundred different kinds of G-proteins might exist. The study of signal transduction—the various biochemical mechanisms by which incoming signals are processed and acted upon inside the cell—is one of the busiest areas in current biomedical research. Thanks to the initial discoveries of Drs. Rodbell and

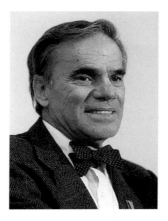

Two Americans, biochemist Martin Rodbell, Ph.D. (above), and pharmacologist Alfred Gilman, M.D., Ph.D. (below), received the Nobel Prize in Physiology or Medicine for their discovery of G-proteins—molecules essential to a wide range of biological activities.

Gilman, there is now a far more detailed understanding of the role of G-proteins as an "on/off switch" for cellular actions. A wide range of biological activities depend on the function of G-proteins.

FUNCTION AND MALFUNCTION

By some estimates, G-proteins play an essential role in as many as one-third of all signal-transduction processes. For example, they form part of the molecular pathway that enables cells to respond to signals from hormones such as epinephrine and glucagon, which help to metabolize fat and glucose. G-proteins also are involved in the cellular processing of acetylcholine and other neurotransmitters, which transmit nerve impulses. Scientists, in examining the biochemistry of vision in humans and other higher animals, are studying the role of G-proteins in the light-absorbing molecules known as visual pigments, which are found in the retina. These proteins help the eyes process light, and transmit visual stimuli to the brain.

In a further indication of the importance of G-proteins, more than half the medications now being used in clinical medicine are targeted at the receptor systems that communicate with G-proteins. These include medicines called beta-blockers, which are used to treat high blood pressure and irregular heartbeat.

When G-proteins fail to function properly, disease often follows. One such instance is cholera, an infectious disease of the gastrointestinal system. The cholera bacteria produce a toxin that acts as an enzyme, altering the function of G-proteins. As a result, instead of fulfilling their usual function of switching on to activate amplifiers and then switching off, the G-proteins remain stuck in the "on" position, like a traffic light stuck on green. With this impairment of cellular function, water and salt in the intestine are not properly absorbed, leading to the severe diarrhea and dehydration by which cholera kills its victims. A similar alteration of G-protein function occurs in cases of infection by *E. coli* bacteria.

G-proteins also have been implicated in other diseases. For example, G-protein malfunction may play a role in symptoms associated with diabetes and alcoholism. In some cases, the formation of tumors also appears to be characterized by overactive G-proteins. Scientists are currently investigating the possible role that G-proteins and similar protein structures in the cell might play in the development of various forms of cancer.

As yet, no specific therapies have been developed as a result of the work of Drs. Rodbell and Gilman. However, these two scientists have laid the foundation for ever-increasing knowledge of the means by which the cell membrane functions as a "switchboard" in processing incoming signals. Gradually, scientists are developing a detailed picture of the cellular pathways—in effect, drawing a wire-by-wire diagram. As Dr. Gilman told a reporter shortly after the Nobel prizes were announced, "When we know the whole diagram, we'll know how every cell is controlled." This knowledge could lead, within a few decades, to the development of drugs designed to target specific molecules within the body, immeasurably improving the accuracy and effectiveness of drug therapy.

Martin Rodbell was born on December 1, 1928, in Baltimore, Maryland. He earned his undergraduate degree in biology in 1949 at Johns Hopkins University in Baltimore, where he also did graduate work in chemistry. He received his doctoral degree in biochemistry from the University of Washington in Seattle in 1954. In addition to his duties at the NIH in Bethesda from 1970 to 1985, Dr. Rodbell was also a visiting professor at the University of Geneva, Switzerland. In 1989, Dr. Rodbell moved to the National Institute of Environmental Health Sciences in Research Triangle Park, North Carolina, where he was head of the signal-transduction laboratory. Dr. Rodbell retired from his post in June 1994.

Alfred G. Gilman was born on July 1, 1941, in New Haven, Connecticut. He earned his bachelor's degree from Yale University in New Haven, and received his M.D. and Ph.D. degrees from Case Western Reserve University, Cleveland, Ohio. After doing postdoctoral research at the National Heart, Lung, and Blood Institute in Bethesda, Maryland, Dr. Gilman became a professor of pharmacology at the University of Virginia School of Medicine in Charlottesville in 1977. In 1981, he moved to the Texas Southwestern Medical Center in Dallas, Texas, where he now heads the school's department of pharmacology.

Christopher King

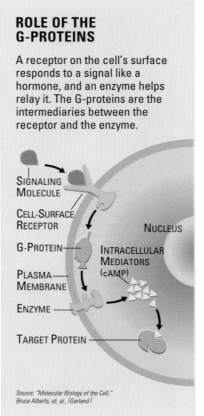

ROLE OF THE G-PROTEINS

A receptor on the cell's surface responds to a signal like a hormone, and an enzyme helps relay it. The G-proteins are the intermediaries between the receptor and the enzyme.

SIGNALING MOLECULE

CELL-SURFACE RECEPTOR

G-PROTEIN

NUCLEUS

INTRACELLULAR MEDIATORS (cAMP)

PLASMA MEMBRANE

ENZYME

TARGET PROTEIN

Source: "Molecular Biology of the Cell," Bruce Alberts, et. al., (Garland)

NUTRITION

DIETING AND INSULIN RESISTANCE

As researchers continue to study obesity, evidence increasingly indicates that a "one size fits all" approach is not the key to successful weight loss. In the 1960s, carbohydrates—such as bread, pasta, and potatoes—were given a bad reputation as a dieter's foe. In more-recent years, fats have been castigated by individuals trying to lose weight as well as by those who want to reduce their risk for diseases linked to a high-fat diet.

Medical experts do not agree on how low in fat the optimal diet should be. Dean Ornish, M.D., extols the necessity of reducing fat intake to 10 percent of total calories for weight loss and heart-disease treatment. The American Heart Association (AHA) offers a more moderate recommendation: lowering fat intake to 30 percent of total calories. Perhaps the same level of dietary-fat intake for everyone is not the answer.

In the past 10 years, a high-carbohydrate, low-fat regime has been the rage for many individuals desiring to lose weight. In fact, many people have eschewed all visible fats, skimming grocery aisles for only fat-free products. This dramatic approach, however, has not resulted in weight loss for everyone. Even though people in the United States have reduced their fat intake over the past decade, they have gained an average of 8 pounds (3.6 kilograms) during that period.

According to some obesity experts, the answer to why many people continue to gain weight following a high-carbohydrate, very-low-fat diet lies in the body's faulty use of insulin, a hormone responsible for metabolizing starches and sugars. Obesity researchers speculate that about 25 percent of the U.S. population may have such a condition, called insulin resistance.

Individuals with insulin resistance particularly have difficulty when they eat refined starches and sugars. After consuming a meal high in starch or sugar, an insulin-resistant person makes too much glucose, which causes an overproduction of insulin. Normally, insulin binds with receptor sites on the surfaces of the body's cells. This binding signals

A high-carbohydrate, low-fat diet may not be the key to weight loss for the one in four Americans believed by obesity experts to have a condition called insulin resistance.

the cells to allow glucose to enter and subsequently be used for energy. In cases of insulin resistance, the receptor sites appear to be less sensitive to insulin; insulin levels remain elevated because the insulin is unable to bind to these sites. The elevated levels of glucose and insulin in the blood signal the liver to convert glucose to fat, resulting in weight gain. To make matters worse, high levels of insulin stimulate the appetite and cause the insulin-resistant individual to eat more frequently.

Insulin research by Gerald Reaven, M.D., of Stanford University Medical School in Palo Alto, California, has led to a better understanding of this condition, which often exists as a cluster of symptoms. According to Dr. Reaven, insulin-resistant individuals may develop high triglyceride (simple fats) levels, low HDL ("good" cholesterol) levels, high blood pressure, and Type II diabetes. Coined "syndrome X," this group of symptoms raises an individual's risk for coronary-artery disease.

A common error for people trying to lose weight is to strive for a nonfat diet and to increase their intake of refined white-flour products and sugars. Research revealing that dietary fat is more readily converted to body fat than are carbohydrates created a myth that one can eat pasta and other low-fat carbohydrates with virtual abandon and not gain weight. Obesity experts dealing with insulin-resistant individuals suggest that the answer does not lie in a full swing back to a high-protein diet. Instead, they suggest that people reduce their intake of sugars and simple starches (such as white-flour products and fat-free cookies), and eat more complex carbohydrates rich in fiber—such as vegetables, legumes, whole-grain bread, pasta, and cereals.

Further research surrounding insulin resistance and "syndrome X" may allow overweight individuals to be screened for the condition, and allow registered dietitians and other health educators to more specifically individualize weight-loss plans.

HEALTH BENEFITS OF CAROTENOIDS

Beta-carotene, a compound occurring naturally in orange fruits and vegetables and in green, leafy vegetables, has become a household word in the 1990s because of its antioxidant properties. Antioxidant nutrients neutralize free radicals (natural byproducts of metabolism) that can damage cell membranes and DNA. Many studies of beta-carotene reveal a correlation between diets rich in this nutrient and a decreased risk for certain cancers and stroke.

Beta-carotene belongs to a family of phytochemicals (plant chemicals) called carotenoids. Carotenoid research is heavily focused on beta-carotene because this compound is well-known for its antioxidant properties, and is more efficiently converted to vitamin A in the body than are other carotenoids. Scientists have isolated 600 carotenoids in plants, with approximately 40 of these found in familiar fruits and vegetables. Attention has been directed at some of these other carotenoids to learn if they also have disease-preventing qualities, as well as to understand how they function in relationship to beta-carotene.

Recent research on humans and in the laboratory indicates that carotenoids probably work most efficiently as a team. Scientists increasingly believe that beta-carotene may not be more important than other carotenoids, and that carotenoids work in concert with other phytochemicals that are found in fruits and vegetables. Individuals who take supplemental beta-carotene rather than eating plenty of foods rich in carotenoids may be missing out on the synergistic effects of these nutrients.

In her research on carotenoids at the National Cancer Institute (NCI), Regina Ziegler, M.D., has found that lycopene, the carotenoid in tomatoes, may decrease the risk for cancers of the colon and bladder. In laboratory studies, lycopene stops the growth of cancer in mice. Preliminary research also suggests that lycopene may also be more effective at preventing cardiovascular disease than are other carotenoids.

MAJOR PLAYERS AMONG MORE THAN 600 CAROTENOIDS

CAROTENOID	MAIN SOURCES	HEALTH BENEFITS SUGGESTED BY STUDIES
ALPHA-CAROTENE	Carrots	Vitamin A activity, decreased risk of lung cancer, decreased growth of cancer cells in mice, improved immune response.
BETA-CAROTENE	Broccoli, cantaloupe, carrots	Vitamin A activity, decreased risk of lung cancer, decreased risk of colon and bladder cancers, decreased risk of skin cancers in rats, decreased growth of cancer cells in mice, improved immune response.
BETA-CRYPTOXANTHIN	Mangos, oranges, papaya, tangerines	Vitamin A activity.
CANTHAXANTHIN	Natural food color added to jellies, salad dressings, soft drinks, tomato juice	Decreased risk of skin cancer in rats, decreased growth of cancer cells in mice, improved immune response.
LUTEIN	Broccoli, spinach, greens (collard, mustard, turnip)	Decreased risk of lung cancer.
LYCOPENE	Tomatoes, tomato products	Decreased risk of colon and bladder cancer, decreased growth of cancer cells in mice.

Source: Environmental Nutrition

Two other carotenoids, lutein and zeax-antin, appear to prevent macular degenera-tion, a degenerative condition of the retina that can lead to blindness. Research at Harvard Medical School, Boston, Massachu-setts, under the direction of ophthalmologist Johanna M. Seddon, M.D., analyzed the diets of 356 people with macular degenera-tion and compared them to the diets of 520 people without the condition. The study revealed that the individuals with the highest intake of these carotenoids were 43 percent less likely to develop macular degeneration than were the people with the lowest intake of carotenoids. The best sources of lutein and zeaxantin are green, leafy vegetables such as broccoli, spinach, collard greens, and kale.

Continued research of phytochemicals will likely reveal the disease-preventing qual-ities of specific fruits and vegetables. Given the present available information, it is clear that taking one carotenoid supplement, such as beta-carotene, cannot provide the desired protection from disease. Nutritional experts now advise the public to eat plenty of fruits and vegetables, especially leafy greens such as spinach, kale, and collards; and yellow-orange and red varieties such as carrots, sweet potatoes, winter squash, man-goes, cantaloupe, apricots, tomatoes, and red peppers.

HOMOCYSTEINE LEVELS, B VITAMINS, AND ATHEROSCLEROSIS

New conclusions from the Framingham Heart Study, Framingham, Massachusetts, have established that high serum levels of an amino acid called homocysteine and low lev-els of two B vitamins—folic acid and B_6—are correlated with an increased risk for carotid-artery atherosclerosis. Results of this re-search, which was headed by Jacob Selhub, Ph.D., were published in the February 1995 issue of the *New England Journal of Medicine.*

Epidemiological studies have concluded that elevated homocysteine levels increase the risk for hardening of the arteries. Researchers conducted a cross-sectional study of 1,041 elderly subjects (418 men and 623 women) from the Framingham Heart Study. Plasma levels for homocysteine, folic acid, and vitamins B_6 and B_{12} were mea-sured in these subjects. In addition, total-cholesterol and HDL ("good")-cholesterol levels were obtained. The degree of occlu-sion of the carotid arteries in all subjects was measured by ultrasound.

Subjects completed a food-frequency questionnaire that estimated their dietary intake of folic acid, B_6, and B_{12}. These B vita-mins are involved in homocysteine metabo-lism, helping to clear the blood of this amino acid. The investigators had previously deter-mined that elevated levels of homocysteine were associated in many cases with insuffi-cient concentrations of these vitamins. Other researchers have shown that vitamin supple-mentation with folic acid, B_6, and B_{12} in patients with elevated homocysteine levels can effectively reduce the serum-amino-acid levels to within the normal range.

The findings of this study reveal that sub-jects with the highest homocysteine levels were twice as likely to have atherosclerosis of the carotid arteries as those with the lowest concentrations. In addition, results show that the subjects with the lowest plasma lev-els of folic acid and vitamin B_6 have the greatest risk for stenosis (narrowing or con-striction) of the carotid arteries. There was only a weak association between plasma lev-els of B_{12} and carotid-artery stenosis.

The researchers also looked at the correla-tion between the dietary intake of these vita-mins and carotid-artery stenosis. Although vitamin B_6 and B_{12} intakes were not linked to the incidence of stenosis, researchers did observe a correlation between low dietary intake of folic acid and the prevalence of clogged carotid arteries. Protection against stenosis appears to occur only when levels of dietary folic acid exceed 475 micrograms per day, a much greater intake than most people in the United States receive. Adults can increase their folic acid intake by eating more green, leafy vegetables; peas; and oranges, or by taking a daily vitamin supplement con-taining folic acid.

The investigators of the study planned to further their research by examining the effects of vitamin supplementation on the incidence of vascular disease in elderly indi-viduals with elevated levels of homocysteine.

Maria Guglielmino, M.S., R.D.

Oceanography

Climate-Prediction Dice

According to the October 28, 1994, issue of *Science* magazine, a broad pattern of North Pacific Ocean temperatures triggers 10-year weather cycles over North America. Researchers Mojib Latif, Ph.D., of the Max Planck Institute for Meteorology in Hamburg, Germany, and Tim P. Barnett, Ph.D., of the Scripps Institution of Oceanography at the University of California, San Diego, describe a large-scale cycle of warmer and cooler ocean conditions in the North Pacific that determines North America's weather about one-third of the time—much like loaded dice.

A distinct pattern of ocean heating and cooling takes about 20 years to run full cycle. Warmer and cooler pools of water, about one-half the size of the entire North Pacific, chase each other around in a clockwise rotation. At one point in the cycle, ocean temperatures tend to be cooler in the northern section of the North Pacific—strengthening the low atmospheric-pressure field just south of the Aleutian Islands and pushing the jet stream to the south. As the cycle runs its course, ocean temperatures gradually warm in the North Pacific, causing the Aleutian low atmospheric-pressure field to weaken and the jet stream to again retreat to a more northerly position.

This decadal air-sea cycle also affects rain and snow patterns in the western third of North America, where the source of most precipitation is North Pacific water. For instance, a jet-stream dip to the south usually is accompanied by increased precipitation. Dr. Barnett compared the ocean effect to loaded "climate-prediction dice."

"The ocean effect loads the climate-prediction dice. Once the state of the ocean has reached one of the two conditions, the dice want to roll a certain weather pattern over North America. This won't happen every time, because other factors, such as El Niños and random weather events, can overwhelm the decadal mode. But there is a definite tendency to roll the same pattern," Barnett says.

The El Niños

Historically, the warming of surface waters off South America's west coast was called El Niño ("the child"), since the phenomenon usually coincided with Christmastime. But El Niño is now recognized as a local manifestation of the global El Niño-Southern Oscillation (ENSO), an irregular cycle during which global wind patterns and pools of very warm surface waters are displaced from one side of equatorial oceans to the other side. The pool's displacement is associated with corresponding shifts in rainfall and winds, both locally and globally.

The famous El Niño has a sibling. Researchers Yves M. Tourre, Ph.D., a meteorologist at Columbia University's Lamont-Doherty Earth Observatory, and Warren B. White, Ph.D., an oceanographer at the Scripps Institution, announced on December 7, 1994, that like the Pacific, the Indian Ocean contains a periodic warm current capable of dramatically affecting the world's weather—for the first time linking the two vast oceans in a related cyclical pattern recurring every three to seven years. The discovery of a more global aspect to the El Niños could advance scientists' understanding of the Pacific El Niño—improving the ability to forecast El Niño-spawned droughts, floods, and storms all over the world.

Drs. Tourre and White discovered an El Niño pattern in the Indian Ocean that is in lockstep with its Pacific sibling. During the same periods when the Pacific warm pool migrated eastward to create the El Niño in 1982-83 and 1986-87, an equivalent El Niño also formed in the Indian Ocean.

Japanese Adventure

On March 1, 1994, an unmanned Japanese vessel called the *Kaiko* descended nearly 7 miles (11.3 kilometers) below the surface of the Pacific into the deepest spot in the world's oceans—sending back the first television pictures of the Marianas Trench (closest landmass: Guam).

Just as it was about to land on the ocean floor, an equipment failure forced the remote-controlled craft to abort its mission. The vessel apparently fell several feet short of setting a record for the greatest depth reached by a human-made vehicle. That record belongs to the *Trieste*, a bathyscaphe manned by Jacques Piccard, a Swiss oceanographer, and Lieutenant Don Walsh, a U.S. naval officer. On January 23, 1960, they descended into the Marianas Trench, reaching a depth of 35,800 feet (10,910 meters).

The *Kaiko*, carrying modern video and sensing equipment, was the first vessel since the *Trieste* to venture into the abysslike Challenger Deep region of the Marianas Trench. Its mission was driven by recent discoveries of microbes, tube worms, and other life-forms that inhabit hot-water vents on the ocean floor. Scientists believe that such organisms could provide a boon of new medicines or chemicals because of their ability to survive under extreme conditions.

NEW HOT-WATER-VENT DISCOVERY

The British journal *Nature* reported in its October 20, 1994, issue a "stunning discovery from volcanic vents in frigid, sunless waters" by a team of researchers from Rutgers University, New Brunswick, New Jersey. The scientists described eerie thickets of snakelike creatures that inhabit these abyssal warm-spring regions, and towering chimneys of rich minerals that can form on the ocean floor—not in eons, centuries, or decades, but in as little as two or three years. In fact, the rates of growth in some cases appear to be among the fastest known anywhere. "This finding is one of the most dramatic underwater discoveries in history," says Robert Corell, Ph.D., of the National Science Foundation (NSF), which financed the research.

The Rutgers team discovered the quick-growing animals and mineral deposits during a study of a 1.5-mile (2.4-kilometer)-deep Pacific Ocean site due west of Costa Rica; the site had been swept by a volcanic eruption in 1991. They were surprised to find that giant tube worms could rapidly colonize a barren area and grow to lengths of nearly 5 feet (1.5 meters) in such a short time. The giant tube worms, which look like clumps of snakes gently swaying in the water, live in symbiosis

with bacteria that metabolize compounds in the water. Despite having no eyes, no mouths, and no obvious means of locomotion or ingestion, the tube worms appear to be the fastest-growing invertebrates on Earth. Similarly, the mineral chimneys were found to grow extraordinarily fast, quickly reaching heights of up to 34 feet (10.4 meters).

Scientists were stunned to find giant tube worms thriving on the ocean floor near deep-sea volcanic vents. The invertebrates grow at an amazingly fast rate, despite their sunless habitat.

Implications abound. For instance, discovery of the chimneys might spur deep-sea mining since they're known to be laced with metallic ores rich in zinc, cobalt, mercury, copper, silver, and gold. More generally, the findings are viewed as important for understanding the nature of the deep-sea hot vents—which were discovered in 1977 and have mesmerized scientists ever since.

Gode Davis

PALEONTOLOGY

AFRICAN DINOSAURS

In an expedition reminiscent of Indiana Jones, a team of paleontologists crossed 1,500 miles (2,400 kilometers) of the Sahara to discover two new types of dinosaurs. The team, led by Paul Sereno of the University of Chicago in Illinois, started its African adventure in Algeria, and drove across the desert to a remote section of Niger. Battling illness, bureaucratic hurdles, and threats of violence from Islamic militants, the scientists managed to unearth a large theropod dinosaur they named *Afrovenator*, or "African hunter."

The 30-foot (9-meter)-long African predator lived during the early Cretaceous period, about 130 million years ago. It resembled *Allosaurus*, a well-known North American theropod from the Jurassic period. Sereno's team also found a large plant-eating dinosaur, not yet named. This sauropod resembled the familiar North American *Camarasaurus*.

Two paleontologists touched off a storm of controversy in 1994 after reporting evidence that Tyrannosaurus rex had a warm-blooded metabolism. Many scientists reject such claims and remain convinced that this celebrated carnivore, and close relatives such as Tarbosaurus (left), were cold-blooded creatures.

The similarities between the African and North American species showed paleontologists how movement of the ancient continents affected dinosaur evolution. Prior to the Cretaceous period, all of the continents were joined together in a massive landmass called Pangaea. Although the supercontinent had splintered some 50 million years before *Afrovenator* lived, this animal shared traits in common with its cousins in North America, suggesting the African species had not evolved in isolation.

HOT-BLOODED DINOSAURS?

A pair of researchers from North Carolina State University in Raleigh made controversial, and widely reported, claims that *Tyrannosaurus rex* had a warm-blooded metabolism more like that of mammals than of cold-blooded reptiles. Scientists Reese Barrick and William Showers reached this conclusion after studying oxygen stored within the bones of a *T. rex* skeleton from the late Cretaceous period, about 65 million years ago.

The researchers analyzed the ratio of light- and heavy-oxygen isotopes—a characteristic thought to record the animal's body temperature when it lived. According to this theory, an abundance of heavy oxygen in the dinosaur's bones would indicate cool body temperatures.

When they analyzed different parts of the *T. rex* skeleton, the scientists found little variation in the oxygen-isotope ratio. They interpreted this data to mean that the dinosaur kept its limbs at nearly the same temperature as the core of its body. They also concluded that the animal's overall body temperature had not varied more than 4° F (2.2° C) throughout its life.

Such results led the scientists to suggest that *T. rex* was warm-blooded, because modern mammals keep their entire body at a relatively stable temperature throughout life. Reptiles allow their body temperatures to vary more.

The methods and findings of the *T. rex* study attracted strong criticism, however. The originator of the oxygen-isotope technique for fossils argues that this procedure does not yield accurate information about body temperature. Meanwhile, other scientists who study the bones of *T. rex* have found growth rings, bands that resemble tree rings. Such bands are common in reptiles and other cold-blooded animals that have fluctuating body temperatures, but they do not develop in mammals. The presence of growth rings in *T. rex* therefore suggests that the animal had a metabolism more like that of a reptile.

ESCAPEE FROM THE SWAMP

Life in Pennsylvania swamps during the late Devonian period, some 365 million years ago, was tough. Many of the fish in this environment had evolved huge teeth and armored bodies, evidence that they were fighting it out in a fish-eat-fish world. But not all animals developed fierce bodies. Some evaded the fray altogether by escaping onto land, report scientists who found the partial remains of an ancient amphibian, one of the earliest known to have conquered the continents.

Discovered in the fossilized deposits of a Pennsylvania swamp, the species *Hynerpeton bassetti* is the oldest known North American tetrapod, or four-legged vertebrate. It is the second oldest known in the world. Despite its antiquity, *H. bassetti* had several adaptations to movement on land that were lacking in amphibians that appeared several million years later. Scientists unearthed a well-preserved shoulder of *H. bassetti* that indicates that the species had surprising muscularity. Its discoverers concluded that *H. bassetti* used its limbs to forage for food on land, instead of competing with the heavies in the swamps. They could not tell whether the animal actually walked or crawled on land.

THE EARLIEST MONSTERS

Paleontologists have discovered a wide variety of giant arthropod-like creatures that terrorized the seas during the Cambrian period, half a billion years ago. These animals, known as anomalocaridids, are the earliest known predators in the fossil record.

Researchers first uncovered elements of an anomalocaridid more than 100 years ago, but they failed to recognize how the various pieces of this odd creature fit together. It took the better part of a century for paleontologists to discover the true shape of these animals. The best-known genus, called *Anomalocaris*, had eyes mounted on stalks, and two jointed feeding appendages in the front of its body. The appendages grabbed animals off the seafloor and carried them back toward *Anomalocaris*' bizarre mouth— a circular arrangement of teeth that worked somewhat like a nutcracker.

With its two jointed appendages and segmented body, *Anomalocaris* resembled an arthropod, the large phylum that includes both insects and crustaceans. But the circular mouth and other aspects of its body were decidedly unlike those of arthropods, suggesting that the anomalocaridids may have belonged to a separate phylum.

Recent finds in China and Australia have turned up several new species of anomalocaridids with different eating habits. With their stalked eyes, some apparently lay on the ocean bottom, buried in the sand, waiting for unsuspecting prey to swim by. Others had rakelike appendages that may have helped in combing through seafloor sediments.

CRAWDADS: LIVING FOSSILS

Freshwater crustacea known as crayfish have scuttled about in North America's streams since before the age of the dinosaurs, report scientists who have found fossils of these animals dating back 220 million years. The discovery pushed back the known origins of North American crayfish, also known as crawdads, by about 170 million years.

Scientists previously thought that crayfish had evolved from marine lobsters, the oldest of which date to approximately 200 million years ago. But the recent fossil discovery has upended these older theories, and suggests that marine lobsters may have actually evolved from even-more-ancient crayfish. These animals have apparently survived so long—while the dinosaurs came and went—because they could successfully adapt to changing conditions on Earth.

Richard Monastersky

PHYSICS

WORLD-RECORD FUSION BURST

During one blink of an eye in November 1994, an experimental fusion reactor at Princeton University in New Jersey generated 10.7 million watts of power, shattering the 9-million-watt world record it had set six months earlier. The short-lived burst of energy from the Tokamak Fusion Test Reactor (TFTR) garnered scientists an extra year's worth of funding for the facility, which had been scheduled to shut down at the end of 1994.

Fusion, the process that powers the Sun, occurs when light atoms—usually isotopes of hydrogen—collide with each other at high temperatures. Under such conditions, these atoms fuse to form larger elements, like helium, and release energy. In contrast, fission, the process used to power today's commercial nuclear reactors, occurs when heavy atoms of uranium or plutonium are split. In both reactions, mass is converted into energy in accordance with Einstein's formula $E=mc^2$.

As a source of power, fusion offers many advantages over fission and fossil fuels. Fusion does not release pollutants into the atmosphere. The fuel for fusion, a mixture of deuterium from seawater and tritium from lithium, is abundant and accessible. And while radioactive elements are produced in a fusion reactor, they are far less hazardous and more easily contained or diluted than the radioactive waste generated in a fission reactor.

The TFTR is a doughnut-shaped magnetic chamber that traps plasma—a super-hot gas composed of free electrons and positively charged nuclei—with magnetic fields. Soviet scientists who invented this type of chamber in the 1950s coined the word "tokamak." Coils of magnets surround the toroidal chamber, and the magnetic fields they produce confine and insulate the plasma. High-energy particle beams heat the plasma to fusion temperatures of more than 90,000,000° F (50,000,000° C).

Researchers at the Princeton University Plasma Physics Laboratory boosted the power output of the TFTR during 1994 by using a plasma with equal parts deuterium and tritium. Although scientists have long known that such a half-and-half mixture would maximize power output, they were concerned that the plasma would become unstable. Instead, they found that this kind of plasma was better behaved than the previous formula of deuterium, mixed on occasion with a touch of tritium.

Researchers also discovered that alpha particles, helium nuclei produced during the fusion reaction, stick around long enough in the plasma to impart their energy. This contributes heat to maintain the fusion process.

In late 1994, the doughnut-shaped Tokamak Fusion Test Reactor produced a record-breaking 10.7 million watts of power, bringing fusion energy a small step closer to becoming a practical power source.

High-energy physicists using Fermilab's 4-mile-long main accelerator were finally able to detect evidence of the top quark, the culmination of a 20-year search for this elusive subatomic particle.

As reported in the October 17, 1994, issue of *Physical Review Letters*, Jorge Rocca and colleagues at Colorado State University in Fort Collins achieved the remarkable transformation by substituting a simple electrical capacitor for the room-sized optical laser traditionally used to lase X rays. The resulting system now takes up the space of a large refrigerator.

To test whether a capacitor could replace the laser's function, the researchers filled a narrow plastic tube with argon gas. Discharging a capacitor between electrodes at either end of the tube produced a current pulse that heated and ionized the gas, stripping electrons from the atoms. The pulse also created a magnetic field that compressed the plasma, reducing energy loss. Collisions between electrons and argon ions in the plasma pumped up the energy of the ions, stimulating photon emissions at X-ray wavelengths.

The wavelengths for X rays—1 to 300 angstroms (1 angstrom equals 10^{-10} meters) are much shorter than those of visible light (380 to 750 angstroms). Consequently, a microscope using X-ray lasers could deliver higher resolution than its optical counterpart, making it an ideal tool for imaging living tissue on an atomic scale. (Scanning electron microscopes offer comparable resolutions, but, unlike an X-ray-based microscope, require specimens to be specially prepared.) Other applications for X-ray lasers include creating holographic views of microscopic objects, etching microcircuitry, and studying plasma conditions in magnetic-fusion reactors.

Ultimately, the goal of the TFTR team is for the Tokamak to reach a state of "ignition," when the energy generated would be great enough to sustain the fusion process in the plasma without additional heating.

Although the experiments breathed new life into the TFTR, the reactions nonetheless consumed far more energy than was produced. With a commercial fusion reactor still decades off, the fusion community is worried that looming budget cuts by the Clinton administration and Congress could introduce further delays.

Researchers hope that by the end of 1995, construction will begin in Princeton on a new fusion-research facility called the Tokamak Physics Experiment (TPX). The TPX, slated to go on-line in 2001, is designed to sustain fusion reactions for periods longer than one minute.

X-RAY LASERS LOSE WEIGHT

Cumbersome, costly, and complex—that is the reputation the X-ray laser has in the scientific community. But scientists intent on harnessing the imaging power of X rays have given the device a makeover by dramatically reducing its size and cost.

TOP THIS

A marriage of high-tech hardware and two competing groups of physicists finally nailed down the evidence of the existence of the top quark at Fermi National Accelerator Laboratory (Fermilab) in Batavia, Illinois. Announced in March 1995, the news ended a 20-year quest for the sixth and last of the quarks—subatomic particles that constitute the building blocks of all matter. The announcement came nearly one year after one of the rival groups, the Collider Detector at Fermilab (CDF) Collaboration, cautiously offered their evidence for the top quark.

At 176 billion to 199 billion electron volts (BeV), the top quark outweighs its counterpart bottom quark by a factor of almost 40, and is 200 times more massive than a proton. Bagging such a hefty beast required smashing protons and antiprotons in Fermilab's 1.8-trillion-electron-volt (TeV) underground Tevatron accelerator and sifting through the debris.

Researchers from the CDF group and the D-zero (D0) Collaboration, both named for detectors used in their experiments, examined trillions of proton-antiproton collisions generated in the Tevatron's 4-mile (6.4-kilometer) ring of superconducting magnets to find familiar decay particles associated with the creation of the top quark. The CDF group found about 21 events pointing to such a quark, while the D0 team turned up 17.

According to the Standard Model, a sweeping theory that physicists use to explain the creation of matter and the forces acting on it, pairs of quarks join with pairs of leptons to form everything in our universe. Quarks classified as up and down combine to form protons and neutrons. Together with the electron and electron neutrino, these particles form the matter of our everyday world.

Strange and charm quarks, together with the muon and muon neutrino, produce more exotic particles found in quasars and cosmic rays. Top and bottom quarks, along with the tau and tau neutrino, form the particles that existed for a fraction of a second after the Big Bang, the cataclysmic explosion believed to have formed our universe.

High-energy physicists are not content, however, to just kick back with a six-pack of quarks. They are pushing to upgrade existing facilities or construct new ones at higher energies to refine the Standard Model. For example, completion of the Tevatron's main injector by 1999 may allow scientists to track the still-missing Higgs boson, a hypothetical type of particle that is believed to orchestrate the masses of quarks and leptons. It is more likely that the Higgs boson will be revealed at Europe's Large Hadron Collider (LHC), scheduled to be operational in 2005, and designed to investigate all mass up to about 1,000 gigaelectron volts (GeV).

Therese A. Lloyd

PUBLIC HEALTH

EMERGING INFECTIONS

Since the Institute of Medicine issued a report on emerging infections in 1992, the world has become increasingly aware of the growing problem of infectious diseases. As recently as two decades ago, the major infectious diseases were thought to have been almost eliminated as serious problems, despite the warnings of a few scientists. Factors that have worked against the control of infectious diseases include: the population explosion; urbanization; increasing rapid worldwide travel; migration and refugees; increasing resistance to antibiotics and insecticides; changes in industry and technology; decreasing diagnostic acuity of new or unfamiliar infectious diseases; changing lifestyle patterns; increasing exposure to new organisms as tropical rain forests are invaded and cut down; and widespread lack of concern about infectious diseases, which, in many areas, has reduced support for public-health measures.

CHOLERA AND DYSENTERY IN RWANDA

Because of the civil war in Rwanda, 3 million to 4 million refugees have fled to nearby

Tanzania and Zaïre, where they have clustered in huge camps with inadequate food, water, and sanitation. Given such bad sanitation, it is hardly surprising that the intestinal diseases known as cholera and shigella dysentery have devastated the camps. Relief workers were calling for help in creating 60,000 latrines and bringing in safe water and food.

A cholera patient is treated with replacement fluids containing salts and sugar. This can be done either by administering intravenous fluids during the peak few days of the diarrhea, or by giving the solution orally, which is almost as effective. If the fluids and salts lost by diarrhea can be rapidly replaced, the patient will soon recover. However, both treatment methods were in short supply. The cases of shigellosis were even more difficult to treat, because the causal organisms were resistant to antibiotics, and more than simple fluid replacement was required for treatment.

BUBONIC AND PNEUMONIC PLAGUE IN INDIA

Few diseases cause as much fear as the great scourge of the Middle Ages, the "Black Death"—bubonic and pneumonic plague. Caused by the bacterium *Yersinia pestis*, plague is fundamentally a disease of small rodents, usually rats in cities, and it is spread from rat to rat, and eventually to human beings, by rat fleas. Because fleas leaving dead rats are likely to bite human beings on the lower limbs, the infection starts there and moves up to the lymph nodes, where the legs join the torso. These lymph nodes become very large and tender (becoming the "buboes" of bubonic plague), and then break down and drain pus. This form of the disease has a moderate mortality rate.

Thousands died when disease swept the camps (left) that house refugees from the brutal civil war in Rwanda. The lack of medical supplies and the squalid conditions worsened the situation.

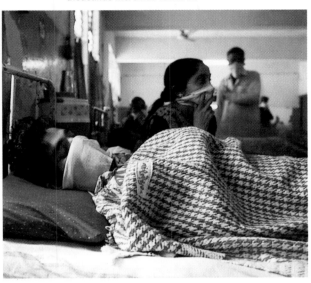

In August 1994, a major outbreak of bubonic and pneumonic plague began in India. By the time it ended two months later, more than 50 people had died and thousands more had fallen ill.

The most dangerous form of plague occurs when the organism gets into the bloodstream and causes a plague pneumonia, known as pneumonic plague, a highly fatal condition. Unfortunately, the victims of pneumonic plague also tend to spread organisms from their noses and mouths by droplet infection, so that those caring for them may get pneumonic plague by direct spread, without going through the bubonic stage first.

Beginning in late August 1994, India suffered a major outbreak of plague. Three major regions of the country were affected: Maharashtra State (which includes Bombay); Gujarat State (including the industrial port city of Surat); and the city of Delhi. Approximately 700 cases of plague with a positive test for antibodies to *Yersinia pestis* were reported to the World Health Organization (WHO) through mid-October 1994, although the actual number of suspected cases was well over 5,000, and the known deaths were more than 50. The human cases began following a reported rat die-off. In some areas, the rodent population was unusually large due to a number of factors: the squalor of shantytowns around big cities; inadequate food-storage facilities, in part due to damage from earthquakes; piles of garbage due to inadequate refuse disposal; and the migration of rodents to higher ground following monsoon rains.

When the bubonic form of the plague was followed by the appearance of the pneumonic form of the disease, which is uniformly fatal if untreated, the population began leaving Surat in a panic, in some cases carrying the disease with them to new areas.

Many nations enacted various levels of quarantine or surveillance of travelers from India until the epidemic was brought under control. No spread of plague was detected by any other country, and the epidemic was brought under control by November 1994. Although it had been almost 30 years since the last plague outbreak in India, no one believes it will be that long again, unless fundamental changes are made.

NEW HUMAN DISEASES

- *New Horse Virus.* In Queensland, Australia, a virus that had never before been known to affect either human beings or horses killed 14 racehorses and their trainer, in addition to making two other people ill. The virus is a member of the paramyxovirus family, to which human measles also belongs. The virus caused an acute respiratory infection.
- *Ehrlichia.* A previously unrecognized strain of Ehrlichia, a tick-borne disease-causing bacterium, was identified by the Centers for Disease Control and Prevention (CDC) in 1994. This organism, which causes a disease called human granulocytic ehrlichiosis, killed several people in Minnesota and Wisconsin in 1994. Among other kinds of damage, the disease destroys granulocytes, an important type of human white blood cell. Symptoms of ehrlichiosis include fever, headache, muscle aches, nausea, and vomiting. It may be confused with influenza or Rocky Mountain spotted fever, but the condition does not produce the spotted fever's characteristic rash. The illness apparently begins 10 to 14 days after a tick bite, the event during which the infectious organism is transmitted to the human host.
- *New Hantavirus.* A young Florida man developed a severe respiratory illness in 1994

that closely resembles the hantavirus pulmonary syndrome first identified in the southwestern United States in 1993. However, tests of his antibodies showed that the virus causing his illness was not the Muerto Canyon virus, which caused the 1993 outbreak, but instead was a new hantavirus. Public-health investigation revealed that the virus probably was spread by the deer mouse (*Sigmodon hispidus*), whose range extends throughout the southeastern and south-central United States. The hantavirus pulmonary syndrome is severe, with an approximately 50 percent mortality rate in young people, making prevention efforts imperative. The infection is apparently spread by rodents and rodent droppings.

GOOD NEWS IN INFECTIOUS DISEASES

There was some good news regarding infectious diseases during 1994, most notably the first drop in the number of new active tuberculosis cases in a decade. The decline was small, but encouraging. It suggested that the major increase in tuberculosis-control efforts over the past few years was beginning to have a positive effect. One of the mainstays of the new approach to tuberculosis control is "directly observed therapy," where a public-health official supervises the taking of medications, so that it is clear the patient is receiving the treatment. One of the causes for the resurgence was that many patients would not take their antituberculosis treatment regularly or at all. Some patients were developing strains of tuberculosis that were resistant to available therapies; these same patients were then infecting other people with the resistant tuberculosis organisms.

In 1994, a special commission from the Pan-American Health Organization, a regional office of WHO, certified the Western Hemisphere free of poliovirus transmission. The last case of infection with wild poliovirus in the Americas was in 1991. Immunization levels and surveillance must be kept high, however, because polioviruses are common in many areas of the world, and may be reimported into the Americas by immigrants or visitors, or by citizens of the Western Hemisphere returning from abroad.

James F. Jekel, M.D., M.P.H

SCIENCE EDUCATION

TEACHERS TEACHING TEACHERS

In the 10 years that have passed since Americans first acknowledged the educational crisis facing their children, many schools have changed the way they teach math and science, and the effort appears to be paying off.

In some cases, schools must first reeducate their teachers before they can implement innovative programs for teaching math and science. One way is to invite university professors into the classroom to develop hands-on exercises that students then carry out. For example, scientists at the University of Arizona in Tucson developed the Marvelous Munching Melanopus Project for Tucson public schools. This program uses grasshoppers to teach basic biology. In another program, two professors at the California Institute of Technology (Caltech) in Pasadena teamed up with the Pasadena public-school system to develop the Science for Early Educational Development program.

The underlying theme in these and similar programs is the need to make learning an interactive experience. Students taught exclusively from textbooks do not retain what they learn as readily as those who actively participate in their education.

For schools without access to university science professors, help is still available—by mail—thanks to a former teacher now living in Brattleboro, Vermont. In 1987, Casey Murrow founded the Teachers Laboratory, Incorporated, a mail-order catalog business that sells materials for teaching math and science through the eighth grade. Two-thirds of the instructional kits Murrow sells, which include suggestions for use, cannot be obtained anywhere else. Teachers Laboratory, Incorporated, also publishes a 20-page newsletter of book and resource reviews, critiques of new classroom strategies, and teacher-authored articles that describe successful classroom experiments. Each bimonthly issue is keyed to a specific math or science theme, which is reflected in that issue's feature articles.

CURRICULUM CHANGES IN NEW YORK

New York City schools are revamping their math and science requirements to further enhance the ability of their graduates to get jobs or enter college. In 1993, New York City hired Ramon Cortines as the new chancellor of schools; less than eight months later, Cortines proposed a sweeping change in the graduation requirements for all New York City high-school students.

The seed for Cortines' plan was planted by his predecessor, Joseph Fernandez. Fernandez dictated that, beginning in 1995, students had to take three science courses to

Advanced mathematics and laboratory science courses have become part of the standard curriculum for high-school students in the New York City school system.

graduate; pupils already were required to pass three math courses. However, under this plan, students could meet their math and science requirements by taking such nonacademic courses as consumer math, which explains how to balance a checkbook or calculate a supermarket discount; or basic human biology, which teaches anatomy, but does not require complex analyses or laboratory experiments. In effect, students in New York City high schools could graduate without ever taking algebra or learning the interdependencies of different species.

The new plan proposed by Cortines, and implemented at the beginning of the 1994 school year, phases out the nonacademic math and science courses, forcing all students to take three *academic*, or college-preparatory, courses in math and science to graduate.

Critics of the plan cite several problems with it: a lack of money to implement it; the need for teacher reeducation; and the effect such a curriculum will have on unprepared students. Indeed, the plan will cost millions of dollars to be successful—$30 million for ninth-grade math and science classes alone, to buy new textbooks and equipment and to retrain teachers.

Opinions differ as to how students will deal with the more challenging coursework. During the 1992-93 school year, only 16 percent of juniors and seniors were enrolled in the now-mandatory math classes; this number was only slightly higher—24 percent—for academic science classes. Some parents fear that when the other 76 to 84 percent of the student population is enrolled in these classes, the high-school dropout rate will increase as some students find themselves unable to keep up in class.

A similar program introduced in a Brooklyn, New York, high school indicates otherwise. Four years ago, Superintendent Joyce R. Coppin began phasing out nonacademic math courses after noticing that students in elementary and high schools were being taught the same arithmetic. She says that students "were being denied the opportunity to take courses they could indeed pass." Today enrollment in academic math courses at her school has doubled, and proficiency has risen sharply.

Cortines says that the students least prepared for the new citywide curriculum— those pupils with standardized test scores in the lowest-third percentile—will be offered summer-school preparatory courses, along with tutoring. And some courses may be taught over three semesters rather than two, or stretched over two periods of the day instead of one, to allow more time to teach and assimilate the more rigorous subject matter. New York City math and science teachers are also being retrained for the shift in curriculum.

SCHOOLS GO ON-LINE

Students in some schools now study math and science with the help of desktop computers and sophisticated multimedia software developed specifically for the classroom. These packages are a far cry from the first educational-software programs introduced 10 years ago. Two multimedia programs released in 1994, *Through the Woods* and *At the Seashore*, allow children from kindergarten to second grade to "explore" a wooded area or a beach from a desktop computer. If a child sees something interesting while "walking" around, he or she can zoom in on it and then print the scene to save in an "electronic album." The student can then add text and other information to the pictures, and teachers can grade the albums using various criteria. During these on-line nature walks, students can also click on pictures to hear recorded descriptions.

The Eduquest division of IBM Corporation and the Children's Television Workshop (CTW), which created *Sesame Street*, are jointly producing *Through the Woods* and *At the Seashore*. The programs can be installed on a school's computer network and then run simultaneously in different classrooms. Single-classroom versions are also available.

The Internet provides another on-line education option for some schools. In Queens, New York, high-school students recently "connected" with students from around the world to discuss how to measure the circumference of the Earth. The program was part of Electronic Partners, which links New York City public schools with other schools in the city, country, or world.

Another Internet program, due to begin in the fall of 1995, will use high-school students to collect scientific data about global change. The Global Learning and Observations to Benefit the Environment (GLOBE) project will be headquartered on the Internet. Students from the 1,500 participating high schools will enter the information they gather—such as daily measurements of water, air, and soil—into a central on-line database. Any school with an Internet connection can access the database and analyze the information it contains.

Abigail W. Polek

SEISMOLOGY

QUAKE DEVASTATES KOBE

On January 17, 1995, a strong earthquake struck near the Japanese port city of Kobe, killing more than 5,300 people. This tremor was the most expensive earthquake in history, having caused an estimated $200 billion in damages. For comparison, the earthquake beneath Northridge, California, a year earlier racked up a damage bill of $20 billion to $30 billion.

Called the Hyogo-ken Nanbu earthquake by Japanese scientists, the Kobe earthquake was the most damaging to hit Japan since the Great Kanto earthquake killed 143,000 people in Tokyo and Yokohama in 1923. The Kobe quake injured more than 26,000 people and destroyed some 50,000 buildings. It left one-fifth of Kobe's 1.5 million population homeless.

The disaster began at 5:46 A.M. when a geologic fault gave way beneath Awaji-shima Island in Osaka Bay, southwest of Kobe City. Rock faces on opposite sides of the fault suddenly slipped past each other by as much as 7 feet (2 meters) horizontally and 4.2 feet (1.2 meters) vertically. The rupture raced northeast along the fault, directly toward Kobe City. In terms of strength, the quake had a magnitude of 6.9, the same size as the Northridge earthquake that struck near Los Angeles on January 17, 1994.

As one of the most seismically active nations in the world, Japan spends considerable effort alerting its population to the dangers of earthquakes and preparing for such disasters. But the Kobe earthquake caught this city and the entire nation off guard because officials had not stressed the seismic dangers in this part of Japan. Instead, scientists and officials had targeted much of their efforts on Tokyo and surrounding areas, where they expect a magnitude-8.0 earthquake in the near future.

Tokyo residents are constantly reminded of the seismic dangers they face by the small and moderate earthquakes that frequently rattle their city. But the Kobe area has far fewer earthquakes, and had not faced any major shock since 1916. As a result, its leaders and populace did not expect damaging tremors.

The primary reason for Kobe's tremendous damage toll was the proximity of the earthquake. The fault ran directly beneath the city, making the quake a direct hit. Damage also ran high because the city had a large number of older structures, built before Japan strengthened its construction codes in

The powerful earthquake that shook the Japanese port city of Kobe in January 1995 killed more than 5,300 people and toppled elevated highways claimed by engineers to be quake-proof.

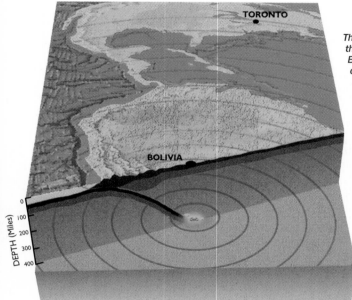

BOLIVIA

TORONTO

DEPTH (Miles)
0
100
200
300
400

The most powerful earthquake in the world in more than five years occurred 400 miles beneath Bolivia, South America. Because of its great depth, the quake's reverberations were felt as far away as Toronto, Canada. Little damage was reported, even in South America, despite the quake's 8.3 magnitude.

GREAT QUAKE BENEATH BOLIVIA

The world's largest earthquake in five years struck deep beneath Bolivia on June 8, 1994. People in cities as far away as Seattle, Washington; Minneapolis, Minnesota; and Toronto, Canada, felt the ground shaking from this giant tremor. The quake measured magnitude 8.3, and occurred at a depth of 400 miles (640 kilometers) below ground. Seismologists say that this is the largest deep earthquake on record.

It shook hard enough to set the planet ringing like a bell for months on end. But because it struck so far below the surface, the quake caused limited destruction in South America.

Most earthquakes occur in the upper 18.5 miles (30 kilometers) of the Earth's crust, where rock is brittle. In deeper layers of the crust and mantle, temperatures are high enough that rock bends rather than breaks. The exception occurs in so-called subduction zones, places where cold pieces of crust dive down into the mantle. The Bolivian earthquake occurred in one of these slabs of crust sinking into the mantle.

Prior to the Bolivian earthquake, seismologists had never received reports of detectable shaking felt so far from the epicenter. The large size and depth of the Bolivian tremor accounted for its widespread shaking.

Following the Bolivian quake, the planet continued to vibrate in a manner imperceptible to people. The extremely long-period seismic waves resembled the overtones produced by striking a bell. By recording these waves, researchers learned more about the density of rock deep within Earth.

COLOMBIAN KILLER

A strong earthquake rocked southwest Colombia on June 6, 1994, triggering avalanches and mudslides that buried sever-

1981. The traditional-style houses, with weak wooden walls and heavy tile roofs, suffered extensive damage.

Although modern structures fared much better, even these did not live up to the expectations of Japanese engineers. Following California's Loma Prieta earthquake in 1989 and the Northridge quake in 1994, Japanese engineers had boasted that their highways and other key structures could withstand powerful earthquakes. The Kobe quake proved them wrong by bringing down part of the Hanshin Expressway, the main traffic artery through Kobe. It also collapsed bridge spans on the Shinkansen, the bullet-train route from Tokyo to western Japan.

U.S. scientists said the Kobe earthquake taught important lessons about how future tremors will affect urban areas in North America. In particular, the geology of the Kobe area bears a close resemblance to that on the east side of San Francisco Bay in California. There the Hayward fault runs directly beneath major urban areas such as Oakland. Like Kobe, these cities have a large number of older buildings. They also sit on soft bayside sediments that can amplify seismic shaking. U.S. seismologists have projected that the East Bay stands a one-in-four chance of experiencing a magnitude-7.0 shock by the year 2020.

al mountain villages. Government officials estimated the quake may have killed as many as 1,000 people and left 13,000 homeless. The quake measured magnitude 6.8.

Centered near the town of Torbio, which lies some 200 miles (320 kilometers) southwest of Bogotá, the earthquake caused landslides of rock and ice to fall from the steep slopes of the Nevado del Huila Volcano, one of the tallest in South America. The avalanche swept away roads and bridges, hindering rescue workers trying to reach this mountainous region.

EARTHQUAKES AROUND THE WORLD

One of the year's largest quakes struck northern Japan on October 4, killing at least 16 people on Russia's Kuril Islands. The quake was centered about 12 miles (20 kilometers) below the Pacific seafloor east of Japan and south of the Kuril Islands. The quake measured magnitude 8.2, but caused relatively little damage because it occurred in a remote area.

The tremor generated 10-foot (3-meter) tsunami waves that flooded coastal regions in the Kuril Islands. Officials sent out a tsunami warning for most of the Pacific Rim, including Hawaii and the West Coast of the United States. As a precaution, Hawaii closed its public schools and evacuated some coastal areas, but the tsunami did not cause major damage there.

Tsunamis generated by an earthquake in Indonesia ripped through snoozing coastal villages in eastern Java on June 3, 1994. The earthquake measured magnitude 5.9. It killed at least 133 people.

A strong tremor shook northwestern Algeria on August 18, 1994, tearing down thousands of homes made from mud brick. The quake had a magnitude of 5.4. It killed at least 164 people and left up to 10,000 homeless. This was the most devastating quake in the area since 1980.

A major earthquake struck under the Pacific Ocean floor off northern California on September 1, 1994. Although the shock measured magnitude 7.0, it caused little damage because it was centered 108 miles (175 kilometers) from the coast.

Richard Monastersky

SPACE SCIENCE

SPACE-SHUTTLE PROGRAM

The National Aeronautics and Space Administration (NASA) launched seven highly successful science and technology missions, for a grand-total flight time of more than 81 days in orbit. In 1994, the shuttle fleet deployed 832 tons of cargo into space, carried an additional 105 tons of cargo to orbit and back, and lofted 42 astronauts into space, including crew members from Russia, Japan, and the European Space Agency (ESA).

Twenty-five years after the first lunar landing, a veteran Russian cosmonaut, Sergei Krikalev, flew aboard a U.S. spacecraft for the first time, as the space shuttle *Discovery* lifted off its pad on February 3, 1994. It was the first space trip jointly staffed by the United States and Russia since 1975, when *Apollo* and *Soyuz* capsules joined and their crews shook hands in Earth orbit.

In April 1994, the space shuttle *Endeavour* carried the international Space Radar Laboratory (SRL) into orbit for the first of two flights in 1994. Comprising two radars and an atmospheric instrument, SRL made unprecedented measurements of Earth's surface and continued observations of the atmosphere that began in 1982.

The space shuttle *Columbia* was launched July 8, 1994, on a 14-day microgravity-research mission designated STS-65. The mission, the second International Microgravity Laboratory flight, was a worldwide research effort into the behavior of materials and life in the microgravity environment of space. The seven-member crew of STS-65 conducted 82 experiments that were developed by more than 200 scientists from 13 different countries.

The second Space Radar Laboratory mission was launched with *Endeavour* on September 30 on a highly successful flight that repeated many of April's SRL investigations. This flight allowed the scientists to observe the changes of seasons in different ecological settings. Both SRL missions carried an instrument to study levels of carbon monoxide in Earth's atmosphere.

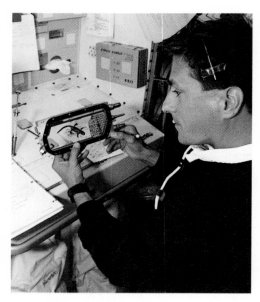

Astronaut Donald A. Thomas studies the effect of microgravity on a salamander during a 14-day mission of the space shuttle Columbia in July 1994. The crew conducted 82 experiments during the long voyage.

NASA's Office of Mission to Planet Earth completed a series of shuttle flights dedicated to studying Earth's atmosphere and its relation to the Sun. Designated the ATLAS series, these flights in 1992, 1993, and 1994 provided scientists with three snapshots of the Sun and the chemistry of Earth's atmosphere, focusing on ozone depletion.

PLANETARY EXPLORERS

In May 1994, the Clementine mission, sponsored by the Department of Defense Ballistic Missile Defense Organization, completed systematic mapping of the lunar surface to produce the first global digital map of the Moon. The digital data set covers 14.7 million square miles (38 million square kilometers) of the Moon mapped in 11 colors in the visible and near-infrared parts of the spectrum during the mission's 71 days in lunar orbit, providing the first view of the global color of the Moon.

The Ulysses spacecraft—the first probe to explore the Sun's environment at high latitudes—completed the first phase of its primary mission when it passed over the Sun's southern pole on November 5. The spacecraft began its traverse of the Sun's northern pole on June 19, 1995. Mission scientists have found that in the Sun's polar regions, the solar wind flows at a very high velocity of

about 2 million miles (3.2 million kilometers) per hour, nearly double the speed at which the solar wind flows at lower latitudes.

At 6:02 A.M. EDT on October 12, 1994, scientists lost radio contact with the Magellan spacecraft; the spacecraft is believed to have burned up in the Venusian atmosphere within two days. The vast database on Venus produced by Magellan includes radar images of 98 percent of the planet's cloud-covered surface, and a comprehensive gravity-field map for 95 percent of the planet.

A propulsion-system failure was the most likely cause of the unexpected loss of the Mars Observer spacecraft, according to a report issued by an independent investigation board. The board concluded that an inadvertent mixing of nitrogen tetroxide and monomethyl hydrazine fuels ruptured a fuel line, causing a pressurized leak that sent the spacecraft into a high spin rate. The Mars Observer spacecraft was to have been the first U.S. spacecraft to study Mars since the Viking missions 18 years ago, but fell silent just three days before entering Martian orbit.

During the third week of July 1994, the United States and the world paused to remember a pivotal moment 25 years earlier, when a voice radioed back to Earth, "Houston, Tranquility Base here. The *Eagle* has landed." The first manned landing on the Moon on July 20, 1969, was marked by observances and lectures in cities across the country, a variety of televised retrospectives, and an appearance at the White House by *Apollo 11* astronauts Neil Armstrong, Buzz Aldrin, and Michael Collins.

EXPLORING THE UNIVERSE FROM AFAR

After five weeks of engineering checkout, optical alignment, and instrument calibration, scientists declared in mid-January that the December 1993 space-shuttle mission to service the Hubble Space Telescope (HST) had been successful in correcting the telescope's faulty vision. The first pictures were also released from the two cameras that received corrective optics.

For the first time, an orbiting astrophysics satellite was put into the "hands" of an artificial intelligence (AI) computer program that operates the spacecraft without people at the controls during overnight shifts, reducing operating costs. During the 14-hour autonomous-operation periods of NASA's Extreme Ultraviolet Explorer (EUVE), the AI-based software conducts health and safety tests on the EUVE science instrument aboard the satellite.

NASA's Wind spacecraft successfully rocketed into orbit aboard a Delta II expendable launch vehicle from Cape Canaveral on November 1, 1994. The main scientific goal of the mission was to measure the mass, momentum, and energy of the solar wind that somehow is transferred into the space environment around Earth.

SPACE STATION FREEDOM

Progress continued on the International Space Station program, which produced almost 25,000 pounds (11,340 kilograms) of flight-qualified hardware in 1994. The program reached a major milestone with the completion of a crucial Systems Design Review (SDR) for the new space station architecture. The SDR resulted in a consensus among its multinational program managers and contractors on the technical validity of the new design, and its capability to support interfaces with the space shuttle and Russian launch vehicles.

At a White House ceremony, President Clinton honored the Apollo 11 *astronauts on the silver anniversary of the first manned Moon landing.*

INTERNATIONAL COOPERATION

As the cooperative efforts between the United States and Russia gained momentum in 1994, significant amounts of spaceflight hardware began flowing between the two nations. In May 1994, NASA shipped the first set of solar-array modules for the International Space Station program. These modules were prototypes of flight units that were delivered later in the year.

Hardware to allow the space shuttle to dock with the Russian *Mir* space station was shipped from the Energia Production Facility in Kaliningrad, near Moscow, to the Rockwell Aerospace facility in California. In November, after integrated checkouts were complete, the entire docking system was delivered to the Kennedy Space Center (KSC). It will be installed in the shuttle *Atlantis* early in 1995.

NASA and the Canadian Space Agency (CSA) reached an agreement in early June 1994 that provides for expanded cooperation in space science, microgravity research, Mission to Planet Earth, and Canada's continuation as a full partner in the International Space Station program.

Representatives of the governments of the United States, Canada, Japan, and several European countries met for the first time with representatives of the Russian Federation to discuss how to bring Russia into the partnership.

NASA and the Russian Space Agency signed two significant documents that underpinned Russian participation in the International Space Station program. The first was an interim agreement that provides for initial Russian participation in the International Space Station until an intergovernmental agreement can be concluded. The second was a $400 million contract for Russian space hardware, services, and data.

Dennis L. Mammana

United States Manned Spaceflights—1994

Mission	Launch/Landing	Orbiter	Primary Payload
STS-60	Feb. 3/Feb. 11	*Discovery*	**Wake Shield Facility:** Deployment of satellite intended to fly behind the shuttle for the purpose of growing high-grade semiconductors in the "ultravacuum" of the shuttle's wake.
STS-62	Mar. 4/Mar. 18	*Columbia*	**U.S. Microgravity Payload (USMP-2):** Materials-science research that included experiments designed to determine the effects of microgravity on the growth of semiconductor crystals.
STS-59	Apr. 9/Apr. 20	*Endeavour*	**Space Radar Laboratory (SRL-1):** Sophisticated radar equipment designed to create a highly accurate 3-D map of Earth's mountains, deserts, forests, oceans, rivers, and volcanoes.
STS-65	July 8/July 23	*Columbia*	**International Microgravity Laboratory:** Included over 80 experiments developed by more than 200 scientists from 13 countries to test the development, reproduction, and adaptation of organisms to long-term spaceflight.
STS-64	Sept. 9/Sept. 20	*Discovery*	**LIDAR In-Space Technology Experiment (LITE):** Global-climate experiment, which involved bouncing laser light off particles suspended in Earth's upper atmosphere and back up to a telescope in the shuttle's cargo bay.
STS-68	Sept. 30/Oct. 11	*Endeavour*	**Space Radar Laboratory (SRL-2):** Second flight of this sophisticated Earth-mapping radar equipment used to generate detailed maps to aid scientists in predicting volcanic eruptions and earthquakes.
STS-66	Nov. 3/Nov. 14	*Atlantis*	**Atmospheric Laboratory for Applications and Science (ATLAS-3):** Instruments to study Earth's atmosphere, particularly the ozone layer and the effects of solar infrared radiation interacting with human-produced chemicals in the stratosphere.

- Sergei K. Krikalev became the first Russian cosmonaut to fly aboard a U.S. shuttle.
- Released six metal spheres for tracking by space-debris experts on Earth.
- Several attempts to release the Wake Shield Facility failed.

- Series of tests focused on new devices that will be used aboard the planned international space station.
- Activated laboratory module in the cargo bay and conducted experiments on new-drug development.
- Refitted shuttle's mechanical arm with a new electromagnetic grappling system.

- Radar system scanned 12 percent of Earth's surface and 25 percent of its land area, generating images of ancient rivers, the "lost city" of Ubar, and other buried archaeological ruins.
- Monitored carbon monoxide levels, enabling scientists to track global air pollution.

- Crew included Chiaki Naito-Makai, the first Japanese woman to fly in space.
- Mission of 14 days, 17 hours, and 55 minutes set a shuttle endurance record—the longest U.S. spaceflight in 20 years to date.
- Several experiments focused on the effect of weightlessness on aquatic animals.

- Laser light-detecting and ranging instrument (LIDAR) used for detailed study of the atmosphere.
- Astronauts engaged in six hours of untethered spacewalking to test NASA's jet pack, which was designed for emergency use by astronauts in the event of a safety-line break.
- Deployment and recapture of the Spartan-201 satellite, which studied the Sun's corona and solar wind.

- Eleven-day Earth-mapping mission part of repeat flight of SRL.
- Environmental instruments detected an intentional oil spill in the North Sea.
- Initial shuttle launch on August 28 aborted 1.9 seconds before liftoff due to sensor problem.

- Most of the mission's experiments were devoted to atmospheric research on the depletion of Earth's ozone layer.
- Deployment and retrieval of German-built CRISTA-SPAS satellite, which was equipped with infrared and ultraviolet telescopes used to make observations of Earth's atmosphere.
- Experiment testing the effect of weightlessness on fetal development centered on 10 female rats, which were the first pregnant mammals to fly aboard a U.S. spacecraft.

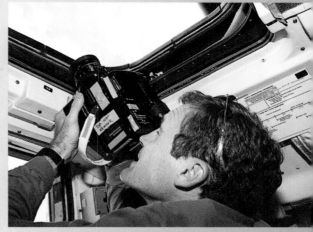

Astronaut James Halsell, Jr., photographs Earth as Columbia *passes over California.*

During the testing of a jet-powered backpack, astronaut Mark C. Lee floats untethered above Discovery's *cargo bay.*

In February 1994, cosmonaut Sergei Krikalev became the first Russian to fly on a space-shuttle mission.

TRANSPORTATION

BIG BOATS

A British firm, the Peninsular and Oriental Steam Navigation Company (P. & O.), announced plans to build the world's largest cruise liner. The ship, anticipated to weigh 100,000 tons, will compete for the weight record with a ship being built for 1996 service by the Carnival Corporation. The P. & O. liner, scheduled for service in 1997, should top the Carnival liner by about 5 tons. Both ships will surpass the size of the now-retired 83,673-ton *Queen Elizabeth*—the heaviest cruise ship ever to sail.

P. & O.'s ship will be built by the Italian firm Fincantieri for $385 million. The ship will be based in Florida and will cruise the Caribbean as part of the Princess Cruise line. The 2,600 passengers will enjoy such features as a simulated golf driving range; a virtual-reality theater; a suspended, transparent swimming pool; and a nightclub that sits above the ocean.

RECREATIONAL BOATS

Designers of recreational sailboats have developed several innovations to achieve greater speeds. Trifoiler Incorporated, a small company in Lakewood, California, began to sell a unique sailboat called a "trifoiler," which lifts off the water's surface when moving at high speeds. The boat, which is 29 feet (8.8 meters) long, appears to be a trimaran, having three parallel hulls attached by struts. Two sails rise above the very thin outer hulls. The two passengers sit in hollowed-out compartments in the center hull.

At high speeds, all three hulls rise above the water, as if the boat were flying. Stability is maintained by two L-shaped foils, which remain submerged and act as underwater wings. As a result, under optimal conditions, the trifoiler's speed can approach 30 knots. A specially formulated prototype of the boat attained speeds just under the record speed for sailboats (46.52 knots). Rough seas slow down the trifoiler, and light winds cause it to operate as a traditional sailboat, with hulls in the water.

A second new recreational sailboat, the *Melges 24*, employs technologies first seen in

the yacht *America³*, which gained fame in the 1992 America's Cup race. Built by the small company owned by Harry "Buddy" Melges, co-skipper of the *America³* in the 1992 race, the *Melges 24* features a 6-foot (1.8-meter) keel at the bottom of which is a 624-pound (283-kilogram) lead bulb. The heavy bulb gives the boat a low center of gravity, and therefore greater stability than a similarly keeled boat without the bulb.

Because the bulb at the bottom of the keel can attract kelp and other plants as the boat moves through the water, the keel has a moving stainless-steel blade to eliminate the plants that otherwise would slow the boat. The *Melges 24* also has a number of parts—including mast, rudder, and tiller—made of carbon composite, a light but strong material that enhances the boat's maneuverability. The *Melges 24* is 24 feet (7.3 meters) long and is capable of speeds approaching 25 knots.

ROUGH SEAS

A large ferry, the *Estonia*, capsized in the storm-tossed waters of the Baltic Sea in the early morning of September 28, 1994. More than 800 of the 1,000 people aboard perished. Jointly owned by the Estonian government and a Swedish shipping firm, the *Estonia* was traveling from Tallinn, Estonia, to Stockholm, Sweden. The scene of the tragedy was close to the southern tip of Finland, and rescue workers from that country helped in efforts that saved about 140 people—pulled from darkness and 50° F (10° C) water in winds higher than 50 miles (80 kilometers) per hour.

The *Estonia*, which was 515 feet (157 meters) long with six decks, was in the middle of a 15-hour trip across the Baltic Sea. Many of the passengers were asleep when the boat went down. Survivors described a sudden lurching of the ship, followed by its sinking in a matter of minutes. Investigators considered the possibility that water had burst into and flooded the ship's hold, perhaps near the large doors through which vehicles and other cargo were loaded.

There was also bad news in the cruise-ship business. In June and July 1994, during trips from New York City to Bermuda, an outbreak of Legionnaires' disease, a rare respiratory-system infection, affected the passengers aboard the Celebrity Cruises ship *Horizon*. About a dozen cases of the disease were confirmed, and one death occurred. The disease is acquired when waterborne Legionnaires'-disease bacteria are picked up by air blowing over the surface of infected water; the contaminated air is then inhaled into the lungs. Hence, the disease has been associated with air conditioners and whirlpool baths.

In Bermuda, the 1,200 passengers evacuated the *Horizon* for 24 hours, during which time the crew cleaned the ship's water systems. The cleaning involved sailing to open sea, dumping millions of gallons of water, and flushing the ship's plumbing system with chlorine. Some passengers elected to fly home from Bermuda; the others reboarded the *Horizon* for the return trip. All passengers received refunds. Celebrity Cruises took the ship out of service for a period in late July. After further inspections and cleaning, the *Horizon* resumed service to Bermuda.

HIGH-SPEED TRAINS

Interest and progress in high-speed trains have dimmed somewhat in the United States in recent years. In Texas, the High-Speed Rail Authority abandoned its plans to build a 200-mile (322-kilometer)-per-hour bullet train—a high-speed conventional train that can attain speeds beyond 150 miles (241 kilometers) per hour—having failed to raise enough money to move forward with construction. As for magnetically levitated trains, or maglevs, the Clinton administration stopped new federal funding of research.

One bright spot is in Germany, where the government announced backing for a maglev train that eventually will run from Berlin to Hamburg at speeds approaching

During a trip from New York to Bermuda in 1994, a severe outbreak of Legionnaires' disease occurred among passengers on the Horizon cruise ship (above). Public-health officials traced the outbreak to a contaminated water system.

300 miles (483 kilometers) per hour. If constructed, the maglev, which travels while suspended by magnets on a cushion of air, will make the trip from Hamburg to Berlin in about one hour—compared to almost three hours by conventional trains. The German government has approved $3.5 billion for this "Transrapid" project; private companies will fund the remaining part of the $5.6 billion total cost. For a number of years, the Transrapid has existed in the form of a 19-mile (30.6-kilometer) demonstration loop in the city of Lathen, Germany. A prototype maglev train on that loop set the world speed record for trains: 281 miles (452 kilometers) per hour.

Another bright spot is in South Korea. A British-French consortium, GEC Alsthom, contracted with the South Korean government to help construct a high-speed train line connecting Seoul to the South Korean port of Pusan. The consortium, which makes bullet trains that currently service Paris, France, will provide a fleet of these trains. As part of a $2.1 billion contract, GEC Alsthom will provide electronic systems in addition to the locomotives. The Korean project is expected to be completed in 2001.

AIRPLANES AND AIRPORTS

Air travelers can take advantage of several new conveniences. Avis, a nationwide car-rental company, began using a system of satellite transmissions and cellular car phones to give geographical information to customers at La Guardia Airport in New York City. The technology can inform a driver of the car's location to within a few feet. As the driver moves away from the airport, the car's location is shown on a video-screen map inside the car.

Airlines have also begun to install interactive video screens for use by passengers. Northwest Airlines is one of a number of companies that have installed systems allowing passengers to play video games, watch movies, send faxes, and dial up such travel information as weather

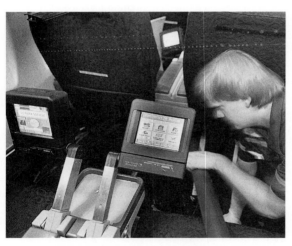

Interactive television on aircraft will allow passengers to play video games, watch movies, or even shop during flight. Northwest Airlines (above) and other domestic and foreign carriers are installing the necessary equipment on many of their planes.

reports and connecting gates—all without moving from their assigned seats. Most features are free, although some, such as Nintendo video games, are not. Future interactive video systems could give passengers the ability to watch live television, make hotel reservations, and even gamble while in the air.

Donald W. Cunningham

VOLCANOLOGY

DISASTER AVERTED IN PAPUA NEW GUINEA

In September 1994, two volcanic cones erupted on the eastern end of Papua New Guinea, covering the port city of Rabaul with a thick layer of ash. Although the town has a population of 30,000, only a handful of people died in the eruption, thanks to careful planning by authorities and more than a bit of geologic luck. Volcanologists successfully forecast the eruptions, allowing the residents to escape the endangered town.

The town of Rabaul, now buried under tons of ash and rocks, was situated within a giant sunken crater called a caldera, which formed during a massive volcanic eruption some 1,400 years ago. Sitting on the edge of a 6.2-mile (10-kilometer)-wide harbor formed by the crater, Rabaul was the largest city on the island of New Britain, part of Papua New Guinea.

Several recently active volcanic cones exist along the edge of the Rabaul caldera. Two erupted violently in 1937, killing more than 500 people. In the 1970s and 1980s, the caldera hosted many earthquakes and produced other ominous signs. Fearing the possibility of a huge eruption like the one that formed the caldera, scientists and civil-defense officials educated the public about volcanic hazards and drew up evacuation plans for the town.

That work bore fruit on September 18, 1994, when a magnitude-5.1 earthquake occurred beneath the harbor. A storm of aftershocks, which averaged two jolts per minute, rocked the city all night. Given that strong geologic warning, the town started evacuating during that night—only hours before two volcanoes erupted early the next morning. The cones, named Vulcan and Tavurvur, sent plumes of ash more than 13 miles (21 kilometers) into the atmosphere, covering the town of Rabaul with more than 8 inches (20 centimeters) of ash. Combined with rain, the ash formed a heavy mud, collapsing many roofs in Rabaul. The evacuation continued during the eruption, forcing 53,000 people from their homes.

The eruption from Vulcan ceased after three days, while Tavurvur continued spouting for weeks. According to press reports, blocks of volcanic rock as big as cars dropped into the harbor. The eruption destroyed a quarter of the buildings in Rabaul and damaged at least half. In terms of size, the blasts ranked about as large as the one from Mount St. Helens in 1980.

VOLCANIC HAZARDS
AROUND THE WORLD

The Indonesian archipelago is known for its intense volcanic activity. In June 1994, an eruption of Indonesia's Rinjani Volcano covered nearby villages in ash. Later that year, water mixed with ash near the summit to create mudflows, or lahars, that killed 30 people.

Merapi is one of Indonesia's most active volcanoes. The summit of Merapi—one of Java's 35 active volcanoes—collapsed during an eruption on November 22, 1994, sending an incendiary avalanche down its slopes. The flow killed 41 people and injured another 43. In total, over 6,000 people were evacuated from the area.

The Klyuchevskoi Volcano erupted in October 1994 on Russia's Kamchatka Peninsula. The ash cloud rose to a height of 9.3 to 12.4 miles (15 to 20 kilometers), and avalanches of glowing rock roared down the mountain's north slope. Interesting images of the eruption were captured by scientists flying on the National Aeronautics and Space Administration's (NASA's) space shuttle *Endeavour*, which carried the Spaceborne Imaging Radar experiment, a radar device capable of detecting changes in the land surface.

The same experiment captured images of Hawaii's Kilauea Volcano, which has been erupting nearly constantly since 1983, the longest-running eruption known. The southern portion of Kilauea is sliding toward the ocean at a geologically fast rate of 4 inches (10 centimeters) per year. Scientists think

the movement of the mountain could produce major earthquakes and tsunamis. It also has the potential to cause catastrophic landslides, although the chances of such an event are remote because they happen only once every 100,000 years or so.

In June 1994, two volcanoes in Zaïre attracted attention with their signs of awakening. The volcano Nyiragongo raised concerns because it looms over the city of Goma, where 1 million Rwandans sought refuge from the bloody civil war in their neighboring country. Situated only 11 miles (18 kilometers) north of Goma, Nyiragongo in the past had erupted lava that nearly reached the city. Also near Goma, another volcano, named Nyamuragira, showed evidence of renewed activity as well. Neither volcano produced a major eruption.

Scientists accurately predicted the eruption of the twin volcanoes Vulcan (at left) and Tavurvur on the island of New Britain in Papua New Guinea, allowing for the evacuation of most nearby residents.

The volcano Popocatepetl near Mexico City grew active in December 1994, threatening tens of thousands of people living near the mountain. Volcanic earthquakes and puffs of ash prompted authorities to evacuate 75,000 people who live nearby. The volcano lies 37 miles (60 kilometers) southeast of Mexico City. More than 30 million people live within view of its summit.

Richard Monastersky

ZOOLOGY

New Species Discovered in Vietnam and Laos

When rumors of a strange cowlike creature living in Vietnam reached scientists, they sat up and took notice. At first, the evidence was only superficial: Vietnamese villagers came forward bearing three sets of long, straight horns belonging to an animal that could not be readily identified. The horns surfaced in the Vu Quang Nature Reserve, a "lost world" of remote mountainous forests straddling the borders of Vietnam and Laos. In 1992, after examining the mysterious horns, British zoologist John MacKinnon and a team of five Vietnamese scientists explored Vu Quang in search of more evidence. A year later, they announced that they had examined the skulls, hides, teeth, and horns of an animal that local villagers called the *saola*, which

A new species of barking deer (above) is just one of the several previously unknown mammal species recently discovered in the remote mountainous forests along the borders of Vietnam and Laos.

translates to "spindle horn." According to the scientists, DNA tests proved that the *saola* was an entirely new genus and species of bovid related to oxen. MacKinnon and his colleagues gave the *saola* the scientific designation *Pseudoryx nghetinhensis*, and described it

as weighing about 220 pounds (100 kilograms), standing about 3 feet (1 meter) tall at the shoulders, and having small hooves adapted for climbing on mountainous promontories. Although the scientists had collected the skulls, hides, teeth, and horns of more than 20 specimens gathered by villagers in the region, a living *Pseudoryx* eluded them.

In 1994, two adult *saolas* were captured by farmers and transported to a botanical garden in Hanoi. Both animals died within a few months. Better news came from the Vu Quang region, where it was discovered that the *saola* was distributed over a larger territory than first suspected, including a large area of Laos that is even less developed and less easily explored than the Vietnamese mountains. Surveys suggested that a few hundred *Pseudoryx* may be found in each country.

More discoveries followed. In addition to *Pseudoryx*, scientists found evidence of two deerlike mammals that had never been identified. The first, a new species of muntjac, or barking deer, was described based on horns and skins, then was seen in the wild by biologists who also examined a specimen that had been captured by farmers. The deer was about 50 percent larger than any known muntjac, and was christened the giant muntjac. DNA testing confirmed it was indeed a new species, and perhaps a new genus. The second deer may prove to be more difficult to identify. Locally named *quang khem*, or "slow-running deer," it is known only from a skull with horns recovered by a Vietnamese biologist while exploring a region north of Vu Quang. Biologists fear it might already be extinct.

In addition to the new mammals, researchers in Vu Quang have thus far discovered a new species of carplike fish, two new birds, a previously unknown tortoise, and a number of birds that are close to extinction.

Unfortunately, the potential habitat for the *saola*, the giant muntjac, and the slow-running deer is far from secure. The region, which John MacKinnon described as "a biological gold mine," is being mined by people who are interested in resources other than rare wildlife. Loggers are harvesting large tracts of old-growth conifers in Laos, and building roads into the heart of the reserves. Hundreds of illegal hunters are entering the reserves to trap animals for food—rare species included—and to poach elephants and tigers. Another ominous threat is the gigantic Nam Theun II dam project, which is expected to flood about 200 square miles (500 square kilometers) of forest.

BOX TURTLES IN TROUBLE

Box turtles have long been popular as pets. They are easy to feed, they live a long time, and, until recently, they were abundant. When conservationists began noticing declining numbers of box turtles in many regions of the United States, they assumed that human encroachment and habitat destruction were to blame. They found that all of the half dozen species and subspecies of box turtles found from the East Coast to the Rocky Mountains were threatened when the woodlands and prairies where they lived were broken up by development. But in recent years, the turtle's numbers were being depleted at a rate greater than could be explained by loss of habitat. The culprit? Collectors supplying pets to Europe and Asia.

Though long-lived—50 to 75 years is not unusual—box turtles have an extremely low reproductive rate. A typical female produces dozens of eggs during her half-century life, yet only two are likely to hatch and survive to reproductive age. When adult turtles are gathered by the dozens and hundreds, it does not take long before an entire population is depleted.

The commercial turtle trade begins at an elementary level, often with children who collect them in neighborhood woods and fields for a fee of about a dollar each. Exporters wait until they have a sizable shipment—often 1,000 or more—before packaging the turtles into cartons and sending them via commercial airplanes to pet-shop dealers in Europe and Asia. Once they reach their destination, the turtles are worth $30 to $50 each as exotic pets.

The British are particularly fond of turtles, and most American box turtles are destined for the United Kingdom. The English like to release turtles into their yards to serve as animate additions to their home gardens. Therein lies the problem. For decades, most of the demand for such garden turtles was

Box turtles, long a favorite pet in the United States (above), have become immensely popular among European gardeners, creating a demand for the creatures that may soon exceed the supply.

supplied by Mediterranean tortoises collected from North Africa and southern Europe. When trade in those turtles was banned in 1984, British pet dealers turned to the American box turtle, assuming that the land-dwelling species, so popular as a pet among American children, would adapt readily to life outdoors in English gardens.

Unfortunately, the cold, damp winters and short summers of the British Isles cause respiratory ailments and disease among box turtles. Even deadlier is the means of transport from the United States. U.S. Fish and Wildlife agents report discovering cardboard boxes and burlap bags stuffed full of turtles that had been left without food or water for weeks. Even those turtles that survive malnutrition and dehydration during the journey overseas have the odds of survival stacked against them. Investigators concluded that half the box turtles shipped to Europe die within the first month after arriving there.

With more than 25,000 turtles leaving North America each year, herpetologists are concerned that wild populations will not remain sustainable very much longer, and that if the trade continues, it is just a matter of time before box turtles will earn a place on the endangered species list. That would halt their sale and shipment, but not before tens of thousands will have perished. In the meantime, conservationists are lobbying to have the trade monitored and regulated, and to require people engaged in the sale and shipment of turtles to apply for permits.

MOUNTAIN LIONS AND PEOPLE

The mountain lion—also known as the cougar, puma, painter, or panther—is the largest of all American cats. This creature was originally found across virtually all of North and South America, making it the land mammal with the most-extensive native territory in the Western Hemisphere. But as European settlers spread across the continents, so did their intolerance of wild cats and other large predators. Mountain lions were routinely shot, trapped, and poisoned to collect a bounty paid by the U.S. government. By 1950, only a few thousand mountain lions remained, and the species was in danger of being wiped out entirely by bounty hunters. Soon after, restrictions on hunting and the establishment of wildlife sanctuaries helped the lions rebound in some portions of the western states, and their population has been growing ever since. Although precise numbers are not known, it is estimated that 9,000 to 12,000 mountain lions now live in California, Idaho, and Colorado, with lesser numbers in adjacent states.

As mountain-lion numbers increased and as people have moved into remote areas inhabited by the cats, encounters between humans and cougars have become more common. Such encounters have attracted the most attention in California, where the cats are perhaps more abundant than in any other state. Following a 1972 ban on hunting them, the population of mountain lions in California has increased from about 2,200 to at least 5,000. But as the number of cats has gone up, so have their tragic encounters with people. Between 1910 and 1986, there were no confirmed cougar attacks in California. Since then, there have been at least eight, two of them fatal. In April 1994, a woman was attacked and killed while jogging in a state park near Sacramento, and, in December 1994, another woman was killed while walking in a park in San Diego County.

Such attacks are still extremely rare—there have been just 12 fatal attacks by mountain lions in North America since 1890—and even sightings of the shy cats are uncommon. California is the only western state to outlaw cougar hunting, although the cats may be killed when they threaten humans or destroy domestic animals. More than 130 of those "problem cats" were destroyed in 1994, most for attacking pets in suburban areas or for making unusually aggressive appearances in places like shopping centers and school playgrounds. A restricted hunting season would certainly reduce the population of mountain

The comparatively frequent encounters between humans and mountain lions in recent years are a sure sign that the population of these normally reclusive cats has increased substantially.

lions, but conservationists point out that cougars have been actively hunted for decades on Vancouver Island, and attacks there are more common than in many places where the cat has been protected.

One expert, Maurice Hornocker, Ph.D., who has been studying mountain lions since the 1960s, told *The New York Times* that the return of healthy cougar populations is "a raging success story. Like the wolf and the grizzly bear, the mountain lion is a majestic and fascinating animal and, to many people, a symbol of wilderness."

ALIEN INVADERS

They come by land, by air, and by sea, intentionally or by accident, and when they arrive in a place to their liking, they take over. By now, the consequences of introducing alien plants and animals to new environments are well-known. Rabbits shipped to Australia as a cash crop nearly destroyed all agriculture in that nation. European gypsy moths were introduced by accident to Massachusetts in 1869, and have since spread gradually westward, denuding millions of acres of forests along the way.

Few places in North America have been affected as much by nonindigenous species as the Great Lakes. Since the early 20th century—when the Welland Canal was opened to bypass Niagara Falls—Lakes Erie, Huron, Michigan, and Superior have been subjected to wave after wave of invaders. First came the sea lamprey, a marine species native to the Atlantic Ocean that feeds on large fish—weakening and often killing them—by attaching to their sides and feeding on their body fluids. The lamprey found the lake trout and whitefish of the Great Lakes easy pickings, and was in large part responsible for the collapse of those fish populations in the 1950s. When the large fish were gone, alewives arrived to take their place. Like the lamprey, these small baitfish entered the lakes through the canal. Once the large predator fish were gone from the lakes, there was no control on the population of alewives. They multiplied until there were so many they died by the millions, fouling beaches with massive die-offs that had to be cleaned up with bulldozers.

Other invaders of the Great Lakes did not swim—they were carried. The zebra mussel, a small mollusk capable of producing 50,000 eggs a year, arrived as a stowaway in the ballast water of an ocean freighter in 1985 or 1986. This native of the Caspian Sea was released, probably in larval form, into Lake St. Clair, and, within a few years, had spread into all five Great Lakes and many of their connecting waters. Without natural predators to keep them in check, the mussels have become a billion-dollar problem. They live in dense clusters glued to any available object, including piers, docks, buoys, and the intake pipes of water-treatment plants. Attached to the hulls of small boats, they have been carried into smaller inland lakes as well. By devouring enormous amounts of phytoplankton, zebra mussels become a significant new member of the food web wherever they appear—an invader whose influence on other animals is yet to be learned.

Another opportunistic invader whose influence is yet to be discovered is the spiny water flea. At just 0.25 inch (0.63 centimeter) long, this innocuous creature would seem to pose no threat. But it is equipped with a sharply barbed tail that makes it unattractive food for fish, and it reproduces so rapidly that it has the potential to crowd out many other animals competing for the same diet of zooplankton.

In 1994, yet another ballast-tank hitchhiker, the Eurasian ruff, made news when it was discovered to multiply faster than previously suspected. Native to the Baltic Sea, this 3- to 6-inch (7.6- to 15-centimeter) member of the perch family first appeared in Lake Superior in 1985 after an oceangoing ship released its ballast water into the harbor in Duluth, Minnesota. At first, scientists did not know whether the newcomer would survive in the cold waters of Lake Superior or whether there was risk of it spreading to the lower lakes. A 1994 study, however, revealed that the ruff comprised 70 percent of the fish population in Duluth Harbor, making it more abundant there than all other species combined. And it seems to be crowding out the competition: the same study showed that while ruff numbers were increasing, populations of native fish had dropped to less than 20 percent of their 1989 numbers.

The ruff is too small for human consumption and too large to be forage for native fish. Large predators like lake trout and northern pike seem little interested in feeding on it, and the ruff's high reproductive rate and longevity increase the potential for explosive population growth, a situation that could be catastrophic for other aquatic life in the Great Lakes. About the same time that scientists revealed their findings from the Duluth Harbor, the ruff was discovered for the first time in the Michigan waters of Lake Superior, 130 miles (210 kilometers) east of Duluth. Many biologists are certain that it is just a matter of time before the ruff invades the lower Great Lakes and enters their connecting waters. If native fish are unable to compete with the little alien from the Baltic, the ruff could prove to be the most devastating invader to date.

Jerry Dennis

In Memoriam – 1994

ALEKSANDROV, ANATOLY (90), Russian-born scientist who led the Soviet effort to design and build graphite-moderated nuclear reactors. The Chernobyl nuclear plant that exploded in 1986 was of this graphite design. He also headed the Kurchatov Institute, Russia's leading nuclear-research center, since 1959 and had served as president of the Soviet Academy of Sciences. d. Moscow, Russia, Feb. 3.

ASCH, TIMOTHY (62), U.S. anthropologist who produced more than 70 documentary films describing the life and rituals of remote societies in Africa, South America, North America, Afghanistan, and Indonesia. Forty of these films dealt with the Yanomamo Indians in the Amazon rain forests of South America. d. Los Angeles, Calif., Oct. 3.

BEAM, THOMAS R., JR. (48), U.S. infectious-disease specialist who gained recognition for his work on drug-resistant bacteria and viruses. He criticized drug companies for abandoning research on new antibiotics, and directed a two-year project to update and streamline the Food and Drug Administration's (FDA's) approval process for new antibiotics. d. Buffalo, N.Y., Aug. 17.

BERGER, STUART M. (40), U.S. author of diet and health books, including the best-seller *Dr. Berger's Immune Power Diet*, in which he described his weight loss from 420 pounds (191 kilograms) to 210 pounds (95 kilograms). He weighed 365 pounds (166 kilograms) when he died. d. New York City, Feb. 23.

BLOCK, GEORGE E. (67), U.S. surgeon who developed new, safer methods of gastrointestinal surgery and was an expert on the treatment of intestinal cancers and other disorders. d. Chicago, Ill., July 17.

CLARK, R. LEE (87), U.S. physician who helped build a small Houston hospital into one of the world's leading cancer facilities, the M.D. Anderson Cancer Center. He served under Presidents Nixon, Ford, and Carter as senior scientist on the President's Cancer Panel, and had been president of the American Cancer Society. d. Houston, Tex., May 3.

CONN, JEROME W. (86), U.S. physician who discovered the cause of, and developed a treatment for, a severe hormonal disorder that affects the kidneys. Now known as "Conn's syndrome," the condition is caused by an adrenal tumor that causes overproduction of a hormone. d. Naples, Fla., June 12.

DAVIS, BERNARD D. (78), U.S. physician who pioneered bacterial genetic research and helped discover how bacteria synthesize proteins, develop resistance to antibiotics, and undergo mutations. He caused a stir in 1976 when he wrote that medical-school standards were dropping because of the admission of unqualified minority students. d. Belmont, Mass., Jan. 14.

ERIKSON, ERIK (91), German-born psychoanalyst who developed the theory that aspects of personality evolve over one's entire life span, from infancy on, and that experiences later in life can alter the effects of earlier experiences. He believed that society, from one's family and friends to the larger societal units, has a significant effect on the successive changes of personality. His 1950 book *Childhood and Society* described his theories and attracted a widespread audience; the book is still in print. Erikson coined the expression "identity crisis" in the 1970s, bringing him even greater recognition among the college and young-adult populations of the time. His psychobiographies of Martin Luther and Mahatma Gandhi were widely praised; the latter won a Pulitzer Prize and National Book Award. d. Harwich, Mass., May 12.

FULLER, CALVIN S. (92), U.S. chemist who helped develop the first practical solar cell for converting sunlight into electricity. d. Vero Beach, Fla., Oct. 28.

GIMBUTAS, MARIJA (73), Lithuanian-born archaeologist who was an authority on prehistoric Europe and its cultures. She postulated that during the Stone Age, the world was at peace, with societies centered on women, and religions based on goddesses. This culture ended about 6,000 years ago when invaded by another culture that glorified war gods instead of women. d. Los Angeles, Calif., Feb. 2.

GORDON, ARCHER (73), U.S. heart specialist acclaimed as the "father of CPR" for developing cardiopulmonary resuscitation. d. Thousand Oaks, Calif., Sept. 18.

HARRIS, HARRY (74), English-born geneticist who was one of the first scientists to determine the extent of molecular genetic differences among people. He also determined that protein variations matched genetic variations in DNA, and found that extreme variations in enzymes and proteins lead to genetic disease. His work led to the Human Genome Project, which seeks to identify and map every gene in the human body. d. Newtown Square, Pa., July 17.

HERRNSTEIN, RICHARD J. (64), U.S. psychologist whose theory that intelligence is largely inherited drew intense criticism from many quarters. His 1971 articles in *Atlantic Monthly* and the *New York Times* held that those with genetically inferior intelligence were unlikely to succeed. His last book, *The Bell Curve: Intelligence and Class Structure in American Life*, was published shortly after his death and ignited another firestorm of controversy. d. Belmont, Mass., Sept. 13.

HIGINBOTHAM, WILLIAM A. (84), U.S. physicist who helped develop the electronics used in early atomic bombs, and soon thereafter helped found the Federation of American Scientists to advocate controlling nuclear weapons. He also developed, but never patented, the forerunner of the early-1970s video game "Pong." d. Gainesville, Ga., Oct. 27.

HIRST, GEORGE K. (84), U.S. scientist who discovered a way to detect viruses in the blood, which, in turn, led to methods for quantifying the amount of viruses and antibodies being produced to fight them. d. Palo Alto, Calif., Jan. 22.

HODGKIN, DOROTHY (84), British scientist who won the 1964 Nobel Prize in Chemistry for using X-ray analysis to study the internal structure of key biochemical compounds. She also discovered the structure of penicillin, Vitamin B_{12}, and insulin. She was only the third woman to be awarded the Nobel Prize. d. Shipston-on-Stour, England, July 27.

HOUK, VERNON N. (64), U.S. environmental-health specialist internationally known as an authority on the effect of toxic substances on human health. Much of his work was done through the U.S. Centers for Disease Control and Prevention (CDC) in Atlanta. One CDC group that he headed found that lead in paint and gasoline poses a substantial health threat to children. This finding initiated government-led efforts in the early 1980s to remove lead from both paint and gasoline. Another CDC group found that radiation from nuclear-weapons production causes cancer. Houk also was involved in studies of dioxin and Agent Orange. d. Atlanta, Ga., Sept. 11.

JAMES, L. STANLEY (69), New Zealand–born pediatric specialist who researched ways of improving the health and welfare of the fetus in the womb. d. Center Harbor, N.H., Aug. 4.

JERNE, NIELS K. (82), British-born immunologist who shared the 1984 Nobel Prize in Physiology or Medicine for research on the human immune system. His theories explained how antibodies are generated to match a specific bacterium or virus; how the immune system develops; and how the immune system fights disease, but becomes inactive when not needed. d. Pont du Gard, France, Oct. 7.

JOHN, FRITZ (83), German-born mathematician who was a leading expert on partial differential equations that can be used to describe the movements of waves or the boundaries of oscillating objects. d. New Rochelle, N.Y., Feb. 10.

KILDALL, GARY (52), U.S. computer scientist who, in 1973, developed the first practical operating system for personal computers, allowing information to be retrieved from a floppy disk rather than being entered with paper tape or by programming toggle switches. In 1974, he and his wife formed the Digital Research company; he served as the firm's chairman until it was sold in 1991 to Novell. d. Monterey, Calif., July 11.

KINZEY, WARREN G. (58), U.S. anthropologist who studied the evolution of New World monkeys and early hominids, and focused on the relationship between diet and tooth-wear patterns. d. Tarrytown, N.Y., Oct. 1.

LEJEUNE, JEROME (67), French geneticist who, in 1959, discovered the chromosomal abnormality that causes Down syndrome. He found that people with Down syndrome have 47 chromosomes, one more than normal. He also described other disorders caused by extra chromosomes or missing pieces of chromosomes. d. Paris, France, April 3.

LUCK, J. VERNON, SR. (87), U.S. orthopedic surgeon who, in 1961, became one of the first physicians to successfully reattach a severed limb—the arm of a construction worker injured in a traffic accident. He also performed a total hip replacement on a person with hemophilia, and, in 1941, developed the first motorized bone saw that could be sterilized without damaging the drivetrain. d. Los Angeles, Calif., Feb. 14.

LUYTEN, WILLEM J. (95), Dutch East Indian–born astronomer who was an expert on stellar motion, dying white dwarfs (extremely dense stellar bodies thought to be the last stage of a star's life), and the origin of the solar system. He was noted for his development of a computerized photographic-plate scanner, a device that helped automate the cumbersome process of studying star motions. d. Minneapolis, Minn., Nov. 21.

LWOFF, ANDRÉ (92), French biochemist who shared the 1965 Nobel Prize in Physiology or Medicine for work in molecular biology. His research showed how some genes control others and how cell metabolism is regulated. He found that some vitamins are vital to proper enzyme function, and studied how viruses can infect bacteria. d. Paris, France, Sept. 30.

MALKIN, MYRON S. (70), U.S. physicist who was the first director of the space-shuttle program for the National Aeronautics and Space Administration (NASA). d. Bethesda, Md., Oct. 24.

MAY, ROLLO (85), U.S. psychologist who studied the human need for self-fulfillment, and proposed that human nature is not based on Freudian principles. He stated that anxiety is a strong motivator of human behavior. May helped found the movement known as humanistic psychology, and authored numerous books, most notably *Love and Will*. d. Tiburon, Calif., Oct. 22.

MORGAN, WILLIAM W. (88), leading U.S. astronomer who discovered the spiral structure of the Milky Way galaxy, developed systems for classifying the brightness of stars and a method to accurately determine distances to an arrangement of stars, and demonstrated the existence of supergiant galaxies. His landmark discovery of the spiral shape of the Milky Way was announced in 1951 to a standing ovation from the American Astronomical Society. d. Williams Bay, Wis., June 21.

NIER, ALFRED O.C. (82), U.S. physicist whose work on radioactive isotopes helped determine the age of Earth. He built a high-resolution mass spectrometer for his studies on isotopes. His research on two uranium isotopes later led to the development of the atomic bomb. In the 1970s, under the auspices of the National Aeronautics and Space Administration (NASA), he studied the composition and structure of the atmosphere of Mars. d. Minneapolis, Minn., May 16.

OLTON, DAVID S. (51), U.S. neuroscientist who studied the biological basis of learning and memory, and focused on arresting the memory loss that often occurs with aging. His work on the hippocampus may hold promise for future research on preventing or treating Alzheimer's disease. d. Bethesda, Md., Feb. 1.

PAULING, LINUS C. (93), internationally known U.S. chemist who won the 1954 Nobel Prize in Chemistry for his research into the nature of the chemical bond, and the 1962 Nobel Peace Prize for his work against nuclear weapons and for advocating peaceful methods of resolving international conflicts. His political activism led to brushes with Senator Joseph McCarthy, who accused him of being a Communist sympathizer; Pauling denied the charges under oath. In 1970, he published *Vitamin C and the Common Cold*, proposing that massive doses of Vitamin C could prevent colds. This led to an unprecedented run on the vitamin, depleting most pharmacies within days. He later said Vitamin C might help treat cancer. d. Big Sur, Calif., Aug. 19.

PFAFFMANN, CARL (80), U.S. physiological psychologist who studied the neurochemical basis for the senses of smell and taste and how certain experiences or conditions can affect preferences or dislikes in odors and taste. He discovered that a specific pattern of brain-cell activity affects the quality of taste. d. Middletown, Conn., April 16.

PLUNKETT, ROY J. (83), U.S. scientist who accidentally created Teflon in 1938. Teflon, the trade name for polytetrafluoroethylene resin or one of its derivatives, is now used on three-quarters of all pots and pans sold in the United States, and in numerous other applications where heat resistance, chemical inertness, and very low surface friction are needed. He was inducted into the National Inventors' Hall of Fame in 1985. d. Corpus Christi, Tex., May 12.

POLLACK, JAMES B. (55), U.S. research scientist with the National Aeronautics and Space Administration (NASA) who, with Carl Sagan and three others, authored the 1983 article "Nuclear Winter: Global Consequences of Multiple Nuclear Explosions." The work led to heated controversy, calming only when the five scientists stated in 1990 that they may have overestimated the severity of a "nuclear winter." d. San Jose, Calif., June 13.

ROOSA, STUART A. (61), U.S. astronaut who, in 1971, flew on the third lunar-landing mission, remaining in orbit while the other two astronauts walked on the Moon. d. Falls Church, Va., Dec. 12.

SCHWINGER, JULIAN (76), U.S. theoretical physicist who shared the 1965 Nobel Prize in Physics for his fundamental work in the field of quantum electrodynamics, which investigates the physics of elementary particles. He helped advance the quantum theory of radiation, leading to a better understanding of the interaction between charged particles and an electromagnetic field. d. Los Angeles, Calif., July 16.

SMITH, HAROLD HILL (84), U.S. geneticist who, in 1976, was the first to fuse a human cell with a plant cell. He also made crucial discoveries about the genetic basis of tumor formation and the genetic effects of irradiating plants. d. State College, Pa., Oct. 19.

SPERRY, ROGER W. (80), U.S. physiologist who shared the 1981 Nobel Prize in Physiology or Medicine for his work on the function of the right and left hemispheres of the brain and his discovery that the left side is not dominant. His experiments helped define the function of the corpus callosum, a bundle of nerve fibers that pass information between the two hemispheres. d. Pasadena, Calif., April 17.

STARR, RICHARD F. (94), U.S. archaeologist who, in 1929, led an expedition to Iraq, where researchers discovered the world's oldest map, dating back to 2500 B.C., and discovered armor and other ancient artifacts. d. Leesburg, Va., March 9.

SWINTON, WILLIAM E. (93), Scottish paleontologist who, in 1934, published *The Dinosaurs*, a classic text on prehistoric reptiles. He also wrote and illustrated science books for children to help spark their interest in extinct animals. d. Toronto, Canada, June 12.

TAGGART, JOHN V., III (77), U.S. physiologist known for his *in vitro* kidney research on the mechanism by which chemicals and hormones move from one cell to another. d. Mount Kisco, N.Y., July 23.

TEMIN, HOWARD M. (59), U.S. cancer researcher who shared the 1975 Nobel Prize in Physiology or Medicine for his discoveries of the interactions between tumor viruses and the genetic material of the cell. He helped discover an enzyme, reverse transcriptase, that was critical to the development of genetically engineered substances such as human insulin, and later played a role in identifying HIV, the virus that causes AIDS. d. Madison, Wis., Feb. 9.

VINE, ALLYN C. (79), U.S. oceanographer who was a leader in developing submersible research vehicles for studying deep-sea life. In 1964, the first submersible built in the United States was named for him. This 22-foot (6.7-meter)-long submarine, *Alvin*, recovered a hydrogen bomb from the Mediterranean Sea in 1968, and reached the sunken *Titanic* in 1986. d. Woods Hole, Mass., Jan. 4.

WALKER, JOHN C. (101), U.S. agricultural scientist who was the first to demonstrate the chemical nature of disease resistance in plants. He developed disease-resistant varieties of onions, cabbages, peas, beets, and cucumbers. d. Sun City, Ariz., Nov. 25.

WERNER, SIDNEY C. (84), U.S. endocrinologist who showed that Graves' disease is caused by a disorder in the body's autoimmune system, leading to excess production of thyroid hormone. He established classifications for the eye changes used to diagnose Graves' disease. d. Tucson, Ariz., April 21.

WIGGLESWORTH, SIR VINCENT B. (94), British biologist who pioneered the field of insect physiology. He specialized in the study of insect hormones and the roles they play in reproduction and development. His 1970 book *Insect Hormones* is considered a classic work in the field, as is his first book, the 1934 *Insect Physiology*. d. Cambridge, England, Feb. 12.

WOLFF, SHELDON M. (63), U.S. physician and expert on infectious diseases who was a leader in crusading for more federally funded research into AIDS. In 1982, he chaired a National Institutes of Health (NIH) committee that found that the use of high-absorbency tampons led to increased risk of toxic-shock syndrome. d. Boston, Mass., Feb. 9.

WYCKOFF, RALPH W. G. (97), U.S. research scientist who used the electron microscope to produce photographs of viruses and other submicroscopic particles, revealing a new world for the first time. He also helped develop the ultracentrifuge and a vaccine against the virus that causes equine encephalomyelitis. d. Tucson, Ariz., Nov. 3.

INDEX

ACKNOWLEDGMENTS

Sources of articles appear below, including those reprinted with the kind permission of publications and organizations.

WOLF SONG, page 29: Reprinted by permission of the author; article originally appeared in the November-December 1994 issue of *Country Journal*, published by Cowles Magazines, Inc.

SCHOOL SPIRIT, page 36: Copyright 1995 by the National Wildlife Federation. Reprinted from the March-April 1995 issue of *International Wildlife*.

BAMBOO IS BACK, page 41: Copyright 1995 by the National Wildlife Federation. Reprinted from the January-February 1995 issue of *International Wildlife*.

ZEBRAS IN TURMOIL, page 48: Copyright 1994 by the National Wildlife Federation. Reprinted from the September-October 1994 issue of *International Wildlife*.

HAVE WINGS, CAN'T FLY, page 54: Reprinted by permission of the author; article originally appeared in the November-December 1994 issue of *International Wildlife*.

CRACKS IN HEAVEN'S VAULT, page 70: Reprinted by permission of the California Academy of Sciences; article originally appeared in the Fall 1994 issue of *Pacific Discovery*.

PLANETARY OCEANS, page 83: Reprinted by permission from *Sea Frontiers*, the magazine of the International Oceanographic Foundation.

THE ASTRONOMICAL NAME GAME, page 87: Reprinted with permission from *New Scientist*.

SECRETS OF THE RINGS, page 91: Dava Sobel/© 1994 The Walt Disney Co. Reprinted with permission of *Discover* Magazine.

DESERT SANCTUARY, page 102: Copyright © 1995 by The New York Times Company. Reprinted by permission.

ON THE BEACH, page 108: Reprinted by permission from *Sea Frontiers*, the magazine of the International Oceanographic Foundation.

RETHINKING THE RICHTER SCALE, page 114: Reprinted with permission from *Science News*, the weekly newsmagazine of science, copyright 1994 by Science Service, Inc.

FIRES OF LIFE, page 120: Copyright 1994 by the National Wildlife Federation. Reprinted from the August-September 1994 issue of *National Wildlife*.

UNDER THE VOLCANO, page 126: © 1994, Kalmbach Publishing Co. Reproduced with permission from *Earth* Magazine.

LIFE FOR LEFTIES, page 154: Reprinted by permission of the author; article originally appeared in the December 1994 issue of *Smithsonian*.

DESIGNER FATS, page 161: Reprinted with permission from *Science News*, the weekly newsmagazine of science, copyright 1994 by Science Service, Inc.

THE MAINSTREAMING OF ALTERNATIVE MEDICINE, page 166: Copyright © 1992 by The New York Times Company. Reprinted by permission.

THE CALL OF THE MERMAID, page 190: Reprinted by permission of the author; article originally appeared in the October 1994 *Wildlife Conservation* Magazine, published by Wildlife Conservation Society.

HOW TO TAME A WILD PLANT, page 195: Jared Diamond/© 1994 The Walt Disney Co. Reprinted with permission of *Discover* Magazine.

ECLIPSES THAT SHAPED HISTORY, page 201: From the May 1994 *Sky & Telescope*. © 1994 Sky Publishing Corp. All rights reserved. Reprinted with permission.

THE MAGIC OF SCIENCE FICTION, page 207: Reprinted by permission of the author; article originally appeared in the October 1994 issue of *Technology Review*.

BEYOND THE TOP QUARK, page 218: Copyright 1994, *U.S. News & World Report*. Reprinted by permission.

THE TIES THAT BIND, page 230: Reprinted with permission from *Popular Science*, copyright 1994, Times Mirror Magazines, Inc. Distributed by the Los Angeles Times Syndicate.

PHYSICS ON THE FAIRWAY, page 239: Reprinted by permission of the author; article originally appeared in the February 1995 issue of *Popular Science* Magazine, copyright 1995, Times Mirror Magazines, Inc.

MAKING MONEY, page 250: Reprinted with permission from *Popular Science*, copyright 1994, Times Mirror Magazines, Inc. Distributed by the Los Angeles Times Syndicate.

THE CHANGING FACES ON MONEY, page 254: Copyright © 1995 by The New York Times Company. Reprinted by permission.

MANUFACTURING FOR REUSE, page 258: Originally published in the February 6, 1995, issue of *Fortune*. Copyright © 1995 Time Inc. All rights reserved.

PRESSING MATTERS, page 266: Reprinted from the February 13, 1995, issue of *Business Week* by special permission, copyright © 1995 by McGraw-Hill Inc.

DOTS OF ILLUSION, page 269: Reprinted with permission from *Popular Science*, copyright 1994, Times Mirror Magazines, Inc. Distributed by the Los Angeles Times Syndicate.

HOW COMPUTERS RECOGNIZE FACES, page 275: Reprinted with permission from *Science News*, the weekly newsmagazine of science, copyright 1994 by Science Service, Inc.

NAVIGATING THROUGH BLINDNESS, page 280: Copyright © 1994 by The New York Times Company. Reprinted by permission.

Manufacturing Acknowledgments

We wish to thank the following for their services:
Color Separations, Gamma One, Inc.;
Text Stock, printed on Champion's 60# Courtland Matte;
Cover Materials provided by Holliston Mills, Inc., and Decorative Specialties, Inc.;
Printing and Binding, R.R. Donnelley & Sons Co.

ILLUSTRATION CREDITS

The following list acknowledges, according to page, the sources of illustrations used in this volume. The credits are listed illustration by illustration—top to bottom, left to right. Where necessary, the name of the photographer or artist has been listed with the source, the two separated by a slash. If two or more illustrations appear on the same page, their credits are separated by semicolons.

3 Clockwise from top left: © David Parker/Science Photo Library/Photo Researchers; © Dr. Jeremy Burgess/Science Photo Library/Photo Researchers; © Paul Shambroom/Photo Researchers; © Sinclair Stammers/Science Photo Library/Photo Researchers
8– © Nancy Siesel/*The New York Times*
9
10 © Fermilab Visual Media Services
11 © Michael Sewell/Peter Arnold
13 Clockwise from top left: © Taheshi Takahara/Photo Researchers; © James Holmes/CellTech Ltd./Science Photo Library/Photo Researchers; © Erich Schrempp/Photo Researchers; © NASA
14– © Flip Nicklin/Minden Pictures
15
16 © Daniel J. Cox/Natural Exposures
17 © Lily Solmssen/Photo Researchers; © Lee Foster/Bruce Coleman
18 © Wendy Shattil & Bob Rozinski
19 © Wendy Shattil & Bob Rozinski; © Tom Brakefield/The Stock Market
20 © Jack A. Barrie/Bruce Coleman; © David Falconer/Bruce Coleman; © Wendy Shattil & Bob Rozinski
21 © Art Wolfe
22 © Wendy Shattil & Bob Rozinski
23 © B. Brander/Photo Researchers
24 © David Hosking/Photo Researchers; inset: © Johnny Johnson/Animals Animals
25 © Mitsuhiko Imamori/Nature Productions; © Edward S. Ross
26 © Dr. Paul A. Zahl/Photo Researchers
27 © Mitsuhiko Imamori/Nature Productions; © Scott Camazine
28 © Mitsuyoshi Tatematsu/Nature Productions; © G.I. Bernard/Animals Animals
29 © Thomas H. Brakefield/The Stock Market
30 © Daniel J. Cox/Natural Exposures; © Jim Brandenburg/Minden Pictures
31 © Art Wolfe
32 © Art Wolfe
33 © Art Wolfe
34 Photo: AP/Wide World Photos; map: © Robert Kemp/*U.S. News & World Report*
35 © Art Wolfe; © Thomas H. Brakefield/Bruce Coleman
36– © Fred McConnaughey/Photo
37 Researchers
38– Left photos: © Fred Bavendam; crossover
39 photo: © Louisa Peterson/Photo Researchers
40 © Mickey Gibson/Animals Animals
41 © David Muench/Tony Stone Images
42 © Frans Lanting/Minden Pictures
43 © Jim Brandenburg/Minden Pictures
44 © George Chan/Photo Researchers
45– All photos: © Jim Brandenburg/Minden
47 Pictures
48 © Tom McHugh/Photo Researchers
49 © Art Wolfe
50 © Karl & Kay Amman/Bruce Coleman
51 © Art Wolfe; © Johnny Johnson/Tony Stone Images
52 © Richard Matthews/Planet Earth Pictures
53 © Carol Hughes/Bruce Coleman
54– © Art Wolfe; crossover photo: © Jan &
55 Des Bartlett/Bruce Coleman
56 © Ben Osborne/Tony Stone Images; © Tui De Roy/Auscape International
57 © Jean-Paul Ferrero/Auscape International
58 © Tom McHugh/Photo Researchers; © Erwin & Peggy Bauer/Bruce Coleman
59 © Diana Rogers/Bruce Coleman; © G.J.H. Moon/Bruce Coleman; © John Cancalosi/DRK Photos

60 © Superstock
62– © Johnson Space Center/NASA
63
64 Hubble Space Telescope Comet Team/NASA
65 Space Telescope Science Institute
66 Richard Gage/*U.S. News & World Report*; inset: H. Hammel, MIT/NASA
67 © Alan Levenson
68 Both photos: Hubble Space Telescope Comet Team/NASA
70 © Dr. Seth Shostak/Science Photo Library/Photo Researchers
71 © Dr. Seth Shostak/Science Photo Library/Photo Researchers
72 Both illustrations: © STSCI/NASA
74 © 1994 by The New York Times Company. Reprinted by permission.
75 Both illustrations: © Laird Close/Donald McCarthy/Fulvio Melia/The Steward Observatory
76 © STSCI/NASA/SPL/Photo Researchers
77 © Julian Baum/SPL/Photo Researchers
78 © The Rohss Museum of Arts & Crafts, Gothenburg
79 © The Granger Collection
80– Crossover photo: © Philip Rosenberg; far
81 right: © David A. Hardy/SPL/Photo Researchers
82 © Dr. Alexander Wolszczan
83 © U.S. Geological Survey/Mark Marten/Science Source/Photo Researchers; inset: © M. Salaber/Liaison
84 © David W. Hamilton/The Image Bank
85 © Michael Carroll/Phototake
87 Art by Chris Murphy
88– Background art by Chris Murphy;
89 crossover Venus photo: JPL; insets: The Bettmann Archive; The Bettmann Archive; AP/Wide World Photos
90 Background art by Chris Murphy; asteroid photo: JPL; inset: Springer/Bettmann Film Archive
91– All photos: JPL
95
97 Mark Showalter/Ames Research Center/NASA
98 © Superstock
100– John Lund/Tony Stone Images
101
102 © David Muench
103 © Sam Roberts; © Tim Davis/Photo Researchers
104– Left column: top: © John Gerlach/Animals
105 Animals; center and bottom: © Frank Balthis; crossover photo: © David Muench; map: © Laszlo Kubinyi
106 © John Eastcott/Yva Momatiuk/Animals Animals; © Jon Mark Stewart
107 © David Muench
108– © James Blank/FPG
109
110 © J. Messerschmidt/Bruce Coleman; © S. Kanno/FPG International; © Lee Rentz/Bruce Coleman
111 Top: © Vince Streano/Tony Stone Images; bottom photos: © Michael Baytoff
113 © Bruce Roberts/Photo Researchers
114 © Reuters/Bettmann
115 © Joe Cempa/Black Star
116 The Bettmann Archive; chart background: © UPI/Bettmann
117 © UPI/Bettmann
118 © Wampler/Sygma
119 Chart background: AP/Wide World Photos
120 © *Seattle Times*/Liaison
121 © Jeff Vanuga
122 © J.B. Diederich/Contact Press

123 © Greg Lovett/*The Palm Beach Post*; inset: © Gail Shumway
124 © Tom Muscionico/Contact Press; © Bart Ah You/Liaison
125 © Jeff Henry
127 © Courtesy of Asia Air Survey Company, Ltd.
128 © Photo Researchers; inset: © Francois Gohier/Photo Researchers
129 Both photos: © Roger Ressmeyer/Starlight
130 © David Weintraub/Photo Researchers
131 © Bill Ingals/NASA
132– Crossover photo: © Carr Clifton; inset: ©
133 Dwight Kuhn
134– Map: © Laszlo Kubinyi; photos: © Carr
135 Clifton; © Frederick McKinney/FPG; © Carr Clifton
136 © Carr Clifton; inset: © Jim Kahnweiler/Positive Images
137 © Martin Miller/Positive Images
138 © Damian Strohmey/f-Stop Pictures; inset: © Bill Silliker
139 © Bill Silliker
140 © Superstock
142– © Comstock
143
144 Dan Winters/© 1994 The Walt Disney Co. Reprinted with permission of *Discover* Magazine.
145 © Peter Menzel
146 © 1995 Ty Ahmad Taylor by The New York Times Company. Reprinted by permission.
148 © Peter Menzel
149 © John Abbott
150 © Dr. Kari Lounatmaa/SPL/Photo Researchers; © Tim Crosby/Liaison
151 © Archive Photos/Express Newspapers
152 Top: © Marta Lavandier/AP Wide World; bottom photos: © Yvonne Hemsey/Liaison
153 © UPI/Bettmann
154 © Peter Simon/Phototake
155 © Nimatallah/Art Resource
156 © Jamie Tanaka/Phototake; © Richard Hutchings/Photo Researchers
157 © Skeet McAuley/The Image Bank
158 © Allan Koss/The Image Works
159 © Focus on Sports
160 © Dirck Halstead/Liaison
161– Artwork by Chris Murphy
165
166 © J.P. Laffont/Sygma
168 Photo: © John Cancolosi/Stock Boston; art: © Richard Gage/*U.S. News & World Report*
169 Photo: © Phillippe Plailly/SPL/Photo Researchers; art: © Richard Gage/*U.S. News & World Report*
170 Photo: © James Schnepf/Liaison; art: © Richard Gage/*U.S. News & World Report*
171 © Francois Gauthier/Sipa
172 © Superstock
174– © Ben Simmons/The Stock Market
175
176 © Jean Clottes/Ministère de la Culture
177 © Jean-Marie Chauvet/Sygma
178 Photo: © Maher Attar/Sygma
179 © Sisse Brimberg/National Geographic Society Image Collection
180 © Jean Clottes/Ministère de la Culture
181 © Jean Clottes/Ministère de la Culture; © Jean-Marie Chauvet/Sygma
182 © Jean-Marie Chauvet/Sygma
183 © SEF/Art Resource
184 © Erich Lessing/Art Resource
185 © Scala/Art Resource
186 © Gianni Giansanti/Sygma

188 © Gianni Giansanti/Sygma; © G.A. Leonards, Ph.D., Purdue University
189 © G.A. Leonards, Ph.D., Purdue University; © Gianni Giansanti/Sygma
190 © Glenn Wolff
191 The Bettmann Archive; © Glenn Wolff
192 The Granger Collection; North Wind Picture Archives
193 © Erich Lessing/Art Resource
194 © Glenn Wolff; The Granger Collection
195 © Erich Lessing/Art Resource; © Walter H. Hodge/Peter Arnold
196 © Klaus D. Francke/Bilderberg/The Stock Market; © Lance Nelson/The Stock Market
197 The Granger Collection; © Barry L. Runk/Grant Heilman
198 © Ronald Sheridan/Ancient Art & Architecture Collection; © Cotton Coulson/Woodfin Camp & Assoc.
199 © Chuck O'Rear/Woodfin Camp & Assoc.
201 © Dr. Fred Espenak/Science Photo Library/Photo Researchers; The Granger Collection
203 Maps: © Sky Publishing Corp. Reproduced by permission; left photo: © Dr. Fred Espenak/Science Photo Library/Photo Researchers; right illustrations: The Granger Collection
204– Left: Yerkes Observatory; crossover
205 photo: © Akira Fujii
206 The Granger Collection
207 Left two illustrations: The Granger Collection; right: © Archive Photos
208 The Granger Collection
209 © The Bettmann Archive
210 © Archive Photos
211 © Archive Photos
212 © Photofest
213 © The Kobal Collection
214 © Superstock
216– © John Madere/The Stock Market
217
218 Skyscape: © John Sanford/Science Photo Library/Photo Researchers; room scene: © Roy Morsch/The Stock Market; superimposed window scenes, from left: © Ian Lawrence/Photonica; © W.G. Allen/Photonica; © Julian Baum/Science Photo Library/Photo Researchers
219 © Ian Lawrence/Photonica
220 © Fermilab Visual Media Services
222 © Julian Baum/Science Photo Library/Photo Researchers
226 © Laura Dwight/Peter Arnold; © Tony Freeman/Photo Edit
227 © M. Antman/The Image Works
228 © Barry L. Runk/Grant Heilman
229 © Lawrence Berkeley Laboratory/University of California
230 Photo: © Mike Morris/Unicorn Stock Photos; art: © Barry Ross
231 Photo: © Jo McBride/Tony Stone Images; art: © Barry Ross
232 © Barry Ross
233 Photo: © Nancy Crisona/UC Berkeley; art: © Barry Ross
234 © Michael Newman/PhotoEdit
235 © Carl Purcell/Photo Researchers
236 © Jonathan Kirn/Liaison

237 North Wind Picture Archives
238 © Trippett/Sipa
239 © John B. Carnett/*Popular Science*/Los Angeles Times Syndicate
240 All illustrations: © Robert Walker/USGA
241 © Robert Walker/USGA; © John B. Carnett/*PopularScience*/Los Angeles Times Syndicate
242 Both illustrations: Courtesy, Donnellon Public Relations
243 © Chuck Savage/The Stock Market
245 © *Popular Science*/Los Angeles Times Syndicate
246 © Superstock
248– © Lonnie Duka/Tony Stone Images
249
250 © Richard Gage/*U.S. News & World Report*
251 © FPG International
252 © Richard Gage/*U.S. News & World Report*
253 © Paul S. Conklin
254– © Joseph Kugielsky
255
256– © Joseph Kugielsky
257
258 © Peter Sibbald
259 Both photos: © Peter Sibbald
260 © Peter Sibbald
261 © Courtesy of BMW; © Courtesy of International Business Machines Corporation
262 © Peter Sibbald; © Photoreporters, Inc.
263 © Laemmerer/Bavaria-Verlag-Bildagentur
265 Top photo: © Phil Matt; other photos: © Steven Rubin
266– All photos: © Robert Hazen
268
269– All illustrations from *Magic Eye: A New*
274 *Way of Looking at the World* © 1993 by N.E. Thing Enterprises
275 © Tom Pantages
276 © Courtesy of Miros, Inc.
277– All illustrations: © Tom Pantages
279
280 © Kim Reierson/University of California, Santa Barbara
281 © 1994 John Papasian by The New York Times Company. Reprinted by permission.
282 © Lawrence Migdale/Photo Researchers
284 © Superstock
287 Clockwise from top left: © Lawrence Migdale/Photo Researchers; © James Holmes/CellTech Ltd./Science Photo Library/Photo Researchers; © Brian Brake/Photo Researchers; © James Bell/Science Photo Library/Photo Researchers
288 © Tom McHugh/Photo Researchers
291 Photo: © B&C Alexander/Black Star
293 © Courtesy of the University of Cincinnati
295 © Michael Stecker
297 © Ford Motor Company
298 © Reuters/Bettmann
299 © Tim Boyle/Wide World Photos
301 © David Young-Wolff/PhotoEdit
302 © Lee Balterman/FPG International
303– Illustrations: John Karapelou/© The Walt
304 Disney Co. Reprinted with permission of *Discover* Magazine.
307 © Courtesy Harvard University Press; © Courtesy Basic Books

308 © Courtesy Alfred A. Knopf; © Courtesy Houghton Miflin; © Courtesy Little, Brown; © Courtesy Random House
309 © Courtesy Viking Penguin; © Courtesy University of Chicago Press; © Courtesy Simon & Schuster
311 Sally Bensusen/© 1995 The Walt Disney Co. Reprinted with permission of *Discover* Magazine.
312 © Richard Shiell/Animals Animals
313 Both photos: © Courtesy Department of Energy
314 © AP/Wide World Photos
315 © AP/Wide World Photos
318 © Courtesy of Thomson Consumer Electronics
320 © Harrison/Gamma-Liaison
322 © Courtesy, Solar Power International; © Courtesy, Pentax
323 © Courtesy, Specialized Bicycle Components
324 © Courtesy, A&H International Products
325 © Switzer, *et al.*/University of Missouri
327 © Roberta Parkin/Spooner/Gamma-Liaison
329 © Tannenbaum/Sygma
331 © Lacy Atkins/AP/Wide World Photos
332 © J. Markowitz/Sygma
335 © Roger Job/Liaison
337 © Jeffrey Friedman/The Rockefeller Center
338 © Hank Morgan/Science Source/Photo Researchers
340 JPL/NASA; © Bruce F. Molnia, Ph.D./USGS
342 Both photos: © Dr. Arthur C. Aufderheide, University of Minnesota
343 © Matt Meadows/Peter Arnold
344 © Louis Bencze/Tony Stone Images; © D. Hudson/Sygma
347 © Sepp Seitz/Woodfin Camp & Assoc.
348 © Daniel Portnoy/AP/Wide World Photos
349 © Dan Groshong/Sygma
351 © Brooks Kraft/Sygma; © Carlo Ellegri/Sygma
353 © Jeffrey Markowitz/Sygma; © Timothy Sharp/Sygma
354 Copyright © 1994 by The New York Times Company. Reprinted by permission.
355 © Jose L. Pelaez/The Stock Market
356 Photo background: © Joseph Kugielsky; table data: *The New York Times*
359 © Norbert Wu
362 © Courtesy of Princeton/Plasma Physics Laboratory
363 © Fermilab Visual Media Services
364 © Thierry Orban/Sygma
365 © Sipa
367 © Nancy Siesel/*The New York Times*
369 © Iwasa/Sipa Press
370 Ian Worpole/© 1995 The Walt Disney Co./Reprinted with permission of *Discover* Magazine.
372 © NASA
373 © Markel/Liaison
375 Top: Johnson Space Center/NASA; center and bottom: NASA
377 AP/Wide World Photos
378 © Tony Gydesen/NYT Pictures
379 Reuters/Bettmann
380 © George B. Schaller
381 © Larry Miller/Photo Researchers
382 © Michael Sewell/Peter Arnold